MANAGING GLOBAL INFORMATION TECHNOLOGY: STRATEGIES AND CHALLENGES

Editors:

Prashant Palvia
Shailendra C. Jain Palvia
Albert L. Harris

Ivy League Publishing, Limited

MANAGING GLOBAL INFORMATION TECHNOLOGY: STRATEGIES AND CHALLENGES

Editors:
Prashant Palvia
Shailendra C. Jain Palvia
Albert L. Harris

IVY LEAGUE PUBLISHING, LIMITED

P.O. Box 680392
Marietta, Georgia 30068, USA

Phone: (770) 649-6718
Fax: (770) 649-6719
Email: admin@ivylp.com

Library of Congress Control Number: 2007010804

ISBN: 0-9648382-4-9

Library of Congress Cataloging-in-Publication Data

Managing global information technology : strategies and challenges / editors: Prashant Palvia, Shailendra C. Jain Palvia, Albert L. Harris.
        p. cm.
  Includes bibliographical references and index.
  ISBN 0-9648382-4-9 (alk. paper)
  1. Information technology--Management. 2. Management information systems. I. Palvia, Prashant. II. Palvia, Shailendra. III. Harris, Albert L.
  HD30.2.M3618 2007
  658.4'038011--dc22

                                        2007010804

Managing Global Information Technology: Strategies and Challenges

Table of Contents

iv

About the Editors

Prashant Palvia is Joe Rosenthal Excellence Professor and Information Systems Ph.D. Program Director at the University of North Carolina at Greensboro (UNCG). He received his Ph.D., MBA and MS from the University of Minnesota and BS from the University of Delhi, India. He is a leading authority in Global Information Technology Management and chairs the annual GITMA world conferences. Prof. Palvia is the Editor-in-Chief of *the Journal of Global Information Technology Management (JGITM)*. His research interests include global information technology, electronic commerce, media choice theory, trust in exchange relationships, and privacy & security. He has published 77 journal articles including in journal such as *MIS Quarterly, Decision Sciences, Communications of the ACM, Communications of the AIS, Information & Management, Decision Support Systems*, and *ACM TODS*.

Shailendra C. Jain Palvia is Professor of MIS at Long Island University, New York (USA). He received his Ph.D. from the University of Minnesota. He has published over 100 articles in referred journals and refereed proceedings. His research has appeared in journals such as *Information Resource Management, Communications of the ACM, MIS Quarterly, Information & Management, JGITM, JITCAR,* and *Journal of Information Systems Education*. Dr. Palvia is Editor-in-chief of the *Journal of Information Technology Cases and Applications Research (JITCAR)*, and in many conferences. He chaired the five international outsourcing (ITO and BPO) conferences. He has been an invited speaker in Boston (USA), Stuttgart (Germany), Singapore, Mumbai (India), Bangalore (India), Anand (India), Napoli (Italy), St. Petersburg (Russia), Bangkok (Thailand), and Indore (India).

Albert L. Harris is Professor of MIS at Appalachian State University and Editor-in-Chief of the *Journal of Information Systems Education*, the leading journal on IS education. Dr. Harris served as Fulbright Scholar to Portugal in 2006. He is a Certified Information Systems Auditor, Certified Computer Professional, and Certified Management Consultant. He received his Ph.D. from Georgia State University, M.S. from George Washington University, and B.S. from Indiana University. He is a Board member of the International Association of Information Management and the Education Special Interest Group of AITP. He has over 75 publications as book chapters and articles in journals and conferences, including *Communications of the AIS* and *Information and Management*. Prior to becoming an educator, he spent 15 years in IT consulting. He served as an officer in the U.S. Marine Corps from 1966-1970.

PREFACE

This is the fourth book we are publishing on the management issues of global information technology. Every time we have edited the book, we felt that the issues will not change dramatically in just a few years and each book will last for a long time. Not so. We have been inundated by calls from our friends and colleagues pleading with us to completely renew the book. Besides the obvious and growing utilization of information technology by firms of all sizes in all parts of the globe, significant changes have occurred in the past few years. Some significant developments are: the increasing use of information technology by firms in less developed countries to improve their business and national economies, the expanding supply chains that are international in scope and depend heavily on information technology, the pervasiveness of offshoring to distant locations by firms in practically all advanced economies, the burgeoning impact of the Internet and e-commerce, and the adaptation of e-government by many government agencies all over the world.

So here it is. This new book not only captures the contemporary global IT issues, but updates the classical issues with updated information. Based on our experience of the three previous books, we were fortunate to know the leading authors and researchers in the global IT field. So we took a different approach in preparing the book and believe, developed a very high quality product. Rather than making a general call for chapters for inclusion in the book, we targeted specific authors for their expertise and invited them to write specific chapters for the book. As you would notice, we have chapters from leading authorities as well as authors from previous books whose chapters were very well received. In addition to the careful screening of authors at the front end, each chapter was further reviewed by the co-editors and went through multiple revisions before final acceptance. We also took extraordinary pains in editing the book so that the book meets the highest standards of professionalism.

The book has twenty five chapters divided into five sections. Each chapter starts off with a chapter summary and is followed by a minicase, listing of important terms, and study questions. The minicase, with its accompanying discussion questions, and the study questions at the end of the chapter can be assigned to students to further illustrate and apply the concepts presented in the chapter. The five sections are: IT in a Global Context, Global Strategies and Policies, Integration of Global Systems, Global IS Development and Outsourcing, and E-Commerce and E-Government.

The first section recognizes that the spread and use of technology has not reached all companies and countries equally. Digital divide continues to persist. Technology flourishes in advanced and newly industrialized countries, but lags in developing and underdeveloped countries. In spite of Thomas Friedman's book "The World is Flat" and using the metaphor of "roads", the roads are still bumpy and not always paved. This section introduces the reader to IT in a global context through a series of six chapters. Chapter 1 looks at the key issues faced by IT executives in four broad categories and provides a model of the global IT environment. Chapter 2 looks at IT environment in Russia, while Chapter 3 examines the use of IT in China. Chapter 4 looks at how Chinese culture has impacted the use of IT in China. Chapter 5 presents a longitudinal analysis of the global digital divide. Chapter 6, the last in this section, presents critical success factors for lesser developed countries to bridge the global digital divide.

The second section examines company strategies and policies, as they evolve from national to global. The policies and procedures that worked well in one country may not work in other countries due to their economy, culture, laws, or other factors. This section presents five chapters that address global strategies and policies. Chapter 7 examines global IT strategies by looking at the issues associated with global, regional, national, corporate, and individual levels. Chapter 8 looks at public information and communication technology (ICT) policies. Twenty-three examples of public ICT policy are presented, along with a framework to evaluate public ICT policies. Chapter 9 looks at global information technology (IT) architecture. A framework for IT architecture is presented and the framework is evaluated using two case studies. Chapter 10 examines the role of global information systems in managing worldwide operations of multinational corporations (MNCs). Finally, chapter 11 looks at governance in the global information economy. Four companies are described in relation to their governance and shaping of their global systems.

The third section deals with the integration of global systems, which not only involves disparate functions within one's own organization, but also the interface with external entities in various parts of the world. Chapter 12 deals with transborder data flows, or the movement of personally identifiable data from one country to another. The chapter first discusses barriers to the flow of data across borders and then looks at privacy legislation around the world. Chapter 13 examines the global supply chain strategy. Supply chains interconnect companies, customers, and vendors around the world. Chapter 14 deals with cultural asymmetries and the challenge of global enterprise integration. The chapter examines national culture, organizational culture, and information culture and presents implications for management. Finally, Chapter 15 looks at the grounded theory in the design and implementation of information systems for multinational enterprises.

The fourth section presents six chapters on GIS development and global outsourcing of IT and IT Enabled Services. The development of a global information system (GIS) is a complex and challenging task. GISs cross national boundaries, cultures, time zones, and established patterns of organizational behavior. In addition, the concept of outsourcing, or hiring a vendor to manage or operate information system functions, is becoming commonplace. Chapter 16 presents a contextual analysis of GIS development strategies. Nine strategies are identified and discussed in the chapter. A framework for GIS development strategies is presented. Chapter 17 discusses best practices for GIS development. Five tactics for implementing the transnational model are presented. Chapter 18 kicks off the discussion of outsourcing by discussing dynamics of control modes in offshored information systems development projects and the role of culture. An integrative framework for control strategies is presented. In Chapter 19, the author develops a sourcing framework and emerging knowledge requirements for offshoring. Chapter 20 presents critical factors for managing offshore contracts. The final chapter in this section, Chapter 21, presents frameworks for selecting countries and companies for outsourcing.

The final section has four chapters on e-commerce and e-government. E-commerce has the ability to make businesses of all sizes, large or small, global. Time and distance are no longer barriers to serving clients. On the same theme, e-government allows government services and information to be available at anytime and from anywhere, thus meeting the needs of the citizens and businesses more efficiently and effectively. Chapter 22 is a comprehensive chapter on organizational e-Commerce capturing statistics and trends, business models, frameworks, and critical success factors. Chapter 23 provides an understanding of the business-to-consumer (B2C) e-commerce diffusion and the underlying infrastructural factors in six important economies of the world: USA, Germany, and the emerging BRIC countries, i.e., Brazil, Russia, India and China. Chapter 24 appraises the changes in industrial organizations propelled by advances in information technology and electronic commerce, and articulates the growth of global alliances. Chapter 25, the last chapter in the book, addresses e-government concepts, discusses its benefits and challenges, provides status of e-government in different parts of the world, and offers several frameworks

The editors would like to compliment and express their gratitude to the authors of the chapters. The authors have indeed worked hard and made quality contributions. While we managed the project and provided extensive comments on various drafts at various stages, we thank them for their diligence and perseverance. They went to extraordinary lengths in targeting the chapters to the needs of our readers, presenting contemporary material, and responding to our revision requirement in a timely fashion.

We would also like to express our appreciation to Dr. Dave Yates for the feedback that he provided. His assistance in editing the chapters helped improve the quality of the book.
As you can see, the book is quite comprehensive. Each chapter has achieved a high level of quality through the efforts of the authors and the editors. Included at the end is a glossary of terms and index for quick retrieval of important topics. The book can be used successfully in graduate classes as well as for undergraduate classes at junior or senior level. If the number of chapters is too daunting, the instructor can select chapters according to the needs of the institution's curriculum. Please contact any of us and we will be happy to provide sample syllabi for graduate and undergraduate classes. Lastly, we welcome any and all feedback from instructors as well as students.

Prashant C. Palvia, Ph.D.
The University of North Carolina at Greensboro, North Carolina, USA
pcpalvia@uncg.edu

Shailendra C. Jain Palvia, Ph.D.
Long Island University, New York, USA
spalvia@liu.edu

Albert L. Harris, Ph.D.
Appalachian State University, North Carolina, USA
harrisal@appstate.edu

Section 1

IT in a Global Context

Information Technology (IT) has had a dramatic effect on business around the world. Worldwide communications networks have allowed companies to go global, have enabled outsourcing to become a worldwide phenomenon, and have created global markets thanks to e-commerce and e-business. Supply chains connect companies in countries all over the world. Customer management and supplier management systems provide detailed records that enable companies to manage their businesses, irrespective of country boundaries.

In spite of the dramatic use of IT by businesses, the spread and use of technology has not reached all companies and countries equally. Technology flourishes in advanced and newly industrialized countries, but lags in developing and underdeveloped countries. This section introduces the reader to IT in a global context through a series of six chapters. Chapter 1 looks at the key issues faced by IT executives in four broad categories and provides a model of the global IT environment. Chapter 2 looks at IT environment in Russia, while Chapter 3 examines the use of IT in China. Chapter 4 looks at how Chinese culture has impacted the use of IT in China. Chapter 5 presents a longitudinal analysis of the global digital divide. Chapter 6, the last in this section, presents critical success factors for lesser developed countries to bridge the global digital divide.

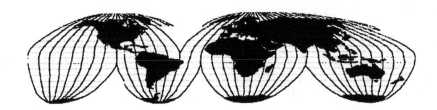

Challenges of the Global Information Technology Management Environment: Representative World Issues[1]

Prashant Palvia
Praveen Pinjani
The University of North Carolina at Greensboro, USA

CHAPTER SUMMARY

As a vast number of businesses continue to expand their operations into international markets, in order to succeed they need to recognize and understand the considerable cultural, economic, political, and technological diversity that exists in different parts of the world. From a technology perspective, it is widely recognized that information technology (IT) is a critical enabler and many times a driver of global business expansion. However, IT is neither uniform nor applied uniformly around the world. This chapter describes and analyzes the key information systems/technology (IS/IT) issues identified during the last few years in different regions of the world. Encouraged by periodic key issues studies in the US, several researchers have done the same for many other countries. This chapter summarizes many of their findings, and provides insights into the various differences and similarities among countries. A model is developed to help understand the nature of the issues and their underlying causes.

INTRODUCTION

During the past decade, the world has witnessed an unprecedented expansion of business into global markets. According to Thomas Friedman (2005), "the world is flat" and this enormous transformation has come about only in the last few years with the turning of the century. There is universal agreement that information technology (IT) has played a crucial role in the race towards globalization. IT has been a critical enabler of globalization in most cases and a driver in many other cases. Today, multinational corporations and governments increasingly rely on IT for conducting international business. Therefore, in order to fully exploit the vast potential of IT, it is extremely

---

[1] This chapter is an adaptation and a major revision of: Global Information Technology Management Environment: Representative World Issues, by Palvia, P., Palvia, S., and Whitworth, J. in *Global Information Technology and Electronic Commerce: Issues for he New Millennium*. Edited by P. Palvia, S. Palvia, and E.M. Roche, Ivy League Publishing 2002, pp. 2-27.

important for corporate executives and chief information officers to understand the nature of the global information technology environment. This chapter provides not only this understanding, but also provides insights into the nature of global IT issues in different economic regions of the world.

Reports of key information systems (IS) issues have continually appeared in the United States. For example, a stream of articles about US issues has appeared in the *MIS Quarterly* (Dickson et al., 1984; Brancheau et al., 1987; Niederman et al., 1991; Ball and Harris, 1982; Brancheau et al., 1996) and the latest one in the *MIS Quarterly Executive* (Luftman and McLean, 2004). Much earlier, a study by Deans et al., (1991) identified and prioritized international IS issues in US based multinational corporations. As technology continues to cross national and international boundaries, researchers have begun to identify IS/IT issues in many other countries. Several such studies have appeared recently; representative examples include: Australia (Pervan, 1997), Canada (Hayne and Pollard, 2000), Hong Kong (Ma, 1999), Taiwan (Chou and Jou, 1999), Thailand (Pimchangthong, 2003), Indonesia (Samik-Ibrahim, 2001), and Nigeria (Badamas, 2004). Such studies are perceived of value as they not only identify issues critical to determining strategies for organizations, but also provide direction for future IS education, practice, and research.

A comparison of the cited studies reveals that the key IS issues in different countries vary to a considerable degree. In order to fully exploit IT for global business, it is imperative that the key IS issues of different countries are identified and dealt with appropriately in the conduct of international business. While an examination of IS issues of the entire world is impractical and infeasible and even the data is not readily available, we summarize issues from a few countries selected on the basis of their level of economic development. Four categories of economic development are defined: advanced, newly industrialized, developing (operational), and under-developed. This classification is somewhat parallel to that used by many international agencies (e.g., the United Nations). The countries discussed in this chapter are loosely categorized using this classification.

While some level of generalization is possible based on the countries discussed herein and is intended, we need to clearly point out the limitations. The chapter does not cover the entire world. Only a few countries are surveyed and while they may represent many other countries, they do not represent them all. Second, the classification of a country into one of the above four classes may be disputable, and furthermore there is a wide range within each class. Some countries may simply defy the classification scheme used here (e.g., Russia and countries of the former Soviet Union) and some others may be in a rapid state of transition from one stage to the next (e.g., India and China).

KEY MIS ISSUES IN ADVANCED COUNTRIES

Advanced and industrialized countries include the United States, Western European countries, Japan, and Australia among others. Key IS issues have been systematically and periodically researched in the United States over the past fifteen years (Ball and Harris, 1982; Brancheau et al., 1987; Dickson et al., 1984; Hartog and Herbert, 1986; Niederman et al., 1991, Brancheau et al., 1996). After a considerable gap of eight years, Luftman and McLean (2004) compiled a list of key IS issues in the US based on a 2003 survey of the Society for Information Management (SIM) members. Rankings from this study are shown in Table 1. While there are many similarities with previous studies (e.g., Brancheau et al., 1996), few new issues have appeared (e.g., security and privacy) and there are some marked differences. There appears to be a shift from technology management to relationship management and governance related issues. Similarities also exist with the Australian issues reported by Pervan (1997) and Canadian issues reported by Hayne and Pollard (2000) (Table 2).

As Luftman and McLean (2004) is the most recent of all advanced nation studies, follows previously established methodological rigor, and is widely distributed, it will be discussed as representative of IS issues of advanced countries.

Key Issue Ranks

The complete ranked list of IS management issues reported by Luftman and McLean, (2004) is shown in Table 1. These issues were captured by a single round survey of senior IS executives in the US.

This was different from previous studies which relied on the Delphi method to capture the issues. In addition to reporting key issues, the study also reported major application and technology developments and enablers and inhibitors of IT and business alignment. These ranks represent the opinions of the members of the Society for Information Management (SIM) and the survey was actually conducted in 2003. The top ten issues in Table 1 are reviewed below. The review draws heavily from the Luftman and McLean (2004) article.

Rank	Description of the Issue
#1	IT and business alignment
#2	IT strategic planning
#3	Security and privacy
#4	Attracting, developing, and retaining IT professionals
#5	Measuring the value of IT investments
#6	Measuring the performance of the IT organization
#7	Creating an information architecture
#8	Complexity reduction
#9	Speed and agility
#10	IT governance
#11	Business process reengineering
#12	Introducing rapid business solutions
#13	Evolving CIO leadership role
#14	IT asset management
#15	Managing outsourcing relationships
#16	Leveraging the legacy investment
#17	Sarbanes-Oxley Act of 2002
#18	Globalization
#19	Offshore outsourcing impacts on IT careers
#20	Societal implications of IT

Table 1. Key Issues for IT Executives - USA (2003)
(Source: Luftman, J. and McLean, E. R. 2004. Key Issues for IT Executives. MIS Quarterly Executive, 3(2): 89-104.)

Rank 1. IT and business alignment: This issue moved to the top from rank 9 in the 1996 study. While not explicitly defined to the respondents, alignment generally means applying IT in an appropriate and timely way in harmony with business strategies, goals, and needs. It is closely linked with IT strategic planning. The importance of this issue warranted the study to further explore the top five enablers and inhibitors of alignment. The top five alignment enablers as specified by the respondents were: IT understanding of the firms' business environment, close partnership between IT and business, senior executive support for IT, linking IT and business plans, and IT demonstrating strong leadership. The top five inhibitors were: lack of senior executives support for IT, lack of influence of headquarters' leadership, lack of business communication with IT, lack of business commitments of budgets to IT investment, and lack of clarity and predictability of corporate goals/direction.

Rank	Description of the Issue
#1	Building a responsive IT infrastructure
#2	Improving IS project management practices
#3	Planning and managing communication networks
#4	Improving effectiveness of software development
#5	Aligning the IS organization within the enterprise
#6	Coping with degree and rate of technology change
#7	Developing and implementing information architecture
#8	Using IS for competitive advantage
#9	Facilitating and managing BPR
#10	Developing and managing distributed systems

Table 2. Key Issues for IT Executives -Canada (2000)
(Source: Hayne, S. C. and Pollard, C. 2000. A Comparative Analysis of Critical Issues Facing Canadian Information Systems Personnel: A National and Global Perspective. Information and Management, 38: 73-86.)

Rank 2. IT strategic planning: Ranked number two in 1991, this issue moved to number ten in 1996 and moved back up to number two in the 2003 study. Strategic planning refers to IT planning that supports the business goals, mission, and strategies of the organization. With the role of IT elevated to a strategic partner for obtaining competitive advantage and achieving superior performance, the need for strategic IT planning is of paramount importance. Over the years, organizations have put processes in place to conduct IT strategic planning on a continuous basis. Yet, strategic planning remains a thorny issue for both senior IS and non-executives. The rate of technological change requires the ability to develop quick courses of action at economical costs, before the innovations become obsolete. Further exacerbating matters is the rapid organizational change as well as environmental change outside of the organization. In spite of the difficulties (perhaps because of them), this issue has remained one of the top issues in the past continues to be a dominant one today.

Rank 3. Security and privacy: This issue was not present in any of the previous studies and appeared strongly at rank 3 in the 2003 study. The tragedy of 9/11 has reinforced the importance of information systems in the United States and their vulnerability to viruses, hackers and terrorists. At the same time there is compelling pressure from the general public demanding greater protection from identity theft and other privacy thefts. Current academic and practitioner literature suggests that security and privacy will remain important concerns for IT executives in at least the short and mid term.

Rank 4. Attracting, developing, and retaining IT professionals: This issue has again gained recognition after moving to number 8 in 1996 from number 4 in 1991. Human resources for IS include technical as well as managerial personnel. The factor includes such concerns as planning for human resources, hiring, retaining, and developing human resources. The economic slowdown of recent years and the dot com crash may have created greater supply than demand for IT skills. Contributing to the demand and supply was also the much reported emphasis by companies on offshore outsourcing. However in 2003, the situation started changing as the economy started to improve and the IS managers began to take a long term view of investing in their professional staff. With offshoring and globalization, different skills are needed to manage international development teams and networks; these skills are new and scarce in the US. Among others, these skills include project management, vendor relationships, and compliance.

Rank 5. Measuring the value of IT investments: Although this issue has appeared in previous key issues studies, the issue was never ranked very high. However, in the 2003 study, it has received significant attention. Information technology has always taken a substantial portion of organizational assets and it is a good sign that executives are now insisting on value. There are at least two reasons for this emphasis on value: the dot com bust at the turn of the century prior to which huge investments were made without regard to returns, and the steep rise in offshore outsourcing to India and China. Because of deep cost savings possible because of offshore outsourcing, corporations have become fiercely competitive in their drive to extract maximum value out of each single dollar.

Rank 6. Measuring the performance of the IT organization: This issue is related to the previous one and it should be no surprise that it ranks next to it. As the adage goes, you cannot manage or improve something which you cannot measure. This issue presents IS executives with questions like, "Are we delivering the applications in a cost effective fashion?" and "Can we measure our contributions in a meaningful way?" After declining steadily over the past decade, IS effectiveness measurement has increased in rank due to a renewed interest in cost justification in light of constantly improving technologies, relentless competition, and inexpensive service provided by countless vendors both within the country and offshore. As a result, many companies are initiating programs to develop and measure IT metrics. The availability of metrics is the first step in their quest to move up the quality ladder as measured by their CMM (Capability Maturity Model) level.

Rank 7. Creating an information architecture: This issue declined somewhat after having been ranked number 4 in 1996 and number 1 in 1991. An information architecture is a high level map of the information requirements of an organization. Also called the enterprise model, it provides the overall framework to guide application development and database development. It includes the major classes of information (i.e., entities) and their relationships to various functions and processes in the organization. The steps included in enterprise modeling are functional decomposition, entity-relationship diagrams, and planning metrics. Many corporations, by and large, today have an acceptable information architecture in place and many have aggressively moved into the areas of data warehousing and data mining.

Rank 8. Complexity reduction: This issue was not included in any of the previous studies. The issue by itself does not refer to any specific item in Information Technology but to the myriad of functional activities involved in IS management. In describing complexity, Luftman and McLean refer to the variety of IT platforms and configurations which make information architectures complex. They also refer to continual changes and upgrades made by the vendors.

Rank 9. Speed and agility: This issue was also not listed in any of the previous studies. Again it does not refer to any specific item in Information Technology. Rather it reflects the heightened pace of business today. As Luftman and McLean state, IT organizations that can respond in cybertime may contribute to the difference between leading and following. Certainly the advent of the Internet has leveled the playing field, and allowed both large and small organizations to respond quickly to new opportunities and changing customer needs. It is increasingly important for IS executives to be able to quickly sense and respond.

Rank 10. IT governance: This issue appeared for the first time in its current form, although different manifestations (e.g., aligning with the organizational) have appeared in previous studies. There are numerous options available to IS executives for organizing and governing IT and there is no universally best answer. Different governance mechanisms (e.g., centralized vs. decentralized, use of steering committees) are suitable based on surrounding contextual conditions.

Other Issues: Ranked at number eleven was business process reengineering (BPR). BPR was also one of the highly ranked issues in the 1994/1995 study. The importance of this issue is attributable to the need for major changes in both internal and external processes in the previous decade to adjust to the ongoing massive changes in the environment and the marketplace. Consistent with speed and agility, "introducing rapid business solutions" came in twelfth place. Another issue that appeared for the first time was the CIO's leadership role and its evolving nature.

Issues that ranked below the top thirteen include IT asset management, managing outsourcing relationships, leveraging the legacy investments, Sarbanes-Oxley Act of 2002, globalization, offshore outsourcing impacts on IT careers, and societal implications of IT. It is apparent that the top issues have a strategic orientation, and relate to planning and successful use of emerging technologies in the organization. What is conspicuous by its absence are any references to Internet related issues and e-commerce. These issues were not present in the 1994/95 study but that was understandable given the fact that the Internet and the Worldwide Web were just beginning to be introduced to the world at that time. But absence of these issues in the 2003 study raises some concerns. Perhaps the Internet related issues were not explicitly expressed by the executives but are indirectly captured by the other issues (e.g., information architecture and security).

KEY MIS ISSUES IN NEWLY INDUSTRIALIZED COUNTRIES

Several countries have made rapid economic growth in just over a decade. These countries have emerged as the "newly industrialized countries (NICs)" and are now beginning to prosper. While the precise categorization of any country into any class is somewhat contentious, and is also subject to movement over time, countries like Taiwan, Hong Kong, Ireland, South Korea, and Singapore fall into this group. Some will argue that the BRIC countries (Brazil, Russia, India, and China) are rapidly approaching this status, although as a whole each of the BRIC countries falls short of the other countries. The latest key issue results that are available from some of these countries are included in the chapter. Hong Kong issues were reported by Ma (1999), Moores (1996), and Taiwan issues by Chou and Jou (1999). The Taiwan issues are presented in Table 3 and Hong Kong issues are presented in Table 4. Once again, there is a certain degree of similarity between these countries' issues. We discuss only the Taiwan issues as representative of issues of newly industrialized countries, as it is the most recent study of all.

Key Issue Ranks

The key IS issues in Taiwan (Chou and Jou, 1999) were obtained by conducting a survey of senior managers in Taiwan, who were well-versed in technology. Responses were obtained from 118 managers on a 10-point Likert scale on 27 issues. The majority of the respondents were IS executives. A wide range of organizations, both in terms of size and type of business were represented in the study. The ranked list is provided in Table 3. Once again, we focus on the top ten issues.

Rank 1. Developing effective communication with end users: This issue has played an important role all through the decade of the 90's in Taiwan. It was also ranked number one in the prior study by Palvia and Wang (1995). Communication between two groups of people: end user and developers is necessary as one group is the user and the other the builder. End users in Taiwan seem to be unable to specify their information needs accurately to the IS group. They also have an unrealistic expectation of the technology's capabilities and expect the IS staff to quickly automate all of their operations. At the same time, IS employees may lack a good understanding of the organization's business processes, and use terminology that end users do not understand. The communication problem between the users and the IS community is further aggravated due to the low level of communication skills among IS graduates.

Rank	Description of the Issue
#1	Developing effective communication with end users
#2	Developing effective communications with senior manager
#3	Satisfying users' needs
#4	Using information systems for competitive advantage
#5	Aligning the IS organization with the enterprise
#6	Making effective use of the data resource
#7	Developing a better promotion channel for IS professionals
#8	Building a responsive information technology infrastructure
#9	Providing better systems interface standards for applications integration
#10	Improving the effectiveness of software development
#11	Planning and managing communication networks
#12	Improving IS strategic planning
#13	Keeping the organization's IT applications portfolio up to date
#14	Recruiting and developing IS human resources
#15	Increasing understanding of IS role and contribution
#16	Keeping close agreement between enterprise's and the IS group's goals
#17	Measuring IS effectiveness and productivity
#18	Helping business reengineering
#19	Facilitating organizational learning
#20	Developing and maintaining an information architecture
#21	Developing and managing distributed systems
#22	Facilitating and managing end-user computing
#23	Implementing and managing collaborative support systems
#24	Developing and managing electronic data interchange
#25	Using object-oriented programming
#26	Planning and integrating multivendor open systems
#27	Outsourcing selected information services

Table 3. Key Issues for IT Executives - Taiwan (1999) (Source: Chou, H. W. and Jou, S. B. 1999. MIS Key Issues in Taiwan's Enterprises. International Journal of Information Management, 19:369-

Rank 2. Developing effective communications with senior manager: This issue though named differently from before deals with the issue of top management support and communication with senior managers. Ranked second in the 1995 study, it stayed at the same rank in the 1999 study also. Top management support is required as IS projects require substantial financial and human resources. They also may take long periods of time to complete. As such, the call for top management support is pervasive in the MIS literature. Taiwan is no exception. Senior management is expected to demonstrate its support by both allocating suitable budget for the IS department, and by showing leadership and involvement. At the same time, top management support will strengthen the IS department by helping acquire the support of other functional departments. Without strong top management endorsement and support, the IS department would have little chance to achieve its mission.

Rank	Description of the Issue
#1	Improving the effectiveness of software development
#2	Building a responsive IT infrastructure
#3	Increasing understanding of IS role and contribution
#4	Making effective use of the data resource
#5.5	Developing and implementing an information architecture
#5.5	Aligning the IS organization within the enterprise
#7	Improving IS strategic planning
#8	Using information system for competitive advantage
#9	Facilitating and managing end-user computing
#10	Managing the existing portfolio of legacy applications
#11.5	Measuring IS effectiveness and productivity
#11.5	Planning and managing communication networks
#13	Improving information security and control
#14	Facilitating and managing business process redesign
#15	Recruiting and developing IS human resources
#16	Establishing effective disaster recovery capabilities
#17	Facilitating organization learning
#18	Implementing and managing collaborative support system
#19	Planning and integrating multi-vendor open system technologies
#20	Developing and managing distributed systems
#21	Facilitating/managing decision and executive support systems
#22	Developing and managing electronic data interchange (EDI)
#23	Outsourcing selected information services
#24	Planning and using CASE technology

Table 4: Key Issues for IT Executives - Hong Kong (1999)
(Source: Ma, L.C.K. Critical Issues of Information Systems Management in Hong Kong, City University of Hong Kong, Working Paper. 1999.)

Rank 3. Satisfying users' needs: End users in the various functional departments of an organization have many informational needs and these needs keep changing and evolving. It is virtually impossible for IS departments to meet each and every request in a timely manner. Many systems are developed late and over-budget and unfortunately, many development efforts still fail. Management frustration with IT costs and backlog of new system requests have led to alternative solutions for centralized system development. These solutions include developing only critical applications as prioritized by a steering committee, small application development by end users themselves, and outsourcing.

Rank 4. Using information systems for competitive advantage: Consistently at fourth place in both 1995 and 1999 studies, this issue deals with deriving competitive advantage from use the of IT in an organization. In the private sector, several retail, wholesale, transportation, and media firms have begun to build information systems that can be utilized to make new inroads, create business opportunities, and enable an organization to differentiate itself in the marketplace. Even public organizations have made progress. Stories of how public organizations (e.g., a government-run hospital and the administrative office of a village) use IT to improve their administrative effectiveness and reduce the waiting time of citizens have been reported. The aggressive promotion of IT by the government has helped to further raise the IS practitioner's consciousness of the competitive impacts of information technology.

Rank 5. Aligning the IS organization with the enterprise: The organizational positioning of the IS department within a company can have a direct impact on its effectiveness. In the early days of computing, IS was relegated to Accounting or Personnel departments and had the image of an overhead function. While this image has changed, there are also issues related to alignment. For those who view IS as a strategic function, the IS department has moved to the top of the organizational hierarchy. Large companies have positions such as Chief Information Officer (CIO), Chief Technology Officer (CTO) and Chief Knowledge Officer (CKO). Another issue related to alignment is whether the IS organization is centralized, decentralized or distributed within the enterprise. A properly aligned IS organization contributes to serving the organizational goals of the company and minimizes potential conflicts and sub-optimization of IS resources.

Rank 6. Making effective use of the data resource: This issue was ranked fourteen in the 1995 study and sharply rose to its current rank in the 1999 study. Data are widely regarded as a vital resource for an organization. Data and information are important corporate resources and not in the domain of an individual or subgroup. Firms collect massive amounts of not only internal data but also from external sources such as customers, suppliers, government, and other firms. Consistent with studies of key issues in developed and advanced countries, recent research emphasizes the notion that organizational data are still largely unrecognized, inaccessible, and underutilized. The IS function must develop a climate within its department and throughout the organization that values data as a corporate asset. The organization must develop a discipline for managing data and get more value out of it. The emergence of this issue at such a high rank denotes a strategic shift in the perceptions of Taiwan's IS organizations and executives.

Rank 7. Developing a better promotion channel for IS professionals: This issue was also ranked low at the eighteen position in the 1995 study. Current and future shortages of qualified IS personnel threaten many organizations' ability to make effective use of information technology. There is also a shift in the types of skills required by the IS professionals. For example, organizations outsourcing their work to other countries have the need to develop project management and vendor relationship skills. Given the rapid pace of changes in the IS field and the many opportunities available to IS professionals worldwide, it is vital for an organization to be able to not only recruit but also maintain the best IS talent that is available. This concern is further underscored in the issue ranked at the fourteenth position.

Rank 8. Building a responsive information technology infrastructure: Ranked at seventh position in the 1995 study, this issue did not move much in the 1999 study. In vibrant economies, a responsive IT infrastructure is vital to the flexibility and changing needs of a business organization. The technology infrastructure issue is exacerbated by a combination of evolving technology platforms, integration of custom-engineered and packaged application software, and the rigidity of existing applications. Many Taiwanese organizations are gradually realizing that building an infrastructure, which will support existing business applications while remaining responsive to changes, is a key to long-term enterprise productivity.

Rank 9. Providing better systems interface standards for applications integration: This issue shifted from rank eight in 1995 study to nine in the 1999 study. Integration of various system components into a unified whole provides benefits of synergy, effectiveness, and added value to the user. Many IS managers in Taiwan are recognizing the need to integrate the "islands of automation" (e.g., data processing, office automation, factory automation) into an integrated single entity. In the past, the execution of systems integration had encountered great difficulty due to lack of IS standards, insufficient technical ability, and inadequate coordination among functional departments. However, open systems, networks, client/server architecture, and standardization of IT products (promoted by the government) are expected to make systems integration easier in the future.

Rank 10. Improving the effectiveness of software development: This issue did not move much either; it was ranked at number nine in the 1995 study. Effectiveness and productivity can be measured by examining both inputs and outputs to the IS function. On both outputs, e.g., the quality and magnitude of software produced, and inputs, e.g., total time to complete a project and the total man-hours, IS had a dismal record. End users (and sometimes IS professionals) complain that it takes excessively long to build and modify applications. The speed of development is not able to keep pace with changing business needs. Possible explanations and reasons include: insufficient technical skills, high IS staff turnover, lack of use of software productivity tools, and inadequate user participation. However, recent years have seen vast improvements in productivity. For example, open software, reusable code and visual programming languages have contributed to rapid software development.

Other Issues: Issues rated just below top ten included: planning and managing communication networks, IS strategic planning, application portfolio, IS human resources and understanding IS role and contribution. Note that some of these were rated among the top issues in the US study. Thus some of the top strategic issues are not as much of a concern in Taiwan. Issues toward the bottom include: using object oriented programming, outsourcing selected information services, managing electronic data interchange, and implementing collaborative systems. These appear to be operational in nature; they seem to be well under control and as such not critical concerns in Taiwan.

KEY MIS ISSUES IN DEVELOPING COUNTRIES

Countries which can be loosely qualified as developing countries include: Thailand, Brazil, Indonesia, Slovenia, India, and Mexico. As commented earlier, the BRIC countries (Brazil, Russia, India, and China) are sharply on the rise in terms of their economic development; however as a whole they each have a long way to go. These countries have been using information technology for a number of years, yet their level of IT sophistication and types of applications may be wanting in several respects. Previous studies indicate that politics, law, culture, economics, technology infrastructure and the availability of skilled personnel have greatly influenced the difference in IS management concerns between developed and developing countries (Pimchangthong, 2003). While organizations in developing countries may have access to the technology for computerization, they do not have carefully prepared plans for developing computerized information systems (Nils, 1998). For example, Pimchangthong et al. (2003) report that, in Thailand, building the IT infrastructure was going to be the top issue for the next three to five years. Many of these concerns are caused by the lack of an integrated policy toward informatics and telecommunication industries, and paucity of quality training programs. Similar obstacles are faced by many other developing countries like Slovenia and Indonesia. As an example, in Indonesia, Samik-Ibrahim (2001) describes IS human resource as the top most concern. With the emergence of many eastern block countries out of closed and guarded environments, and the general trends towards globalization, information is now available about the IT readiness of these countries. While the information is derived from individual experiences, general observations, and case studies (e.g., Chepaitis, 2002; Goodman, 1991), many of these countries seem to face similar problems.

Russia and several former Soviet Union countries defy a natural classification into any of our four classes. In fact, the World Bank places the former socialist countries in a separate category in and of itself. Traditionally, there were two sectors of Soviet computing: the state sector which included development and deployment of a full range of highly sophisticated computers, and the mixed sector of private, state, foreign and black-marketing activities which were struggling in the sustained use of information technology. While giant centrally planned enterprises were created that emulated technological developments of the West, little computer equipment was either designed for or used by management and consumers. Thus, while Russia and former Soviet Union countries made great strides in selected technological areas (e.g., space program, and aerospace industry), the general consumer sector and management lagged behind significantly in IT utilization. Back in 2002, Chepaitis (2002) observed that the lack of adequate supply of quality information and poor information culture were IS issues reflective of Russia. However many things have changed in Russia since then. The country and its entrepreneurial leaders are beginning to enjoy the advantages of its highly trained workforce in engineering and technology. In fact, all four countries: Brazil, Russia, India, and China are reaping the benefits of offshore IT outsourcing. Nevertheless, the underprivileged masses in these countries have not been able to participate in this revolution (Friedman, 2005).

Examples of recent key issue studies in developing countries are in Thailand (Pimchangthong et. al., 2003) and Indonesia (Samik-Ibrahim, 2001). Their results are shown in Tables 5 and 6 respectively. The later study in Thailand provided a prioritized list of ranked issues based on a systematic methodology. We present the Thailand results as an example of issues from a developed country.

Key Issue Ranks

The key IS issues in Thailand were obtained by Pimchangthong et al., (2003) and were based on data collection using a custom made online, web-based, three-tier survey system from Thai IS academics and practitioners. One hundred and sixty one subjects participated representing a 64% response rate. Respondents were located through a network of friends and associates and for each participant an account was created on the survey system, which automatically sent them a customized e-mail invitation to participate at the survey website and also provided them an automatically generated personal access code to the survey. The issues considered were selected from the literature and the study followed the Q-sort ranking technique. The following discussion draws primarily from their study.

Rank	Description of the Issue
#1	Building IT infrastructure
#2	IS strategic planning
#3	IS human resources
#4	Quality of software development process
#5	Electronic data interchange
#6	IS organizational alignment
#7	Data resources
#8	IS disaster recovery
#9	Telecommunication and network systems
#10	IS architecture

Table 5. Key Issues for IT Executives – Thailand (2003) (Source: Pimchangthong, D., Plaisent, M., and Bernard, P. 2003. Key Issues in Information Systems Management: A comparative study of Academics and Practitioners in Thailand. Journal of Global Information Technology Management, 6(4): 27.

Rank 1. Building IT infrastructure: The issue of building IT infrastructure was ranked in first position by IS academicians and practitioners in Thailand. This issue has also been ranked high by advanced countries like Canada and Australia. It was ranked number eight in the Taiwan study. In Indonesia, it was ranked at number two. The IS professionals in Thailand believe that the lack of necessary infrastructure limits their ability to effectively build and use information systems. However, the meaning of infrastructure can be different in different economies. In the developed countries, it could mean the building of technologically advanced and highly efficient capabilities, while in the developing economies it could mean the development of more basic levels of support.

Rank 2. IS strategic planning: This issue is about aligning the IS plan with the strategic plan of the organization to help achieve organizational goals. The high ranking of this issue indicates a shift of IS importance to more strategic concerns within organizations in developing countries. However, this issue is ranked much lower in the Indonesian study, which points to the difference in economic growth and IS orientation of managers in the two countries. It appears that once the IS function is able to support the operational and service needs of a company, executives begin to find ways to use IS as a strategic tool for further business growth and advancement.

Rank 3. IS human resources: More of an operational issue, IS human resources was ranked the third most important issue by IS professionals and academicians in Thailand. It was perceived by managers that the current and future shortages of qualified IS personnel will threaten the organization's ability to make effective use of information technology. Firms need to have appropriate plans in place to recruit qualified professionals and at the same time minimize turnover by providing incentives and a higher quality of work life. The IS professionals believe that career paths need to be clarified and emphasis be placed on developing effective business skills along with the development of IT skills.

Rank 4. Quality of software development process: The IS managers and professionals in Thailand are concerned about the quality of the software and the development process to build software. Many believe that more effective software tools and techniques are needed to improve the development of software and satisfy the system demands of the users. More skilled system analysts and project managers are needed who understand the systems development life cycle (SDLC) and quality control techniques. In fact, many developing countries which are IS outsourcing destinations, e.g., India, China, and Russia, have undertaken major efforts to improve their software processes in order to achieve higher levels of CMM certification.

Rank	Description of the Issue
#1	IS human resources
#2	Responsive IT infrastructure
#3	Software licenses / free software
#4	Multivendor open system
#5	Communication network
#6	IS effectiveness measurement
#7	Software development
#8	Collaborative systems
#9	IS role and contribution
#10	Organizational learning
#11	Business process redesign
#12	IS strategic planning
#13	Data resource
#14	End user computing
#15	IS organization alignment
#16	Outsourcing
#17	Distributed systems
#18	Information architecture
#19	Legacy applications
#20	Electronic data interchange

Table 6. Key Issues for IT Executives – Indonesia (2001) (Source: Samik-Ibrahim, R. M. 2001. Key Issues in Information Management: Indonesia. http://rms46.vlsm.org/1/22.html.)

Rank 5. Electronic data interchange: One of the key ingredients for IS success in business is electronic data interchange (EDI). EDI involves exchanging inter organizational data in a predefined format through telecommunications systems, such as for e-commerce with consumers and business-to-business (B2B) transactions. EDI has evolved over the years. Traditional EDI solutions used to be expensive and only large firms and trading partners could participate. However, now web-based EDI systems using emerging technologies like XML and JAVA are within the reach of even small and medium-sized customers, partners and suppliers. The importance of this issue in Thailand demonstrates the need for automation of communication between customers and business partners in order to compete in the global economy.

Rank 6. IS organizational alignment: The IS organizational alignment issue is about the proper placement of the IS department in the organizational hierarchy of the enterprise. The organizational positioning of the IS department can have a direct impact on the effectiveness of the IS function. The alignment of IS in the organization is also reflected by who represents IS at the highest executive level (e.g., a Chief Information Officer). Additionally, the IS resources need to be aligned with the enterprise structure, making proper use of centralized, decentralized, and distributed alternatives.

Rank 7. Data resources: The data resource pertains to the organizational data, its size, complexity, and value for the business. Data is increasingly regarded as a vital resource for an organization, especially for the information systems function and application development. This issue appeared at number six in the Taiwan study and although it did not appear in the latest US study, it was among the top ten in prior US studies. As developing countries march into the global world and compete with counterparts in the western world, they seem to face similar IS management issues. They must manage the data resource so that it can be accessed, properly harnessed and leveraged for maximum benefit to the organization. The importance of this issue also implies that there will be greater demand for better data storage systems and database management systems in the coming years.

Rank 8. IS disaster recovery: Ranked at number eight, this issue has gained importance in the wake of recent natural catastrophes in South Asia. The Thai IS professionals realize that their business depends increasingly on information technology and the risks from potential losses due to a disaster are too great to ignore. These risks become proportionately greater as enterprise applications grow and become more integrated. Effective recovery plans must be in place and tested regularly to ensure that losses are minimized.

Rank 9. Telecommunication and network systems: Telecommunication systems provide the backbone for an organization to do business anywhere, anytime, without being constrained by time or distance. Telecommunications networks have become a major resource in the competitive world. Historically, the developing world has lagged behind in the development of telecommunication and network systems. However, recent years have seen a dramatic improvement in both the quality and quantity of such systems. Telecommunication rates have steadily declined and the number of telephones (either land line or cell) has increased substantially in much of the developing world. Nevertheless, implementation of telecommunication systems poses challenges for organizations in terms of huge financial investments and lack of common industry standards.

Rank 10. IS architecture: IS architecture was ranked at number ten by Thai IS academicians and professionals. This issue has consistently remained in the top ten in the US studies, although it has seen a small decline in recent years. It is typically associated with sound planning practices in an organization. The IS architecture is an analysis of the information requirements of a firm and it guides long-term application and database development. It also facilitates the integration and sharing of data both internal and external to an enterprise. The emergence of this issue in the top ten in Thailand suggests that the developing world has begun paying attention to planning and long-term issues in IS management.

KEY MIS ISSUES IN UNDERDEVELOPED COUNTRIES

Underdeveloped or basic countries are characterized by low or stagnant economic growth, low GNP, high levels of poverty, low literacy rates, high unemployment, agriculture as the dominant sector, and poor national infrastructure. While precise categorization is difficult, subjective and arguable, countries like Bangladesh, Cuba, Haiti, Jordan, Kenya, Nigeria, Iran, Iraq, and Zimbabwe may be included in this group. Note that countries may move in and out of a particular class over time. In this chapter, we use an African country, namely Nigeria, as representation for underdeveloped countries. We were unable to locate a published report on information management issues in at least the last ten years from any under developed nation. The Nigerian study is a working paper and was obtained directly from the author.

Key Issue Ranks
The key MIS issues of Nigeria were reported by Badamas (2004) in an unpublished working paper. The methodology used by Badamas was based on an exploratory survey of seventy six IS managers in Nigeria. The sample consisted of IS managers employed in banks, manufacturing, and service industries in Lagos, the commercial capital of Nigeria, where most organizations have their headquarters. A list of the key issues was compiled from existing literature and respondents were asked to rate these issues on a scale of 1-5.

Like many under-developed countries, Nigeria can be classified as poor in the information technology resource and its use by local firms. There is a general lack of computing technologies in private firms and government agencies and their exploitation is inadequate. Many seem to be in the early stages of computing, some even in the pre-computing stage (Tiamiyu, 2000). There are significant obstacles to progress in information technology, e.g., unsatisfactory power supply, lack of technology infrastructure, and inadequate government policy or initiatives. The situation is exacerbated by the virtual absence of skilled IS human resources and an inadequate educational system that produces trained IT undergraduates and graduates. The Nigerian results represent the concerns of some of the poorest countries in the world. Table 7 presents the ranking of 29 issues faced by Nigerian IS managers. The discussion of the top ten issues borrows heavily from the Badamas' study.

Rank 1. Power supply: Power supply is considered the most important key issue in Nigeria because of the erratic nature of electricity supply by the government-owned electricity company. The constant disruptions of operations caused by power cuts are major concerns to management information systems managers. The alternative sources of electricity are generators which are installed for nearly all the major companies and organizations. However, constant shortage of diesel and oil for generators make these alternative sources also unreliable. The developed world may take power supply for granted, but in the under-developed countries it becomes a matter of great concern to IS managers.

Rank 2. Information system and data security: Information system and data security are rated next to the need for continuous power supply. Information security is important for managers, especially in an environment where there are no established information security policies. MIS managers are always unsure about the activities of fraudulent employees using computer and information technology. Data contained in prior manual systems was not very vulnerable to breach of security due to either unavailability of ready access or inordinately long access times. As a result, many information workers have developed poor habits in data handing. This attitude can cause severe security and integrity problems in computerized systems. Furthermore, there is no doubt that cybercrime is an image nightmare for Nigeria. The classic example is the infamous "Nigerian Scam" or "419 Scam" where the sender asks for an advance fee in return for substantial amounts of money.

Rank	Description of Issue
#1	Power supply
#2	Information system and data security
#3	Availability of skilled human resources
#4	Hardware maintenance
#5	Planning communication networks
#6	Telecommunication and network security
#7	Quality of input data
#8	IS strategic planning
#9	Top management support for info. system
#10	IS dept. and end-user communication
#11	Opportunities for professional development
#12	Improvement of IS productivity
#13	User friendliness of systems
#14	Telecommunication infrastructure
#15	IT infrastructure
#16	System integration
#17	Establishment of professional standards
#18	IS funding level
#19	User participation
#20	Availability of software packages
#21	Placement of IS dept. in the organization
#22	Computerization of routine work
#23	Government influence in computer market
#24	Proliferation of vendors
#25	Level of economic development
#26	Obsolete software
#27	Cultural and traditional influences
#28	Obsolete hardware
#29	Political instability

Table 7. Key Issues for IT Executives – Nigeria (2004) (Source: Badamas, M. A. 2004. Critical issues in the Management of Information Systems in Nigeria. Working Paper.)

Rank 3. Availability of skilled human resources: Availability of skilled human resources is ranked high because of the need to have the necessary manpower. There is a shortage of people with computing and system skills. Finding trained personnel and keeping existing information systems people current with the latest advances in IT are vital concerns of information system managers in less developed countries. The IT professionals must understand that they work in an organization that has broad responsibility to plan, develop, implement and manage computers, communication facilities, data and enterprise information processing systems. While the concepts of business process design, e-business design and change management must be understood by the IT professionals, they must also have sound technical knowledge of hardware, software and communications.

Rank 4. Hardware maintenance: Ranked at fourth position, this issue is related to lack of skilled manpower to support and maintain the available hardware in Nigerian organizations. A related concern is the availability of state of the art computing equipment and required services for this equipment. There is only one plant assembling personal computers in the country, and the brand of its product is not very well known. There are various makes of IT equipment imported from all over the world and there are not enough maintenance facilities. If the hardware breaks down and cannot be repaired in a timely manner, it compounds the problem of inadequate computing infrastructure.

Rank 5. Planning communication networks: Planning communication networks is the next critical issue. Telecommunication networks are essential in this age and time, and they provide the backbone connectivity in order to conduct business. Even today, the underdeveloped countries are the farthest behind in their telecommunications infrastructure. With the lack of public sector support and inadequate and unreliable infrastructure, planning and managing these networks becomes extremely difficult, and is a source of concern for many managers. With privatization of the telecommunication sector on the horizon, firms should be able to see improvements coming their way soon. For example, six firms have been short-listed in an attempt to privatize the Nigerian Telecommunications Plc. (NITEL) and it is expected that the privatization of NITEL would be concluded sometime in 2006.

Rank 6. Telecommunication and network security: Security shows up again as a critical issue, this time in the form of telecommunication and network security. Related to the previous issue, it also requires adequate communication infrastructure and public sector support. Poor and unreliable telecommunication and networks cannot provide the needed security for developing, exchanging and managing electronic communications and data interchange. Many concerns make up this issue, e.g., service outages, improper access, data integrity, disclosure of sensitive information, and damage to the infrastructure. Cyber security remains an obstacle to a society's development and can perpetuate the digital divide in less developed countries if the under-privileged segments cannot be (securely) connected to the rest of the world.

Rank 7. Quality of input data: Information systems rely on accurate and reliable data. The age-old adage of GIGO (Garbage In Garbage Out) is well known in MIS, and directly impacts the quality of IS. This issue has also been seen in Russia and India (Chepaitis, 2002; Palvia et al., 2002) and other developing countries. While not reported as a key issue in US studies, it appears that less developed countries have inferior input data due to several reasons: lack of information literacy and information culture among workers as well as a less-than-adequate infrastructure for collecting data. Some managers reported experiences of excessive errors in data transcription as well as deliberate corruption of data. The underlying causes may be mistrust and intimidation caused by computer processing, resulting in carelessness, apathy and sabotage.

Rank 8. IS strategic planning: While being used to automate manual and laborious processes, it is recognized that information technology can be utilized to achieve higher level organizational goals and strategic needs. Information systems strategic planning is important, but lack of familiarity with

IS planning methodologies, rapidly changing economic and business environment and the constant change of technology make information system strategic planning difficult in Nigeria. Many of the organizations operating in the country are beginning to rely on information technology. However, long term business plans are not aligned with IS plans. This issue is almost always present in advanced and newly industrialized countries. But its emergence in under-developed countries signifies that they are beginning to look beyond their short-term operational needs.

Rank 9. Top management support for information systems: Top management support for information systems is another issue that IS managers in Nigeria considered critical. Top managers in most of the organizations were not familiar with information technology during their entry level days and in earlier functions. They seem to still consider IT and IS as necessary nuisances in an organization. Since IS has not proven its strategic relevance in Nigeria, it has been difficult for IS managers to receive support from top managers. Top management support is essential as many IS projects require substantial commitment of financial and human resources. In order to succeed, senior management must demonstrate its support by both allocating suitable budget for the IS department, and by showing leadership and involvement. At the same time, top management support will strengthen the IS department by helping acquire the support of other functional departments.

Rank 10. IS department and end-user communication: An appreciation of the benefits and potential applications of MIS is absolutely necessary for successful IT deployment. There is a general lack of knowledge among Nigerian managers as to what MIS can do for their business and adding to the problem is the lack of communication channels between IS department and other departments within an enterprise. For example, personal computers are part of the "furniture" for end-users who do not see the relevance of IS in their functions. Communication between the IS department and end-users is critical so that useful applications are developed and used for the benefit of the organization. Specific end-user roles and communication channels must first be defined to allow the IS department to communicate effectively with them. At the same time, the IS employees need to develop an understanding of the organization's business processes and learn to speak the language of the end-users.

OTHER KEY MIS ISSUES

Some regions of the world have special characteristics and defy the four-way classification suggested above. One region is the countries of the former Soviet Union and the other is the Arab world. We briefly describe key IS issues from recent studies conducted in Estonia (Table 8), representing the former Soviet Union, and in Kuwait (Table 9), representing the Arab world.

The Estonia study (Ifinedo, 2006) was conducted in 2005 using the established Delphi method. Forty seven IS managers were surveyed which resulted in a list of 25 key issues. It was concluded that half of the critical issues present in 1990s, such as "Improving information security and control," "Building and maintaining reliable information systems," and "Promoting standards for hardware, software and data" are important for the 2000s as well. Further, many of the higher-ranked issues in the top ten list for Estonia are operational in nature, which might be a reflection of the country's economic development level.

The Kuwait study (Alshawaf, 2002) interviewed 62 IS managers and comprised a list of 25 IS issues for professionals in Kuwait. The findings depict that IT is not used to its full potential, as in many developing countries. Disaster recovery and information security were the top ranked concerns (possibly due to the country's vulnerability in the light of current events). These were followed by effective management of data resources, building an effective IT infrastructure, and educating senior management. Planning issues came next. In a sense, the issues were mixed between operational and strategic factors. It was concluded that managers in Kuwait should leverage their investments in IT by focusing on the effective use of IT and measurement of its impacts.

Rank	Description of Issue
#1	Improving information security and control
#2	Making effective use of data resource
#3	Building and maintaining reliable information systems
#4	Assuring software quality
#5	Enterprise systems e.g. ERP and EDI
#6	Promoting standards for hardware, software and data
#7	Using IT satisfy the needs of users/organizations
#8	IT awareness among top management/leaders
#9	Improving the general IT skills of end-users
#10	Improving inter-organizational IS planning
#11	Recruiting and developing IS human resource
#12	Keeping updated with new trends in IT
#13	Improving link between IS strategy and business strategy
#14	Implementing IT for e-commerce/e-government
#15	Measuring IS effectiveness and productivity
#16	Ensuring the physical security of computer systems
#17	Implementing and improving computer networks
#18	Using IT for competitive advantage
#19	Organizational learning and the use of IS technologies
#20	Planning and implementing a telecommunication systems
#21	Developing an information architecture
#22	Alliances and linkages with other Western (EU) organizations
#23	Legislating software copyright protection
#24	Building and controlling a responsive IS infrastructure
#25	Loss of skilled IT workers to foreign countries

Table 8. Key Issues for IT Executives –Estonia (2006) (Source: Ifinedo, P. 2006. Key Information Systems Management Issues in Estonia for the 2000s: A Comparative Analysis. Journal of Global Information Technology Management, Vol. 9, No 2, 22-44)

A MODEL OF GLOBAL INFORMATION TECHNOLOGY ENVIRONMENT

The prior review and discussion show that there are major differences between issues of different countries, and few commonalties. There were more common issues between USA and Taiwan, and fewer between other countries. As an overall impression, it seems that advanced countries are driven by strategic needs, developing countries by operational needs, and under-developed countries by basic survival needs. Based on this observation, Palvia et al., (1992) posited an initial model of country specific MIS issues based on economic development of the country. This model classified countries into three categories based on the level of economic growth. These categories are: advanced countries (e.g., United States, Canada, Japan), developing/operational countries (e.g., India, Russia, Argentina, Brazil), and under-developed/basic countries (e.g., Kenya, Chile, Iran, Nigeria). They acknowledged that the placement of a country into a particular category is subject to some debate, and that countries may change categories over time. Nonetheless, they were able to make some broad generalizations on the nature of IS issues based on economic growth of a nation. According to the model, the level of IT adoption increases from one stage to next, i.e., from underdeveloped to developing to advanced countries. Quite striking are the types of IS issues at each stage of economic development. In the underdeveloped countries, the survival issues dominate (e.g., power supply, availability of computer hardware, operating and applications software, and human resources for MIS). In the developing countries, operational issues are paramount (e.g., human resource development for MIS, the quality of software development, telecommunications, and disaster recovery. Advanced country issues are characterized by strategic needs (e.g., IT strategic planning, information architecture, IT and business alignment, data resource management, measuring the value of IT).

While the Palvia et al., (1992) model appears to be generally sound, the Taiwan study and experience from other countries like Hong Kong led us to refine the model (Palvia et al., 2002). Another class of countries was added to the original three-way classification (Figure 1). Several countries have emerged as the newly industrialized countries in the last decade and are now prospering. Examples of such countries include Taiwan, South Korea, Hong Kong and Singapore. Once again, the BRIC countries (Brazil, Russia, India and China) are closing in on this status. If we extrapolate the Taiwan issues to NICs in general, then many of the NIC issues are similar to the advanced country issues but there are also many differences. Representative NIC issues include strategic issues like: information systems for competitive advantage, aligning the IS function with the business, making effective use of the data resource, and building a responsive IT infrastructure. But they also include operational issues like: communication with end users,

Rank	Description of Issue
#1*	Establishing effective disaster recovery capabilities
#1*	Improving information security and control
#3	Making effective use of data resources
#4	Building a responsive IT infrastructure
#5	Educating senior management
#6	Improving IS strategic planning
#7	Planning and managing communications network
#8	Recruiting and developing human resources for IS
#9	Increasing understanding of the role and contribution of IS
#10	Legislating information intellectual property protection
#11	Measuring IS effectiveness and productivity
#12	Reengineering business processes through IT
#13*	Using information systems for competitive advantage
#13*	Integrating data processing, office automation, telecommunication and image technology
#15*	Developing and implementing an information architecture
#15*	Aligning the IS organization within the enterprise
#15*	Facilitating organizational learning and use of IS technologies
#18	Improving the quality of software development
#19	Facilitating/managing decision and executive support systems
#20	Facilitating and managing end user computing
#21	Determining appropriate IS funding level
#22	Developing and managing distributed systems
#23	Outsourcing selected information services
#24	Using IS to influence organizational structure
#25	Information technology transfer
*	Denotes a tie for Issues

Table 9. Key Issues for IT Executives – Kuwait (2002)
(Source: Alshawaf, A. and Delone, W. H. 2002. IS Management Issues in Kuwait: Dimensions and Implications. *Journal of Global Information Management*, 10(3): 72-80.

communication with senior managers, satisfying user needs, promoting channels for IS professionals, and improving software development. Overall, the NIC issues appear to be lower in their strategic orientation as compared to the advanced countries. These issues then can most appropriately be labeled as "management and control" issues reflective of growing technology adoption. In a sense, the refined "global information technology environment" model is correlated with the Nolan stage model (1979), which posited the need for a control stage to contain and manage the proliferation of IS activities in an organization. The main difference is that our model explains the nature of IT conditions and practices based on economic conditions in different countries.

Palvia, Palvia, and Whitworth (2002) attempted to empirically verify the above model by performing a cluster analysis on a sample of ranked IS issues from sixteen different regions of the world. Their analysis supported a linkage between the level of economic development of a region and the ranking of various types of IS issues. However, it provided stronger support for the three-way classification of regions as developed, developing, and underdeveloped as proposed by Palvia and Palvia in 1992 rather than four-way classification reported here as: developed, newly industrialized, developing, and underdeveloped countries. Thus the labeling of the NIC country issues as "management and control" may be a little fuzzy; they may as well be called a mix of strategic and operational issues. In any case, we see a transitioning of issues from operational to strategic as countries advance the economic ladder and may witness a combination of issues during the transition.

Thus the model depicted in Figure 1 provides an attempt to understand the complex global IT environment. We recognize that there are limitations and other elements may be necessary for a finer understanding of the global IT environment, or the environment of any particular country. For example, the inclusion of Russia and socialist countries under the "developing/operational" country class may be of concern to some. The BRIC countries and the flattening of the world (Friedman, 2005) may bring forth interesting dynamics. The Arab countries may have unique concerns of their own. Singapore might also be a special case, as it is not really a country, but a city-state, and has a benevolent ruler form of government. Nevertheless, the above model may be a good point for an organization considering expansion into far way world markets, and attempting to evaluate the role and use of information technology in unfamiliar locations.

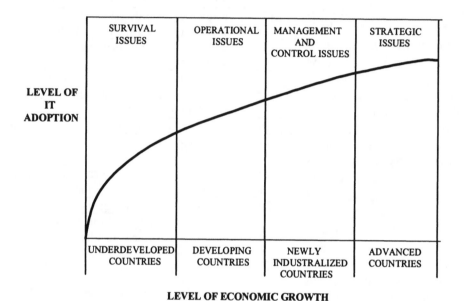

Figure 1. A Model of Global IT Management Environment

An Extended Model

The above model links the key IS issues to economic development. For a deeper understanding of the key issues, we need to examine a fuller range of antecedents as well as consequents of the key issues. Besides the level of economic development, antecedents may include political, cultural, industry and firm-specific factors, while consequents may include factors related to business and IT strategies. A model for analyzing global IS issues is shown in Figure 2 – as proposed by Palvia, Palvia and Whitworth (2002). The model is based on current (and somewhat eclectic) literature on global IT and observations of many authors. The key variable in the model is "key IS management issues" of firms in a country or in a homogeneous region of the world. This is the oval at the center of the figure. Variables that influence these issues are divided into two major categories, country specific (environmental) and firm-specific factors. The country-specific factors are largely uncontrollable, at least in the short term, but may influence the IT management priorities in a country. Finally, the IS management issues themselves influence the global IT strategy as well as the business strategy adopted by the firm. We have already discussed the "economic" variable at length; a brief description of the remaining factors in the extended model follows.

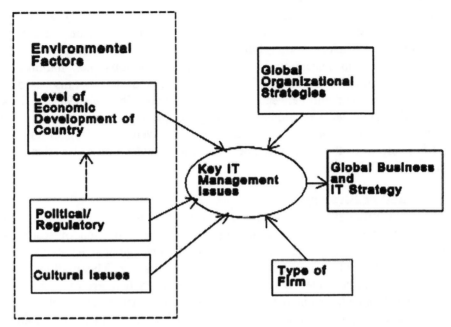

Figure 2. The Palvia, Palvia, Whitworth Model for Analyzing Key IT Issues

Political/Regulatory

This factor covers a broad spectrum of issues emanating from the political and governance philosophy (e.g. socialism, capitalism, communism, democracy, dictatorship) of a country. These issues may directly or indirectly influence different IT related areas, e.g. transborder data flow restrictions, governmental technology initiatives, privatization trends, enactment and enforcement of standards, technology investments tariffs, and trade and customs regulations. This phenomenon is highlighted by Chepaitis (2002) in her reporting of data quality and information poverty problems in Russia. These problems are exacerbated by the impact of the political system that include control and pressure by the authorities, poor public data stores, and a lack of competitive market experience. Furthermore, the political/regulatory practices may also affect the economy of the country, as shown by the dotted line relationship.

Cultural

Culture has been repeatedly cited as an important factor in the study of global IT, and frameworks have been developed that incorporate culture explicitly in the study of global IT (D'Aubeterre, 2005, Ein-Dor et.al., 1993). The work of Hofstede (1980) is classical in understanding national culture and is being used by many IS researchers; for example, Shore and Venkatachalam (1995) analyzed differences in systems analysis and design based on culture. Recent studies assess the impact of culture on technology adoption (McCoy et al., 2005) and IT outsourcing (Gurung and Prater, 2006). Culture can affect IT practices in subtle ways; its effects need to be examined in many areas of information technology using a variety of culture dimensions and newer models.

Type of Firm

The "type of firm" or "industry" has long been used as an antecedent factor in IS research. Among the key IS issues studies, Niederman (1991) studied three types of organizations: manufacturing, service, and non-profit, and found considerable differences among the three sectors. By the same token, the Deans et al., study (1991) of international IS issues showed a statistically significant difference in the rankings of service and manufacturing firms. It is therefore important that this factor be appropriately measured and accounted for in future studies.

Global Organizational Strategies

Organizational strategies may be classified according to Porter (1985) as cost leadership, differentiation, or focus. Miles and Snow (1978) distinguish firms based on strategy as analyzers, defenders, prospectors and reactors. The evolving global IT literature has considered four strategies of multinational corporations in managing HQ-subsidiary relationships, i.e., multinational, global, international, and transnational (Bartlett and Ghoshal, 1989). One of the most discussed and analyzed issue in global IT literature is the fit between the four Bartlett and Ghoshal (1989) business strategies and global IT architectures. Most previous work suggests that the IT architectures of global firms should be aligned with their business strategies (Ives and Jarvenpaa, 1991). In addition to global architecture, it is likely that other IT management strategies would need to be aligned to the global structures (Janz, et al., 2002)

Global Business and IT Strategy

The main reason to identify key IS management issues in a firm is to use them in the formulation of its IT strategy. They assist IS and senior management in the allocation of scarce resources to competing priorities. Additionally, we contend that key IS management issues may also have an impact on the formulation of the overall global business strategy. The traditional model of IT utilization was the cost/service center focus, which is increasingly being replaced by more proactive uses for business development. As noted at the beginning of the chapter, information technology has been a critical enabler of globalization in most cases and a driver in an increasing number of instances.

It is our hope and intention that the extended model will be the subject of further discussion, evaluation and enhancement.

CONCLUSIONS

Reports of information systems management issues in different parts of the world are useful to organizations as they begin to plan and implement IT applications across the world. In this chapter, we have presented IS issues for many countries, and have examined the issues in USA, Taiwan, Thailand, and Nigeria in greater depth. The world is a large place, and attempting to understand the critical issues in every single country, or even selected countries, would be an arduous, perhaps an imprudent task. Instead, we divided countries into four classes, and provided an example in each class. A parsimonious model for the global IT environment was postulated based on this categorization. An extended model was also presented to enhance our understanding the relationship between the antecedents and consequents of the key IS issues.

In closing, we would like to offer some suggestions for the conduct of future key IS issue studies. Future studies should adhere to the following principles in order to build a unified and cumulative body of knowledge:

- Use a common framework for data collection and analysis, such as the extended model proposed in this chapter.
- Use a common methodology across studies.
- Use common instruments.
- Conduct the studies in a pre-defined set of countries, thus providing a good representation of the world.
- Conduct the studies at periodic intervals.
- Make the data and the results available to the global community in a responsive manner.

MINI CASE

Public-Funded Communal Computing Among the Urban Poor: The Case of Cape Town

Introduction

One of the proposed ways of bridging the digital divide is a setup where the population are accorded access through shared facilities (universal access). These shared facilities, referred to as "communal computing," come in different forms including low cost computing such as Simputers and Volkscomputer, telecentres and the like. Presented are the results of a case study which identifies the critical factors for the success of communal computing among the urban poor in Cape Town, South Africa.

To appreciate the current distribution of access to Information and Communication Technology (ICT) among different racial groups in South Africa, one has to appreciate that up until 1994 the country had an apartheid policy. Due to the legacy of apartheid, locations which are predominantly non-white still have minimum access to technology. While 90% of all whites have telephone in their homes, the figure for blacks stands at 10%. Smart Cape (www.smartcape.org.za) is one of the many initiatives which have been undertaken to address this imbalance.

Smart Cape, a project aimed at providing free computer access and internet connectivity to the residents of Cape Town, is an initiative of the Cape Town City Council. The access points for the initiative are located in public libraries in the city. To access the facilities one needs to be a member of the library. In order to keep operating costs low, the initiative uses open source software. Each centre has five internet-enabled computers available to the public. At the time of this writing, the project had established access points in six libraries in the city, of which three were selected for this research namely: Grassy Park, Guguletu, and Brooklyn.

The Guguletu centre serves a largely black community; Grassy Park serves a predominantly coloured community, while Brooklyn serves a community in which many refugees from central Africa reside. While all three centres are within disadvantaged areas, they are also at different levels of development. Guguletu is characterized by extensive informal housing, Grassy Park is mostly formalized low cost high-density housing. The Brooklyn area is characterized by formalized low cost single unit housing.

Findings

Several key factors which contribute to the success of communal computing facilities were evaluated. The key success factor identified was usefulness expressed as using the computers for typing up resumes and applying for jobs. This is due to the high unemployment rate in underprivileged communities all over South Africa. The biggest negative factor expressed by both users and staff is that the Internet at each site is too slow, followed by the fact that learning how to use Linux based systems is difficult. It was also evident that, although capacity is insufficient; users still use the facility as there is nowhere else in the community where these services are offered free of charge.

Local Buy-in and Local Champion

Although the implementers of the project did not try hard to achieve local buy-in, this factor does not seem to play a role. A reason for this contradiction could be that the centers are set up in local libraries, which already had the support of the respective communities. Starting up a centre within an operational community organization such as a library, using existing staff members to run the centre, seems to be a huge benefit. People are familiar with the organization and its staff and therefore the initial barrier, of adapting to new surroundings and new people is eliminated. The centre is seen as an extension of this existing system to expand the knowledge resources to include those offered by ICTs and people may therefore view the centre as additional resources to use within the library, not a foreign resource at an unknown location, with unknown staff.

Location

Communal computing centres need to be positioned centrally in the community, lie on routes that are well serviced by public transport networks or be located in or near places where people already tend to come together. An interesting observation was that the libraries are not within apparent retail or commercial areas. This means that users wishing to access the computer facilities are required to commute to the library specifically. It can be concluded, therefore, that these neighboring services need not be retail or commercial.

One Guguletu (predominantly black community) respondent focused on the importance of the sociable aspect of the location of the library, favoring the presence of numerous people. In contrast, two Grassy Park (predominantly black community) respondents noted that they felt their safety was compromised when visiting the centre because of the high volume of people using the adjacent taxi rank.

Computing Capacity and Reliability of Facilities

Capacity was one of the bottlenecks of the project. It was hypothesized that a centre with a smaller capacity will be less appealing to users and so will be less successful. The results support this proposition as both users and staff (except the Brooklyn centre) feels that there are insufficient computers at the respective centres and that usage would increase if there were a greater number of computers. Although capacity correlates positively to the success of a communal computing centre, users are still willing to wait for the service rather than go elsewhere and be required to pay.

Most users wait for computers to become available or return later if "the system is down" simply because they cannot find this free service anywhere else. Thus reliability is not as important to users as the price of the service. Reliability does not seem to affect the long term perceptions of the centre since most users come back to the centre. However, if there was another facility nearby offering free services, the competition would force the centre to pay closer attention to the reliability of its systems.

Pricing and Affordability

Many development organizations believe demand for ICT access to be almost perfectly elastic at a zero price. At Grassy Park, one user claimed that "The true cost of charging for this service would be suffered by the government in the total loss of usage, and wastage of these computer resources because people will stop using the facility completely as they cannot afford to pay."

Contrary to this prevalent view, the finding was that the users, even those in urban areas, felt that the service warranted a substantial "fair price". Admittedly, it is difficult for people to attach a price to something they have always received for free, but most still felt that the service was worth a monetary value. An important observation was that this "fair price" correlates with the general income level of the community. This correlation poses an important question regarding the use of ICTs in development. Is the value lower in more disadvantaged communities because these people have less money available for expenditure on ICT, or is it because ICT realistically presents negligible value in the struggle to put bread on the table?

Discussion Questions
1. What issues should a firm pay attention to when setting up an IT based business in an economically disadvantaged community?
2. Discuss the importance of critical factors in the success of communal computing?
3. Is the value of ICT lower in disadvantaged communities because people cannot afford ICT services, or is the value negligible to the struggle to put bread on the table? Discuss the above question and provide arguments to support your answers.

Source: Adapted from: Chigona, W., Van Belle, J., Arellano, N., Euvrard, K., and Heslop, R. "Success Factors of Public-Funded Communal Computing Among the Urban Poor: The Case of Cape Town" *Proceedings of the 6th annual Global Information Technology Management Association World Conference*, June 5-7, 2005, Anchorage, Alaska,

KEY TERMS
BRIC countries
Business Process Reengineering (BPR)
Business-To-Business (B2B)
Chief Information Officer (CIO)
Capability Maturity Model (CMM)
Data Security
Delphi method
E-commerce (EC or Electronic commerce)
Electronic Data Interchange (EDI)
GIGO (Garbage In Garbage Out)
Information architecture
Privacy
Sarbanes-Oxley Act of 2002

STUDY QUESTIONS
1. Describe the key IS management issues in advanced countries and the underlying causes for these issues. What other issues do you see emerging in the advanced countries in the next few years?

2. Describe the key IS management issues in newly industrialized countries and the underlying causes for these issues. What other issues do you see emerging in these countries in the next few years?

3. Describe the key IS management issues in developing countries and the underlying causes for these issues. What other issues do you see emerging in these countries in the next few years?

4. Describe the key IS management issues in under-developed countries and the underlying causes for these issues. What other issues do you see emerging in these countries in the next few years?

5. Select any of the BRIC countries. What are their key issues? How are they different from or similar to any of the four classes discussed in this chapter?

6. Discuss the proposed comprehensive model for global IT environment. Do you agree? Are there other factors that might influence the IT environment?

7. Select a country and conduct research into finding its IS management issues. How do your findings compare with this chapter's findings?

8. The following hypothesis is examined: *There is a correlation between the rankings of IT management issues and the level of economic growth or development of a region/country.* What is this correlation? Is it justified? Discuss why or why not?

9. Briefly describe several ways that IT can serve as an "enabler" and "driver" of global business expansion.

REFERENCES

Alshawaf, A. and Delone, W. H. "IS Management Issues in Kuwait: Dimensions and Implications," *Journal of Global Information Management*, (10:3), 2002, pp.72-80.

Badamas, M. A. "Critical issues in the Management of Information Systems in Nigeria," *Working Paper*, 2004, Available from the author.

Ball, L. and Harris, R. "SMIS Members: A Membership Analysis," *MIS Quarterly*, (6:1), March 1982, pp.19-38.

Bartlett, C. A. and Ghoshal, S. *Managing Across Borders: The Transnational Solution*. Boston: Harvard Business School Press, 1989.

Brancheau, J. C. and J. C. Wetherbe. "Key Issues in Information Systems Management," *MIS Quarterly*, (11 :1), 1987, pp. 23-46.

Brancheau, J. C., Janz, B. D., and Wetherbe, J. C. "Key Issues in Information Systems: 1994-95 SIM Delphi Results," *MIS Quarterly*, (20:2), 1996, pp. 225-242.

Chepaitis, E. V. E-Commerce and the Information Environment in an Emerging Economy: Russia at the Turn of the Century. In P. Palvia, S. Palvia, and E.M. Roche (Eds.), *Global Information Technology and Electronic Commerce*. Pp. 53-72: Ivy League Publishing, 2002.

Chou, H. W. and Jou, S. B. "MIS Key Issues in Taiwan's Enterprises," *International Journal of Information Management*, (19), 1999, pp. 369-387.

D'Aubeterre, F., Palvia, P., and Stevens, J. "A Meta Analysis of Current Global Information Systems Research," *Proceedings- AMCIS 2005 Conference*, Omaha, Nebraska, USA, August 2005.

Deans, P. C., Karawan, K. R., Goslar, M. D., Ricks, D. A., and Toyne, B. "Identification of Key International Information Systems Issues in U.S. based Multinational Corporations," *Journal of Management Information Systems*, (7:4), 1991, pp. 27-50.

Dickson, G. W., Leitheiser, R. L., Nechis, M., and Wetherbe, J. C. "Key Information Systems Issues for the 1980s," *MIS Quarterly*, (8:3), 1984, pp 135-148.

Ein-Dor, P., Segev, E., and Orgad, M. "The Effect of National Culture on IS: Implications for International Information Systems," *Journal of Global Information Management*, (Winter), 1993, pp. 33-44.

Friedman, T.L. 2005. *The World is Flat: A Brief History of the Twenty-First Century*. Farrar, Straus and Giroux, 2005.

Goodman, S. E. and McHenry, W. K. "The Soviet Computer Industry: A Tale of Two Sectors," *Communications of the ACM*, (34:6), 1991, pp. 25-29.

Gurung, A., and Prater, E. "A Research Framework for the Impact on Cultural Differences on IT Outsourcing," *Journal of Global Information Technology Management*, (9:1), 2006, pp. 24-43.

Hartog, C. and Herbert, M. "1985 Opinion Survey of MIS Managers: Key Issues," *MIS Quarterly*, (10:4), 1986, pp. 351-361.

Hayne, S. C. and Pollard, C. "A Comparative Analysis of Critical Issues Facing Canadian Information Systems Personnel: A National and Global Perspective," *Information and Management*, (38), 2000, pp. 73-86.

Hofstede, G. *Cultural Consequences: International Differences in Work Related Values*. New-bury Park, CA: Sage, 1980.

Ifinedo, P. "Key Information Systems Management Issues in Estonia for the 2000s: A Comparative Analysis," *Journal of Global Information Technology Management*, (9:2), 2006, pp. 22-44.

Ives, B. and Jarvenpaa, S. L. "Application of Global Information Technology: Key Issues for Management," *MIS Quarterly*, (15:1), 1991, pp. 33-49.

Janz, B.D., Vitalari, N.P., and Wetherbe, J.C. Emerging Best Practices in Global Systems Development. In P. Palvia, S. Palvia, and E.M. Roche (Eds.), *Global Information Technology and Electronic Commerce*: 332-355: Ivy League Publishing, 2002.

Luftman, J. and McLean, E. R. "Key Issues for IT Executives," *MIS Quarterly Executive*, (3:2), 2004, pp. 89-104.

Ma, L.C.K. Critical Issues of Information Systems Management in Hong Kong, City University of Hong Kong, *Working Paper*. 1999.

McCoy, S., Everard, A., and Jones, B. M. "An Examination of the Technology Acceptance Model in Uruguya and the US: A focus on Culture," *Journal of Global Information Technology Management*, (8:2), 2005, pp. 27-45.

Miles, R. and Snow, C. *Organization strategy, structure, and process*. New York: McGraw-Hill, 1978.

Moores, T. T. Key Issues in the Management of Information Systems: A Hong Kong Perspective. *Information and Management*, (30), 1996, pp. 301-307.

Morgado, E. M., Reinhard, N., and Watson, R. T. "Adding Value to Key Issues Research through Q-Sorts and Interpretive Structured Modeling," *Communications of the AIS*, (1), 1999, pp. 1-24.

Niederman, F., Brancheau, J. C. and Wetherbe, J. C. "Information Systems Management issues for the 1990s," *MIS Quarterly*, (17 :4), 1991, pp. 475-500.

Nils, A. K., Lin, T. W., and Muntoro, R. K. "A Study of the Attitudes of Indonesian Managers toward Key Factors in Information System Development and Implementation," *Journal of Global Information Management*, (6:3), 1998, pp. 17-28.

Nolan, R. L. "Managing the Crisis in Data Processing," *Harvard Business Review*, (57:2). 1979, pp. 115-126.

Palvia, P., Palvia, S., and Roche, E. *Global Information Technology and Electronic Commerce*. Ivy League Publishing, 2002.

Palvia, P., Palvia, S., and Whitworth, J. "Global Information Technology: A Meta Analysis of Key Issues," *Information and Management*. (39:5), 2002, pp. 403-414.

Palvia, P., Palvia, S., and Zigli, R. M. Global Information Technology Environment: Key MIS Issues in Advanced and Less Developed Nations. In S. Palvia and P. Palvia and R. M. Zigli (Eds.), *The Global Issues of Information Technology Management*: Idea Group Publishing, 1992.

Palvia, P. and Wang, P. "An Expanded Global Information Technology Issue Model: An Addition of Newly Industrialized Countries," *Journal of Information Technology Management*, (VI:2), 1995, pp. 29-39.

Palvia, P. and Palvia, S. Global Information Technology Environment: Representative World Issues. In P. Palvia, S. Palvia, and E.M. Roche (Eds.), *Global Information Technology and Electronic Commerce: Issues for the New Millennium*: 2-27: Ivy League Publishing, 2002.

Palvia, P., Palvia, S., and Whitworth, J. E. "Global Information Technology: A Meta Analysis of Key Issues," *Information and Management*, (39), 2002, pp. 403-414.

Pervan, G. "Information Systems Management: An Australian View of Key Issues 1996," *Australian Journal of Information Systems*, 5(1), 1997, pp. 55-68.

Pimchangthong, D., Plaisent, M., and Bernard, P. "Key Issues in Information Systems Management: A comparative study of Academics and Practitioners in Thailand," *Journal of Global Information Technology Management*, (6:4), 2003, pp. 27.

Porter, M. E. *Competitive Advantage: Creating and Sustaining Superior Performance*. New York: Free Press, 1985.

Samik-Ibrahim, R. M. Key Issues in Information Management: Indonesia. http://rms46.vlsm.org/1/22.html, 2001. Accessed April 21, 2006

Shore, B. and Venkatachalam, A. R. "The Role of National Culture in Systems Analysis and Design," *Journal of Global Information Management*, 3(3), 1995, pp. 5-14.

Tiamiyu, M. A. "Information technology in Nigerian federal agencies: problems, impact and strategies," *Journal of Information Science*, 26(4), 2000, pp. 227-237.

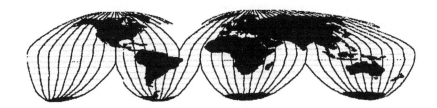

Managing Information Assets in a Low Trust Russian Environment

Elia V. Chepaitis
Fairfield University, USA

CHAPTER SUMMARY

This research examines the relationship between culture, institutionalized secrecy, and historic mistrust and its impact on knowledge creation and decision management in Russia. Russia is rich in strategic natural resources, such as natural gas and oil, and GDP growth is in excess of 6%. Yet, in contrast with emerging economies in Central Europe and Asia, Russia lags in entrepreneurship. Russia's business environment contains a high degree of risk and uncertainty for business partners such as the Rayter group. It is difficult to manage information assets in Russia's low-trust environment. Not only the Soviet past, but also dynamic economic, political, and socio-cultural factors perpetuate mistrust and risk avoidance in this transition economy, with a pernicious impact on management learning. Russia's economy, stability, and information infrastructure have improved in the past decade, but heavy-handed policies and the ensuing business uncertainty not only create top-down unethical behavior, but also compromise the effectiveness of information and communication technologies (ICTs). Mistrust and uncertainty perpetuate the existence of "information classes" and information poverty, and inhibit robust international and intercultural alliances. The author contrasts the lack of initiative and risk among business managers with the creativity, recklessness, and bravado of world-class cybercriminals in Russia. The author justifies Russia as a model for emerging economies that also are constrained by mistrust and cronyism, and suggests strategies to enhance trust and knowledge management.

INTRODUCTION

Russia's Economy and Putin's Role

Russia's GDP in 2006 increased by more than 6%, and the prospects for prosperity are excellent. Oil and natural gas prices are soaring and the ruble is strong and stable. However, free market forces have reversed over the past three years. In late 2006, Thomas Friedman coined the term "petro-authoritarianism" to explain the inverse relationship between freedom and the price of oil (Friedman, 2006). The heavy-handed policies of Putin against Gazprom, political opponents, the free press, and international aid agencies perpetuated a climate of uncertainty and risk avoidance in Russia and for potential business partners (Reed and Bush, 2006). Although polls show Putin's popular approval in excess of 70%, his regime curtailed not only market development but also entrepreneurship and information resource management profoundly. Under Putin, the prosecution and partial nationalization of Yukos Oil, the curtailment of a free press, the imprisonment of the businessman Khordovsky, the executive order that provincial governors will be appointed rather than elected—all perpetuate and deepen a climate of mistrust and business uncertainty. Yet 75% of Russians approve of Putin's performance, and support for the stability and cultural congruence of his regime contrasts sharply not only with Yelstin's 20% approval rating in 1995 but also President Bush's 30% in May, 2006 (Zakaria, 2006).

Under Putin, information continues to be mismanaged, hoarded, and distorted in the interests of stability and personal security: to prevent performance assessments, for control of distribution and supply channels, for fraud, to transfer assets abroad, for egregious personal aggrandizement, for deception and unfair advantage, and for tax avoidance, even though tax reform has reduced taxation to a flat 15%. In turn, these machinations distort the economy. Popular information, by contrast, is plentiful, but unreliable for different reasons: a plethora of rumor mills, astrological influences, fraud, and competing non-professional sources with an eye to self-aggrandizement and sensationalism. At both ends of the data quality spectrum, robust ICTs depend upon not only the availability of information technology (IT), but also on equitable and honest information-handling behaviors and other moral considerations. Habits of mistrust and misinformation are deep-rooted and difficult to eradicate.

Internet/ICT Growth

Although telephony has improved dramatically since liberalization and privatization began in 1997, and Internet usage has increased exponentially to 16 million websites, e-business and information development are constrained by a culture of caution, uncertainty, and mistrust. Although domestic e-business is limited, telephony and advanced communications are expanding outsourcing opportunities exponentially. B2B and B2C sales are relatively modest for numerous reasons: shifting government policies, a popular lack of trust in financial institutions, a reluctance to accept credit cards, fear of fraud and chicanery, and culture-based impediments to management learning (Ruth et al., 2005).

The Rise of Cybercriminals in Russia

By contrast, Russia provides a haven for the most brazen and global cybercriminals in the world (Ante and Grow, 2006). In areas such as customer relation management (CRM), knowledge creation is limited by both systemic and organization-based barriers. Not only piracy, a lack of early stage funding, a lag in e-business management experience and global networking, but also a fear of capricious government regulation and taxation under Putin perpetuates "information poverty" in critical areas. This lack of confidence and experience in information sharing limits the effectiveness of open, integrated, and extended ICTs in knowledge creation.

Obstacles to Knowledge Creation

In some transition economies, obstacles to knowledge creation are not only contemporary but also historic and culture-based. In Russia, proprietary access to information predates the advent of ICTs (information and communication technologies), and information was one of many resources reserved for the political, social, and economic privileged classes. However, when information stores lack integrity, contextual authenticity, and discovery capabilities, a cyclical pattern emerges. A lack of information ethics, often regarded internally not as immoral, but as prudent and time-honored mores, increases information poverty, misinformation, and a proprietary view of information. The intercultural and international "static" caused by conflicting definitions of ethics and of justifiable caution inhibits information alliances and robust partnerships.

CHALLENGES TO MANAGING INFORMATION ASSETS IN RUSSIA

General Challenges

In spite of deep-rooted political and economic changes in the post-Cold War era, information management is constrained by habits of secrecy and prevarication, by habits of caution, and by loyalty to cronies and peers rather than the system. Where popular opinion regards change with pessimism, as probably for the worse, the traditional inclination to avoid any appearance of imprudence or impudence through information sharing makes sense. Although this posture protects the interests of the group, the organization, and the individual, three negative consequences preserve the legacies of the Imperial and Soviet period: market development lags, information resource management is constrained, and customs of mistrust are perpetuated,

Russian business is characterized by high power distance, risk avoidance, in-group collectivism, and focus on short-term goals that marked the Soviet era (Map, Puffer, and McCarthy, 2005). Ironically, uncertainty avoidance constrains information gathering and shared decision support, and reinforces tendencies to hide and manipulate data to perpetuate a lack of assessment and accountability. Above all, Russian managers protect their organizations and own tenure; they have succeeded by circumventing rules and directives, and hoarding not only information but also materials, labor, and other capital resources.

In Russia, information resources mirror systemic instability: political cronyism, widespread corruption, the lack of rigorous commercial law, unstable banking, widespread tax evasion, and habits of deference and of taciturnity. Information resources reflect what Gaddy and Ickes (2002) call "a virtual economy" - a unique hybrid with distinct non-market institution and behaviors, congruent with the Rayter experience. It is particularly difficult, even when information is shared and accurate, to develop strategic information because the information itself reflects an irrational market - valuations remain artificial and divorced from market forces (Chepaitis, 2002b and 2004; Freeland, 2002; Gaddy and Ickes, 2002). When the information environment is characterized not only by poor connectivity but also by misinformation, arbitrary pricing, suspicion, and resentment, ICTs cannot deliver benefits in this unstable information environment. Customer relationship management, agile enterprises, business resource planning - all cannot be developed to full potential in contemporary Russia. Instability and market immaturity compounds and is compounded by profound ethical problems and by low expectations that business ethics are feasible.

Challenges for the Rayter Group

A decade of management training experience has taught the Raytor group, a U.S.-Russia cross-cultural management training organization, that external business models and strategies fail in Russia (Map, Puffer, and McCarthy, 2005). The Rayter Group found resistance to training across industries ranging from banking to manufacturing to energy, foods, and pharmaceuticals, with leaders such s Gazprom and Avtovaz. Russian managers focused on individual goals, and depended upon organizational inefficiency and ambiguity to hide mistakes and shortcomings.

The Rayter Group's experience supports research conducted by the author from 1991 to 2001 by the author. Extensive interviews in Russia revealed the impact of low trust on information ethics, the digital divide, and information quality. Reinforced by more recent studies, this chapter illustrates the pernicious relationship between ethics, culture-based information mismanagement, and crony capitalism (See Figure 1).

The Rayter Group incrementally resolved the conflict between traditional and emerging values for Russian managers through three strategies for knowledge transfer and management recognizing traditional Russian values as a Foundation for Knowledge Transfer, Incorporating Emerging Values for Knowledge Transfer, and Applying a Culturally Based Approach to Knowledge Transfer (Table 1).

Rayter's tactics to support these strategies included: combat denial that change was unavoidable, correct the naiveté of trainers who failed to realize the importance of self-interest and self-aggrandizement for managers, and build acceptance using emerging catalysts for change such as concrete business opportunities supported by linear planning featuring tacit, rather than non-tacit, knowledge (Table 2).

Political Corruption	Government control of media
Economic Corruption	Economic uncertainty and controls
Legal privilege	Political cronyism: imperfect competition Wasted financial, material and labor resources Obstacles to information access
Information elites	Irrational market behavior Lack of demand as a primary driver Institutionalized imperfect competition
Socio-cultural norms	Information hoarding as a survival technique Duplicity accepted as a prudent, respectful, loyal, to avoid attentions, prevent embarrassment, and preserve leverage for future strategies Fear of attracting attention, taciturnity Routine tax and regulation avoidance

Figure 1. Soft Factors That Promote Mistrust and Unethical Information Habits

Recognize Russian values Incorporate emerging values Apply a culturally-based approach

Combat managers' denial Erase trainers' naiveté Build acceptance: Use opportunities as catalysts Use linear planning using tacit information

Table 1. Rayter's Knowledge Transfer Strategies   **Table 2. Rayter Tactics to Support Knowledge Management Strategies**

CYBERCRIMINALS, INITIATIVE AND GLOBAL SUCCESS

The resistance to change, reluctance to invest in e-business, and lack of initiative among business managers contrasts sharply with the creativity, recklessness, and bravado of world-class cybercriminals in Russia. While Putin's popularity stems from stability and decent living conditions, the tolerance for not only arbitrary autocracy and secrecy but also the limited rule of law and boundless global opportunity promotes and protects cybercrime.

Russians lead the world in the $67 billion a year business of credit card fraud, malware, spyware, network intrusions, spamware, and identity theft (Ante and Grow, 2006). There is no security periphery, and Russian cybercriminals have a global reach: global drop houses for illicit purchase deliveries, reshipping rings, and cybercrime websites such as *vendorsname* for intrusions, *ratsystems.org*. for spyware, *carderplanet*, *DarkMarket.org*, and *theftservices.org*. Tan Systems' Security Leak specifically invades German companies. The Russians-based International Association for the Advancement of Criminal Activity's (IAACA) website brazenly recruits, rains, and coordinates cybercriminals. Stolen data is sold and swapped like baseball cards (Ante and Grow, 2006).

The risk of doing business in emerging nations similar to Russia is well-founded. However, numerous emerging economies that were once in the Soviet bloc have evolved into free markets and have developed effective business law. Unlike Central Europe, from the Baltic states to the Balkans are booming. The European Union's expansion and venture capital have enabled small businesses from Latvia to Czechoslovakia to Hungary to enter global markets as serious players. To the east, a striking contrast exists between Russia and China; unlike China, Russia lacks a vast and growing population, lags in low cost manufacturing and market-oriented leverage for strong technical talent, and has not experienced a similar tsunami of foreign capital by investors afraid to be excluded from a promising future. Yet Russia has not only attracted but also spawned native criminal elements that have taken advantage of e-business on a scale unknown elsewhere.

LITERATURE REVIEW

Crime and the Culture of Cybercrime

Comrade Criminal (Hendelman 1995), Gaddis and Ickes' *Virtual Economy* (2002), Freeland's *Sale of the Century* (2002), and Montaigne's *Reeling in Russia* (1998) portray the disregard for law and the climate of criminality and opportunism that spawns cybercrime in Russia in 2006. Ante and Grow (2006) provide a current description of cybercrime, but neglect the cultural and political roots of this unique brand of successful entrepreneurship. An ocean of consistent and reliable data is available through common search engines on increasing connectivity and e-business in Russia. Popular business periodicals such as the *Wall St. Journal* and *Business Week,* such as the article by Ante and Grow (2006), provide the most current information on cybercrime and Russia's global reach.

Developing Countries and Information Quality

Research on ICTs and economic development, both those that discuss culture and technology transfer and also those that treat information systems as social systems, typically proceed along one of two tracks. The first track emphasizes ICT diffusion rather than information and communications development. Information *per se*, the main component of an information system, is seldom discussed extensively. For example, a recent study of the twenty-five top issues for information systems managers in Kuwait lists better use of data resources as the third most important issue, but the research investigated only the management of hard factors in the ICT infrastructure (Alshawaf, 2002).

The second track considers the impact of ICTs on culture, politics, economies, and other local conditions, but seldom discusses the impact of those soft factors on ICT effectiveness (Castells, 2000). Exceptions include the article by Ruth et al. (2005), "Transferring management knowledge to Russia: a culturally based approach" that examines the challenges faced by the Raytor group. During 1992-2002, Raytor found that "conflicting values presented barriers to knowledge transfer and limited mangers' absorptive capabilities to receive knowledge (Ruth et al., 2005). Managers accustomed to reward systems based on central planning rather than demand factors "froze" and resisted learning market-oriented practices.

In addition to the Rayter study, scores of field-based studies of ICT diffusion investigate knowledge creation through tangential issues, such as: learning to use information (Lopez and Vilaseca, 1996), the integrity of informal and formal information resources (Volkhow, 2000), the problem of language in information handling (Hall, 2000), and the custom of deference to elites and traditional protocol when using information resources (Rohitratana, 2000). In a pair of insightful articles, Mennecke and West (2001, 1998) illustrate how imported knowledge-based systems, such as a Geographic Information System, drive information quality; the authors describe the challenge of codifying political and socio-economic data in developing countries. Harris (2002) and Raman and Yap (2000) discuss the criticality of government commitments to the IT infrastructure (to create an information-rich society in Malaysia)—their intent is not only to improve the hard information infrastructure but also to leapfrog past obstacles in the infrastructure.

Russia: Instability, Initiative, and Culture

Graham's classic *The Ghost of the Executed Engineer: Technology and the Fall of the Soviet Union* (1997) illustrates historically the impact of political terror and intimidation on scientific achievement, truth sharing, and technology design. This masterpiece is a superb introduction to the problem of information resources, ethical culture and technology. Handelman's (2005) sensational *Comrade Criminal: Russia's New Mafiya* is the definitive description of cowboy capitalism. Gustafson discuss contemporary Russia's information poverty, and Brand (1998) and Zisk (1998) not only describe both the rigidity and ineffectiveness of Soviet planning, and also misinformation in the 1990s. Aslund (1995) describes inadequate and unreliable data in Russia, and provides a list of unreliable internal sources. A continuous stream of investigations in periodicals such as *The Wall Street Journal, The New York Times, and The Economist* provides a critical mass of material on the current economic instability in Russia. Gaddis and Ickes' *Virtual Economy* (2002) masterfully describes and evaluates the disconnect between market aspirations and overriding non-market forces in culture and institutions that inhibit knowledge management, discourage foreign investment, encourage criminality in both real and virtual markets, and perpetuate a disregard for law.

Trust

Surprisingly, few scholars address the problem of trust. Francis Fukuyama (1995) offers a large study, in *Trust: The Social Virtues and the Creation of Prosperity*. His terse observation that "a low trust society may never be able to take advantage of the efficiencies that information technology affords" (pp. 25) was a major stimulus for this article. Fukuyama (1996) links the necessity of trust for successful electronic relationships in a subsequent article.

The criticality of trust and other soft factors surfaces in a broad range of research on Russia: international partnerships, emergent e-commerce, information quality, and the telecommunications infrastructure (Chepaitis, 2001a; 2001b; 2002a). Beyond Russia, the significance of soft factors in four areas are investigated: e-market impacts, ICT design, expert and knowledge-based systems, and the criticality of information ethics for information development (Chepaitis, 1997; 1999; 2001a; 2001b).

RESEARCH METHODS

The Rayter Group engaged in a decade-long transition from normative to more Russia-specific, culturally congruent management training approach. This approach to knowledge management incrementally builds trust and effective behaviors in their clients. Their research addresses the problem of change, and the necessity to pursue limited goals through cautious transitions to primarily assure the personal well-being of managers.

The Rayter study complements the author's experience and research as a business consultant in Russia from 1991 to 2001, and a Fulbright fellow in 1994 and 1998. The sets of interviews involved eighty subjects: the *first* set, in Moscow and cities in western Siberia from 1991 to 1996, and the *second* set, in the Rostov region, in the city of Taganrog from 1998 to 2003 (Chepaitis, 1996; 2002a; 2004). In simple but structured conversations, participants were asked to identify their organizations' critical success factors and information needs. Interviews were preferred to questionnaires by Russian respondents in both the initial studies and follow-up studies. Subjects were not only reluctant to write information, they were also visibly uncomfortable during interviews if the researcher took notes, used a laptop, or displayed schedules or records. Reticence especially characterized the 1991-1996 interviews in the Western Siberian cities of Kemerovo, Tomsk, and Irkutsk, even though the author worked and socialized with many of the respondents for several years both in Russia and abroad. Subjects were less taciturn in Taganrog, Peter the Great's prime warm water port with commercial relationships dating back to the classical era, and an ideal base for the 1998-2003 research. A former weapons research and development center, the city of Taganrog suffers from unemployment and recession but has vast human capital, significant commercial connections ranging from expatriate Armenian and other minority connections to a massive investment in agribusiness through the European Union (Belton, 2002). The city benefits from a decade of extensive foreign partnerships: a sister city project with the Netherlands, an EU assistance program (Technical Assistance to the Community of Independent Sates or TACIS), multi-project EBRD (European Bank for Reconstruction and Development) funding, and an extensive academic exchange program with Michigan State University.

The project's original purpose was to assess Russia's telecommunications infrastructure, and not to investigate the role of culture, law, politics, or other soft factors in ICT development. However, interviewees drove the research toward ethics and information quality as salient issues; the significance of "soft" factors such as information hoarding, patterns of misinformation, mismanagement, and corruption surfaced. The interviews yielded significant insights into cultural attitudes toward information sharing and the ongoing need for Soviet style middlemen (tolkachi) for survival in the gray economy.

In a set of interviews from 1991 to 1996, twelve foreign managers were struck by the Soviet legacies in information management, by the disdain for work ethics, and by the lack of attention to demand and customer preferences. Interviews with twelve foreign managers working in Russia were also conducted from 1991 to 1995 using the same questions, yielded significant insights into the lack of change in cultural attitudes toward information sharing in Russia. These participants were struck by the legacies of the Soviet system: secrecy, a popular mistrust of business success, the disregard for business ethics, and the widespread popular attitude that change will probably be for the worse. The Russian subjects were more pessimistic about reform and stabilization than their foreign counterparts. Several referred to the vision of a business environment with robust information as "utopian". Representatives of different occupations, generations, and classes varied on the respectability of business as a profession. There was an interesting correlation between a belief in the accuracy of business information in advanced economies and a belief that the transition from Russia's Wild Capitalism (dikii capitalism, as the 1990s are called) to normalcy would succeed.

In the 1998-1999 research, twenty subjects discussed plans for open and extended information partnerships both across and outside their organizations, for growth, cost-savings, and competitive advantage (Chepaitis, 2002b). This group noted that information partnerships and connectivity were critical, to link business processes, and for information discovery, market analysis, customer reach, and resource sharing.

One interesting strategy for dealing with information poverty was to secure foreign partners, and move human resources to information-rich environments. For example, a mammoth oil and gas conglomerate sent 1,000 interns abroad for business education and internships, to environments with mature business practices, information plenitude, and a high degree of social cohesion and veracity. More often, enterprises learn to do local business with minimal but accurate data and trusted partners until conditions improve.

Data quality is affected by the type and ease of data gathered personal fortunes, established internal alliances, foreign aid, and other material and intellectual resources. Foreign businesses often accept information poverty as part of the high risk of direct investment in the huge untapped market and maintain highly speculative portfolio investments. These businesses operate at risk in an environment characterized by weekly currency, regulatory, and market shifts.

IS THE RUSSIAN ENVIRONMENT SIMILAR TO SOME DEVELOPING ECONOMIES?

Is the Russian environment of a low-trust, poor information quality, and scant regard for ethical issues similar to that in other developing economies, especially those outside of the former Soviet Bloc? Russia has seminal differences in resource endowments, international relations, history and politics as follows:

- Massive natural resources: mineral and agrarian wealth
- Vast human capital: pre-19986 world-class investments in science, health, education, military expertise, sports, performing arts
- No post-colonial or post-imperial adjustments
- Little MNE impact until the 1990s
- A millennium of recorded history and political traditions
- A history of membership in the European family of nations

However, Russia has yet to capitalize on vast natural resources, international leadership, or traditions of excellence in the arts and sciences to attack the digital divide and ameliorate economic instability because of a climate of mistrust and mismanagement. Intrusive and ineffectual government planning and regulation, barriers to fair market entry, volatile price controls, currency restrictions, and habits of clandestine entrepreneurship, black markets, and barter systems not only encourage secrecy and duplicity, but also perpetuate information poverty and inequities that bear a marked resemblance to developing economies.

Additional characteristics include: chronic political uncertainty, unstable financial institutions, and rigid, hierarchical management styles that exacerbate the digital divide: a marked reluctance to share or divulge information, proprietary attitudes toward data ownership, within socioeconomic and political elites, and a reluctance to divulge information without compensation or reciprocity. Some information characteristics, such as an emphasis on quantity and price to the exclusion of quality and cost-effectiveness, bore a unique Soviet stamp, and appear to be dynamic and improving, as customer demands drive quality and cost-containment. Certainly, other characteristics, such as a reliance on oral traditions in retailing, or the use of more than one language for business relations and record-keeping, are existent in Russia, but are more common in developing economies.

The criticality of the soft factors that Russia shares with developing economies suggests that the common list of characteristics descriptive of developing economies be expanded, beyond economic factors such as GDP per capita and literacy and infant mortality rates, to include more political and socio-cultural factors relevant for ICT adoption. Research into ICTs and economic development may be overly focused on the diffusion of hardware and software, and microeconomic impacts, rather than on information itself and on the information environment. Across multiple levels and through varying sectors of economic development, a low trust environment compromises the effectiveness of ICTs, and widen the gap between the information "haves and have-nots" (Chepaitis, 2000).

RUSSIA'S PROSPECTS

Friedman's (2005) *The World is Flat* occasionally referred to Russian activities in the new competitive and collaborative global environment, but the stars in outsourcing and entrepreneurship are nations such as India and China, not Russia. Friedman notes that, in the past two years, in spite of massive leverage as an international oil supplier, Putin's Russia has fallen behind nations such as China and India. No one asks whether the 21st is the Russian Century—the question is whether it is China's century or India's century. Although software engineering and other information services are outsourced routinely to Russia, Russia at present lacks the shared norms and expectations, based on regular, honest, and cooperative behavior, which are vital for optimal growth, equity, and prosperity (Fukuyama, 1995; Chepaitis 2002b), yet stability has been achieved since the panic of 1998. Contemporary businesses prefer to release minimal data, even to allies, for numerous reasons: for leverage, to avoid the tax police, and to maintain a low profile. Russian entrepreneurs also maintain minimal accounting data not only because of exorbitant and shifting taxes and fees, but also because of enduring popular resentment of profits. Also, numerous commercial and financial advantages are transitory and optimized by secrecy. In Russia, numerous liquid or scarce assets, such as capital, extra apartments, automobile parts, or luxury items, often are kept off the books, because of fears of confiscation or theft. The long-standing prejudice against data sharing, rooted in the belief that power and security are eroded if data is shared, is reinforced by fear of revealing assets. The ethical environment reinforces widespread cynicism. One obstacle to the development of a social contract is the subjective definition of the common good, as well as of stockholders, stakeholders, and political duty—particularly in an era of survivalist, ad-hoc business practices.

Russia lacks clear-cut ethical traditions to provide an appropriate philosophy or model for building a consensus on moral behavior (Donalson, 1996). Orthodox Christianity is more ethereal and other-worldly than Western Christianity, and, at any rate, church leaders have demonstrated a striking unwillingness to speak out and demand reform conforming to Christian values. Western traditions of individualism, of human rights, or of political participation differ markedly from Russian traditions and experience. Unlike China, no Confucian school with an emphasis on duty and decorum predates the Communist system. Perhaps the simple theory of the greatest good for the greatest number will emerge as the pivotal point for a consensus on ethics, linking communal and syndicalist values and modern moral behavior. The Japanese concept of Kyosei - working together for the common good--is perhaps nearest to post-Communist ideals.

Ironically, entrepreneurs, who reject the viability of business ethics, concur vigorously when asked whether political candor and public debate would reduce risk and idiosyncratic behavior in the economy. For example, an egregious housing shortage often determines where consumers work, travel, and study, and also deeply affects family structure, disposable income, and eating preferences. In many cities, workers, including professionals, cannot be hired unless their domestic passports are tamped to prove that they have secured an apartment. Yet timely and reliable data on housing is unavailable, and productivity, labor mobility, and market development are deeply affected by unofficial data from underground housing markets. (Data brokers would find ripe areas for e-commerce if public and private data stores were accessible and trustworthy.)

Entire industries, from automobiles to housing, could not rely on official statistics in 2002. After state enterprises were auctioned, privatization data became inaccurate when businesses split up, declared bankruptcy, changed their names, hid production, and changed locations frequently to avoid taxation (*Wall Street Journal*, February 9, 2000). .

Authorities know that private production is underreported for tax-avoidance and that many enterprises fail to register with national and local authorities to avoid taxes; as many as 50% of private enterprises were unregistered in 1994. Financial and monetary data is especially sparse, a legacy of the perennial neglect of monetary and financial data in the Soviet era, when the budget, monetary supply, and foreign debt were unpublished. The state has failed to collect critical data on the impact of inflation, bank failures, massive and unrecorded inter-enterprise borrowing, soaring bankruptcies, and privatized assets (Gustafson, 2000; Aslund, 1995). In addition, foreign trade statistics are unreliable because of widespread smuggling, bribery, and irregular registration procedures. Interstate trade statistics between members of the Commonwealth of Independent States are especially poor. Similarly, intra-organizational commerce, especially intra-company loans and shared ownership are not tracked (Aslund, 1995).

Finally, managers, academics, and foreign partners frequently complain about irrational government planning, and the inability to secure quality data because of ongoing policy shifts, currency devaluation, and arbitrary tax assessments, tariffs, and non-tariff barriers. Future costs cannot be calculated because of inflation, unexplained price increases, and interruptions in supply and distribution. Western models perform poorly in other areas also; for example, ICT decision support probably cannot succeed in areas such as environmental auditing using imported models, techniques and technologies developed in Western firms whose primary objective is compliance with existing regulations. Given her massive economic dislocations, Russia needs data and decision support that is not intended to measure legal compliance, but to provide the tools for massive damage assessment, policy formulation, and clean-up processes.

CONCLUSION

Using Russia as a model, twelve relatively malleable factors affect trust, ethics, and the information environment. These factors limit the emergence of professionalism, equal opportunity, and information sharing - creating deep pockets of local and systemic information poverty. They include:

1. Unsuccessful and intrusive government planning and regulation;
2. Barriers to entry and dictated pricing in distribution, supply, or production;
3. Clandestine entrepreneurship, black markets, and barter;
4. Singular methods of managerial accounting, (for example, omission of various overhead, depreciation, and maintenance costs, a common practice in Russia);
5. Unanticipated shortages and other tactics that inhibit consumption and disguise demand;
6. Political fear and widespread avoidance of information disclosure and sharing;
7. Inconvertible and unstable currency, nascent financial regulations, and a dearth of financial services;
8. A reluctance to divulge information without compensation or reciprocity;
9. Proprietary attitudes toward data ownership, IT, and IS training, by socioeconomic and political elites, including multinational and foreign controllers;
10. Rigid, hierarchical management styles featuring a marked reluctance to share information or to empower partners or employees through data sharing;
11. Communication behaviors such as a reliance on oral traditions in retailing, or the use of more than one language for business relations and record-keeping;
12. An emphasis on price and availability to the exclusion of quality, which discourages proximity to the customer and attention to preferences and trends.

Obviously, both Soviet traditions and the post-Soviet disregard for the rule of law, as well as an uneven telecommunications infrastructure, combine to shape mistrust and the ethical argument.

However, market maturation, political reform after Putin, an increased popular respect and understanding of business as a profession, together with rising popular and external pressures for equity—all may contribute to an ongoing dialogue on ethics. This malleability suggests that the information poverty and the climate of mistrust may dissipate over time, interrupted by occasional crises and cyclical volatility. Freeland believes that a younger "millennium" generation must come to power before success is achieved (2002).

The acceptance of broad responsibility and the delivery of multi-level commitments through systemic political, legal, and socio-economic reforms may be the key to trust and equal opportunity. Russia's GDP is growing and should continue to grow, despite waste and under investment in capital equipment and infrastructures. Optimism (as well as foreign investment and assistance) is buoyed by the realization that she posses vast natural resources such as oil, natural gas, gold, diamonds, and other minerals, and also an educated population and an undeveloped internal market. The author expects in the first decade of the twenty-first century, Russia's digital divide may narrow through internal push factors and external pull factors. These include global partnerships and the demonstrated success of former client states in the Baltic and Eastern Europe, who joined the European Union in May, 2004.

MINICASE

IT Comes to Russia

Russia, a country known for its limited funds and crime, is looking to information technology (I) to help its economy and bring hi-tech investment to the country. Long dependent on natural resources like oil for its economic prosperity, Russia is set to invest $650 million in hi-tech initiatives, including: infrastructure growth, an e-Russia initiative, and regional "technoparks" to help attract hi-tech investments. As a result, Russia has made IT development one of its top priorities, with plans for and industry-friendly legislation. The plans stress the importance of providing as many Russian citizens as possible with increased information access, through telephone and Internet connectivity.

Russia still faces significant challenges in its infrastructure. While there are over 40 million land-based telephones, there are still about 46,000 communities that lack a single fixed telephone line. That translates into a prime market for mobile services to 'leapfrog' the fixed line deficiencies. By the end of 2005, the Russian government expected to have 100 percent of the Russian Federation to be covered by a GSM (Global System for Mobile Communications) network. To do this, the government is putting a universal service guarantee into law and establishing a service fund, as well as enticing local operators to take on the initial financial burden of spreading phone access, with the promise that they will be rewarded by market growth later on. The government is pointing to the growth in mobile phone use to underscore the nation's IT appetite and encourage investors. Mobile phone use has grown from just 3.4 million users in 2000 to around 120 million users in 2005, giving Russia a national penetration rate of 84 percent. In Moscow and St. Petersburg the penetration is over 100 percent.

The e-Russia initiative, also a major program under development, is attempting to extend the Internet to a vast majority of Russian citizens. This initiative intends to expand the country's Internet infrastructure and provide Internet access to remote communities. It also makes a big push for e-government and services such as putting medical records online.

To spur further growth, Russia hopes to develop regional, government-sponsored IT research and development centers, or "technoparks," similar to areas in Bangalore, India. The technoparks will be geared at developing areas of technical expertise. Software development is a major part of this plan, given the country's strong base of local programmers. Software exports are already growing at 40 percent to 50 percent annually, and by 2010, the government hopes that Russian programmers' contributions will make up 7 percent of global software exports, and a $40 billion market. Proponents of the technoparks point out that Russian programmers have substantial experience in the development of complex solutions since much of Russia's application software has historically been developed in-house by IT departments of large organizations. Along with government investment, private sector businesses must also invest in the technoparks. There has also been some interest expressed by foreign IT companies that want to strengthen their presence in Russia with local RandD. For example, Germany's Siemens already has about 3,000 employees and seven regional offices in Russia. Recently they opened two RandD centers in Russia. Other global hi-tech companies also see great opportunities and growth in IT in Russia over the next few years.

There are enormous challenges to the infusion of IT in Russia. Computer crime, concerns over government intrusion, and emerging market competition are three of the major issues in bringing IT to Russia. Russia may have some of the best software programmers in the world, but it also has some of the best hackers. Computer crime flourished in Russia from 200-2003 doubled each year. However, the telecommunications and Internet service providers have been fighting cyber crime in an effort to increase Internet usage in the country. Businesses are fighting cyber crime in an effort to increase Internet usage in the country. Businesses have been pushing for new international laws that define cyber crime and set out similar penalties and sanctions across borders, so that countries can work together to locate and punish hackers. A certification program for IT security companies is also being pushed to eradicate unscrupulous consultants posing as security consultants.

The Russia government is hoping to reassure investors by cutting red tape and amending the tax code to create simplified regimes favorable to the IT industry. It is also developing a set of laws governing intellectual property, e-commerce and information exchange.

While these efforts are moving Russia in the right direction, Russia faces competition from a growing list of emerging market competitors. Eastern European countries like the Czech Republic, Poland, Hungary and Estonia are also trying to get their piece of the IT pie. World powers like India and China are also vying for more IT business.

Russia's low labor costs and new industry-friendly legislation may help it win some of the new competitive IT. Political stability is still a concern. While Russia may have come late to the IT game, it is playing to win.

Discussion Questions:

1. Why has Russia been slow in developing outsourcing capabilities in IT?
2. What other obstacles, not discussed in the case, might have slowed or prevented IT development in Russia?
3. Research the concept of technoparks. What other countries have developed technoparks to spur IT development? Have these other countries been successful with the concept?
4. If Russia can develop an IT capability, how might they compete for business against Eastern European countries? How might they compete for business against India and China?
5. What factors should be considered when developing an e-Russia initiative? What areas might this initiative be applied to in Russia?

KEY TERMS

Cybercriminals
Digital divide
Economic corruption
Identity theft
Information and communication technologies (ICTs)
Legal privilege
Malware
Political corruption
Spamware
Spyware
Trust

STUDY QUESTIONS

1. Describe the business climate in Russia.

2. Why is there a general atmosphere of mistrust and unethical information habits in Russia? What actions must be taken for the atmosphere to change?

3. How can an intrusive government impact business and e-commerce? Give some instances where a government could be considered intrusive.

REFERENCES

Alshawaf, A. "Critical issues of information systems management in Kuwait," *Journal of Global Information Technology Management*. 4(1), 2002, pp. 5-26.

Ante, S. and Grow, G. "Meet the Hackers," *Business Week*. May 26, 2006, pp. 58-63.

Aslund A. *How Russia Became a Market Economy*. The Brookings Institution, Washington, D.C. 1995.

Belton, C. *Meet the New Global Grain Giant. Time*. November. 2002, pp. 66.

Brand H. Why the Soviet economy failed: consequences of dictatorship and dogma. In *Global Studies: Russia, the Eurasian Republics, and Central/Eastern Europe*, 6th ed., Moldman M. (ed.). Dushkin Press, Guilford, CT, 1998.

Castells M. *The Rise of the Network Society*. Blackwell, Oxford, UK, 2000.

Chepaitis E. "After the command economy: Russia's information culture and its impact on information resource management," *Journal of Global Information Management* 2(1), 1994, pp. 5-11.

Chepaitis E. The problem of data quality in a developing economy: Russia in the 1990s. In *The Global Issues of Information Technology Management*, Palvia, PC, Palvia, SC, Roche, EM(eds.). Idea Group Publishing, Harrisburg, PA, 1996.

Chepaitis E. "Information ethics and information cultures," *Business Ethics: An European Review* 6(4), 1997, pp. 195-200.

Chepaitis E. "Ethics across information cultures," In *International Business Ethics*, Enderle, G(ed). University of Notre Dame Press, Notre Dame, In, 1999.

Chepaitis E. "The criticality of information ethics in emerging economies: Beyond piracy and privacy," *Journal of Information Ethics* 9(2), 2000, pp. 5-7.

Chepaitis E. "It's alive! Life and death in an international information infrastructure," In *Proceedings: 2001 International Information Resource Management Conference*. Toronto, 2001a.

Chepaitis E. "Soft information infrastructures and e-commerce," In *Proceedings: Global Information Technology World Conference*. Dallas, TX, 2001b.

Chepaitis E. "Soft Barriers to ICT Application in Development: Trust and Information Quality.," *Journal of International Development*. 14, 2002a , pp. 51-60.

Chepaitis E. E-Commerce and the information environment in an emerging economy: Russia at the turn of the century. In *Global Information Technology and E-Commerce: Issues for the New Millennium*, Palvia, PC, Palvia, SC, Roche E.M. (Eds). Idea Group Publishing, Harrisburg, PA, 2002b.

Chepaitis E. Non-technical barriers to Robust ICT Development in Emerging Economies: The Problems of Information Quality and Trust in Russia, *Journal of International Development: Special Issue on Information and Communication Technologies*. Ed. Richard Heeks. Spring: 14, 2002c, pp. 51-60.

Chepaitis E. Business Identity, Credibility, and Strategies in Russia: The Limits of Impressions Management, *Managing Impressions with Information Technology* Ed. Jon Beard. Praeger, 2004.

Donalson, T. Values in Tension: Ethics Away from Home. *Harvard Business Review*. Sept-Oct., 1996, pp. 4-11.

Friedman, T. *The World is Flat*. Farrar, Strauss, and Giroux, 2005.

Friedman, T. "The Really Cold War," *New York Times*. October 25, 2006, pp. A19.

Freeland, C. *Sale of the Century*. N.Y.: Crown Business, 2002

Fukuyama F. *Trust: The Social Virtues and the Creation of Prosperity.* Simon and Schuster, New York, 1995.

Fukuyama F. "Trust still counts in a virtual world: issues of security and control," *Forbes ASAP* 158(13), 1996, pp. S33-4.

Gaddy, C. G. and Ickes, B. W .*Virtual Russia.* Brookings Institution Press. 2002.

Graham L. *The Ghost of the Executed Engineer: Technology and the Fall of the Soviet Union. Harvard University Press, Cambridge, Ma.* 1997.

Gustafson T. *Capitalism Russian-Style.* Cambridge University Press, Cambridge. 2000.

Hall P. Local language software in South Asia. In Avgerou C, Walsham E, *Information Technology in Context.* Avebury, Aldershot; 2000, pp. 56-69.

Handelman, S. *Comrade Criminal: Russia's New Mafiya.* New Haven: Yale University Press. 1995.

Harris R. Malaysia's multimedia super corridor: an experiment in employing information and communication technologies for national development. In *Global Information Technology and E-Commerce: Issues for the New Millennium,* Palvia, P.C., Palvia, S.C., Roche, E.M. (eds.). Idea Group Publishing, Harrisburg, PA; 2002, pp. 28-52.

Lopez E, Vileseca M. IT as a global development tool. In *Information Technology, Development and Policy,* Roche E. M., Blaine, M. (Eds.). Avebury, Aldershot; 1996, pp. 57-76..

Matlack, C. "Go East Young Man" *Business Week.* October 30. 2006, pp. 46-47.

Map, R. C., Puffer, S. M. and McCarthy, D. J. "Transferring management knowledge to Russia: A Culturally based Approach.,"*Academy of Management Executive.* 19:3, 2005, pp. 24-35.

Mennecke B. E., West L. "Geographic Information Systems in developing countries: issues in data collection, implementation, and management," *Journal of Global Information Management* 9(4), 2001, pp. 44-54.

Mennecke B. E., West L. "Geographic Information Systems in developing countries: opportunities and options for decision support," *Journal of Global Information Management* 6(3), 1998, pp. 14-15.

McConnell International. Risk E-Business Report. www. mcconellinternational.com. 2000.

Montaigne, F. *Reeling in Russia.* N.Y.: St. Martins. 1998.

Raman K. S., Yap C. S.. "From a resource rich country to an information rich society: an evaluation of Information Technology policies in Malaysia," *Information Technology for Development* 7(3), 1996, pp. 109-129.

Reed, S. and Bush, J. "A Gusher for Big Oil Is Drying Up". *Business Week.* October 2. 2006, pp. 44.

Rohitratana, K. "The role of Thai values in managing information systems: A case study of implementing a MRP system". In Avgerou C., Walsham G. 2000. *Information Technology in Context.* Ashgate, Aldershot, 2000, pp. 3-39.

Ruth, C., May, S., and McCarthy, D." Transferring management knowledge to Russia: A culturally based approach". *Academy of Management Executive.* 19(2), 2005, pp. 24-35.

Volkow N. Strategic use of information technology requires knowing how to use information. In *Information Technology in Context,* Avgerou C, Walsham G (eds.). Avebury, Aldershot; 2000, pp. 56-69.

Zakaria, F. What the World Really Wants. *Business Week.* May 29, 2006, p. 35.

Zisk K.M. *Weapons, Culture, and Self-Interest: Soviet Defense Managers in the New Russia.* Columbia University Press, New York. 1998.

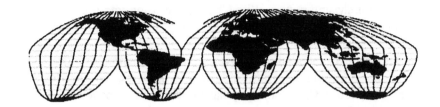

Adoption and Use of Information Technologies in China: Assessing the Modified Technology Acceptance Model

En Mao
Nicholls State University, USA

Prashant Palvia
University of North Carolina - Greensboro, USA

CHAPTER SUMMARY

In this chapter, we describe the status of information technology and trends in China. Specifically discussed will be the telecommunications industry, PC and IT industry, software and IT services industry, and the Internet and e-commerce. While a sound IT infrastructure is a prerequisite, there are many factors that influence organizational adoption of technology. In order to effectively manage technology adoption and use in Chinese organizations, managers constantly face the challenge of applying theories that were developed in the Western countries. However, theories developed in the context of one country may not necessarily work well in a distinctly different culture. It is therefore wise to test these theories before relying on them in any significant manner. We will, therefore, describe the results of a research study that examines IT acceptance and adoption by individuals in Chinese organizations. The study incorporates several factors from existing theories about IT adoption. Comparisons will be made with published studies in the West.

INTRODUCTION

China (officially known as The People's Republic of China or PRC) has increasingly been the focus of attention of the entire world as the country has made phenomenal leaps in economic development. It seems that every sector in China is being characterized as "the fastest growing" and "one of the largest" when compared with the global marketplace. The feelings you get walking on the streets of major cities in China are nothing short of awe and excitement. What is amazing is how fast China has risen to become a major competitor in the midst of fierce global competition. In the late 1980s, the personal computer (PC) was a rare find in China and was available only in prestigious research institutions. Few could have imaged that a Chinese company named Lenovo would buy IBM Corporation's PC division in 2005 and become the third largest PC vendor on the globe. Today,

China is one of the largest economies in the world, regardless of whether it is measured by gross domestic product or purchasing power. With China's accession into the World Trade Organization in 2001 and Beijing to host the 2008 Olympics, the prominence of China is gaining increasing momentum.

China has made tremendous improvements in its national infrastructure of information technology (IT). Its telecommunication industry is growing at the fastest pace since 1985 (Farhoomand and Tao, 2005). China currently has limited Internet penetration (7.3% estimated July 6, 2005 by Internet World Stats (2005)), yet maintains the second largest number of Internet users in the world after the United States. Like the rest of the world, Chinese organizations must adopt and use IT to compete in the global marketplace. Foreign companies and multinational corporations, in order to take advantage of the Chinese market, have been boosting their local presence in China. In the process, foreign companies are increasingly hiring local employees who are required to use IT.

INFORMATION TECHNOLOGY IN CHINA

The Telecommunications Industry

Advanced telecommunications infrastructure and electronic switching systems are the backbones of emerging information technology. Information technology diffusion is strongly dependent on the capacity of the IT infrastructure. The Chinese government played a significant role in jump starting the telecommunication industry. The commercialization of telecommunication was first planned in 1979 and the major development and growth started in late 1980s (Farhoomand and Tao, 2005). Through carefully planned and regulated growth, China has registered an explosive growth rate in its telecommunication industry. To better manage the growth, the Ministry of Information Industry (MII) was created by the State Council (the central government of China; also known as the Central People's Government) in 1998. Today, MII is the key government ministry that plans and manages the development and growth of China's telecommunications industry. MII stimulated growth by creating competition through a multi-staged reorganization and division of China Telecom. The industry grew from the monopoly of China Telecom to include a number of other major players: China Netcom, China Mobile, China Unicom, China Railcom, and China Satcom. The annual revenue of the telecommunications industry was approximately $65 billion in 2004. The largest operator is China Mobile (35.6%), followed by China Telecom (31.4%), China Netcom (16.3%), China Unicom (14.6%), China Railcom (2.0%), and China Satcom (.1%) in 2004. In 2005, the industry continued to grow at an impressive 11% rate, with over 30 million new subscribers of fixed phone lines, and over 37 million new mobile phone subscribers in the first 8 months of 2005 (as reported by MII). Mobile connectivity is excellent and dropped calls are rare. The number of mobile phones surpassed the number of fixed lines in 2003; by the end of the second quarter 2005, there were 370 million mobile phones compared to 346 million fixed lines.

Foreign operators are preparing to join in the competition which would bring more growth to the Chinese telecommunication industry. The competitive landscape is ever changing. The government, in an attempt to grow the market, announced the development of a proprietary wireless LAN standard in 2003. The proponents for implementing the new standard argue that it would encourage domestic intellectual development and help the Chinese to rely less on foreign technologies. The standard, called Wired Authentication and Privacy Infrastructure (WAPI), would not be compatible with the commonly established wireless LAN standard Wi-Fi, 802.11. As a result, this standard would have forced foreign competitors to collaborate with Chinese companies to compete in the wireless market. It would have also required manufacturers of wireless components that support Wi-Fi to make drastic changes in their products and design. The WAPI standard was scheduled to become effective by June 2005; however, in April 2005, the Chinese government under pressure from US companies agreed to postpone the imposition of the standard indefinitely. As the growth of the world-wide wireless market continues, the role of the Chinese market will be exciting to watch.

The IT Industry and Education

IT growth in China is evident in the personal computer (PC) sector, IT education, software development, IT services, and outsourcing. China is the world's fastest growing PC market and second largest in the world after the United States. Computer use in China is growing rapidly. Based on Internet World Stats, in 2003, 22 million PCs were sold in China, second only to the US.

China is not only a large consumer of PCs; it is also becoming a world-class PC manufacturer. Lenovo, the third largest PC maker in the world after acquiring IBM PC, held 25% of the Chinese PC market in 2005. It was founded in 1984 at Beijing University and quickly became a major market player. Lenovo reached world standing in the 1990s, and by 2001 was ranked the 13th largest PC vendor in the world. Partly owned by the Chinese Academy of Sciences, Lenovo is facing fierce competition from the largest PC maker in the world, Dell Corporation, which is determined to increase its market share in China which is currently about 8%. Dell is known for its lean structure and efficient direct sales method. Competition from Dell has forced Chinese PC makers to become more efficient. But they are showing the desire to become global players and the desire to learn. While Lenovo is facing severe competition, its rise in the industry is impressive.

The IT industry's growth is fueled by China's emphasis on education. Education is highly valued in the Chinese culture. Currently, China is building 200 research centers a year. College enrollment continues to grow. The country is producing on average 200,000 engineers each year. In addition, large multinationals are pouring investment into research and development. Microsoft, Infosys Technologies, and Wipro Technologies are among those who have positioned themselves to capitalize on the intellectual resources in China. In 2000, Neusoft Information Technology Institute of Northeast University, China's first privately funded IT education institution, was funded.

The Software and IT Services Industry

China's software and IT services industry is growing at an astonishing rate. The growth is evident in many perspectives: the demand from domestic businesses is exploding, foreign investment in research and development centers is increasing, and domestic software development and outsourcing capabilities are strengthening. The total market value of IT services reached $1.62 billion in 2001, as reported by IDC Research. It is projected that the software market in China will grow at a compound annual growth rate of 36.9% to $7.8 billion by 2006. Gartner Dataquest reported that the Chinese IT services market is expected to reach $8.9 billion in 2006. According to a January 2005 report from Yu Guangzhou, Vice Minister of the Ministry of Commerce in China, the software industry revenue and export value totaled $19.3 billion and $2 billion respectively in 2003. In October 2005, Analysys International, a leading Internet-based research firm in China, reported that the Chinese software outsourcing market was valued at $8.71 billion in 2005 and expected to reach $29.43 billion in 2009. Some key domestic outsourcing companies include BeyondSoft, ShineTech, Worksoft, and Objecitiva. Many are certified at CMM-3 to CMM-5 levels. Many of the companies were founded only recently, since 2000. The world's leading software vendors and IT services firms like Microsoft, Accenture, IBM, SAP, and Oracle continue to develop close relationships with China through joint-ventures and investment in IT research centers.

The growth in the software industry is fueled by the government's commitment and focus on the industry. The State Council recognizes the necessity to deploy infrastructure to support domestic software development and is positioning itself as the next major outsourcing provider to the global market. The Ministry of Science and Technology together with MII and other government agencies oversee what is called the High-Tech Torch Plan. Approved by the State Council in 1988, the plan has successfully launched regional and national high-tech development projects. The primary objective is to create environments for high-tech development by establishing and improving infrastructure, policies, governance structure, information availability, R&D capabilities, high-tech education, and high-tech labor resources. Another key objective is to globalize the high-tech sector through partnership with foreign countries, technology transfer, and high-tech import and export.

The torch plan has led to the establishment of a set of national high-tech, industrial, and software centers that have attracted foreign corporations, increased technology export, stimulated software development and cultivated intellectual IT resources. As of September 2005 there are 53 National New & High Tech Industrial Development Zones: 12 overseas student's pioneer parks, 22 university science parks, and 28 national software parks. These centers and regional zones have preferential policies from the government; thus they have been successful in attracting investment and development. The development zones are designed to develop general infrastructures for high-tech and industrial research and development. Often the software parks are located in the high-tech development zones. The overseas student's pioneer parks attract overseas Chinese students to return to the country. The university science park is another incubator for R&D in science and technology in leading Chinese universities.

The major cities leading the software industry development include Beijing, Shanghai, Dalian, Guangzhou, Shenzhen, and Xi'an. Currently, among the 28 software centers, five are considered "National Software Export Bases." The five designated export bases are Tianjing, Shanghai, Dalian and Shenzhen, and Xi'an. The majority of the centers are clustered in the north and northeastern China. These Silicon Valley like software centers, called "Ran Jian Yuan," house many of the new multinational's R&D offices and regional offices for leading software companies. The centers serve as bases for domestic software development and IT outsourcing. In fact, the 2100 companies in those centers account for over 80% of the software industry sales. Most of the software centers went into operation in 2000. Many of the software centers are now in their second expansion phase where additional structures and facilities are being constructed. Some notable centers include Beijing's Zhongguancun Software Park, which is known as "China's Silicon Valley." Another major software center is Shanghai Pudong Software Park (SPSP), founded in 1998 by the MII and the city of Shanghai.

Dalian Software Park (DLSP), established in the Liaoning province in northeastern China in 1998, is known for outsourcing. The State Committee of Planning & Development and Ministry of Information Industry named DLSP a "National Base of Software Industry." DLSP is strategically positioned. The city of Dalian's economic success and its strategic location at the heart of trade zone with Japan and Korea make it an excellent location. Japanese investors have a significant stake in DLSP. In 2004, Japanese outsourcing to Dalian reached $375 million (Thibodeau, 2005). Its modern facilities, state of the art technologies and infrastructure, and aggressive multi-phase development plan backed by the city officials have attracted over 300 foreign companies. There is a large concentration of Japanese-speaking and Korean-speaking workers in Dalian. Although India leads China in IS/IT outsourcing, the unique language capability of the Chinese IT workforce in Dalian make it an excellent alternative to India. Foreign multinational IT services corporations are using Dalian as an offshore hub for their Japanese and Korea markets. Similarly, Chinese software companies are setting up export operations to Japan and Korea. For example, one of the largest Chinese software companies, China National Computer Software & Technology Service Corporation has an office in Dalian serving as its gateway to Japan and Korea.

The software industry's future is bright in China; however it is not free from challenges. While China is looking to become a leader in the global software market, its software industry remains highly domestic with only 20% of the revenue coming from outsourcing (Thibodeau, 2005). It is forming strategic alliances with other nations, especially companies in the Silicon Valley and Bangalore. Malaysia is eyeing possible entry into the software centers. China and India are forming one of the most important alliances in the software industry. Having seen India's impressive rise to be the world's leader in IT services and the software market, young Chinese software engineers are eager to learn from India.

The domestic software growth is limited to the gaming industry. The growth in this sector is exemplified by Shanda Interactive Entertainment Limited (Nasdaq: SNDA), which went public on the

NASDAQ in May 2004. Growth in other areas is less evident. While there are an increasing number of universities and technical colleges training software engineers, companies are finding that there is a labor shortage. Particularly, qualified managerial IT staff and project managers are difficult to find. Some companies in Dalian are already recruiting such talent in Japan (Balfour and Tashiro, 2005).

Software piracy is a major and wide-spread problem. Almost 90% of all software in China is counterfeit. The government is intensifying its commitment to fight software piracy. The results are showing up in the streets of China where sales of counterfeit software are on the decline. In December 2004, the Chinese highest courts released a more stringent interpretation of the intellectual property rights laws in China.

The Internet and E-Commerce

According to the Internet World Stats, the number of Internet users in China reached 103 million in 2005 (7.9% of the population). In 2005, China had 43 million broadband Internet users, the largest number in the world, surpassing the US. Although most of the users go online for e-mail, news, and information access, e-commerce is taking off. The potential of e-commerce growth is tremendous given the population base and economic gains. The e-commerce market is ranked as the second largest in the world. Yet it is in its infancy and projected to grow at 50% annually. China's e-commerce market was projected to reach 620 billion Yuan ($76.5 billion) in 2005, according to estimates by Analysys International.

Some of the large online content providers are Netease.com, Sohu.com, and Sina.com. Baidu.com is the largest search engine followed by Yahoo and Google. Both Yahoo and Google are strengthening their presence in China. In August 2005, Yahoo purchased a 40% share of the Chinese company Alibaba.com, which operates the world's largest online marketplaces for both international and domestic trade, to become a dominant player in China. Google opened its offices in China in October 2005. eBay is a dominant e-commerce site in China. Few people have credit cards; the payment method remains dominated by cash paid at the time of delivery or through banks and post offices. The most popular online payment system is AliPay, operated by Alibaba.com.

To ensure healthy growth of e-commerce, China recognizes the importance of establishing a legal framework. The PRC Electronic Signatures Law was passed in August 2004 and became effective on April 1, 2005. The law defines digital messages and signatures and provides legal validity to messages that are digitally signed. This law is setting the foundation for a more comprehensive set of regulations for e-commerce.

The Chinese government is aggressively implementing Internet access in the school systems. In October 2005, the Chinese government awarded a $42 million contract to Sun Wah Linux for 104,000 PCs in the Chinese primary and elementary schools as a part of the initiative to connect 90% of schools to the Internet by 2010.

As the Internet and E-Commerce continues to grow in Chinese organizations, security is increasingly important. In the 2005 *InformationWeek* Research's Global Information security survey, 700 Chinese business professionals agreed that IT security would require significant improvement. Forty seven percent had security breaches that compromised confidential information. Many could not assess the value of the damage. Almost half indicated that their companies lacked IT security strategy. The major challenges identified were complexity of security, lack of user awareness, and budget constraints.

IT ACCEPTANCE IN ORGANIZATIONS

Background and Prior Research

In light of the vast advances made in the deployment of IT infrastructure in China, it is instructive to examine the organizational adoption of the technology. As organizations increasingly embrace IT, organizational management of information systems and technologies will become more important.

Determinants of adoption/usage of information systems and technology are of great interest to IS researchers. In the 1970s and 1980s, numerous scales and measures were developed pertaining to systems and technology use; however, many of them failed to correlate with the usage construct because of lack of theoretical foundation and poor measurement. More recently, research that has focused on significant theories and models include the technology acceptance model (TAM) (Davis 1986; 1989), theory of reasoned action (TRA) (Fishbein and Ajzen, 1975), and innovation diffusion theory (IDT) (Rogers, 1995).

Innovation diffusion theory and theory of reasoned action serve as theoretical foundations for the technology acceptance model. Innovation diffusion theory focuses on innovation attributes, namely: relative advantage, complexity, compatibility, observability, trialability, and image. Innovation attributes are treated as behavioral beliefs, a key concept in the theory of reasoned action. TRA focuses on predicting behavioral intention and actual behavior based on behavioral beliefs and subjective norms (Figure 1). Its strong predictive power has drawn attention from multiple disciplines, such as psychology, sociology, marketing, and MIS (Sheppard et al., 1988). However, TRA's normative beliefs and subjective norms constructs have received inadequate attention by IS researchers. It is reasonable to assume that norms play an important role in shaping behaviors in a collectivist culture, such as China (Hofstede 1980).

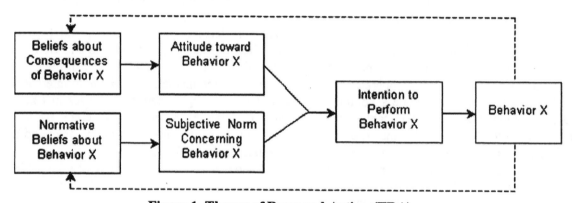

Figure 1. Theory of Reasoned Action (TRA)

While IDT provides the framework for behavioral beliefs in technology acceptance models, TRA supports the underlying causal relationships among behavioral beliefs, subjective norms, attitude, and behavior. In the technology acceptance model, Davis (1986, 1989) validated two key determinants of technology use: perceived usefulness (PU) and perceived ease of use (EOU). The perceived usefulness construct parallels relative advantage and perceived ease of use parallels complexity (Davis et al., 1989; Karahanna et al., 1999). These two constructs constitute the major determinants of user attitude, which mediates the relationship to user intention (Figure 2). There is

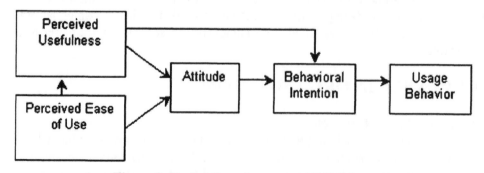

Figure 2. Technology Acceptance Model

also a direct link between perceived usefulness and behavioral intention. The rationale is that irrespective of attitude, positive belief of usefulness can lead to positive usage intention (Taylor and Todd, 1995b). While relative advantage and complexity are studied consistently in TAM research, other behavioral beliefs including compatibility are rarely included. These beliefs and constructs constitute important concepts and are worth investigating further.

IT Acceptance across Cultures

Most of the research in technology acceptance has been conducted in North America. It has been long recognized that culture has a significant impact on organizational theories (Hofstede, 1994; Hofstede, 2001) including IT acceptance (Straub, 1994; Straub et al., 1997). It would be preposterous to assume that IT acceptance theories predict equally well in other cultural settings. Thus the robustness of the models may vary across different cultures. In a practical sense, as multinational companies continue to penetrate China, the question of how IT should be managed in Chinese organizations must be answered. In this chapter, we examine a research model, based on existing innovation theories, applied to China.

We expect to find differences based on the considerable disparity between cultural values and clusters between China and the western nations. The United States is placed in the Anglo cluster while China is in the Far Eastern cluster, and the countries are rated on five cultural dimensions (see Table 1; for a complete discussion of cultural dimensions and clusters, see Hofstede, 1994 and Hofstede, 2001). Briefly, the five cultural dimensions are: power distance, individualism-collectivism, uncertainty avoidance, masculinity-femininity, and long-term orientation. Power distance is the degree of inequality among people, from relatively equal (small power distance) to extremely unequal (large power distance). Individualism-collectivism contrasts a social fabric in which each individual takes care of himself or herself with a fabric where groups take care of the individual. Uncertainty avoidance is the extent to which a society is threatened by uncertain situations and attempts to avoid such situations. Masculinity-femininity reflects whether the dominant values are associated with the collection of money or things (masculinity), as contrasted with the caring for others and quality of life (femininity). Long-term orientation focuses on the degree the society embraces or does not embrace long-term devotion to traditional values.

Country	Cultural Cluster	Power Distance	Individual-ism	Uncertainty Avoidance	Masculinity	Long-Term Orientation
United States	Anglo	40	91	46	62	29
China	Far Eastern	80	20	30	66	118

Table 1. Culture Dimensions and Their Values of the United States and China (Adapted from Hofstede et al., 2002). (100 = highest; 50 = middle)

The U.S., an Anglo culture, has a low degree of power distance and uncertainty avoidance and an extremely high degree of individualism. The degree of masculinity is relatively high for the Anglo culture. It is also short-term oriented. China on the other hand is classified under the Far Eastern cluster. Compared with the U.S., it has a higher degree of power distance and uncertainty avoidance, much lower degree of individualism, and a slightly lower degree of masculinity. China has the highest score in long-term orientation among all countries investigated by Hofstede. Clearly, the Chinese culture is quite different compared to the U.S. and we expect findings to be different from the U.S.-based studies. More specifically, differences are expected in the effects of the determinants of attitude and behavioral intention.

Research Model

In this research study, the TAM was extended and modified significantly. Most current studies are limited to testing technology acceptance models in North America. TAM, in particular, has been found to be less applicable in several countries, such as Japan, Switzerland, and the Arab countries (Rose and Straub, 1998; Straub, 1994; Straub et al., 1997). Furthermore, the non-U.S. studies test only a sub-set of the TAM constructs. Therefore, a more comprehensive model was developed and tested in the cultural context of China.

IDT, TRA, TAM, and other key studies contributed to the development of a comprehensive research model, shown in Figure 3. The model combines TAM's perceived usefulness, ease of use, attitude and behavioral intention constructs, IDT's innovation attributes (treated as behavioral beliefs), and TRA's normative beliefs and subjective norms constructs. The variables and their linkages are discussed further below. They are accompanied by plausible hypotheses.

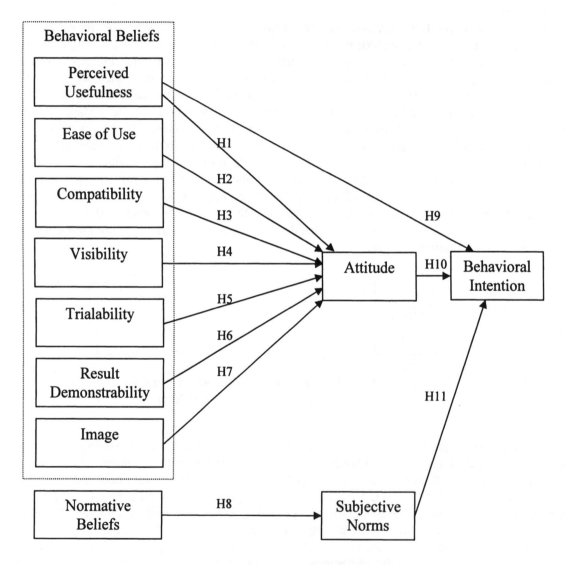

Figure 3. Research Model

Behavioral Beliefs

Dimensions of behavioral beliefs include usefulness, ease of use, image, compatibility, trialability, visibility, and result demonstrability (e.g., Agarwal and Prasad, 1997; Davis, 1989; Davis et al., 1989; Karahanna et al., 1999; Rogers, 1995). These constructs have seldom been tested simultaneously. Table 2 provides succinct definitions of these dimensions. Based on TRA and previous studies, behavioral beliefs lead to attitude, defined as "a learned, implicit anticipatory response" (Doob 1947, in Fishbein and Ajzen 1975, p. 24). Hypotheses 1 to 7 investigate the effects of behavioral beliefs on attitude.

> H1: IT users' perceived usefulness has a positive effect on attitude.
> H2: IT users' perceived ease of use has a positive effect on attitude.
> H3: IT users' perceived compatibility has a positive effect on attitude.
> H4: IT users' perceived visibility has a positive effect on attitude.
> H5: IT users' perceived trialability has a positive effect on attitude.
> H6: IT users' perceived result demonstrability has a positive effect on attitude.
> H7: IT users' perceived image has a positive effect on attitude.

Behavioral Beliefs	Definition
Perceived Usefulness	The subjective probability that using a specific application system will increase his or her job performance within an organizational context.
Ease of Use	The degree to which using a particular system is free of effort.
Compatibility	The degree to which using the IT innovation is compatible with what people do.
Trialability	The degree to which one can experiment with an innovation on a limited basis before making an adoption or rejection decision.
Visibility	The degree to which the innovation is visible in the organization.
Result Demonstrability	The degree to which the results of using the IT innovation are observable and communicable to others.
Image	The degree to which usage of the innovation is perceived to enhance one's image or status in one's social system.

Table 2. Perceived Innovation Attributes (Behavioral Beliefs) (Adopted from Karahanna et al., 1999)

Normative Beliefs and Subjective Norm

Normative beliefs of an individual refer to his/her perceptions of what his salient referents expect him to do. The IS literature indicates that normative beliefs are formed from the following sources: top management, friends and peers, IS department, and IS specialists (Karahanna et al., 1999). Normative beliefs shape a person's subjective norm, which is the perception of social pressure to perform the behavior (Mathieson, 1991). Thus,

> H8: IT users' normative beliefs have a positive effect on subjective norms.

Behavioral Intention

Behavioral intention is a good predictor of both self-reported and actual usage (Agarwal and Prasad, 1999; Jackson et al., 1997; Szajna, 1996). Therefore, intention is a meaningful surrogate for behavior. According to TRA, both attitude and subjective norms affect behavioral intention. Particularly in the context of IT use, perceived usefulness has a direct effect on behavioral intention (Davis et al., 1989). Thus,

H9: IT users' perceived usefulness has a positive effect on behavioral intention.

H10: IT users' attitude has a positive effect on behavioral intention.

H11: IT users' subjective norms have a positive effect on behavioral intention.

Research Methodology

E-mail was used as the target technology for evaluating the research model. From the time e-mail was introduced in China (late 1980s to early 1990s), sufficient time has elapsed to allow its widespread diffusion in organizations, thus allowing us to study users with various levels of experience. E-mail is one of the most accessible computer applications in China and its use is predominantly voluntary, making it a good candidate for target technology.

The constructs were operationalized using existing scales from previous studies. Fully anchored 7-point Likert scales were used with end points being "strongly disagree" and "strongly agree". Because the majority of Chinese employees are not proficient in English, the instrument was developed in English and was translated into Chinese and back translated to English to ensure that the instrument was equivalent. The instrument was validated and refined through a pilot test with Chinese employees. The final instrument demonstrating adequate reliability contains 44 items for the 11 constructs. Appendix A shows these items. The instrument asked the respondents about their e-mail training, usage pattern, and primary purpose in using e-mail. The final survey was carried out in 30 Chinese companies.

Five hundred and thirty three (533) usable surveys from employees in these companies were returned. Approximately 40% of the respondents were between the ages 23 and 28, representative of the young work force in China. Approximately 72% were males. Most were college graduates. The survey covered every level of the organization, including professionals, technical staff, managers, and executives. The average length of e-mail use in the study was two and a half years.

Analysis

Scale reliability of the instrument was assessed using Cronbach's alpha (α). Table 3 shows the reliability coefficients, ranging from .76 to .93, above the accepted cutoff of .70 (Nunnally, 1967). In addition, construct validity was assessed through convergent and discriminant validity. Finally, the risk of multicollinearity was assessed. The instrument met all recommended criteria.

Construct (# of Items)	Cronbach's α
Perceived Usefulness (6)	.88
Perceived Ease of Use (4)	.82
Compatibility (3)	.83
Trialability (4)	.84
Visibility (5)	.86
Result Demonstrability (3)	.76
Image (4)	.91
Normative Believes (6)	.93
Attitude (4)	.89
Subjective Norm (2)	.93
Behavioral Intention (3)	.84

Table 3. Reliability Coefficients

The associations between the constructs were evaluated with structural equation modeling, a technique for discovering potential latent structures (Jöreskog, 1993). The estimation procedure used was maximum likelihood (ML). A two-step approach (Anderson and Gerbing, 1988) was followed: the evaluation of the measurement model followed by the structural assessment. The measurement model fit statistics were satisfactory (Table 4). Given a satisfactory measurement model fit, the structural model was assessed. The eleven structural paths of the model were entered into the assessment. The indices again indicated good fit of the data (Table 4).

The structural model results including the estimated parameters, their t-values, significance level, and R^2 values are shown in Figure 4. Eight of the eleven structural paths are significant in the hypothesized direction lending support to H1, H3, H5, H6, H8, H9, H10, and H11. Table 5 provides a summary of the standardized path coefficients estimated in the structural model and the hypothesis testing results.

Fit statistics	Measurement Model	Structural Model	Recommended Value
χ^2 (df)	2887.78 (847)	3031.76 (863)	
Root Mean Square Error of Approximation (RMSEA)	.067	.069	about .06
Comparative Fit Index (CFI)	.95	.94	$\geq .90$
Normed Fit Index (NFI)	.93	.92	$\geq .90$
Incremental Fit Index (IFI)	.95	.94	$\geq .90$

Table 4. Fit Indices for the Measurement Model and Structural Model

Structural Path	Path Coefficient	Hypothesis	Hypothesis Support
Perceived Usefulness→Attitude	.31**	H1	Yes
Ease of Use→Attitude	-.06	H2	No
Compatibility→Attitude	.26**	H3	Yes
Trialability→Attitude	-.05	H4	No
Visibility→Attitude	.10*	H5	Yes
Result Demonstrability→Attitude	.22**	H6	Yes
Image→Attitude	.01	H7	No
Normative Belief→Subjective Norm	.52**	H8	Yes
Perceived Usefulness→Behavioral Intention	.29**	H9	Yes
Attitude→Behavioral Intention	.13*	H10	Yes
Subjective Norm→Behavioral Intention	.20**	H11	Yes

Table 5. Summary of Estimated Path Coefficients and Hypothesis Testing (Note: * $p < .05$; ** $p < .01$)

Discussion of Findings

The above study extends current IT acceptance research across cultures. It supports prior studies conducted in North America as well as provides evidence of differences. It confirms the applicability of TAM, TRA, and IDT as theoretical foundations for IT acceptance among Chinese employees, particularly in the context of e-mail use. Our model seems to be robust and generally supportive of existing theories.

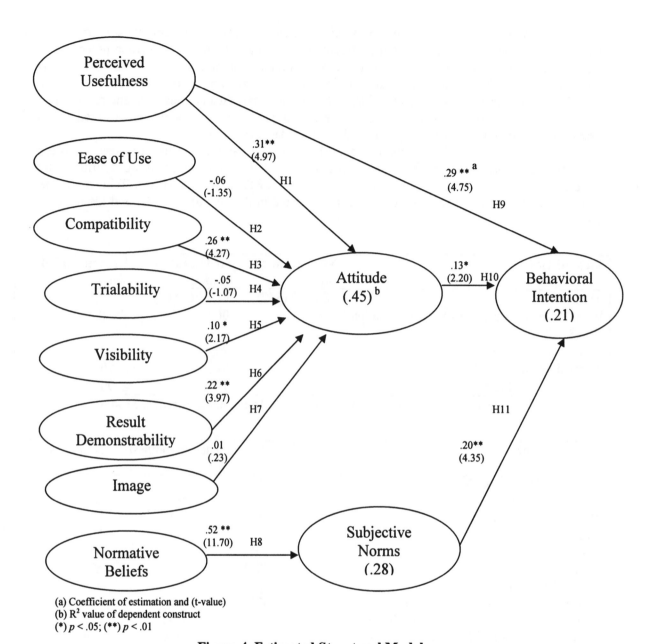

Figure 4. Estimated Structural Model

(a) Coefficient of estimation and (t-value)
(b) R² value of dependent construct
(*) *p* < .05; (**) *p* < .01

        Overall, the results show that the model demonstrates good predictive power and explains behavioral intention of Chinese e-mail users well. The model fit indices were comparable to North American studies of technology acceptance models (e.g., Agarwal and Prasad 1998; Bagozzi et al., 1992; Doll et al., 1998; Igbaria et al., 1997; Taylor and Todd, 1995a; 1995b). Note that in prior studies, when TAM was considered by itself, its applicability was relatively low in several cultural contexts.

        More specifically, the underlying theoretical themes that "behavioral beliefs" → "attitude" and perceived "usefulness+attitude+subjective norms" → "behavioral intention" are supported. We believe that the cultural dimensions such as individualism, uncertainty avoidance and long-term orientation, help to explain our findings. These are discussed in greater detail below.

Formation of Attitude

The salient behavioral beliefs that influence attitude toward IT adoption are: perceived usefulness, compatibility, visibility, and result demonstrability. Ease of use, trialability, and image were not significant determinants of attitude.

The effect of perceived usefulness is significant on attitude among Chinese IT users. More importantly, its relationship is the strongest among all beliefs. Some studies have demonstrated that the effect of perceived usefulness become stronger over time (e.g., Davis, 1989; Szajna, 1996). In studies conducted in other cultures, e.g., Switzerland (Straub et al., 1997), Arab countries (Rose and Straub, 1998), and Hong Kong (Hu et al., 1999), the effect of usefulness has also been significant. By nature, the Chinese culture does not favor uncertainties and changes. Therefore, it seems that they would commit to a change to a new technology only if the perception of usefulness is strong.

The effect of ease of use in our study was similar to many studies where its impact quickly diminishes after short period of usage (e.g., Adams et al., 1992; Davis, 1989; Hu et al., 1999; Igbaria, et al., 1995). The lack of a direct relationship between ease of use and attitude has also been observed in other cultural contexts (e.g., Hu et al., 1999; Strau et al., 1997). We suspect that because ease of use is a short-term belief, it may not be salient for the Chinese who tend to focus more on long-term beliefs resulting in delayed gratitude. In addition, "ease of use" may have a negative connotation in that it undermines the importance of learning. Respect for learning is one of the most treasured long-term values of the Chinese culture (Hofstede, 2001). Thus ease of use may be an implicit but not an explicit requirement for technology acceptance.

Compatibility was significant in our study, in accordance with both Agarwal and Prasad (1997) and Moore and Benbasat (1991) studies. The Chinese IT users are conscious about the fit between technologies and their work style and environment. When the technology is harmonized with work, they tend to have a more favorable impression of it. Harmony is a norm expected in almost every aspect of human behavior in the Chinese society (Hofstede, 2001).

For Chinese users, it seems trialability was not important; consistent with the results of Karahanna et al. (1999). The ability to try out a technology is only salient before adoption because the experimentation helps the users overcome uncertainties and makes the change process less demanding (Karahanna et al., 1999). For users, trialability may be obsolete or irrelevant after adoption.

Visibility was a significant determinant of attitude. Among Chinese users, using a new technology provides visibility among fellow employees and adds to positive opinions about oneself among peers and proximate work groups. This is consistent with the Chinese culture, classified as collective (Hofstede 1980), where a person's attitude and behavioral are greatly affected by others.

Result demonstrability was a significant factor as well. When the results of a new technology can be clearly communicated to others, the result is a more favorable attitude. However, result demonstrability had no impact on users' attitudes in U.S. studies (e.g., Agarwal and Prasad, 1997; Karahanna et al., 1999). This can be explained by the uncertainty avoidance dimension of culture (Hofstede, 1980). The Chinese culture is characterized high on uncertainty avoidance, where in the U.S., people are more risk tolerant. When the outcome of a certain behavior is clear and certain, it reduces uncertainty leading to greater acceptance. In addition, the Chinese do not hold abstract principles and concepts in high regard (Hofstede, 2001). They need demonstrable results in lieu of concepts or promises.

Few studies in IS have examined the effect of image. Our results contrast those of Karahanna et al. (1999). In our study, the IT users' perceived images of using e-mail had no impact on attitude. One explanation is people in collectivist cultures are less conscious of their own image than in individualistic cultures. Another explanation emerged in informal interviews with some employees. It was suggested that e-mail lacks authority and is not perceived as a status symbol. If something is really important, it would be reinforced with handwritten notes.

Formation of Behavioral Intention

Our results support the notion that perceived usefulness has a direct impact on behavioral intention as professed by TAM. It also confirms TRA, where behavioral intention is influenced by attitude and subjective norms.

While usefulness, attitude, and subjective norms all impact behavioral intention, the comparative strengths of the three constructs are different. Usefulness has the highest strength, followed by subjective norms and attitude in that order. There are two important conclusions in the Chinese context from this observation. First, perceived usefulness is the most important to the Chinese, even more than own personal attitude. The Chinese people are results oriented and are more willing to adopt something when they clearly see its value. This is consistent with their tendency to minimize risk.

The second finding is the significance of subjective norms and is even more revealing. When prior studies compare the strengths of attitude and subjective norms, it is found that users form attitude based on direct experience rather than subjective norm; thus a closer relationship between attitude and behavioral intention is expected (Fazio and Zanna, 1981; Karahanna et al., 1999). However, in the Chinese culture, subjective norms play a more important role than attitude in influencing intention. This is a strong indication that in a collectivist culture, people tend to base their behavior more on what others think rather than their own attitude.

Other Observations

In our research, we also asked employees about e-mail training, usage pattern, and the primary purpose of using e-mail. We asked the Chinese employees to indicate whether they received training before and after they started using e-mail. Results show that training was not widely conducted (Table 6). Only 5.1% indicated that they received training before adoption and 6.0% were trained after adoption. In fact, six organizations in our study provided no training at all.

Response	Training Before Adoption	Training After Adoption
No	62.9%	61.9%
Yes	5.1%	6.0%
Not reported	32.1%	32.1%

Table 6. Employee E-Mail Training

In addition, we interviewed several organizations about their IT practices. The interviews confirmed that most of the organizations lacked IT training and support. While some organizations offered training before implementing the technology, training was voluntary. Formal policies were absent in general. The common model was that when new technologies were introduced, each functional area would send its computer person, unofficially appointed, to attend the training (if it was provided). Vendor-offered training dominated the scene. Following the training, the computer person would train the rest of the members in the functional area. However, the responsibility was never mandatory nor compensated.

The main form of IT support was self-provided. Employees attempted to troubleshoot and resolve problems by themselves first. Only when they failed, would they ask for help from the computer person. Only in situations such as hardware failures would employees contact the IT supporting staff. The average IT staff was small. For example, in a research institution that had over 600 employees, there was only one IT specialist. Many firms reported relying on vendor support.

Thus, management of IT is largely neglected in Chinese organizations. IT training is greatly lacking. Users are expected to learn technologies on their own. Little organizational resources are devoted to support and maintenance of IT, and IT departments are non-existent in some organizations.

While this laissez-faire approach of IT management may not seem to have impeded the adoption and effective use of IT, it should be noted that the use of e-mail in the organizations we studied is still in the early stages of assimilation. The average length of use is only two and a half years. The penetration in most Chinese employees' work is still shallow. About half of the users are not using e-mail on a daily basis. Heavy users of e-mail are rare. When e-mail becomes more prevalent in the workplace, training and support would be necessary to promote more wide-spread and effective use.

CONCLUSION

China's telecommunications, PC, software, and IT outsourcing markets are experiencing historical growth and reaching exciting milestones in the new millennium. The support and commitment from the government and foreign multinationals will continue to pave a bright future for IT development in China.

While the macro environment for IT growth is positive in China, little research has investigated the dynamics of individual IT use in organizations. The research study reported in this chapter is one such attempt and makes an important contribution to cross-cultural research in the IT literature. Cultural factors have a significant impact on IT users and should be considered when theories are applied across cultures. While the comprehensive research model developed for this study was based on U.S. based theories, it explained the IT acceptance behavior well in the Chinese culture but some differences were also observed. Previous attempts using simpler models found little support in other cultures, such as in Japan (Straub, 1994). Our study has strong implications for the applicability of IT acceptance theories and models. In essence, the theoretical validity of western models simply cannot be assumed away in other cultures and needs to be confirmed empirically.

Practical implications of our research are twofold. First, for multinational organizations managing IT in China, the study points out that perceived usefulness is the most important element of technology perception. Therefore, IT intervention programs need to focus on promoting perceived usefulness. Other important aspects of the technology, such as compatibility, visibility, and result demonstrability should also be addressed in efforts to encourage IT usage. Second, it is important to recognize that social influences bear a strong impact on why people adopt technologies in certain cultures. Managers need to provide channels to encourage social exchange of IT experiences.

Appendix A. List of Items, Abbreviations, and Descriptions

Construct (Abbreviation) /Item	Item Description
Perceived Usefulness (PU)	
1 PU1	Using E-Mail helps me to accomplish tasks more quickly.
2 PU2	Using E-Mail improves the quality of my work.
3 PU3	Using E-Mail enhances my effectiveness on the job.
4 PU4	Using E-Mail makes my job easier.
5 PU5	Using E-Mail in my job increases my productivity.
6 PU6	I find E-Mail useful in my job.
Ease of Use (EOU)	
7 EOU1	Learning to use E-Mail was easy for me.
8 EOU2	E-Mail is easy to use.
9 EOU3	My interaction with E-Mail is clear and understandable.
10 EOU4	It is easy for me to become skillful at using E-Mail.

Construct (Abbreviation) /Item	Item Description
Compatibility (COM)	
11 COM1	Using E-Mail is compatible with most aspects of my work.
12 COM2	Using E-Mail fits my work style.
13 COM3	Using E-Mail is very compatible with the way I like to work.
Trialability (TR)	
14 TR1	Before I started using E-Mail, I was able to use it on a trial basis.
15 TR2	Before I started using E-Mail, I was able to properly try it out.
16 TR3	I was permitted to use E-Mail long enough to see what it can do.
17 TR4	I had E-Mail for a long enough period to try it out.
Visibility (VI)	
18 VI1	In my organization, one sees E-Mail on many computers.
19 VI2	In my organization, I have seen many people with E-Mail on their computers.
20 VI3	I have seen what other people do using E-Mail.
21 VI4	It is easy for me to observe others using E-Mail in my company.
22 VI5	I have had plenty of opportunity to see E-Mail being used.
Result Demonstrability (RD)	
23 RD1	The results of using E-Mail are apparent to me.
24 RD2	I could communicate to others the pros and cons of using E-Mail.
25 RD3	I have no difficulty telling others about the results of using E-Mail.
Image (IM)	
26 IM1	People who use E-Mail have high status in the organization.
27 IM2	People who use E-Mail have more prestige than those who do not.
28 IM3	Using E-Mail is a status symbol.
29 IM4	Using E-Mail improves my image within the organization.
Normative Beliefs (NB)	
30 NB1	Top management thinks I should use E-Mail.
31 NB2	My supervisor thinks I should use E-Mail.
32 NB3	Peers think I should use E-Mail.
33 NB4	Friends think I should use E-Mail.
34 NB5	MIS department thinks I should use E-Mail.
35 NB6	Computer Specialists in the company think I should use E-Mail.
Attitude (A)	
36 A1	Using E-Mail on my job is extremely good … extremely bad.
37 A2	Using E-Mail on my job is extremely harmful…extremely beneficial.
38 A3	Using E-Mail on my job is useless ….. Useful.
39 A4	Using E-Mail on my job is worthless ….valuable.
Subjective Norms (SN)	
40 SN1	Most people who are important to me think I should use E-Mail.
41 SN2	Most people who influence my behavior think I should use E-Mail.
Behavioral Intention (BI)	
42 BI1	I intend to continue using E-Mail.
43 BI2	Assuming I had access to E-Mail, I intend to use it.
44 BI3	Given that I had access to E-Mail, I predict that I would use it.

MINICASE

How Governments Matter to Digital Economy Creation: China's Golden Card Project (GCP)

Background and State of the Art of GCP

Golden Card is one of the three Golden projects launched by the Chinese central government and the former Ministry of Electronic Industry as a series of information infrastructure initiatives aimed at developing a digital economy and promoting the government's administrative capabilities. GCP's objective was to allow monetary circulation by electronic information transfer through a unified payment clearance system.

GCP was initiated by the State Council (Chinese Central Government Cabinet), initially aimed to develop China's electronic monetary system and accelerate the informatization of the banking industry. By using the information technology and communication infrastructure, this project was designed to allow currency circulation by electronic information transfer through a unified payment clearance system. China's fragmented banking system has traditionally made it extremely difficult to clear transactions, and this was recognized as a major barrier to the development of digital economy. The Blueprint for the Golden Card Project (*Jin Ka Gong Cheng Zong Ti She Xiang*) formulated in 1994 set the target of issuing 0.2 billion integrated circuit (IC) cards among 0.3 billion people in 400 cities within ten years. By the end of 2002, the total number of IC cards issued was 1.1 billion, far exceeding the planned number. In particular, 4.56 billion high end IC cards - CPU IC cards – were issued by the end of 2003. These cards were mainly applied in mobile telecommunication, social welfare, motor vehicle, utility and network security (Table 1).

Application Industry	Mobile Telecom	Social Welfare	Motor Vehicle	Utility	Network Security	Others	Total
No. of Cards Issued	414.3	19.9	7	4.35	3	8	456.55

Table 1

Chinese Government's Impacts on the Supply of IC Cards

The implementation of GCP spanning a period of more than 10 years was divided into three stages: the pilot stage, the dissemination stage and the popularization stage. At the pilot stage, ten provinces were chosen where the communication network facilities were comparatively well developed and the local government leadership was strong. During the three years of this stage, the cards issued were mainly by banks in the first chosen 12 cities. Also, the cards issued at this stage were magnetic stripe cards instead of IC cards. Although the Chinese government started a project to develop the card operating system (COS) for IC cards in 1994, progress of the project was described as "really slow". The two main reasons were the number of organizations involved was too small and government funding dedicated to these projects was limited. COS development was charged mainly to three companies - Beijing Cast Information Systems Technology Co. Ltd., Beijing Watchdata Co. Ltd. and Great Wall Computer Software and System Co. Ltd. On the other hand, the demand for IC cards was not high enough and there was no IC card standard. These factors impeded private companies to invest in this area. The slow progress of domestic IC card development prevented some industries from applying IC cards due to security concerns.

At the end of 1997, the National Golden Card Project Office issued the Standard for Chinese Financial Integrated Circuits. This official document served as a benchmark for China's CPU development. It lured a number of Chinese companies to invest in the design of IC cards following the standard. It was from then on that non-banking industries, such as social welfare, started to apply IC cards. The popularization stage started from 1999. With the lower cost and better security of CPU cards and many more organizations and cities participating in GCP, the total number of CPU cards issued increased dramatically (Table 2). The complete value-adding chain ranging from chip design, development and production, large scale production of various cards, the research and development of card reading machines (ATM and POS machines), component and material supply, to the development of operating systems and application software, system integration and technical support services has come to existence. By 2003, there were 13 chip-design companies registered with China's Integrated Circuit Registration Center. These companies had about 30% share of the Chinese chip market. All the domestically designed and manufactured electronic information products accounted for more than 80% of China's market by 2004.

Year	Number of CPU cards issued (in millions)
2000	57
2001	82
2002	106.5
2003	133.2

Table 2. Number of Cards Issued

Chinese Government's Actions to Spur the Demand of IC Cards

For the demand side of IC cards, the Chinese government exerted influence by requiring government agencies and state-owned organizations to develop application programs. Examples of these organizations were hospitals, public transportation companies, Tourism Bureau, Industrial and Commercial Administration, Taxation Bureau, Public Security Bureau and utility companies. Since these companies received funds directly from the government, they were obligated to carry out what was advocated by the government. Also, the Chinese government set up an Informatization Office in every city participating in GCP. These local government agencies were charged with the responsibility to coordinate the collaboration among companies within and across industries. Coupled with this, the Chinese government used the media to disseminate information on how other countries were using IC cards and how citizens could benefit from using IC cards. Also, the IT infrastructure built by the government, especially the Internet, provided Chinese opportunities to learn how other people lived their lives and how digital economy was popular in foreign countries. In addition, the Chinese government lifted the restriction on citizens' visiting foreign countries, which allowed Chinese people to witness and experience how digital economy could affect their daily lives. All this information and experiences made Chinese people willing to adopt IC cards.

Discussion and Conclusion

The study of how the Chinese government facilitated the digital economy creation by GCP reveals that governments in transitioning economies have large scope and impact. In particular, governments in transitioning economies still have the power to change private behavior and a nation's social structure. Therefore, many activities that governments in developed economies leave to the market are provided directly by governments in transitioning economies. In addition, the digital technologies used are at their imitation stage for transitioning economies. This status of technologies facilitates development of digital economy in two ways. At the supply side, organizations in transitioning economies have better ideas about what technologies to develop and how they can be applied, based on the experience of developed countries. Thus, transitioning economies may enjoy the late-mover advantage. At the demand side, learning about the benefits of a digital economy achieved in developed countries enhances companies' and citizens' predisposition to accept digital economy and it's related technology. Therefore, it is easier for governments in transitioning economies to mobilize user's acceptance of the technologies.

Adapted From: Ke, W., Xu, W., and Tang, J. "How Governments Matter to Digital Economy Creation: An Exploratory Case Study on China's Golden Card Project," *Proceedings of the 7th Annual Global Information Technology Management Association World Conference*, June 11-13, 2006, Orlando, Florida, USA.

Discussion Questions
1. How is the role of government for facilitating information technology different in developed and transitioning economies, and why?
2. In transitioning economies, what roles can government play to influence organizations and their behavior in developing new technologies?
3. In transitioning economies, how can the government influence the society's and its citizens' behavior in accepting new technologies?
4. Provide philosophical and economic arguments for the role of government in the growth of its country's IT industry.

KEY TERMS
Bandwidth
Broadband
CMM
IC Card (integrated circuit card or ICC)
WAPI
Wi-Fi
Wireless LAN (WLAN)

STUDY QUESTIONS
1. Describe the current status of the Chinese IT and telecommunications industry. What are its strengths and weaknesses?

2. Describe the key factors that drive the Chinese software industry growth.

3. What role does the Chinese government play in stimulating IT industry growth?

4. What role does the foreign multinationals play in China's IT industry?

5. What are some strategies for the future growth of the Chinese IT industry?

6. Describe potential challenges IT managers may face in Chinese organizations. Discuss strategies they may use to promote the use of IT.

7. What is your vision of IT development in China in the next 5 years?

REFERENCES

Adams, D. A., Nelson, R. R., and Todd, P. A. "Perceived Usefulness, Ease of Use, and Usage of Information Technology: A Replication," *MIS Quarterly,* 16(2), 1992, pp. 227-247.

Agarwal, R., and Prasad, J. "The Role of Innovation Characteristics and Perceived Voluntariness in the Acceptance of Information Technologies," *Decision Sciences,* 28)3), 1997, pp. 557-582.

Agarwal, R., and Prasad, J. "A Conceptual and Operational Definition of Personal Innovativeness in the Domain of Information Technology," *Information Systems Research,* 9(2), 1998, pp. 204-215.

Agarwal, R., and Prasad, J. "Are Individual Differences Germane to the Acceptance of New Information Technologies?," *Decision Sciences,* 30(2), 1999, pp. 361-391.

Anderson, J. C., and Gerbing, D. "Structural Equation Modeling in Practice: A Review and Recommended Two-Step Approach," *Psychological Bulletin,* 103(:3), 1988, pp. 411-423.

Bagozzi, R. P., Davis, F. D., and Warshaw, P. R. "Development and Test of a Theory of Technological Learning and Usage," *Human Relations,* 45(7), 1992, pp. 659-686.

Balfour, F., and Tashiro, H. "GOLF, SUSHI -- AND CHEAP ENGINEERS," *Business Week,* 39(26), 2005, pp. 54.

Davis, F. "A Technology Acceptance Model for Empirically Testing New End-User Information Systems: Theory and Results," Doctoral Dissertation, Massachusetts Institute of Technology, Cambridge, MA, 1986.

Davis, F. D. "Perceived Usefulness, Perceived Ease of Use, and User Acceptance of Information Technology," *MIS Quarterly,* 13(3), 1989, pp. 319-339.

Davis, F. D., Bagozzi, R. P., and Warshaw, P. R. "User Acceptance Of Computer Technology: A Comparison Of Two Theoretical Models," *Management Science,* 35(8), 1989, pp. 982-1003.

Doll, W. J., Hendrickson, A., and Deng, X. "Using Davis's Perceived Usefulness and Ease of Use Instruments for Decision Making: A Confirmatory and Multigroup Invariance Analysis," *Decision Sciences,* 29(4), 1998, pp. 839-869.

Farhoomand, A., and Tao, Z. *China's Telecommunication Industry in 2004,* Asia Case Research Centre: The University of Hong Kong, 2005.

Fazio, R. H., and Zanna, M. P. "Direct Experience and Attitude-Behavior Consistency," In *Advances in Experimental Social Psychology,* L. Berkowitz (ed.) 14, Academic Press, New York, 1981, pp. 161-202.

Fishbein, M., and Ajzen, I. *Belief, Attitude, Intention, and Behavior: An Introduction to Theory and Research,* Addison-Wesley, Reading, MA, 1975.

Hofstede, G. *Culture's Consequences: International Differences in Work-Related Values,* Sage Publications, Beverly Hills, 1980.

Hofstede, G. "Management Scientists are Human," *Management Science,* 40(1), 1994, pp. 4-13.

Hofstede, G. *Culture's Consequences: Comparing Values, Behaviors, Institutions, and Organizations across Nations,* Sage Publications, Inc., Thousand Oaks, CA, 2001.

Hofstede, G., Hofstede, G. J. and Pedersen, P. B. Exploring Culture: Exercises, stories and sythetic cultures,Yarmouth, Maine: Intercultural Press. 2002.

Hu, P. J., Chau, P. Y. K., Sheng, O. R. L., and Tam, K. Y. "Examining the Technology Acceptance Model Using Physician Acceptance of Telemedicine Technology," *Journal of Management Information Systems,* 16(2), 1999, pp. 91-112.

Igbaria, M., Guimaraes, T., and Davis, G. B. "Testing the Determinants of Microcomputer Usage via a Structural Equation Model," *Journal of Management Information Systems,* 11(4), 1995, pp. 87-114.

Igbaria, M., Zinatelli, N., Cragg, P., and Cavaye, A. L. M. "Personal Computing Acceptance Factors in Small Firms: A Structural Equation Model," *MIS Quarterly,* 21(3), 1997, pp. 279-302.

IWS "Top 10 Countries With the Highest Number of Internet Users," October 2, 2005,

Jackson, C. M., Chow, S., and Leitch, R. A. "Toward an Understanding of the Behavioral Intention to Use an Information System," *Decision Sciences,* 28(2), 1997, pp. 357-389.

Jöreskog, K. G. "Testing Structural Equation Models," In *Testing Structural Equation Models*, K. A. Bollen and J. S. Long (eds.), Sage, Newbury Park, CA, 1993, pp. 294-316.

Karahanna, E., Straub, D. W., and Chervany, N. L. "Information Technology Adoption Across Time: A cross-Sectional Comparison of Pre-Adoption and Post-Adoption Beliefs," *MIS Quarterly,* 23(2), 1999, pp. 183-213.

Ke, W., Xu, W., and Tang, J. "How Governments Matter to Digital Economy Creation: An Exploratory Case Study on China's Golden Card Project," *Proceedings of the 7th Annual Global Information Technology Management Association World Conference*, June 11-13, 2006, Orlando, Florida, USA.

Mathieson, K. "Predicting User Intentions: Comparing the Technology Acceptance Model with the Theory of Planned Behavior," *Information Systems Research,* 2(3), 1991, pp. 173-191.

MII "January-August 2005 Growth Statistics," October 2, 2005,

Moore, G. C., and Benbasat, I. "Development of an Instrument to Measure the Perceptions of Adopting an Information Technology Innovation," *Information Systems Research,* 2(3), 1991, pp. 192-222.

Nunnally, J. C. *Psychometric Theory*, McGraw-Hill, New York, 1967.

Rogers, E. M. *Diffusion of Innovation*, Free Press, New York, 1995.

Rose, G., and Straub, D. "Predicting General IT Use: Applying TAM to the Arabic World.," *Journal of Global Information Management,* 6(3), 1998, pp. 39-46.

Sheppard, B. H., Hartwick, J., and Warshaw, P. R. "The Theory of Reasoned Action: A Meta-Analysis of Past Research with Recommendations for Modifications and Future Research," *Journal of Consumer Research* (15), 1988, pp. 325-343.

Straub, D. "The Effect of Culture on IT Diffusion: E-Mail & Fax in Japan and the U.S.," *Information Systems Research,* 5(1), 1994, pp. 23-47.

Straub, D., Keil, M., and Brenner, W. "Testing the Technology Acceptance Model Across Cultures: A Three Country Study," *Information and Management,* 33(1), 1997, pp. 1-11.

Szajna, B. "Empirical evaluation of the revised technology acceptance model," *Management Science,* 42(1), 1996, pp. 85-92.

Taylor, S., and Todd, P. "Assessing IT Usage: The Role of Prior Experience," *MIS Quarterly,* 19(4), 1995a, pp. 561-570.

Taylor, S., and Todd, P. A. "Understanding Information Technology Usage: A Test of Competing Models," *Information Systems Research,* 6(2), 1995b, pp. 144-176.

Thibodeau, P. "China Starts IT Services Push," *Computerworld,* 39(33), 2005, pp. 10.

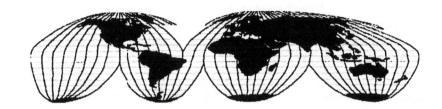

Cultural Mediation in the Global Transfer of Information Technology Systems: The Case of China

Carol Pollard
Appalachian State University, USA

Yan Nee Ang
University of Tasmania, New Zealand

CHAPTER SUMMARY

Globalization and improvements in telecommunication technology are creating different experiences for people of different cultures, including conflict with traditional beliefs because of ambiguous meanings, hidden agendas and diversity of entrenched traditions across cultures. It is anticipated that there will be a cultural price ascribed to the dissemination of information technology artifacts to countries with contexts that are socially, ideologically, philosophically, and historically different. This chapter analyses the impact of embedded ideologies and philosophies in IT models and how they fail to consider a cross-cultural perspective (e.g. Western vs. Eastern philosophies and ideology). To exemplify, we provide a mini-case on the influence of the ti-yong paradigm, used by the Chinese since the second century, as a strategy for adopting foreign technology. We emphasize the need to make necessary adjustments in IT models that need to be made before disseminating into different culture and take into consideration the influence of IT on traditional cultural values in the systems development process.

INTRODUCTION

IT as an artifact plays an important role in affecting societal interests and values. This becomes particularly important when technology is developed in one culture and adopted for use in another culture that has dissimilar cultural values. In 2001, the Software and Information Industry Association reported that the top 100 software companies in the United States made 50% or more of their sales to other countries and that it was common for software products to be released simultaneously in 10 or more languages. A growing list of examples of poor IS design for global use provided by Isys Information Architects (http://homepage.mac.com/bradster/iarchitect/global.htm) in their "Hall of

Shame" (see Table 1) illustrates the need to better understand even the most obvious of cultural assumptions embedded in IS development efforts given the growing "global reach" of technology.

This chapter begins to dig a little deeper to explore the diffusion of meanings, politics and laws along with the cross-cultural transfer of IT artifacts in the context of transfer of IT systems developed in western countries to China.

- Software translated into foreign language, BUT error messages appearing in English.
- Incorrect translation of terms from one language to another, e.g., "Browse" to choose another starting directory, translated to "Scrub"; "Find now" to find a file translated to "Start".
- Inadequate consideration of differences between US zip codes and European/Australian postal codes that vary in composition and length
- Spelling checkers that only support "American" English
- Translations of functions truncated because of space limitations based on "American" spelling

Table 1. "Hall of Shame" Poor IS Designs for Globalization

In China, the understanding a new technology often takes the form of understanding the practical and functional aspects of the "Information Technology" object. However, understanding IT comes at the price of cultural change. Understanding a specific information technology requires interpretation and engagement of the embedded ideology and philosophy of the IT artifact and the conflicts between ideologies that can often arise. These engagements with IT artifacts manifest themselves not only in the meaning, politics and governance but also in how IT is used and developed across cultures. The basis of this chapter is that philosophical differences, such as Confucian values that have been embedded in the lives of the Chinese people for 4000 years, are very different from the IT philosophical underpinnings of the West. This gives rise to two important questions:

1. How do cultural perspectives of the embedded ideologies and philosophies of IT differ across nations?
2. What mechanisms are being used to mediate embedded ideologies and philosophies in the IT artifact during the process of IT transfer from one culture to another?

This chapter seeks to explore the properties of the IT artifact, differences in ideologies and philosophies embedded in the IT artifact and encourages a new way of thinking about information technology vis-a-vis culture.

First, we explain the concept of cultural dimensions. Second, we describe the embedded ideologies and philosophies in IT artifacts, through examining the five premises of theorizing the IT artifact. Third, we discuss a number of national paradigms that are being used to mediate the effects of technology on cultural norms and propose a conceptual model of mediation that is explained by the specific example of the Ti-Yong paradigm (used by the Chinese since 1500) used in China. In conclusion, we suggest that IT artifacts need to be changed to make allowances for differing cultural values to facilitate cross-cultural adoption and use of IT and minimize the decline of traditional cultural norms.

CULTURAL DIMENSIONS

Extensive data have been collected on world cultures and the ways in which they differ. The pre-eminent authority on cultural dimensions is Geert Hofstede who conducted one of the most comprehensive studies of how values in the workplace are influenced by culture. Hofstede (1991) analyzed responses from 116,000 IBM employees, collected between 1967 and 1973. Although the responses represented more than 70 countries, his initial dimensions were based on analysis of the 40 largest countries. He later extended his analysis to 50 countries in 3 geographic regions. More recently Hofstede, Hofstede and Pedersen (2002) reported scores for 74 countries and regions, partly based on replications and extensions of the IBM study on different international populations.

From the initial results, and later additions, Hofstede developed a model that identifies four primary dimensions to assist in differentiating cultures. These are: Power Distance - PDI, Individualism - IDV, Masculinity - MAS, and Uncertainty Avoidance – UAI. Comparing the USA, China and world average across Hofstede's five dimensions (5D) reveals some interesting differences, as shown in Table 2.

COUNTRY\DIMENSION	PDI	IDV	MAS	UAI	LTO
USA	40	91	62	46	29
CHINA	80	20	66	30	118
WORLD AVG.	55	43	50	64	45

Table 2. Comparison of Hofstede's 5D

Clearly, there are considerable differences on Power Distance (PDI), Individualism (IDV) and Long-Term Orientation (LTO) that might have significant effects on the development of technology in the USA and its assimilation into culturally different countries. These differences have been and still are a source of concern for countries that are significantly different, e.g., the USA vs. China, relative to preserving their culture. In a recent study of nearly 50 countries, Erumban and De Jong (2006) explored the connection between ICT adoption and national culture. They reported that power distance and uncertainty avoidance seem to be the most important cultural dimensions affecting ICT adoption. These differences in cultural values in different countries raise a number of IT-related questions:

- Can a company in a country be characterized as high in individualism find it easy to engage collaboratively in a close working relationship with data sharing (partnership model) as it can in a competitive relationship with minimal data sharing (arm's-length model)?"
- Can a company from a country characterized as high in collectivism find it as easy to engage in an arm's-length relationship as it can with a partnership relationship?
- How can these relationships be facilitated by accommodating these cultural differences in the information systems that are developed in one culture and deployed in another culture?

American manufacturers who are typically high on individualism and low on uncertainty avoidance primarily follow the arms-length model whereas the opposite would be expected of Chinese manufacturers who are low in individualism and high on uncertainty avoidance.

EMBEDDED IDEOLOGIES AND PHILOSOPHIES IN THE IT ARTIFACT

In their article entitled, "Desperately seeking "IT" in IT research - A call to theorizing the IT artifact", Orlikowski and Iacono (2001) propose five premises of IT (p. 131):
1. not natural, neutral, universal or given;
2. always embedded in some time, place, discourse and community;
3. usually made up of a multiplicity of often fragile and fragmentary components;
4. neither fixed nor independent;
5. not static or unchanging, but dynamic.

Hofstede Dimensions – An Overview

Power Distance Index (PDI) is the extent to which the less powerful members of organizations and institutions (like the family) accept and expect that power is distributed unequally. This represents inequality (more versus less), but defined from below, not from above. It suggests that a society's level of inequality is endorsed by the followers as much as by the leaders. Power and inequality, of course, are extremely fundamental facts of any society and anybody with some international experience will be aware that 'all societies are unequal, but some are more unequal than others.

Individualism (IDV) on the one side versus its opposite, collectivism, is the degree to which individuals are integrated into groups. On the individualist side we find societies in which the ties between individuals are loose: everyone is expected to look after him/herself and his/her immediate family. On the collectivist side, we find societies in which people from birth onwards are integrated into strong, cohesive in-groups, often extended families (with uncles, aunts and grandparents) which continue protecting them in exchange for unquestioning loyalty. The word 'collectivism' in this sense has no political meaning: it refers to the group, not to the state. Again, the issue addressed by this dimension is an extremely fundamental one, regarding all societies in the world.

Masculinity (MAS) versus its opposite -femininity, refers to the distribution of roles between the genders which is another fundamental issue for any society to which a range of solutions are found. The IBM studies revealed that (a) women's values differ less among societies than men's values; (b) men's values from one country to another contain a dimension from very assertive and competitive and maximally different from women's values on the one side, to modest and caring and similar to women's values on the other. The assertive pole has been called 'masculine' and the modest, caring pole 'feminine'. The women in feminine countries have the same modest, caring values as the men; in the masculine countries they are somewhat assertive and competitive, but not as much as the men, so that these countries show a gap between men's values and women's values.

Uncertainty Avoidance Index (UAI) deals with a society's tolerance for uncertainty and ambiguity; it ultimately refers to man's search for Truth. It indicates to what extent a culture programs its members to feel either uncomfortable or comfortable in unstructured situations. Unstructured situations are novel, unknown, surprising, and different from usual. Uncertainty avoiding cultures try to minimize the possibility of such situations by strict laws and rules, safety and security measures, and on the philosophical and religious level by a belief in absolute Truth; 'there can only be one Truth and we have it'. People in uncertainty avoiding countries are also more emotional, and motivated by inner nervous energy. The opposite type, uncertainty accepting cultures, are more tolerant of opinions different from what they are used to; they try to have as few rules as possible, and on the philosophical and religious level they are relativist and allow many currents to flow side by side. People within these cultures are more phlegmatic and contemplative, and not expected by their environment to express emotions.

Based on data collected with Chinese employees and managers, Hofstede added a fifth dimension, based on Confucian dynamism, which he labeled Long-Term Orientation - LTO.

Long-Term Orientation (LTO) versus short-term orientation: this fifth dimension was found in a study among students in 23 countries around the world, using a questionnaire designed by Chinese scholars. It can be said to deal with Virtue regardless of Truth. Values associated with Long Term Orientation are thrift and perseverance; values associated with Short Term Orientation are respect for tradition, fulfilling social obligations, and protecting one's 'face'. Both the positively and the negatively rated values of this dimension are found in the teachings of Confucius, the most influential Chinese philosopher who lived around 500 B.C.; however, the dimension also applies to countries without a Confucian heritage.

In short, their proposal emphasizes that the IT artifact should not be viewed as being neutral, since it has embedded within it the values and interests of its interest group relative to time, place, discourse and community. The IT artifact also requires activities such as "bridging, integration and articulation" to work together. This requires that we understand how IT needs to change to "accommodate a diversity of evolving interest, values, assumptions, cultures and other new technologies". It also requires an understanding of how and why IT artifacts have become "stabilized in certain ways at certain times and places" depending on the social and economic aspect associated with different socio-historical contexts. Neither should IT be discussed as if it were "whole, uniform and unified". IT is rarely full integrated; it usually consists of a number of interlinked components that must be considered as independent pieces. Nor is it fixed, independent, static or unchanging – consider the World Wide Web and its ever changing dynamic nature and content.

Where are Ideologies and Philosophies Embedded?

IT is shaped by the interest, values and assumptions of its developers, investors and users. Ideologies such as Western market interest (capitalism), values (ethics and freedom of choice) and assumptions (how things ought to be) are obvious. Systems designed in an organization often take into consideration the power structure of the organization and the technology structure consequently reflects structures of domination. These expressions of power in resource allocation are similar to Bray's (1997) description of technology as "a form of cultural expression and as such plays a key role in the creation and transmission of ideology." In considering the case of IT-enabled supply chain management, Shore (2002, p.122) discusses the need to consider both relationships and data and the need for information systems developers to consider the level of authority and responsibility in the execution of tasks when developing for use in countries other than the country of origin

What Happens When East Meets West?

IT adoption has been primarily examined through the lens of the Western world. As such, the ethnocentricity of such view fails to reflect the realities of other cultures that are different from the Western ideology and philosophy. For example, China's ideologies [i.e. Confucius to Marxism] that provide the framework for the formation of structure and distribution of labor in China are in sharp contrast to Western philosophies.

In China, relationships, not rules, govern the availability of information in organizations. Any technology that has the potential to change the power structure of organizations would consequently be viewed with caution. Acquiring reliable information in China requires years of personal relationship cultivation (e.g. guanxi) - the more reliable or valuable the information, the more difficult it is to cultivate the relationship. Thus, it can be proposed that the introduction of IT, with its' embedded power structure, will have two kinds of influences: changes in the organization structure (which is explicit) and changes in the power structure (which is implicit). Thus, technological systems that reflect structures of domination do not suit non-Western cultures.

It would appear then that a different framework is needed when adopting technologies developed in Western cultures into cultures that are significantly different from the West. Embedded interests, values, assumptions, ideologies and philosophies in IT that are foreign to Chinese philosophy and designed in an economic system different from China have to be modified to allow for the effective use of information technology, with an emphasis on its fit within the Chinese context. These differences and problems are discussed below in terms of cultural implications and problems in knowledge acquisition.

Cultural Implications: From the Western point of view, any cross-cultural transfer of models needs to take the realities in China into account. Development of IT for China requires an understanding of a number of currently prevailing cultural conditions:

1. *Chinese rationality* – the influence of the Chinese value systems in guiding how they make decisions;

2. *Economic structure* - the 'birdcage theory' with emphasis on the role of central planning (as the 'cage' to regulate economic activities and creation of space) and 'bird' as the economy (a form of liberation). Although they are opening up their economy, key structures such as the networks are state-owned, which is in line with the government's insistence that the country's communications infrastructure remain under government control (Hartford 2000);

3. *Political climate* - the growing influence of the conservatives in the Chinese Communist Party who are intent on rolling back reforms (Sargis 1999), as the digital divide correlates with the number of have and have nots, the greater the gap between the rich and poor and the greater the influence of the conservatives;

4. *Availability of institutional support* - greater support from the Chinese government means that the state will most likely be the driver of the market which in turn guides the enterprises (Sargis 1999), hence any form of influence, e.g., Foreign Direct Investment or Joint Venture, that may shift the balance towards a market driven approach would be questioned.

These prevailing cultural conditions and the differences with Western conditions are evident in the following example by Zhou (2004):

Establishment of Research and Development (R&D) facilities by Multinational Companies (MNCs) were welcomed as a form of improvement of technological levels in China, however, their underlying strategies of 'getting returns on their investment' by dominating the foreign market were met with skepticism by the 'Chinese government agencies, academic institutions and national industries'. To remain in control of China's direction, control policies such as the "24-character direction for China's informatization[1]" that include overall planning (*tongchou guihua*), state dominance (*guojia zhudao*), unified standards (*tongyi biaozhun*), joint construction (*lianhe jianshe*), links between government units (*hulian hutong*), and shared resources (*ziyuan gongxiang*). These informationization policies culminated in adoption of "Three Goldens" projects in 1994. Golden Bridge would build networked economic information, Golden Customs would network international trade information, and Golden Card would network financial and banking information. These proved golden in so many ways that more than 20 other smaller "Golden" projects have since sprung up to join them, thus shaping the social landscape of the technological environment in China.

According to Bernard Carlson (1992:177) assumptions, as to who will use the technology and the meanings users might assign to it, constitute a frame of meaning that directly links the inventor's unique artifact with larger social or cultural values. Success in this sense lies in the inventor's interpretation of "the values, institutional arrangements, and economic notions of that culture". Hence to succeed in another culture, these factors must be taken into account by system developers.

Problems in Knowledge Acquisition: The issues pertaining to engagement of IT in both intended and unintended ways, bound by historical and cultural aspects, provide a cross-cultural perspective on the complexity of predicting how IT artifacts will be used. No matter how technology is used, it has, of itself, a number of positive and negative consequences. As such, these have impacted on non-Western cultures in their engagement with IT artifacts as well as in knowledge acquisition.

Engagement in IT Artifacts (Corruption of Intent)

From the IT developers and providers' (based in a western country) point of view, the 'bottom line' of their IT engagement is to utilize China's huge reserves of raw material, human resources and huge market potential to create a return on their investments. This is done with a view to lowering the cost of production and provides another source of revenue for the company. This engagement in trade and production usually involves the transfer of home country technologies to host country. However,

---

[1] A set of policies designed to direct the "informatization" of China.

dilemmas faced in this engagement have been described as the four issues of the information age -- "Privacy, Accuracy, Property and Access" (Mason 1986). The most important of these is the question of intellectual property rights. The lack of trust in the systems of a foreign country to protect their intellectual property rights is one of the high-risk areas. More often than not, organizations in China rely on the loyalty of their employees and management to minimize these risks. Home country companies exercise their rights through new rules and policies and by limiting what can be transferred. The effect of such policies results in technology being transferred piecemeal rather than as a coherent and consistent whole.

These practices often change the intrinsic intent of IT before it even reaches the recipients. Consequently, IT recipients often question whose interests are being served in this kind of filtering process, since in practice the original interest, value and assumptions of the developers, investors and users, discussed in the first premise, have been lost. In reality, then IT deviation from its intended use lies not in the technology, but rather in the organization and process of its transfer. This raises the critical question of corruption of intent in the transfer process and the actions that can be taken by providers of IT with respect to reducing such deviations.

The Chinese interaction with technology utilizes the knowledge that they are operating in an imperfect information environment, where decision making and choice will be based not on rational choice, as in the Western context, but will be based more on reputation and guanxi-rationality. and through their network to provide them with a more certain outcome. This reputation and guanxi-based rationality often undermines the activation or appropriation of IT which is created in the Western context simply because it does not contain any meaningful role in fulfilling the objectives set by the host organization company.

Managing Cultural Expectations

From the Chinese point of view, their main concern would be whether they are getting what they paid for (i.e., to have access to sources of information-intellectual property assets). These assets are normally knowledge-based, especially tacit knowledge, embedded in complex organizational routines (e.g. skilful use of appropriate technical infrastructure - eProcurement) and developed from experience.

Acquiring knowledge through experiences takes time, and recipients are limited in how much they can accelerate their learning merely through greater investments. Moreover they have to work through a filtration process to introduce what they have learned and apply it to traditional Chinese attitudes and environments. For example, McFarlan in an interview reported by Rockart (2004) gave the example of how a Chinese company established an innovative email/postal service to receive email messages on behalf of individual residents in rural areas and deliver them via "snail mail" to overcome the problems experienced by those who live in rural areas and don't have facilities to communicate through the Internet (Rockart 2004). Clearly, the Chinese are experiencing and interacting with IT differently from their Western counterparts and consequently their evaluation of IT will most likely be based on their unique experiences. Hence, it is difficult for anyone to take a detached view of his own culture, because he can only use culture-bound ideas to judge it" (Daniel, 1975: 16). It is clear that "what" and "how" technology is shaped by available cultural resources. It has been suggested that technology is not universally valid and culturally neutral, in that "there are always room for culture variation and for the adaptation of whatever was culture-transferable' (Daniel, 1975:5).

Historical Role of Technology in China

According to Bray (1997), technology embodies power relations and serves as a means of transmitting values. For example, in ancient China:

> *Basic productive technologies define the everyday work and material lives of large number of people; they are one important way in which ordinary members of society 'live through' ideology and through which hegemonic values are transmitted. (pp:37)*

Such transmission of ideology is deemed more important than using latest technology. Even in modern Japan, traditional rice farming systems have not been replaced by more efficient methods of production. This ideological conservatism enables continuity in ideology that signifies the aspirations of the people to preserve their traditions and social values. For example, Francesca Bray (1999) in her article "Towards a critical history of non-Western technology" states that:

> *...when a modern Japanese family sit around the supper table eating their bowls of Japanese-grown rice, they are not simple indulging a gastronomic preference but they are eating and absorbing a tradition- in the sense of an invented and re-invented past...each mouthful of rice offers communion with eternal and untainted Japanese values, with a rural world of simplicity and purity, inhibited by peasants tending farms in harmony with nature and ruled over by the emperor...family rice farm lives on as a powerful symbol of national identity (pp: 204).*

To guard against these embedded ideologies and philosophies, cultures are implementing various mechanisms to mediate their effect (Figure 1). One of these mechanisms is the ti-yong paradigm that has been used in China for near two thousand years, however other countries with similar concerns might use similar paradigms to balance culture and IT adoption. This mediation concept is described next.

CULTURAL MEDIATION OF TECHNOLOGY

The word "mediation" is used to symbolize the need for a balance between adopting a technology for its survival and controlling the influence of foreign values and meanings. We live in a world of multiple realities and accordingly, cultural mediation may come in various forms. We also acknowledge that different paradigms are used in different cultures to mediate the influence (i.e. values and philosophies foreign to their culture) of IT adoption.

Some, like the indigenization of technology endeavor by Malaysia (Wan and Shaharir, 1999) believe that such formal processes could provide the necessary mechanism to filter out cross-infection of values and meanings. While others like those of Iran (Fatemeh, 1996) mediate such influence through "preventing the import of alien and non-essential technologies in[to] the country" and selecting appropriate technologies that have "greater conformity with the socio-cultural and economic conditions". Hence it is posited in this chapter that such mediation activities reflect the prevailing paradigm of how IT is acquired, understood, employed and why there is this need to incorporate a country's own values into IT (e.g. through indigenization). To formalize our ideas, we developed the *model of cultural mediation on impact of IT* (Figure 1) to explain mediation activities. The various aspects of the model are described next.

Internal Environment

In the internal environment of cultural mediation on the impact of IT, there are two main influencing factors. The first is the cultural norm and the second is the cultural paradigm. Both reside within the internal environment of the culture. In this model (figure 1) cultural norm is defined as:

> *"a society's propensity towards certain ideals; their aversion from others; and their standard, ritualistic practices. Essentially what the 'norm' is a summation of typical activities and beliefs of group of people." (Wikipedia online dictionary)*

Enforcement of Cultural Norms Through IT: Each culture has different methods of enforcing its cultural norms which are "the basis on which members of a society interpret their experience and structure their relationships with one another, their environment, their past, and their future into a coherent way of life" (Vanderburge, 1985: xxiii). Examples of such methods of enforcing cultural norms were evident in strategies such as those proposed by Wan and Shaharir (1999) on indigenization of technology in Malaysia where they lamented that the learning and use of technology in Malaysia is heavily influenced by the values and philosophy foreign to their culture. They call for the indigenization of technology where they can integrate their values systems into the technology through strategies such as:

> "...indigenisation [sic] by nurturing indigenous pride in its own history of ethno science and ethno technology, adaptation of the Malaysian-Malay-Islam value system in teaching and education of science and technology, the integration of Malaysian-Malay-Islam culture in the implementation and management of technology, more empowerment of the indigenous scientists and technologist to plan their own course of technological change and less dependence on corporate leaders on the direction of technological development." (Pg.110)

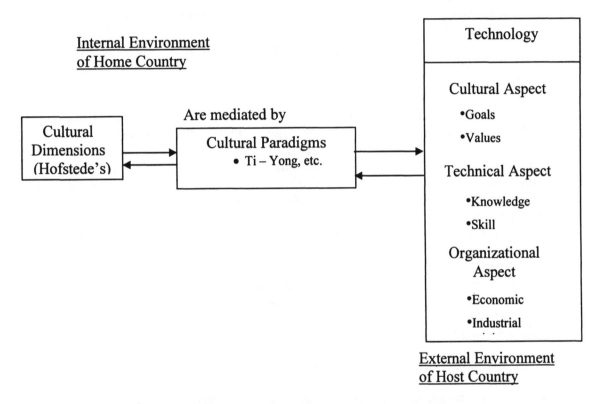

Figure 1. Model of Cultural Mediation on Impact of IT

The indigenous users of Western technologies are often criticized for deviating from its intended use, however the failure may lie with the observer who views the IT artifact as "relatively stable, discrete, independent and fixed" (Orlikowski and Iacono, 2001) and does not grasp how IT and its embedded values are being reworked in the context of local practice. This chapter argues that local cultures do not passively receive the ideologies and philosophy, but rather they are discriminatory and selective (e.g. In Iran, Malaysia and China) in their use of technology. They can adapt and transform these technologies for their own purposes as in the indigenization activities in Malaysia), or they can reject their values. Charles Ess (2002) in 'Culture in Collision' stated,

> "...technologies do not simply reshape their users to conform with those embedded values and preferences. Rather, diverse people and cultures are capable of (re) designing systems more in keeping with their own cultural values and communicative preferences."

The argument is that when IT is reconceptualized in another culture, a new meaning is given to the IT artifact. As such, there is no guarantee that the original intent of the designer will be recognized. Hence, it can be said that the process by which a new meaning is given to the IT artifact is very much influenced by the prevailing cultural paradigm held by these cultures. To illustrate this point, the ti-yong paradigm is used to explain this process in China.

Mediating Cultural Paradigms - The example of the Ti-Yong Paradigm: The ti-yong paradigm has been used as an evaluation strategy in China for nearly 2000 years. Traditionally Wang Bi (226-249) is credited as the first to use ti-yong as a philosophical term. It allows the Chinese to strategically employ objective evaluation of technology rather than as a derivative from western knowledge, which embodies a relationship of political domination. An example of its usage can be found in the use of the "ti-Yong" framework as a means of survival to withstand foreign aggression. By prioritizing Chinese learning as the *goal* and Western learning as the *means,* they hoped to assimilate foreign military technology, while at the same time retaining Chinese systems of governance at the core (Schwarcz, 1986). However, we will describe below the difficulty of this approach as the Chinese discovered the inseparability of the embedded ideologies and philosophies of the IT artifact.

The meaning of 'ti' refers to 'essence', whereas 'yong' refers to 'function'. Together, 'ti-yong' refers to the essence-function of any person, thing or situation. Hence, it can be interpreted that the Chinese values take priority to preserve the cultural values that are essential to social stability. The ti-yong framework is often used in the practice of technological adoption in the Chinese context. Such practices enable the Chinese to prioritize what they deem as most essential. The practice of prioritizing and emphasizing values in the Chinese context (e.g. using the ti-yong concept) as a mediator is relatively unexplored in the West. However, Muller (1999) points out that "it [ti-yong framework] is by no means a radically new theory or discovery ... It has been expressed by the leading Confucian, Taoist and Buddhist thinkers for over two millennia". However, in doing so, it creates a dilemma

> *"Political reformers [nineteenth century Chinese officials] discovered that embedded in Western 'means' that is to say in technological expertize, were distinctive goals that were inimical to the fundamental values of Chinese, or more precisely Confucian civilisation. The inseparability of means and ends in both western and Chinese learning posed an awkward and lasting dilemma for cultural conservatives." (Schwarcz, 1986: 5)*

The Chinese Paradox: The inseparability of the means from the goals in the adoption of IT artifacts could be explained through the 'tung-ta' or interpenetration concept. According to Muller, the interpenetration (or tung-ta concept) can be explained as "both passing through that which is already open, and piercing through that which has been heretofore closed." Hence, it could be argued that one cannot learn the technical aspect of the IT artifact without having to also engage in the cultural aspect (goals and values) and the organizational aspect (economy and industrial activities) of the IT artifact as describe by Pacey (1983) in technological practice. The interpenetration concept in the ti-yong paradigm explains that the values learned through technological practice both infuse and diffuse into the consciousness of the users. Both [ti and yong] also mean to "apprehend, "understand" and "grasp" and their etymology indicates that in the consciousness of their original users, such terms actually reflect the operation of some form of "penetration" or "permeation". To understand how essence-function works "it is necessary to see the human being as a continuum from inner to outer". Such interconnectedness is reflected in Figure 2. This stance may be viewed as being similar to Bostrom and Heinen's (1977a, 1977b) socio-technical perspective of IT Systems Implementation.

In contemporary China, adopting foreign technology has taken on a different purpose, one of which is to catch up with the developed world. However, they have not abandoned the 'ti-yong' formula. This is apparent in their concern about cross-cultural transfer of meanings through technology, e.g., the fear of increasing dependency on imported foreign technology for the revolution

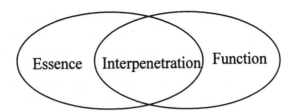

Figure 2. Essence-Function and Interpenetration Model (adapted from Muller, 1997)

and innovation of the economy. This dependence has been referred to as the 'technology opium' that is driving the economy in most of the Western economy. This focus on technology, instead of social-cultural values of society, has created a new dilemma for the government. Their main concerns are cultural change, loss of meanings, change to power base, a new worldview and breakdown of society. These threats are real and can be explained in the 'technological imperative' described by Pacey, (1983) as a means of securing and maintaining power, mainly western power, over others and is a major concern for the Chinese Government. Hence their emphasis on Chinese learning as priority and western learning as a means to achieve the status that most western society are currently enjoying in the world arena.

The cross-cultural transfer of meanings, truth and knowledge carried by IT, is especially germane in terms of adoption and use of the Internet (Yang, 2003). In China, internet users are forbidden from debating the 'Four Cardinal Principles'. These principles are: the principle of upholding the socialist path; the principle of upholding the People's Democratic Dictatorship, the principle of upholding the leadership of Communist Party of China, and; the principle of upholding Marxist-Leninist-Mao Zedong thought. This fear of citizens criticizing the government on the Internet through the means of anonymous communication are not unfounded as Mulgan's (1997) theory of connexity states:

"Connexity means more knowledge about other lives, places and possibilities, and this is always the starting point for freedom... connexity makes it harder for those in power to contain new ideas... Boundaries and borders are more easily bypassed" (pp: 40)

China is a collective society (Hofstede, 1980) and any deviation from mainstream thoughts is not likely to be tolerated. Hence their reservation of the social implications associated with the use of the Internet that might divide the nation and dilute the power of the state.

Paradoxically, the current Chinese leadership believes that communism can never be attained if China remains technologically backwards, hence, they can't avoid technological determinism, assuming that technology is the central element in the discourse of Western superiority. Daniel (1975) reminds us of the danger of a technologically deterministic view, in that it could result in "some danger that people ... will be mesmerized into thinking that they can create conditions that favor development by adopting Western culture ..." (pp: 84) and also adopt what the western culture has discarded as bad for their society. As explained earlier, IT has inherent in-built values and skills sets that may not be evident to the adopter (Bunker, 2001). Its hidden values often undermine the mediation process, which makes it harder for these cultures to control the course of technological change and its impact on their cultures. Hence, in their quest for survival in the era of Information Technological reality, their technological discourse often engages in learning from more advanced technology producer. The paradox is that these engagements are impact both on their concerns and their survival. As Edward Hall (1976) would have said "the various facets of culture are interrelated - you touch a culture in one place and everything is affected" (Pg.16). Such evidence can already be seen in China.

External Environment

There is a prevailing perception in the East that technology constitutes the reality of this current time and age and that modern technology is often perceived as a product of Western civilization. In the article "Interface of Cultural Identity Development: Culture and Technology", Fatemeh (1996) writes: "...technology is a product of the Western industrialized communities which owe their present position to the attempt made by their ancestors within certain traditional culture patterns." These concerns were also expressed by Wan and Shaharir (1999), "Science and technology education in accordance to the Western interpretation that there is only a diffusion of science and technology from the West would only produce enthusiastic worshipers of the West." There is this underlying perception that countries adopting these western IT artifact runs the risk of the endangering their "cultural identity" (Fatemeh, 1996) or an attempt by the West to colonize through commercialization (e.g. Charles Ess, 2002 on the example of Korea). Hence, this may explain why these cultures would often choose to engage only in the technical aspect (e.g. skills and knowledge) when selecting foreign technological practices (i.e. the desire by these cultures to preserve their traditional culture values against the onslaught of foreign ideologies and philosophies from their own culture). However, in reality, Pacey (1983) proposes that the practice of technology often engages the users with the values that lie behind technology even though they may chose to identify with only the technical aspect of technology.

Aspects of Technology

It has been suggested that the general meaning of technology includes cultural and organizational aspects of technology as well as the technical aspect:

- Technical aspects-concerns with the knowledge and skills-deals with how to make and operate technology;
- Organizational aspects-concerns with the economic and industrial activities-deals with the management and administration of technology;
- The cultural aspects-concerns with the goals and values in the use of technology.
  (Source: Adapted from the Diagrammatic definition of 'technology' and 'technology practice' in Pacey (1983:.6)

People identify with this technical aspect because "that have to do with machines, techniques, knowledge and the essential activity of making things work.". This focus on the technical aspect often discounts other aspect of technological practice such as the cultural aspect (goals and values) and the organizational aspect (economic and industry). However, the engagement with the technological aspect of technology does not mean that technological practice is "value-free" or "politically neutral" (Pacey, 1983:5). Thus technical solutions that do not involve social and cultural measures are impossible.

Thus the model presented in this chapter is designed to raise an awareness of the need to consider the potential influence of embedded ideologies and philosophies inherent in the IT artifact (typically developed in a Western culture) on national cultural values and the mediating effects of cultural paradigms.

SUMMARY

This chapter seeks to engage the reader in a discourse on the need for IS developers and researchers to appreciate and understand the mechanisms that are available to protect cross cultural values. Through the example of the ti-yong paradigm we have attempted to demonstrate how these effects are being mediated in China and urge the developers of information systems to consider the potential impact of those paradigms on IT development for cross-cultural adoption and use.

Typically, the different levels of cross-cultural uptake of IT are explained in terms of differences in cultural values using classifications of culture provided by Hofstede (1980) and others. Little, if any, previous consideration has been given to the mediating effects of paradigms, such as ti-yong, that enunciate the means by which traditional cultural values can be maintained in the face of adoption and use of new technologies. Having said that, we have also indicated that in the case of China, the situation is complicated by the interpenetration concept in the ti-yong paradigm where they could not separate Western values from the function (i.e. yong). Hence there is a need to learn more and understand the role of the ti-yong paradigm and their effectiveness in filtering unwanted ideologies from IT artifacts.

We contend that there is an opportunity to be gained by understanding these paradigms and by making an attempt to recognize and embrace their objectives in IT development and implementation. The aim is to enable more successful IT adoption and use through a closer alignment of the embedded ideologies and philosophies of the IT artifact and the traditional cultural values of countries around the globe.

MINICASE

Clashes in Culture: The 'Ti-Yong' Distinction and the Digital Revolution

The digital technology revolution has had a profound effect on entertainment media consumption in China. In the mid-1990s, virtually overnight, waves of pirated CDs, software, computer games, and Video-CDs became available through underground bootleg channels. China was suddenly inundated with a veritable tsunami of foreign-made intellectual products. Outdoor stalls in the open-air markets began to offer counterfeit versions of software, music CDs from Mozart to Megadeth, and movies from *Bambi* to *Basic Instinct*. Pirated versions of Western first-run movies could be purchased almost the same week they were released overseas, making Chinese movie fans instantly familiar with current film trends.

The Chinese who lived in one of the most culturally-isolated locations in the world now had unimaginable access to a wide variety of mainstream Western entertainment products, and at a very affordable price. Suddenly current Western notions, images and cultural trends were directly and *immediately* available to virtually anyone, not just the Party elite, the super rich or the Westernized. In addition, this consumption was now *individually* mediated, rather than a shared, collective experience. In the privacy of their own homes, Chinese people suddenly had more freedom to map out their own media space, to sample and collect entertainment products according to their own idiosyncratic tastes, and to create sub-cultures based only on connections between like-minded individuals.. Most importantly, the Chinese were now culturally in step with the rest of the world.

At this point, the Party instinctively resorted to a variation on an old approach dating back to China's first shock of Western contact in the Qing Dynasty: the *ti-yong* dichotomy – retaining Chinese "essence" (*ti*), while employing Western "practice" (*yong*). To update the strategy, the Chinese would have preferred to borrow western hardware, while disabling the social and moral software that came bundled with it. The attempt was no more successful in the 90s than it had been 100 years earlier.

The problem with this new digital revolution was that it enabled the channelling of potentially dangerous foreign attitudes and ideas *directly* into the psyches of Chinese people, on an unprecedented scale. It was as if the feared "spiritual pollution" was now being *injected* into the very bloodstream of Chinese culture. A cultural cataclysm was taking place virtually in the blink of an eye, as the Chinese populace suddenly enjoyed easy access to western VCDs and violent video CD-ROMs from Hong Kong. And at this point the ongoing battle being waged against bourgeois liberalization and peaceful evolution was effectively lost.

The rise of a middle class and disposable incomes combined with a new plugged-in worldliness was setting the stage for massive cultural shifts. In particular, a new youth culture had begun to emerge that was as contemptuous of traditional values as the youth cultures of the 1960s in the US and other industrialized countries. Chinese young people, at long last connected to the vibrant global youth network, also began to sport outlandish hair styles, get tattoos, form rock bands and take drugs - developments that would have been unthinkable just a few years earlier. The Party's thought control apparatus was apoplectic – but the genie could not be put back into the bottle.

Discussion Questions:

1. Why did pirated CDs, software, computer games, and Video-CDs become available in China?
2. What is meant by the phrase "retaining Chinese "essence" (*ti*), while employing Western "practice" (*yong*)?
3. How has a growing middle class impacted *ti-yong*?

Adapted from:
http://www.danwei.org/media_and_advertising/media_schizophrenia_in_china_b.php

KEY TERMS

Arm's-length relationship
Artifact
Collectivism
Connexity
Guanxi
Individualism:
Masculinity (MAS) versus Femininity
Mediation
Partnership Model
Power Distance Index (PDI)
Ti- "essence"
Ti-Yong
Uncertainty Avoidance Index (UAI)
Yong

STUDY QUESTIONS

1. Do you agree or disagree with the need to consider embedded ideologies and philosophies in information systems vis-à-vis cultural differences? Explain your position.

2. What factors do you think explain why IT developers need to accommodate different cultures in software development?

3. What are the differences between the cultural dimensions of China and USA? What are the implications of these differences?

4. How should IT companies proceed when developing software for "foreign" markets?

5. You have been hired by a large manufacturing company whose home office is in New York, NY, USA to implement SAP, a complex enterprise integration software package into their operations throughout China. Some of these locations have no technology and currently keep their records by paper and pencil. Other locations have varying levels of information technology in place. Consider the culture of the home office of the company vis-à-vis the China operations and the German developers of SAP. How would you proceed as the project manager?

REFERENCES

Bostrom, R. and Heinen, S. "MIS Problems and Failures: A Socio-Technical Perspective. Part I - The Causes," *MIS Quarterly,* 1(3), September 1977a, pp. 17-32.

Bostrom, R. and Heinen, S. "MIS Problems and Failures: A Socio-Technical Perspective. Part II - Solutions," *MIS Quarterly,* 1(4), December 1977b, pp. 11-28.

Bray, F. Towards a Critical History of non-Western Technology in *China and Historical Capitalism,* eds Brook, T and Blue, G.., Edinburgh, Cambridge University Press. 1999.

Bray, F. *Technology and Gender: Fabrics of Power in Later Imperial China,* Berkeley, University of California Press. 1997.

Bunker, D. A Philosophy of Information technology and Systems (IT & S) as Tools: Tool Development Context, Associated Skills and the Global Technology Transfer (GTT) Process. *Information Systems Frontiers,* 3(2), 2001, pg. 185-197.

Carlson, W. B. Artifacts and Frames of Meanings: Thomas A. Edison, His Managers, and the Cultural Construction of Motion Pictures in *Shaping Technology/Building Society: Studies in Sociotechnical Change,* eds Bijker, E. W. and Law, J., Cambridge, The MIT Press. 1992.

Daniel, N. *The Cultural Barrier: Problems in the Exchange of Ideas.* Edinburgh, Edinburgh University Press. 1975.

Erumban, A. and deJong, S. B. "Cross-Country Differences in ICT Adoption: A Consequence of Culture?," *Journal of World Business,* 41(4), December. 2006, pp. 302-314.

Ess, C. "Cultures in Collision: Philosophical Lessons From Computer-Mediated Communication.," *Metaphilosophy,* 33(1/2), 2002, pp. 229-253.

Fatemeh, F. Interface of Cultural Identity Development: Culture and Technology in *Interface of Cultural Identity Development,* eds Baidyanath Saraswati, 1996, p. 290.

Hall, E., (1976). Beyond Culture. New York, Anchor Books

Hartford, K. "Cyberspace with Chinese Characteristics." *Current History,* 99(638), 2000, pp. 255-263.

Hofstede, G., *Culture's Consequences: International Differences in Work-Related Values,* Beverly Hills, California, Sage Publications. 1980.

Hofstede, G. Culture's Consequences, Comparing Values, Behaviors, Institutions, and Organizations Across Nations, Second Edition. Newbury Park, California, Sage Publications. 2003.

Hofstede, G., Hofstede, G. J. and Pedersen, P. B. *Exploring Culture. Exercises, stories and sythetic cultures* Yarmouth, Maine: Intercultural Press. 2002.

Michael Ing. Zhu Xi's Ti-Yong: Context and Interpretation, *Confucisionstudies.com,* http://www.confucianstudies.com/ingzhustiyong.html (accessed 28 February 2007).

Mason, R. "Four Ethical Issues of the Information Age." *Management Information Systems Quarterly* 10(1), 1986, pp. 4-13.

Mulgan, G. *Connexity: How to Live in a Connected World*. London, Chatto and Windus. 1997.

Muller, C. A. Asia's Unexplored Pivot of Metaphysic and Hermeneutics: Essence-Function/Interpenetration. *Chapter Presentation at the 1997 Annual Meeting of the American Academy of Religion,* Nov 22, 1997.

Muller, C. A. Tiyong, Interpenetration and Sincerity in the Great Learning and Doctrine of the Mean. *Annual Meeting of the American Academy of Religion,* Boston, Nov. 2, 1999.

Orlikowski, W.J. and C. S. Iacono "Research Commentary: Desperately seeking "IT" in IT research-A Call to Theorizing the IT Artifact." *Information Systems Research,* 12(2), 2001, pp. 121-135.

Pacey, A. *The Culture of Technology*. Oxford, England, Basil Blackwell Publisher Limited. 1983.

Rockart, J. "China and Information Technology: An Interview with Warren McFarlan from the Harvard Business School." *MIS Quarterly Executive,* 3(2), 2004, pp. 83-88.

Sargis, A. Ideological Tendencies and reform policy in China's Primary Stage of Socialism," *Nature, Society, and Thought,* 11(4), 1999, pp. 391-398.

Schwarcz, V. *The Chinese Enlightenment: intellectuals and the legacy of the May Fourth movement of 1919 Berkeley,* University of California Press. 1986.

Shore, B. "IT Strategy in International Supply Chain Management". *Global IT and E-Commerce,* Marietta, Georgia, Ivy League Publishing, pp. 120-137. 2002.

Vanderburg, W. H. *The Growth of Minds and Cultures: A Unified Theory of the Structure of Human Experience.* Toronto: University of Toronto Press. 1985.

Wan, Ramli Wan Daud and Shaharir, Mohamad Zain, Indigenisation of Technology and the Challenges of Globalisation: The Case of Malaysia. *Journal of Islamic Science,* 15(1-2), 1999, pp. 109-126.

Yang, G. "The Internet and Civil Society in China: A Preliminary Assessment." *Journal of Contemporary China,* 12(36), 2003, pp. 453-475.

Zhou, X. "E-Government in China: A content Analysis of National and Provincial Web Sites", *Journal of Computer-Mediated Communication,* 9(4), 2004.

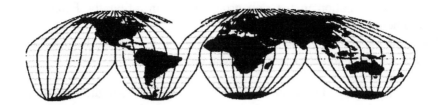

Global Digital Divide: A Longitudinal Analysis

Kallol Bagchi
Godwin Udo
The University of Texas at El Paso, USA

CHAPTER SUMMARY

This chapter introduces a modeling scheme containing several new indicators that are relevant for global digital divide. The major contributions of the chapter are:

- A set of related technologies has been identified that can contribute to digital divide, and a large set of nations has been examined.
- The findings suggest that the global digital divide is not increasing with respect to the U.S. index.
- The factor values that are responsible for such divide are not all common for the OECD (Organization for Economic Cooperation and Development) and (ECLAC Economic Commission for Latin America and the Caribbean) sets of nations.
- Indicators of digital divide as well as digital divide itself undergo substantial changes over the years.
- Trust building and income improvement of a nation may reduce the digital divide.

Several propositions are evaluated through correlation, regression analysis, ANOVA and Wilcoxon Signed-Rank tests. The important implication of the results is that for the digital divide to be eliminated or minimized, the factors identified in this study need to be properly addressed.

INTRODUCTION

Digital Divide (DD), the gulf between users and non-users in digital technology use, has drawn the attention of researchers and policy makers alike, in recent times (Ge and Jain, 2003; Hoffman et al., 2000; OECD, 2001; NTIA, 2001). Controversy exists regarding the nature and extent of digital divide. For example, some scholars claim that divide is a fact of life and will continue to remain; others claim that the divide is dangerous to our society and should be bridged (Novak and Hoffman, 2001).

Take the example of Internet use. When assessed by region, Internet use was dominated by North Americans in 2003 (World Bank, 2005):

- More than 50% of the population in the United States and Canada are using Internet.
- 43% of the population in the rich group of Organization for Economic Cooperation and Development (OECD) nations is on-line.
- 1.4% of the population in least developed nations is accessing Internet.
- 10.6% of the population in Latin American nations is on line.

Even among highly developed nations, there existed vast differences in the number of Internet users per 1000 population in 2003. Iceland ranks as the nation with the highest number of Internet users per 1000 population at 674; Spain has 239 (World Bank, 2005). Take the example of the PC (personal computer) in the year 2002: 65.88 % of the U.S. population used a PC, whereas the figure for the least developed nations was 0.42% and the world-wide figure was 10.08% (World Bank, 2005). Similar results are found if an old technology such as the telephone is considered. The figures for per 1000 telephone users for the US was 645.8, for the least developed nations was 7.06 and for the world was 175.93.

Although many studies exist that explore this problem within a society, empirical studies that deal with this problem at a global level between various nations are few. The status of digital divide is not uniform across all societies. DiMaggio et al., (2001) call for research to determine digital inequality among users, groups, organizations and nations. In an effort to understand the problem better, the present chapter builds on past research to develop a set of factors that are responsible for digital divide.

WHAT IS THE DIGITAL DIVIDE?

Digital divide (DD) is a multidimensional phenomenon encompassing three distinct aspects (Norris, 2001). The global divide refers to the divergence of technology access between industrialized and developing societies. The social divide is concerned with the gap between information rich and poor in a given nation. The democratic divide within the online community denotes the difference between those who do, and do not, use the digital resources. The present article focuses on the global divide aspects of the digital divide. The global digital divide is measured as the difference in the value of the information and communication technology (ICT) index. This measure is derived from a factor analysis of adoption data for four ICTs: the Internet, PCs, mobile phones and telephone adoption per 1000.

Digital divide research can be grouped into three categories (Bagchi, 2005). First, the digital divide studies can be grouped based on whether the focus of the study is a single nation or multiple nations. Usually, multiple nation studies refer to the gaps between first world and third world countries. Single nation studies refer to differences among various population groups within an industrialized country (such as the United States). Global inter country empirical analyses of digital divide are rare (Kiiski and Pohjola, 2002; Lu, 2001; Sciadas, 2002; Wolcott et al., 2001). Lu (2001) discusses it in terms of developing nations; Kiiski and Pohjola (2002) and Petrazini and Kibati (1999) discuss the Internet growth using a number of nations. Sciadas (2002) did a digital divide study on Canada and other developing nations and showed that the gap in digital divide is bridging. On the other hand, studies exist that discuss digital divide within a nation. Kvasny and Keil (2002) discuss digital divide in relation to inter-city situations. Ge and Jain (2003) analyze the divide situation in China while Peha (1999) discusses Haiti's Internet development situation. For the purpose of this paper, the focus will be on inequities among multiple nations or societies.

The second category of digital divide research discusses the divide in terms of a specific technology or a group of technologies. Early articles discussed general computer penetration among households. Later, as the Internet/web became more predominant, Internet access by individuals became the measure. Now, with free Internet access available through most public libraries, experts discuss the quality of access and usage (Kiiski and Pohojola, 2002; Hoffman et al., 2000; Katz, 2003).

Telecommunication technologies may help to bridge the digital divide. In recent times, some scholars have argued that the characteristics of mobile technologies and emergence of mobile commerce (m-commerce) offer the prospects of bridging the global digital divide if proper policies are put in place at various levels in the public and private sectors (Dholakia and Kshetri, 2001; Zhang and Wolff, 2004).

Even with respect to telephones, the divide has been investigated and found to persist. The divide exists even between racial groups in the U.S. About 6.3 million or more American households were still not connected to the plain old telephone services in 2000 (World Bank, 2005). The condition is far worse in developing nations. About 80% of the world population is without telephone connections (World Bank, 2005). Therefore, the level of access to PC/computer, Internet/Web, telephone and mobile phone technologies can be used to measure digital divide. Many of the studies mentioned above, except Ge and Jain (2003) and Sciadas (2002), were related to access of one technology, the Internet. The present chapter investigates the problem using a group of related technologies.

The third category of the divide studies is about how the divide is growing. This is actually done by either studying the growth rate or growth level. When considering the growth rate, some researchers have come to the conclusion that the gap is bridging and that the developing nations are leapfrogging (Corrocher and Ordanini, 2002; Sciadas, 2002). This chapter investigates the level of divide in various nations and provides several conclusions. It may also be noted that except for a few studies, most studies are not longitudinal in nature. The present chapter is based on a longitudinal analysis. Kaufman (2005) has presented several interdisciplinary perspectives of digital divide that mirror the classification discussed above.

A logical extension of the many divide studies discussed above is needed to answer such questions as: What factors contribute to the digital divide and how are they different in various regions of the world? What constitutes the current divide gaps for the computer and communication technologies and what might realistically be done to close the gap? These are some of the questions that need to be empirically investigated and addressed, as has been pointed out by several scholars (Digital divide Network, 2002). This chapter explores the digital divide problem from a global perspective and finds major factors that address the divide in "access to information technology."

A MODEL OF MEASUREMENT

As illustrated in adoption research, social, economic, political, and linguistic factors have been cited as major factors in Internet usage (Katz, 2003; Rogers, 1986). It is well-known that the digital divide is more than just "digital." It is a sociological phenomenon reflecting broader contextual factors such as existing social, economic, cultural, and learning inequalities. Drawing from previous studies, a simple model is proposed that explains factors contributing to the digital divide that exist between different countries. The proposed model is shown in Figure 1 and uses several types of factors (measured at various levels) which have been discussed in the literature (Corrocher and Ordanini, 2002; Sciadas, 2002, Wolcott et al., 2001). The proposed model can be applied to a set of technologies.

The proposed model also contains several new and important indicators that have not been considered previously. The set of indicators is listed below:

Economic indicators: GDP per capita, inflation, income inequality, ICT expenditure as % of GDP

Social indicators: Secondary education average, illiteracy level, interpersonal trust, urbanization level, ethno-linguistic fractionalization (ELF)

Basic infrastructural indicators: The level of infrastructure

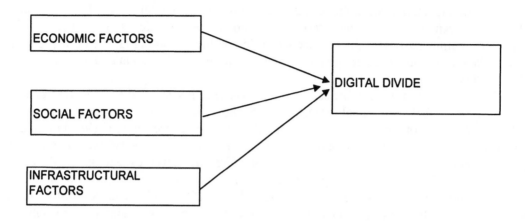

Figure 1. The Digital Divide Model

SOME PROPOSITIONS FOR THE DIGITAL DIVIDE

Economic Indicators

The major economic indicator, GDP per capita (the income variable) has been shown to be positively correlated to ICT (information and communication technology) infrastructure growth (Bagchi, 2005; Dijk and Hacker, 2003; Hargittai, 1999), and thus is expected to be negatively related to digital divide. The National Telecommunications and Information Administration (NTIA) study (2002) found that among American families making over $75,000 a year, 60 percent have Internet access, while only 20 percent of families making under $35,000 a year have access.

Proposition 1a. The higher the GDP per capita level of a nation, the smaller is the digital divide of that nation.

Inflation sometimes plays a negative role in economic growth and consequently in ICT growth (Davis and Kanugo, 1996). So inflation is expected to be positively related to divide.

Proposition 1b. Higher inflation level is positively related to the digital divide of a nation.

The amount of GDP spent on ICT expenditure is also an important economic factor to consider and it is expected to negatively impact the divide growth (Corrocher and Ordanini, 2002).

Proposition 1c. The higher the spending level on ICT budgets, the smaller the digital divide.

The Economic Commission for Latin America and the Caribbean (ECLAC) nations have the most unequal distribution of wealth (ECLAC, 2002). This factor can negatively impact the ICT infrastructure growth and thus the increase of divide gap. If there is a gap in income equality in society, that may be reflected in ICT adoption and usage, which can again aggravate the inequality problem (Hargittai, 1999).

Proposition 1d. The higher the income inequality level in a nation, the more is the digital divide in that nation.

Social Indicators

Primary evidence exists that supports the conjecture that higher educational levels of individuals are correlated to high ICT use, irrespective of the income level of a person, especially in ECLAC nations (Corrocher and Ordanini, 2002; Dijk and Hacker, 2003; NTIA, 2002). For example, the NTIA study (2002) found that the Internet-use pattern between Americans at the highest and lowest education levels widened by 25 percent from 1997 and 1998. Kiiski and Pohjola (2002) found that tertiary education has an influence on ICT diffusion. However, Hargittai (1999) and Norris (2001) found evidence to the contrary: education did not influence ICT diffusion. Lee (2001) and Caselli and Coleman (2001) found that education influences ICT adoption. Higher educational level could be a contributing factor in bridging the divide and this fact needs to be empirically tested.

Proposition 2a. The higher the level of education of a nation, the smaller the digital divide is.

Interpersonal trust (or simply trust) among members of a society may play a significant role. Informal communication channels may be much stronger in high trusting societies and may in turn aid the economic growth as well as the adoption process of an ICT product (Bagchi, 2005; Huang et al., 2003; Inglehart et al., 1998). Huang et al. showed that trust is important for Internet adoption, using a set of twenty two nations. Bagchi (2005) empirically showed the role of trust in technology adoption. Based on these works, it is conjectured that high trust will be negatively related to digital divide growth.

Proposition 2b. The higher the level of trust in a nation, the smaller the digital divide is in that nation.

Digital divide can also be broken up along the level of urbanization as differences in access may exist among different urbanization levels (Katz, 2003). Nations with a low urbanization level can reflect a larger gap in divide (Hugguns and Izushi, 2002).

Proposition 2c. Nations with high level of urbanization are likely to have smaller digital divide.

Similarly, ethnic heterogeneity could be another source of digital divide prevalent in nations (Dijk and Hacker, 2003). The majority group in a nation has a stronger probability to have computers and telecommunication gadgets at home than the minority groups (Hoffman et al., 2000; Katz, 2003, Novak et al., 2001). NTIA surveys (2002), on the other hand, found that the gap due to ethnic division is diminishing. So heterogeneity of a nation may contribute to growth of divide and this has to be empirically verified.

Proposition 2d. The higher the ethnic diversity level of a nation, the larger the digital divide.

Infrastructural indicators

In many poor nations, basic infrastructural facilities such as electricity are lacking. As basic infrastructural elements such as electricity are essential in any ICT related work, a lack of basic infrastructure such as a low level of electrification may further increase the digital gap between nations (Cecchinia and Scott, 2003; Dholakia and Kshetri, 2001).

Proposition 3. Nations with good infrastructure level experience smaller digital divide.

Digital Divide in Developing and Developed Nations

Internet growth studies exist that attempt to compare digital divide between developing and developed nations (ITU, 1999; Kenney, 2001). These studies have noted differences in digital divide among these nations. Building upon these works, the present work investigates the digital divide phenomenon among developed (OECD) and developing nations (ECLAC) over a set of technologies using a number of above-mentioned indicators. Specifically, we believe that:

Proposition 4. *The factor levels that contribute to digital divide in developing nations are different from those factor levels in developed nations.*

Digital Divide over Time

Factors of digital divide may change over time. It is postulated that digital divide factors will differ over time.

Proposition 5a. *For the group of nations, the digital divide factor levels change significantly over the years.*

Studies exist that demonstrate that digital divide is decreasing as developing nations are showing a better ICT growth rate than developed nations (Corrocher and Ordanini, 2002; Ge and Jain 2003). On the other hand, the divide (in terms of the level or absolute difference in adoption) may have increased considering the level of adoption. However, a nation such as the U.S. may have slowed down in ICT growth compared to many developed nations and a few developing nations; thus, considering the level of ICT adoption of nations, the digital distance of other nations from the U.S may not be on the increase. Considering it all,

Proposition 5b. *The digital divide level is not increasing over time.*

DATA

In order to empirically verify the relationships between digital divide and factors described above, the data were obtained from the World Bank database. Since the interest was in observing how digital divide is progressing over the years and how various factors are contributing to the divide over the years, two years, 1995 and 2001, were used in our analysis. The main indicators are shown in Table 1. A sample set of data for five nations is depicted in Table 2. As shown, there is enough variability in data. Three sets of nations were considered in this study: first the OECD (Organization for Economic Cooperation and Development) set of 30 rich nations (www.oecd.org); second, the ECLAC (Economic Commission for Latin America and the Caribbean) set of nations (www.eclac.org) consisting of a total of 33 nations; and third, the combined set of OECD and ECLAC nations.

To measure ICT development as defined in this work, a factor was extracted after Principal Component Analysis (PCA) of four ICTs: telephone, mobile phone, PC and the Internet level per 1000. It is worth noting that PCA is a technique typically used to simplify a dataset, by reducing multidimensional datasets to lower dimensions for analysis. The contribution of individual ICT components of this factor (named ICTIndex) extracted from each ICT varied from .88 to -.97. The difference in value of this index between the U.S. and a nation can measure the magnitude of the digital gap or the digital distance (DD) between the nation and the U.S., the U.S. being the base nation in the present study. The digital distance is the dependent variable of interest.

The income inequality index (GINI) was measured using the Gini Index. The Gini Index is equal to the Gini coefficient multiplied by 100. The Gini coefficient can be used to measure income inequality. (A Gini coefficient value of 0 denotes perfect income equality and a value of 1 denotes perfect income inequality). The ethnic factor was measured using the ELF index. The ELF index, a measure of ethnic diversity, is based on the probability that two people of a nation chosen at random will be from different ethnic groups (Mauro, 1995).

Indicators (Abbreviations)	Type	What it denotes
Inflation Rate (CPI)	Economic	Consumer price index (1995 = 100). Range: 1-100.
GDP per capita (GDP)	Economic	Base GDP per capita per nation.
Ethnicity (ELF)	Social (Ethno-linguistic)	ELF index quantifies ethno-linguistic fractionalization in countries and represents the probability that two individuals drawn randomly will be from different groups. Low value→less ethnic fragmentation. Range: 1-100.
Income Inequality (GINI)	Economic	Gini Index. Low value→less inequality. Range: 1-100.
ICT Expenditure (ICT/GDP)	Economic	Information and communication technology expenditure (% of GDP).
Illiteracy Rate (ILLITERACY)	Social	Illiteracy rate, adult total (% of people ages 15 and above).
Sec. Education Average (EDU)	Social	Average of school enrollment, secondary (% net), 1990-1997.
Interpersonal Trust (TRUST)	Social	Average trust index values of three years per nation. The trust index value is generated from percentage of respondents in each nation who replied that "most people can be trusted." High value→high trust. Range: 1-100
Infrastructure Level (INFRA)	Infrastructural	Television sets (per 1,000 people) to capture electrification level of a nation.
Urbanization Level (URB)	Social	Rural population (% of total population). Low value→more urbanization.
PC	A component of ICT index from which DD is derived	Personal computers per 1000
TEL	Same	Telephone per 1000
INTERNET	Same	Internet hosts per 1000
MOBILE	Same	Mobile phone per 1000
Digital Divide (DD)	Calculated	First, the ICT Index is calculated from PC, the Internet, mobile phone, and telephone adopted per 1000 population, using PCA. Next, digital gap of a nation is calculated from its ICT index distance from the U.S. (the base nation).

Table 1. Variables Related to Digital Divide

The ICT expenditure factor was measured by "Expenditure in ICT as a percentage of GDP." The infrastructure variable (INFRA) was measured as TV adoption per 1000. This is a rough surrogate measure of infrastructure level (such as level of electricity) of a nation, in absence of real data. The urbanization variable (URBANIZATION) was reverse coded as it represented the percentage of rural population. We had two variables representing education level of a nation: secondary education average (EDU) and adult illiteracy rate (ILLITERACY).

Nations/ Year 1995	PC	TEL	Mobile	Internet	ICT Index	GDP	ELF	GINI	EDU	URB
The U.S.	328.09	607.2	128.44	22.88	1.85	28279.67	32	40.81	88.8	23.85
The U.K	201.32	501.7	97.86	7.50	.6702	20445.76	50	35.97	89.4	10.78
Germany	178.45	513.3	45.53	5.798	.385	22495.03	3	38.22	91.79	13.51
France	146.94	560	22.52	2.6002	.237	21425.64	26	32.74	79.32	25.29
Brazil	17.33	85.1	8.25	.1291	-.962	6516.41	7	60.66	32.71	21.92

Table 2. Sample Data for Five Nations (The numbers are in units per 1000 population)

RESULTS

The results are first presented on a Kiviat Diagram (Kolence and Kiviat, 1973) with each "spoke" representing one of the dimensions. Values of factors for one or more set of countries at one or more times can be plotted on the same diagram or compared side-by-side on several diagrams. The results of two years of factor values are shown on each spoke. The higher the distance of the point in a spoke from the center, the larger is the value of the factor representing the spoke. The status of divide was compared using three sets of nations, OECD and ECLAC and the overall set, consisting of all nations from ECLAC and OECD (Figure 2).

Figure 2 describes the status of various factor level values for three groups of nations. The indicator values are averaged for each group for that year and then divided by the highest value of that indicator in that year from the overall set used in the study. For all three groups of nations, inflation consistently shows a significant difference between 1995 and 2001. When considering Latin American nations, all factor levels except education (and of course inflation) seemed to display the same factor values between 1995 and 2001. When considering the second group of nations (All Nations), in addition to inflation, infrastructure and GDP seem to have significant difference in factor values between the two years in view. Finally, for the third group of nations, the OECD, GDP (in addition to inflation) seems to be the only digital divide factor level with difference between 1995 and 2001. The rest of the factors levels seem to display the same values in 2001 as they did in 1995.

Correlation shows the strength and direction of a linear relationship between two random variables, but does not indicate causality between the two variables. Table 3 shows the results of Pearson's correlation coefficient values between digital divide and the factor levels of interest, as described above. Propositions 1-3 are largely supported with the exception of factors such as ethnicity level (ELF), income inequality level (GINI), illiteracy level (ILLITERACY) and inflation level (CPI), which are not significantly correlated across all the years. All other factor levels show significant correlations in the predicted direction over the years.

A preliminary regression was performed and the digital divide for year 2001 was used as the dependent variable. Due to paucity of data, only a few major indicators (at least one indicator from each major group: economic, social and infrastructural) were used as independent variables. The results are shown in Table 4. (The adjusted $R^2 = .90$, F=48.99 (p<.000), df=26). Trust index and GDP come out as significant with expected signs in predicting digital divide.

ANOVA Analyses of Dimensions of Digital Divide

It is instructive to examine whether significant differences among regions exist in various digital divide dimensions. Table 5 summarizes the ANOVA comparison results for the means for the various dimensions. Post-hoc Hochberg's GT2 test was used to compare means of groups which had largely differing sizes. Since the sample sizes were quite different, Hochberg's GT2 test works better instead of Gabriel's procedure. When population variances were equal (detected by Levene test), Games-Howell's procedure was used instead (Field, 2002).

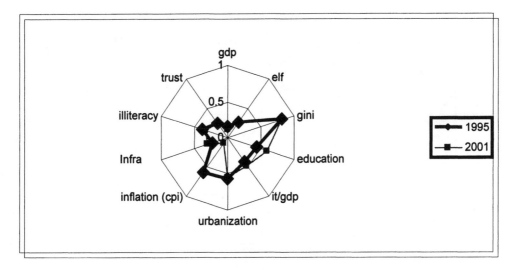

(a) Latin America

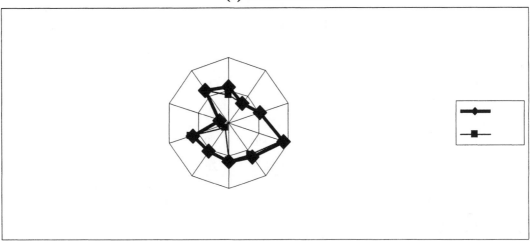

(b)OECD

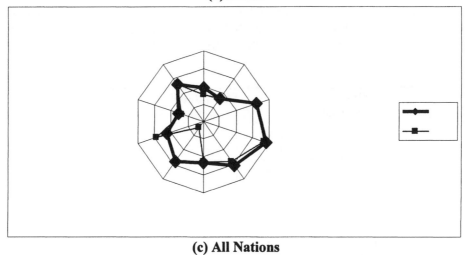

(c) All Nations
Figure 2. Kiviat Diagrams for the Group of Nations

Indicators of DD	Set of Nations	ECLAC		OECD		ALL		Remark
	Year	DD95	DD01	DD95	DD01	DD01	DD95	
GDP	Pearson Correlation	-.811**	-.786**	-.763**	-.901**	-.777**	-.860**	Supported
	N	12	15	27	43	28	39	
ELF	Pearson Correlation	.734*	.599*	0.013^{NS}	0.312^{+}	0.16^{NS}	0.216^{NS}	Weakly Supported
	N	11	14	20	35	21	31	
GINI	Pearson Correlation	$.014^{NS}$	$.016^{NS}$	$.131^{NS}$	.715**	$.134^{NS}$	.584**	Weakly Supported
	N	13	16	26	43	27	39	
EDU	Pearson Correlation	-.561*	-.503*	-.496**	-.804**	-.521**	-.686**	Supported
	N	13	16	27	44	28	40	
Illiteracy	Pearson Correlation	-789**	.550*	$.315^{NS}$	.491*	-395^{NS}	.546*	Weakly Supported
	N	13	16	8	24	8	21	
ICT/GDP	Pearson Correlation	$-.774^{+}$	$.088^{NS}$	-.713**	-.435*	-.471*	-.776**	Supported
	N	6	6	27	33	27	33	
CPI	Pearson Correlation	$.216^{NS}$	$.262^{NS}$	.452*	$.287^{+}$	.458**	.443**	Weakly Supported
	N	13	16	27	44	28	40	
TRUST	Pearson Correlation	$-.736^{+}$	$-.573^{NS}$	-.891**	-.905**	-.901**	-.912**	Supported
	N	7	7	19	26	19	26	
INFRA	Pearson Correlation	-.774**	-.704	-.602**	-.85**	-.753**	-.759**	Supported
	N	13	12	27	26	21	40	
Urbanization	Pearson Correlation	.794**	.584*	.388*	.434**	.530**	.316*	Supported
	N	13	16	27	44	28	40	

** Correlation is significant at the 0.01 level (2-tailed). + Correlation is significant at the 0.1 level (2-tailed) * Correlation is significant at the 0.05 level (2-tailed). NS—Not significant

Table 3. The Pearson Correlation Results (DD VS indicator levels)

Variables	Unstandardized Coefficients		Standardized Coefficients	t	Sig.
	B	Std. Error	Beta		
Constant	1.024	.968		1.058	.302
TRUST	-.035	.006	-.603	-5.393	.000
GINI	.012	.013	.125	.911	.372
EDU	.003	.008	.055	.355	.726
GDP	-5.758E-05	.000	-.452	-3.548	.002
INFRA	.001	.001	.128	1.349	.192

Dependent Variable: Digital Divide (DD)

Table 4. Regression Results of Digital Divide

Individual dimensions	Nation Groups			F	p	Hochberg's GT2 Means Comparison Test Between Groups+		
	U.S. and Canada(3)	OECD(1)	ECLAC(2)			1 and 2	2 and 3	1 and 3
GDP+	31102.55	23615.3	6385.07	31.32	0.000	17229.2*	-24716.5	-7487.3
N (Sample size)	2	26	19	47				
ELF	62.5	18.15	28.61	5.27	0.01	-10.46	-33.89	-44.35*
N (Sample size)	2	20	18	40				
GINI	36.16	31.11	55.11	53.47	0.000	-24*	18.95*	-5.04
N (Sample size)	2	26	6	34				
EDU+	90.23	85.4	49.21	41.34	0.000	36.2*	-41.01*	-4.82
N (Sample size)	2	26	21	49				
ILLITERACY	1	3.95	11.09	3.07	0.060	-7.14	10.09	2.95
N (Sample size)	2	8	20	30				
IT/GDP	8.3	8.16	6.6	0.99	0.383	1.56	-1.7	0.14
N (Sample size)	2	26	6	34				
CPI	175.8	205	111	0.184	0.833	-29.13	94.0	64.88
N (Sample size)	2	26	19	47				
TRUST	47.4	16.1	38.9	8.34	0.002	22.77*	-31.28*	-8.5
N (Sample size)	2	18	7	27				
INFRA+	257.2	155.3	42.1	7.95	0.001	113.24*	-215.16*	-101.93
N (Sample size)	2	25	13	40				
URB+	24.58	34.41	21.83	3.09	0.055	-9.83	12.58	2.75
N (Sample size)	2	26	21	49				
Note 1 *: The mean difference is significant at the .05 level								
Note 2+: Games-Howell's Test is adopted in case when the homegeneity of variance is detected via								
Levene's test								

Table 5. ANOVA results of Digital Divide Dimensions

For effective comparisons, the nations were divided into three regions: US and Canada, ECLAC and OECD nations. In comparing the regions, it became clear that there were several significant differences along the digital divide factor levels. In particular, ECLAC and the OECD regions differed in GDP, income inequality (GINI), education (EDU), trust (TRUST) and infrastructure (INFRA). Interestingly, the US-Canada and ECLAC regions also differed in the same variables: GDP, GINI, EDU, Trust and INFRA. OECD and US-Canada differed in ethnicity level (denoted by ELF index). This result implies that Proposition 4 is supported which states that the factor levels that contribute to digital divide in developing nations are different from the factor levels in developed nations.

To test whether digital divide factor levels changed over time, two years, 1995 and 2001 were selected. Table 6 shows the empirical tests of the comparison results over two different years using Wilcoxon rank test. Most of the indicators showed significant change over the years including digital divide indicator (DD). The results showed that for 37 out of 39 nations, the DD score of 1995 was greater than the DD score of 2001, indicating lesser DD values in 2001 compared to 1995. Thus Proposition 5a is supported.

Factors	URB	Illiteracy	EDU	IT/GDP	TV	DD
Statistics/ Years	2001-1995	2001-1995	2000-1995	2001-1995	2000-1998	1995-2001
Z	-5.595(a)	-4.623(a)	-2.656(b)	-4.941(b)	-4.552(b)	-5.025(b)
Asymp. Sig. (2-tailed)	0.000	0.000	0.008	0.000	0.000	0.000
N	49	28	19	33	50	39
a	Calculation based on positive ranks.					
b	Calculation based on negative ranks.					

Table 6. Wilcoxon Signed Ranks Test Results of Digital Divide Dimensions Over Years

As shown in Figure 3, relative to the U.S. ICT index values in 1995 and 2001, all nations are showing decreased digital distance in 2001 when compared to year 1995, except for three nations: Denmark, Sweden and Norway. The U.S. was trailing these nations in ICT index, in 2001. It must be mentioned that these nations have higher ICT index values than the U.S. in 2001. In general, the U.S. ICT index value has increased less in comparison to other nations during this period. Thus in general, digital divide level is not increasing and Proposition 5b is supported (in terms of digital divide level). Table 7 summarizes the results obtained.

DISCUSSION

Propositions 1-3 address the significance of various indicators to the digital divide growth. As correlation results from Table 3 show, most of the indicators are significantly correlated with digital divide. Many of these relationships are significant and are in the expected direction. The relationship

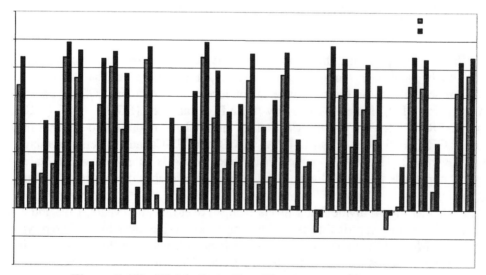

Figure 3. The Divide Over Two Time Periods, 1995 and 2001

Proposition	Correlation	Regression/ANOVA/ Other statistical tests
Proposition 1a: The higher the GDP per capita, the lower the digital divide adoption	Supported	Supported
Proposition 1b: The higher the inflation, the higher the digital divide	Weakly supported	Not used
Proposition 1c: The higher the ICT expenditure/GDP per capita, the lower the digital divide	Supported	Not used
Proposition 1d: The higher the income inequality the higher the digital divide	Weakly supported	Not supported
Proposition 2a: The higher the percentage of secondary education enrollment of nation, the lower the digital divide	Supported	Not supported
Proposition 2b: The higher the level of interpersonal trust, the lower the digital divide	Supported	Supported
Proposition 2c. The higher the urbanization level, the lower the digital divide	Supported	Not used
Proposition 2d. The higher the ethnic difference level, the higher the digital divide	Weakly Supported	Not used
Proposition 3. The higher the infrastructure level, the lower the digital divide	Supported	Not used
Proposition 4. Factor levels of the digital divide differ between developing and developed nations		Supported (ANOVA)
Proposition 5a. Factor levels of the digital divide differ over time		Supported (Wilcoxon Signed-Rank test)
Proposition 5b. Digital divide level is not increasing over time		Supported (Wilcoxon Signed-Rank test)

Table 7. Summary of Research Findings

with ethnicity index (ELF) is significant only for ECLAC nations. The relationship with income inequality index (GINI) is significant only for the set of "all nations." The relationships with GDP, trust, education, infrastructure level and urbanization level are significant for all groups. For the year 2001, the relationships with ICT index for OECD and ECLAC differ significantly in three dimensions: ethnicity, illiteracy level and trust. The relationships for ECLAC nations denote influence of lesser trust, more heterogeneity and more illiteracy level, when compared to the OECD nations.

The preliminary regression also showed that trust and GDP are strong predictors of digital divide. This implies that increasing the level of trust and economic condition of a nation may lead to a reduction of the digital gap between nations. The estimated magnitude of the effect of trust on digital divide is statistically significant. This is also supported in literature where growth of information technology product and associated phenomenon (such as software piracy, telecommuting) are associated with high interpersonal trust (Bagchi, 2001; Huang et al., 2003). Thus, increased interpersonal trust building activities in a society may reduce the digital distance of a nation from that of the U.S. to a reasonable degree.

Proposition 4 addresses the issue of whether the digital divide factor levels remain the same or different for developing and/or developed nations. These indicators are quite different for the different sets of nations. This conclusion is a confirmation of earlier research (ITU, 1999; Kenney, 2001). ECLAC nations and OECD (as well as US-Canada) nations differ on several important aspects in 2001. Compared to the OECD nations, ECLAC nations have lower GDP, lower education level, lower trust, high income inequality index value, low infrastructure level, higher ethnicity and high illiteracy level. The ECLAC region's investment in ICT as a percent of GDP is favorably comparable to OECD, as also its recent low inflation level. Table 5 additionally shows the empirical proof of such differences through individual ANOVA analyses.

Proposition 5a addresses the issue of what factor levels of digital divide change significantly over the years and is supported from results of empirical tests. Two years, 1995 and 2001 are considered. For the OECD nations, average GDP per capita, ICT investment as a percent of GDP, and inflation reduced, whereas infrastructure level increased. For the ECLAC nations, inflation went down, whereas education level, ICT investment as a percentage of GDP and infrastructure level increased. For all nations, inflation went down significantly, average GDP per capita went down; however, the infrastructure level went up. Table 6 shows the statistical significance of changes in factors over the years. Considering all nations, digital divide indicator (DD) as well as other indicators registered statistically significant changes over time.

Proposition 5b also addresses the issue of whether the digital divide gaps are increasing over time. From Figure 4 and Table 6, it could be concluded that the levels of digital divide are not growing for most of nations over time. So, proposition 5b is supported.

CONCLUSIONS

This study is a logical extension of the previous digital divide studies and was aimed at answering such questions as: What factors contribute to digital divide and how are they different in various regions of the world? What constitutes the current divide gaps for the computer and communication technologies and what might realistically be done to close the gap? These questions needed to be empirically investigated and addressed as already called for by some scholars of digital divide. This chapter discussed the digital divide problem from a global perspective and explored major factors that affect the digital divide.

This longitudinal study introduced a modeling scheme with several new indicators that are relevant for global digital divide. One of the major contributions of this study includes: using a set of related technologies that may contribute to digital divide, unlike previous studies, and use of a larger set of nations. The findings of the present study have led to the conclusion that global digital divide may not be increasing with respect to the U.S. index. The factor values that are responsible for digital divide are not all common for OECD and ECLAC set of nations. There seems to be substantial changes over the years in the indicators of digital divide. The findings also conclude that trust building and income improvement of a nation may lead to reduction in the digital divide gap. Table 7 summarizes our findings.

The limitations of the study include the fact that some other factors (e.g. demographics such as the number of young people in a nation, percentage of female in the population) which could be relevant to digital divide were not considered due to lack of data. The sample size used, due to non-availability of data, can make some of the results less stable in nature. However, while cross-national studies when done over time are often plagued with this problem, the results are still insightful. Nevertheless, an exhaustive regression analysis can be conducted to investigate more indicators with more data and make the results more robust. Future research efforts should be directed towards this goal.

MINICASE

Analyzing the Digital Divide in Individual ECLAC Nations

The concepts of the article are illustrated by selecting three sample nations from the ECLAC set of nations and discussing how the digital divide has evolved in these nations. These nations are Uruguay, Costa Rica and Argentina. They are classified as developing by the World Bank (2005).

Table M1 shows several digital divide-related statistics for these nations. Argentina has the lowest inflation, highest percentage of secondary educated people and highest income inequality. Its infrastructure (INFRA) and GDP per capita are second highest. Uruguay has highest infrastructure (INFRA) and GDP per capita values. Inflation in Uruguay is highest and its income inequality level is lowest. Costa Rica has lowest infrastructure (INFRA) and GDP values, as well as lowest education. The average trust index values for all three nations are in the low 20s, which is an indication of low interpersonal trust among the publics of the three nations. The ethnic heterogeneity (ELF index value) is highest in Argentina, followed by Uruguay and is substantially low in Costa Rica.

Indices/Nations	Uruguay		Costa Rica		Argentina	
	Year 1995	Year 2001	Year 1995	Year 2001	Year 1995	Year 2001
CPI	128.342	196.8453	117.5225	201.8771	100.1557	98.4231
EDU		69.9339	40.7735	49.2181	73.6639	79.0638
GDP	12457.37	12801	6816.093	8543.28	10608.96	11544.1
GINI	44.836	44.836	45.88	45.88	54	54
INFRA	532.9153	530.4166	225.2252	231.1708	276.1001	325.7514
ELF	20		7		31	
URB	9.457	7.8818	43.64	40.4824	12.55	11.6561
ICT/GDP	--	--	--	--	3.6	4
TRUST	Low		Low		Low	

Note: -- denotes missing data; blank denotes average data

Table M1. Various Indicator values for 3 ECLAC Nations

The Kiviat graphs of two of the nations for normalized values (normalized with respect to the values of the U.S.) of some of these parameters are shown in Figure 4.

The changes that have taken place over the years from 1995 to 2001 are noted as follows. Inflation in Costa Rica has soared (72%) as well as its GDP per capita (25%) and educational level (21%). For Argentina the noticeable change has been in infrastructure improvements (18%). Inflation has gone down 2%, whereas education and GDP registered slight increases. For Uruguay, the only noticeable change has been in inflation which increased by 54%. Table M2 presents information on ICT–related changes. Four ICT level per 1000 values (Internet, Mobile phones (Mobile), PC and Telephones (TEL)) for two years 1995 and 2001 are shown.

For the Internet, the most rapid growth has taken place in Uruguay followed by Costa Rica and Argentina. For mobile phones, the growth rates from highest to lowest are in Argentina, Uruguay and Costa Rica. For telephones, the growth rates are from highest to lowest in Uruguay, Costa Rica and Argentina. It can be noted that in 2001 Costa Rica enjoyed the highest penetration of PCs, Uruguay the highest in Internet and telephones and Argentina registered the highest penetration in mobile phones (Table M2).

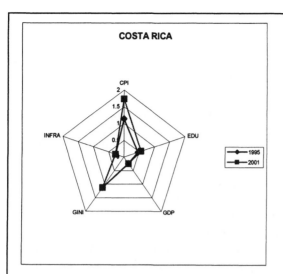
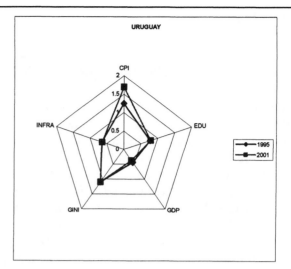

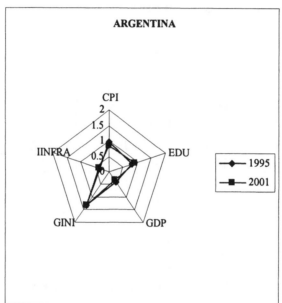

Figure 4. Kiviat Graphs for 3 ECLAC nations

COUNTRY/ Variables	Internet 95	Internet01	Mobile95	Mobile01	PC95	PC01	Tel95	Tel01
Argentina	0.86	88	9.8	192.55	24.45	91.1	161.7	223.83
Costa Rica	4.23	98.81	5.63	75.69	--	170.19	143.8	229.75
United States	75.47	502.9	128.44	450.76	328.09	625.01	607.2	667.14
Uruguay	3.11	119.08	12.51	154.71	21.94	110.09	194.9	282.91

Note: -- denotes missing data

Table M2. Digital Divide Indicator Values for 3 ECLAC Nations

Uruguay has the highest GDP per capita, lowest income inequality, highest urbanization and highest infrastructure level or infrastructural development. Based on the propositions stated above, these values imply that Uruguay has the lowest digital divide. Argentina reduced its relative digital divide gap from 1995 to 2003 by reducing inflation (2%) and increasing the level of education (7%), among other measures. Finally, the digital gap has decreased from 1995 to 2003 for the nations considered in this study. This observation is consistent with the results depicted in Figure 3.

Discussion Questions:
1. Discuss the digital divide concept for Costa Rica and Uruguay. Is the digital divide gap high or low for these countries?
2. Why are the average trust index values for Uruguay, Costa Rica and Argentina so low?
3. Look up the three countries in the Transparency International's Corruption Perceptions Index (http://www.transparency.org). Where are they ranked? Discuss their relative ranking with all of the other South American countries. Does their ranking surprise you?
4. What is a Kiviat graph? What does it show?

KEY TERMS
Basic Infrastructural Indicators
Digital Divide
ECLAC
Economic Indicators
ELF index
Interpersonal Trust
OECD
Social Indicators

STUDY QUESTIONS
1. Can the concept of measuring the digital divide as outlined above also be extended to other developing regions such as the African or Asian regions?

2. Using the results presented in Figure 2, compare the three groups of nations in terms of how various factors influence digital divide.

3. A number of things have changed in 2006. The mobile penetration, in particular, has been spectacular in many developing nations including some of the ECLAC nations in recent times. How will that impact (if at all) the digital distance among nations?

4. What other social, political, cultural, and institutional factors can be taken into consideration in a digital divide study such as this?

5. Can the Scandinavian nations (Denmark, Finland, Iceland, Norway and Sweden) be taken as a whole as the base set of nations from which the digital distances can be calculated? What are the advantages and disadvantages of having the U.S. as a base nation for calculating the digital divide index?

6. What other technologies can be included in designing a digital divide index?

7. Will the digital distance among nations increase or decrease in future? Discuss.

REFERENCES

Bagchi, K. "Factors Contributing to Digital Divide," *Journal of Global Information Technology Management (JGITM)*, 8(3), 2005, pp. 47-65.

Caselli, F. and Coleman, W. "Cross-country Technology Diffusion: The Case of Computers," *American Economic Review*, 81, 2001, pp. 328-35.

Cecchinia, S. and Scott, C. "Can information and communications technology applications contribute to poverty reduction? Lessons from rural India," *Information Technology for Development*, 10, 2003, pp. 73-84.

Corrocher, N. and Ordanini, A. "Measuring the digital divide: a framework for the analysis of cross-country differences," *Journal of Information Technology*, 17, 2002, pp. 9–19.

Davis, G. and Kanago, B. "On measuring the effect of inflation uncertainty on real GNP growth," *Oxford Economic Papers*, 48, 1996 pp.163-175.

Dholakia, N. and Kshetri, N. "Will M-Commerce Emerge to Dilute Digital Divide?," *RITM Working Paper Series*, 2001. Available at: http://ritim.cba.uri.edu/working%20papers/Global-Digital-Divide-M-Commerce-draft-9[1].pdf.

Digital Divide Network. "Digital Divide Basics Fact Sheet". Available at: http://www.digitaldividenetwork.org. 2002.

Dijk, J. V. and Hacker, K. "The Digital Divide as a Complex and Dynamic Phenomenon," *The Information Society*, 19, 2003, pp. 315–326.

DiMaggio, P., Hargittai, E., Neuman, R., and Robinson, J. "Social Implications of the Internet," *Annual Review of Sociology* 27, 2001 pp. 307-336.

ECLAC Statistical yearbook for Latin America and the Caribbean. Available at: http://www.eclac.org. 2002.

Field, A. Discovering Statistics using SPSS for Windows, SAGE Publications. 2002.

Ge, W. and Jain, H. "Internet Diffusion and Digital Divide in China: Some Empirical Results," 2003, pp. 1095-1103, *Proc. AIS 2003*.

Hargittai, E. "Weaving the Western Web: Explaining Differences in Internet Connectivity among OECD Countries," *Telecommunications Policy*, 23, 1999, pp. 701-18.

Hoffman, D. L., Novak, T. P., and Schlosser. The Evolution of the Digital Divide: How Gaps in Internet Access May Impact Electronic Commerce. *Journal of Computer Mediated Communication* 5(3), 2000. Available at: http://www.ascusc.org/jcmc/vol5/issue3/hoffman.html.

Huang, H., Keser, C., Leland, J. and Shachat, J. "Trust, the Internet, and the digital divide," *IBM Systems Journal*, 42(3), 2003, pp. 507-517.

Hugguns, R. and Izushi, H. "The Digital Divide and ICT Learning in Rural Communities: Examples of Good Practice Service Delivery," *Local Economy*, 17(2), 2002, pp. 111-122.

Inglehart, R., Basanez, M. and Moreno, A. "Human Values and Beliefs," *A Cross-sectional Sourcebook, Findings from 1990-1993 World Values Survey*. The University of Michigan Press, 1998.

ITU Challenges to the Network: Internet for Development, International Telecommunications Unit, Geneva. 1999.

Katz, J. "Road Maps Towards an Information Society in Latin America and the Caribbean," *Economic Commission for Latin America and the Caribbean (ECLAC) Report, Santiago, Chile*, 2003. Available at: http://www.eclac.org, pp. 1-119.

Kaufman, R. "Interdisciplinary Perspective on the 'Digital Divide' Part I: Economic Perspectives," *Journal of the Association for Information Systems*, 96(12), 2005, pp. 293-297.

Kenney, C. "Prioritizing Countries for Assistance to Overcome the Digital Divide," *Communications and Strategies*, 41, 2001. pp.17-36.

Kiiski, S. and Pohjola, M. "Cross-Country Diffusion of the Internet," *Information Economics and Policy*, (4(2), 2002, pp. 297-310.

Kolence, K. and Kiviat, P. "Software Unit Profiles and Kiviat Figures," *ACM SIGMETRICS: Performance Evaluation Review*, 1973 pp. 2-12.

Kvasny, L. and Keil, M. "The Challenges of Redressing the Digital Divide: A Tale of Two Cities," 2002, pp. 817-828, *Proc. AIS 2002*.

Lee, J-W. "Education for Technology Readiness: Prospects for Developing Countries," *Journal of Human Development*, 2, 2001, 115-51.

Lu, M. "Digital Divide in Developing Countries," *Journal of Global Information Technology Management*, 4(3), 2001.

Mauro, P. "Corruption and Growth," *Quarterly Journal of Economics*, (110: 3), 1995, pp. 681–712.

Mineta, N. Y., Rohde, G. L. and Shaprio, R. *Falling Through the Net: Toward Digital Inclusion. A Report on Americans Access to Technology Tools, Washington, DC: U.S. Department of Commerce, Economics and Statistics Administration and National Telecommunications and Information Administration*, 2000.

Norris, P. *Digital Divide? Civic Engagement, Information Poverty and the Internet in Democratic Societies*, New York: Cambridge University Press, 2001.

Novak, T. P. and Hoffman, D. L. Bridging the Digital Divide: The Impact of Race on Computer Access and Internet Use, *Science*, 17 April 1998, Elab Manuscripts Ecommerce Research Center Online, 2 February 1998, Vanderbilt University, Nashville, TN, 21 March. . 2001. Available at: http://ecommerce.vanderbilt.edu/papers/race/science.html.

NTIA"A Nation Online: How Americans Are Expanding Their Use of the Internet", National Telecommunications and Information Administration, Washington, DC, U.S. Department of Commerce. Available at: http://www.ntia.doc.gov/ntiahome/digitaldivide. 2002.

OECD *Understanding the Digital Divide*, Washington, DC: OECD Publications. 2001.

Peha, J. M. "Lessons from Haiti's Internet Development," *Communications of the ACM*, 42(6), 1999, pp. 67-72.

Petrazzini, B. and Kibati, M. "The Internet in Developing Countries," *Communications of the ACM*, 42(6), 1999, pp.31-36.

Rogers, E. *Communication Technology*, New York: The Free Press. 1986.

Sciadas, G. "Monitoring the Digital Divide," *Orbicom Report*, ISBN 2-922651-01-0. 2002.

U.S. Department of Commerce's Digital Divide Web site, Available at: http://www.digitaldivide.gov/

Wolcott, P., Press, L., McHenry, W., Goodman, S., and Foster, W. "A Framework for Assessing the Global Diffusion of the Internet," *Journal of Association for Information Systems*, (6:2), November 2001, pp. 1-50.

World Bank data base .http:// www.devdata.worldbank.org. 2005.

Zhang, M. and Wolff, R.S. "Crossing the Digital Divide: Cost-Effective Broadband Wireless Access for Rural and Remote Areas," *IEEE Communications Magazine*, 42(2), 2004, pp. 99-106.

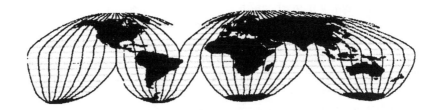

Bridging the Global Digital Divide: Critical Success Factors for Lesser Developed Countries

Steven John Simon
Mercer University, USA

CHAPTER SUMMARY

Developing countries are at a distinct disadvantage when competing with developed countries in the electronic commerce domain. Electronic services hold both peril and promise for developing countries as a means to expedite their entry into the world of cyber commerce, create value-added jobs within their economies, and attract much needed foreign investment. This chapter examines critical success factors (CSFs) developing countries encounter as they develop their cyber economy and explains challenges and potential solutions. Anecdotal evidence and "lessons learned" from developed and developing countries are investigated as well as implications from the World Trade Organization's (WTO) General Agreement on Trade in Services (GATS) negotiations and Organization for Economic Cooperation and Development (OECD) proceedings. The study develops a framework of technical and societal CSFs whose synergy can expedite the entrance of developing countries into the cyber economy.

GLOBAL DIGITAL DIVIDE

The growth of Electronic Commerce (EC) has been staggering and was expected to reach $6.2 trillion US by 2004 (Forrester Research 2003). In the developed world, especially the United States and Western Europe, businesses have leveraged the Internet to deliver lower transaction costs, reduced paperwork, and created fluid sourcing that results in improved profitability. Consumers in developed countries have used the Internet as a means to gather information, becoming more informed resulting in changed consumer behavior. Additionally, the advent of EC has opened new sources of products and greater choices for consumers paralleling efficiencies achieved by business. Unfortunately, Internet adoption and gains in efficiency and productivity from the Internet have not yet been replicated in the developing world and has led to the coining of the term Digital Divide – referring to the disparity in Internet access and technology between developed and developing countries or the gap between Internet/technology "haves" and "have-nots."

Digital Divide is a very serious matter for those who are currently behind in Internet access, for they are not able to enjoy many benefits of being wired and are handicapped in participating fully in society's economic, political and social life (Howland 1998, Office of the Press Secretary 1999). These benefits include finding lower prices for goods and services, working from home, acquiring new skills using distance learning, making better-informed decisions about healthcare needs, and getting more involved in the education of their children. These are only some of the myriad benefits conferred by Internet access. Thus, for citizens of developing countries, lagging behind in Internet access entails further lagging behind in economic progress in the quality of life. Developing countries lagging in EC find themselves in an increasingly difficult position as they attempt to promote their exports, attract capital investment and jobs, and transform their economies. A variety of reasons have been suggested for the digital divide from lack of telecommunications infrastructure, dearth of computer skills on the part of business and consumers, failure of regulatory reform and standards, as well as the poor state of physical infrastructure, e.g. roads, rail, etc.

Technology Adoption in Developing Countries

The literature on e-commerce adoption in developing countries is extremely limited, although some evidence exists describing the impediments (Travica 2002). Petrazzini and Kibati (1999) report on e-commerce impediments characterizing Argentina, Kenya, India, and Armenia. These include limited Internet accessibility, a lack of competition in international telephone traffic that makes access to the international network expensive, a lack of intra-regional infrastructure, and a disproportionate penetration of the telephone in the urban as opposed to less populated rural areas. South Korea has had a problem with customers' lack of trust in online transactions (Lee 1999). Plant (1999) identifies obstacles to e-commerce in Latin America, such as the lack of customer protection laws, tradition of remote shopping, and methods of non-cash payment. Montealegre (1999) draws on King et al. (1994) and suggests that both society and culture must be considered for successful adoption in developing countries. He illustrates examples of Latin American countries that successfully adopted technology using varying combinations of government, non-governmental, and business organizations. Other cases (Peha 1999, Clark 1999) cite examples from Haiti and China, respectively, where successful adoption of telecommunications technology had been achieved as a result of competition between government agencies (that formerly controlled the telecommunications networks) and private entities. Davis (1999) indicates that accessibility to technology is the limiting factor, while in reality it is a combination of infrastructure and organizational culture.

In recent years, economists have analyzed the impact of a technology developed in an industrialized country which is copied by a developing country. They have shown that the rate of growth of the developing country depends on its initial stock of knowledge and the costs of imitation (Barro and Sala-I-Martin 1995). They have further argued that if the costs of imitation are lower than the costs of innovation, the poorer country can grow faster than the richer one by leapfrogging technologies development through participating and competing in global trade and sharing information globally (Srikantaiah and Xiaoying 1998). For instance, countries with an underdeveloped telecommunications infrastructure can implement a digital telecom network and avoid the costs many developed countries incurred in first laying out an analog system. Yet, even when developing countries adopt electronic commerce, the technologies are not always optimized. A recent survey by the International Trade Center (ITC) discovered that businesses in developing countries view their Internet connectivity as a valuable communications tool, but failed to incorporate the technology as an aspect of their competitive strategy (Barclay and Domeisen 2001). Business perception contributes to the fact that less than a third of the surveyed countries included electronic trade as a component of their national export development strategies, an excellent indicator of the need for close cooperation between government and business during this technology adoption. The next section examines the technical critical success factors required to bridge the global digital divide.

CRITICAL SUCCESS FACTORS – TECHNICAL

Communication Infrastructure

A country's readiness for e-commerce depends on network infrastructure and technology diffusion. EC growth is fostered by strong growth in infrastructure, including narrow and broadband access, hardware investment and Internet use, but it depends also on growth of mobile applications, price reductions, service improvement, ease of use, speed, and reliability. A key lesson from OECD experience is that telecommunications reform has been a major determining factor in the emergence of the so-called "new economy" (OECD 2000b). Faster and more reliable network infrastructure associated with new ways of pricing, both for consumers and for the leased lines used in B2B transactions, have led to increased Internet connection in homes and businesses. Low access costs are an important factor, while competition among infrastructure providers and among ISPs has led to innovative pricing structures.

In low-income developing countries, the first priority is to attain greater telecommunication penetration. There are just 14 million copper phone lines, for example, serving Africa's population of 800 million, whereas the United States has 169 million lines. Approximately 80 per cent of the world's population (almost all living in developing countries) has no access to reliable telecommunications (Panos, 1998). Historically, a major reason for the slow pace of basic telecommunications network expansion has been the unfavorable economics of connecting rural areas, especially remote ones, in low-income countries. By one estimate, assuming capital costs of US$ 1,000 per line, a telecom operator would need to generate revenues of US$ 330-400 per line to be profitable, above the average *per capita* income of quite a few poor countries (Ernberg 1998). Telecommunications reform can be a positive-sum game in which customers, existing and new operators, employees, domestic and foreign investors, and government all gain. Some rules that will enhance those benefits include sorting out conflicting objectives early – especially the conflict between maximizing revenue and delivering more, better, and cheaper services; using market mechanisms rather than individual negotiations to select the partners and determine the right sale price; and establishing and following clearly defined processes for sale of assets and regulation that are open to participation and review by all interested parties, including the general public. Nonetheless, it is a well-known lesson from almost two decades of regulatory reforms worldwide that even while private participation takes place in increasingly competitive market structures, poor performance of regulatory agencies may limit the benefits of reform.

Implementing wide Internet access requires the emergence of local Internet service providers (ISPs) and portals that can arrange a reliable, low-cost connection to the Web, develop sites with useful, local language content, and offer a range of other services demanded by local Internet users. Once telephone density is sufficiently high, it should be possible to offer access to most users at local call rates. This presumes that an ISP can lease a high-capacity line from a telecom service provider at a competitive rate. At present the cost of such leased lines varies widely across countries, but it is generally several times higher in developing countries than in the United States.

- Physical telecommunications infrastructure
- Providing universal access at a reasonable cost
- Achieving interconnection and interoperability of telecommunications
- Networks and services

Exhibit 1. Infrastructure Development Challenges

Legal and Standards Issues

The lack of required maintenance on aging telecommunications equipment - most of which is unable to support high-speed Internet connections - is another reason for infrastructure initiatives. In many cases, poor service and loss of revenues can be blamed directly on the maintenance of outdated equipment and the shortage of trained personnel (Mbarika 2002). These problems are exacerbated with the existing problems associated with routing and interconnections. It is not unusual for Internet connections initiated in one South American country to be routed through the United States instead of going directly to another South American country. Problems of this nature decrease the reliability of the service.

Assuming the physical infrastructure bottlenecks to Internet expansion are overcome and access prices become more affordable in developing countries, a number of other significant policy challenges must be met if governments are to create an environment conducive to e-commerce. E-commerce requires legal norms and standards (e.g., covering contract enforcement, consumer protection, liability assignment, privacy protection, and intellectual property rights). Additional issues that governments are examining include recognition of digital signatures and electronic documents, taxes and tariff collection, and compliance with global trading commitments. Most developing countries have not examined or created policies or laws to address the issues originating as a result of EC. Perhaps the key question for developing countries involves the role of governments to intervene and regulate or let market forces make adaptations to the new electronic environment. Many developed countries (e.g. the United States and Canada) have opted for a mixed approach, particularly for promotion of EC, privacy, and intellectual property rights. In developing countries, for instance in Latin America, governments have yet to define a governance approach and as a result this section will examine the GATS and actions taken by the international community. Many of these countries' legal traditions require notarized paper-based documents and signatures, which creates a disincentive for companies seeking to adopt electronic contracts and documents for business transactions.

General Agreement on Trade in Services (GATS)

GATS defines trade in services as the supply of a service through any of four modes: cross border supply, consumption abroad, commercial presence and presence of natural persons (Article I). These modes distinguish between service transactions on the basis of the territorial presence of the supplier and the consumer of the service. The agreement makes no distinction between the different technological means by which a service may be delivered - whether in person, by mail, by telephone or across the Internet. The supply of services through electronic means is therefore covered by GATS in the same way as all other means of delivery. Because of the way it can render the distance between supplier and consumer virtually irrelevant, it is perhaps natural to think of electronic commerce essentially in terms of cross-border supply. [A detailed review of the GATS and Global Electronic Commerce is found in Simon (2002) and at www.wto.org]

Article VIII (related to the infrastructure issues previously discussed) requires each member to ensure that any monopoly supplier of a service does not 'in the supply of the monopoly service in the relevant market' act in a manner inconsistent with the MFN (Most Favored Nation) obligation and the member's specific commitments. There are at least two respects in which Article VIII is relevant to electronic commerce. First, where the basic telecommunications service is still monopolized but market access has been granted to competitive Internet access providers, Article VIII would require governments to ensure that the monopolist does not discriminate against rival Internet access providers. Secondly, Article VIII requires that exclusive suppliers of Internet services do not frustrate commitments made on other services which are being supplied by Internet. This article enhances competition and should lower access prices and improve availability. There probably is a need to establish at least some intergovernmental guidelines on what is permissible regulation of EC content services. After all, government regulations protecting basic public interests like public health and safety, consumer and data protection, and the security of transactions ought to apply equally in both the virtual and physical worlds. There is nothing sacred about the Internet that should or will preclude governments from regulating, for example, the on-line supply of medical or educational services to their citizens. And if governments are going to establish such regulations, then there should be some level of multilateral agreement about what kinds of regulations are GATS legal.

- Adapting national juridical and regulatory systems to Electronic Commerce
- Introduce changes to accommodate electronic transactions and transmissions
- Develop public policies to maximize EC benefits without compromising policy objectives
- Recognize and certify electronic signatures
- Protect intellectual property through a guarantee of electronic copyrights and trademarks
- Understand tax implications and insure fair treatment with traditional commercial activities
- Ensure enforcement of electronic contracts and provide for recourse in dispute settlement.

Exhibit 2. Legal Challenges

Standardization

A related issue explored in the EC work program is technical standardization, which presents a special problem in the electronic environment. Clearly there is a need to ensure that governments and private firms do not establish standards that are unduly trade restrictive. But judging whether standards have that effect using the GATS' language could be a difficult task. The issues of domestic regulation and non-discrimination are intrinsically linked in this regard. Under the status quo even admittedly "like" products might be denied entry by technical choices that are not clearly driven by discriminatory intent. Standards can create critical positive momentum during the early phases of Internet and EC adoption and in some cases - Ecuador and Peru (Montealegre 1999) - can actually speed adoption.

Standardization issues can be extremely complicated and assessing them often requires a high level of technological expertise. Moreover, the GATS language on standards is very broadly framed. It therefore is obvious that dispute settlements panels would not have an easy time rendering well grounded judgments if, as it seems reasonable to expect, conflicts arise with the expansion of EC. One of the greatest impediments to the general adoption of EC in developing countries is the issue of electronic documents and digital signatures. Within this discussion of new contracts and payment methods, governments must create adequate mechanisms to protect their consumers if they are to have confidence that on-line transactions are as safe as those in the physical world. These issues are currently being resolved in developed countries and can provide an existing model for a developing country.

Privacy and Consumer Protection

New methods of processing vast amounts of data, such as data mining techniques, make it possible to identify new kinds of purchasing relationships and unusual associations, and, in some cases, to make statistical inferences. While they raise some potentially serious privacy issues, they can also be used to detect fraud, especially for large-volume, small-value e-commerce transactions. They are already being used for this purpose by credit-card companies, cellular communications providers, and law enforcement agencies. Both the public and private sectors must help adjudicate the trade-off between protecting privacy and obtaining the benefits of electronic commerce that users value, while fostering consumer confidence. European countries have agreed upon principles for the protection of privacy and personal data. These principles include assurances to consumers that personal information will not be collected or used without their knowledge, made available to parties other than their initial correspondents, or linked to other data about them without their consent.

While many governments have the legal tools to control such conduct effectively in their own markets, electronic commerce requires international mechanisms. National consumer law enforcement authorities will have to cooperate in fighting international swindlers by conducting joint investigations, sharing confidential information, seizing swindlers' assets, and organizing redress for victims. Technology also offers new ways to resolve some of the issues. The Internet is distinct from other kinds of media in that there are technological tools that allow consumers to protect themselves. Some technological solutions for helping consumers protect themselves in the on-line environment are certification mechanisms, such as labeling systems that certify that an on-line business meets certain good standards of business, or mechanisms for notifying consumers of the legal jurisdiction or venue for resolving disputes arising from a transaction. In addition, consumers can access consumer education messages that describe their rights in the context of electronic transactions. Consumer education is a key component of consumer protection. However, technological solutions must be underpinned by common criteria and organizational procedures to ensure that the information provided to consumers is correct and true. Such coordination could be achieved by industry self-regulation. Government input, when required, should consist of simple and predictable legal tools that are sensitive to the technology and to the pace of change in the on-line environment.

Intellectual Property Rights

Intellectual property rights (IPRs) have been crucial in providing security and trust with respect to investment and trade in ideas and cultural activities by guaranteeing commercial returns. The growing importance of intellectual content in the global information infrastructure-global information society (GII-GIS) means that such rights are crucial for the development of electronic commerce. Yet, the digital nature of the content and the availability of new technologies make it relatively easy to circumvent many controls, owing to the possibility of making exact duplicates. At the same time, new technologies (digital watermarking and encryption) can help protect against or prosecute rights violations. In a number of cases, the private sector has made significant progress in agreeing to common standards for the protection of IPRs in new multimedia goods and services. Through the TRIPS (Trade Related Aspects of Intellectual Property Rights) and recent WIPO (Copyright Treaty) agreements on intellectual property rights, governments have also made progress in agreeing to common international standards of protection; it is important for the development of electronic commerce that countries move rapidly to implement these agreements in national legislation. The issue of IPRs and copyrights are of greatest concern to developed countries whose companies hold many of the legal rights. Theft of these rights has become a growing concern across many industries (e.g. software, music and video, luxury items [watches], etc.). As developing countries become more integrated into the global EC arena, they will come to hold and benefit from IPRs and it is therefore in their best interest to support and enforce legislation.

Taxation[1]

Assessment and collection of taxes on e-commerce transactions are an issue that concerns both government and business. Governments are concerned about the potential loss of revenue and businesses are concerned about the possible impacts of government regulation. In the physical world, collecting taxes is a challenge that, by and large, governments have met. They will probably be equally successful in the "virtual" world insofar as countries interpret and apply existing rules in an internationally consistent fashion. If they succeed in this, they will not need to create new taxes specifically for electronic commerce.

---

[1] It is important to note that there is a difference between taxes - income and sales - charged by a government and tariffs - fees assessed by a government on goods or services entering their country. The WTO members have temporarily agreed not to impose any new tariffs on electronic transfer of information, but countries still assess taxes on EC.

The ability to digitize physical products and sell them over the Internet raises issues that fall under the income characterization rules of tax treaties. Any information that can be digitized - computer programs, books, music or images - can be transferred electronically between countries for a fee. In a transaction involving a downloaded digital image, for example, it may be argued either that this is equivalent to purchasing a physical photograph and results in business profits or that it is a service and results in royalty income taxable in the source country. The problem here is that if the internet transmission is downloaded as goods or service, or used as either a good or a service in electronic form, then issues related to internal sales taxes or value-added-taxes (VAT) immediately present themselves. As the WTO secretariat pointed out in its 1998 study (www.wto.org), "If Internet transactions are not taxed, this would give the medium a considerable advantage over other means of commerce that are taxed. If a VAT of 20 percent, or corporate income tax of 30-50 percent, could be circumvented via the Internet, the latter would be made more attractive for sellers and buyers alike."

CRITICAL SUCCESS FACTORS – NON-TECHNICAL

Education -Developing Education Programs

Assuming that a developing country is able to create an accessible and inexpensive infrastructure and that legal issues are overcome, individual users and businesses must be trained, educated, and encouraged to use the Internet and adopt EC. Davis (1999) reports that the typical Latin American user is not unlike that of the typical North American user, which suggests that training and education methods from the developed countries might be transplanted successfully in developing countries. He goes on to suggest that the profile of the first time Latin American Internet user is changing rapidly to a demographic user that is younger, female, and unilingual Spanish-speaking. The rapid growth of these first time users indicates the need for education and training of these and more experienced users. Since the use of EC presents new experiences and a different business environment, training and education must extend beyond the desire to introduce users to the technology and ensure they are familiar enough to operate it efficiently. This education should encompass issues related to consumer rights - which in turn builds consumer trust - credit and electronic payment options, and training to utilize the medium for advancement and as a gateway to new job opportunities. In part, education should lead to some fundamental cultural changes in the users and society.

Workforces in developing countries, as in developed countries, are changing from labor intensive to knowledge-based work. In developed countries, surveys have shown Internet use is associated with higher education. The same principle applies in developing countries. The key players in a plan to educate and train Internet users are institutions of higher education, secondary education institutions, technology support centers (sponsored by a combination of the public and private sectors), industry supported projects, and government institutions. In the developed world, institutions of higher education launched, introduced, and have acclimated users (their students) to the new technology. Those students in turn adapted the technology and their training while spreading the medium throughout their countries. Today in developed countries, the secondary institutions are taking the lead in the use of the Internet for education purposes, while in many cases primary school students have already obtained a mastery of Internet skills upon entering grade school. This movement from higher to primary educational institutions has taken place in part due to the ability of the Internet to create a self-education environment. Since there is generally minimal limitations to site access, barring language barriers, developing world users have ready access to all the information already developed and in place. Given the ability of the Internet to provide formatted educational/training material, the training programs offered by the key players listed above should focus on providing the basic tools of the Internet and education on the advantages/pitfalls of EC, while informing consumers of their rights. Governments working in conjunction with industry groups within each developing country should create a program of study that accomplishes these objectives. Additionally, these programs could demonstrate to the users places to obtain information from government and government-sponsored web sites designed to advance their education and improve their overall access to information. An entirely different set of programs should be developed and targeted towards small and medium businesses which inform them about the opportunities using the Internet for EC, government-sponsored programs and web sites to help them develop sites and promote themselves (particularly outside their country), legal matters, and general business knowledge.

Change Management (Trust)

The essential challenge facing developing countries is to create a climate of trust which makes it possible for agents to conduct business online without need for face-to-face contact. A best solution is to put in place a legal and judiciary framework that meets certain minimum standards of transparency, impartiality and timeliness. In many countries, however, this remains a distant goal. In the medium term, self-regulated codes of conduct currently under discussion in many OECD countries may provide a model from which business in developing countries could take inspiration; the OECD's (2000a) *Guidelines for Consumer Protection in the Context of Electronic Commerce* also serves as a model. Eventually, it may not be too far-fetched to imagine that non-OECD businesses could subscribe to such codes, either individually or as part of a group of like-minded entrepreneurs (e.g., associations or co-operatives). Insofar as independent compliance accreditation is required, the costs could be partly or fully borne by development funds.

Weaving a web of trust is the most important issue for extending the use of electronic settlements. Trust is needed at many levels, including hardware and software security, the regulatory regime, familiarity and users' perceptions. Factors affecting the level of trust required and provided include (ODEC 2000a):

1) where and how payment takes place (whether real or virtual – for virtual settlement, data circulated over the network are recognized as having monetary value or contain payment instructions);
2) when settlement takes place (prior to, at the time of, or after the transaction);
3) who settles (established incumbents or new entrants);
4) whether the transaction is B2B or B2C; and
5) whether settlement can be traced

Establishing trust in the eminently impersonal environment of the Internet is not straightforward. Traditional paper-based rules and regulations may create uncertainties as to the validity and legal effect of electronic transactions. In many societies, especially in the developing world, trust is established and reinforced through family association, repeated personal contact and interaction. Modern societies have devised ways of extending the basis for trust through the impartial enforcement of the law and its adaptation to a new technological environment. This is the basis of the trust that underpins e-commerce in the developed world. Where legal and juridical institutions are not advanced, as in much of the developing world, e-companies find themselves at a disadvantage because of insecurity, whether real or perceived. The reluctance to entrust sensitive personal information – like credit card numbers – to businesses operating on the Web remains strong. Surveys of e-commerce users in developing countries suggest a low willingness to provide sensitive financial information over the Web.

Users in developed countries may be reluctant to entrust such information to businesses operating in developing countries that have a weak reputation for rule of law and prosecution of business fraud. A broader issue of confidence arises with respect to the accuracy of product descriptions and claims and the enforcement of contracts. This is a general consumer protection issue, but the newness and relative anonymity of e-commerce presents new challenges (Panos 1998). New entrants have generally not had time to build reputations for honesty and reliability, and low entry and exit costs also weaken incentives for honest dealing. For this reason, as noted above, brand recognition may matter even more in the world of e-commerce than in the real world. To some extent, the problem of trust is being addressed through private sector innovation. For example, an effort is underway to develop a system of collaborative ratings that small e-businesses could display on their websites to reassure consumers. In the case of electronic exchanges, those transacting through the exchanges can rate suppliers on the basis of quality of service, speed of delivery and other measures. Even here, there is clearly scope for fraud. So certain safeguards are built into the rating system; e.g., evidence of a purchase is required for one's rating to count, and ratings of regular customers are assigned a higher weight. Trends in ratings would be available to users as well as comments by specific customers. Such initiatives, however, do not address fully consumer protection concerns. Thus, regulators in OECD countries see it as incumbent upon themselves to offer e-consumers a level of protection on a par to that afforded other consumers, and business is currently thrashing out self-regulation guidelines to pre-empt more restrictive legal measures. Relevant issues in this context are full disclosure of the terms of sale; the opportunity to review the transaction and all costs (including shipping); standards for cancellation, return, refund and warranty; and security for customers' personal records.

- Establish reliable, secure, and accessible electronic payment systems
- Protect consumer privacy without creating barriers to trade
- Protect consumers from deceptive practices (e.g. fraud and unlawful content)
- Create training/education programs for consumers and business managers

Exhibit 3. Trust Building Challenges

Business and Government Awareness

Business Awareness: Managers in developing countries are faced with great challenges and opportunities. It is their responsibility to ensure that their companies are prepared to compete in this new environment. However, they cannot simply make fashionable investments for the company without making responsible and systematic analysis of its needs, its individuals and its environment. It is true that the emerging global information infrastructure has within it the capacity to go a long way toward solving many of the problems confronted by developing country companies. However, if managers fail to understand how to use it in accordance with their situation and idiosyncrasies, it will only create new barriers, limitations, and foreign necessities in their societies. They need to strengthen the capacity to understand the technological advances and learn how to improve the transfer and assimilation of these advances. Companies, research centers, and universities in developing countries have worked together to gain access to the Internet. Now managers need to devise new joint strategies for mobilizing the scarce resources, including science and technology, in the most effective way to promote endogenous development to understand the implications of doing business on the Internet. Even for companies that seem unlikely to fully utilize these emerging technologies at this point in time, it is still necessary for their managers to understand and assess the potential impact of the new technologies on the company's future strategies and economies. Managers need to be prepared to cope with innovation and must not be submerged by it, especially in the earliest phase when little input can be made and a near-passive receiver role of imported technology is adopted. Countries with strong managerial capabilities, such as the newly industrializing economies of South-East Asia, have been able to acquire and retain competitiveness and build adequate bases to keep up with the headlong pace of progress by devoting major efforts to investigating new managerial trends. In particular, Singapore - a small, resource poor country - has become a regional powerhouse as a result of government and business commitments to the development of a "wired" society.

It appears that managers attempting to effectively implement Web applications in developing country organizations face one stumbling block right from the start. Although these technologies rapidly and seemingly effortlessly permeate the economic and production systems of the world, they are not available 'off the shelf'. They have to be absorbed, mastered, and controlled. Their application calls for preexisting capabilities that are not easily available in developing countries, such as the preexisting capacity to insert new ideas, new practices, and new elements into a flexible system. This raises an important question about the overall ability of developing countries to exploit the malleability of the Internet and to implement Web applications - nurtured in the proper social, cultural, and technological environment - to capitalize on their full potential (Montealegre 1996). As more individuals and organizations connect to international networks, they are coming to expect an enhanced level of performance from service and information providers. A customer who is used to instant response time from around the globe is no longer willing to wait days or even hours for a query to be acknowledged. Tomorrow becomes too late to find the answer or deliver the product. If one company cannot meet these expectations, a competitor with a network connection will be happy to oblige. To gain competitive advantage through information, Porter and Millar (1991) advise that managers must understand not only the technology but also the 'value chain' in which their company operates. To uncover and evaluate new avenues for competitive advantage through the use of the Internet, companies need to analyze their relationship with suppliers and vendors, the existing role of information in the organization of the company, internal production mechanisms, and the points of contact with customers. This can permit companies in developing countries to leverage two of the key advantages of the Internet: 1) the ability to reduce transaction costs and 2) the use of an inexpensive and flexible means to promote themselves (while entering new markets) and satisfy customers.

- Support small and medium enterprises in adopting new technology
- Stimulate the use of EC between individuals and businesses with government organizations
- Increase efficiency and transparency of government and in supply of government services via EC
- Promote efficiency in acquisition of goods and services by governmental departments

Exhibit 4. Challenges for Skill and Business Awareness

Government Awareness - An interesting parallel is that of the government's managers, civil servants. Like managers in the business sector, these government officials must not only encourage and support the use of the Internet by business and consumers but actively use it themselves. Governments in developed countries have made extensive use of the Internet as a means to promulgate information to their constituents and have recently embarked on programs to transform and streamline their procurement processes. In developing countries, governments could post information to the Internet as part of their training and education programs. This would demonstrate to their people a commitment to use the Internet themselves while encouraging use, and perhaps reduce costs while providing improved services. Models can be taken from former developing countries such as Singapore, whose government has not only embraced the Internet but created programs that speed development and implementation of a "wired" society, giving the country competitive advantage in the region as it became a regional power for transportation and services. Their programs permeate their society and provide incentives for government departments, businesses, and individuals to utilize the Internet for both business and education.

CSF DISCUSSION AND CONCLUSION

A country's readiness for e-commerce/service depends on network infrastructure and technology diffusion. EC is fostered by strong growth in infrastructure, including narrow and broadband access, in hardware investment and in Internet use, but it depends also on price reductions, service improvement, ease of use, speed, and reliability. A key lesson from OECD experience is that telecommunications reform has been a major determining factor in the emergence of the so-called "new economy" (OECD 2000b). Faster and more reliable network infrastructure, associated with new ways of pricing, both for consumers and for the leased lines used in B2B transactions, have led to increased Internet connection in homes and businesses. Low access costs are an important factor driving uptake, while competition among infrastructure providers and among ISPs has led to innovative pricing structures. In low-income developing countries, the first priority is rather obviously to attain greater telecommunication penetration.

It is important to note that the term developing country refers to a large category of nations, of which no two are alike (Austin 1990). The same strategy, therefore, cannot be applied across the board, though groups of countries with the need for similar strategies could perhaps be identified. Thus, greater country-to-country cooperation to take the maximum advantage of the broad range of lessons, managerial advances, and technological options should be a primary goal. All development strategies should facilitate management of networks to exploit the whole range of technological and societal options now becoming available. Given the differences among developing countries – each with their corresponding strong and weak attributes – the application of CSFs will most likely vary as will the importance and implementation difficultly to various county situations.

MINICASE

Using Information and Communications Technology to Reduce Poverty in Rural India

The World Bank's *World Development Report 2000/2001: Attacking Poverty* identifies three crucial elements of poverty reduction efforts: opportunity, empowerment, and security. Experiences in rural India show that information and communications technology can enhance poor people's opportunities by improving their access to markets and health care. It can empower them by expanding their use of government services. And it can increase security by widening access to microfinance.

In Gujarat computerized milk collection centers are helping ensure fair prices for small farmers who sell milk to dairy cooperatives. The fat content of milk used to be calculated hours after the milk was received; farmers were paid every 10 days and had to trust the manual calculations of milk quality and quantity made by the staff of cooperatives. Farmers often claimed that the old system resulted in malfeasance and underpayments, but such charges were hard to prove. Computerized milk collection increases transparency, expedites processing, and provides immediate payments to farmers.

In Andhra Pradesh handheld computers - provided under the InfoDev-sponsored India Healthcare Delivery Project - are enabling auxiliary nurse midwives to eliminate redundant paperwork and data entry, freeing time to deliver health care to poor people. Midwives provide most health services in the state's vast rural areas, with each serving about 5,000 people - typically across multiple villages and hamlets. They administer immunizations, offer advice on family planning, educate people on mother-child health programs, and collect data on birth and immunization rates. Midwives usually spend 15-20 days a month collecting and registering data.

But with handheld computers they can cut that time by up to 40 percent - increasing the impact and reach of limited resources.

Since January 2000 Gyandoot, a government-owned computer network, has been making government more accessible to villagers in the poor, drought-prone Dhar district of Madhya Pradesh. Gyandoot reduces the time and money that people spend trying to communicate with public officials and provides immediate, transparent access to local government data and documentation. For minimal fees, Intranet kiosks provide caste, income, and domicile certificates, enabling villagers to avoid the common practice of paying bribes. The kiosks also allow small farmers to track crop prices in the region's wholesale markets - enabling them to negotiate better terms for crop sales. Other services include online applications for land records and a public complaint line for reporting broken irrigation pumps, unfair prices, absentee teachers, and other problems. Kiosks are placed in villages located on major roads or holding weekly markets, to facilitate access by people in neighboring villages. The network of about 30 kiosks covers more than 600 villages and is run by local private operators along commercial lines.

Smart cards that hold information on low-cost access to clients' credit histories are lowering transaction costs for Swayam Krishi Sangam information (SKS), a microfinance institution in the Medak district of Andhra Pradesh. One of the main problems facing SKS - which uses the group lending model developed by Bangladesh's Grameen Bank - is the high cost of delivering services to poor borrowers. All cash transactions occur at village meetings, and each takes about 90 seconds per person. Considerable time is spent completing paperwork, discussing loan terms and conditions, and counting money. Office computerization alone would not save much time because SKS staff would have more free time during the day but not in the morning and evening, when villagers are available for meetings. Smart cards lower the cost of delivering services by eliminating paperwork, reducing errors and fraud, and expediting transactions during meetings. As a result, SKS's operational costs could be cut by nearly one-fifth once the cards are fully implemented. Once all its transactions are conducted with handheld computers, SKS plans to leave a read-only device in each village so that clients can check the information stored on their smart cards.

These examples show that information and communications technology can help reduce poverty. But the diffusion of such benefits remains limited because poor and rural areas suffer from widespread illiteracy, high access costs, and insufficient information and communications infrastructure - creating a digital divide. Poor people in India have very limited access to information and communications technology. A recent survey of five villages in Andhra Pradesh, Uttar Pradesh, and West Bengal found that radios are the only type of such technology owned by most poor households (Marwah, in Pigato 2001). Few families have access to a computer or Internet connection, and some have never viewed television, read a newspaper, or used a telephone. Poor people rely on information from family, friends, and local leaders - but these informal networks do not satisfy their information needs. The digital divide can be addressed by policies that increase connectivity and by projects that take into account the constraints facing poor people.

Low-cost access to information infrastructure is the basic (but insufficient) necessity for reaching poor people. Inadequate or nonexistent connectivity and unstable power supplies reduce the economic viability of projects promoting information and communications technology. Competition in telecommunications can slash service costs, improving poor people's access. In India, market reforms significantly increased the number of telephone mainlines between 1997 and 2000. But because telecom privatization permitted prospective operators to bid for the right to operate in an entire state, only large corporations could participate. Indian states are large, and bids of more than $1 billion were common. Large telecom operators tend to limit their operations to higher income urban areas because poor rural areas have lower revenue potential and higher service costs. Privatization should be opened up to allow small entrepreneurs to supply telecom services in rural areas. Though revenues are lower, small entrepreneurs can - and want to - earn profits in such markets. In India cable television micro-entrepreneurs sell connections, install dish antennas, provide services, and visit subscribers to collect fees and fix problems. Customers know these operators personally. For these reasons cable services are considered superior to telephone services.

Allowing entry by small entrepreneurs is unlikely to be sufficient to provide basic connectivity to the poorest, most isolated rural areas. In urban India a telephone connection costs $650 for phone booth operators, and operators must earn $190 a year to break even. Telephones are more expensive in rural areas: a line can cost $1,500-1,700, so operators must earn $425 a year to break even. Because most information and communications technology projects are recent, experience on sustainability is limited. Few of the Gyandoot kiosks (see above) have achieved commercial viability. Regulations and subsidies can increase access to information infrastructure. Examples include geographic coverage requirements and universal access funds. Private operators can be invited to bid to provide services in areas that are not commercially viable in return for a subsidy financed from a universal access fund. A concession contract is then awarded to the company that requests the smallest subsidy. In Chile this approach has leveraged $40 million in private investment in telephone lines based on just over $2 million in public subsidies. As a result 1,000 public telephones have been installed in rural towns - at about 10 percent of the cost of direct public provision.

Even if information infrastructure reaches rural areas, there is no guarantee that poor people will access information and communications technology. Many projects that provide Internet access in rural India end up favoring middle-class and educated men. Rural women in particular tend to be excluded because of their restricted mobility, lack of education, and in some cases male control over information and media. But successful projects show how project design can help reach the poor. Information and communications technology projects that succeed in reducing poverty are generally run by organizations with a proven track record in working with poor people. Gujarat's dairy cooperatives have reached small farmers for years.

Applications developed by or in collaboration with local staff are more likely to suit local conditions and to be sustainable. Outside control and top-down approaches, by contrast, often waste resources. Rajasthan's state-sponsored e-governance program has failed even though the software is easy to use and delivered in Hindi - because centralized planning did not take into account local conditions.

Illiteracy and knowledge only of local languages are powerful obstacles to people's use of information and communications technology. To be relevant for poor people, applications must be available in local languages and, to the extent possible, be visually oriented and use voice interfaces. For example, the handheld computers used in the India Healthcare Delivery Project use software designed in line with the literacy levels of health care workers. In addition, content provided through information and communications technology should not be limited to knowledge from outside sources, but extended to draw on knowledge held by poor people.

Training is another important aspect of successful information and communications technology projects. Because learning is more effective through practice, innovative and interactive training is more successful. India's Self-Employed Women's Association has trained poor women to use video cameras and audiovisual equipment. A team of 8 full-time and 20 part-time members is now producing videos as a tool for learning, education, development, and policy action. Raising awareness about the potential of information and communications technology is also important. Providing content not directly related to development goals - such as news, matrimonial ads, and entertainment information-can increase the use of Internet kiosks.

Discussion Questions
1. How do illiteracy and knowledge only of local languages help create a digital divide?
2. How can information and communications technology help reduce poverty? Give at least one specific example.
3. How can privatization of telephone and communications services provide economic opportunities to poor and underprivileged people?

(Adapted from World Bank case files)

KEY TERMS

Critical Success Factors (CSF)
Digital Divide
General Agreement on Trade in Services (GATS)
Intellectual Property Rights (IPR)
Lesser Developed Country (LDC)
Most Favored Nation (status) (MFN)
OECD - Organization for Economic Cooperation and Development
Value Added Tax (VAT)
World Trade Organization (WTO)

STUDY QUESTIONS

1. Discuss the concept of Digital Divide. What actions would you recommend to overcome this problem in LDCs?

2. Discuss some key barriers of implementing technology solutions in LDCs.

3. Pick one of the barriers identified in the previous question and provide a potential solution with example.

4. Identify the critical success factors for LDCs to implement eService solutions.

5. Which critical success factors do you believe are the most difficult to implement? Justify your answer.

6. Using the Internet, search for a LDC that has successfully used technology solutions to improve the situation for their businesses and people. Create a one page paper explaining how this was accomplished.

REFERENCES

Barclay, B. and Domeisen, N. "E-Trade Opportunities: Are Developing Countries Ready?," *International Trade February,* 13, 2002 Forum, 1, pp. 16-19.

Barro, R. J. and Sala-I-Martin, X. *'The Diffusion of Technology' in Economic Growth.* New York: McGraw Hill. 1995.

Bhatnagar, P. "Electronic Commerce, Trade and Development," *Development Policy Review*, 17(3), 1999, pp. 281-292.

Budge, E. C. "E-Government Experiences and Lessons," In *Digital Opportunities for Development.*

Academy for Educational Development, 2003, pp. 369-382.

Clark, T. Electronic Commerce in China. in Sudweeks, F. and Rom, C.T. (Eds.), *Doing Business on the Internet: Opportunities on the Internet*. London: Springer. 1999.

Davis, C. H. "The Rapid Emergence of Electronic Commerce in a Developing Region: The Case of Spanish-Speaking Latin America," *Journal of Global Information Technology Management*. 5(1), 1999, pp. 25-40.

Davis, C. H.. The Wiring of India. *Economist*, 355:8172, 27 May 2000, pp. 63-64.

Edwards, S. Openness, Productivity, and growth: What Do We Really Know? *Economic Journal*, 108(44), 1998, pp. 383-398.

Edwards, S. Online Invaders from a Neighbor to the North. *Financial Times*, 17 November 1999.

Edwards, S. Many Crossed Wires in Tanzania. *Financial Times*, 01 June 2000.

Edwards, S. Bank in Control of Turkey's Internet Explosion. *Financial Times,* 11 March 2000b.

Fontaine, M. Power to the People: Entering the Information Age, In *Digital Opportunities for Development*. Academy for Educational Development, 2003, 42-55.

Forrester Research, Inc. *Projections for Global E-Commerce*. http://www.forrester.com, 2003.

Goldstein, A. and O'Connor, D. E-Commerce for Development: Prospects and Policy Issues. Working Paper, OECD Development Center, Paris. 2001.

Hutzler, C. "Internet Use in China Gains Breadth," *The Wall Street Journal*, 292(99), 2003, B4.

Howland, J. S. "The 'digital divide': Are we becoming a world of technological 'haves' and 'have-nots?," The *Electronic Library*, 16(5), 1998, pp. 287-289.

International Telecommunication Union. *World Telecommunication Development Report* (Geneva: ITU). 1997.

Iyer, L. S., Taube, L., and Raquet, J. "Global E-Commerce: Rationale, Digital Divide, and Strategies to Bridge the Divide," *Journal of Global Information Technology Management*. 5(1), 2002, pp. 43-68.

King, J. L., Gurbaxani, V., Kraemer, K. L., McFarlan, F. W., Raman, K. S., and Yap, C. S. "Institutional Factors in Information Technology Innovation," *Information Systems Research*, 5(2), 1994, pp. 139-169.

Lee, Ook An Action Research Report of an E-Commerce Firm in South Korea in Sudweeks, Fay, and Celia T. Rom (Eds.), *Doing Business on the Internet: Opportunities on the Internet,* pp. 246-258. London: Springer. 1999.

Lu M. "Digital Divide in Developing Countries," *Journal of Global Information Technology Management*, 4(3), 2001, pp. 1-4.

Ministry of Foreign Affairs and Trade, Commonwealth of Australia, Global Trade Reform: Maintaining Momentum. Canberra. 1999.

Montealegre, R. "Implications of Electronic Commerce for Managers in Less Developed Countries," *Information Technology for Development*, 7(3), 1996, pp. 145-153.

Montealegre, R. "A Temporal Model of Institutional Interventions for Information Technology Adoption in Less-Developed Countries," *Journal of Management Information Systems*, 16(1), 1999, pp. 207-232.

Mould-Iddrisu, B. "Introduction to Intellectual Property Rights: A Developing Country's Perspective," United States Department of State, http://usinfo.state.gov/products/pubs/prp/ 2003.

New York Times. Three Roads in China: B2B, B2C, and C2C. *New York Times*, June 7, 2000.

Nikolova, I. Bulgarian Public Computer and Communications Centers (PC3s), In *Digital Opportunities for Development*. Academy for Educational Development, pp. 72-86. 2003.

OECD. Communications Outlook 1999, Telecommunications: Regulatory Issues, Mexico (Paris: OECD). 1998.

OECD, *Guidelines for Consumer Protection in the Context of Electronic Commerce*, Paris. 2000a.

OECD, *Information Technology Outlook 2000*b, Paris.

Office of the Press Secretary. The Clinton-Gore Administration: *Working to Bridge the Digital Divide*, The White House, December 9, 1999.

Peha, J. M. Lessons from Haiti's Internet Development. *Communications of the ACM*, 42(6), 1999, pp. 67-72.

Petrazzini, B. and Kibati, M., "The Internet in Developing Countries," *Communications of the ACM*, 42(6), 1999, pp. 31-36.

Plant, R. *eCommerce: Formulation of Strategy*. Upper Saddle River, NJ: PrenticeHall. 2000.

Porter, M. E. and Millar, V. E. *How Information Gives You Competitive Advantage. In, Revolution in Real Time: Managing Information Technology in the 1990s*, Harvard Business Review Press: Boston. 1991.

Razeen, S. "Developing Country Trade Policy and the WTO," *CATO Journal*, 19(3), 2000, pp. 403-424.

Rayport, J. F. and Sviokla, J. J *"Exploiting the Virtual Value Chain*," Harvard Business School, November-December, 1995, pp. 75-85.

Richman, L. S. "The Real Toll of Tariffs," *Fortune*, 128(15), 1993, pp. 1-4.

Rockart, J. F. "Chief Executives Define their own Data Needs," *Harvard Business Review*, March-April, 1979, pp. 81-93.

Sachs, J. and Warner, A. Economic Reform and the process of Global Integration, In Brainard, W. and Perry, G. (Eds.) *Brookings Papers on economic Activity*, 1, 1995, pp. 1-118.

Simon, S. J. "The Dilemma of Global E-Services: Solutions for the General Agreement on Trade in Services (GATS)," *International Journal of Business and Economics*. Summer 2002.

Srikantaiah, T. K. and Xiaoying, D. "The Internet and Its Impact on Developing Countries: Examples from Chain and India," *Asian Libraries*, 7(9), 1998, pp. 199-209.

Stephenson, S and Ivascanu, D. "Electronic Commerce in the Western Hemisphere," Organization of American States, Trade Unit Working Paper. 2001.

Tetelman, M. "Foundations of Electronic Commerce," In *Digital Opportunities for Development*. Academy for Educational Development, 2003, pp. 275-309.

Travica, B. "Diffusion of Electronic Commerce in Developing Countries: The Case of Costa Rica," *Journal of Global Information technology Management*. 5(1), 2002, pp. 4-24.

United Nations. Standard country or Area Codes for Statistical Use. Series M, No. 49, Rev. 4, 2003.

USAID. USAID Leland Initiative. http://www.usaid.gov/regions/afr/leland/project.htm, 2003.

White, L. J. *Reducing the Barriers to International Trade in Accounting Services: Why It Matters, and The road Ahead*. World Trade Organization Working Paper. 2000.

World Bank. *World Development Indicators*. Washington, DC: World Bank. 1997.

World Economic Forum. *Jordan Education Initiative to Roll Out e-Learning across Kingdom and Beyond*. New York: WEF. 2003.

World Trade Organization. *Electronic Commerce and the Role of The WTO*. WTO Special Studies 2. Geneva: WTO. 1998.

World Trade Organization. Annual Report, 1997. Vols. I and II. Geneva: WTO. 1997.

Section 2

Global Strategies and Policies

As companies evolve from national to global, the strategies and policies that are used must be reexamined. The policies and procedures that worked well in one country may not work in other countries due to their economy, culture, laws, or other factors. As a result, companies must reevaluate their strategies and policies when becoming multinational. This section presents five chapters that address global strategies and policies.

Chapter 7 examines global IT strategies by looking at the issues associated with global, regional, national, corporate, and individual levels. Several theories are used to look at global IT strategies, including Porter's Competitive Forces Framework, the National Diamond Model, Bartlett and Ghoshal's business strategy model, concentration and diversification strategies, and the use of virtual teams. Chapter 8 looks at public information and communication technology (ICT) policies. Twenty-three examples of public ICT policy are presented, along with a framework to evaluate public ICT policies. Chapter 9 looks at global information technology (IT) architecture. A framework for IT architecture is presented and the framework is evaluated using two case studies. Three propositions are presented and evaluated using the case studies. Chapter 10 examines the role of global information systems in managing worldwide operations of multinational corporations (MNCs). The authors examine competition, productivity, and access paradoxes and develop a framework for global information systems. Finally, chapter 11 looks at governance in the global information economy. Four companies are described in relation to their governance and shaping of their global systems.

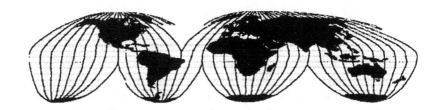

Corporate IT Strategies in the Global Economy

Charlie C. Chen
Albert L. Harris
Appalachian State University, USA

CHAPTER SUMMARY

Companies in all countries of the world are going global. As they do, they are challenged by a multitude of forces. To be successful in this age of multinational corporations, it is imperative that a global information system strategy be developed to overcome the complexities of global business. This chapter examines corporate information technology strategies in the global economy from five levels: global, regional, national, corporate, and individual. To do this, we first look at global information technology issues for four general categories of countries: Developed, Newly Industrialized, Developing, and Underdeveloped. We use several well known models and frameworks to examine information technology strategy development for multinational companies. We conclude by assessing the impacts of virtuality and virtual teams in global information technology strategy development.

INTRODUCTION

Multinational enterprises (MNEs) relentlessly seek business solutions to the impacts of a saturated domestic market, slowed domestic market growth, increased labor costs, and shortage of specialized labor. One solution is to enter international markets. Other forces are also accelerating the degree of globalization, such as the rise of global standards, global products, global services, and global customers, privatization, advances in information and telecommunication technology (ITT), the growing trade investment, emerging economies, and the emergence of world trade organizations. The degree of interconnection among the world economies continues to grow with the increased ubiquity of telecommunication and networking technology. More than 95% of the Fortune 500 companies have some type of global operations. Many companies in their home countries, particularly in emerging economies, are facing the threats from overseas competition. The dynamics of international competition has given many companies only two strategic options: "go global" or "go bankrupt." This is in conformance with the then Labor Secretary in the Clinton administration, Mr. Robert Reich, who said "Companies that globalize will make history; those who do not will become history."

In today's global world, almost every business is an information business. Information processing activities, such as capturing, storing and processing information, are indispensable for the normal operation of a business. To some businesses, such as airlines and retailers, effective information management has become an important core competence. Information technology (IT) is an enabler and a weapon to supply critical information to help MNEs compete in the international economy. IT used to support the global operation of an MNE is comprised of many global information systems (GISs). GISs are now used to support all business functions, such as international marketing, human resources, research and development, accounting, distribution, and finance. National conditions, such as culture, politics, economy, legal regulation and demographics, differ greatly among the different regions of the world: Asia Pacific, Europe, the Middle East, Africa, Latin and North Americas regions. In addition, IT infrastructures, skills, diffusion, and policy vary by region. MNEs need to understand these differences and leverage IT services accessible in the different regions to provide competitive products and services to local marketplaces. When working in the global community, businesses and IS professionals need to be aware of cultural differences. Learning to improve cultural intelligence is important for an international manager. The growing popularity of virtual teams, with members located around the world, further substantiates the importance of cultural understanding.

Take India for example. This country is growing to become a major outsourcing provider of information technology services to companies throughout the world. McKinsey-NASSCOM projected that IT services revenues in India would grow up to $78 billion by 2008. The 2005 Summit on Indian Manufacturing Competitiveness discovered that keys to the success of Indian companies operating in global industries include the urban infrastructure, fair competition and access to markets, favorable import regulations, incentive import duties, quality vocational and educational systems, R&D budgets, and other conditions to support small and medium-sized enterprises (Deloitte Research, 2005). This global benchmark study substantiates that national competitiveness is the underpinning for the success of a nation's multinational enterprises.

It is vital for a multinational enterprise to formulate an information system strategy to support the growing complexity of global business. A seven-year study surveying CEOs of 150 companies located in 20 countries and 25 industries discovered that some organizations do not have a global IS strategy and the others do not align their IS strategy with international business strategy (King and Sethi, 2001). An IS executive needs to learn how to formulate an effective global IS strategy to support global operation of a business.

Information systems have strong influences on the formation of a borderless economy by promoting free and unfettered exchange of information across different geographical areas. The process of moving ideas, information, decisions, business processes, and business operations across countries is made easier with global information systems. Our world is becoming closer because we can transcend physical boundary with the light speed of digital transmission, rather than physical transportation. Information systems are a conduit and an agent for frictionless exchange of information. To join the international community, nations and business communities alike need to learn how to assimilate information systems into their enterprises and use them to their advantage.

FRAMEWORK FOR FORMULATING GLOBAL CORPORATE IT STRATEGY

Business and IS executives need to be competent in analyzing a global strategy from at least five levels: Global, Regional, National, Company and Individual. This multilevel approach is useful to provide a thorough review of macro- and micro-conditions before formulating a competitive international strategy. Knowing how to assess these conditions at different levels and their relationships is an important skill to acquire for any executives. Figure 1 is a framework for exploring the complexity of working in the global economy. This depicts the various levels and some of the strategies and frameworks used to analyze the levels. Global is on the bottom because it is the broadest. As one goes up the levels, the issues and strategies become narrower. In this chapter, we look at global, regional, national, company, and individual (managerial) issues faced when creating global strategies for MNEs.

Before looking at the issues faced in each of the five areas shown in Figure 1, we will examine how information systems have created a borderless economy.

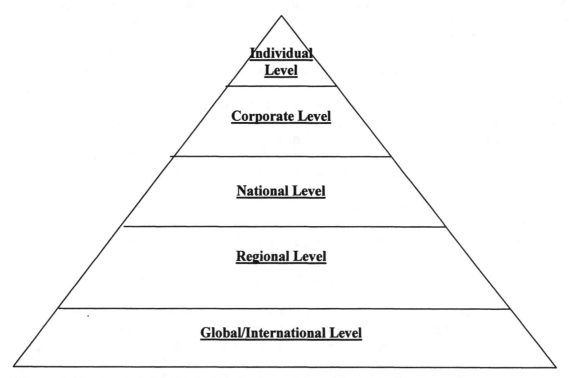

Figure 1. Framework for Exploring the Complexity of Working in the Global Economy

One of the biggest impacts on global business has been the Internet. The Internet is an open system that allows people of the world to interact with each other anytime from anywhere; all you need to have is connectivity. Its influences on how people interact with each other have significantly minimized the importance of physical borders. A borderless world brings many benefits to business communities, such as increased opportunities for innovation, collaboration, and communication. At the same time, many technical, social, and economic challenges have resulted from this interconnectivity. One major technical challenge for the global use of the Internet is international standards. The Internet builds on seven layers of the Open Systems Interconnection (OSI) model, enabling smooth communications across interconnected systems. Differences in hardware and software have not stopped the widespread use of the Internet. International standards have been one major factor contributing to the increased use of the Internet. Many not-for-profit organizations (e.g. the Organization for the Advancement of Structured Information Standards) are promoting universal standards to further increase the degree of our interdependence. These organizations are comprised of international organizations, regional and international coordinating bodies, as well as collaborative partnership of government, companies and nonprofit organizations. The American National Standards Institute (ANSI) develops global Internet infrastructural standards (e.g. data, transmission medium, protocol and topologies). The Organization for the Advancement of Structured Information Standards (OASIS), a nonprofit and international consortium, facilitates the development of interoperable web languages, such as HTML, XML and SGML, to improve communication efficiency. The Internet Corporation for Assigned Names and Numbers (ICANN), a private sector, nonprofit corporation, manages IP addresses, domain names, and root server systems. Many of these standards are evolving to meet the growing needs of diversified applications. A borderless economy will be further distributed with a higher degree of standardization.

The decreasing influence of physical borders creates numerous social challenges, including diversity, educational divide, digital divide, social isolation, social disparity, income distribution, privacy intrusion, and e-crimes. You can virtually meet or conduct business with anyone who has access to the Internet. Those who do not have the basic IT infrastructure are at a disadvantage when competing with those that do have an IT infrastructure. The imbalance of IT infrastructures is widening the gap between the "haves" and the "have nots." The emergence of the virtual society creates new social problems, such as privacy intrusion, copyright infringements, illegal files sharing, and security breaching. A borderless economy needs to welcome and address these social challenges to make a better interconnected world. Economic challenges range from the creation of new business models, creation of new life styles (e.g. telecommuters, virtual teams), changing employment and labor access, and emerging new standards and regulations. These challenges are affecting every facet of business. An important task for a global information systems manager is to understand these challenges and assess what and how information systems can affect global business operations.

Given a borderless economy, we now need to look at a framework for analyzing the global level issues. This is done in the next section.

ASSESSING GLOBAL/INTERNATIONAL LEVEL ISSUES

IT issues vary with the development of a country, which is often measured with statistical indexes, such as income per capita (GDP), literacy rate, international trade volume, and investment dollars. Based on these statistics, a country is classified into one of four general categories (Palvia, Palvia, and Whitworth, 2002). The highest category is *Developed Countries* (e.g. the United States, most European Union countries, Japan, and Australia). Key IT issues in developed countries are about the strategic use of information systems to support the global operations of a business. The next category is *Newly Industrialized Countries* (e.g. South Korea, Hong Kong, Taiwan, and Singapore). The key IT issues in newly industrialized countries concern the infrastructure and the management and planning of the IT function. The third category is that of *Developing Countries* (e.g. India, Czech Republic, Brazil, and Russia). Major IT issues of developing countries are to improve operational efficiency and effectiveness of the IT function. Finding qualified personnel is a major problem for IT managers in developing countries. The final category is *Underdeveloped Countries* (e.g. most African countries, Cambodia, and Laos). Many underdeveloped countries are stricken by poverty, disease, and war over many years. Basic hardware, software, and IT infrastructure needs are of primary concern to IT managers in underdeveloped countries. Many basic IT infrastructures, such as a working telephone network, water, power, and other support systems, are not available to support business operations. There are some key issues that are common to countries of all categories. These include data security, the productivity paradox and the Internet infrastructure.

Global information systems are IT applications that are global in scope. GISs are comprised of four major components: strategic, infrastructural and management, operational and organizational. The strategic component includes the integration and maturity stage of IS growth and using information systems to achieve international competitiveness. Infrastructural and management issues are the foundation for advanced IT management and lay the groundwork for IT becoming a strategic tool for a MNE. These issues deal with the design of information architecture, such as information and telecommunication technology, networks, and database, and the management of personnel, security, and standards to support the international operation of a business. When entering a developing country, a MNE needs to overcome many operational and organizational issues.

Operational and organizational issues include such things as culture, technology adoption, training of IS professionals, and the country's laws and regulations. Basic issues include just getting the hardware, software, and support services needed to survive. Table 1 lists the global information technology issues faced by developed, newly industrialized, developing, and underdeveloped countries.

Country Classifications	Predominant IT Issues
Developed countries: United States, Canada, most European Union countries (United Kingdom, Ireland, Germany, France, Italy, Spain, etc.), Switzerland, Japan, and Australia	**Strategic Issues**: Alignment of IT strategy with global strategy of the company, development of effective inter-organizational systems that span across many countries.
Newly industrialized countries: China, South Korea, Hong Kong, Taiwan, and Singapore	**Infrastructural and Management Issues**: Information, computing, and telecommunication (ICT) infrastructure and standards: specific computers, networks, databases, and other facilities, and their relationships.
Developing countries: India, most East European counties (Czech Republic, Hungary, Poland, Greece, Turkey, etc.), most South American countries (e.g. Brazil, Chile, Argentina, etc.), South Africa, Mexico, Philippines, and Russia	**Operational and Organizational Issues**: Patents; contractual controls on information; privacy; security; data export control; encryption policy; technology adoption and transfer; rationalization; logistical control; government policies; censorship; criminal liability of information services; dissemination of government information; regulation of financial; education services; interoperability and standards; dispute settlements and digital divide.
Underdeveloped countries: Most sub-Sahara Africa (Angola, Cameroon, Kenya, Nigeria, Rwanda, Somalia, Zimbabwe, etc.), Vietnam and Laos	**Basic IT Issues**: Quantity, quality, and timeliness of hardware, software, and support services; IT platforms; capture and processing of data; access to qualified IS people; Educational divide.

Table 1. Global Information Technology Issues

ASSESSING REGIONAL LEVEL DIFFERENCES

Industry characteristics pose varying constraints on the operation of an international business. Companies in airline, telecommunication, pharmaceutical and biotechnology industries need to invest enormous capital in R&D or capital equipment to survive. An efficient way to make a profit from these investments is to expand the customer base by entering new markets. Most products and services from these industries are in a standardized form. It is easier for MNEs to enter global markets with standardized products and services. At the other end of the spectrum are products and services that must be tailored and customizable for customer acceptance in multiple markets, such as the retail sales, food, arts and publication industries. Customers in one region can require very different products from customers in another region because of cultural norms and tastes. These industries favor domestic companies and pose high entry barriers for MNEs, such as uncooperative local distribution channels, differing requirements, established customer base, and legal systems. Most companies fall into the middle of these two extreme classifications, having to balance some local differences and global efficiency. Many standard industry-level analyses are available for a company to assess an industry's characteristics, including Porter's (1980) Competitive Forces analysis and Prahalad and Doz's (1987) global integration and local responsiveness framework.

Geographical Scope of Industry-Level Analysis

When formulating an international business strategy, a company needs to take the geographic scope of the industry into consideration because industry characteristics can differ significantly from one region to another. Four major categories of forces are shaping the stance of international competition in a region: market factors, scale factors, comparative advantage, and regulatory factors. Figure 2 presents a model of this interaction for the four globalization drivers. Within the same region, the market conditions, in terms of customer tastes, political environments, and communication channels, may have a higher degree of similarity, compared to other regions. Managing the supply chain within a close physical proximity creates the advantage of increasing economies of scale in the production process for companies within the same region. Some regions have comparative and/or competitive advantages over other regions in natural resources. Regulatory environment, such as tariff and non-tariff barriers, can siphon away many foreign direct investment opportunities.

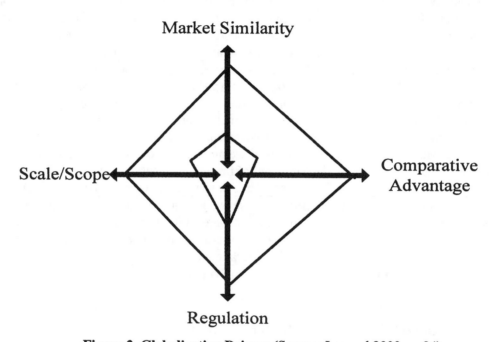

Figure 2. Globalization Drivers (Source: Lessard 2003, p. 84)

Secondary information about an industry in a region is useful to map the degree of globalization along with the four dimensions. Take the North American region, for instance. The United States, Canada, and Mexico all adhere to the same industry code system, the North American Industrial Classification System (NACIS) (U.S. Census Bureau, 2005). A company outside this region would have to adapt its classification system to NACIS if it wanted to compare products with respect to the four globalization drivers. After mapping, a bigger diamond shape on the globalization map indicates that the industry is more receptive to global competition pressure. The degree of reach in those four dimensions indicates that different forces pose varying pressures to globalize an industry in a particular regional market.

Telecommunications industry in the U.S. is privatized, much more diversified, and receptive to competition. Hardware, software and content providers in this industry are more competitive due to the intense competition in the regional market. In contrast, this industry in the Asian region is highly regulated. As such, global competitive barriers and pressures are higher in Asian than in the U.S. The success story of many Chinese companies in entering the international market has aroused the interest of many American companies to acquire the assets of Chinese companies. However, due to market dissimilarity and different regulations, such as Chinese tastes and different accounting practices, many acquisitions have stumbled and failed to materialize.

The European amusement parks industry is projected to generate $3.6 billion in revenue by 2007 with a stable growth of 5.7% since 2003, according to PricewaterhouseCoopers (Koranteng, 2005). Despite the rosy prospect, Disneyland Paris and Walt Disney Studios Park, as the only Disney theme parks in the European region, continue to lose money. In contrast, Disney parks in Asian and North American regions post impressive revenue gains and profits. Denmark-based Lego Group declared a $36 - $72 million loss in 2004. The group is planning to sell off its theme parks in Denmark, the United Kingdom and Germany, while keeping the profit-making toy business. These examples characterize how the product for a single company can be accepted differently in different parts of the world; sometimes it is successful and sometimes not as successful.

Industry Structure Analysis

Porter's Competitive Forces framework can assist in analyzing the industry structure from five perspectives: (1) buyer's bargaining power, (2) supplier's bargaining power, (3) substitute products, (4) threat of entry, and (5) rivalry of competitors. System openness and standards are two major factors that can alter the strengths of these five forces. Figure 3 depicts the impacts of system openness and standardization on Porter's five forces. A company needs to assess the impact of system openness and standards on an industry structure when assessing the impacts of Porter's five forces (Porter, 1980).

Buyer's Bargaining Power - When a buyer has a strong ability to influence purchase conditions, such as price, quality, and terms of delivery, a higher degree of system openness and standards equips a firm with ability to:

- Increase bargaining leverage
- Improve buyer information transparency
- Reduce the threat of backward integration
- Product similarity
- Remove buyer concentration
- Improve substitutes availability
- Increase buyer's incentives

As a result, a firm can have a higher degree of flexibility to meet customer's demanding needs. This can increase the operational agility of a firm to enter a new market.

Supplier's Bargaining Power - EDI networks are proprietary and limited to the use of a few suppliers. RosettaNet is an open system that interconnects innumerous consumer electronics suppliers and provides buyers a one-stop sourcing solution. Suppliers of proprietary EDI systems have a stronger bargaining power than RosettaNet. In an industry where suppliers have strong bargaining power, open system can weaken the bargaining power to favor the buyer by:

- Removing supplier concentration
- Decreasing differentiation of inputs
- Reducing impacts of inputs on cost of differentiation
- Lowering switching costs of firms
- Improving visibility of substitute inputs
- Lowering threat of forward integration
- Reducing cost relative to total purchase

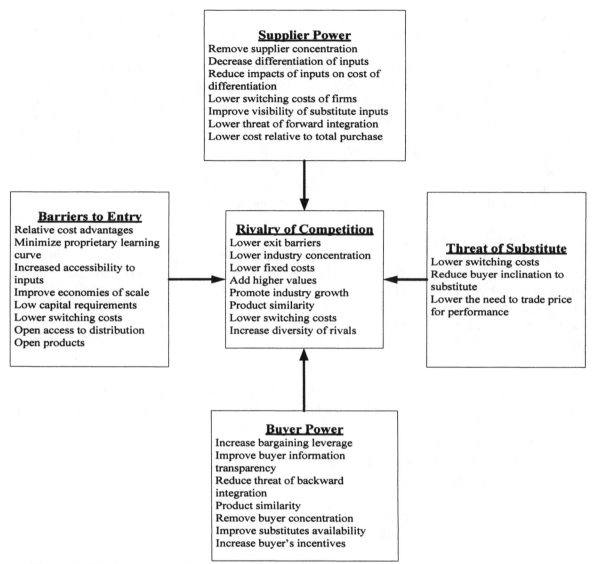

Figure 3. The Impacts of System Openness and Standardization on an Industry Structure
(Source: Porter (1980))

Barriers to Entry - Many firms deliberately immobilize their strategic assets to create high entry barriers in order to sustain their competitiveness in an industry. Wal-Mart's complex distribution channels, Toyota's close network relationship with suppliers, and Coca Cola's brand values are great barriers to dissuade the entry of competitors. These intangible assets are hard to imitate and have attracted many firms to construct them. A short cut for small- and medium-sized firms to compete head-to-head with large MNEs is to adopt the system openness and standards. It does not require heavy capital investment for an online company to compete with big companies. Increasing the degree of system openness can lower the entry barriers by:
- Minimizing the influence of proprietary assets in an industry
- Increasing accessibility to inputs
- Improving economies of scale
- Lowering capital requirements
- Lowering switching costs
- Increasing accessibility to distribution channels

Threat of Substitutes - In an industry where proprietary products and services dominate, the switching cost for a firm to find alternative products is high. Buyers are less inclined to substitute existing products and services. Systems openness and standardization can lower switching costs, increase the buyer's inclination to substitute products/services, and decrease the need to trade price for performance.

Rivalry of Competition - In an industry where the competition intensity is high, industry concentration and diversity of rivals are high. Open systems allows a firm to ally with other firms and innovate business models in order to stay competitive in the industry. Increasing the degree of system openness can:

- Lower exit barriers
- Lower industry concentration
- Lower fixed costs
- Add higher values
- Promote industry growth
- Increase product similarity
- Lower switching costs
- Increase diversity of rivals

When entering a new market, a MNE needs to be aware of industry structure and needs to assess the impacts of system openness and standardization. A higher degree of system openness can promote a fair competition, lower the bargaining power of buyers and suppliers, increase the number of substitute products and services, and lower entry barriers. However, system openness does not benefit firms of all kinds. A careful analysis of the industry structure can prepare a firm to better compete in the international marketplace.

Competitors' Identification

The competitive intensity of an industry, products, or services is not the same in all regional markets due to the differences in globalization drivers. It is important for a company to identify and diagnose consistent symptoms of competition when entering a regional market. In the ancient strategic management book "The Art of War," Chinese strategist Sun Tzu stated, "You must be guided by the actions of the enemy in attempting to secure a favorable position in actual warfare." He further commented, "If you know the enemy and know yourself, you need not fear the result of a hundred battles. If you know yourself but not the enemy, for every victory gained you will also suffer a defeat." Identifying competitors in the entry region is the first important strategic exercise needed to formulate a regional business strategy. The exercise is comprised of five sequential steps to analyze potential competitors in a region. Table 2 describes the steps.

After a few rounds of answering questions in these five steps, the benchmarking areas between regions can be identified and listed. Table 3 shows an example to provide a systematic view of regional differences in these benchmarking areas.

ASSESSING NATIONAL LEVEL DIFFERENCES

After identifying regional competitors, a company can narrow its analysis to the "how" and "what" of competition by identifying the competitive levers. When operating in its host country, a company has relative advantages over other companies from another country because of national differences. An effective framework to assess cross-country differences can aid business and IT executives in the decision-making process when penetrating into a foreign country. With time constraints, many country managers turn to reputable ranking information on national competitiveness, such as the Index of Economic Freedom, the World of Competitiveness Yearbook, and the Global

Competitiveness Report. Although these reports are easy to use, too many variables are used to construct the indexes for the national competitiveness of a nation. Such a complexity is difficult to articulate and can complicate the communication and decision-making process, thereby making the final indices hard to discern. For instance, the Index of Economic Freedom uses 50 variables and the World of Competitiveness Yearbook uses 321 variables to produce indexes for a nation. Some international managers broadly classify these variables into cost conditions as determined by exchange rate, and the institutional and systematic conditions, such as by legal, governmental and technological policies (Thompson, 2004).

Step 1	Initial market selection: Define the product markets of interests – presumably a list of the markets in which the firm competes. This is essentially a list of broad product markets. Each of these markets will be narrowed by following steps 2 to 5.
Step 2	One product market or several? Assess whether the competitors are likely to be the same for all the products you have selected. If you are not sure, then do not assume they are. If you believe the set of competitors is likely to be the same, then choose one product to study. Otherwise, be sure to repeat steps 3 to 5 for each product.
Step 3	One geographic market or several? Identify the different geographic regions in which the product is sold. If you believe the set of competitors is likely to be the same in each region, then pick one region to study. Otherwise, repeat steps 4 to 5 for each region. (Note. If competition varies by product and by region, the number of distinct markets to study can rapidly proliferate. This is not an excuse for pretending that competition is the same in each product/region, however.)
Step 4	Identify the key product performance characteristics. What does the product do for the consumers? Here you should specify the features that drive customer choice: • Do customers prefer a "one stop shop" or do they prefer to deal with multiple vendors? • How might the product be segmented by attributes like: look and feel, ease of use, warranties, durability, availability of complementary goods as well as other relevant factors that consumers consider in choosing among industry offerings? • What types of service contracts are firms offering? • What different channels is the product distributed through? • Does brand matter and why? • How intimate are relationships between firms and customers? What are the switching costs? • How much price dispersion is there in the market? What drives this price dispersion?
Step 5	Competitor identification: Identify the set of firms whose products deliver comparable specifications on the key product performance characteristics. These firms constitute the market.

Table 2. Competitor Identification (Source: Darnove and Marciano 2005, p.105)

Benchmark Area	Asian	North America	European	Middle-East	Africa
Market similarity					
Production scale/scope					
Institutional barriers					
Comparative Advantages					

Table 3. Benchmark Results

Other researchers sensitive to the impacts of technology on national economies suggest that the determinants of national competitiveness need to encompass techno-economic factors, such as national resources, technologies, organizations, product markets, external business activities, institutional framework and government (Hämäläinen, 2004).

Analysis with the National Diamond Model

Among the frameworks to assess national competitiveness, Michael E. Porter's National Diamond model perhaps is a more suitable tool to analyze a nation's competitiveness from a practical business perspective. This model provides a holistic and systematic view about key determinants of national competitiveness. According to this model, a nation could leverage four sources to improve its competitive advantages over other countries: factor conditions, demand conditions, related and supporting industry, and firm strategy, structure and rivalry. Figure 4 depicts the Diamond of National Advantage model. Factor conditions are natural resources, such as land, labor and raw materials. Upgrading the stock of these national endowments can help sustain a nation's competitiveness. A more demanding local market can pressure local companies to offer innovative products and services to satisfy domestic customers. These demand conditions can naturally lead to national competitiveness. Related and supporting industries, such as industry cluster with a physical proximity, are effective inputs and convenient resources to the successful business operations. The chance of having innovative outputs, such as unconventional business models and innovative business models, are more likely with the presence of these supporting industries. The other three conditions affect the formation of the firm strategy, structure and rivalry. The corporate structure of German and Japanese companies is more hierarchical in nature due to their tradition in labor unions and Keiretzu (company consortium). In contrast, the history of extended family has resulted in the emergence of many Italian companies. A successful business strategy is an agent and a key ingredient of national competitiveness to leverage, upgrade, and innovate the other three conditions. These four sources have an effect on each other and as a whole can contribute to the national competitiveness.

Take McDonald's franchising strategy, for instance. McDonald's is a global food service retailer with more than 30,000 stores in more than 100 countries servicing millions of customers each day. Maintaining a consistent supply of quality food ingredients, meat, fish, bread, potato and vegetables to local McDonald's stores is indispensable for the global operation of the business. It is also important for McDonald's to be aware of religious and eating habits in a country and customize its food and service offerings for local customers. Income levels and consumption ability of local customers are other important demand conditions to consider when devising a pricing strategy for product offerings. McDonald's stores in Muslim countries cannot have pork on their menu. To make sure that the serviced food is fresh and well served, it is important to ensure that transportation infrastructure is robust, production control can meet certain standards, and waiters receive adequate training. A country manager of McDonald's can decide conditions to approve a local franchise based on a thorough analysis of other three factors.

Assessing IT Infrastructure in Different Countries

A strong information, communication, and telecommunication (ICT) infrastructural constituent is required for the continuous growth of the national economy and global IT diffusion. The widespread use of information and communication technology in local area network, metropolitan area network, wide area network, wireless area network, the World Wide Web, and grid computing depends on the support of the information and telecommunications infrastructure. When entering an international market, a common issue facing all MNEs is the availability and accessibility of information and telecommunication technology. The Internet accessibility probably is the most pertinent issue facing all industries to date. A company from the U.S. will have a hard time communicating with its subsidiary in the part of India where a telephone network is not a viable option. As the number of different networks increase and cross country borders, their incompatibility becomes a bottleneck for global and open communication. The ideal is to have a global network of networks smoothly communicating with each other takes the minimum of ICT infrastructures (such as Public Switched Telephone Network or Satellite).

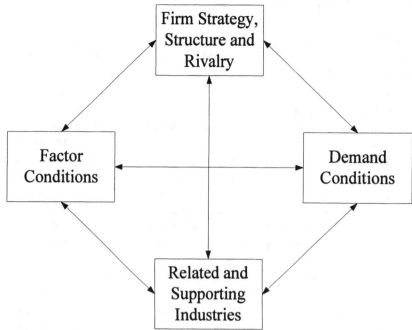

Figure 4. Diamond of National Advantage (Source: Porter 1990)

Many parties are contributing to the development of an interconnected global network that is not controlled by any single government. These parties are comprised of many not-for-profit international organizations, regional and international coordinating bodies, as well as collaborative partnership of government, companies and nonprofit organizations. As mentioned earlier, ANSI institutionalizes the development of standards for the global Internet infrastructure that includes data, transmission medium, protocol and topologies. OASIS devotes its energies to creating interoperable industry specifications based on public standards such as XML and SGML, as well as others that are related to structured information processing. The most popular web languages, such as SGML, XML, HTML, and CGM are all the innovations of OASIS. ICANN is in charge of the technical coordination of the Internet activities on the worldwide basis. This includes: IP address space allocation, protocol parameter assignment, domain name management, and root server system management functions.

The global telecommunication industry is another key player in the movement of global information systems. This industry can be generally classified into four key players: communication providers, distribution providers, content providers and tools providers (Grover and Vaswani, 2000). Communication providers include local phone, cellular phone, PCS, and other wireless service providers. Distribution providers include broadcast, Internet service provider, cable TV, and long-distance phone service. Tools providers are manufacturers and suppliers of communication hardware and software. Networking devices, such as routers, bridge, firewall and Ethernet card, are communication hardware. Operating systems, antivirus software, and browsers in wired and wireless devices are examples of communication software. Companies, such as Time Warner, Cox Communications, AT&T, and Oracle, provide entertainment programs and online applications and are content providers.

These four key players of the telecommunication industry are acquiring other players in the telecommunications industry resulting in increased efficiency in the industry. Take the merger and acquisition between Time Warner and America Online, for instance. This partnership between content providers allowed the resultant company to realize the benefits of economic scale and scope. Many companies rely on the alliance between communication and distribution providers to offer customized and innovative products and services for their customers. For instance, AT&T acquired Media One and TCI in order to have immediate access to the local cable and cable Internet service providers market. Long-distance companies can provide DSL services by bypassing local loops. Tools providers of hardware and software can help streamline the production process to create a more efficient supply chain. This trend is creating many opportunities for the telecommunication industry in different countries. Customers can anticipate the introduction of better and innovative telecommunication services and products. Many governments need to decide on the degree of deregulation and privatize the regulated telecommunication industry to provide a more competitive and fair environment. A country needs to formulate a clear policy to dictate the changes to the telecommunication industry to benefit not only its people, organization, and region, but the world as a whole. Table 4 charts the partnership distribution of these four telecommunication players from 1999 to 2001 in the U.S.

The telecommunication industry is undergoing the global convergence of communication networks, computing hardware, software, contents, and IT education. The convergence creates many opportunities for (1) newer and better telecommunication service and products, (2) fair, but intense global competition, (3) more affordable innovative products, and (4) deregulation of monopolized telecommunication industry of some countries. The deployment of global Internet infrastructure can increase the bandwidth of data transmission across different countries. UUNET (UNIX to UNIX Network), a major international Internet service provider, has already deployed T1, T3, and OC3 across continents. These are the major backbones of today's Internet. Studies indicate that a single fiber optic could deliver 1,000 billion bits per second. When the global Internet infrastructure can deliver at least the bandwidth of one fiber optic within and across all countries, the entire world will be able to enjoy multimedia presentation of the Internet as TV today.

However, not all countries can benefit from the telecommunication convergence and global telecommunication infrastructure. Information technology infrastructure is relatively primitive in

Partnership	Overall (N = 589)		1999 (N = 319)		2000 (N = 216)		2001 (N = 54)	
	Total	%	Total	%	Total	%	Total	%
Network Provider Landlines								
Network Provider Landlines	102	17.32	70	21.94	25	11.57	7	13.0
Network Provider Wireless and Satellite	13	2.21	11	3.45	1	0.46	1	1.85
Hardware Provider	44	7.47	29	9.09	11	5.09	4	7.40
Software Provider	15	2.55	9	2.82	4	1.85	2	3.70
Service Provider	31	5.26	28	8.78	2	0.93	1	1.85
Transaction Service Provider	15	2.55	12	3.76	3	1.39	0	0
Content Provider	8	1.36	6	1.88	1	0.46	1	1.85
Internet Content Provider	3	0.51	2	0.63	1	0.46	0	0
Network Provider Wireless and Satellite								
Network Provider Wireless and Satellite	41	6.96	17	5.33	5	2.31	19	35.18
Hardware Provider	7	1.19	7	2.19	0	0	0	0
Software Provider	6	1.02	6	1.88	0	0	0	0
Service Provider	6	1.02	2	0.63	1	0.46	3	5.55
Transaction Service Provider	6	1.02	1	0.31	5	2.31	0	0
Content Provider	0	0	0	0	0	0	0	0
Internet Content Provider	0	0	0	0	0	0	0	0
Hardware Provider								
Hardware Provider	182	30.9	64	20.06	104	48.15	14	26.00
Software Provider	46	7.81	30	9.40	16	7.41	0	0
Service Provider	14	2.38	8	2.51	4	1.85	2	3.70
Transaction Service Provider	5	0.85	3	0.94	2	0.93	0	0
Content Provider	1	0.17	0	0	1	0.46	0	0
Internet Content Provider	0	0	0	0	0	0	0	0
Software Provider								
Software Provider	39	6.62	10	3.13	29	13.43	0	0
Service Provider	0	0	0	0	0	0	0	0
Transaction Service Provider	5	0.85	4	1.25	1	0.46	0	0
Content Provider	0	0	0	0	0	0	0	0
Internet Content Provider	0	0	0	0	0	0	0	0

Table 4. Partnership Relationships Between Telecommunication Partners (Source: Grover and Saeed 2003, p. 122)

many underdeveloped and developing countries. This imbalance has contributed to the slow diffusion of global IT. Many factors contribute to the unavailability of IT infrastructure, including funding, management and technical expertise, awareness of available technologies, training, electricity, transportation, banking, etc. Without the operating environmental factors, many businesses cannot sustain themselves in these countries, and will hinder the technological diffusion on the global basis. Countries like Norway, Singapore and the U.S. have more than 50% Internet penetration rate. In contrast, the penetration rate of the Internet in countries such as India, Egypt and China is lower than 10%. More than half the population of the world does not have a telephone and four of every 10 African adults cannot read. Some 90 percent of Internet hosts are located in the developed countries with only 16 percent of the world's population, according to the United Nations. Lack of basic ICT infrastructure and support of many complementary assets in developing and underdeveloped countries are barriers to the global diffusion of IT. The "digital divide" and "educational divide" phenomena are hindering the realization of a true global society. A firm needs to take the educational and digital divide issues into serious consideration when entering an international market where IT infrastructure and complementary assets are not yet developed. A firm can use the parameters in Table 5 to measure the digital divide. A systematic assessment of these parameters can prepare a firm to make a conscious decision before entering a foreign country and its marketplace.

Survival Strategies for Local Companies in Developing and Underdeveloped Countries

The rapid influx of MNEs into the developing and underdeveloped countries to grab a large market share is posing unprecedented threats to the survival of local businesses. More than 80% of the world's population currently lives in developing and underdeveloped countries. These markets account for more than 40% of the world's purchasing power. Although some local businesses in these countries are large in scale, they have been long protected from real competition and do not know how to compete with MNEs. Take state-owned enterprises in China, for instance. The Chinese government passed a reform in 2005 to require local ownership of Chinese companies listed on the Shanghai and Shenzhen Stock Exchanges. Most local businesses in developing and underdeveloped countries are small in size. They are in an extraordinarily disadvantageous position because of limited financial resources, poor technological infrastructure, poor management skills, and poor local brand awareness, when competing with giant MNEs from developed countries. How to survive from the cut-throat competition with domestic and international companies is a strategic question for many companies to answer. A major strategic concern to a company in developing and underdeveloped countries is how to devise an effective IS strategy to support their survival in the face of MNE competition. Open systems' portability, interoperability, and scalability will enable a firm to quickly adjust its posture in response to the threatening of MNEs.

Figure 5 is a strategic matrix to guide companies in developing and underdeveloped countries in their fight for survival against MNEs. The horizontal dimension is the degree to which a company's assets can be transferred to non-home countries. The vertical dimension is the strength of globalization pressure in the industry. A company can employ the *defender* position if globalization pressures are weak and a company's assets are not transferable. Companies taking the defender position should try to avoid direct confrontation with MNEs and make their products and services appealing to customers who favor local brands. Local companies should concentrate their resources and focus on customers who appreciate the local touch. With this strategy, they will have a higher chance of operational success against MNEs.

When facing globalization pressure and company assets are tailored for local markets, a company is in the *dodger* position. The major strategic goal is to avoid the head-to-head competition. To defend or dodge the deep entrenching of MNEs, one secure way to avoid the direct confrontation is to rely on proprietary information supplied by an information system that is difficult to duplicate by MNEs. Baidu.Com is the largest search engine in China and primarily offers the searching of information in Chinese. Google is enticed with the growing online population in China and has penetrated the search engine market in China. Faced with the feverish threats of Google, Baidu has, so far, successfully defended its position with its search capability, specialized in searching for information in Chinese. Leading enterprise resource planning (ERP) solutions providers, such as Oracle and SAP, have not successfully acquired a large share of ERP market in China because they are not flexible in integrating with the existing systems of Chinese enterprises and they are not familiar with the corporate rules. This gives many local Chinese ERP solution providers room to defend their unique positions by customizing applications to integrate with the existing systems of local customers.

Parameters	Questions Asked
Tele-density	What is the number of telephone lines per 1000 people? Used to gauge how many people have telephone access.
Compu-density	What is the number of computers (PCs) per 1000 people? Where are the computers (PCs) located (homes, workplace, Internet cafes, community centers, etc.)? Used to gauge how many people have computer access.
Internet suppliers	What is the number of ISPs? Used to gauge the access to the Internet.
Internet users	How many citizens use the Internet in some form? What percent of the population use the Internet in some form? Used to gauge how many people are actually using the Internet.
Bandwidth	What types of connections (modem dialup, ISDN, DSL, cable modems, etc.) are available for data transmission? Used to gauge speed and quality of data transmission.
Infrastructure access	What telecommunications networks are in place? What is telephone coverage outside urban areas? Used to gauge the availability of communications services.
Literacy rate	What percent of the population is literate? Used to gauge the ability to read and write.
Training	Do people know how to use the technology? Is technology use taught in schools or vocational programs? Is training affordable? Used to gauge ability to use technology.
Relevant content	Is Internet content available in local languages? Does the Internet content address interests of the local population? Used to gauge the accessibility of relevant content.
Geography, age, religion, gender, and culture	What percent of the population lives in rural vs. urban areas? What is the age distribution of the population? Does religion impact Internet use? Does gender impact Internet use? Does culture impact Internet use? Used to gauge impact of "other" items on Internet use.
Affordability	What is the per capita income of the population? What is the per capita GDP of the population? Is there an income divide? Used to gauge the affordability of the Internet to the population.

Table 5. Parameters to Measure Digital Divide (Adapted form Sharma and Gupta 2003, p.10)

The ideal situation for a company to directly contend with MNEs is when assets are transferable to another country and global competitive pressure is high. Since there is no way to sidestep or avoid the direct competition, the best policy is to engage or become a contender. Tata Consultancy Services (TCS) is a great contender overcoming the entrenched competition from MNEs. IT software and services is an industry with enormous international pressure because of the transferability of software. This industry is highly competitive with competent providers (e.g. Accenture, EDS, and other global companies) from developed countries, and developing countries, such as East Asia, South America, and Eastern Europe. IT services is one of the fastest growing industry of international trade. This industry is projected to grow up to $142 billion in 2008, according to The Economist.

Competitive Assets

	Customized to Home Market	Transferable Abroad
High	**Dodger** Focuses on a locally oriented link in the value chain, enters a joint venture, or sells out to a multinational Examples: *Skoda from the Czech Republic; Vist from Russia; Baidu.Com from China* *System standard: low proprietary*	**Contender** Focuses on upgrading capabilities and resources to match multinationals globally, often by keeping to niche markets Examples: *Tata from India, Indah Kiat Pulop and Paper (IKPP) from Indonesia; Sundaram from India* *System standards: low openness*
Low	**Defender** Focuses on leveraging local assets in market segments where multinationals are weak Examples: *Bajaj from India; Jahwa from China; Grupo Industrial Bimbo from Mexico* *System standard: high proprietary*	**Extender** Focuses on expanding into markets similar to those of the home base, using competencies developed at home Examples: *Lenovo from China, Jollibee Foods from the Philippines; Televisa from Mexico; Asian Paints from India* *System standard: high openness*

Pressure to Globalize in the Industry (left axis label)

Figure 5. Positioning for Emerging-Market Companies (Source: Dawar and Frost, 1999)

Tata's low-cost strategy is facing the head-on competition with application developers from developing countries and developed countries. International customers contribute to the vast majority of Tata's business revenues, with companies in the United States as its primary customers, accounting for more than 50% of its revenues. By partnering with Tata, American companies enjoy the benefits of Tata's large, highly skilled, and low cost software developers, and time-zone (7-10 hours difference) advantages. Seeing the success of Tata's low cost strategy, large-scale software developers from the U.S. began entering the Indian market to take advantage of the production factors. In 2004, IBM acquired Daksh, one of India's largest call-center companies. Moreover, the domestic IT industry is highly fragmented and crowded with different sizes of IT services providers, such as Wipro, Infosys, Satyam, HCL Tech, and Intel India. Tata's low cost strategy is facing a great challenge with the same strategy used by both domestic companies and international companies, primarily from developing countries. To counter these threats, Tata shifted its strategic focus from being a low-cost solution provider to a quality service provider by providing near-shore facilities in Canada and on-shore facilities in the U.S.

An *extender* company transfers its company assets to another emerging market to replicate its successful experience, where global competition pressure is not having imminent threats. Adopting the open systems and standards allows a firm to quickly scale up to match MNEs. The personal computer (PC) is a standardized product with little variations inside components. It is easy to transfer assets, such as assembly line, brand and technical support, from one country to another country. Dell's reputable direct sales strategy works very well in most economies. Its close relationship with major, single suppliers for each component around the world allows fast assembly of a PC based on the specific requirements of users, avoids intermediaries' markups, reduces inventory, and delivers a low cost strategy. When making inroads into the China market, this low-cost strategy comes head to head with the strategy of local competitor Lenovo. Dell's direct sales strategy cannot function in China because it violates Chinese government regulations that ban direct sales activities, and the ICT and transportation infrastructures in China are not well established. While institutional barriers help Lenovo defend the fierce competition of Dell, Lenovo aggressively acquired IBM's PC business to become the world's third-largest PC seller. By reaching U.S. customers in the home base of Dell and by capitalizing on the brand name, R&D capability, financing and service of IBM, Lenovo changed the rules of game to its advantage.

Formulate International Business Strategy to Enter or Compete In Foreign Markets

Three major enablers for international competitiveness of a business are operational efficiency, local differentiation, and worldwide innovation (Bartlett and Ghoshal, 2003). Each enabler requires an enormous amount of coordination among headquarters, subsidiaries, and suppliers across countries to resolve differences in the factors of socio-politics, economy, language, culture, currency, and IT infrastructure. A company expands internationally by first entering a new market, followed by local market expansion and global rationalization. The degree of coordination and information processing increases with each stage of the international expansion. Information technology is an effective leverage for MNEs to efficiently produce accurate, timely and relevant information, and to simplify and automate the coordination process. International marketing experts assert that a well-designed information system needs to produce information on at least three levels: (1) macro-environment of a nation, (2) market-specific products and competitive structure, and (3) company sales and performance (Douglas and Craig, 2002).

Strategic alignment between businesses and IT strategies can lead to international competitiveness of a company (Zwass, 1992; Ives and Jarvenpaa, 1991). Four major business strategies to direct the global operation of a business are: multinational, international, global and transnational strategies (Bartlett and Ghoshal, 2000). The choice of an international business strategy can help determine a mode of entry into the international marketplace, such as exporting, foreign direct investment, licensing, strategic alliances, acquisitions and joint venture. A trade-off, between local-responsiveness and global-efficiency, needs to be made when deciding on an international business strategy. Table 6 shows corporate strategies and roles of MIS in the global business environment.

Information Systems for Multinational Organizations - Firms adopting information systems for multinational organizational strategy attempt to customize product and service offerings for country or regional differences. The strategic concern of this strategy is to differentiate products and services from local markets. This differentiation effort can not only potentially capture new markets, but also increase the survival rate in that market. According to a 1984-1993 study on the effectiveness of brand stretching, using another brand for the same product and service can increase its survival rate in a new market from 30 to 65 percent (Koch 2000). Despite the advantage, the multinational strategy is more likely to cost more to produce products and services. Foreign operations in a country are part of a grant portfolio to optimize local responsiveness rather than global efficiency. Decision-making processes of a business unit are independent and decentralized to subsidiaries. The relationship between headquarters and subsidiaries is informal. The major function of a global information system is to track and report information on customers, market and financial performance of subsidiaries to headquarters for control purposes. Most databases of subsidiaries are independent from each other.

Quest International is a Holland-based producer of flavors, textures, and fragrances. These products are extremely sensitive to the needs of local customers. A global strategy to mass-produce and mass-market these products often leads to failure in market penetration. Multinational information systems are a key to customized products and services based on the needs of local markets. To understand customers and country-specific tastes and needs and to create new products based on this information, Quest adopted a CRM solution along with a database to gain insights to its local customers. Quest also played as a broker by feeding customer and market information from the CRM system to its manufacturers and sales offices among different countries. System features, such as online discussion forums, sample and product ordering, and online information gathering, have been assimilated to collect information for Quest to better understand its customers.

Business Strategy And Structure	Principal Characteristics	Decision-making Characteristics	MIS Role	MIS Structure
Multinational (Decentralized federation)	Foreign operations regarded as a portfolio of relatively independent businesses	Decision making decentralized to subsidiaries; informal relationships between headquarters and subsidiaries	Financial reporting by subsidiaries to headquarters for control purposes	Decentralized; primarily stand-alone systems and dispersed databases
International (coordinated federation)	Foreign operations regarded as appendages to domestic corporation, where core competencies are honed	More vital decisions and knowledge in general developed at headquarters and transferred to subsidiaries	Formal planning and control systems coordinate the entire operation	Largely centralized planning and control systems implemented on a variety of hardware architectures that ensure links among units
Global (centralized federation)	Foreign operations regarded as pipelines for delivery of goods and services to a unified global market, in search of economies of scale and scope	Decisions made at the center; knowledge developed and retained at the center	Tight central control of subsidiaries through centralized planning, control, and general decision making	Centralized systems and databases
Transnational (integrated network)	Differentiated contributions by all units to integrated worldwide operations	Decision making and knowledge generation distributed among units	Vital coordination role at many levels; knowledge work, group decision making, planning and control	Integrated architecture with distributed systems and databases, supporting management and knowledge work across the organization

Table 6. Corporate Strategies and Roles of MIS in the Global Business Environment (Source: Zwass (1992), p.470.)

Information Systems for International Organizations - Information systems for international organizations are a form of coordinated federation of business units. Headquarters is the brain of the global operation of a business. Subsidiaries wait for the commands from headquarters and act on those commands. There are limited adjustments in business decisions about marketing strategies in overseas markets. Headquarters has primary interests in the control, rather than flexibility. As a result, value chain activities and core competences are honed in the headquarters. This is a compromised approach to reap the benefits of local responsiveness and global efficiency. Optimization of either benefit is not the goal of these information systems. A formal planning and control system to coordinate the global operations of a business is imperative for the success of this business strategy. All information is centralized and processed at headquarters. Subsidiaries are more likely to have limited computing power to receive information, instead of processing information.

Citibank employs over 250,000 people across more than 100 countries. The bank has its tradition in making a strong commitment to local communities. Financial products are global by nature, yet require a minor adjustment based on specific financial needs of local customers. Citibank's e-business initiative to empower local, regional and global customers and the B2B2C marketplace to conduct transactions online is an excellent example of the use of information systems to support international business strategy. In 2000, Citigroup formed a high-level Internet Operation Group committee to gradually infuse Internet systems for different functions, such as e-customer, e-business, e-capital market, e-asset management, into business units of Citibank around the world.

Strategic alignment is a practical exercise to ensure that an adequate information systems structure is designed to support an international business strategy. IT is very likely to miss the target when entering into an international market unless it relies on the supply of accurate information. Many changes to the international communities, such as SARS, bird flu, terrorism and natural disasters, are requiring shifts to today's international strategies. A MNE needs to constantly evaluate the strategic fitness of information systems against its international business strategy and structure. MNEs need to be prepared to make any changes to their information systems structure when formulating a new international business strategy to sustain international competitiveness.

Information Systems for Global Organizations- The global business strategy is to ensure the consistence in business operations across countries. This strategy allows an MNE to conduct business in a similar fashion throughout the world. McDonald's, Gucci, Dior and Hang Dos are typical example companies that adopted a global business strategy. Brand recognition is a key approach to differentiate the company's products or services from local products or services. MNEs attempting to achieve international competitiveness by the economies of scale and scope often adopt the global business strategy. Information systems are tightly controlled at headquarters to plan, coordinate, and control information flows and decision-making processes for subsidiaries. The GISs are not affected by the adjustment to local information needs. Whether information and knowledge generated at headquarters can be capitalized on a worldwide basis and distributed to foreign subsidiaries is a major consideration.

Information Systems for Transnational Organizations- The primary goal of the transnational strategy is to achieve worldwide innovation and global efficiency, in addition to quickly sensing and responding to local needs for differentiation. The decision to adopt this strategy is to maximize the gains in both local responsiveness and global efficiency. Businesses adopting this strategy are in virtual or fluid form to allow quick assembly and disassembly of its value chain activities to supply the best and cheapest resource. The success of this strategy relies on the cross-fertilization of information and knowledge residing in headquarters and subsidiaries. Each subsidiary is autonomous in making an independent decision by relying on the integrated information fed from local subsidiary and headquarters. An information system that supports the transnational strategy needs to accommodate virtual planning, decision-making, control and coordination roles at the local, national and regional levels. Transnational information systems rely on integrated system architectures to network with disparate systems distributed across organizational units of the MNE. The transnational business strategy is an optimal solution to enable firms to out-perform foreign competitors in today's turbulent international environment. Unlike the other three international business strategies, transnational business strategy has the option to accomplish strategic objectives of operation efficiency, differentiation and worldwide innovation at the same time. Information systems can be deployed at different geographical locations and managerial levels to coordinate knowledge and information creation autonomously. However, this is the most complex business strategy to implement.

Nokia has the tradition of being flexible, and nimble in creating new ideas and products in the hyper-competitive mobile phone and telecommunication network industry. To support the tradition, Nokia demands that all business units constantly interact with and cross-fertilize ideas, talent, and knowledge formally and informally. To accomplish this, ad-hoc and cross-business teams are constantly formed to address important issues. The Digital Convergence unit of Nokia was a natural product of an ad-hoc team designed to deliver a joint project between phone and electronic organizer business units. A knowledge management system to support the organizational learning was an effective system solution to support the transnational business strategy of Nokia.

ASSESSING COMPANY LEVEL ISSUES

Concentration Strategy

Any strategic resource of a company in its home base will become insignificant after being stretched across international boundaries. Concentrating limited resources on a particular geographical scope, market, or competitive area is a commonly adopted international business strategy to mitigate this potential problem (Pearce, 1982). Figure 6 lists the top 30 Global Fortune 500 firms that have a large concentration on one or two major industries. However, this strategy is not suitable for products, services and markets of all kinds. Furthermore, this strategy poses many threatening complications, such as higher risks. In a market where seasonal or cyclical factors have minimal influences on the profitability, this concentration strategy often prevails and can help a firm to diversify its businesses. Products in this category include food, utility, automobile, insurance and electronics. Four conditions conducive to the concentration strategy are (Pearce and Harvey, 1990):

- High industry entry barriers, such as high capitalization, institutional barriers, products in late growth and maturity stage of the product life cycle
- Room for future growth of a firm's target market
- Distinctive product-markets that are hard to be substituted
- Abundant and stable inputs, such as price, capital, quantity and supply

Diversification Strategy

When a company diversifies its products and service according to the needs of different markets, the chance to succeed in the international competition and to make more profit is higher (Grant, 1987). This market diversification strategy is practical when a company:

1. Has advantages in location-specific factors (e.g. labor costs, tax incentive and trade barriers of host government),
2. Produces unique products and services that cannot be obtained from the local market,
3. Has a competitive advantage in technological skills, marketing knowledge, or an oligopolistic market structure, compared to local competitors (Hood and Young, 1979).
4. Can easily reproduce the production process in other locations.
5. Has unlimited access to capital, in the form of franchisees (Darnove and Marciano, 2005).
6. Can create a portfolio of related products/services to reduce risks and achieve synergy.

McDonald's can easily replicate its production process and has experience in operating the franchising business model. The diversification strategy is a feasible one for McDonald's. Diversifying business according to geographical scope creates enormous demands for information exchanging, sharing, processing and integration, communication and coordination across business units of a company in different locations. Lack of information processing capability will undermine the effectiveness of a diversification strategy. IT is a vital lever to provide the information processing capability. Communication channels, such as video-conferencing, IP phone and instant messaging, are effective tools to facilitate the inter-company communication.

| 2003 Rank | | | | | | | Profit | |
Fortune Global 500 Rank (Revenues)	BusinessWeek Global 1000 (Market Value)	Company Name	Main Industry	Headquarters Country	Revenues $ million	Market Value $ billion	$ million	Rank
1	5	Wal-Mart	General Merchandisers	USA	246,525.0	232.22	8,039.0	8
2	184	General Motors	Motor Vehicles & Parts	USA	186,763.0	19.81	1,736.0	>50
3	3	Exxon Mobil	Petroleum	USA	182,466.0	244.93	11,460.0	3
4	8	Royal Dutch/Shell Group	Petroleum	UK/Netherlands	179,431.0	158.48	9,419.0	5
5	9	BP	Petroleum	UK	178,721.0	153.24	6,845.0	12
6	194	Ford Motor	Motor Vehicles & Parts	USA	163,871.0	19.22	(980.0)	>50
7	115	DaimlerChrysler	Motor Vehicles & Parts	Germany/USA	141,421.1	31.86	4,460.6	27
8	26	Toyota Motor	Motor Vehicles & Parts	USA	131,754.2	86.32	7,752.7	10
9	1	General Electric	Diversified Financial	USA	131,698.0	286.10	14,118.0	2
10	156	Mitsubishi	Trading	Japan	109,386.1	23.19	494.6	>50
11	538	Mitsui	Trading	Japan	108,630.7	7.31	255.5	>50
12	123	Allianz	Insurance	Germany	101,930.2	29.61	(1,103.3)	>50
13	6	Citigroup	Finance	USA	100,789.0	210.86	15,276.0	1
14	24	Total	Petroleum	France	96,944.9	103.78	5,616.8	19
15	36	ChevronTexaco	Petroleum	USA	92,043.0	75.79	1132.0	>50
16	60	NTT	Telecom	Japan	89,644.0	55.58	1,915.1	>50
17	108	ING Group	Insurance	Netherlands	88,102.3	32.41	4,254.5	>50
18	NA	Itochu	Telecommunications	Japan	85,856.4	NA	164.8	>50
19	11	IBM	Computers, Office Equipment	USA	83,132.0	148.80	3,579.0	41
20	263	Volkswagen	Motor Vehicles & Parts	Germany	82,203.7	14.23	2,443.0	>50
21	78	Siemens	Electronics	Germany	77,205.2	42.20	2,386.5	>50
22	870	Sumitomo	Trading	Japan	75,745.2	4.14	232.1	>50
23	NA	Marubeni	General Merchandisers	Japan	72,164.8	NA	248.8	>50
24	25	Verizon	Telecom	USA	67,625.0	103.55	4,079.0	34
25	10	American Intl. Group	Insurance	USA	67,482.0	150.97	5,518.9	20
26	284	Hitachi	Electronics	Japan	67,228.0	13.12	228.7	>50
27	NA	U.S. Postal Service	Mail, Package, Freight Delivery	USA	66,463.0	NA	(676.0)	>50
28	100	Honda Motor	Motor Vehicles & Parts	Japan	65,420.4	35.11	3,501.5	43
29	113	Carrefour	Food & Drug Stores	USA	64,978.6	32.07	1,299.1	>50
30	28	Altria Group	Tobacco	France	62,182.0	85.43	11,102.0	4

Sources: Adapted from; BusinessWeek Online 2003; Forbes 2003 and Fortune 2003.

Figure 6. Top 30 Global Fortune 500 Firms That Have Concentration on One or Two Major Industries

Guidelines to Formulate Concentration and Diversification Strategies

Concentration and diversification strategies are useful strategies for a firm to compete in international markets. Each strategy has its strengths and weaknesses. Knowing the conditions conducive to the use of these two strategies is important for their successful execution. A company can use the IT demand/supply planning process as a guide in deciding how to leverage IT to support the business strategy. Figure 7 shows planning drivers for the concentration and diversification strategies. The objective of this planning practice is to "produce an actionable strategic plan for it, consisting of a statement of business strategic requirements (demand) and its strategic response (supply)" (Benson, Bugnitz and Walton 2004, p.184). Conditions favorable for the use of a concentration or diversification strategy are business drivers for these two strategies.

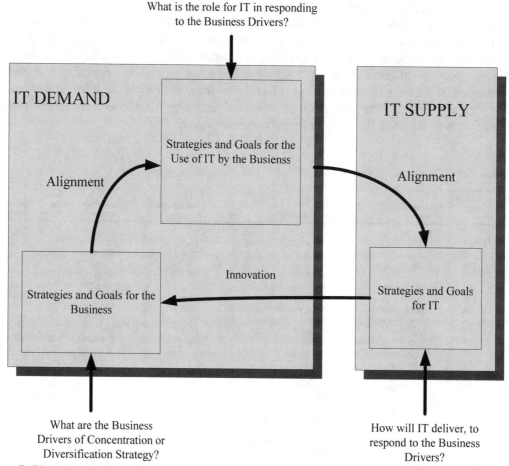

Figure 7. Planning Drivers for Concentration and Diversification Strategies (Source: Modified from Benson, Bugnitz and Walton 2004, p. 182)

ASSESSING INDIVIDUAL LEVEL ISSUES

Global IS Managers

Many changes in organizational work patterns are occurring in the global economy. One major change is the growing disproportionate distribution of labor forces with IT skills. It has been proven that IT investment can significantly improve national economy. Countries without enough people with IT skills and robust IT infrastructures are more likely to have poor economic performance. A growing shortage of IT skills in the developed countries is increasing their demand to import IT laborers from developing countries. An immigration policy is imperative to encourage the flow of IT labor forces from developing to developed countries. The shortage of the IT labor force has also brought about the fast formation of virtual teams.

Information and communication technologies (ICT), such as IP phone, mobile devices, and instant messaging, enable people to work and learn remotely and virtually. The trend of globalization has pressured many firms to locate the best talent around the world. For some projects, people are grouped into a virtual team to collaborate with each other. The number of virtual teams is increasing and growing to become a working norm, particularly in the field of information technology.

A higher degree of virtuality poses a higher degree of challenges for the delivery of teamwork because discontinuity factors, such as geography, time zone, national culture, corporate culture, work practices, and technology, can make conflict resolution and social interactions difficult (Chudoba,

Wynn, Lu and Watson-Manhelm, 2005). A virtual team needs to address both technical and cultural issues. These factors can have a strong influence on team performance if not properly managed. An IS professional working in a global organization is more likely to have these challenges. How to assess the influence of these discontinuity factors on the job performance is an important task for global IS managers and professionals.

Geography
1. Work at home during normal business days
2. Work while traveling, e.g. at airports or hotels
3. Collaborate with people in different sites or geographies
4. Collaborate with people you have never met face to face
Temporal
5. Work extended days in order to communicate with remote team members
6. Collaborate with people in different time zones
Cultural
7. Collaborate with people who speak different native languages or dialects from your own
8. Collaborate with people from different cultural backgrounds
Work practices
9. Work on projects that have changing team members
10. Work with teams that have different ways to track their work
11. Work with people that use different collaboration technologies and tools
Organization
12. Collaborate with people from different business groups
13. Work at different sites
14. Have professional interactions with people outside the organization
Technology
15. Work with people via internet-based conferencing applications
16. Participate in real-time online discussions, such as chat or instant messaging
17. Meet with people via video-conferencing tools
18. Work with mobile devices

Table 7. Assessment to Measure the Degree of Virtuality (Source: Chudoba, Wynn, Lu and Watson-Manhelm 2005, p. 303)

Assessing the Impacts of Virtuality on Team Performance

A virtuality index is a good surrogate to perform this assessment task. This index logically separates discontinuity factors into categories of geography, temporal, cultural, work practices, organization, and technology. An IS manager can ask his/her subordinates who have been working with partner organizations in the virtual form to report their individual working experiences. Table 7 is the assessment to measure the degree of virtuality in six dimensions. The six-point frequency scale has options of "never", "daily", "weekly", "monthly", "quarterly", and "yearly". A higher ranking in each question item indicates a higher virtuality. Team members are more likely to lose sight of team goals when working in a dispersed working environment, which can lead to poor learning performance.

Teams in physical and virtual forms need to address some common factors to operate successfully: clear and measurable goals, appropriate team size, operating guidelines, effective communication processes, and team interactions. However, dysfunctional factors have made many IS managers aware that more active team roles, effective leadership, cultural intelligence and a higher degree of trust are essential for the success of virtual teams. Virtual team members adopt varying synchronous and asynchronous vehicles to carry out interpersonal communications, collaboration, and coordination. Synchronous media have different degrees of social presence and information richness factors. Richer synchronous media include text-, audio- and video-conferencing systems. E-mails, discussion forums, bulletin boards, workflows, scheduling systems, and project management applications are useful asynchronous media to support the global operations of virtual teams. An IS manager needs to fully utilize these media to his/her advantage. Table 8 compares key challenges facing virtual teams and traditional teams.

Challenges	Virtual Teams	Traditional Teams
Communication	• Multiple time zones can lead to greater efficiencies when leveraged, but can also create communication difficulties in terms of scheduling meetings and interactions. • Communication dynamics such as facial expressions, vocal inflections, verbal cues, and gestures are altered	• Teams are collocated in same time zone. Scheduling is less difficult. • Teams may use richer communication media, including face-to-face discussion.
Technology	• Team members must have proficiency across a wide range of technologies: VT membership may be biased toward individuals skilled at learning new technologies. • Technology offers an electronic repository and may facilitate building an organizational memory. • Work group effectiveness may be more dependent on the ability to align group structure and technology with the task environment.	• Technology is not critical for group processes. Technological collaboration tools, while possibly used, are not essential for communications. Team members may not need to possess these skills. • Electronic repositories are not typically used. • Task technology fit may not be as critical.
Team Diversity	• Members typically come from different organizations and/or cultures. This makes it: • Harder to establish a group identity • Necessary to have better communication skills • More difficult to build trust, norms, and shared meanings about roles, because team members have fewer cues about their teammates' performance.	• Because members are more homogeneous, group identity is easier to form. • Because of commonalities, communications are easier to complete successfully.

Table 8. Key Challenges Facing Virtual Teams and Traditional Teams (Source: Pearlson and Saunders 2001, p.125)

Leadership of a Virtual Team

Effective leadership is more important in a virtual team than in a traditional team. Nevertheless, it is harder to establish strong leadership in a virtual team. A shared or distributed leadership among team members rather than centralized leadership is more likely to achieve team success (Lipnack and Stamps, 1997). This means that team members need to have autonomy to manage their team project in a collaborative fashion. To manage a virtual team in a charted direction, the support of internal and external mechanism is essential. Internal group mechanisms include job traits, operating procedures, relationships among team members, team processes and team internal leadership. External supporting mechanisms include educational systems, reward systems, high-level leadership style, tools and technology and communication styles.

The behavioral complexity theory of leadership stresses the importance of a leader exhibiting diversified leadership roles in order to improve team effectiveness (Kayworth and Leidner, 2002). Leadership has been defined in many ways as follows:

- Leadership is the behavior of an individual...directing the activities of a group toward a shared goal. (Hemphill and Coons 1957, p.7)
- Leadership is a process of giving purpose (meaningful direction) to collective effort, and cause willing effort to be expected to achieve purpose (Jacobs and Jaques 1990, p.281).
- Leadership is the influential increment over and above mechanical compliance with the routine directives of the organization (Katz and Kahn 1978, p.528).
- Leadership is the process of influencing the activities of an organized group toward goal achievement (Rauch and Behling 1984, p.46).

Effective leadership in a virtual team needs to address issues of change management, inspiration, motivation and influence, which is quite different from traditional management (Kotter, 1982). To cope with behavioral complexities, a leader needs to be capable of exhibiting different leadership roles in different situations. A leader can perform at least three types of leadership roles: 1) interpersonal contact, (2) information processing and (3) decision making (Mintzberg, 1973). Leadership roles in the category of interpersonal contact include the roles of figurehead, leader, and liaison. Monitor, information disseminator and spokesperson are leadership roles of information processing. Decision making leadership includes entrepreneur, disturbance handler, resource allocator, and negotiator. An efficient leader has to play diversified and sometimes competing leadership behaviors to respond to rapid changes of internal and external environments (Denison, Hooijbert and Quinn, 1995).

Leaders in virtual teams are facing new challenges, such as IT-enabled communications, cross-cultural communications, global logistical design, technological complexity, information overload, lack of social cues, and creation of camaraderie. In a virtual setting, the need for an effective leader to recognize differences among team members is even greater than that in face-to-face settings. Employing members' talents to achieve synergy and communication synchronization as well as managing member and leader expectations in an effective way is a task that cannot be underestimated.

Cultural Influences on the Adoption of Information Systems

Cultural differences are an important issue that needs to be addressed when forming a virtual team. When people from different countries collaborate with each other virtually, unprecedented communication and coordination challenges emerge. Social anthropologists consider culture as the "collective programming of the mind" to distinguish one group of people from another one. Hofstede (1997) states, "Culture is learned, not inherited. It derives from one's social environment, not from one's genes." (p. 182) According to Hofstede (1997), culture should be separated from an individual's personality and human nature. Culture should not be measured in real and absolute values because cultures cannot be compared.

Culture manifests itself in symbols, heroes, rituals, and values. Symbols represent the most superficial and deepest manifestations of culture, with heroes and rituals in between. Legacy about heroes can be written and told while rituals and symbols can be observed. Values, however, have their intrinsic virtues and can hardly be observed or told. One way to measure people's values is to interpret statements about desires. In 1983, Hofstede, designed a questionnaire to ask IBM employees from 55 countries about how they thought the world ought to be (the desirable) versus what they want for themselves (the desired). Hofstede identified four cultural dimensions to represent values of different cultures: power distance, individualism, masculinity, and uncertainty avoidance. Each cultural dimension is quantified with a specific indicator to illustrate countries' differences.

The Power Distance Indicator (PDI) stands for "the extent to which the less powerful person in a society accepts inequality in power and considers it as normal." Malaysia (PDI=104), Mexico (81), India (77), Singapore (74) and Brazil (69) are good examples of high power distance culture. In contrast, the countries with lower power distance culture include Austria (11), Israel (13), Ireland (22), Great Britain (35), Australia (36), Canada (39) and USA (40).

The high Individualism Index (IDV) pertains to a "society in which the ties between individuals are loose" while the low IDV or high collectivism refers to a "society in which people from birth onwards are integrated into strong, cohesive in-groups, which continue throughout peoples' lifetimes and continue to protect them in exchange for unquestioning loyalty." USA (IDV=91), Australia (90), Great Britain (89), Canada (80) and South Africa (65) are good examples of high individualism culture. In contrast, the countries with lower individualism or high collectivism culture include Guatemala (6), Taiwan (17), Thailand (20), Mexico (30), Arab countries (38), and Japan (46).

People who live in the high Masculinity Index (MAS) society are more "assertive, tough, and focused" and people with a low MAS are more "modest and tender." Role differences between genders are not so distinct in the femininity society. Japan (95), Austria (79), Italy (70), Mexico (69), and USA (62) have higher MAS. Sweden (5), Denmark (16), Thailand (34), South Korea (39), and Taiwan (45) have lower MAS or stronger femininity culture.

Uncertainty avoidance is the extent to which the members of a culture feel threatened by uncertain or unknown situations. The feelings of nervous stress, predictability, and a need for written rules are good indicators for uncertainty avoidance. Countries with high uncertainty avoidance index (UAI) include Greece (112), Japan (92), France (86), Mexico (82), Israel (81), and Germany (65). The low UAI countries are Singapore (8), Denmark (23), Great Britain (35) and USA (46).

Straub (1994) researched how culture can influence peoples' attitudes towards using IT in achieving individual and organizational productivity gains. He found that people from low IDV countries tend to avoid using IT in supporting individual and organizational productivity. Igbaria, Anandarajan and Chen (2005) also confirm the evidence by studying computer usage in Nigeria, a country with the low IDV culture (IDV=20) in relation to the U.S. (91). Since low IDV people often come from culture where indicators of PDI, MAS, and UAI are low, Straub formulated a CMSI (Computer-Mediated Support Indicator) index to represent cultural influences to the perceived usefulness of IT and its actual use. Straub's research findings recommend considering cultural factors (e.g., CMSI) when deploying GIS.

All nationalities possess unique cultures that have to be integrated into the design and deployment of information systems. A study by Marcus and Gould (2000) on the awareness of cultures in the global web user-interface design showed that Hofstede's cultural considerations can significantly improve the performance and the receptivity of the Web on the worldwide basis. Marcus and Gould suggest that a web design with cultural sensitivity can attract more real and global customers, not visitors, and improve the bottom line. The above discussion suggests that culture influences GIS designs (symbols) and adoption (values). When deploying GIS, cultural impacts have to be carefully assessed and well integrated into GIS.

CONCLUSIONS

We are becoming a global economy connected with each other via international trade, information and communication technologies, global products/services, cross-cultural activities, and keen interests of knowing each other from another part of the world. Information is particularly important for the successful operations of a multinational enterprise. The geographical chasm creates differences in culture, business norm, educational system, legal system, and ethical values in the global economy. It is vital for an MNE to formulate a global information system (GIS) strategy to overcome the complexity of global business. GIS strategy is a core element of global business strategy that can be devised from four levels: regional, national, corporate and individual levels. Challenges vary with each geographical level.

Four major categories of forces are shaping the regional differences: market similarity, comparative advantage, scale/scope and regulation. These regional differences create demands for a business and IT executives who are competent of assessing the geographical scope of industry-level analysis, analyzing industry structures in different regions, identifying regional competitors, and understanding the digital divide among regions. Major challenges at the national level are the ability of an executive to assess cross-country differences, including information and telecommunication infrastructure, soft resources and governmental policies. Porter's Diamond of National Advantage model addresses four major issues at the national level: factor conditions, related and supporting industries, demand conditions and firm strategy, and structure and rivalry. A company can use the framework to assess these issues before entering an international market. To many local companies facing the intense competition of MNEs, they can tailor their survival strategies based on the dimensions of competitive assets and pressure to globalize in the industry. Four forms of effective survival strategy can help a business sidestep international competition or engage in head-to-head competition with MNEs. No companies have unlimited resources to compete internationally. When constrained with limited resources, a smart business must concentrate and refocus the use of these resources to areas that can promise the highest return.

Three major enablers for international business competitiveness are operational efficiency, local differentiation, and worldwide innovation. Information systems strategy is one of major sources for the creation of these enablers. In the global business environment, a business can formulate its information systems strategy to align with one of four business strategies in order to achieve those competition enablers: multinational, international, global and transnational business strategies. A higher degree of virtuality brings greater challenges for managing an organization with geographically dispersed virtual teams. A GIS manager needs to learn how to lead and manage virtual teams with diversified backgrounds.

MINICASE

H.J. Heinz Company - An Evolving International Company

The H.J. Heinz Company has been a pioneer in the food industry for 137 years. It possesses one of the world's best and most recognizable brands—Heinz©. In 1869 Henry J. Heinz and L. Clarence Noble launched Heinz & Noble, thus laying the groundwork for today's global company. The first product is Henry's mother's "pure and superior" grated horseradish, bottled in clear glass to show its purity. In 1867, ketchup was added to the company's condiment line, which also includes celery sauce, pickled cucumbers, sauerkraut and vinegar. The company has continued to grow since then.

Heinz operates in three core categories of food products: Ketchup and Sauces, Meals and Snacks and Infant Food. The company operates primarily in six major developed markets, including the U.S., Canada, U.K., Italy, Western Europe and Australia/New Zealand. They are developing an Asia operation and entering the China, India, and Indonesian markets. The organization chart, as of the end of 2006, for the operating divisions and the executive in charge of strategy is shown below.

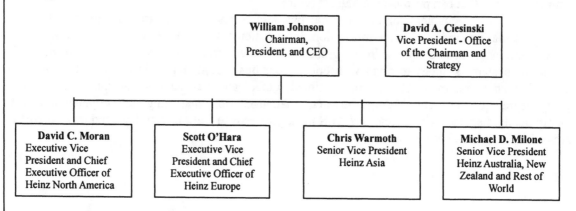

Worldwide Strategies

Under the leadership of William R. Johnson, Chairman, President, and Chief Executive Officer since September 2000, the company has adopted "focus on the core" operating direction. This has since evolved into two operating strategies: a Transformation strategy and a Profitable Global strategy. These strategies are aimed at global operations to improve the competitiveness of the company in all areas of operation.

This Transformation strategy began with the spin-off of non-core U.S. businesses in December 2002, and continued through 2006. Since that time, Heinz has been making great progress in simplifying and focusing the Company on its three core businesses. This has resulted in the divesture of approximately 20 non-core product lines/businesses and generated proceeds of approximately $1 billion. Although the company is divesting non-core businesses, it continues to look for valuable new acquisitions. In August 2005, Heinz acquired HP Foods Limited, HP Foods Holdings Limited, and HP Foods International Limited (collectively referred to as "HPF") for a purchase price of approximately $877 million. HPF is a manufacturer and marketer of sauces which are primarily sold in the United Kingdom, the United States, and Canada. The Company acquired HPF's brands including HP©, Lea & Perrin©, and a perpetual license to market Amoy© brand Asian sauces and products in Europe. In March 2006, the British Competition Commission formally cleared this acquisition, concluding that the acquisition may not be expected to result in a substantial lessening of competition within the markets for tomato ketchup, brown sauce, barbeque sauce, canned baked beans and canned pasta in the United Kingdom. As a result of the Transformation strategy, more than 90% of Heinz's sales are in their three core categories of food products and approximately 60% of sales are generated by the top 10 brands, making Heinz one of the most focused companies in the packaged food industry.

The Profitable Global strategy puts quality assurance professionals in a direct reporting role to the head of each Heinz affiliate, as well as World Headquarters. This strategy has five initiatives:

1. Drive Profitable Growth by devoting energy and resources to increase consumer insights to improve value to customers and consumers in its six major developed markets. As part of this initiative, the company plans to focus on the key emerging markets of Russia, India, China, Indonesia and Poland. These markets represent over 40% of the world's population and 15% of the world's GDP growth. Heinz has good, profitable businesses in each of these markets and will be looking to drive strong growth with products designed for local tastes and cultures.

2. Further Simplify the Business by continuing to improve the effectiveness of the three core categories of food products and reduce complexity by divesting any remaining businesses that do not fit with the long-term strategy; Eliminating non-value-added facilities and SKU's; Continuing to de-layer the organization; and Establishing best-in-class processes and systems around the globe.

3. Reduce Costs to Improve Margins that include initiatives to drive efficiency in trade spending, enhance sales mix, accelerate global procurement, improve supply chain processes/tools and reduce general and administrative costs. All of these initiatives are expected to improve operating margins and provide the fuel for additional growth.

4. Achieve Operational Excellence by attracting, developing, and retaining great leadership and talent.

5. Drive Cash Flow to Improve Shareholder Value by continuing to driving cash flow to leverage value.

Worldwide Operations

The following table lists the number of the Company's principal food processing factories by region:

Factories	Owned	Leased
North America	27	4
Europe	27	0
Asia/Pacific	18	2
Rest of World	11	3
Total	83	9

Heinz Global Innovation and Quality Center

To enhance its global operations, the Company opened the Heinz Global Innovation and Quality Center in September 2005 and announced a significant commitment to product development and quality to better align with consumer desires. Located north of Pittsburgh, the facility is Heinz's global hub for research and development and home to more than 100 chefs, food technologists, researchers and package designers, plus experts in nutrition and quality assurance. The center provides technical direction, assistance and advice to Heinz business units worldwide.

Revenues

The Company's revenues are generated via the sale of products in the following categories (Dollars in thousands) (Source: 2006 Annual Report):

Fiscal Year Ended	May 3, 2006 (53 Weeks)	April 27, 2005 (52 Weeks)	April 28, 2004 (52 Weeks)
Ketchup and sauces	$3,530,346	$3,234,229	$3,047,662
Meals and snacks	3,876,743	3,680,920	3,309,831
Infant foods	863,943	855,558	908,469
Other	372,406	332,749	359,869
Total	$8,643,438	$8,103,456	$7,625,831

Risk Factors

In its 2006 Annual Report, Heinz identified several risks and uncertainties were identified. The following are risks and uncertainties that are a result of Heinz's global operations:

- Competitive product and pricing pressures in the food industry worldwide.
- Economic and political conditions in the U.S. and in various other nations where the Company does business.
- Increases in the cost and restrictions on the availability of raw materials throughout the world.
- Higher energy and fuel costs and other factors affecting the cost of acquiring raw materials and producing, transporting, and distributing the Company's products worldwide.
- The impact of various food safety issues, environmental, legal, tax, and other regulations in the U.S. and other countries.
- The failure to successfully integrate acquisitions and joint ventures into our existing operations or the failure to gain applicable regulatory approval for such transactions.
- The Company's operations face significant foreign currency exchange rate exposure.

Conclusions

The H.J. Heinz Company is a global company with factories and operations in many countries throughout the world. Heinz has the number-one or number-two branded businesses in more than 50 world markets. It has established strategies for an expanding global company.

Discussion Questions

1. How has the H.J. Heinz Company adapted to its operations and markets as it has become a global company?
2. Applying Bartlett and Ghoshal's structure to the H.J. Heinz Company, which structural category would you put Heinz into? Why?
3. Has H.J. Heinz Company used more of a Concentration strategy or a Diversification strategy? How did you reach your conclusion of the strategy used?
4. Apply Porter's Competitive Forces to Heinz's food products. How would you rate each force?

KEY TERMS

Digital Divide
Global Information Systems
Multinational information systems
International Information Systems
Virtual Team

STUDY QUESTIONS

1. Describe the multilevel approach that business and information systems executives should adopt when analyzing a global strategy

2. Discuss major information technology issues faced by countries in four general categories.

3. How does the system openness and standardization impact an industry structure based on Porter's Five Forces Model?

4. Choose a country that your company plans to enter. Name at least five parameters to help systematically assess the potential influence of the "Digital Divide" problem on the business operation of your company.

5. Discuss how to align international business and IT strategies.

REFERENCES

Bartlett, C. A., and Ghoshal, S. Transnational Management: Text and Cases, Irwin/McGraw-Hill. 2000.

Bartlett, C. A., and Ghoshal, S. *"What is a Global Manager?,"* Harvard Business Review. 2003.

Benson, R. J., Bugnitz, T., and Walton, W. *From Business Strategy to IT Action Right Decisions for a Better Bottom Line*. Hoboken, N.J., Wiley. 2004.

Chudoba, K. M., Wynn, E., Lu, M., and Watson-Manheim, M.B. "How Virtual are We? Measuring Virtuality and Understanding Its Impact in a Global Organization," *Information Systems Journal* 15(4), 2005, pp. 279-292.

Darnove, D., and Marciano, S. *Kellogg on Strategy: Concepts, Tools, and Frameworks for Practitioners*. New York, John Wiley & Sons, Inc. 2005.

Dawar, N., and Frost, T. "Competing with Giants: Survival Strategies for Local Companies in Emerging Markets," *Harvard Business Review*, March-April 1999, pp. 119-129.

Deloitte Research. *Indian Manufacturing in a Global Perspective: Setting the Agenda for Growth*. Retrieved December 2, 2005, from http://www.deloitte.com/dtt/research/, Nov 2005.

Denison, D. R., Hooijberg, R., and Quinn, R. E. "Paradox and Performance: Toward a Theory of Behavioral Complexity in Managerial Leadership," *Organization Science* 6(5), 1995, pp. 524-540.

Douglas, S. P., and Craig, S. *International Marketing Research*. New York, John Wiley & Sons, Ltd. 2000.

Grant, R. M. "Multinationality and Performance among British Manufacturing Companies," *Journal of International Business Studies* 18(3), 1987, pp. 79-89.

Grover, V., and Vaswani, P. "Partnerships in the U.S. Telecommunications Industry," *Communications of the ACM* 43(2), 2000, pp. 80-89.

Grover, V., and Saeed, K. "The Telecommunication Industry Revisited: The Changing Pattern of Partnership," *Communications of the ACM* 46(7), 2003, pp. 119-125.

Hämäläinen, T. J. 'The Changing Determinants of Economic Performance in the World Economy: National Competitiveness and Economic Growth," Journal of Socio-Economics 33(3), 2004, pp. 377-380.

Hemphill, J. K., and Coons, A. E., Ed.. *Development of the Leader Behavior Description Questionnaire. Leader Behavior: Its Description and Measurement*. Columbus, OH, Bureau of Business Research of Ohio State University. 1957.

Hofstede, G. *Cultures and Organizations: Software of the Mind*. New York, McGraw-Hill. 1997.

Hood, N., and Young, S. *The Economics of Multinational Enterprise*. London, Longman Group. 1979.

Igbaria, M., Anadarajan, M., and Chen, C. C., Ed. Global Information Systems, The Encyclopedia of Information Systems. 2005.

Ives, B., and Jarvenpaa, S. L. "Applications of Global Information Technology: Key Issues for Management," *MIS Quarterly* 15(1), 1991, pp. 32-49.

Jacobs, T. O., and Jaques, E., (Ed.) *Military Executive Leadership. Measures of Leadership.* Greensboro, NC, Center for Creative Leadership. 1990.

Katz, D., and Kahn, R. L. *The Social Psychology of Organizations.* New York, Wiley. 1978.

Kayworth, T. R., and Leidner, D.E. "Leadership Effectiveness in Global Virtual Teams," Journal of Management Information Systems 18(3), 2002, pp. 7-40.

King, W. R., and Sethi, V. "Patterns in the Organization of Transnational Information Systems," Information and Management 38(4): 2001, pp. 201-215.

Koch, R. *The Financial Times Guide to Strategy: How to Create and Deliver a Useful Strategy.* New York, Prentice Hall. 2000.

Koranteng, J. "Euro threesome gear up for '05," *Amusement Business* 117(1), 2005, pp. 10-11.

Kotter, J. P. The General Managers. New York, Free Press. 1982.

Lessard, D. R. *Frameworks for Global Strategy Analysis.* Journal of Strategic Management Education 1(1), 2003, pp. 81-92.

Li, Z. "Chinese Firms' Overseas M&A Value Likely to Reach USD14bn in 2005," *SinoCast China Business Daily News.* London: 1. April 29, 2005.

Lipnack, J., and Stamps, J. *Virtual teams: Reaching Across Space, Time and Organization with Technology*, John Wiley &Sons, Inc. 1997.

Marcus, A and Gould, E. W. "Crosscurrents: Cultural Dimensions And Global Web User-Interface Design," *ACM Interactions* 7(4), 2000, pp. 32-46.

Mintzberg, H. *The Nature of Managerial Work.* New York, Harper and Row. 1973.

Palvia, P., Palvia, S., and Whitworth, J. Global Information Technology Management Environment: Representative World Issues. In Palvia, P., Palvia, S., and Roche, E. *Global Information Technology and Electronic Commerce.* Ivy League Publishing, 2002.

Pearce II, J. A., and Harvey, J. W. "Concentrated Growth Strategies,". *Academy of Management Executive* 4(1), 1990, pp. 61-68.

Pearce II, J. A. "Selecting Among Alternative Grand Strategies," *California Management Review* 30(2), 1982, pp. 23-31.

Pearlson, K. E., and Saunders, C. S. "There's No Place Like Home: Managing Telecommuting Paradoxes," *The Academy of Management Executive* 15(2), 2001, pp. 117-128.

Porter, M. *The Competitive Advantage of Nations.* Harvard Business Review: pp. 73-93. 1990.

Porter, M. Competitive Strategy: Techniques for Analyzing Industries and Competitors. New York, The Free Press. 1980.

Prahalad, C. K., and Doz, Y. L. The Multinational Mission: Balancing Local Demands and Global Vision. New York, McGraw-Hill. 1987.

Rauch, C. F., and Behling O., (Ed) *Functionalism: Basis for an Alternate Approach Study ff Leadership. Leader Managers International Perspectives on Managerial Behavior and Leadership.* Elmsford, N.Y., Pergamon. 1984.

Sharma, S. K., and Gupta, J. N. D. "Socio-Economic Influences of E-commerce Adoption," *Journal of Global Information Technology Management* 6(3), 2003, pp. 3-21.

Straub, D. "The Effect of Culture on IT Diffusion: E-Mail & Fax in Japan and the U.S.," *Information Systems Research* 5(1), 1994, pp. 23-47.

Thompson, E. R. "National Competitiveness: A Question of Cost Conditions or Institutional Circumstances?," *British Journal of Management* 15(3), 2004, pp. 192-218.

U.S. Census Bureau. *North American Industry Classification System (NAICS).* Retrieved December 5, 2005, from http://www.census.gov/epcd/www/naics.html. 2005.

Zwass, V. Management Information Systems, William C. Brown Publishers. 1992.

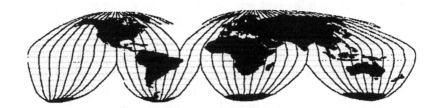

Public ICT Policy Initiatives and Deployment: Theories, Stakeholders, Success Factors, and Regulatory Tools

Yide Shen
Detmar Straub
Georgia State University

Eileen M. Trauth
The Pennsylvania State University

CHAPTER SUMMARY

This chapter looks at public information and communications technology (ICT) policy initiatives and deployment from several perspectives. It presents many of the stakeholders of ICT policy initiatives and introduces twenty three examples of Public ICT Policy. Four categories of ICT policy are presented, including: Information Flow Policies, Economic Policies, Societal-Human Equity Policies, and Governance Policies. The chapter also presents four major frameworks/theories that have been used in empirical public ICT policy studies and identifies five other frameworks/theories. Understanding public ICT policy is important when considering global IT strategies.

INTRODUCTION

Information and communications technology (ICT) has been held up as a source of national wealth and as a solution to cycles of poverty and economic deprivation, both in developing and developed world (Kraemer and Dedrick 1994). In order to leverage national economic and social development by employing ICT, certain public ICT policies need to be enforced. For example, in the domain of IT copyright protection and other forms of intellectual property, countries that lack legal protection for a nation's intellectual property are not likely to create a native industry because firms cannot profit with only one sale of a new product (Checchi et al., 2005), the remainder of the diffusion being pirated copies.[1] Laws and enforcement of such policies can reverse this effect by encouraging entrepreneurship in developing and marketing locally-owned intellectual property.

---

[1] Naturally, a nation can institute any policy it chooses, and one way this can be done to retain/encourage a native industry is to punish violations of copyrights internal to the nation but not those external to the nation. In other words, pursue a policy that differentiates between native-owned and foreign-owned copyrights. Some

Motivated by the importance to enforce public ICT policy, the purpose of this chapter is to introduce public ICT policy initiatives and deployment from several important perspectives. The chapter is organized in six sections. Section two introduces different types of public ICT policy. Section three identifies various stakeholders that are involved in public ICT policy making process and public environment for ICT policy. Section four describes the regulatory tools and success factors of public ICT policy. Section five reviews the theories or explanatory models that have been employed in empirical public ICT policy studies. Section six suggests several theories that are potentially useful for empirical research in public ICT policy domain.

NATIONAL ICT POLICY CATEGORIES

Before presenting detailed discussion about public ICT policy, it will be helpful to introduce different categories of polices and see some examples for each category. In a research forum on Advancing Theory on National IT Policy[2], participants[3] generated a list of public ICT policies (as shown in Table 1) that have been or can be implemented in various countries. Based on each policy's purpose orientation, they were mapped into a parsimonious set of four categories.

Table 2 summarizes these four categories. The policies falling into the first category (*information flow policies*) either encourage or protect against the free flow of information. *Economic policies* intend to increase the wealth of entities or stakeholders. *Societal-human equity policies* aim to achieve equitable distribution of citizenship privileges. *Governance policies* aim to create and sustain the environment for economic and social development, and maintain continued economic investments in national ICT.

Stakeholders and Public Environment for Public ICT Policy
The stakeholders that influence and are influenced by public ICT policies and the public environment in which ICT policies are formulated and deployed are probably the most important factors shaping a nation's ICT policies. To illustrate the interactions between various stakeholders and the public environment for public ICT policies, as well as to facilitate researchers to position future studies in this domain, an integrative framework was created by Checchi et al. (2003), as shown in Figure 1. The dotted lines in the figure show the relationship between stakeholders, and the arrows indicate the bi-directional interaction between stakeholders and public environment.

Stakeholders for Public ICT Policy
When trying to identify the various stakeholders that are involved in public ICT policy making, we cite King et al.'s (1994) taxonomy of institutions having an influence over IT innovation. King et al. (1994) put forward a general definition of institution, which considers institutions as social entities that exert "influence and regulation over other social entities" (p. 148). Concerning the dissemination of IT, King et al. (1994) identified the following key institutions, as listed in Table 3.

Asian countries seem to be pursuing this strategy at the time of this writing. As with any other negotiated position in trading relationships, this policy does not breed trust and promote cooperation and in the long run could lead to retaliatory trade practices.

[2] The forum was entitled "Forum on Advancing Theory on National IT Policy," October 2-4, 2004. The forum was sponsored by NSF grant INT-032250. Parts of the current chapter are based upon work supported by the National Science Foundation under grants DST-0082473 and INT-032250. Any opinions, findings, and conclusions or recommendations expressed in this material are those of the author(s) and do not necessarily reflect the views of the National Science Foundation.

[3] Participants included Detmar Straub, Elieen Trauth, Karen Loch, Ken Kraemer, Khaled Wahba, Lynette Kvasny, Michael Best, Peter Meso, Peter Wolcott, Philip Musa, Ricardo Checchi, Roberto Evaristo, Sherif Kamel, and Victor Mbarika.

#	Policy	Description	Country Where Practiced
1	Technology Clubs	Locally-oriented, low-cost access points for users, including children and their families	Egypt
2	Telecommunications liberalization	Privatizing publicly owned Post and Telegraph systems	India, Ireland (Trauth and Pitt, 1992)
3	eRate or school access	Provide cheap Internet access for libraries and schools	N/A*
4	Censoring regulations	Making Internet Service Provider (ISP) responsible for content that is delivered; controlling flow of information	Several Arab counties; China, Singapore
5	Privacy Legislation	Provides protection for specific types of personal information, in response to European Union regulations	Ireland
6	Laws protecting individuals and companies against Internet fraud	Limitation of individual liability for transactions on the Internet	Worldwide
7	Anti-circumvention	Making it illegal to circumvent intellectual property (IP) protection	USA
8	Export control-encryption technology	Permitting exports of older forms of encryption	USA formerly
9	File sharing (IP)	Regulation of peer-to-peer networks	USA
10	Telecommunication Regulatory Agency	Creation of an independent regulatory agent for ICT, especially data communications	Tanzania; Kenya
11	Creation of an IT ministry	Centralizing the government and private sector efforts to promote IT	Egypt
12	Outsourcing initiatives	Government procurement restricted to buying technology good and services domestically	Australia
13	Taxation of Internet transactions	Monitoring and assigning tax structure to e-Commerce	N/A
14	Software engineering training	HR efforts to increase skilled pool of workers	Egypt, Irealand (Trauth, 1993)
15	Immigration policy	Opening immigration to deal with shortage of IT workers	Canada, US
16	Internet telephony regulation	Opening up market to Voice-over-IP (VOIP)	N/A
17	Spectrum Regulation	Licensing bandwidth frequencies	N/A
18	Foreign Direct Investment promotion	Offering incentives for foreign firms to invest in domestic IT	Singapore, Ireland
19	National Security	Collect data on individuals via Internet	USA
20	Universal service	Requiring telecomm operators to balance high accessibility against ability to pay	N/A
21	Market concentration/ ownership issues	Monopoly regulations to prevent concentration of power in IT markets	N/A
22	Infant industry protection	Tariffs on certain IT goods and services that do not have domestic content	Brazil
23	Equality policy	Policies that are related to gender equality (see also Trauth, 2000)	EU and European countries

* N/A indicates no example was offered during the discussion.

Table 1. Examples of Public ICT Policy

Category	Policy
Information Flow Policies	5, 6, 7, 8, 10, 17, 18, 20, 22
Economic Policies	2, 3, 9, 13, 14, 16, 19
Societal-Human Equity Policies	1, 4, 15, 21, 23
Governance Policies	11, 12

The values in the Policy column correspond to the policy number in the first column of Table 1

Table 2. Four Categories of National ICT Policy

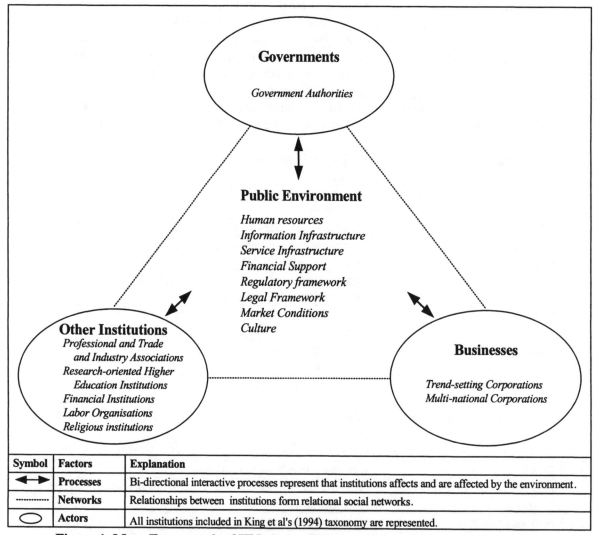

Figure 1. Meta-Framework of IT Policies (Based on Checchi et al. (2003), p. 57)

Consistent with Checchi et al. (2003), we consider these institutions to be actors or stakeholders involved in the process of public ICT policy formulation and deployment. In addition, another type of stakeholder not identified in King et al.'s taxonomy is economic development agencies in a country or region. These agencies influence on national and regional economy will inevitably impact ICT policy.

Checchi et al. (2003) recognized that various stakeholders' influences on public ICT policy have different levels of importance across contexts. For example, religious institutions have much stronger influence in Arab countries than they do in Latin American countries. Especially, regarding government's interventions when making national ICT policy, the literature suggested several aspects that distinguish less developed countries from developed countries (see Table 4).

Public Environment for Public ICT Policy

Other variations arise from the public environment in which public ICT policies are formulated and deployed. According to Checchi et al. (2003), there are eight public environment components that vary across countries: human resources, information infrastructure, services infrastructure, financial support, regulatory framework, legal framework, market conditions and culture. Table 5 summarizes the differences between less developed and developed countries with respect to public environment.

Regulatory Tools and Success Factors of Public ICT Policy

Once a nation's ICT policies have been established, the next question would be: How can policies be successfully initiated via regulatory tools and other mechanisms? Based on Lessig (1998), this section introduces four regulatory tools and four success factors of public ICT policy.

REGULATORY TOOLS OF POLICY

According to Lessig (1998), the regulatory effects of any policy are fulfilled by one or more of the four regulatory tools (or modalities): law, norms, markets, and architecture. *Law* structures people's behavior in certain ways; otherwise strict punishments have to be enacted. Similar to law, *norms* regulate by threatening punishment, but punishment resulting from norms is not a centralized act.

Institution	Description
1. Government authorities	National government agencies, provinces, prefectures, states, municipalities, etc.
2. International agencies	Mission agencies of international organizations such as the United Nations, the World Bank and the International Monetary Fund, plus international "outreach" agencies of developed countries (e.g., US-AID).
3. Professional and trade and industry associations	Scientific and technical societies, organizations of professionals such as physicians and lawyers, and trade and industry associations.
4. Research-oriented higher education institutions	Influential organizations that typically have strong international, institutional ties.
5. Trend-setting corporations	Powerful domestic companies performing important functions that influence innovation.
6. Multi-national corporations	Cross-national companies that influence the movement of technology where they operate.
7. Financial institutions	Banks, non-bank lending institutions, equity markets, venture capital funds and informal financing arrangements (e.g. kin- or ethnic-based ties).
8. Labor organizations	Unions that influence the use of technologies in particular industries.
9. Religious institutions	Religious authorities that raise moral or ethical questions regarding use of technology.

Table 3. Influencing Institutions in IT Innovation (Based on King et al. (1994), p. 148)

Government Intervention Component	Less Developed Countries	Developed Countries
Initiator for policy making (mostly)	Regional or international Agencies	Domestic government
Government attitude	Passive or reactive	Proactive
Investment purpose	Invest mostly in IT infrastructure	Invest in both research knowledge and IT infrastructure
Typical capabilities of the government	Lack of technical skills, financial limitations	Has both technical and financial capabilities
Position with respect to standards	Standards following	Standards setting

**Table 4. Differences with Respect to Government Intervention
(Based on Checchi et al. (2003), p. 54)**

Public Environment Component	Less Developed Countries	Developed Countries
Human resources	Lower demand and supply of knowledge workers	Higher demand and supply of knowledge workers
Information infrastructure	Low teledensity, poor connection quality, and insufficient power supply	High quality information infrastructure
Service infrastructure	Inferior services infrastructures (e.g., lower credit card usage, unreliable e-logistic services)	Superior services infrastructures
Financial support	Subsidized by international agencies, with few investments in research	Governments support technology research program
Regulatory framework	Highly regulated contexts (e.g., state-owned monopolized communication services), less attention to regulatory issues in e-commerce related policies	Less regulated contexts, more attention to regulatory issues in e-commerce related policies
Legal framework	Incomplete laws protecting intellectual property, higher software piracy level	More complete laws protecting intellectual property, lower software piracy level
Market conditions	Lower purchasing power and lower customer readiness to adopt IT innovation	Higher purchasing power and higher customer readiness to adopt IT innovation
Culture	Non-industrialized cultures respond in conflicting way with industrialized features embedded in technologies	Industrialized cultures more likely to resonate well with technologies designed for those from industrialized countries

**Table 5. Differences with Respect to Public Environment
(Based on Checchi et al. (2003), p. 58)**

Successful IT Policies	Unsuccessful IT Policies
Long-term oriented	Short-term oriented
Capability-building	Resource-consumption
Adaptive	Less-responsive
Collaborative	Non-collaborative

**Table 6. Characteristics of Successful and Unsuccessful National ICT Policy
(Based on Checchi et al. (2003), p. 54)**

That is, norms are not enforced by a centralized government, but by a community. Given the constraints of law (property and contract law governing markets) and social norms (markets operating within the permitted domain of social norms), *markets* regulate by price and present another set of constraints on individual and collective behavior. *Architecture* refers to the physical world surrounding people. For example, a town square with easy accessibility to a diversity of shops in a town is likely to increase the integration of residents in that town.

As inherent in the definitions, these four modalities are not independent of each other; instead, they work together. Lessig (1999) pointed out that "the 'net regulation' of any particular policy is the sum of the regulatory effects of the four modalities together. A policy trades off among these four regulatory tools" (Lessig, p. 507). Thus, policy makers should select among these four modalities depending upon what works best. Most of the examples of policies in Table 1 are legal in nature, but norms and market are subsequent effects. Regulation of the information flows on the Internet, though, can sometimes be handled through technology architectures, such as censoring and restricted file sharing (enforced by policy numbers 4 and 9 in Table 1).

Success Factors for Public ICT Policy Making
Based on public ICT policy literature, the successfully deployed ICT policies share similar patterns across countries (Checchi et al., 2003), as shown in Table 6.

First, successful policies commit to long term capability building, such as emphasizing human resources development, infrastructure, and coordination between policies. Second, the countries with successful IT policies are able to build their own capability and rely less on foreign expertise. In contrast, less successful policies focus on consumption rather than production of ICT, which creates over reliance on foreign assistance. For example, in Ireland a concerted effort was undertaken on several fronts to develop a qualified IT labor force. First, existing universities added new curricula. Second, new universities and institutes of technology were created. Finally, expertise was 'imported' in the form of multinational IT companies (Trauth 1993; Trauth 1996; Trauth 1999).

Third, flexible policies that are adaptive to shifting environment are more likely to succeed than less responsive policies. Empirical evidence has been observed in various countries such as Singapore (Wong 1998), Ireland (Montealegre 1999; Trauth 2000), and Latin American countries (Tallon and Kraemer 2000).

Fourth, the alignment between ICT policies and other concurrent activities – such as infrastructure construction programs, education programs, economic development projects, and funding mechanisms – is another critical success factor. The alignment of these components generate a cohesive building force, which helped countries like Ireland (Trauth 2001), Singapore, Korea, and Costa Rica achieve successful economic development. To the contrary, unsuccessful ICT policy deployment cases in Ukraine (Jennex and Amoroso 2002), Pakistan (Hassan 1998), and Africa (Mbarika et al. 2002) showed a distinctive pattern of a disconnection between ICT policies and other concurrent activities.

THEORIES/FRAMEWORKS IN EMPIRICAL PUBLIC ICT POLICY RESEARCH

As one major stream in the emerging field of global ICT, some empirical work has been done in examining public ICT policy formulation and deployment. It will be helpful for practitioners to be aware of the frameworks/theories that have been used in empirical public ICT policy studies, in order to better understand the results from these studies.

IT Diffusion and Adoption Models
The most frequently referenced models in public ICT policy research are IT diffusion and adoption models. Tan and Teo (2000) derived an Internet banking adoption framework, mainly based on the

theory of planned behavior (Ajzen 1985) and the diffusion of innovation theory (Rogers 1983). The framework hypothesized three types of factors influencing consumers' intention to use Internet banking: (1) attitudinal, (2) social, and (3) perceived behavioral control factors. Among the perceived behavioral control factors, government support is found to be an influential factor for intention to use Internet banking in Singapore. Brown and colleagues (2004) tested the same framework in South Africa and found government support has no significant influence on Internet banking adoption. Montealegre (1999) derived a temporal model of institutional intervention in IT adoption in less developed countries. The analysis showed IT adoption as a five-phase process and identified the institutional interventions that contribute the most for each phase. Wong (1998) developed an integrated value chain framework to analyze the structure and growth dynamics of Singapore's information economy. This research identified four generic chronological stages in the development path of Singapore's information economy and suggested a staged, leveraged, learning strategy in making IT industry development policies.

Trauth (2000) developed a framework of environmental influences and impacts in her investigation of the development of an information economy in Ireland. The factors include: culture, economy, policy and infrastructure. Subsequent research has applied this model to the diffusion of electronic data interchange in The Netherlands (Trauth et al., 1993), exogenous and endogenous factors influencing the evolution of the software industry in Ireland (Heavin et al., 2003), and socio-cultural factors influencing the development of a sustainable knowledge economy in central California (Yeo and Trauth 2004; Yeo 2004).

Institutional Frameworks

Another framework that has been often used in public ICT policy research is King et al.'s (1994) framework of institutional actions and IT diffusion. The framework was constructed on two dimensions of potential institutional action: (1) influence and regulation that institutions might exert and (2) "supply-push" and "demand-pull" forces that drive those actions. Linking the two dimensions, this framework provides a schema of possible institutional actions that can stimulate or hinder IT diffusion. The authors then identified six general kinds of institutional actions (knowledge building, knowledge deployment, subsidy, mobilization, standard setting, and innovation directive), which can be mapped into four cells of this two-dimensional framework.

Using King et al.'s (1994) framework, Silva and Figueroa (2002) examined the institutional interventions that influenced the adoption of ICTs in Chile. The institutional perspective of the framework bridges the gap between the conception of development and policies for the diffusion of ICT. Drawing on the framework, the authors theorized why some national ICT policies achieve their goals while some others may not. They concluded that national ICT diffusion policies should be grounded on an understanding of the forces that forge society, in order to increase the likelihood of introducing sustainable social changes. Papazafeiropoulou (2004) employed King et al.'s (1994) framework to examine how the government and policy makers in eight South Eastern European countries used certain policy measures to diffuse electronic commerce. Raman (1996) analyzed the Malaysia government's actions relating to IT during the period 1980-1988 and mapped these actions to King et al.'s (1994) framework.

Intellectual Capital Model

Edvinsson and Malone's (1997) model of intellectual capital has shed some light on research related to public ICT policy making, more specifically, national information resource management policy making. Due to the increasing emphasis on aligning national information resource planning, design and implementation with growth and the performance needs of nations, better understanding of new valuation and assessment techniques is necessary for information resource management policymakers (Malhotra 2000). Malhotra (2000) applied the model of intellectual capital to develop the need for assessing knowledge capital at the national economic level, and evaluated case evidence to show how one popular method for assessment of national intellectual capital was used in Israel.

Specialized Models

Besides utilizing these generic models, some researchers also developed specialized and unique models of institutional influences and applied them to study public ICT policy issues (Checchi et al., 2003). For example, Nidumolu et al. (1996) derived three theoretical perspectives (functional, political/symbolic, and social information processing) from past research and employed these theoretical perspectives to explain IT adoption by Egypt local governorates. Based on their findings, the researchers identified three stages of the IT adoption project (implementation, evaluation, and transformation), and found the three theoretical perspectives have varying explanatory power across the adoption stages of the system.

Meso and Duncan (2000) utilize an information infrastructure index to measure national information infrastructure, and a national development index to measure social development. The results of their study show a clear correlation between levels of information infrastructure and social development, and between growth rates of information infrastructure and social development (Meso and Duncan 2000). Pook and Pence (2004) expanded this model by explicitly including technology and suggesting that both models can be used to study the interactions of national policy and social, economic, and technological factors. Based on their study of Visegrad-4 countries (the four Central European post-communist countries of the Czech Republic, the Republic of Hungary, the Republic of Poland, and the Slovak Republic), Pook and Pence (2004) suggested that public policy makers need to create a regulatory environment in these countries that will foster the growth of their respective information industries.

ADDITIONAL THEORIES FOR PUBLIC ICT POLICY RESEARCH

Although several theories or models have been used in empirical national ICT policy research, there is little theory development in this domain (Checchi et al., 2003). More specifically, most of the empirical research to date is either single-case studies that examine contingencies of policy formulation, implementation and consequences (Checchi et al., 2003) or surveys sans explicit theory bases. Despite their valuable contributions to the literature, the results from these studies are scattered and not easily accumulated to provide concrete guidance to various stakeholders of national ICT policy.

What are the possible theoretical bases for explaining the formulation and deployment of ICT policy? What different perspectives can stakeholders take to examine national ICT policy formulation and deployment? A brainstorming exercise that was held at the Forum on Advancing Theory on National IT Policy in Cairo in October of 2004 generated numerous candidate theories. These are discussed next.

Stakeholder Theory

Stakeholder theory was originally articulated by Freeman (1984). This theory argues that strategy formulation should consider and balance the conflicting claims of diverse stakeholders in order to be successful. Stakeholders are defined as those that "affect or are affected by the achievement of ...objectives" (Freeman, p. 46). Although stakeholder theory was originally developed for organizational context, Freeman (1984) implies that the concepts of stake and influence can also be applied to entire governments and to macro-institutional entities such as non-governmental organizations (NGOs).

Stakeholder theory is a relevant theory base to study the relationships between actors involved in formulating and executing public IT policies. Public policies, whether they focus on IT or not, convey a set of goals for a country or a region, and these policies are influenced by groups of stakeholders. Due to lack of resources, a nation's government cannot satisfy all of its stakeholders. Thus, the stakeholder theory base is clearly instrumental in solving key issues such as: Who are the appropriate stakeholders and to what extent do these stakeholders become involved in the stated goals

(Loch et al., 2005)? Knowledge of and consideration of those with a stake in the outcomes in the formulation and executive of policy should produce higher levels of success (Freeman 1984).

Governance Theory

Governance theory is another candidate theory to explain public IT policy making. The concept of governance goes beyond the halls of government, and is related with the concept of autonomous self-governing networks of institutions (Checchi et al., 2005). That is, governance recognizes that the capability to achieve objectives does not depend solely and simply on the power of the government's authority. Thus, governance involves a coalition of stakeholders from government, non-governmental organizations, and business working together to achieve mutually agreed goals (King et al., 1994; King and Kraemer 1995; Leftwich 1995; Kazancigil 1998; Stoker 1998).

As summarized in Checchi et al. (2003), researchers have realized that the role played by government in the development of public ICT capabilities varies from country to country. In less developed countries, government is usually the most active agent, and domestic profit organizations are typically less involved in the process. While in most of the least developed countries, regional or international agencies have played the most significant role in shaping IT infrastructure and capabilities. One way or the other, government is not the only influential institution who formulates national ICT policies. It is crucial to recognize what government can and cannot realistically do, and shift from government-directed to government-partnered coalition of stakeholders.

Transactional Cost Theory

Transaction cost theory (Williamson 1981; Williamson 1985) is concerned with the minimization of a cost function consisting of transaction costs and production costs. It also concerns the risk of opportunism arising from un-trusted parties involved in the relationship. Transaction cost theory has been found to be a useful conceptual lens through which to study many aspects of strategic alliances, including structure, continuity, and stability or survival (Young-Ybarra and Wiersma 1999). Information systems researchers have used this theory to study the impact of information systems on firms and markets (Gurbaxani and Whang 1991), interorganizational systems (Kumar et al., 1998), and suppliers' benefits of using supply chain management systems (Subramani 2004).

Although it has not been applied at the national or regional level to our knowledge, transaction cost theory could conceivably offer many insights to public ICT policy study. For example, transaction cost economists suggest utilizing economic constraints such as the investment in specific assets and hostage arrangements to reduce opportunism potential by locking partners into a strategic alliance (Williamson 1985). This could apply to the alliances established among the various stakeholders of public ICT policy as well. It could perhaps also apply to regional-level policies.

Institutional Theory

Institutional theory has increasingly been employed as a theoretical lens for examining the interaction between organizations and their environment. The theory entails a conceptualization of the environment focusing on the social and culture features of the environment, as opposed to the technical-rational perspective (Bada et al., 2004). According to DiMaggio and Powell (1983), institutional theory identifies three sources of pressure that drive organizational change: (1) mimetic pressure (the pressure to make an organization change to become more like other organizations in its environment), (2) coercive pressure (both formal and informal pressures exerted on an organization by other organizations upon which it depends and by the cultural expectations in the society), and (3) normative pressure (the pressure that stems mainly from professionalization). We believe that the concepts of mimetic pressure, coercive pressure and normative pressure identified by institutional theory are applicable to study national governments' reaction to the changing environment, in terms of the needs for ICT policies.

Colonial Theory

Colonial systems have been presented as an alternative to the mechanistic and organic systems paradigm to explain how human systems (such as organizations and social institutions) grow, evolve, and persevere (Porra 1999). A colonial system is defined as "a collection of individuals who share a history and an environment and who cooperate directly or indirectly for the maintenance of the colony" (Porra 1999, p. 56). Porra (1999) suggested that the colonial viewpoint supplements the mechanistic or organic systems because it attempts to explain how history, local refinement, and radical change are all required to operate in periods of both homeostasis (stability) and radical change. Porra (1999) further compared the differences between colonial systems with mechanistic and organic systems from ten axioms. Researchers may consider studying how involved stakeholders of public ICT policy react to environmental change from the perspective of colonial systems. For example, various stakeholders of a national ICT policy may be viewed as a colony. In the case when the policy's existence is threatened, who will choose to stay or leave the colony may be of great interest to researchers and practitioners.

SUMMARY

This chapter gives an overview of public ICT policy initiatives and deployment from several perspectives: stakeholders of public ICT policy; public environment under which public ICT policy is formulated and deployed; types, regulatory tools, and success factors of public ICT policy; and a few theories used in empirical public ICT policy studies. Motivated by the paucity of theory in the area of public ICT policy, this chapter also suggests several candidate theories that have potential application to this domain, based on a discussion at the Forum on Advancing Theory on National IT Policy. We hope these theories will help researchers cumulating results from future empirical research and provide concrete guidance to parties related with public ICT policy.

MINICASE

The Development of National Information and Communications Technology (ICT) Policy: The Experience in Egypt

Countries take different avenues in creating (and implementing) national IT policies, and Egypt is no exception to this general observation. A Georgia State University study team was funded by two US National Science Foundation grants to investigate this process[1] and to derive theoretical and practical observations about the manner in which policy-making occurs.

Historically, Egypt has been interested in the use of ICTs to advance social and economic goals. As described in Nidomolu et al. (1996) and Kamel (1995; 1997a; 1997b), the main impetus for change in this regard was a Cabinet-level agency known as the IDSC (Information and Decision Support Center). This agency developed systems that allowed governorates, the civil units that represented government at the local or provincial level, to plan and to report their progress to a central agency, i.e., the IDSC. Some of the planning systems that were put into place were geared to construction, the expansion of roads and public utilities, and the measurement of economic activity.

For well over a decade, the IDSC was a primary means by which the national government sponsored the governmental use of IT in Egypt. But further changes were in the making when the Internet became an international force for profound alterations of societies. At first, the entire Egyptian nation was served by a single 256K POP administered by the IDSC. When it became clear that the needs for widespread Internet diffusion were far outstripping the ability to service these needs with this thin a bandwidth, pressures for change mounted. By the late 90's, new forms of Internet access were being developed, including satellite uplinks and point-to-point dedicated lines to foreign hosts, and the centralized control of the bandwidth by IDSC was becoming a thing of the past.

Besides forces for change emerging from the desire to engage in e-commerce, there were other movements to launch ICTs boldly into the national life. Liberalization (aka privatization) of the telecommunications industry, for instance, was one of these emerging forces. The intent was to drive down the cost of bandwidth and exponentially expand the use of telecomm networks and the Internet. Internal and external pressure for protecting intellectual property, including copyright of software, was another such force. Near the end of the nineties, the government of Egypt determined that a new ministry to create and implement new ICT policies was required. The new ministry was formed as the Ministry of Communications and Information Technology (MCIT) and it was headed up by a Cairo University professor who was later appointed to the Prime Minister's position.

Besides the creation of this ministry, the government engaged in an ambitious program of policy and regulatory activities. Some policies, such as those that sponsored systems to catalogue and capture key information of the nation's cultural treasures, were extensions of existing programs in place. Others were wholly new.

A partial listing of the central policies rolled out by MCIT is shown in Table MC1. Government policies or efforts related to IT went beyond this set, to be sure, but these were the headliners for the overall initiative.

From the very inception, the new ministry decided to involve key stakeholders in the formulation and deployment of policies. Under the efforts to expand Egypt's human capital capacity, for example, MNCs like IBM, Microsoft and Ericcson were involved as partners in the venture. Trend-setting Egyptian firms such as ClickGSM and NileOnline were also consulted and had a major influence on the policies. In fact, MCIT officials often described their role as "catalysts" in the process rather than "funders," "leaders,"or "directors."

This is clearly a shift from government-directed change to government-partnered change, which, as Checchi et al. (2003) indicate, speaks of a maturing attitude toward what government can and cannot realistically do in developing countries. Where little to no ICT infrastructure exists, government and NGOs may have no choice but to lead (and fund) the entire build-up of ICT. Once ICT infrastructure is generally present, as was the case in Egypt by the late 1990's, the private sector and NGOs become a crucial part of the fabric of development.

Egypt today is looked upon by other countries in the Arab world, the Gulf region, and Sub-Saharan Africa as a model of success in ICT policy formulation and IT diffusion. The program in Egypt was very ambitious and, as funding in developing countries is chronic, it is not clear that there was enough funding to carry out this ambitious program on such a broad front. Nevertheless, even if all policies do not meet with equal success, there is a clear indication that the involvement of key stakeholders has galvanized support for government efforts (Meso et al. 2005). Given that the diffusion of IT is such a thorny issue in nearly all developing countries, the fact that Egypt has met with success in certain arenas is encouraging for all counties that are currently in this process.

Within Africa itself, for instance, Tanzania has just disseminated a draft set of policies for the nation and is at the beginning stages of implementing them. Kenya has made initial efforts in drafting policies, and after a suitable period for discussion and revamping, may also begin the process of deployment (Loch et al. 2005). The point is that both countries seem to view Egypt as a model for where they would like to be. This speaks highly of the perceptions of the developing world with respect to the role of national ICT policy in changing a nation's socio-economic development.

[1] This paper/material is based upon work supported by the National Science Foundation under grants DST-0082473 and INT-0322501. Any opinions, findings, and conclusions or recommendations expressed in this material are those of the author(s) and do not necessarily reflect the views of the National Science Foundation.

How should policy-making evolve? The experience in Egypt suggests that nations should capitalize on their inherent resources. The view in Egypt is that their young people are capable of learning the new technologies and energizing business and the public sector with their increased understanding. Hence a lot of investment in HR development was a critical hallmark of MCIT early initiatives. The effort had both a broad objective, to increase computer literacy, and a set of narrower objectives, such as the creation of systems network specialists. It is obvious that immediate utilization of these new pools of human capital is a challenge, and the nation may have to export these talents for a period to places of need within the region, but the parallel evolution of Egyptian infrastructure should eventually mean a more extensive market for these talents at home. Time will tell as to the success of the ICT policies in Egypt. What can be said is that this is certainly an auspicious start.

Discussion Questions

1. What would you surmise was the goal of the IDSC program for linking the governments in Egypt with the central government? Is this model exportable to other developing countries? Why or why not? Give examples from countries you are familiar with.
2. How does a country prioritize its national ICT policies?
3. What are the measures of success for a given ICT policy such as the 7 listed for Egypt? When these measures involve human judgment, who should be consulted to determine success?
4. Are there stages nations go through regarding the most effective ways to develop ICT policies?

Policy	Description
1. e-Government I: online forms	The Egyptian government is encouraging e-commerce initiatives within the government itself, in part to stimulate the movement of the entire private sector to e-commerce. One of the initiatives involves making government forms, such as tax and driver license forms, available to citizens on the Internet and the World Wide Web.
2. e-Government II: information sharing	The Egyptian government is computerizing the sharing of information between government agencies.
3. Smart Villages	The Egyptian government is granting tax-free status to IT and high-tech firms that locate their operations in incubator cities or villages, known as "Smart Villages." One of these villages will be located beyond the pyramids. High speed Internet connections and other high-tech capabilities will be built into these villages by the private sector.
4. Custom Duties	The Egyptian government reduced the tax on importation of computer hardware from 15% to 5% in 2000. This reduced the cost of a 2000LE PC to organizations, for example, by 200LE.
5. Intellectual Property	The Egyptian government is putting in place legislation to support e-commerce and a software industry within Egypt. Copyright laws as well as digital signature and digital certificate laws are part of this initiative.
6. Human Development Efforts	The Egyptian government is working with the private sector to greatly increase public computer and Internet literacy. Training programs underway articulated the goal of graduating 100,000 persons per year with heightened computer literacy, IT professionals and network engineers. A more computer literate workforce is a goal of the program.
7. Liberalization (privatization)	The Egyptian government is privatizing the telecommunications industry in Egypt. Begun over ten years ago, this government policy initiative will lead to government minority ownership of the industry within another few years. The formation of MobiNile, ClickGSM, and EgyNet are all part of this privatization initiative. Made up of private and public sector members, the Telecomm Regulatory Authority (TRA) was a body formed as part of the transition.

KEY TERMS

Economic Policies
Governance Policies
Information Communication Technology (ICT)/Information Technology (IT)
Information Flow Policies
Societal-human Equity Policies
Public ICT Policy
Public ICT Policy Stakeholder

STUDY QUESTIONS

1. Discuss the role of national ICT policy in developing a country's IT industry.

2. Discuss the influences placed by various stakeholders on national ICT policy development. Other than the ones identified in section three, are there other stakeholders that have influential impact on national ICT policy?

3. Discuss the insights offered by theories in section five. Do you think they are valuable for researchers and policy makers interested in national ICT policy?

4. Select a country and conduct research into its national ICT policy making, using one of the theories recommended in this chapter. How do your findings compare with findings in research that used other theories?

5. Select a national ICT policy in your country and conduct research to find how it is developed and implemented, who the stakeholders are and what influence they've placed, and which theory can best explain the policy implementation process.

REFERENCES

Ajzen, I. "From Intentions to Actions: A Theory of Planned Behavior," *Action Control: From Cognition to Behavior.* New York, Springer Verlag: , 1985, pp. 11-39.

Bada, A. O., M. C. Aniebonam and V. Owei. "Institutional Pressures as Sources of Improvisations: A Case Study from a Developing Country Context." *Journal of Global Information Technology Management* 7(3), pp. 2004, 27.

Brown, I., R. Hoppe, P. Mugera, P. Newman and A. Stander "The Impact of National Environment on the Adoption of Internet Banking: Comparing Singapore and South Africa." *Journal of Global Information Management* 12(2), 2004, pp. 1-26.

Checchi, R. M., J. P. Hsieh and D. W. Straub "Public IT Policies in Less Developed Countries: A Critical Assessment of the Literature and a Reference Framework." *Journal of Global Information Technology Management* 6(4). 2003, pp. 45-64.

Checchi, R. M., K. D. Loch, G. R. Sevcik and D. W. Straub. The Effectiveness of National ICT Policy: Extending Theory from Egypt to Other Developing Nations. Georgia State University working paper. 2005.

DiMaggio, P. and W. W. Powell " The Iron Cage Revisited: Institutional Isomorphism and Collective Rationality in Organizational Fields." *American Sociological Review* 48(2), 1983, pp. 147-160.

Edvinsson, L. and M. S. Malone *Intellectual Capital: Realizing Your Company's True Value by Finding Its Hidden Brainpower*. New York, HarperCollins Publishers, Inc. 1997.

Freeman, R. E. *Strategic Management: A Stakeholder Approach*. Boston, MA, Harper-Collins. 1984.

Gurbaxani, V. and S. Whang "The Impact of Information Systems on Organizations and Markets." *Communications of the ACM,* 34(1), 1991, pp. 59-73.

Hassan, S. Z. "A Framework for IT Industry Development: A Case Study of Pakstan." *Journal of Global Information Technology Management,* 1(4), 1998, pp. 38-55.

Heavin, C., B. Fitzgerald and E. M. Trauth Factors Influencing Ireland's Software Industry: Lessons for Economic Development through IT. *Information Systems Perspectives and Challenges in the Context of Globalization.* M. Korpela and R. Montealeagre. Boston, Kluwer Academic Publishers, pp. 235-252, 2003.

Jennex, M. E. and D. L. Amoroso "E-Business and Technology Issues for Developing Economics: A Ukraine Case Study." *Electronic Journal on Information Systems in Developing Countries,* 10(5), 2002, pp. 1-14.

Kazancigil, A. "Governance and Science: Market-like Modes of Managing Society and Producing Knowledge." *International Social Science Journal,* 155, 1998, pp. 69-79.

King, J. L., V. Gurbaxani, K. L. Kraemer, W. F. McFarlan, K. S. Raman and C. S. Yap "Institutional Factors in Information Technology Innovation." *Information Systems Research,* 5(2, June): 1994, pp. 139-169.

King, J. L. and K. L. Kraemer "Information Infrastructure, National Policy, and Global Competitiveness." *Information Infrastructure and Policy,* March 1995.

Kraemer, K. L. and J. Dedrick "Payoffs from Investment in Information Technology: Lessons from the Asia-Pacific Region." *World Development,* 22(12), December, 1994, pp. 1921-1931.

Kumar, K., H. G. Van Dissel and P. Bielli "The Merchant of Prato--Revisited: Toward a Third Rationality of Information Systems." *MIS Quarterly* 22(2), 1998, pp. 199-226.

Leftwich, A. "Bringing Politics Back In: Towards a Model of the Developmental State." *Journal of Development Studies* 31, 1995, pp. 400- 427.

Lessig, L. "The New Chicago School." *Journal of Legal Studies,* 27, pp. 661-666. 1998.

Lessig, L. "The law of the horse: What cyberlaw might teach." Harvard Law Review, 133(12), pp. 501-546. 1999.

Loch, K., G. Sevcik, P. Meso and D. Straub *Stages of ICT Development and IT Transfer: A Stakeholder Theory Approach.* Georgia State University working paper, NSF proposal submitted in May, 2005.

Malhotra, Y. "Knowledge Assets in the Global Economy: Assessment of National Intellectual Capital." *Journal of Global Information Management,* 8(3), 2000, pp. 5-15.

Mbarika, V. W., P. F. Musa, T. A. Byrd and P. McMullen "Teledensity Growth Constraints and Strategies for African's LDDs: 'Viagra' Prescriptions or Sustainable Development Strategy?" *Journal of Global Information Technology Managemen,t* 5(1), 2002, pp. 25-42.

Meso, P. and N. Duncan "Can National Information Infrastructure enhance social development in the Least Developed Countries? An empirical investigation." *Journal of Global Information Management,* 8(4), 2000, pp. 30-42.

Montealegre "A temporal model of institutional interventions for information technology adoption in less-developed countries." *Journal of Management Information System,s* 16(1), 1999, pp. 207-232.

Nidumolu, S. R., S. E. Goodman, D. R. Vogel and A. K. Danowitz. "Information Technology for Local Administration Support: The Governorates Project in Egypt." *MIS Quarterly,* 20(2), 1996, pp. 197-224.

Papazafeiropoulou, A. "Inter-Country Analysis of Electronic Commerce Adoption in South Eastern Europe: Policy Recommendations for the Region." *Journal of Global Information Technology Management,* 7(2) 2004, pp. 54-69.

Pook, L. A. and N. E. Pence. "Evaluation of Information Infrastructures and Social Development Among the Visegrad-Four Countries of Central Europe." *Journal of Global Information Management,* 12(2), 2004, pp. 63-83.

Porra, J. "Colonial Systems." *Information Systems Research,* 10(1), pp. 38-68. 1999.

Raman, K. S. and C. S. Yap "From a Resource Rich Country to an Information Rich Society: An Evaluation of Information Technology Policies in Malaysia." *Information Technology for Developmen,* 7(3), 1996, pp. 109-131.

Rogers, E. M. <u>Diffusion of Innovation</u>. New York, New York, USA, Free Press. 1983.

Silva, L. and E. Figueroa "Institutional intervention and the expansion of ICTs in Latin America: The Case of Chile." *Information Technology & People,* 15(1). 2002, pp. 8-25.

Stoker, G. "Governance as Theory: Five Propositions." *International Social Science Journal,* 155, 1998, pp. 17-27.

Subramani, M. "How do Suppliers Benefit from Information Technology Use in Supply Chain Relationships?" *MIS Quarterly,* 28(1), 2004, pp. 45-73.

Tallon, P. P. and K. L. Kraemer "Information Technology and Economic Development: Ireland's Coming of Age with Lessons for Developing Countries." *Journal of Global Information Technology Management,* 3(2), 2000, pp. 4-23.

Trauth, E. M. "Educating Information Technology Professionals for Work in Ireland: An Emerging Post-industrial Country," *Global Information Technology Education: Issues and Trends.* M. Khosrowpour and K. Loch. Harrisburg, PA, Idea Group Publishing: pp. 205-233. 1993.

Trauth, E. M. "Impact of an Imported IT Sector: Lessons from Ireland," *Information Technology Development and Policy: Theoretical Perspectives and Practical Challenges.* E. M. Roche and M. J. Blaine. Aldershot, UK, Avebury Publishing Ltd.: pp. 245-261. 1996.

Trauth, E. M. "Leapfrogging an IT Labor Force: Multinational and Indigenous Perspectives." *Journal of Global Information Management,* 7(2), 1999, pp. 22-32.

Trauth, E. M. *The Culture of an Information Economy: Influences and Impacts in the Republic of Ireland.* Dordrecht, The Netherlands, Kluwer Academic Publishers. 2000.

Trauth, E. M. "Mapping Information-sector Work to the Workforce: The Lessons from Ireland." *Communications of the ACM,* 44(7), 2001, pp. 74-75.

Trauth, E. M., F. E. Derksen and H. M. Mevissen "The Influence of Societal Factors on the Diffusion of Electronic Data Interchange in the Netherlands," *Information Systems Development: Human, Social and Organizational Aspects.* D. Avison, J. Kendall and J. I. DeGross. Amsterdam: North-Holland, pp. 323-337. 1993.

Williamson, O. E. "The Economics of Organization: The Transaction Cost Approach." *American Journal of Sociology,* 87(2), 1981, pp. 233-261.

Williamson, O. E. <u>The Economic Institutions of Capitalism: Firms, Markets, Relational Contracting</u>. New York, The Free Press. 1985.

Wong, P. "Leveraging the Global Information Revolution for Economic Development: Singapore's Evolving Information Industry Strategy." *Information Systems Research,* 9(4), 1998, pp. 1047-7047.

Yeo, B. and E. M. Trauth E-business Potential in California's San Joaquin Valley: An Investigation of Societal Influences. *IFIP WG8.4 Working Conference on E-business.* S. Elliot, K. V. Andersen, E. M. Trauth and S. Reich. Laxenburg, Austria, Trauner Druck. 2004.

Yeo, B. T., E.M. and Wong, P. "Infrastructural Challenges in Developing an Information Economy in Humbolt County, California," *Americas Conference on Information Systems,* New York. 2004.

Young-Ybarra, C. and M. Wiersma "Strategic flexibility in information technology alliances: The influence of transaction cost economics and social exchange theory." *Organization Science,* 10(4), 1999, pp. 439.

 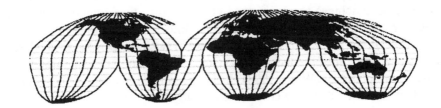

Global Information Technology Architecture: Foundations and Organizational Issues

Prashant Palvia
Naveed Baqir
The University of North Carolina at Greensboro, USA

Sharm Manwani
Henley Management College, UK

CHAPTER SUMMARY

A carefully designed global IT architecture is an important organizational enabler for the successful implementation of the business and IT strategy of a multinational corporation. Essentially, an information technology architecture is the design of the various IT elements that work together to achieve organizational goals. Included among these elements are hardware and software, databases, telecommunications, IT standards, and the IT organization. A model for global IT architecture is presented in this chapter focusing on two key processes of integration: control and coordination. Many business factors are examined which impact the architecture. These include: Multinational Corporation (MNC) strategy and structure, strategic disposition, organizational culture and personnel practices. Also described are key steps in IT architecture planning and the role of business strategy and IT strategy in such planning.

A key component of the IT architecture is the IT organizational structure itself. Various management roles are involved in the creation and evolution of the IT organization. These roles range from corporate, business unit, to group services. Among broad choices for IT organizational structure are single corporate department, decentralized IT units, and federal structures. Depending on the management style and MNC structural form, specific roles will be determined in the formation of the IT organizational structure. Two detailed case studies of large MNCs provide further insights into these issues.

INTRODUCTION

A global information technology (IT) architecture provides a vision for how a multinational firm will select and deploy its many corporate IT resources. The global IT architecture is the overall framework and design that acts as a guide in satisfying business needs via a blueprint of computing, data, communications, and applications (Earl, 1989). Once the vision is established, then various approaches are used to achieve the envisioned global architecture, including policies, standards, and funding allocations. Specifically, the enterprise IT architecture has both logical and physical elements (Sandoe et al., 2001). The architecture generates a set of business-driven IT standards as a policy tool for the effective application of the technology (Cook, 1996), and is an important element in creating the IT infrastructure platform (Weill, 1993). In fact, senior IT managers have consistently regarded the creation of an IT architecture as a critical issue in IS management (Luftman and McLean, 2004).

Creating and implementing a global IT architecture is challenging in a multinational corporation because of the inherent complexities present in a vast global organization. If misaligned, the existing IT infrastructure can represent a significant barrier to implementing international business strategies (Daniels and Daniels, 1993). There are many issues related to the development and implementation of a global IT architecture in a firm, which are discussed in this chapter. The chapter begins with a definition of the IT architecture and an introduction to its various elements. The IT architecture's role in meeting the control and coordination needs among the IT resources deployed by the firm is discussed. The links between corporate business strategy, IT strategy and IT architecture are explored. A major part of the chapter is devoted to management and organizational factors that affect the choice of IT architecture. Several propositions based on different management styles and their impacts on IT architecture are offered. Two case studies and their analysis are presented to evaluate the propositions.

WHAT IS AN INFORMATION TECHNOLOGY ARCHITECTURE?

An information technology architecture is the design of various IT elements (e.g., network topology, servers, software, users, internet, intranet, extranet, IT management structure, and IT organization, but not limited to these elements alone) that work together to achieve organizational goals. The scope of the architecture may even extend beyond to customers and suppliers as seen in Figure 1. The basic purpose of an IT architecture is to develop, realize, sustain, and use these IT elements and services to achieve organizational operations. The IT architecture addresses issues such as the streamlining of business activities, processes, data sets, information flows, applications, software, and technology. While it is easy and tempting to restrict the architecture to simply hardware and software issues, broader issues must be considered for the effective utilization of it even in the case of simple and small organizations.

While the architecture refers to the design of IT elements, the IT infrastructure represents the current state of IT resources in the firm, and may or may not reflect the realization of the design. The infrastructure includes such components as computers, telecommunication networks, databases, operating systems, systems software, and business applications. In practice, the two terms are often used interchangeably, although we will make the distinction wherever possible.

The existence of an IT architecture even with the description of specific goals does not necessarily mean that an organization will be able to immediately update its systems and applications, and achieve efficiency and effectiveness in the use of its IT resources. An important aspect of the architecture plan is to guide the future development of the IT infrastructure gradually and steadily leading to improved efficiency and effectiveness. In today's increasingly complex global world, organizations simply cannot afford to ignore the development of a sound IT architecture and its continuous refinement. In multinational MNCs whose partners, suppliers and customers are spread all around the world, the difference between exploiting the true potential of IT infrastructure and ignoring it could mean thriving business or challenges to their very existence.

A MODEL FOR GLOBAL IT ARCHITECTURE

As the purpose of the IT architecture is to integrate the various IT resources in the firm, it is instructive to examine two key processes of integration: control and coordination. Briefly, control is a process which brings adherence to goal or target through the exercise of power or authority. While control is a more direct intervention, coordination is seen as an "enabling process" which allows for linkages between sub-units in the accomplishment of tasks, resulting from smooth flow of information. While important concepts in their own right, to some extent control and coordination can work as substitutes for one another in their role of providing integration among the subsidiaries of an MNC.

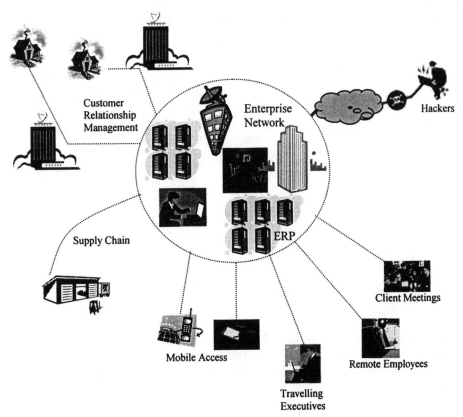

Figure 1. Scope of IT Architecture

Steve Simon (1996) used the concepts of control and coordination as the driving mechanism for designing the global IT architecture. He proposed a framework for examining the alignment of a multinational corporation's structure and strategy, and other practices with its information infrastructure. This framework focuses on the processes of coordination and control, and discusses the impact of coordination and control strategies on IT infrastructure. Figure 2 depicts the information architecture model proposed by Steve Simon. It shows the relationship between business driven IT factors, control and coordination needs, and the organization's information architecture. The business factors such as corporate structure, strategic predisposition of the firm, organizational culture and personnel practices act as the independent variables in the model affecting the control and coordination needs. The information architecture defined by the computer location, database structure, telecommunication, and IT organization structure and technology standard acts as the dependent variables affected by coordination and control needs.

Control is achieved through centralization, formalization, output and behavior control, performance tracking systems, standardization, and reporting systems. Coordination on the other hand is achieved by decentralization, departmentalization, planning systems, lateral and cross-departmental relations, informal communication and socialization. There is, however, a need to trade off between control and coordination in the case of MNCs due to their very nature. MNCs working in different geographical locations have to operate under the local laws, regulations, economic circumstances, political situations, social customs and cultural conditions in order to achieve the goals and targets shared by other units in various parts of the world. In addition, an MNC has to operate with people with different value systems, competencies, varying national market structure, population and geography (Burn and Cheung, 1996). These factors impact the control and coordination structure of an MNC differently from an organization operating in only one geographic location or country. Since an MNC is by definition an organization operating in geographically dispersed environment to achieve a common goal, development of an IT architecture that caters to the control and coordination needs becomes essential.

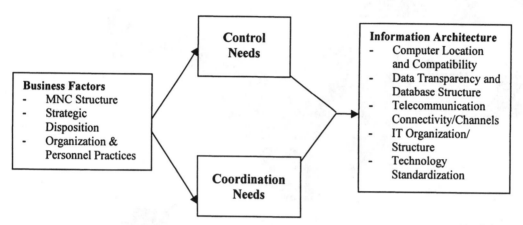

Figure 2. Simon's (1996) Information Architecture Model

According to Simon's model, control and coordination mediate the impact of business factors on the IT architecture. Whether via mediation or otherwise, the point is that ultimately business factors should influence the design of the IT architecture. Among the business factors included in the model are:

MNC Structure: A number of topologies have been proposed to classify overall organizational structure of a multinational. The most widely recognized topology is based on the global/transnational framework developed by Bartlett and Ghoshal (1998). According to this classification, there are four structures. In the *Global* structure, the organization is driven by global efficiency while having structures that are centralized in their strategic and operational decisions. In the *International* structure, emphasis is placed on transferring and adapting the parent company's knowledge or expertise to the foreign subsidiaries. In the *Multinational* structure, sensitivity and responsiveness to different organizational environments is achieved by decentralization and giving independence to the subsidiaries. Finally, in the *Transnational* firm, the organization seeks a balance between the pressures of global integration and local responsiveness by having both centralization and decentralization.

Strategic Predisposition: Four distinct predispositions based on Heenan and Perlmutter (1979) are offered. In *Ethnocentrism*, all strategic decisions are guided by the values and interests of the parent. In *Polycentrism*, strategic decisions are tailored to suit the cultures of the various countries in which the MNC operates. *Regiocentrism* tries to blend the interests of both the parent and the subsidiaries at least on a regional basis. *Geocentrism* attempts to integrate the diverse subsidiaries through a global systems approach.

Organizational Culture and Personnel Practices: Four organizational cultures are described (Simon 1996). In the *Home Country Culture*, the mindset would most likely develop home country nationals for positions everywhere in the world and apply home standards for evaluation. In the *Host Country Culture*, people of local nationality would be developed for key positions in their own country with local standards for evaluation. The *Regional Culture* performs the same way as the host country but uses regional standards in place of host country standards. Finally, the *Global Culture* seeks to promote the best people everywhere in the world and the standards for evaluation are usually universal but weighted to suit local conditions.

According to Simon's model, the information architecture itself is composed of the following elements:

Computer Location and Compatibility: Various options exist for the location of the MNC's data centers ranging from centralization at one location, decentralization at the subsidiaries, regional data centers, to highly integrated networks. With various standards and vendors, the issues of compatibility of the hardware, software, data, and information exchange are of concern to many IT managers. Given the advent of the open source software (Meyers and Oberndorf 2001), some firms are moving in that direction and others are at least evaluating their options.

Data Transparency and Database Structure: The structure of the database and the type of database management system have the power to link dispersed parts of the organization while providing information in varying degrees to corporate subunits. The options for the structure of the database management system are many and include: centralized databases, decentralized databases, subsidiary databases linked to the central database, and highly integrated databases.

Telecommunication/Connectivity Channels: Given the environment of high uncertainty in multiple markets and increasing interdependencies, MNCs are likely to have multiple telecommunication channels with high bandwidth capable of handling massive amounts of data. Numerous options exist for the configuration and topology of the channels, their bandwidths, media characteristics, intra and inter organizational networks, use of private and public networks, and the types of data to be transmitted (e.g., numeric and textual data, audio, image, and video). As an illustration, just for bandwidth, there are a whole variety of alternatives among narrow, medium, and high bandwidth channels, which range from T1 to T4 lines and utilize frame relay and ATM technologies.

Technology Standardization: Technology standards can significantly affect the interconnectability of an organization's information system. The degree of standardization will be driven by the desired level of exchange of data or knowledge among the headquarters and the subsidiaries. The choices are not simple as many of the standards and systems are proprietary. While the organizational commitment to one set of proprietary systems facilitates the exchange of data and information, it can be expensive and can also limit the organization's ability to innovate and add flexibility to its operations. On the other hand, in recent years open source software (OSS) has significantly matured. Open Source Software is software for which the underlying programming code is available to the users so that they may read it, make changes to it, and build new versions of the software incorporating their changes (Meyers and Oberndorf 2001). Many firms are beginning to consider the use of OSS in their development efforts.

IT Organization/Structure: Strategic alignment of a firm's IT organization and its business strategy is of critical concern for both domestic and multinational firms. Senior managers have consistently ranked it as a key issue in IS management (Luftman and McLean 2004; Luftman et al., 2006). A single model does not work for every multinational firm. Several topologies exist for the organizational structure of an MNC, including the one by Karimi and Konsynski (1991). Their topology categorizes IT structures into the following four types: centralized federation, decentralized federation, coordinated federation, and integrated network. Many nuances exist and will be the subject of a later section.

BUSINESS STRATEGY, IT STRATEGY AND IT ARCHITECTURE

While the IT architecture of a global organization is driven by its IT strategy, the IT strategy itself is determined by the business strategy, industry trends and the strengths and weaknesses of the IT function in the MNC (Valanju and Jain 2002). Additionally, IT strategy has to respond to business partners' business and IT strategies, which lead to various IT initiatives. These initiatives determine the need for and funding of various IT infrastructure projects (e.g., the global communication network, applications development, etc). Valunju and Jain depicted relationships between IT strategy, its drivers, influencers, determinants and outcomes, as shown in Figure 3.

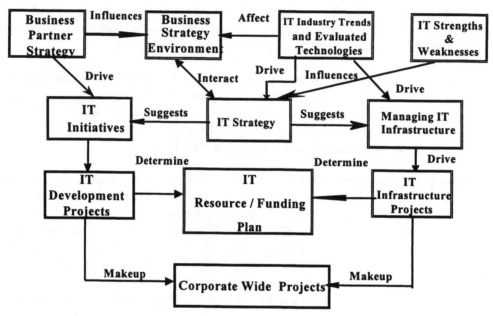

Figure 3. Valanju and Jain's (2002) Context Diagram for IT Infrastructure

As seen in Figure 3, business strategy of an MNC is directly influenced by its business partners' strategies. Even though IT strategy dictates IT initiatives and infrastructure management, business partners' strategies are important drivers that help prioritize IT initiatives. Another influential factor in determining the business strategy and IT strategy in today's environment is IT industry trends and new technological capabilities that become available in the marketplace. Based on the IT strategy and projects that are identified thereby, an IT resource and funding plan is established. The plan leads to the approval of various corporate wide development and infrastructure projects.

Valanju and Jain (2002) also described a process and framework for the ongoing managing of IT infrastructure as shown in Figure 4. This model can be used for making a compelling case to achieve strong management commitment for financial funding and resource investment in order to stay competitive and build business value for the global organization. IT infrastructure vision must be based upon the sound understanding of business environment for the MNC including geographic mapping of business locations, business linkages across the supply chain and major application systems requirements to support the business with other partners. The vision must include feasibility analysis and a consideration of conceptual and logical design elements. Once the IT strategy is developed and IT infrastructure vision is formed, the architectural planning phase begins. This phase involves the creation of an organization structure consisting of internal experts and consultants to facilitate the development of a detailed architectural plan. Technology evaluation, technology selection, vendor selection and cost allocation to units are parts of this phase. Acceptable performance levels are developed using performance simulations and service level agreements. More details about the architecture planning stage are described in the next section. The deployment phase covers issues such as global rollout, managing the acceptance curve and standards enforcements. Once the global IT architecture is in place, it is necessary to provide resources and funding for the on-going maintenance of this architecture including future iterations aimed at reactive and proactive enhancements to the architecture.

IT Architecture Planning

After obtaining management commitment for the infrastructure vision, the formal planning for the IT architecture begins. As described by Valunju and Jain, the entire IT architecture can be divided into logical components such the network topology, servers, desktops/laptops, software, internet, intranet, extranet and the IT management organization. The architecture should be designed with the goal of streamlining business activities, processes, data sets, information flows, applications, software, and technology. At the same time, it should address important issues such as the need for future growth and expansion, and the need for requisite levels of security and defense against malicious attacks from hackers and viruses. The architecture planning involves project planning, technology evaluation and selection, vendor selection, performance monitoring, and budgeting decisions. At the outset, a planning team consisting of representatives from each division in the geographical regions should be formed. Prioritization of various logical components and segments shown in Figure 1 is critical.

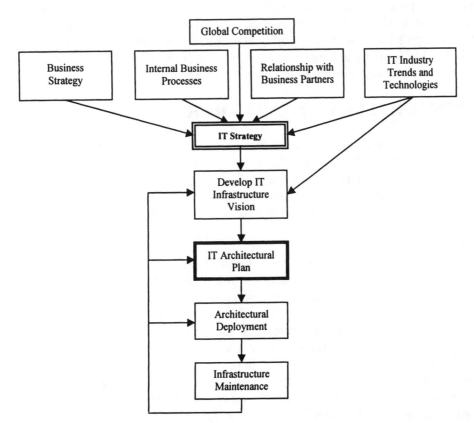

Figure 4. Framework for Managing IT Infrastructure (Adapted from Valanju and Jain 2002)

For technology evaluation and selection, technologies from different parts of the world and trends need to be evaluated. Information needs to be gathered from top IT vendors, research organizations (such as Gartner Group, Forrester Research, and Meta Group) and consulting firms. A careful and structured process should be laid out for evaluating the technologies. The vendor selection process can be fairly involved and complex. There is no single vendor that can meet all the needs of a large MNC. Even for individual segments of the infrastructure, such as a wide area network, there are no global providers. Reliance on multiple vendors including vendor alliances and use of intermediaries may be necessary for effective sourcing decisions.

Key considerations in vendor selection include performance evaluation and service level agreements. Performance evaluation provides the ability to predict performance of the IT infrastructure by creating several "what if" scenarios of expected workload in a controlled/lab environment. Either live testing or simulations can be conducted to evaluate performance. Typically, changes in the infrastructure are recommended based on the results of the evaluation.

Performance evaluation serves as the basis for developing service level agreements. Service level agreements (SLAs) are critical in establishing contractual linkage between the MNC's expectation of infrastructure performance and the vendors' commitments. SLAs typically include such areas as up-time availability, service coverage (such as 24x7), response time, problem resolution time, pro-active monitoring, and management reporting of important performance statistics.

Since the IT architecture is a critical corporate-wide initiative, budgeting, funding, and top management support are critical to its successful deployment. Appropriate levels of funding should be allocated with contingency plans to cover any overruns. Given the multi-year nature of the implementation plan, it is absolutely necessary that top-level executives act as champions for the project and provide the necessary resources in times of hardship. Preferably, the whole initiative should be treated as one program (with sub-allocations as necessary). Such an approach allows more leverage in dealing with vendors for volume discounts. Several approaches exist for infrastructure funding. One approach puts the entire responsibility and funding with the corporate headquarters. In another approach, the headquarters assumes responsibility for the backbone and common elements, while the other parts are divided up among the individual business units.

MANAGEMENT CHALLENGES IN IT ARCHITECTURE PLANNING

An important influence on global IT architecture planning is the form of the IT function or the IT organization itself. The structure of IT organization varies considerably in global organizations and as well as by organizational levels. The roles of the IT function at various levels of the organization change depending on its structure. This section first looks at possible structures in diversified domestic firms and then examines IT department structures in multinationals.

IT Roles in Diversified Domestic Firms

The Corporate and Business Unit roles vary under different IT organizational forms as noted by Earl, Edwards, and Feeny (1996). Specifically, three levels of roles are defined: the corporate/headquarters level, the business unit level, and the group level. The group level is an interesting phenomenon in which various business units combine and share their capabilities to achieve efficiency and effectiveness in the usage of their combined resources. Earl et al.'s list of IT structures provides a useful classification and is shown in Table 1. It moves top-down from centralized to decentralized functions. They also remark on the increasing prevalence of the federal structure that combines a centralized corporate department with IT-competent sub-units. Their research concluded that the bureau would not remain a dominant structure although it could become one of the sources of supply in a federal IS structure, by operating as an IT Services Group. This differentiation is shown in Table 1 with the two middle rows representing examples of federal structures and a column representing the group role. Note that the roles of the corporate level, the group level, and the business unit level are different in the four IT structures. In this table, the group role is effectively a separate entity that provides shared services and consolidates IT operations such as the data center, hardware, software, telecommunications, web, and email services.

Multinational IT Structures

The distinction between the corporate policy and group IT services roles is supported by various research studies. While the centralized and decentralized models respond to the needs of control and coordination respectively, the group model seems to take the middle ground on both control and coordination. In large multinationals, such as IBM and Shell, a degree of granularity applies primarily due to the dimensions of distance and geography. An MNC has business units that may or may not be located in the home nation, as well as local area units that service a specific geographic area and may report to a regional area unit for coordination (Lehrer and Asakawa 1995). In a decentralized or federal IT structure, there will be IT departments in the business units, the local area units and the regional units. MNCs assign some IT management functions to IT departments in different subunits, which implies that there is a challenge to align conflicting goals.

Brown and Magill (1994) classified IT structures in six large companies as centralized, decentralized, and shared, and found a wide variation in their IT structures. This supports a contingency approach in defining the IT organization. Jarvenpaa and Ives (1992) also found evidence to support a contingency view when they were able to map IT department structures to organizational forms. Four IT configurations were matched to the different MNC strategies (Table 2). However, they found less than expected fit between the IT configurations and business structure of MNCs (about 56 percent). There are additional contingency factors, for example senior management support, subsidiary resistance and prevailing national IT infrastructure, which could influence the direction and pace of change of the IT configuration.

A framework needs to be developed to help design the detailed IT architecture so that it matches with the organizational form and the overall IT configuration. Managers need to align IT approaches based on the type of "global" strategy adopted since the IT architecture chosen will have major implications for the IT organizational form. Table 3 shows some basic elements of this

Structure	Corporate Role	Group Role	Business Unit Role
Single corporate department	Sets policies and standards - manages total IT function	Not separate – included in Corporate role	Minor role as link between Corporate IT and Business Unit
Internal bureau separate from Corporate department	Sets policies and standards for business units and service bureau	Unified Service bureau acting as IT service provider to all internal business units	IT Buyers who have competence to specify needs and 'buy' from internal bureau
Externally competing IT Service provider	Sets policies and standards for business units – advises head office on Service business venture	Unified service company acting as IT service provider to internal business units and competes externally	IT Buyers who have competence to specify needs and make external purchase vs. in-house decisions
Decentralized IT operations in Business Units	Small or non-existent Corporate Unit focused mainly on identifying total IT costs and providing a service to head office	No central bureau	IT Manager competence in all IT functions including strategy, development, and operations

Table 1. IT Organizational Forms (Adapted from Earl, Edwards, and Feeny 1996)

Strategic Orientation	Business Structure/Strategy	IT Configuration
Responsiveness	Multinational	Independent operations
Efficiency	Global	Headquarters-driven
Transfer of Knowledge	International	Intellectual synergy
All of the above	Transnational	Integrated IT

Table 2. Business Structure and IT Configurations (Adapted from Jarvenpaa and Ives 1992)

	Multinational	*Global*	*Transnational*
Technology	Local facilities at HQ and subsidiaries	Central shared facilities	Interdependent facilities at HQ and subsidiary
Databases and Processes	Decentralized, low level of integration	Large centralized databases	Distributed/shared databases
Telecommunications	Direct HQ – subsidiary links	Multiple networks between HQ and subsidiary	Global networks for Enterprise-wide connectivity
IT Management	Local, minimum HQ influence	Centrally managed	Shared responsibility and team orientation

Table 3. MNC Organizational Forms and IT Architecture

alignment (Alavi and Young 1992). This table does not include the international strategy, which can be viewed as an intermediate step between the multinational and transnational strategies, and so its architecture will have elements of both.

Towards An Integrated Framework for IT Management Roles
The simple MNC form has a corporate head office and operating business units where the former drives the strategy and policy, and the latter implements IT applications and services. Large firms typically create a senior level of hierarchy that coordinates the activities of several lower level subunits. The coordinating body for business units is called a business sector while the coordinating body for several local geographical units is called a regional area.

What factors determine the degree of influence held by the different coordinating bodies? Table 4 summarizes the influences on sub IT units within a multinational based on the management style and organizational form. Three management styles are shown: strategic planning, strategic control, and financial control. The table shows that a global MNC with a strong strategic planning style is much more likely to have an influential corporate IT unit than a multi-domestic MNC with a financial control style. There is an implication here that the management style will match the MNC organizational form, although there may be non-aligned transition states when a new executive team is appointed.

The above discussion leads us to an integrated framework of IT management roles. Figure 5 includes the above management style and organizational form drivers that determine which are the most influential of the three business-linked IT roles: corporate, sector, business unit. It also shows how the fourth IT role of Group IT can support each of the core roles as a service provider assuming that it has the requisite capabilities. Corporate IT will have a stronger chance of implementing its *standards* if the Group IT service bureau supports it with the *controls* in these areas. The often newly formed Sector or Region will be looking for the right *competencies* from Group IT in delivering on its *strategy* role across business IT subunits. At the business unit level, the core relationship is that Group IT provides agreed *services* at minimum *cost*.

Management Style	MNC Organizational Form	Major IT Influence
Strategic Planning	Global	Corporate
Strategic Control	Transnational	Sector and/or Region
Financial Control	Mult-domestic	Business Unit

Table 4. MNC Organizational Forms and IT Architecture (Derived: Goold and Campbell (1986), Ramarapu and Lado (1995))

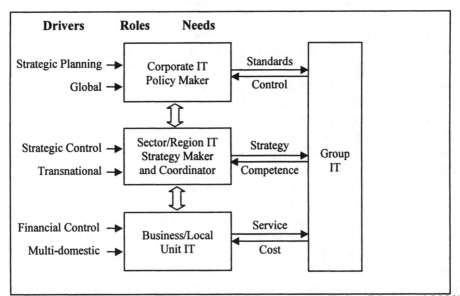

Figure 5. Integrated Framework of IT Management Roles (Manwani 2002)

In federal structures discussed earlier, it is more likely that no one unit will continue to have a dominant influence over time. Hence an understanding of the different roles and the potential for conflict is essential to maximize the chances of a successful IT architecture.

In summary, from this framework and preceding discussion we can postulate that:

Proposition I: There are multiple IT stakeholders with different roles in the global IT architecture development.

Proposition II: The IT stakeholder influence varies depending on the corporate style and MNC organizational form.

Proposition III: Conflict between the IT subunits will arise from multiple stakeholders with different roles.

The validity of these propositions is evaluated by conducting two case studies. Several findings and implications are drawn from these cases.

THE CASE STUDIES

The integrated framework is evaluated using case studies in two leading multi-national multi-business companies: Household AB and Food&Drinks PLC, both operating in the consumer product sector (Manwani 2002). This approach allowed for qualitative data collection and an insightful examination of the facts. There is an inherent flexibility in the case research method where data collection times and methods can be varied as the study proceeds (Miles and Huberman, 1994). The selection of these companies is justified by the impact on their global IT architecture resulting from significant business and IT changes. During the 1990s, Food&Drinks-Europe made a number of IT investments to support new business and systems structures resulting from acquisitions, mergers and divisional restructuring. Similarly Household Europe implemented new IT systems and created new IT structures during 1995-1999 due to business drivers such as mergers and restructuring. All the data were categorized by IT unit policies, investments, and compliance in order to evaluate the propositions.

Food&Drinks

Food&Drinks in the 1980s comprised ten relatively stand-alone companies. There was a strong emphasis on financial control in this period.

> "Food&Drinks is a very financially driven company...it's a very tough organization...anyone who did not achieve budget two years in a row would be out."
> Comments from Group Finance Director (reported Hodgkinson 1991 – A28/9)

At the same time, there was a strong focus on strategic opportunities across business sectors. This balance indicated and was confirmed using the Goold and Campbell's instrument that the corporate management style was Strategic Control. The following comment was made on the corporate IT function in the late 1980s/early 1990s.

> "It is apparent that the Group IS Director has no formal authority over the IS Directors – if they have a good business case for acting outside the policy guidelines then they may do so. As they have all agreed to the guidelines themselves... this seems not to be a common occurrence." Hodgkinson (1991: A-41)

Thus the IT function represented a federal structure which mirrored the firm's management style and organizational form. This finding supports the predicted relationship from Table 4.

In the mid 1990s, a new IT service operation was created to separate policymaking and service provision. The Group IT Services manager stressed that standards were defined for telecommunications and electronic mail to allow companies and people to communicate with each other, not just from head office to the operating companies. With the right standards, acquired companies could be quickly integrated into the organization by installing standard business systems. Cost was another driver for the IT policy in that there was an opportunity to negotiate hardware deals such as IBM AS400 purchasing agreements. However there was a sense that setting standards was more of an expectation than a demand since business units were allowed to choose another product if they could identify a reason for not following the standard.

By the mid 1990s it was clear that Food&Drinks was no longer a conglomerate; instead it had become highly focused on premium, international brands within three major sectors, Food, Drink and Retailing. There was a change that prompted some political conflict between subunits in Food&Drinks as sectors became larger.

> "They were big companies and wanted to have a higher level of standardization – what they all became was global... and each of those sectors became more willing to prescribe what their own IS policy would be on a global basis – at the same time using a common (group) infrastructure." IS Director

From a corporate viewpoint the main sectors were regarded as the business units, although in practice the sectors each had multinational operations with strong business unit and local managers who considered that they had full operational responsibility. The corporate CIO perspective in the mid 1990s was that there should be different roles at group and subunit levels. At the Group level the tasks were to: share best practices, develop standards and guidelines, conduct research into new technology and telecommunications, develop architecture and infrastructure plans, and be active in management development. In contrast the subunits needed to be close to the customer and develop business systems locally, which would facilitate process, redesign and support major change programs.

In corporate IT there developed a vision of a common platform of systems. According to the Group IT Services Director, recent developments in enterprise resource package (ERP) solutions such as SAP and JDE offered more flexibility and functionality. Where a package was a feasible solution it was desirable to set up a central team with the skills to implement across different companies. This was more of a goal than a reality, as in practice sectors were able to define their own ERP solutions, reflecting the increased power of sector units relative to corporate IT.

Foods Sector standardized on SAP, however Drinks had a more flexible approach, recommending AS400 application packages but not enforcing a standard supplier. Drinks Europe, with its powerful, profitable brands preferred market responsiveness to the efficiency benefits of a single solution. Subunit managers were encouraged to select integrated IBM AS400 package solutions that met local business needs and had a strong local supplier. France, Belgium, Greece, and Italy all moved from a mix of bespoke and stand-alone packages on different hardware to integrated solutions on the AS400 hardware. This policy did enable a subsequent move to implement standard software when European function and support became available.

Senior IT managers recognized the difficulties in implementing corporate IT standards. Generally major changes could not be implemented at the same time as this was too costly; one could aim to standardize over a period of 3-4 years, providing everyone agreed to change. Mergers needed to be treated as a special case. If standards of the acquired company were in conflict, one needed to change immediately. If differences existed but there were no major conflicts, then interfaces could be developed as an interim measure. Similarly divestments caused a problem when services needed to be maintained for the departing company.

When the software product was common and used in a consistent way, there were few obstacles to implementing a common system. However implementing a standard system did not guarantee standard data. One sector implemented SAP as a standard software in its operating companies; yet the data categories such as product codes were not common. In theory, shared decision support data could be achieved through transferring operational data into a single data warehouse; in practice this was a complex activity with translation tables and interfaces.

A challenge to standards compliance arose from the diversity of stakeholders. Within IT, there were five units – Corporate, Group IT Services, Drinks Sector, European Region, and national business units. Many standards were defined at too high a level for them to be useful. For example, defining a supplier is not enough - there must also be a support structure. Occasionally standards set by technical people working in a sophisticated head office environment were detrimental to some subunits, or not understood. Smaller companies were more likely to focus on the purchase cost of a PC rather than total cost of ownership.

In summary, during the research period Food&Drinks experienced many changes and the creation of the major sectors and regions as new organizational forms was in line with the management style. There was an evolution of the IT architecture and of the IT departments each with a unique role in the management of IT. As suggested by the framework, IT department stakeholders all had a say in the development and implementation of the IT policy and architecture, with varying degrees of influence and conflict during the 1990s.

Household

In 1997, Household had more than 100,000 employees and revenues in excess of $10 billion; it focused on three core areas: Household Appliances, Commercial Appliances, and Outdoor Products (Nordicum 1997). Household Appliances had grown through a series of over 400 acquisitions. Appliance Europe was the largest sector and the market leader in household appliances. The CEO of Appliance Europe was promoted to corporate CEO and maintained both roles. As a result of this, the corporate style towards Appliance Europe in the early-mid 1990s was one of strategic planning (Bartlett and Ghoshal 1998). Even though the company history meant there was great diversity, the stated goal was to operate as 'one company'.

In 1996, the corporate IT manager had responsibility for both IT policy and services, giving guidance and support to the business units who had varying levels of IT competence depending on their history prior to acquisition. In line with the corporate management style, the group IT policy, created during this initial period, defined and communicated detailed standards in order to achieve the integration goal both internally and customer-facing. It specified the reasons as:

> *The most fundamental reason for faster cross functional and external information flow is that the direct connection of businesses for reporting, ordering etc. has become imperative for effective process work, i.e. customer care, order to delivery, delivery to payment, product development and supplier management. As the Group strives to integrate, the large customers do the same and internationalize. All this requires smooth exchange of information, and at the present the most effective and simplest way to achieve this is with standardized systems. The standardized systems together with uniformly and coordinated standardized data will form an important part of our common business and working language within the Group. Basic IT Directives - June 03, 1996.*

The Corporate CIO confirmed and expanded on the IT Policy.

> *"if we look upon cost parameters, of course we have group purchasing agreements ... we have to look upon this not only for cost potential reasons but also business reasons – look upon our present and future customers – they are looking for a lot of commonality out from a group like Household even with different business sectors." (Corporate CIO, January 1998)*

The reaction to the corporate IT policy and standards was mixed. Some units followed the standards, however other local units effectively suspended major IT investments where they did not agree with the standard. For example, Household UK retained multiple order processing systems leading to internal inefficiency and customer issues.

> *During 1997 there was a change of corporate CEO with an external appointment. The new perspective was to focus on shareholder value, giving the business sectors autonomy providing that the financial results were delivered in line with the required goals. The result was a different management style, more linked to control rather than planning.*

This shift towards a control perspective caused some uncertainty among Household executives. Synergies were still expected across business sectors, however this would be achieved in a different way by sectors seeking help due to tough targets or working together to support a common customer need.

With the new Corporate CEO management style, the role of Corporate was more focused on protecting shareholder value and the sectors had a stronger influence on strategy and operations linked to target profit goals. This gave the new sector managers a stronger say in the setting of the IT standards, leading to potential conflicts. For example within Appliance Europe, the CEO was a believer in shared data rather than shared applications. His aim was to standardize on a supply chain planning and the profitability data model across Europe, rather than enforcing common ERP systems. Yet the continued corporate management influence meant that it was difficult to choose another ERP system, leading to longer delays in implementing new solutions.

During a latter period, the corporate IT role was split and the goal was articulated to create a Global IT Services organization from all the different IT units across the organization, resulting in a separation of the policy and service roles, as predicted by prior research. Sectors were asked to appoint 'IT Buyers' who understood the business needs and were competent to evaluate and purchase IT components. This structure and responsibility is in line with the revised business unit role predicted by Earl, Edwards, and Feeny (1996) when an internal bureau is set up.

In Appliance Region West Europe a new IT architecture was implemented. This was based on a largely common JDE application with interfaces to the 'shared data' supply chain and profitability applications on a central computer. As part of this new 'IT model', Appliance Europe chose a data warehousing solution prior to Corporate IT defining a standard. Approval for this solution was obtained from all the IT stakeholders: Corporate IT, Group IT Services, Region West, and Local Business units.

An interview with the corporate CIO identified a number of factors explaining why the Household companies did or did not follow standards. His view was that the Basic IT Directives addressed the need for *communication* of standards explaining clearly the associated logic and the benefits. However he acknowledged the multiple stakeholder viewpoints commenting that there was always *'a political dimension in a big organization.'* In particular, the change of corporate leadership had meant a reduced focus on central direction that had made the policy enforcer job more difficult. As a consequence he needed to rely more heavily on his network of IT subunit managers but there was a lack of support due to some of these IT managers taking a *narrow technical view*. While he recognized that the subunit IT managers had a responsibility to deliver to *business goals* he was disappointed that they were selecting other systems solutions given the corporate choice of JDE as a flexible, integrated application package.

The corporate CIO noted that *cost* was often raised as an issue for not following a standard; however his view was that the companies were taking a short-term perspective, for example in choosing a local PC where the total cost of ownership was higher due to integration issues. On this specific point, Household initiated a group purchasing agreement with two major PC suppliers. *Timing* was another factor linked to *motivation* - local companies needed a reason to change in a specified period or the solution needed to be imposed. In fact corporate IT provided little direction in this area. From the Appliance Europe sector viewpoint, there was also limited *support in implementing* key policies such as sharing common data; as highlighted above there was no data warehouse standard. The corporate IT manager also accepted that the IT policy was focused on components rather than how to integrate these into an overall business-driven architecture.

In summary, during the investigation Household had a change of corporate leadership resulting in the creation of large sectors/regions as new organizational forms, which was consistent with the new strategic control management style. In parallel, there was a growing role for the IT subunit departments each linked to their position in the Household organization. At the start of the period Corporate IT had created what it considered to be a comprehensive and justified IT policy. However the degree of compliance with the policy varied both by subunit and by the IT architecture element. One major positive outcome was the partnership between the different IT departments in creating a new IT architecture that was successfully piloted in the Appliance Europe Region West area. The results in Household support the conceptual frameworks derived in this chapter and suggest how a partnership approach can deal with the inherent conflicts arising from multiple stakeholder positions.

ANALYSIS

Evaluation of Proposition I – Multiple IT Stakeholders

Evidence was found in both case studies of the five expected IT management stakeholder groups: Corporate IT, Sector IT, Region IT, Business Unit IT, and the internal bureau, Group IT Services.

There were some specific differences in the two organizations.

- In Drinks, Group IT Services reported to Corporate IT while Household had a separate reporting line to the Chief Financial Officer.
- At the Sector/Region level, Drinks had a global Sector product role while in Household, Appliance Europe had the Sector role with combined business product group and regional responsibility
- Within the sector, the Regions were different – in Drinks the region comprised all of Europe, while in Appliance Europe there were four geographical areas.

These are minor variations, yet as shown in Figure 6, the two MNC organizational forms had evolved to represent similar structures.

The cases demonstrate that each of the five unit types had their own IT competence and that their roles had developed as expected from the framework.

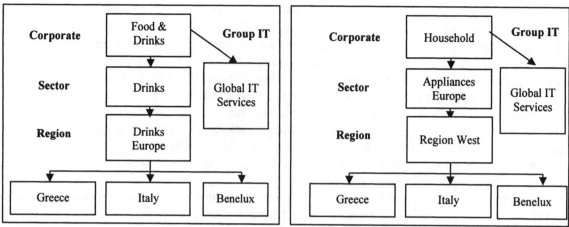

Figure 6: IT Management Structures

Evaluation of Proposition II – Determinants of IT Stakeholder Influence

Evaluating this proposition involves assessing the roles of the different IT stakeholders in the development of the Global IT architecture. The case studies show that the corporate management style had an impact on the Group IT Policy in both organizations. Food&Drinks had a strategic control style in the 1990s. The evidence for this intermediate position is that while Corporate IT set the technology standards, it had less direction on application standards, particularly as the Sectors grew in size and importance.

In Household, the strategic planning style led to a detailed Group IT Policy covering both technology and applications. While both organizations had a corporate communications infrastructure and central IT purchasing agreements, Household had a noticeably stronger stance on application standards. With the change to a strategic control style, Corporate IT became less directive as the Sectors gained more influence on applications, exemplified by Appliance Europe selecting its own data warehouse solution.

The growth of the Sector as an MNC organizational form was a noticeable feature in both companies. Food&Drinks moved earlier than Household to a Sector structure with strong co-ordination over the Business units and a policy link with Corporate. This change mirrored the management style and is consistent with the derived framework. In contrast, Household had a strong global 'one company' vision and took longer to move to a full Sector structure, an initiative driven by the new corporate CEO with a stronger 'control' style. As a result, Sector IT directors had major influence in the two organizations both in the setting and the implementation of IT policies. In Food&Drinks, the policy of IBM AS400 application packages was a switch from the previous corporate mainframe standard.

The role of the Region was also vital in both cases. Drinks Europe IT had the key role of coordinating the implementation of the Sector policy of integrated AS400 packages, as well as strongly recommending when local suppliers should be selected. In Appliance Region West, the managing director adopted a 'one company' approach in Household, perhaps due to his corporate background. Consequently his region played a major part in coordinating the implementation of the new Appliance Europe architecture. At the European level there was evidence of a transnational approach which prior research has suggested is a common occurrence with international consumer product companies that have strong local brands. Major drivers in Europe for integration were the single market, the Euro currency, and cross-border retailers. At the same time the need to satisfy differences in local markets caused by channel, language, and purchasing processes required a responsive approach.

The creation of Group IT Services as a separate IT entity changed the nature of the IT stakeholder relationships in both organizations. Specifically it reduced the influence of corporate IT by separating the policy and service roles. In Food&Drinks, the focus was more on implementing a corporate IT infrastructure including a global network for office communications. Household had a more encompassing vision that all IT professionals would move to Group IT Services and it would become the major provider of IT to internal units, although it took time for it to build the competence in the components and integration tools required to build the global IT architecture.

This evaluation demonstrates significant support for the proposition that management style and MNC organizational form were key factors in the type and level of influence exercised by the IT departments in the creation of the global IT architecture.

Evaluation of Proposition III – IT Stakeholder Conflicts

The cases covered a period of major change in both organizations. IT was a key enabler for much of the restructuring that occurred as a result of the major acquisitions. Therefore the business management of the different units was keen to influence the development of the global IT architecture through their IT managers. Given the limited resource, this led to conflicts about where the major investments should be made. For example, in Household there were two separate camps promoting 'shared data' or 'common applications', and this was a source of considerable debate in both business and IT forums.

There were many reasons highlighted for non-compliance by the IT units, including: not considering total cost of ownership, lack of understanding of benefits, and taking a narrow technical view. Of course, as highlighted by the Household CIO, there is a political dimension with multiple stakeholders and the challenge is to address both the objective and the subjective concerns.

In both cases Corporate IT highlighted cross-sector synergies, as there were important common international customers across the main sectors. This was more explicitly recognized within Household as part of the Group IT Directives and a common database system of codes was established. Yet these cross-sector synergies were not sufficient for the Corporate CEOs to demand a global strategy. It is worthy of note that both Corporate CIOs determined that the best approach to resolving the conflicts with the strong Sectors was to attempt to build a partnership.

The decision taken by Household in 1998 was that, in the future, standards would be created through a cross-business sector group, comprising Corporate and Sector IT, with an optional invitation to Group IT Services. This recognized the corporate devolution and the growing role of the Sectors following the change of Corporate CEO and new management style. It can be compared with an earlier Food&Drinks initiative to create a cross sector group of IS directors for major IT decisions. This organizational approach to developing global IT architecture is consistent with a style of strategic control. Summarizing, there was evidence of conflict due to the multiple stakeholders and there was a consistent response that it could only be resolved by the most influential IT unit managers working together.

A common element of the two organizations is the history of acquisitions and mergers. This resulted in a high degree of change as these groups sought to integrate their new acquisitions, with Food&Drinks acting more aggressively in this goal. Both companies are in the business of making and selling consumer products. While the findings are useful and provide many insights, their common background may be a limiting factor in the generalizability of the findings and a wider base of organizations would provide an opportunity for further research.

CONCLUSIONS

A carefully crafted global IT architecture is critical to the successful implementation of the business and IT strategy of a multinational corporation. An information technology architecture is the design of the various IT elements (e.g., network topology, servers, software, users, internet, intranet, extranet, IT management structure, and IT organization, but not limited to these elements alone) that work together to achieve organizational goals. In this chapter, we defined the various components of the IT architecture. A model for global IT architecture was presented which focused on two key processes of integration: control and coordination. Many business factors were examined which impact the design of the architecture. These included: MNC strategy and structure, strategic disposition, organizational culture and personnel practices. Also described are key steps in IT architecture planning and the role of business strategy and IT strategy in such planning.

A key component of the IT architecture is the IT organizational structure itself. Various management roles are involved in the creation and evolution of the IT organization. These roles range from corporate, business unit, to group services. Among broad choices for IT organizational structure are single corporate department, decentralized IT units, and federal structures. Depending on the management style and MNC structural form, decisions are made on the formation of the IT organizational structure. Two detailed case studies of large MNCs provide further insights into these issues.

Ultimately, there is a huge and sometimes hidden investment in time and money to create the IT architecture. Without a coordinated management effort, the result may be a non-aligned collection of inappropriate components. While Simon's (1996) information architecture model provides a conceptual basis for building an IT architecture in a global organization, only through a deep understanding of the roles and potential conflicts can an organization make effective use of its IT resources. This chapter has provided both the basic foundations as well as many intricacies in developing the global IT architecture.

MINICASE

GlobalManufacturing

GlobalManufacturing is a Fortune 500 company headquartered in Atlanta, Georgia. It has five manufacturing plants in California, Illinois, North Carolina and Texas. Three of its manufacturing plants are located in England, Germany and Spain in addition to the ones located in South Africa and Australia. The company has its operations in Asia as well and to facilitate the demand from this geographic region, the company has three more manufacturing plants in Malaysia, China, and United Arab Emirates (UAE). In order to enhance its delivery time to its customers, the company maintains a network of 25 warehouses all around the world. In this global company, about sixty percent of business comes from outside the US. Even though the company has centralized marketing, accounting and financial management systems, in different countries it has to cater for the local business environments and needs. The company has also grown through mergers and acquisitions. Different management structures exist in different parts of the world such as in China and UAE. Most of the business is partnerships and join-ventures whereas in England and Germany, the company has wholly owned subsidiaries. In many other countries, the company has different marketing and distribution networks. Additionally, government legal regulations change in different parts of the world that dictate different modes and means for the operations. Different countries have different levels of availability of telecommunication infrastructure.

The company's products are sold internationally as OEM products and to customers through different distribution networks. The company's sales force in most countries travel around the country to visit customers and take orders. Due to differences in both managerial and technical infrastructure components that exist at different locations, it is a challenge to coordinate and control operations for this global company. On top of everything else, fast changing nature of business, competitive pressures, and integration needs driven by electronic commerce are forcing the company to re-think its computing strategy.

If you were to be appointed as a consultant to the Chief Information Officer of *GlobalManufacturing,* your recommendations will be very critical for the success of the company. Use your imagination and information given above to assume the existing organizational and other environment of the company for your planning. Also assume the exact locations of the plants, warehouses etc. If you can make a strong enough case, the company is willing to replace all its current hardware software and systems with a new Internet based distributed computing environment, which should serve the company well into 21st century. This means that the company is willing to acquire state-of-the-art technology such as: wireless, distributed object technologies, computing grid, intelligent agents, etc. Should the company consider investing in intranet, extranet, Internet and e-business technologies?

Propose a medium term infrastructure strategy (plan), which will allow efficient and effective development and operation of new applications to keep the company competitive. You must specify the following in your plan.

Discussion Questions:
1. How will you create a global IT architecture vision for the company? What components will you include in this infrastructure and how will the standardization effort take place? Specify the method and criteria you will use to identify and choose various components of this architecture.
2. How will the system be implemented? Will there be a need to suggest a change in the organizational structure? If yes, what changes will be needed to effectively deploy and use the global IT infrastructure?
3. How will you evaluate the extent to which your plan will be considered a success after its implementation? Given the speed of change in the global business environment, how will the architecture meet change management due to legal regulations, business models in different companies, growth factors such as future mergers and acquisitions and improvement in the hardware/software components of the architecture?
4. What kind of IT structure or organization will you suggest at corporate level and group IT level?
5. Provide a cost analysis of the architecture that you recommend. Also provide justifications for the choices you made.
6. Address cultural, social, legal and country specific issues and their impact on the design of the architecture that you proposed.

KEY TERMS
ATM Technology
Control
Coordination
Ethnocentrism
Federal IS Structure
Geocentrism
Global Culture
Global IT Architecture
Global Structure
Home Country Culture
Host Country Culture
Information Technology (IT) Architecture

Information Technology (IT) Infrastructure
International Structure
Multinational Corporation (MNC)
Multinational Structure
Network topology
Open Source Software (OSS)
Polycentrism
Regiocentrism
Regional Culture
Service Level Agreement (SLA)
Transnational Corporation

STUDY QUESTIONS

1. How would you create and sell a compelling global IT architecture vision for an organization? Give a brief example of the need for a global IT architecture in the light of changing global business environment due to global competition and its impact on the IT architecture.

2. Describe major components of a global IT architecture including their interdependencies and interrelationships. How would a global IT architecture differ from IT architecture for a local company that operates in a city of less than 10,000 people?

3. What strategies for a match between architecture vision and implementation compliance will you suggest?

4. How do various IT roles impact IT architecture? Discuss the importance of corporate, business unit, and group roles in the implementation of the IT architecture. What are the trade-offs between control and coordination when the vision for the architecture is developed at the headquarters of an MNC and the implementation is done by the local IT units?

5. What would you suggest to manage architecture changes due to reasons such as business model change (reconfiguration of basic elements), technology change (drop in the prices of hardware/software, network bandwidth, etc.) and local legal compliance (evolution of local laws and regulations)?

6. Conduct research and evaluate the capabilities of existing tools for global architecture, and innovative approaches to interoperability.

REFERENCES

Alavi, M., and Young, G. Information Technologies in International Enterprise: An Organizing Framework. *The Global Issues of Information Technology Management* (editors Palvia, S., Palvia, P., and Zigli, R.M.), Idea Group Publishing, 1992.

Bartlett, C. A. and Ghoshal, S. *Managing Across Borders* (2nd Edition), Random House, 1998.

Brown, C. V. and Magill, S. L., "Alignment of the IS functions with the Enterprise: toward a model of antecedents", *MIS Quarterly*, 18(4), 1994, pp 371-403.

Burn, J. M. and Cheung, H. K. *Global Information Technology and Systems management: Key Issues and Trends* (editors Palvia, P., Palvia, S., and Roche, E.), Ivy League Publishing, 1996.

Cook, M. A. *Building Enterprise Information Architectures: re-engineering information systems,* Prentice-Hall PTR, 1996.

Daniels, J. L. and Daniels, N. C. *Global Vision: Building New Models for the Corporation of the Future*, McGraw-Hill, 1993.

Earl, M. J., Management Strategies for Information Technology, Prentice-Hall, 1989.

Earl, M. J., Edwards, B. and Feeny, D. F. *Configuring the IS Function," Information Management: The Organizational Dimension* (editor M J Earl), Oxford University Press, 1996.

Goold, M. and Campbell, A. *Strategies and Style: The role of the centre in managing diversified corporations,* Oxford: Blackwell, 1986.

Heenan, D. A., and Perlmutter, H.V. Multinational Organizational Development: A Social Architecture Perspective. Reading, MA: Addison-Wesley, 1979.

Hodgkinson S. L. *'The Role of the Corporate IT Function in the Large Multi-Business Company',* Unpublished thesis submitted for the degree of Doctor of Philosophy, Linacre College, Oxford University, 1991.

Jarvenpaa S. L., and Ives B. "Organising for Global Competition: The Fit of Information Technology," *Decision Sciences*, 24(3), 1992, pp. 547-575.

Karimi, J., and Konsynski, B. R. "Globalization and Information Management Strategies," *Journal of Management Information Systems*. 7(4), 1991, pp. 7-26.

Keen P. G. W. *Shaping the Future - Business Design through Information Technology*, Harvard Business School Press, 1991.

Lehrer, M. and Asakawa, K. "Regional management and regional headquarters in Europe: A comparison of American and Japanese MNCs", Insead working paper 95/01/SM, January 1995, 1995.

Luftman, J., Kempaiah, R., and Nash, E. "Key Issues for IT Executives 2005," *MIS Quarterly Executive*. 5(2), June 2006, pp. 81-99.

Luftman, J, and McLean E. R. "Key Issues for IT Executives," *MIS Quartely Executive*. 3(2), June 2004, pp. 89-104.

Manwani, S. "Global IT Architecture: Who Calls the Tune," *Journal of Global Information Technology Management*, 5(2), 2002, 38-59.

Meyers, B. C., and Oberndorf, P. *Managing Software Acquisition: Open Systems and COTS Products*. Addison Wesley Professional, 2001.

Miles M. B. and Huberman A. M. Qualitative Data Analysis, Sage, 1994.

Nordicum "First Among Equals: The Swedish Manager Leads Without Leadership," *Scandinavian Business Review*, 1997.

Ramarapu, N. K. and Lado A. A. "Linking information technology to global business strategy to gain competitive advantage: an integrative model," *Journal of Information Technology,* 10(2), 1995, pp 115-124

Sandoe, K., Corbitt, G., and Boykin, R., *Enterprise Integration*, John Wiley & Sons, 2001.

Simon, S. J. *An Information Perspective on the Effectiveness of Headquarters-Subsidiary Relationships: Issues of Control and Coordination',* Global Information Technology and Systems management: Key Issues and Trends (editors Palvia, P., Palvia, S., and Roche, E.), Ivy League Publishing, 1996.

Valanju, S. and Jain, H. *Global Information Technology Infrastructure for Transactional Corporations: Developing, Deploying and Maintaining, Global Information Technology and Electronic Commerce* (editors Palvia, P., Palvia, S., and Roche, E.), Ivy League Publishing, 2002.

Weill, P. "The Role and Value of Information Technology Infrastructure," *Strategic Information Technology Management*, (editors Banker R D, Kauffman R J, Mahmood M A), Idea Group Publishing . 1993.

10

The Role of Global Information Systems in Managing Worldwide Operations of Multinational Corporations

Luca Iandoli
The University of Naples Federico II, Italy

Anil Kumar
Central Michigan University, USA

CHAPTER SUMMARY

Information Technology (IT) advances in the last two decades have enabled and accelerated the process of globalization. IT continues to be a critical success factor for effective management and profitability of multinational corporations (MNCs). In this chapter we analyze the role of IT in globalization and emphasize the need to design and develop global information systems (GIS). GIS are complex applications used by organizations that operate in the global environment to help support decision-making, manage organizational data, support and enable organizational business processes, facilitate organizational communications, and support global business strategy. A framework is proposed to comprehend the domain of global information systems. This framework helps understand the characteristics of a GIS. Practitioners can use the framework to guide them in designing and developing a GIS whereas students can use the framework to identify skills they need to successfully design and develop a GIS.

INTRODUCTION

Information Technology (IT)[1] advances in the last two decades have enabled and accelerated the process of globalization. Globalization necessitates that companies continually adapt their business models to stay competitive in the global economy. IT based systems become a critical success factor for effective management and profitability of multinational companies (MNCs). These systems referred to as global information systems (GIS) help a MNC to control and coordinate their global operations.

---

[1] We use IT to imply information communications technology (ICT). These technologies are used for storing, processing, retrieving and disseminating information.

The Role of IT in Globalization

Today we live in a global economy in which companies routinely cross established national boundaries to compete for markets and customers (Taylor and Weber, 1996). This is a matter of fact largely confirmed by economic data and statistics about the world economy. For instance, the turnover of many big corporations is higher than that of many national economies. Not only MNCs but also small and medium enterprises (SMEs) are required to deal with opportunities provided by globalization and to cope with competitive threats due to globalization.

In global competition, information systems play a major role. Information systems are used as a tool to coordinate global operations and manage worldwide business relationships. These systems enable companies to cross organizational and national boundaries, to effectively coordinate international supply chains, to set up or enter in new markets, and to advertise and sell through the internet on a global scene. In the next section we provide an overview of how globalization and information technology change business strategies and organizational models for global companies.

The Emerging MNCs and Multinational Alliances

Information Technology is producing deep social, technological and business transformations in the world economy. For instance, the growth of IT has been crucial for the growth of some emerging economies, such as China and India. Companies that want to operate at the global level are more and more interested in establishing their operations directly in foreign countries and in building international alliances both with local partners and international partners. Alliances with local partners can be built both to produce and/or to commercialize products locally as well as for export to other countries. Alliances with international partners are often built to achieve economy of scale or to share risks related to the development of new products. Surprisingly these alliances can emerge also between competitors, as is often the case in the automotive industry (see for instance the recent agreement between FIAT and FORD for the production of a new city car).

In the formation of such alliances MNCs have to deal with many factors that ultimately influence their choice to operate in one country or the other. Then, once a partnership has been finalized, global technology-based systems have to be designed and developed to manage operations and transactions at the international level. For these reasons, it is important to study how IT grows and thrives in the world economy and how it is changing the way MNCs do their business. There is a huge body of research examining IT related factors that play a key role in facilitating the decision of a MNC to invest in a foreign country. We classify these factors in the following clusters: *infrastructure, legal system, social development and education*, and *cultural environment* (Bruno et al., 2004*)*.

Infrastructure: Beyond traditional infrastructure such as transportation networks, the availability of effective communication infrastructure is crucial for MNCs, in particular for value added services such as outsourcing and electronic commerce (Mann et al., 2000). Relevant aspects include physical access to telecommunication infrastructures and networks, and economic access so that the price structure is not prohibitive. Both are crucial for firms to manage their transactions and operations at the global level.

Legal System: One of the critical factors for MNCs to manage worldwide operations is the availability of an adequate legal framework. For instance, inefficient intellectual property protection laws can discourage MNCs from investing in a foreign country. Other relevant factors related to legal aspects are international and local trade regulations as well as the fiscal policies of local governments.

Education: Social development is beneficial for the overall growth of the IT enabled economy. A key element for creating positive opportunities is to integrate IT development policies to overall development policies. Palvia (1998) has classified such factors broadly into economic, technological, cultural and political categories. The availability of human resources will continue to be an overriding issue in the development of an IT enabled economy both in developing and developed economies. In this respect, it is not accidental that the most successful countries in the IT industry, such as India, South Korea and more recently China, have been successful in to training a substantial number of ICT professionals.

Cultural Environment: Differences among cultures may play a key role for MNCs when they have to decide to establish presence in a foreign country (Hofstede et al., 1990). Language differences may represent an obstacle, especially for the Internet (Fagan, 2001; OECD, 1998 b). Cultural barriers, coupled with cultural resistance, may put a serious constraint on the actual use and growth of IT (Shore and Venkatachalam, 1995).

The Dawn and Maturity of Global Outsourcing Industry

The lack of positive levels of infrastructure, legal system, education and cultural incompatibility can, prevent an MNC from investing in a given country from developing effective global information systems for the coordination of off-shore facilities and operations. On the contrary, the presence of positive levels of these factors and cultural compatibility encourages the presence of foreign firms, laying the foundation for the establishment of off-shore partnerships among MNCs and indigenous firms.

Off-shore partnerships can offer benefits to both indigenous client firms and foreign vendor firms. On the one hand, local companies can expand their market through international exposure and enjoy considerable increase in their technological competences through technology transfer. On the other hand, foreign companies can obtain two advantages: a) to access local qualified and often low-wage workforce; b) to enter strategic and developing markets. Global outsourcing helps create partnerships among MNCs and local firms. Success of these partnerships depends upon "effective relationship management" (King, 2005) between the partners. The main driver, at least initially, for these partnerships was the availability of low-cost and skilled workforce in developing countries such as India. However, globalization is fostering competition and both MNCs wuth headquarters in developed nations and national companies located in developing countries can no longer rely on low costs to gain competitive advantages both domestically and internationally. As global outsourcing matures, outsourcing goes beyond movement of non-core activities to low-cost countries to a way to access specialized skills and competencies. Consequently, MNCs are transforming into international networks of competencies with central coordination to manage development, production and selling of new products at the global level (Doz et al., 2001). ST Microlectronics (STM), an Italian MNC leader in the micro processors industry, is a point in case. STM manages production facilities are located in several areas of the world including Europe and North Africa, as well as a network of R&D centers dispersed around the globe from India, to Italy and USA, each specializing on a specific research area.

It is possible to identify four different types of partnership models in outsourcing (Bruno et al., 2004):

- Direct ownership;
- Off-shore development;
- On site/Off-shore development;
- Commercial partnership.

With <u>direct ownership</u>, firms establish their own off-shore center to lower costs and maintain complete control over operations. The goal is to establish presence in developing markets with good growth potentialities. In this model, the control over the whole value-chain is in the hands of the MNC. In the <u>off-shore</u> model, MNCs agree with off-shore suppliers to outsource some non core activities. For the software industry, the off-shore model is evolving rapidly into a more sophisticated form of partnership called <u>on site/off-shore</u> model. In this case, the supplier's staff works at the client's site in MNC's own country and perform high-value-added services, such as consultancy services. In the <u>commercial partnership model</u>, the role of local firms is limited to selling products and /or services entirely implemented by a MNC.

Complex Management Issues of MNCs

Globalization and the diffusion of IT enabled network technologies have radically changed the way companies run their businesses in traditional or in hi-tech industries, in manufacturing or in the service sector. Many experts recognize that the integration between globalization and technology-driven economy has contributed to create a complex competitive environment showing many paradoxical characteristics (Davis and Meyer, 1998). In the following sections, we focus on three paradoxes that have been observed in the last 10-15 years:

a) The Competition Paradox
b) The Productivity Paradox
c) The Access Paradox.

The Competition Paradox: Does IT increase competition or collaboration among companies? A MNC struggles with aggressive competitors and operates in turbulent markets characterized by fast changes in customers' needs and continuous innovation. Liberalization policies such as simplification of customs procedures, opening up to foreign investments, abandoning of protectionism, and creation of free trade areas -- make access to international markets easier and faster than ever before. This reduces entry barriers to a foreign country market. According to the well known Porter's Five Forces model, this means increasing competition intensity (Porter, 1980). Within an open market, where powerful players compete with one another in an attempt to provide customers with advanced and high quality products, power is in the hands of customers. On the internet, competitors are just one click away. Though e-commerce sales still represent a small percentage of total sales in the retail sector, the global competition for products and services has become hyper intense.

Companies show pervasive customer focus in the attempt to increase loyalty and retain highly profitable customers. Capturing customer life time value, i.e. the amount of money that a customer will potentially spend during his/her lifetime for a product, is the target. This scenario is true for both mature and emerging economies. The opening of new huge markets due to the adoption of a capitalist system in the former Soviet Union and the rise of new country giants such as China and India, have almost doubled the number of potential customers for the products and services produced in the these countries.

MNCs based in different parts of the world can use IT based global systems to increase cooperation by creating strategic alliances. For example two global chemical companies based in US and Asia compete for customers in different parts of the world. The US based MNC is a global leader in the industry and the Asian based MNC is a new entrant to the global marketplace. The competition paradox viewpoint would argue that with the entry of the Asian MNC in the US market, prices will fall due to increase of supply. An alternate view to this argument is that the two MNCs may decide to use global IT to create a strategic alliance. The new alliance will provide access to global markets for the smaller Asian MNC and it would help the US MNC to optimize their cost by moving their production to Asia. Both the strategic partners will benefit from the alliance that is based on global IT.

The Productivity Paradox: Productivity is the capability of companies to produce more with less. Investments in information technology based systems can lead to streamlining of business processes by eliminating non value-added tasks. This reduces costs in the long run as fewer people accomplish the same tasks in less time. While this impact on productivity may be visible in an organization it is often missing in productivity statistics when viewed from a national perspective. Investments in information technology based systems have continued to increase since the 1960s in the US though there has been limited improvement in national productivity statistics. This phenomenon is referred to as the 'productivity paradox' and Nobel Prize winner economist Robert Solow is credited with coining this term.

Any disruptive technological revolution, such as railways and electricity in the 19th and 20th century, brought up a discontinuous improvement in the productivity of the overall economic system. As regards IT however the debate about the so called productivity paradox (Harris, 1994) is still far from reaching a consensual conclusion. For example, many reasons make difficult to evaluate the return on investment in IT (Brynjolfsson, 1998), such as the wide temporal lag between investment and outcomes, the pervasiveness of IT systems that can be employed virtually in any company function or value chain activity, the fact that IT investments must be accompanied by relevant change in work organization and business process re-engineering.

Many productivity gains are related uniquely to IT use, such as:
- Reduction of telecommunications costs
- Diffusion of e-government initiatives resulting in efficiency and effectiveness gains.
- better coordination of supply chain and logistic activities though ERP systems;
- easier and faster access to information and knowledge through Knowledge Management and Decision support systems;
- Cheaper access to market and customer information through Customer Relationship Management (CRM) tools;
- Disintermediation costs due to the possibility of cutting out some intermediaries in the B2C and B2B platforms just to mention a few applications. Such applications and tools IT not only contribute to increase productivity but also foster a global economy by shrinking communication barriers, linking value chains and empowering Business intelligence.

The Access Paradox: According to Rifkin (2000) we live in the "age of access". In the age of access we are not referring to tangible properties and assets, but to intangible information assets and to the use of these assets only when we really need them. Internet allows virtually anyone to enter an incommensurable patrimony of knowledge and data which is constantly updated. In the first days of e-commerce the dominant view was that the internet was opening the market by lowering entry barriers to any industry: anyone could then be able to connect and make its business global.

Later, facts and experience showed that this was not true for many reasons: high costs for infrastructures and technology, skills shortage and high labor costs, necessity of deep organizational changes for companies going on-line, etc. More than opening the market, the internet changed the global economy by:
- Allowing for the emergence of new businesses and companies (e.g. Google, Yahoo, e-Bay) or of new ways to make existing businesses (e.g. Amazon, Dell, etc.)
- Changing the supplier-customer relationship, in general by allowing disintermediation and higher transparency about product information and prices
- Allowing companies to know ever more about their customers by facilitating the gathering and analysis of huge amount of data about customer preferences, behavior, satisfaction factors, etc.
- Promoting the diffusion of open standards thereby allowing different operating systems and users to be connected to the same global network by inventing new ways of value exchange and creation (peer to peer, open source communities, consumer to consumer transactions)
  There is no doubt that many people in the age of access can obtain more information at a very low cost than ever before, and that this availability contributes to making better decisions and saving money and time. On the other hand many factors limit universal access.

  - First, the digital divide, i.e. the disparities in terms of opportunity to access the internet and the information economy between developed and developing countries is still very high (ITU, 2001).

- Second, competing in internet economy requires huge amount of resources and investments. This implies in many businesses the presence of few big players, market closure and the reduction of diversity. Diversity is also reduced because of what might be called the "Google effect". This popular search engine uses an algorithm to look for web sites that are based on a reputation-based mechanism: the more a web site is linked by others, the more it is considered reliable and relevant. Undoubtedly, this helps web surfers to look for information in a more effective way but at the same time promotes homogeneity and conformism, and, ultimately, a "rich-gets-richer" effect.

- Third, products and services in the global information economy become more and more sophisticated and technologically complex, so that the "average" customer is less and less capable to make objective and informed choice between two or more products. Fourth, concerns for privacy, security and intellectual property rights limit free circulation of information and knowledge on the internet.

In order to manage the above three paradoxes, companies can exploit the operational and strategic advantages offered by IT. They have to face <u>two</u> challenges. The <u>first</u> challenge is of technological nature and consists in developing IT systems that are able to work effectively at the global level. The <u>second</u> challenge is of organizational nature and consists in designing effective organizations able to operate and compete in the global economy. In order to be "effective" companies must develop IT systems and organizational models to support them to face the three paradoxes: 1) compete and at the same time cooperate in complex changing market networks, 2) enhance productivity and at the same time contribute to realize extra-rents to finance research, innovation and huge investments in IT; 3) make internal knowledge accessible to and sharable with customers and partners, and, at the same time, protect critical know-how and gain rents form copyright and intellectual property.

FRAMEWORK TO COMPREHEND DOMAIN OF GLOBAL INFORMATION SYSTEMS

In one of the earlier works on global IS Ives and Jarvenpaa (1991) state that: "A global information technology application contributes to achieving a firm's global business strategy by using information technology platforms, to store, transmit and manipulate data across cultural environments." Since then, there have been various researchers (Alavi and Young, 1992; Deans et al., 1991; Deans and Ricks, 1991; Ein-Dor et al., 1993; Kumar and Palvia, 2002; Palvia, 2002; Palvia, Palvia and Whitworth, 2002; Tetteh and Burn. 2002) that developed research frameworks for global IS though no consensus was reached on defining the term global IS.

In one of the recent studies Kumar and Basu (2002) highlighted the key characteristics that they said should be incorporated in the definition of global IS. These characteristics though not comprehensive include the following; "(1) Global IS systems should help an organization achieve its global business strategy, (2) Global IS systems can be built on multiple technology platforms, (3) Global IS systems should enable organizations to collect, process, and analyze data from worldwide locations, (4) Global IS systems should facilitate transmission and sharing of information and knowledge to all people both inside and outside the organization, (5) Global IS systems pose unique challenges with respect to their development, use, management, and operation in different environments, (6) Global IS systems add value to the processes, strategy, operations and management of these organizations."

As is evident from these definitions a global IS refers to a system that supports data collection, processing, and analysis in organizations that span multiple nations. These organizations often have headquarters in one nation and subsidiaries worldwide. For example companies such as Microsoft, GE, Coca-Cola, IBM, Wal-Mart, Procter and Gamble, Dow Chemical etc. have their headquarters in the US but subsidiaries worldwide. Similarly companies such as British Petroleum (UK), Toyota (Japan), Siemens (Germany), Nestle (Switzerland), Samsung (Korea), Infosys (India) have their headquarters in Europe and Asia but subsidiaries exist worldwide.

In this chapter the term global IS refers to a computer-based system that collects, stores and processes data from worldwide subsidiaries, at the subsidiary or regional offices or worldwide headquarters level, to provide relevant and timely information for the people working in the global organization. The global IS uses worldwide computers and communications networks to facilitate the flow of information within the global organization. These networks also aid the flow of information between the global organization and worldwide business partners, customers, and national governments where the organization has business operations.

Multiple information system applications are designed, developed and used by global companies to manage organizational data, support business processes and facilitate organizational communications promoting knowledge sharing. These applications are developed using multiple technology tools and platforms. It is crucial to ensure that the global IS applications help the business achieve its global business strategy. Figure 2 presents a framework that is useful in understanding the domain of global information systems.

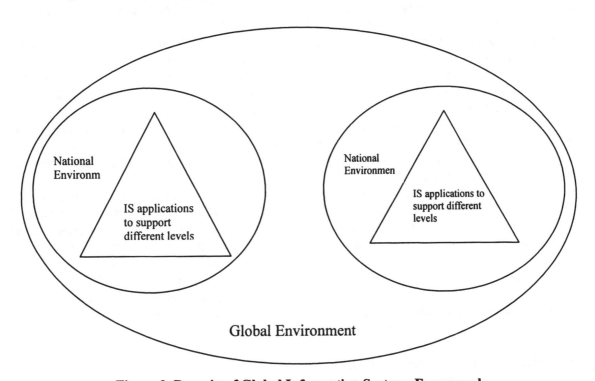

Figure 2. Domain of Global Information Systems Framework

National Environments and Global Environment

The national environment represents the environment that the company functions in and includes various entities such as customers, suppliers, competitors, potential new entrants, and potential substitute products etc. A company has to continually interact with these entities to stay in business. Also included in this environment are legal and regulatory regimes that govern how business is conducted, the political philosophy of the nation, the social norms, and cultural values etc. Since a multinational company operates in multiple nations, host country environment also influences its activities. Adding to the complexity of this situation is the fact that there are multiple international treaties and agreements in the global environment that a business needs to conform with. Examples include NAFTA, ASEAN, Pan-Pacific etc. Keeping all this in view a global business needs to design and develop IS applications that will help it to manage organizational data, support business processes and facilitate organizational communications from a global perspective.

Global IS Manages Complex and Diverse Organizational Data

As a business goes global the complexity of data needed to make decisions multiplies. Executives and managers in global organizations need access to both external and internal data for decision-making. Examples of external include data on international markets, cross-border regulations, international reporting standards, and international governance regulations (Sarbanes-Oxley in the US and Basel II rules proposed to be introduced in Europe that will apply to most EU banks from 2007) etc. Examples of internal data include organizational performance data, both financial and operational, and human resources data etc. This data needs to be collected from worldwide subsidiaries. After data integrity standards have been established, data can be collected, stored, processed, analyzed, and finally distributed to corporate decision-makers across the world.

Information technology based systems play an important role in each step of the data management process. Initially data needs to be collected at source and then stored using an IT tool such as a database management system. At this time care should be taken to ensure that global data standards are followed in data collection and all data are validated before it is stored for use in the organization. Data processing can occur at multiple levels in global organizations depending on the information needs of decision-makers. For example a company may prefer to process data at the subsidiary level for local reporting and then have individual subsidiaries or regional offices transmit reports to corporate headquarters where information is created by integrating processed data from around the world. In other cases companies may use IT based systems to integrate their worldwide systems enabling worldwide employees to use a common system for data processing. In this case all data irrespective of its origin is processed online and in real time to create information. Such systems have been made possible as a result of the diffusion of the Internet and the merging of computers and communications technologies.

Decision-makers in global organizations usually do not have access to organizational data that resides in production databases. The data stored in worldwide organizational databases is imported to a central repository such as a corporate data warehouse that can be accessed by all employees. The internal organizational data from the data warehouse can then be merged with external data to create a global data warehouse. The global data warehouse allows decision-makers to slice and dice the data for different types of analysis such as creating what-if scenarios. The advantage of using a data warehouse is that data is modified during analysis and it does not impact production data in organizational databases. Once data has been processed and analyzed it can be distributed to all subsidiaries based on need.

Global IS Supports Business Processes

To provide goods and services to customers work needs to be carried out in organizations. This work is often carried out by organizational employees and is referred to as business processes. The complexity of business processes in global organizations increases because of the following: (1) business processes in global organizations often span multiple nations, (2) the number of business processes that need to be managed can be overwhelming, (3) the large number of global business processes generate information that needs to be managed along with the flow of goods and services adding to the complexity, and (4) employees in global companies work from different parts of the world and invariably have different work culture that is determined by their national culture often overriding corporate culture. Multiple approaches and technology based tools are used by global organizations to support, enable and manage the business processes.

A global organization may decide to design and develop an in-house global IS to support, enable and manage its business processes. In such an organization, other IS applications may be used to support the business processes. Often times these systems are designed for organizational functions (departments), product divisions, or regional subsidiaries. Integrating information generated by such systems is often challenging because of multiple technologies used. Another approach that a global organization may choose is to purchase an integrated system that supports, enables and manages enterprise wide business processes. Such systems referred to as ERP (Enterprise Resource Planning) systems are becoming very popular around the world and are being implemented by a large number of global corporations. The ERP systems are based on industry best practices and there are several technology vendors such as SAP (Germany), and Oracle (U.S.A.) that provide ERP systems.

There are several factors that are critical to ensure that a global IS optimizes business processes helping employees perform their work better, faster and cheaper. It is critical that people in the organization are involved with all decisions relating to the design and development or the purchase of such a system to ensure that they are comfortable with it and will indeed use it when implemented in the organization. Technical and cultural issues that impact implementation of such a system should be identified and addressed early on in the process. Top management should demonstrate their commitment to using such a system and should ensure transparency when championing the system. They should highlight additional value that is generated for employees in performing their work and value added for both customers and the organization.

Global IS Facilitates Organizational Communications

In a global organization that scans multiple nations' information and knowledge resides in two places. The first one is the formal corporate knowledge repository created using technology based systems and the second one is the informal repository that resides as tacit knowledge of employees in the organization. It is critical that all employees working in the organization have access to this knowledge when they need to perform their work. As employees are spread across the world, a global IS can be a very useful tool for enabling the process of sharing information and knowledge. The diffusion of the Internet has facilitated the process of global organizational communication and knowledge sharing. Now employees in a global organization are able to work 24/7/365. For example employees of a global company headquartered in Europe working on a project after completing their work on a given day store all their documents in a corporate repository that is then accessed by their colleagues in the US where the work day is just beginning. The same process is repeated in the US and work is handed over to employees in the eastern part of the world. In this manner work continues around the clock and an organization benefits tremendously from using the Internet based global information systems. This has been termed as work that follows the sun.

Not only do organizational communications improve using a global IS, knowledge sharing is also facilitated. Challenges that employees face in one part of the world can easily be solved by sharing knowledge of experts in another part of the world. Employees can simply access the corporate repository and search for the expertise in the system irrespective of where they are located. Further if a project requires expertise of employees located in multiple locations around the world a global IS can be used to create a virtual project team. This team works on the project in a virtual environment for the duration of the project and then the team can be disbanded. Virtual teams can be a powerful tool for global companies to solve organizational problems. Information and knowledge sharing and creation of virtual teams using a global IS can lead to significant gains in productivity of organizational employees.

One potential negative consequence is breach of security of these systems. While the Internet facilitates the process of communications and knowledge sharing it also creates the likelihood that people can break into these systems and disrupt the workflow in these organizations. To prevent this from happening global organizations need to invest heavily in the security of these systems. Organizations that realize that information systems are organizational resources that need to be protected and take appropriate measures will succeed in stopping intruders who intend to harm these systems. Investing in security of global information systems is a long term investment that is bound to add value to an organization's key resource, its information and knowledge.

Successful use of global IS applications in MNCs will depend on proper alignment (Mann, 2005) of the various components of the framework as shown in Figure 2. For example, IT policies and national priorities of host countries need to be carefully studied and understood before investing in a GIS application. Further the GIS applications need to be designed with a view to enable the global business strategy of a MNC. If proper alignment exists, MNCs will be able to overcome organizational challenges of operating in the global economy. This would lead to an integrated consistent and uniform offer of products and services to customers worldwide and to the global customer as the organization become a truly globally networked organization.

COMPETING IN THE GLOBAL INFORMATION ECONOMY

How do companies deal with the paradoxes of the global information economy? What are the emerging trends? In this section we discuss how GIS applications enable companies operating in the global economy to meet organizational challenges and stay competitive. A global company that uses GIS effectively becomes a networked organization that is able to provide an integrated offer to its global customers. In what follows, we discuss the details of integrated offer and networked organization.

The Integrated Offer

In order to illustrate the concept of "integrated offer" we quote two examples from Davis and Meyers (1998):

1) Mercedes is testing a systems that will connect cars with a remote center for assistance to car drivers through on-line fault diagnosis (and in some case repair too), maintenance and assistance.

2) In a partnership involving America Express and IBM, Hilton Hotel's customers will be able to book on-line their room from all over the world, enter their preferences and make the check-in through automatic machine that will release an electronic key for the room having the requested characteristics.

Whether or not these programs have been implemented and successful after the testing phase, they provide ingenious examples of the way companies offer their products in the global information economy. Figure 3 shows that an integrated offer from a global company offer is a mix of five components (Davis and Meyer, 1998):

1) **Product**: Tangible part of the offer (e.g. the car)
2) **Services**: Often provided using IT (e.g. remote assistance)
3) **Customization**: Both product and ensuing services are more and more tailored to a single customer's needs and preferences. IT and Internet based applications help to collect information from each single customers and to interact with him/her (e.g. answering to special service requests from a customer)
4) **Content**: Each product or service always provides certain amount of information (e.g. think of an hotel web site containing relevant information about the hotel but also about the city ad its surroundings)
5) **Community**: Keep in constant touch with communities of loyal customers by offering them special services and privileges. Communities are made up of customers sharing preferences, life-style, status, and in many cases opinions and values.

By enhancing information sharing and diffusion, interaction and communication, remote 24x7x365 services and contents delivery, IT contributes to make an integrated offer realizable. The integrated offer is a way through which companies try to create a long term relationship with customers. In this relationship, focus is beyond the immediate transactions to gain as much lifetime value of the customers as possible. For a mobile phones company what really matters is not how much a client has spent on that call but how much that client will spend during all his/her life and trying to retain him/her as much as possible. In fact, this is a fundamental change from the past. Very often a product (e.g. a mobile phone) is no more than a bridge to reach the customer while the real aim is to sell customers life long value added services. In this sense, it is possible to say that nowadays economy is a dematerialised economy. It does not mean that products are disappearing, but the major contribution to value creation is provided by services.

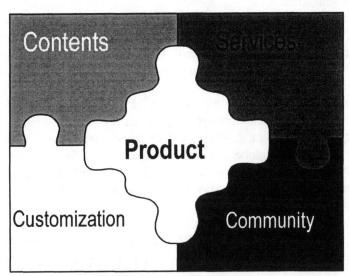

Figure 3. The Concept of Integrated Offer (Elaboration from Davis and Meyers, 1998)

The Networked Organization

The role and importance of networking for a firm has been recognized and analyzed by economists. Spatial networks allow companies to exploit advantages derived from physical proximity to critical resources (Marshall, 1965), membership to a localized production system ensure specialization, knowledge exchange as well as the sharing of culture and tradition (Becattini, 2000; Scott, 1995). In the global information economy, the motivation to enter into or to build business networks is more and more compelling for many trends (Iandoli et al., 2004).

- First, market internationalization and the availability of large amounts of data and information, facilitated by Internet-based collaborative systems have made it possible for organizations to search for partners on a global scale.

- The second trend is the challenge of off-shore outsourcing to coordinate activities that are geographically and globally dispersed. The result is a complex value chain extending across continents in which many of the links among members are increasingly based on strategic relationships and focus on core competencies. In these complex and articulated inter-organizational networks, information systems play a major role in linking activities to ensure a smooth and economic flow from suppliers to customers.

- The third trend is of collaboration among new forms of inter-organizational cross-boundary alliances that are based on sharing of product research and development, and sharing of ordering, manufacturing and logistics processes.

As a result of above trends, market globalization and the diffusion and growth of technology have modified companies' structures and their inter-organizational relationships. Companies belong more and more to transnational networks made up by quasi independent units operating on the global market. A new organizational paradigm, the so called extended enterprise, is often evoked to describe this transition (Kinder, 2003). An extended enterprise employs enterprise global information systems to provide excellent integrative capability among different functional enterprises in an industry and information localization and delivery within the entire network.

Global IS contributes to provide the extended enterprise with useful tools for the coordination and management of both intra and inter organizational networks, Global ISs aid in managing and analyzing large quantity of data derived from computer and network transactions in globally dispersed areas. These systems also support decision making at the operational, tactical and strategic levels for the global organization.

However, there are costs involved in managing massive amount of global data. Interfacing and coordinating different networks systems belonging to different companies create new management problems. Information management becomes very complex and difficult of both syntactic and semantic aspects which require an approach more oriented to knowledge management than to traditional information management.

The following case study related to Ducati, a global manufacturer of sports motorcycles, exemplifies some trends outlined above. First, it gives an idea of the complexity of the business network the company is involved in. It also provides some examples of how IT systems can be developed and used to manage a global network. Second, Ducati is not a multinational giant but represents a good example of those small and middle-sized multinational companies that have redesigned their organizational model and have adopted global IT systems to enable them to operate effectively in the global economy.

CASE STUDY: DUCATI – USING IT TO BUILD VIRTUAL VALUE CHAIN FROM SUPPLIERS TO VIRTUAL COMMUNITIES OF CUSTOMERS[2]

Ducati is an Italian company that leads in the production of high performance motorcycles. Ducati sells motorcycles, accessories and sport/merchandising wear in more than 40 countries and is one of the most competitive racing team of the world in the superbike class. The use of IT-enabled management systems at Ducati is pervasive in all segments of the company's value chain.

Motorcycle production is enabled by MRP systems aimed at monitoring the information flow from customers' orders to material planning and stock management. An IT platform has been built to ensure high integration and synchronization with suppliers. On the selling side, Ducati developed an Extranet called DesmoNet™ in 2000 that connected sellers and assistance points all over Europe allowing the company to monitor in real time its sale network.

But IT does more than helping companies to coordinate their operations. Many products in the global information economy are more than tangible objects merely satisfying material needs of buyers. Companies increasingly practice the concept of Integrate Offer i.e., they try to build an integrated combination of services, contents, customization and community around a product. For customers, belonging to a community means not only to share the ownership of the same product but but also common languages, life-styles, and values and aspirations. For certain kind of products, their symbolic value, i.e. the perception of the customers, is by far more important than what they actually are or how they are concretely made or perform. This is particularly true in the motorcycle industry. For a motorcycle owner, his/her preference for one model over another is often influenced by factors that are not merely related to technical performances or costs, but to cultural and social factors such as their reputation in sport competition (Honda, Yamaha, Ducati), or lifestyle and fashion (Harley Davidson, Piaggio with the famous Vespa).

On the B2C side Ducati has developed a web site that is visited on average by more than one hundred thousands web surfers per day. More than 20,000 fans are registered worldwide. They

---

[2] This case study has been adapted by us from Prandelli and Verona (2002), Internet Marketing, McGrawHill

receive a company newsletter about racing competition, new products, and other company promotional initiatives. E-commerce activity was initially limited to auctions of special products for collectors and fans such as vintage products or special accessories. Then customers were encouraged to buy some special models in limited production, such as the MH900. However, the company strategy was not to build an e-commerce site but a virtual meeting place for the community of Ducati customers and fans aimed at enhancing brand recognition and to "feel the pulse" of the clients. For this reason the web site was developed as a portal hosting vertical sites such as ducaticorse.com, memorabilia.ducati.com, ducatistore.com where customers can find detailed information, merchandising and news about Ducati products and activities.

The model MH900 has been the first model sold on-line. After the opening of the on-line selling in 2000 on January 1st the company was able to sell in few minutes the equivalent of one year production. Customers were required to pay on line only 10% of the total price. The remaining payment was made at the time of delivery in the nearest Ducati store.

In the future Ducati's objective is to become the main vertical portal for motorcyclists, in particular for those interested in racing. The virtual community serves also as a C2C virtual market allowing customers to buy used motorcycles from other customers and using the Ducati web site for transactions. The virtual community site offers many entertainment services and contents to visitors, such as forum, FAQ, chat, games, news, and the Desmo Card. The Desmo Card permits customers to store on the card's chip technical and historical data of their own motorcycle, so that any Ducati store will be able to have immediate access to information such as previous problems, past maintenance interventions, and so on.

The integration of services to the community through the Ducati web site allows company to build a huge database concerning customers' needs, habits, and preferences. Using this database, customer relationship management software can be effectively implemented.

Overall it is possible to say that the availability of a pervasive IT infrastructure like in the Ducati case, allows companies, in particular those operating in traditional manufacturing industry to build a digital value chain on top of the traditional value chain aimed at creating, producing and distributing contents, services and at building virtual community of users, as showed in Figure 4.

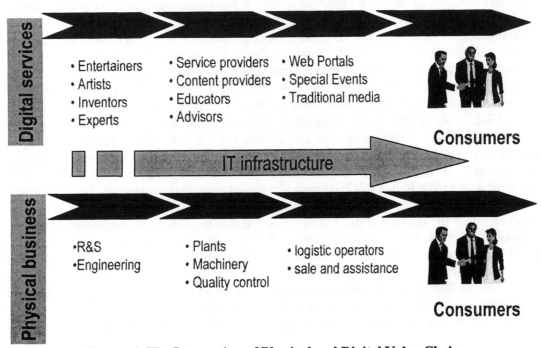

Figure 4. The Integration of Physical and Digital Value Chain

CONCLUSION

In this chapter we introduced and discussed the concept of a global information system. These systems are used by organizations that operate in the global environment to help support decision-making, manage organizational data, support and enable organizational business processes, facilitate organizational communications, and support global business strategy. The impact of the increasing number of global information systems in organizations will be felt by all stakeholders in the system. Organizations will need more people with skills who are willing to travel across national boundaries and cultures. Managers in companies will have to retrain themselves to ensure that they understand the issues involved in managing a global IS. Information system workers in organizations will have to reeducate themselves to sharpen their skills so that they can work in virtual teams with people from diverse backgrounds. Future information system managers will need to understand the challenges involved in managing a global IS. Management information systems (MIS) programs across the world need to redesign their programs to incorporate the global dimension in their curriculum. Students of information system need to make sure they understand how these systems are designed, developed, used and managed. In addition to taking courses in MIS they will have to take language (Spanish, French etc.) courses, acquire soft skills that help them communicate with people from around the world and be aware of and sensitive to multiple cultures. Are you ready to be a participant in the global economy? If yes, make sure that you understand the issues, and know what needs to be done to meet the challenge to be a IS professional in the global world.

MINICASE

CHL: Exploiting the Virtual and Real Value Chain for Global Business

This case represents an interesting example of how in the global information economy companies try to exploit the advantages offered by on-line commerce and the benefits of IT use in building and controlling a virtual value chain. At the same time, however the new IT based business model has to be integrated with the real physical world and with more traditional issues such logistics and post sale assistance. While IT-enabled management systems permit companies to operate globally without limitations in time and space, IT alone is not sufficient to deal with many processes requiring face-to-face interaction with the customers or physical delivery of products.

CHL is an on-line Italian company founded in the early nineties whose business was initially assembling personal computers and on-line selling. Later CHL started to sell on-line many kinds of electronic devices such as mobiles phones, digital cameras, computer accessories, and equipment for digital entertainment such as home theatre, hi-fi, etc. Today CHL can be considered as the main Italian B2C companies in digital consumer equipments. In the first half of the nineties, when Internet use was still relatively scarce in Italy, CHL adopted a pioneering system based on the Bulletin Board System (BBS) technology allowing customers to access the company product database, insert an order and buy a PC. The first initial market target was formed by undergraduate students of technical faculties wanting to customize their PC. In 1995 the company started its own e-commerce web site. In 1996 CHL opened its first Popitt (POint of Presence In The Territory). A Popitt was not a shop where goods were exposed for customers but a place where customers could go to use available PC to connect with the CHL web site and make an order. In those years internet diffusion in Italy was relatively scarce and many people still did not have a connection at home. For the same reasons, in the same period there was in Italy, like in other countries, a tremendous growth of the so-called internet café, public places where people could go and access the Internet while possibly enjoying a cup of coffee or another drink.

The Popitts were also created to allow customers to get post-sale or technical assistance or to pick up their PC after delivery to the mail-boxes of an express courier. The logistic model developed by CHL through the Popitts is depicted in Figure 5.

The main advantage derived from the adoption of such a model is not delivery cost reduction. Actually for the company the cost for delivering goods at a Popitt or at customer's home is more or less the same in most of the cases. Rather, the Popitt model was aimed at making customers confident with on line purchase, providing them with a tangible local reference point where to get assistance and face-to-face interaction, facilitating payment for the purchased goods without credit card for on-line transaction. At the beginning of the internet era this model facilitated and encouraged customers to buy on-line. And this still happens in many developing economies where internet access is problematic and customers' and sellers' diffidence is quite high toward electronic business or, more in general, toward business virtualization and dematerialization through IT.

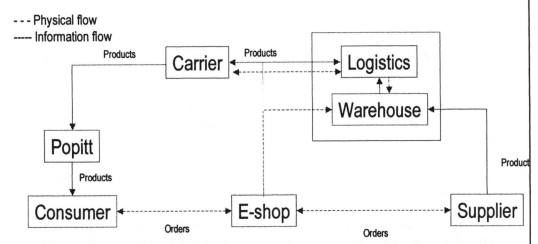

Figure 5. The Pick-up point model (adapted from Prandelli e Verona, 2002)

The Popitt model actually helped the company to build a physical sale network, i.e. to integrate a traditional business model with a new one. Today, due to internet diffusion and e-commerce growth the Popitt model has lost its initial role and the company is more oriented to a pure e-commerce model with the strategic objective to be the first Italian vertical portal for consumer electronics.

Discussion Questions:
1. Describe the business network in which CHL operates.
2. Outline the characteristics of the integrated offer in the case of CHL.
3. Using figure 5 as a framework, try to illustrate and describe the value chain of CHL.

KEY TERMS
Access paradox
Business process
Competition paradox
Data Warehouse
Database
Database Management System
Enterprise Resource Planning (ERP)
Global information system (GIS)
Knowledge sharing
Multinational
Organizational networks
Outsourcing
Production database
Productivity paradox
Virtual teams

STUDY QUESTIONS

1. What role does technology play in global corporations? Define a global information system (GIS)?

2. Identify and discuss the main changes that globalization and IT diffusion have on companies operating in the global economy. What are the major implications of such changes for these companies?

3. Describe the characteristics of a global information system (GIS) and illustrate how global IT management can help companies to compete effectively in the global economy.

4. In the global economy the role of Multinational corporations and of outsourcing has evolved and changed through time. Describe such evolution and provide an explanation for these changes.

5. Identify and describe examples of multinational companies that have been able to set up and manage effective networked organizations? Discuss these networks by using the framework suggested in this chapter?

6. What is an integrated offer? Provide examples of integrated offers and discuss them in the context of the framework suggested in the chapter?

REFERENCES

Alavi, M. and Young, G. *Information Technology in an International Enterprise: An Organizing Framework in The Global Issues of Information Technology Management* by Palvia, Palvia, and Zigli (eds). 1992, pp. 495-516.

Becattini, G. *Il Distretto Industriale, Rosenberg e Sellier,* Torino, Italy. 2000.

Brynjolfsson, E. "Beyond the productivity paradox," *Communications of the ACM,* 41(8), 1998, pp. 49-55.

Davis, S. and Meyer, C. BLUR- The Speed of Change in the Connected Economy, Capstone, Oxford. 1998.

Deans, P. C., Karawan, K. R., Goslar, M. D., Ricks, D. A., and Toyne, B. "Identification of the key international information systems issues in U.S. based multinational corporations," *Journal of Management Information Systems*, 7(4), 1991, pp. 27-50.

Deans, P. C., and Ricks, D. A. "MIS research: A model for incorporating the international dimension," The Journal of High Technology Management Research, 2(1), 1991, pp. 57-81.

Doz, Y., Santos, J., and Wiliamson, P. "From global to metanational: How Companies Win in the Knowledge Economy," *Harvard Business School Press*, Cambridge, MA. 2001.

Ein-Dor, P., Segev, E., and Orgad, M. "The Effect of National Culture on IS: Implications for International Information Systems," 1(1), Spring 1993, pp. 33-44.

Harris, D. H. (Ed. by), *Organizational Linkages: Understanding the Productivity Paradox*. Washington, DC : National Academy Press. 1994.

Hofstede, G., Neuijen, B., and Sanders, G. "Measuring Organizational Cultures: A Qualitative and Quantitative Study across Twenty Cases," *Administrative Science Quarterly*, 35, 1990, pp. 286-316.

Iandoli, L. Shore, B., Venkatachalam, A. R., Zollo, G. "Towards a Learning Organization Perspective to Supplier Selection for Global Supply Chain Management: an Integrated Framework", Journal of Information Science and Technology, 1(1), 2004, pp. 26-43.

ITU. World Telecommunications Indicators. Geneva, Switzerland. 2001.

Ives B., and Jarvenpaa S. L. "Applications of global information technology: Key issues for management," *MIS Quarterly,* 15(1), 1991, March, pp. 33-49.

Kinder, T. "Go with the flow—a conceptual framework for supply relations in the era of the extended enterprise", *Research Policy*, 32, 2003, pp. 503–523.

King, W. R. "Outsourcing and Offshoring: The New IS Paradigm." *Journal of Global Information Technology Management*, 8(2), 2005, pp. 1-4.

Kumar, A. and Basu, S. C. "Towards a Deeper Examination of Global IT Theory and Frameworks." *Journal of Global Information Technology Management,* 5(4), October 2002, pp. 4-17.

Kumar, A. and Palvia, P. C. *Developing Global Executive Information Systems in Global Information Technology and Electronic Commerce: Issues for the New Millennium* by Palvia, Palvia and Roche (eds.), Ivy League Publishing, Limited Georgia, USA, pp. 408-429. 2002.

Mann, C. L., Eckert S. E., and Knight S. C. *Global Electronic Commerce*. Institute for International Economics, Washington DC. 2000.

Mann, J. "Global Issues and the Importance of Fit*." Journal of Global Information Technology Management,* 8(1), 2005, pp. 1-5.

Marshall, A. Principles of Economics. London: Macmillan. 1965.

Palvia, P.C. "Global Information Technology Research: Past, Present and Future," *Journal of Global Information Technology Management*, 1(2), 1998, pp. 3-14.

Palvia, P. C. *Strategic Applications of Information Technology in Global Business: The 'GLITS' Model and an Instrument in Global Information Technology and Electronic Commerce: Issues for the New Millennium* by Palvia, Palvia and Roche (eds.), Ivy League Publishing, Limited Georgia, USA, 2002, pp. 100-119.

Palvia, P. C., Palvia, S. C., and Whitworth, J. E. *Global Information Technology Management Environment: Representative World Issues in Global Information Technology and Electronic Commerce: Issues for the New Millennium* by Palvia, Palvia and Roche (eds.), Ivy League Publishing, Limited Georgia, USA, pp. 2-27.

Porter, M. E. *Competitive Strategy: Techniques for Analyzing Industries and Competitors*, New York: the Free press. 1980.

Prandelli, E., Verona, G. *Marketing in rete. Analisi e decisioni nell'economia digitale*, McGraw-Hill. 2002.

Rayport, J. F., Sviokla, J. J. "Exploiting the virtual value chain", The McKinsey Quarterly, 1, 1996, pp. 21-37.

Rifkin, J. *The Age of Access*, Penguin Putnam. 2000.

Scott, W. R. *Institutions and Organizations,* Thousand Oaks (CA): Sage. 1995.

Shore, B., and Venkatachalam, A. R. "he role of national culture in systems analysis and design," *Journal of Global Information Management,* 3(3), 1995, pp. 5-14.

Taylor, W. and Webber, A. *Going Global,* New York: Viking, 1996.

Tetteh, E. O. and Burn, J. M. *A Framework for the Management of Global e-Business in Small and Medium-Sized Enterprises in Global Information Technology and Electronic Commerce: Issues for the New Millennium* by Palvia, Palvia and Roche (eds.), Ivy League Publishing, Limited Georgia, USA, 2002, pp. 275-293.

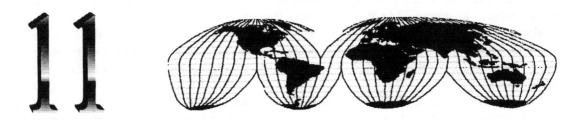

Governance in the Global Information Economy

F. Warren McFarlan
Harvard Business School, USA

CHAPTER SUMMARY

In the early 21st century, IT has become more important than ever. Technology evolution, the creation of new channels to global resource pools, increased corporate operational dependence on IT, and enhanced application opportunities have combined to drive this topic much higher on many companies' agendas. Different companies are impacted in different ways. Embedded in this chapter are two analytical frameworks often used by managers to understand this different impact; namely, the strategic grid and technological learning.

Some aspects of IT have remained unchanged over a 40-year period. These include the constant emergence of new technologies, the obsolescence of technical skills, and the need for strong leadership. For many firms, however, this technology now has a much deeper impact on the transformation of their operations than could have been conceived several decades ago. The chapter successively describes how Otis, World Bank, COSCO and Cathay Pacific have each been utterly transformed by IT.

INTRODUCTION

In the field of information technology, governance has been a timeless and enduring problem. The first Harvard Business School case on the subject was prepared in 1961 entitled "Harmony Life of Hartford"(Overman, 1961) and the issues in that case are still worthy of discussion today. In my first IT book in 1965, a chapter was devoted to the topic, (Dearden & McFarlan, 1965) and it was the primary topic in 1967 in *Computers and Management* (Leatherbee, 1967). In short, the historical roots of the area are deep.

However, the topic turns out to be even more important as we complete the first decade of the 21st century. In numerous organizations, IT is such a critical component of competitiveness and value added that its oversight now extends to the board of directors in companies such as Home Depot, Novell and Procter & Gamble (Nolan & McFarlan, 2005).

What are the factors that made the topic so important today? The first and foremost is the relentless improvement of new hardware and software technologies whose underlying cost effectiveness is not only improving at 35% + per year, but will continue to do so at the same rate for the next several decades. The art of the possible keeps changing as chip performance, telecommunications bandwidth, and enabling software capabilities which can effectively use these characteristics continue to improve. At the same time, the way of delivering these resources has powerfully changed from the "build and run" paradigm that dominated the 1970s to the package "source and tailor" mode and similarly operations have changed from running your own to being increasingly outsourced. All of this has called for both modifications in and increased visibility of the IT governance process.

Furthermore, in the networked world, the ability to access resources now takes place on a global basis. No author has been more influential in describing this phenomenon than Thomas Friedman in his book, "The World is Flat" (Friedman, 2005). He notes the combination of the fall of the Berlin Wall, the Internet boom and, the rush of telecommunication companies to build massive cheap fiber networks around the world created the opportunities for insourcing, outsourcing, offshoring, open sourcing, supply chaining and informating - topics which consume today's IT practice. The fiber optic links have become digital highways which arbitrage the global labor markets as India, China, and others and now vital interlinked components of the global economy.

The development of these new technologies for many firms has created an unprecedented level of operational dependence on IT and major risks exist if the organization can not run 24/7 with sub-second response time virtually all the time. In a world where global warming is being replaced by the concerns relating to "Peak oil" and rolling blackouts (Simmons, 2005), this level of operational dependence must be managed in a much more sophisticated way. Similarly, the possibility of "force majore" means one's global operations must be carefully tuned so that if several elements of the supporting global IT infrastructure collapse, the organization can continue operating.

On the other hand, fundamental new applications have emerged which have deeply impacted organization's competitiveness and service not only in the for-profit world, but in the field of government and non-profits. These applications range from growth companies like Otis to challenged ones like Lucent (Otis, 2004, Lucent, 2003). In each company, the new infrastructure now allows work to be done five-times faster than previously. Business process outsourcing as a way of managing cost and improving service has exploded across the globe. A company like Cathay Pacific Airlines (Cathay, 2003) headquartered in Hong Kong now has its data center located 4,000 miles away in Sydney, Australia where it is currently outsourced to IBM/Australia.

Product structures have been deeply impacted with the electronic component of the automobile now being higher in value than the steel and safety components which are in the car. Finally, courtesy of satellites, information service can be reliably driven to the farthest corners of the world. For example, the World Bank (World Bank, 2003) today now supports 109 data-intensive operations in the third world through their satellite-based network.

While these potential opportunities all stand in front of a firm, the management question of when and how to invest vis-à-vis competitors remains a burning issue. Does one want to be a first mover like Charles Schwab (Schwab, 2001) in the brokerage industry on online Internet service, or is it better to be a fast follower like Merrill Lynch (Merrill Lynch, 2001) was. These are not easy questions to answer as the risks are often very finely balanced. At the same time, a whole series of services have simply become strategic necessities and there is no choice but to invest to create and maintain them, if one wants to survive (Clemons, 1986).

Looking beyond the world of IT, recent new standards of governance and accountability in arenas such as accounting, courtesy of Sarbanes-Oxley, have surged forward. The wretched excesses of Enron and WorldCom combined to create important new tighter standards of corporate accountability and closer control over data flows. These issues converge to make IT governance an area of heightened importance. The opportunity for IT to create customized and differentiated outputs makes it sharply different at this stage from the commodity "electricity" (with its long history), and it cannot be ignored by management as a potential source of added competitive value. The IT Governance Institute (ITGI) was established in 1998 to provide focus on and study the critical issues on IT governance (IT Governance, 2003).

How do organizations go about thinking about these issues? There are two important frameworks brought to this task that shape the approach an organization undertakes for its IT governance. The first one is the strategic grid (Pyburn, 1983) and the second is the Levers of Governance (Nolan, 2005).

STRATEGIC GRID FRAMEWORK

Different organizations are challenged by IT at different points in time in different ways. One governance structure will not work for all. Exhibit 1 is a framework which has been used since the mid-1980s for thinking about this phenomenon. Exhibit 2 suggests some of its macro governance implications. The different quadrants can be described as follows (Nolan, 2005).

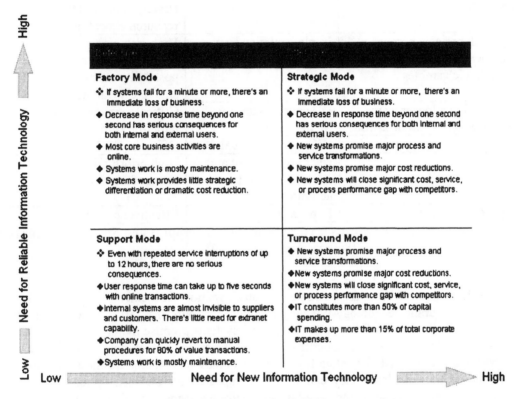

Exhibit 1. Strategic Grid Framework

Support: Firms in this quadrant have both a relatively low need for reliability and a low need for strategic IT; technology fundamentally exists to support employees' activities. The Spanish clothier Zara, which began as a small retail shop, is a good example; the company keeps strict control over its supply chain operations by designing, producing, and distributing its own clothing. Though IT is used in these areas, the company won't suffer terribly if a system goes down (Zara, 2004). Core business systems are generally run on a batch cycle; most error correction and backup work is done manually. Customers and suppliers don't have access to internal systems. Companies in the support quadrant can suffer repeated service interruptions of up to 12 hours without serious bottom-line consequences, and high-speed Internet response time isn't critical.

Factory: Companies in this quadrant need highly reliable systems but don't really require state-of-the art computing. They resemble manufacturing plants; if the conveyor belts fail, production stops.

Airlines and other businesses that depend on fast, secure, real-time data response fall into this group. These companies are much more dependent on the smooth operation of their technology, since most of their core business systems are online. They suffer an immediate loss of business if systems fail even for a minute; reversion to manual procedures is difficult, if not impossible. Factory-quadrant firms generally depend on their extranets to communicate with customers and suppliers. New IT service innovation is not part of this quadrant's activities.

Support	Activity	Strategic
Middle level management	Organization integration mechanisms	Active senior management involvement key
Less urgent; mistakes in resource allocation not fatal	Planning	Critical; must link to corporate strategy; careful attention to resource allocation vital
Avoid high-risk projects because of constrained benefits; poor place for corporate strategic gambles	Implementation risk profile project portfolio	High-risk/high-potential benefit projects appropriate if possibility exists to gain strategic advantage
Can be managed in a looser way; operational headaches less disastrous	IT capacity/security Management	Critical to manage; 24/7 bullet-proof reliability
Can be lower	CIO reporting level	Office of CEO
Lower priority Difficult standards tradeoff	User involvement and control over systems activities	High priority/difficult standards tradeoff
Efficiency – cost control	Expense control	Effectiveness key word

Exhibit 2. Different Managerial Strategies for Companies in Support and Strategic Quadrants
(Source: Applegate, 1999)

Turnaround: Companies in the midst of strategic transformation frequently bet the farm on new technology. In this quadrant, technology typically accounts for more than 50% of corporate capital expenditures and more than 15% of corporate costs. New systems promise major process and service improvements, cost reductions, and a competitive edge. At the same time, companies in this quadrant have a comparatively low need for reliability when it comes to existing business systems; like companies in the support quadrant, they can withstand repeated service interruptions of up to 12 hours without serious consequences, and core business activities remain on a batch cycle. Once the new systems are installed, however, there is no possible reversion to manual systems because all procedures have been captured into databases. Over time, the reliability of systems becomes more of an issue and many firms leave this quadrant as they go higher on the operational reliability axis.

Strategic: For some companies, total innovation and total uptime reliability is the name of the game. New technology informs not only the way they approach the marketplace but also the way they carry out daily operations. Strategic-quadrant firms do this, but they also aggressively pursue process and service opportunities, cost reductions, and more competitive advantages. Like turnaround firms, their IT expenditures are large.

Technology Learning

From the beginning of the field in the early 1970s, it was noted that new technologies required very different management approach to assimilate than ones which the organization was familiar with. Nolan and Gibson (1974) in their "Stages of DP Growth" identified these stages as discovery, contagion, control and steady state. Technologies in each of these stages required a different governance and management approach. The need to manage different technologies in a company in different ways depending on the organization's understanding of them remains a dominant issue today.

WHAT HAS STAYED THE SAME?

As we look back over the last 40 years, there are some governance issues and challenges which have remained intact. The best-selling 1966 *Harvard Business Review* article was entitled "The Myth of Real Time Management Information" (Dearden, 1966). This article was widely acclaimed by business executives and even academics. The reality in the early 21st century is that almost everything that John Dearden attacked has become standard operating procedure today. Nearly 40 years later, however, the best selling article in the *Harvard Business Review* was Nick Carr's "IT Doesn't Matter." (Carr, 2003) This article attracted a stream of heated attacks. What has remained constant over the 40 years is that when you are trying to execute massive organization change, it is too much to ask to be liked for it by those whose lives you are changing. Often only the passage of time allows the full impact of a new technology to be seen and the world to accept it as an accomplished reality.

As noted earlier, rapid technology change has been an enduring feature of the past. Less well understood but perhaps more important is that organizational resistance to change has been a dominant reality of life for the past 40 years. The author of this chapter noted in 1968 that the primary discipline in the IT arena was applied organizational psychology as opposed to that of technology. Nothing in these intervening years has caused him to change his mind. The governance processes must deal with overcoming substantial internal hostility and organizational inertia; phenomena which have remained intact over the forty years.

Technology skill obsolescence and concern about how to maintain an organization skill base have been an enormous challenge which governance has had to address. Sometimes for firms like Pfizer, the problem of doing this inside the firm has been seen to be so complex and risky that outsourcing was seen to be the most viable solution (Pfizer, 2004). Similarly, many organizations have failed to understand the negative impact of cost structures and the information silos created by legacy processes and the consequent drag they pose to the organizations' adaptiveness.

Most importantly, throughout the entire forty years, the need for capable IT leadership (in the form of what we call today a CIO) has been a vital element of governance. Similarly, while the urgency is higher today, efficiency, capacity, reliability, and security issues have always been key topics to be addressed in the governance process. Finally, for over 25 years, the application development portfolio as a way of thinking about the total thrust of investment and its implementation risks have been well understood and an approach focused on by governance (McFarlan, 1981). In short, there are many aspects of the governance challenge which have remained the same over a long period of time. This is not a new field.

WHAT HAS CHANGED?

While a number of things have remained constant over the last 40 years, there have also been some dramatic changes for some firms in applications and operational dependence, which have triggered major changes in governance processes. These dramatic application and operational dependence changes have particularly been felt in the arena of fundamental infrastructure transformation. Many of the changes have driven firms into the strategic quadrant and have forced extraordinary governance methods to ensure success. The following paragraphs describe four of these companies.

Otis Elevator (Otis, 2004)
Otis is the world's largest elevator company, founded more than 150 years ago. It is currently both the world's most profitable elevator company as well as the one earning the highest return on assets.

For more than 20 years, IT has been at the heart of the transformation of Otis. In 1985, the Otis field service organization was a 4-level hierarchical structure with its 122 branch offices being at the base of the hierarchy. These branch offices were responsible for receiving all elevator service calls, dispatching mechanics to handle the service calls, as well as attending to the bookkeeping and other activities after the call was completed and its results reported by the mechanic back to the branch. Monthly, the branches would report levels of activity up through the hierarchy. This led to repeated situations where often through bad reporting (often deliberate), major service problems were hidden at the base of the organization and senior management was not aware of the quality performance of any of the offices, specific product lines or individual mechanics.

In 1986, under the leadership of CEO, George David, they installed a new organization unit at corporate headquarters called Otisline. Staffed by over 160 people, it operated on a 24/7 basis. All service telephone service calls were routed immediately to corporate headquarters where they were logged in on the central computer through a terminal. A dispatch operator at Otisline then routed the specific call to the appropriate mechanic, who had a computer device on his belt to receive the call. The mechanic would receive the call, go to the site, fix the elevator, and then report the results back to Otisline. With this reporting system, Otis was quickly able to evaluate:

Which branches were good both in fast response to calls and fixing the elevator so it didn't break again?
Which mechanics were good with fixing elevators so they stayed fixed?
Which product lines were causing an excessive amount of failure, thereby allowing new design work to be undertaken by Otis to permanently alleviate the problem?

These features led to a number of staffing and product changes. A system which was simple on the surface, in fact, caused a dramatic upheaval in the company's operations and performance. A long-time *bottoms-up* organization structure with an empowered set of mechanics and branch office managers (largely unsupervised) suddenly became a *top-down* measurement organization. Troubled mechanics and branch offices were quickly flagged for management performance reviews; product lines that were not doing well were subject to similar initiatives. In the process, the 4-level hierarchical organization, with 800 people in the middle two layers, was flattened with two layers being eliminated. The installation of this system destroyed every norm of what was seen to be appropriate practice in the company while also producing a 50% reduction in elevator service calls because of the sharp improvement in quality that resulted from fixing elevators right the first time. This project was aggressively managed by the President, George David. He not only conceived the project, but provided the hands-on guidance for its development and shot personal videotapes on the project's importance that all people in the company had to see. A key part of the implementation process was the visible unswerving support of the CEO. Otis, a division of United Technologies, handled this work on an independent basis with the key person in the governance process being their active impatient CEO. The turnaround and its financial impact were so complete and thorough that George David was ultimately promoted and today is Chairman of United Technologies, Otis's parent.

Twenty years later, the company is in the midst of another dramatic information-enabled shift in its infrastructure. This initiative is designed to dramatically speed up the processing of orders in the field and sharply reduce product inventories. The name of the project is e*Logistics and has consumed to date over 300-person years of effort in design and implementation. The project reports directly to Ari Bousbib, the current Otis CEO, who every two weeks chairs the Review Committee looking after the project. The main achievement of the project has included a reduction of the 340-day cycle from quoting an order, to installing an elevator, and completing the billing to 68 days. This is a 5-fold improvement. A dramatic reduction in inventory in the field construction sites is a result of changing the manufacturing strategy from a push strategy to a pull strategy. In the previous approach, Otis concentrated on running smooth, efficient factories, whose inventory levels of $140 million turned ten times a year. Totally neglected was the $2-1/2 billion of inventory, which was scattered over thousands of sites, waiting to be installed, and turning at a rate of one-turn per year (Bousbib, 2004). It has been dramatically reduced. Simplification of the preparation of elevator price quotes to customers was so dramatic that, for example in the U.K., they were able to do five times more quotes, leading to a 16% increase in revenue.

The technology and change management problems of e*Logistics were extraordinary as the system had to run reliably on a standardized basis across 20,000 PCs hooked to 1,000 local area networks scattered across 200 countries. These initiatives helped Otis to recently jump 5% points in terms of its return on sales. Otis now generates 40% of all of United Technology's profits.

This was only made possible by a broad-based visionary CEO who, coming from outside the company, was able to conceive both an understanding of the problem and then drive the necessary changes in the company's systems and processes to help the firm reach 21st century performance standards. In a dramatic way in his words, "…. led Otis from being a manufacturing company to being an information-enabled logistics and service firm where factories were only kept if they could produce superior products at a better cost than outsourced alternatives." In fact, twenty-six of fifty two factories were closed. Today Otis benchmarks their service against companies like FedEx and the Ritz Carlton Hotel. In short, for 20 years, the key to Otis's success in performing well in the strategic quadrant has been the unabashed leadership of two CEOs in conceiving and driving transformation by their personal energy and involvement. Often the CIOs, while good at implementation, did not understand the totality of what they were doing.

World Bank (World Bank, 2003)

The World Bank is a venerable Washington based organization committed to providing financial aid and financial resources to the third world. When Jim Wolfensohn became its CEO in 1995, the World Bank operated in 109 countries. It was a large bureaucratic organization with all its data files and much of its staff located in Washington, D.C. far away from the problems in the local countries.

Jim's vision was that the major challenges of the World Bank lay out in the field and that was where he wanted his leadership and staff to be physically located. This led to an aggressive effort to develop a world-class centrally managed information system, whose full knowledge and content could be easily accessed in the farthest corners of the world. This system would support the information needs of onsite country managers, which sharply reduced the need for their physical presence in Washington.

Over five years, the World Bank transformed itself from primitive, silo-oriented, Washington-based batch-processing systems to a full online state-of-the-art capability where the entire database and knowledge base became instantly electronically accessible 24/7 through three satellite based networks to the 109 offices, primarily located in the most impoverished parts of the globe. Often driven by local electric generators to get power, these low offices now had high-speed access to the latest reports and information from Washington. Indeed, their information is so comprehensive that the local governments have requested (and received) access to this information to better manage their own activities, which are not supported by data and information services of this quality. Delivered on a 24/7 basis, this information capability allowed the World Bank to reposition both its staff and its leadership from Washington to the field. Today, more than 70% of the country managers are now resident in the countries as opposed to Washington (up from 0% five years earlier). Also, substantial amounts of staff have been redeployed from Washington to the countries where the real problems are.

The key to making this happen was first the unabashed leadership and vision of Jim Wolfensohn, who saw a fundamentally different way of the organizational model, which would dramatically improve the World Bank's performance and the role IT would have to play to make it happen.

The second key was his selection as CIO of Mohamed Muhsin. Mohamed was a long-term, extraordinarily well-connected staff member at the World Bank, who had served widely across the globe in a variety of financial jobs. Under him, Mohamed Muhsin built a very strong technical team to develop this leading-edge system. The major challenges the World Bank faced in developing and installing the system was first deep change management in the organization's operations. Global redeployment of both managers and staff was very complex. The second challenge was managing the movement of the technology to parts of the world that had never before been supported in this way.

It was the unusual combination of Jim Wolfensohn's vision and Mohamed Muhsin's user language skills, combined with the acquisition and management of great technical talent that enabled the World Bank to fundamentally rebuild itself over five years as an enhanced information-enabled organization; with key staff moved from Washington to the field where the real problems were. It is startling to see in a world where we talk about the digital divide to see an organization where the most sophisticated databases and knowledge sets are delivered to the most impoverished parts of the globe in a way that not only improves the operations of the World Bank's local offices, but also supports local government operations who do not have data of this quality.

Again, this is a strategic quadrant organization. At the core of this story are a strong CEO leader and a strong user-oriented CIO who have combined to solve the major problems on change management. In this case, however, unlike Otis, the technologies were extraordinarily complicated for the environment where they were being deployed requiring the management of a different set of challenges.

COSCO (COSCO, 2005)

COSCO, a China state-owned enterprise, is the #2 shipping company in the world with over 550 ships, whose headquarters are based in Dalian, China. Their objective is to be the largest shipping company in the world in the next 2-3 years; a goal which increasingly seems doable. Shipping and port management is a deeply information intensive operation as global tracking systems have emerged across the industry which track and guide the movement of a container from the moment it leaves the customer until it lands in the recipient's intended hands, allowing quick redeployment if necessary.

COSCO did not come to this problem with great technical strength. Indeed in 2000, the Chinese Academy of Science prepared a deeply critical report which benchmarked COSCO's service and performance against its leading competitors and found that they were very backward and not operating at either 21st century service or cost standards. This report was delivered to Capt. Wei Jiafu, CEO of COSCO, one of the rising stars in both state owned enterprise and the government. As a result of this report, he made COSCO's IT reinvention his #1 priority.

The IT activities of the company were moved to report directly to him, new leadership hired, a major increase in staff was authorized, and a number of packages were acquired. Additionally, to gain further insight into what the best of the best were doing, they were the first company to buy a container dock in Singapore in a joint partnership with PSA (Port of the Singapore Authority), the leading port authority in terms of IT service in the world (PSA, 2002). Today, COSCO, with an average IT staff age of 28, is well on its way to being an IT leader in its industry. At great expense they have been able to reposition themselves from a lower support quadrant company to one which is steadily moving up towards the strategic quadrant and improving its customer service. Additionally, they have moved from IT ship enabled operations to running IT activities in various ports around the world as the port operations industry centralizes around a few providers.

At every step along the way, the combined impetus of the outside benchmark study and the CEO has driven this transformation. They have aggressively dealt with new technologies and willingly undertaken new levels of operational risk as they have transformed their business model. New alliances (like PSA) have been an important part of their governance strategy as they expand their reach to the best of new technologies.

Cathay Pacific (Cathay, 2003)

Cathay Pacific, a midsized Hong Kong based national air carrier, illustrates another set of issues. Founded in 1947, Cathay Pacific was an early and aggressive user of IT in the 1970s and 1980s, as it grew to encompass routes across six continents, and sold its software packages to other Asian carriers.

During the 1980s, however, the IT department at Cathay Pacific evolved from one which designed systems, wrote code and installed systems to one which acquired packages and tailored them to the company's needs. While Cathay Pacific still possesses substantial amounts of legacy code, an aggressive plan to eliminate it in the next two years is now underway. With high reliance on 24/7 operations, they settled into the factory quadrant and became a fast follower of the innovations by carriers like American Airlines.

By 1997, they had already outsourced much of their systems development work through the acquisition of packages. However, in the mean time, another opportunity had emerged. In 1995, the most expensive real estate in the world was in Hong Kong and Cathay Pacific had five data centers located there. Concerned both with cost and the underlying quality of the operations, their board commissioned the CIO to lead a broad review of how they could reduce IT operating costs while remaining in control. The final recommendation was to move 67% of all of their IT staff (and costs) including all data centers from Hong Kong to Sydney, Australia (only two time zones away, but 4,000 miles away as well). After studying the new possibilities opened in the networked world, they came to the conclusion this was completely viable with low operational risk. They then proceeded to move substantial numbers of staff and all the data center operations activity from Hong Kong to Sydney. Two years later, focusing more clearly on what their core competencies were, they outsourced the Australian operation to IBM-Australia, who runs it today. The story is a fascinating one. The Hong Kong airline reliably runs its IT service, 4,000 miles away from home.

The challenge the company faces today is even more interesting. As a result of history, in 1984, Cathay Pacific was denied landing rights in China (with the recent exceptions of one daily round trip to Beijing), which is today the world's fastest growing air market. Over the past ten years in China, as a result of national policy, fiber-based communication networks have exploded in number and reliability as their costs have sharply gone down. Additionally, large numbers of technically trained graduates are emerging from their universities (as many as are graduating from the Indian universities) with the result that today China has extraordinary IT technical capabilities. The question today for Cathay Pacific then has become, could they relocate the processing service (which have already been moved once) from Australia to a city such as Shenzhen or Shanghai to take advantage of the new robust technology infrastructure, their skills and low salaries. If such a friendly act were done and if Cathay Pacific helped share their expertise with other Chinese airlines, what might the implications be in terms of being granted additional route structure in China for Cathay Pacific? Strategic issues of this sort can only be hammered out at the board and CEO level. This case is indicative of the very different set of strategic issues which face the delivery of IT services in 2006 as a factory quadrant firm not only positions itself to maintain reliable operations, but also position itself to drive costs down and extend marketing reach.

Summary

These four cases paint a vivid picture of the extraordinary IT-enabled changes that are occurring in a number of old-line companies along with the governance approaches they are using. These changes are often so powerful that their implementation involves the combined efforts of the Board, the CEO and divisional management as well as the CIO.

Not addressed in these examples is, of course, the question of timing. As a new set of industry technology innovations emerges, does one want to be the first mover or fast follower? In the brokerage industry, a particularly significant story involved Charles Schwab in the late 1990s, which built on its deep technology friendly management culture, and rode the waves of the Internet boom through online trading so successfully that for a time their market capitalization exceeded that of Merrill Lynch, a competitor three times their size. Merrill Lynch, however, (having both deeper financial resources and a powerful brand) was able to have the luxury of seeing the direction that Charles Schwab was moving, see their success, and after feeling the pain in Merrill's diminished market share numbers invest with force and power to recover completely their market position (incurring significantly less risk than Schwab because the market receptivity to online trading had been proven). Both companies acted off their particular strengths appropriately (Westerman, 2006).

LEVERS OF GOVERNANCE (Nolan, 2005)

There are at least four groups that play an active role in the governance of IT. These are the Board of Directors, the CEO, the CIO, and user line management. Exhibit 3 is a list of questions asked to ensure that the overall governance of IT is adequate. The groups who should respond to these questions depend on where the firm is on the strategic grid.

A	B	C
Has the strategic importance of our IT changed?	Has anything changed in disaster recovery and security that will affect our business's continuity planning?	Are our strategic IT development plans proceeding as required?
What are our current and potential competitors doing in the area of IT?	Do we have in place management practices that will prevent our hardware, software, and legacy applications from becoming obsolete?	Is our applications portfolio sufficient to deal with a competitive threat or to meet a potential opportunity?
Are we following best practices in asset management?	Do we have adequate protection against denial of service attacks and hackers?	Do we have processes in place that will enable us to discover and execute any strategic IT opportunities?
Is the company getting adequate ROI from information resources?	Are there fast-response processes in place in the event of an attack?	Do we have processes in place to guard against IT risk?
Do we have the appropriate IT infrastructure and applications to exploit the development of our intellectual assets?	Do we have management processes in place to ensure 24/7 service levels, including tested backup?	Do we regularly benchmark to maintain our competitive cost structure?
	Are we protected against possible intellectual-property-infringement lawsuits?	
	Are there any possible IT-based surprises lurking out there?	

Exhibit 3. Governance Questions

The Board of Directors

The Board of Directors, for example, has a critical role to play in strategic quadrant firms, and would be expected to address all the questions in columns A, B and C of Exhibit 3. The normal method for doing this is to set up an IT governance committee of the Board, as has been done by firms like Procter & Gamble, UPS, FedEx and Mellon Bank. For firms in the factory quadrant, the Board would be concerned primarily with the items in column A and B. The oversight of this can be delegated to the Audit Committee of the Board, which would need a certified IT expert on it (someone with deep IT application skill, who can also relate effectively with the other Board members, as a peer. Ruth Bruch, CIO of Lucent, and member of Mellon Bank's Technology Committee is a good example of such an expert). For firms in the turnaround quadrant, the questions in columns A and C need to be addressed at the Board level through an IT Committee, while for firms in the support quadrant, it would be enough for the Audit Committee to simply address the questions in column A. In the examples talked about in this chapter, the Board for the most part, did not fully play the role that is suggested here. It should also be noted that both the Board and the CEO are particularly critical at times of significant transition when a company is moving from one quadrant to another.

The CEO

The CEO plays a critical role in strategic quadrant firms and must be involved in directly understanding and triggering appropriate action on questions raised in columns A, B and C. This was true for Ari Bousbib and George David at Otis, and Jim Wolfensohn at the World Bank. Ari Bousbib, George David and Jim Wolfensohn were absolutely critical through their time and interest in helping to drive these terribly important wrenching organization transformation initiatives forward. For the turnaround quadrant, the CEO need not worry a great deal about the operations activity but must be focused on the items in columns A and C. In the factory quadrant, however, because of the huge operational vulnerability, they must have a clear view on the items in both columns A and B. For the support quadrant, it is enough that they be involved in the questions in column A unless, like Captain Wei at COSCO, opportunities to fundamentally transform the positioning of the company exist through new applications of IT.

The CIO

The CIO conversely is a critical person in the implementation process and must be fully active and on top of the issues in columns A, B and C in all cases. The type of appropriate background that a CIO should bring to bear depends a lot on the dimensions of the task and what they are trying to execute. The World Bank situation, for example involved both a massive creation of the global networks where nothing existed there before and also dramatic organization changes. Mohamed Muhsin, with deep user background, was the key person in managing the organization transformation part of the process. He had, however, to recruit a very strong technical team and use outside consultants to make sure they were on top of the technical challenge, areas where he was not personally strong.

A similar situation existed at Otis, except their CEO, Ron Beaver, carried much deeper technical skills and relied on Ari Bousbib to do much more of the change management issues; while he and his team focused on the technology implementation issues. Two other people are of interest. The first is the CIO at Lucent Technology, Ruth Bruch, who has been charged with rebuilding the total infrastructure at an IT intensive company. She brought an extraordinary three-company CIO technical background to the task. She has both great technical depth and also strong upwards communications skills reporting directly to the CEO. As noted earlier, she also chairs the Board's IT Committee at Mellon Bank, one of the nation's largest financial institutions. In short, she is close to being a renaissance CIO.

The second person is the CIO of a major European telecommunications company, which is in the process of both massive organization and technical change to deal with the reality of voice over IP, which has blown the company's century-old value generation model to smithereens. To lead the transformation the firm selected a CIO from investment banking, who was deeply skilled in mobilizing both the right technical resources and IT management processes, but who also counts on the CEO for substantial support as he drives significant organization change through the company. So far, it is working.

User Leadership

The final critical group involved in the governance process is the users, particularly, division presidents and senior functional leaders. In a very real way, for the strategic and turnaround quadrant firms, these individuals' ability to execute their broad strategies depends on the successful implementation of initiatives that have come out of the IT priority-setting process. The Board and the

CEO have a strong vision as to where the company should be going. The CIO provides great insight on technical architecture and the underlying technologies. In the end, however, the practical hands-on assessment on what is feasible and on what time schedule lies heavily in the users' hands. This is why an articulated planning process is absolutely critical as the shape of the applications development portfolio is firmed. For more on this, see *"Connecting the Dots,"* (Benko & McFarlan, 2004) which focuses on IT planning and the roles of the various players.

Outputs of the Governance Process

In defining the totality of the outputs to be addressed by the governance process, six come to the surface as being particularly important. Assessment of the appropriate level of IT investment needs to be made in aggregate and by each business unit. This is an intrinsically complex process, which must take into account multiple factors such as the potential strategic value of the investment and the need to be reasonably assured of continuity in day-to-day operations. The issue, however, is further complicated by the fact that some organizations are extremely tight in their availability of funds, while others have much looser capital constraints. One of the most innovative organizations studied by the author is a healthcare organization, whose capital investment was nearly one-tenth that of their major leading competitor. Because of the great skill of their management and technical team, however, the overall operations of the IT application organization have not been harmed and they remain one of the leaders in their industry.

Assessment and Acceptance of Priorities and Risks

The risk in the portfolio of development work is of two natures. The first is the implementation risk. How likely are the projects to go wrong? The early work on portfolio risk done in the late 1970s remains relevant today (McFarlan, 1981) In later years, organizations have taken major steps to move from the highly expensive, often risky, waterfall method of project implementation to an unfolding process of small hot house designs. (Austin, 2003) This focus on fast-cycle iterative development with each piece being completed within 90 days can sharply reduce implementation risk and is doable in a variety of settings. The other risk, however, is that the portfolio of planned work is inadequately aligned with the real competitive needs of the company. The combination of the internal lobbying process, flawed judgments on the feasibility of different technologies, etc. mean a sub-optimal set of priorities emerges in relation to the firm's needs. The issues to be worried about in aligning corporate strategies to the portfolio were addressed comprehensively in the *"Connecting the Dots"* book.

Assessment and Management of Operational Vulnerability to 24/7 Operations

Vulnerability to "force majore," rolling blackouts, etc. must be carefully examined. Significant operational exposure exists in this area today for firms in the factory and strategic quadrants. These basic issues of reliability and stability are unglamorous, but turn out to be absolutely critical in these settings.

Striking the Appropriate Balance between Innovation and Stability

The further one goes across the innovation dimension, the more likely things are to go wrong. Conversely, not to take a fair amount of innovation for companies where technology is strategic is to open the doors to sub-optimal business performance and ultimately substantial business risk as competitors move into the vacuum.

Legal risk Assessment

It is critical to understand the multiple potential legal problems facing the organization and taking a profile consistent with the organization's tolerance for risk. While legal exposure cannot be totally eliminated, an intelligent portfolio approach can reduce many of the potential problems.

Matching the IT Control and IT Project Management Processes
The last point concerns the matching of the IT control process and the IT project management process in a way which is consistent with the broader culture of the firm. Good IT controls help the project management process. Good governance of IT involves dealing with the internal realities of corporate values and processes and trying to adapt the IT ones to be consistent whenever possible.

CONCLUSION

Successful implementation of IT transformation activities requires a sharply increased level of governance activities where the board, the CEO, the CIO, and senior user leadership all now play a role. This new governance process is aimed at ensuring that the appropriateness of the total IT investment is analyzed and that the risks and priorities of the applications development portfolio are assessed and accepted. The governance process balances the tension between innovation and stability; in a world where legal risks must be managed. Additionally, the governance process must shape discussion on the amount of IT operational vulnerability that is acceptable. Finally, the governance process must be appropriately linked to the broader corporate planning and control systems.

MINICASE

CareGroup (CareGroup, 2003)

CareGroup was a team of healthcare professionals dedicated to providing the best quality care to patients in a highly personalized manner. CareGroup and its members offered a broad spectrum of health services to residents of Eastern Massachusetts, in a variety of settings, ranging from world-renowned academic health centers and outstanding community hospitals, to physician offices and community health centers. CareGroup hospital members included: Beth Israel Deaconess Medical Center in Boston; Mount Auburn Hospital in Cambridge; and the New England Baptist Hospital in Boston. With more than 13,000 employees and 2,000 medical staff, CareGroup offered community-based primary care and a wide range of specialty services close to where individuals live or worked.

CareGroup had been formed in a three-way merger on October 1, 1996. The Beth Israel Hospital, the Deaconess Hospital, and the Mount Auburn Hospital came together on that day. The Beth Israel and Deaconess Hospitals, which were physically adjacent, merged into a single hospital; every department was merged and headed by one individual. (i.e., the two surgical units were merged and a head of surgery appointed.) The Mount Auburn Hospital, located in Cambridge, reported in to CareGroup management as a separate entity, as did four other hospitals, which had formerly been a part of the Pathway Network, assembled over the previous decade by the Deaconess Hospital. (See Exhibit 1 for the organization chart of CareGroup, and Exhibit 2 for descriptions of the different hospitals.)

The CareGroup Board consisted of twelve individuals who had come from the previous hospital Boards. It was organized into an Executive Committee, Audit Committee, Nominating Committee and Compensation Committee. It had no IT Committee, but had one certified IT expert on the Board.

This merger produced a hospital group with $1.6 billion revenue, the second-largest group of hospitals in Eastern Massachusetts. The merger was driven by the intense competitive environments which existed in the mid-1995 period. Specifically, the factors that brought CareGroup together were:

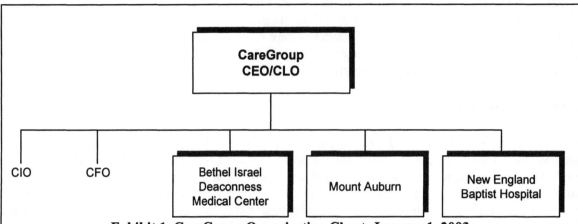

Exhibit 1. CareGroup Organization Chart, January 1, 2003

1. The contracting power needed by the hospitals against the HMOs.
2. The possibility of developing integrated services across the hospitals that could improve quality of care and drive down costs.
3. The need for a strong balance sheet in a complex price war, in which there were more than 40% excess hospital beds in the region; because of this excess supply, some hospitals were closing their doors.

Over the next seven years, under the leadership of two CEOs, CareGroup sought to deal with these issues.

A brief summary of progress would include the following observations:

1. It was a time of extraordinary financial pressure for CareGroup. First the Mount Auburn Hospital, which had been profitable or over 15 years, suddenly produced a $10 million loss and had to re-engineer its operations. Just as it recovered, Beth Israel Deaconess began losing significant amounts of money. Not until mid-2002 did they begin to recover. At about that same time, the Baptist Hospital suddenly incurred a $20 million loss, which led to the appointment of new management there. By early 2003, these problems were largely behind CareGroup. Each hospital in the group was headed by a different CEO than at the time of the merger, and financial stability issues were fading into the past.
2. Operational coordination across the hospitals had turned out to be extremely difficult because of their history of independence. Financial synergy in terms of lower debt costs, however, had been a strong feature. Similarly, joint contracting with the HMOs had been very successful.
3. An unexpected glittering success was the development of an integrated technology system, which linked the entire group together. The system was widely touted nationally; it was considered not only the best in health care, but also one of the very best in the industry.

On November 1, 1998, John Halamka became CIO of CareGroup as it was systematically working through a $41 million project to deal with the Y2K problem. By the time, the IT organization had 380 staff members and annual expenditures in excess of $50 million. Halamka brought an extraordinary background to the task. An undergraduate at Stanford University, majoring in Computers and Economics, he had founded a software company in his dorm room at age 18. After Stanford, he enrolled simultaneously at UCSF Medical School and Berkeley Enginering School, where he completed a combined mechanical/electrical/ engineering and medical school program. At residency time, he sold his software company, which had by then grown to 35 people, and became an emergency medicine specialist in Los Angeles. In his spare time, he authored several books on computing subjects and wrote a hypertext system to coordinate all clinical information in the county hospital in Los Angeles. In 1996, he moved to Harvard to practice emergency medicine at the Beth Israel Deaconess Medical Center and undertook post-doctoral work at the Massachusetts Institute of Technology in Medical Infomatics. He also headed a group of 50 data analysts and web specialists, developing web applications for CareGroup.

Halamka, in 2000, assumed the additional role of CIO of the Harvard Medical School. (Mt. Auburn and Beth Israel/Deaconess were both Harvard teaching hospitals.) In talking about his background, Halamka observed:

"The reason why I've been successful is because I know all the technologies, I program in 12 languages, and I've written books on UNIX system administration. I'm a doctor, so I understand the clinical domain and the technical requirements."

CareGroup IT. The IT organization that Halamka took over in October of 1998 was a decentralized, non-standardized operation. Each of the hospitals ran their own homegrown legacy systems that predated the merger. At the Beth Israel Deaconess Medical Center, computer operations were complicated by having to run a mish-mash of the systems from each of the merged hospitals. In addition to internal IT staff, Care Group employed an additional 78 consultants. NEBH had $500,000 per year outside consultants, a problematic lab system, a self-developed payroll system, a failed OR system installation, and a limited network incapable of remote access. Mount Auburn Hospital, the most sophisticated of the non-medical center hospitals, was running on its own homegrown system built around the Meditech package.

By 2002, all of these hospitals had been brought together on a common system with the Meditech software at the center. All had state-of-the-art email, networking, PCs, and clinical/financial information systems at costs similar or reduced from those at the time Halamka took over. For example, NEBH's IT budget dropped $135,000 in fiscal year 2002, and it was expected to drop another $400,000 in fiscal year 2003. By 2003, CareGroup believed it had the most advanced network in healthcare, the most advanced email system in healthcare, the most advanced voice/wireless system in healthcare, the most advanced data center in healthcare, and the most advanced web infrastructure in healthcare. It served 3,000 physicians, processed 40 terabytes of data per day, and handled 900,000 patient records dating back to 1977, all supported by a staff of 200.

All applications were web enabled. In late 2002, the case author, using Halamka's password, was able to access all of his own personal health records, x-rays, and records of office visits for the past decade on a PC five miles away from the hospital where he had received those services (he was delighted to find that they were accurate). The IT organization ran a complete "lights-out" data center with three back-up generators, and had not suffered a data center power outage in three years. In the first quarter 2003, the final IBM mainframe was scheduled to be decommissioned, and the network would be exclusively built around clustered Unix/Linux servers. Storage was 100% EMC (with no local server based storage). Paired CPUs for development, testing, and production assured that new software performed well by the time it was in use

HP was the primary supplier of the UNIX boxes and Compaq (now HP) was the primary supplier of Wintel boxes; Dell supplied machines for Linux clusters. Following a McKinsey Study at Harvard, IBM came in with a bid that undercut Dell prices for PCs by 50%. As a result, over a five-year period, all desktops (including at CareGroup, because it included Harvard teaching hospitals) were being replaced by IBM PCs. The data center housed tape backup systems that did incremental backups on the 40 terabytes of daily data, transferring them onto 3 Gigabyte tapes. Every night those tapes were taken to an Iron Mountain storage facility that had once been a missile silo. Peoplesoft software handled HR, payroll, accounts payable, and general ledger. Physicians were provided free email accounts and they had begun experimenting with wireless messaging devices such as Blackberry text pagers. As of the first quarter of 2003, all networks became IP based; Novell IPX would be replaced by year-end 2002, and AppleTalk would be gone by the end of the following quarter.

CareGroup had cut capital budget expenditures by nearly 90% in the three years prior to 2003 from $30 million to nearly $4 million. The Meditech installations in the various hospitals were done without consultants in half the usual time, at 20% of the cost. Exhibit 6 shows CareGroup's operating expenses vis-à-vis, Partners and Gartner standards. In September 2001, the CareGroup IT organization was ranked #1 in American by Information Week, and it has been in the *Information Week* top 100 companies for the last three years. By November 2002, CareGroup's IT systems and services were widely viewed as critical to building clinical loyalty and they were believed to provide the best knowledge management service in the United States

MAJOR CAREGROUP MEDICAL FACILITIES

Beth Israel Deaconess Medical Center. Beth Israel Deaconess Medical Center is a Harvard-affiliated, research-intensive teaching hospital located in Boston's Longwood Medical area. Serving as the principal academic and clinical resource of CareGroup, Beth Israel Deaconess Medical Center is home to several nationally recognized clinical centers of specialized expertise, including solid-organ transplantation; diabetes/vascular surgery; obstetrics; cardiology and cardiac surgery; gastroenterology: trauma: cancer (with a particular interest in breast cancer): and AIDS. Complementary, state-of-the-art inpatient and outpatient facilities, in addition to two regional outpatient centers, primary-care offices in more than 30 communities, and transitional and palliative care units, enhance the broad array of clinical services available.

Mount Auburn Hospital. Mount Auburn Hospital in Cambridge is an acute-care, Harvard-affiliated community teaching hospital, serving the healthcare needs of residents of Arlington, Belmont, Cambridge, Lexington, Medford, Somerville, Watertown and Waltham. The hospital offers comprehensive inpatient and outpatient medical, surgical, obstetrical and psychiatric services and is a leading provider of advanced, specialized care in cardiology, cardiac surgery, oncology, orthopedics, neurology and vascular surgery. In addition, Mount Auburn Hospital offers an extensive network of satellite primary-care practices in seven communities, as well as a broad range of community-based programs including Mount Auburn Home Care; outpatient specialty services; and occupational health. The hospital's Prevent and Recovery Center is a provider of education, intervention and support programs for public health issues such as substance abuse and violence. The Mount Auburn Center for Problem Gambling is the first such outpatient clinic in the state.

New England Baptist Hospital. Established in 1893, New England Baptist Hospital is a 150-bed adult medical/surgical hospital, located in the Mission Hill neighborhood of Boston, with specialty services in musculoskeletal care, sports medicine, occupational medicine and cardiology. New England Baptist Hospital ranks among the nation's foremost providers of hip and knee replacement surgery. To solidify its commitment to musculoskeletal care, the hospital in 1995 formed the New England Baptist Bone & Joint Institute. The Institute is the region's leading resource for a full range of prevention and education, diagnostic, treatment and rehabilitation services in orthopedics and rheumatology, joint replacement, spine care, foot and ankle care, hand surgery, occupational medicine and sports medicine. The hospital has a 40-bed skilled nursing unit, specializing in rehabilitative care for the orthopedic patient, in addition to post-surgical medical patients. NEBH is the sports medicine hospital of the Boston Celtics.

Exhibit 2. CareGroup Medical Facilities

IT Operating Expenses as a Percentage of Organization Revenues

CareGroup	1.9%
Partners (largest Boston competitor)	2.3%
Gartner benchmarks for 1B IDNs	2.7%

Range for 2nd/3rd quintiles – 1.9%-2.9%

IT as a Percentage of Total Hospital Capital Expenditures

CareGroup	10.0%
Partners (largest Boston competitor)	25.0%
Gartner benchmarks for 1B IDNs	21.0%

Range for 2nd/e4d quintiles – 10%-26%

Exhibit 3. CareGroup Benchmark Comparisons, FY-'01

Discussion Questions:
1. Is John Halamka's background appropriate for a CIO? Where might he be weak?
2. How should the individual hospitals relate to the CIO?
3. What role should the Board of Directors play in overseeing IT?
4. Is CareGroup's IT advantage sustainable? Why?
5. As a board member, what would you be most worried about by IT?

KEY TERMS
Board of Directors
CEO
CIO
Factory Mode
Strategic Grid
Strategic Mode
Support Mode
Turnaround Mode

STUDY QUESTIONS
1. How would you go about assessing whether an IT Committee of the Board was doing a good job? What questions would you ask? Be as specific as possible.

2. How hard is it to move from one quadrant of the strategic grid to another? What areas would you have to address in making this move?

3. Which CEO, George David, Ari Bousbib, Jim Wolfensohn, or Captain Wei had the hardest job in relation to IT conceptualization and execution? Why?

4. How would you go about assessing your firm's applications development portfolio against those of your closest competitor?

5. How would you decide if a firm's operational dependence on IT was appropriately managed? Can Cathay Pacific be adequately protected if they have all their operations activities in Australia?

REFERENCES

Applegate, L. M., McFarlan, F. W. and McKenney, J. L., Adapted from Page 446, "Corporate Information Systems Management," Irwin McGraw-Hill, 1999.

Austin, R. D., and Devin, L. "Artful Making: What Managers Need to Know about How Artists Work." Prentice Hall, Upper Saddle River, N. J., 2003.

Benko, C. and McFarlan, F. W., "Connecting the Dots," *HBS Press,* 2004.

Bousbib, A., Interview with [DVD #305706, VHS #305707], HBS Publishing, Boston, MA. 2004.

CareGroup, #303-097, Adapted from, President and Fellows of Harvard College, 2003.

Carr, N. G., "IT Doesn't Matter" With Letters to the Editor #3544, *Harvard Business Review,* 2003.

Clemons, E., "Information Systems for Sustainable Competitive Advantage," *Information and Management,* 11, November 1986, pp. 131-136.

Cathay Pacific: Doing More with Less, #303-106, President and Fellows of Harvard College, 2003.

COSCO, #305-080, Information Technology at, President and Fellows of Harvard College 2005.

Dearden, J. and McFarlan, F. W., *Management Information Systems*, Richard D. Irwin, 1965.

Dearden, J., "Myth of Real Time Management Information," *Harvard Business Review* May-June 1966.

Friedman, T. L. *The World is Flat: A Brief History of the 21st Century*, Farrar, Straus and Giroux, New York, 2005.

Harmony Life of Hartford, Glenn Overman University, Arizona, 1961.

IT Governance Institute, 3701 Algonquin Road, Suite 1010, Rolling Meadow, IL. (See http://www.itgi.org for publications including "Board Briefing on IT Governance (2nd edition, 2003)

Leatherbee, G. H. lectures, *Computer and Management,* Harvard Business School, Boston , 1967.

Lucent's Quote-to-Cash System, #304-050, President and Fellows of Harvard College, 2003.

Merrill Lynch: Integrated Choice (Abridged), #301-081, President and Fellows of Harvard College, 2001.

McFarlan, F. W., "Portfolio Approach to Information Systems," *Harvard Business Review, #81510* September-October 1981.

Nolan, R. and McFarlan, F. W., "Information Technology and the Board of Directors," *Harvard Business Review*, October 2005.

Nolan, R., and Gibson, C. F., "Managing the Four Stages of EDP Growth," *Harvard Business Review,* January-February 1974.

Otis Elevator: Accelerating Business Transformation with IT, #305-048, President and Fellows of Harvard College, 2004.

Pyburn, P., McFarlan, F. W. and McKenney, J. L., "The Information Archipelago – Plotting a Course," *Harvard Business Review,* January-February 1983.

Pfizer's Virtual CIO (Abridged) #305-018, Presidents and Fellows of Harvard College, 2004.

PSA: The World's Port of Call, #802-003, President and Fellows of Harvard College, 2002.

Charles Schwab Corporation (A) #300-024, Charles Schwab Corporation (B) #300-025, President and Fellows of Harvard College, 2001.

Simmons, M., "*Twilight in the Desert,*" John Wiley & Sons, (2005).

Westerman, G., McFarlan, F. W. and Iansiti, M., "Organization Design and Effectiveness of the Innovation Life Cycle," *Organization Science,* 17(2), March-April 2006, pp. 230-238.

World Bank, Enabling Business Strategy with IT at the #304-055, President and Fellows of Harvard College, 2003.

Zara, Ferdows, K., Lewis, M. A., and Machuca, J. A. D., "Rapid-Fire Fulfillment," *Harvard Business Review,* November 2004.

Section 3

Integration of Global Systems

One of the hardest things to do when managing the information systems function of a global company is the integration of the systems into useable global systems. The integration not only involves disparate functions within one's own organization, but also has to interface with external entities in various parts of the world. Many factors can impact this task. This section looks at the issues associated with the integration of global systems.

The first chapter in this section, Chapter 12, deals with transborder data flows, or the movement of personally identifiable data from one country to another. The chapter first discusses barriers to the flow of data across borders and then looks at privacy legislation around the world. Chapter 13 looks at global supply chain strategy. Supply chains interconnect companies, customers, and vendors around the world. The issues of change management and culture in supply chain relationships are examined. Chapter 14 deals with cultural asymmetries and the challenge of global enterprise integration. The chapter examines national culture, organizational culture, and information culture and presents implications for management. Finally, Chapter 15 looks at a grounded theory of the design and implementation of information systems for multinational enterprises.

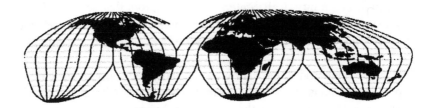

Transborder Data Flows in the Global Economy

Albert L. Harris
Appalachian State University, USA

CHAPTER SUMMARY

This chapter examines the impacts that transborder data flows have had on the digital economy and on multinational enterprises. Transborder data flow deals with the movement of personally identifiable data from one country to another. Transborder data flows are impacted by many things, the biggest being country laws on personal privacy. After an introduction and background discussion, this chapter will look at the barriers to the flow of data across borders. The barriers are discussed in three categories: technical, cultural, and legal. This is followed by a discussion on the privacy laws in numerous countries as they impact the movement of data across borders. Next, the impacts of transborder data flows in the online world are discussed. The Internet is all pervasive and allows easy flow of personal data across country boundaries. In many cases people do not know where the data that they provide on the Internet is being sent. The next section will cover the historical impacts of transborder data flow legislation on multinational enterprises. The final section presents some concluding thoughts on transborder data flows in the global economy.

INTRODUCTION

Business today is becoming borderless. Global information systems (GISs) are a necessity for multinational enterprise (MNEs) and have transformed the way MNEs operate. Information and communications technology (ICT) have advanced to give MNEs unparalleled abilities to exploit business functions and units on a global level. If businesses are to operate on a global level, they must be able to move data on a global level and this means that data must travel from one country to another.

In today's world of globally operating companies, computers through telecommunication links have replaced all other methods as the conduit of information flow. Every spot on earth can be reached with some type of telecommunications signal. Companies and governments are becoming critically dependent on telecommunications to transact business (Culnan, 1993). Data are being collected across the globe on almost all aspects of life in unprecedented amounts and at lightning speed. These data, in turn, are being used by companies for a multitude of purposes. Today, a company can transact business with other companies or individuals anywhere in the world. For instance, a traveler can access his or her bank account from an ATM in a foreign country as easily as they could in their home city. Call centers and help desks that service clients all over the world are increasingly being relocated to India and other countries throughout the world. E-commerce allows consumers to buy goods using the Internet regardless of where the consumer or the company proving the goods is located.

This interconnectivity has allowed virtually any involved entity to capture and build electronic profiles of consumers and potential consumers (for example Market Place, a software company, has a database that tracks the purchasing behavior of more than 200 million individuals in the U.S.). Data that are collected by any organization can then be manipulated and/or matched with data from other databases to extract information and profiles. This information can severely impact a person's life. As a result, "decisions having major impacts on individuals (such as whether or not to grant a loan, offer a sensitive job, or accept a life insurance proposal) are all too often made on the basis of these electronic profiles, almost regardless of their accuracy and without the knowledge of the individual(s) concerned" (Lee, 1994, p. 3).

Not only has the computerization of a society resulted in immense benefits to individuals, it also has the potential to threaten the privacy and economic well being of those same individuals. The threat is even greater when sensitive information can be transmitted across country borders to foreign entities that are not regulated. As a result, governments are reacting to make the purveyors of private data more accountable and responsible for the collection and distribution of name linked information (Culnan, 1993). Businesses must comply or they will have trouble operating in multiple markets. For example, US based credit reporting agencies have been denied licenses in Europe, and companies in nations with lax privacy laws are being threatened with economic sanctions by their trading partners.

Transborder data flow (TBDF) has been defined in previous literature as the movement of data across national boundaries (Guynes and al., 1990) and the exchange of computer readable data across national boundaries using electronic means (Waples and Norris, 1992). Most types of data can move across borders with little or no interference, limited only by the technical capabilities on either side of the transmission. Problems arise, however, when the transborder data flows (TBDFs) contain personally identifiable or name linked information.

While the ICT has increased the ability to disseminate information, there has also been an equal expansion of various types of barriers to information dissemination (Jarvenpaa and Ives, 1993). These barriers, which are often in the form of transborder data flow legislation, have the potential to limit the flow of data across national boundaries (Ajami, 1990; Boehmer and Palmer, 1993, Walczuch, Singh and Palmer, 1995) and, thusly, inhibit the ability of MNEs to operate on a global basis. TBDF of data with personally identifiable or name linked information have been the subject of numerous guidelines, directives, and laws over many years and these have been designed to protect the privacy of individuals.

TBDF legislation may have started in earnest with the Organization for Economic Co-operation and Development (OECD) Guidelines on the Protection of Privacy and Transborder Flows of Personal Data, which was adopted September 23, 1980. The guidelines identified eight basic principles related to protection of privacy and transborder flows of personal data. They are:

1. Collection Limitation Principle - There should be limits to the collection of personal data and any such data should be obtained by lawful and fair means and, where appropriate, with the knowledge or consent of the data subject.
2. Data Quality Principle - Personal data should be relevant to the purposes for which they are to be used and, to the extent necessary for those purposes, should be accurate, complete and kept up-to-date.
3. Purpose Specification Principle - The purposes for which personal data are collected should be specified at or before the time of data collection and the subsequent use of personal data should be limited to the fulfillment of those stated purposes.

4. Use Limitation Principle - Personal data should not be disclosed, made available or otherwise used for purposes other than those specified in accordance with the Purpose Specification Principle, except: with the consent of the data subject; or by the authority of law.

5. Security Safeguards Principle - Personal data should be protected by reasonable security safeguards against such risks as loss or unauthorized access, destruction, use, modification or disclosure of data.

6. Openness Principle - There should be a general policy of openness about developments, practices and policies with respect to personal data. Means should be readily available of establishing the existence and nature of personal data, and the main purposes of their use, as well as the identity and usual residence of the data controller.

7. Individual Participation Principle - An individual should have the right: (a) to obtain from a data controller, or otherwise, confirmation of whether or not the data controller has data relating to him; (b) to have communicated to him, data relating to him, within a reasonable time; at a charge, if any, that is not excessive; in a reasonable manner; and in a form that is readily intelligible to him; (c) to be given reasons if a request made under subparagraphs (a) and (b) is denied, and to be able to challenge such denial; and (d) to challenge data relating to him and, if the challenge is successful to have the data erased, rectified, completed or amended.

8. Accountability Principle - A data controller should be accountable for complying with measures which give effect to the principles stated above. (OECD, 1980)

The guidelines were published as minimum standards, capable of being supplemented by additional country-specific measures for the protection of privacy and individual liberties. (OECD, 1980)

The driving force for TBDF legislation has been the concern for the privacy of the citizens, although some countries have cited economic reasons for their legislation of TBDFs (Guynes, and al., 1990). The privacy issue is essentially dependent on the cultural doctrines of a society (Buchholz, 1992). Privacy legislation generally makes it harder to do business across borders, especially where the laws are not consistent.

In this chapter, we first look at the barriers to the flow of data across borders. Next, we will look at the status of privacy legislation in selected countries around the world. We will then look at the use of transborder data flows in the online world, especially in Electronic Data Interchange (EDI) and the Internet. This is followed by a discussion of the impacts of TBDF on MNEs. Some conclusions are presented in the final section of the chapter.

BARRIERS TO THE FLOW OF DATA ACROSS BORDERS

Before looking at the impacts of transborder data flow on multinational enterprises, we need to look at the barriers that inhibit the flow of data from one country to another. These barriers are summarized in Table 1 and presented in four broad categories: technical, cultural, political, and legal.

Technical
Technical barriers have to do with the communications technology and the worldwide telecommunications infrastructure that carries data across country borders.

Connectivity: Connectivity deals with an MNE's ability to connect to an established communications network. In the developed and newly industrialized countries, connectivity has been largely resolved; however, in developing and underdeveloped countries, connectivity can be a problem. Many countries in Africa, South America, and Southeast Asia still have a connectivity problem. The basic communications infrastructure is not present in those countries. Table 2 shows the Internet hosts and the number of Internet hosts per 1000 people in selected countries in the world. Notice the wide range of numbers of hosts in the countries and the large differences per 1000 people, ranging from .00 (less than .005 per 1000 people) in many African and Asian countries to a high of 653.85 in the United States. The lack of connectivity in many countries of the world is contributing to the "Digital Divide."

Technical		
Connectivity	Some countries of the world barely connected	
	Small number of hosts in some countries	
	Lack of basic telephone communications	
Bandwidth	Narrow bandwidth in many countries	
Security	Growing concern with individuals sending personal information over the Internet	
Cultural		
Language and dialects	6912 languages in the world	
	Many dialects of some languages (Spanish and Portuguese)	
Alphabets	Many alphabets in the world, including: • Chinese, Japanese, and Korean • Arabic • Cyrillic • Greek • Hebrew	
Other Coding differences	Distance measure Temperature Dates Addresses Postal codes Use of periods and commas in numbers	
Political	Accessibility	
Legal	Privacy laws among the countries of the world in disharmony	

Table 1. Transborder Data Flow Barriers

Bandwidth: Bandwidth refers to the amount of data that can be transferred over a set period of time. The availability of sufficient bandwidth is always a concern when transmitting data. The increasing use of the Internet has exacerbated the problem with bandwidth, even in the developed and newly industrialized countries. Even in the U.S. bandwidth is a concern, as companies continually increase the amount of data that is transmitted in the conduct of their businesses. Many countries in the world have only a narrow bandwidth available, which means that large amounts of data can not be easily transmitted to or from the country.

Security: Security is a growing concern throughout the world. Security includes the safekeeping of data and the transmission of data. Over the past few years, large amounts of personal data (names, addresses, credit card number, etc.) have been stolen or lost. This places a huge responsibility on IS executives to ensure that stored data is safe from intrusion. Security regarding the transmission of data has been largely resolved due to widespread use of encryption.

Cultural
Cultural barriers to the flow of data across borders relate to people and their characteristics. Some of the cultural barriers are discussed in the following paragraphs.

Country	Internet hosts	Per 1000 people	Country	Internet hosts	Per 1000 people
World	316,407,593	48.49	**Europe**		
Africa			Belgium	2,238,900	215.71
Angola	2,502	0.21	Bosnia and Herzegovina	8,525	1.89
Botswana	1,621	0.99	Bulgaria	95,539	12.94
Cameroon	34	0.00	Croatia	19,369	4.31
Chad	7	0.00	Czech Republic	819,773	80.09
Egypt	1,702	0.02	Denmark	2,110,002	387.11
Ethiopia	87	0.00	Finland	1,503,976	287.49
Iran	5,246	0.08	France	2,922,040	48.00
Iraq	4	0.00	Germany	7,657,162	92.90
Israel	1,069,088	168.30	Greece	414,724	38.80
Kenya	11,645	0.34	Ireland	238,706	58.76
Nigeria	1,535	0.01	Italy	1,246,253	21.44
Rwanda	1,588	0.18	Netherlands	6,781,729	411.23
Saudi Arabia	10,335	0.38	Norway	1,342,667	291.20
Somalia	2	0.00	Poland	366,898	9.52
South Africa	460,572	10.42	Portugal	845,980	79.77
Uganda	2,496	0.09	Romania	56,188	2.52
United Arab Emirates	118,495	45.53	Spain	1,380,541	34.17
Zimbabwe	6,582	0.54	Switzerland	1,823,012	242.30
			Turkey	753,394	10.70
Asia			United Kingdom	4,688,307	77.35
Afghanistan	76	0.00			
Bangladesh	266	0.00	**North America**		
Burma	43	0.00	Canada	3,525,392	106.51
Cambodia	1,315	0.09	Cuba	1,918	0.17
China	187,508	0.14	Mexico	2,026,633	18.86
Hong Kong	859,926	123.90	United States	195,138,696	653.85
India	787,543	0.72			
Japan	21,304,292	167.14	**South America**		
Korea, South	5,433,591	111.24	Argentina	1,233,175	30.89
Malaysia	151,239	6.20	Brazil	4,392,693	23.36
Pakistan	38,309	0.23	Chile	335,445	20.79
Philippines	96,500	1.08	Colombia	386,610	8.87
Russia	1,306,427	9.14	Costa Rica	12,578	3.09
Singapore	679,369	151.23	Ecuador	16,217	1.20
Taiwan	3,838,383	166.62	Honduras	4,763	0.65
Thailand	786,226	12.16	Nicaragua	12,628	2.27
Vietnam	3,611	0.04	Panama	7,013	2.20
			Paraguay	10,206	1.57
Oceania			Peru	205,532	7.26
Australia	5,351,622	264.09	Uruguay	112,968	32.92
New Zealand	751,719	184.42	Venezuela	57,875	2.25

Table 2. Internet Hosts for Selected Countries (Source: CIA Factbook, 2006)

Language and Dialects: There are approximately 6912 languages in the world (Ethnologue, 2005). Even within languages, there may be many dialects. Take Spanish for example. In South America most countries have Spanish as their official language, but in different countries, different words are used for the same thing - e.g. router: different word in Spain Spanish than in Latin American Spanish. In addition, translation from one language to another is not always accurate. English may eventually become a universal language, but the great majority of people in the world do not know English (Wallraff, 2000).

Alphabets: The many alphabets in the world cause a problem in cross border data flows. Some examples of alphabets and their idiosyncrasies include:

- Chinese, Japanese, and Korean alphabets have more than 256 characters, they require special coding. To store 1 character in those languages, we need more than 1 byte of storage.
- The Arabic alphabet is composed of 28 basic letters and is read from right to left, top to bottom. All dialects of Arabic, Farsi, Urdu, Kurdish, Pashto, Persian, and other similar languages use the Arabic alphabet. There is no difference between upper and lower case nor between written and printed letters.
- The Cyrillic alphabet is used to write six natural Slavic languages (Belarusian, Bulgarian, Macedonian, Russian, Serbian, and Ukrainian) and many other languages of the former Soviet Union. It is spoken mostly in Asia and Eastern Europe. It contains 44 basic letters. The non-Slavic and Arabic dialects contain additional letters. Several computer encoding systems are available for data held in the Cyrillic alphabet.
- The Greek alphabet contains 24 letters. There are no separate numbers; they are made with Greek letters. As with the Cyrillic alphabet, special encoding systems are available for the Greek alphabet.
- The Hebrew alphabet is a set of 22 letters and used in the Hebrew and Yiddish languages. Hebrew is read from right to left.

Other Coding Variations: There are many other cultural variations that cause problems for transborder data flow. How data is represented in computer systems can impact its readability and usability when it crosses borders. Some of the coding variations are as follows:

- **Distance Measure** - We have two major measuring systems in the world for distance and weight: Metric and Imperial.
- **Temperature** - Temperature is measured in Celsius and Fahrenheit. Conversion can be a problem.
- **Dates** - In the U.S., dates are usually shown as month, day, and year. In most other parts of the world, dates are shown as day, month, and year. In China, the most populous country in the world, dates are shown as year, month, and day. So, is 05/07/06 really May 7, 2006, July 5, 2006, or July 6, 2005?
- **Addresses** - In the U.S. most addresses are shown as number, followed by street. In most of the other parts of the world, addresses are shown as street, followed by number.
- **Postal codes** - Postal codes differ in every country. In the U.S. it is a ZIP code, with five or nine numbers. In other countries, it is a postal code with differing numbers of numbers and letters. Many countries have no postal codes.
- **Use of periods and commas in numbers** - In the U.S., dollars and cents are separated by a period, a comma used to separate every three numbers, and the dollar sign would appear at the beginning (e.g. $30,000.01). In the EU, a comma separates Euros from cents, a space separates every three numbers, and the Euro sign appears at the end (e.g. 3 000,01 €). Other variations appear elsewhere in the world.

Lack of confidence in the Internet: This is a hidden cultural barrier to transborder data flows. Many people throughout the world do not trust the Internet and believe that data that travels over the Internet is subject to theft. As a result, they will not enter personal data, such as a social security number or a credit card number, into an e-commerce form. This comes from a cultural lack of confidence or mistrust of the Internet.

Political

The free flow of information depends on accessibility. An individual or company's ability to communicate depends on accessibility - the ability to access the technology needed to communicate. This includes the access to a computer, the Internet, or communications networks, such as a satellite or communications channel. As a result, it is easy for a government to restrict access to a communications network. Quite a few governments have used their power over communications networks to control how their citizens can communicate with others outside of the country.

The government of China, for example, continues to block access to web sites that it deems "subversive." The government of Singapore blocks web sites that it considers objectionable. North Korea does not let its citizens have any access with outside parties. The government of Tibet allows no access to the Internet for its citizens. In these cases political constraints are stronger than any technical, cultural, or legal barriers.

Legal

Laws regarding privacy legislation differ throughout the world. Different countries have different approaches to the issue of privacy, as reflected in their laws. Most laws apply only to the host country, with little reciprocity, and apply to a person's privacy. Some countries such as Austria, Denmark, and Luxembourg, have laws that protect the privacy of some types of corporations. These countries believe that it is difficult to separate data about individuals from business data. For example, financial information about many small businesses reveals financial information about the owners. Legal barriers remain as the biggest inhibitor to transborder data flows. As a result, they are dealt with in more detail in the next section of this chapter.

PRIVACY LEGISLATION AROUND THE WORLD

Countries around the world continue to pass laws that impact transborder data flows. These laws seem to be in reaction to privacy restrictions imposed by countries with which they want to trade (e.g. countries in the EU). Herald (2004) is said to have identified over eighty worldwide privacy-related laws that impact transborder data flow so far, and there are likely many more in existence not yet discovered.

European Union

The European Union (EU) published Directive 95/46/EC "on the protection of individuals with regard to the processing of personal data and on the free movement of such data" in October 1995. The EU Directive was intended to ensure the right of privacy to EU citizens and was binding on all member states. This was one of the most significant statements of data privacy of its time because it covered so many countries. It set the standards for the collection, storage, processing, use, disclosure, and transfer of personal data within the EU. The EU Directive was designed to protect the privacy of European Union citizens, while allowing the free movement of data. It applied to any public or private organization and foreign entities that process personal data within the EU. Law enforcement agencies were excluded.

Article 6 of the EU Directive stated that Member States shall provide that personal data must be:
1. Processed fairly and lawfully;

2. Collected for specified, explicit and legitimate purposes and not further processed in a way incompatible with those purposes.

3. Adequate, relevant and not excessive in relation to the purposes for which they are collected and/or further processed;

4. Accurate and, where necessary, kept up to date; every reasonable step must be taken to ensure that data which are inaccurate or incomplete, having regard to the purposes for which they were collected or for which they are further processed, are erased or rectified;

5. Kept in a form which permits identification of data subjects for no longer than is necessary for the purposes for which the data were collected or for which they are further processed.

Article 7 of the EU Directive said that Member States shall provide that personal data may be processed only if:

1. The data subject has unambiguously given his consent; or

2. Processing is necessary for the performance of a contract to which the data subject is party or in order to take steps at the request of the data subject prior to entering into a contract; or

3. Processing is necessary for compliance with a legal obligation; or

4. Processing is necessary in order to protect the vital interests of the data subject; or

5. Processing is necessary for the performance of a task carried out in the public interest or in the exercise of official authority or in a third party to whom the data are disclosed; or

6. Processing is necessary for the purposes of legitimate interests by the third party or parties to whom the data are disclosed. (Directive 95/46/EC, 1995)

Article 25 of the EU Directive requires that data transfers from an EU member country to a country outside the EU take place only if the recipient country ensures an "adequate" level of protection for the data. If the recipient country does not have any privacy laws, or the existing privacy laws of the recipient country fail to satisfy the EU adequacy test, EU member countries cannot allow the transfer of the personal information. But what is an adequate level of protection? Adequate level of protection can be different for different types of data and different types of processing. According to the EU Directive, adequacy is determined depending on the nature of the data, the purpose and duration of the proposed processing operation, the country of origin, the destination country, and security measures in force in the third country. This presents a very real concern about the EU Directive's impact on organizations within EU countries that need to export, import or supply personal information to organizations in third world countries. Article 25 also gives the European Commission (the executive arm of the EU) the power to determine whether a third country provides an inadequate or adequate level of protection.

If a third country has been determined to have an inadequate level protection of data protection, Article 26 of the EU Directive allows transfers to the third country on condition that the:

1. Data subject consents to the transfer;

2. Transfer is necessary for performance of a contract with the data subject;

3. Transfer is necessary for performance of a contract for the data subject's benefit;

4. Transfer is necessary or legally required on important public interest grounds or in exercise or defense of legal claims;

5. Transfer is necessary to protect the vital interests of the data subject; or

6. Transfer is made from a source which by law is intended to provide information to the public.

Any EU citizen may file a complaint about a company's noncompliance if it appears that their personal information was not adequately protected.

The United States

The U.S. is one of the countries not considered to have comprehensive personal data protection laws. Therefore, unless other measures are taken, the transmission of personal data to the U.S. from an EU country is subject to the EU adequacy test. There are two major ways for a U.S. company to meet the adequacy test. The first way is for the sender to have entered into a written agreement with the U.S. company, whereby the U.S. company agrees to abide by the standards of the EU. The second way is under the safe harbor framework (described below).

In 2000 in response to the EU Directive, the US Department of Commerce (DoC) developed the 'safe harbor' framework which was approved by the EU. The Safe Harbor framework allows individual companies to comply with EU data privacy provisions by adhering to seven 'safe harbor principles.' The EU has certified that the seven principles provide adequate protection. This finding of adequacy is binding on all EU member states. The US has jurisdiction over complaints by EU citizens against US organizations. US organizations annually must 'self certify' to the US DoC that they agree to adhere to the safe harbor requirements. By adopting the safe harbor provisions, the US organization agrees to treat information in accordance with seven privacy principles:

1. **Notice** – at the time of collection, organizations must indicate:
    (i)   the purpose for collection and use;
    (ii)   the means by which the individual can contact the organization;
    (iii)   the types of third parties to which the organization discloses the information; and
    (iv)   the choices and means the organization offers for limiting its use and disclosure.

2. **Choice** – organizations must give the individual the opportunity to opt out from having their information disclosed to a third party or used for incompatible secondary purposes. For sensitive information, this choice to disclose or use for secondary purposes must be explicit and affirmative (i.e. an opt-in).

3. **Onward Transfer** – before disclosing to a third party, organizations must apply the notice and choice principles. If the organization is acting as an agent, it may transfer the information if the third party recipient also subscribes to the safe harbor principles or is bound by the Directive or another finding of adequacy. Alternatively, contractual obligations to provide equivalent protection may be sought from the third party recipient.

4. **Access** – organizations must provide individuals with access to their information. They must also provide the ability to correct, amend or delete information that is inaccurate.

5. **Security** – organizations must take reasonable precautions to protect personal information from loss, misuse and unauthorized access, disclosure, alteration or destruction.

6. **Data Integrity** – personal information must be relevant to the purposes for which it is used and an organization should ensure it is reliable.

7. **Enforcement** – the organization must have:
    (i)   Recourse mechanisms in place to handle complaints and disputes;
    (ii)   Procedures for verifying implementation of the principles;
    (iii)   Obligations to remedy problems arising out of failure to comply with the principles.

The safe harbor principles are enforced indirectly, via a self regulatory approach. The US policy encourages private sector enforcement of the principles, primarily through internal dispute resolution systems.

The DoC then publishes a list of organizations that have self-certified. Some of the companies that self-certify yearly include well known companies like Apple Computers, Disney, Eastman Kodak, Ernst and Young, General Motors, Intel, Johnson and Johnson, Monsanto, Proctor and Gamble, Boeing and Pepsico.

Canada

Canada has closely adopted the EU privacy guidelines. In 1996, the Canadian legislature passed the Model Code for the Protection of Personal Information. This legislation sought to balance trade interests and business needs with consumer rights to privacy. Two main concerns were addressed in this legislation:

1. The way in which organizations collect, use, disclose, and protect personal information, and

2. The right of individuals to have access to personal information about themselves and to have it corrected if necessary.

Australia

The Australian Privacy Act of 1988 regulates handling of personal information in Australia and originating from Australia. Under Australian Law, if an organization's overseas activity is required by the law of a foreign country, then it does not interfere with the privacy of an individual under Australian Law. An organization may transfer personal information overseas provided that one of the following conditions is satisfied:

1. The individual consents to the transfer
2. The organization reasonably believes a law or contract applies at the destination which effectively delivers privacy standards substantially similar to Australia's
3. The transfer is for the benefit of the individual and it is impracticable to obtain consent, but it is likely consent would be given;
4. The transfer is required by a contract between the individual and the organization, or a contract between the organization and a third party in the interests of the individual; or
5. The organization has taken reasonable steps to ensure the information will not be held, used or disclosed by its recipient inconsistently with Australia's privacy laws.

Australia's privacy laws relating to transborder data flow have been deemed to be equivalent or to at least be deemed adequate by EU standards.

New Zealand

New Zealand's Privacy Act was an "omnibus data protection law" which covers all "personal information" (not just computerized data) and both the public and private sectors (with limited specific exceptions, the only notable private sector one being the news media in their news activities). The New Zealand law set out 12 information privacy principles modeled on the OECD Guidelines and established a Privacy Commissioner. The New Zealand Privacy Act complies with the EU's definition of adequate data protection measures. (Stewart, 2000)

India

India has had to address the issue of transborder data flow because of its outsourcing industry. As a result, data protection is now a hot political issue. As can be expected, the lack of data protection laws in India has not affected Indian companies' ability to handle personal information from the United States. However, the growing market of outsourcing from EU countries has placed enormous pressure for India to comply with the EU's data privacy directive. As U.S. companies have done, Indian outsourcing companies can use the EU standard contractual clauses to provide "adequate" levels of data protection.

The existing Indian privacy law focuses on an implicit right of privacy in the Indian Constitution, but the Indian *Information Technology Act 2000* did not directly address the privacy rights issue. Naturally, with India's position the world's outsourcing market, the issue had been at the heart of many political debates. The first proposals were to model India's privacy laws on the EU's privacy Directive. However, the Indian Government's position has changed to look more like the U.S.'s Safe Harbor Agreement that would give Indian organizations flexibility and an appearance of regulatory simplicity. (Sainty, 2004) This issue continues to be a hot item for the Indian Government. It was expected to be on the legislative agenda for 2005.

China

China does not have wide ranging data protection laws, as their concepts of a planned economy and collective society are generally inconsistent with broad privacy rights. There are no specific privacy laws applicable to data protection in the People's Republic of China as a whole. As China moves to a more capitalist economic model, its citizens have a greater interest in privacy rights.

Hong Kong, which was under British control for many years, does have the regulations concerning personal data privacy. The regulations were enacted in 1996 and broadly provide rights for informed consent at the time of collection, a right of access and correction of inaccurate data, an obligation of accuracy, openness and security, and limitations on the use of personal data. The regulations also have an employee record exemption. These personal data privacy laws are only binding in the Special Administrative Region of Hong Kong and not in the rest of China. (Sainty, 2004)

Pacific Rim

The eleven-member Asia-Pacific Economic Cooperation (APEC) Privacy Sub-Group developed a Privacy Framework for the eleven members in 2004. (Herald, 2004) The Privacy Framework impacts transborder data flow in the Pacific Rim as it regards e-commerce. Member countries have also been working to achieve secure "Paperless Trading" in the region that addresses transborder data flows. Other regulations in this region cover electronic information or particular economic sectors.

TRANSBORDER DATA FLOWS IN THE ONLINE WORLD

Two major capabilities have impacted the amount and kind of data that flows across borders: electronic data interchange (EDI) and the Internet. These topics are discussed separately.

EDI

EDI is the electronic transfer of business documents between business partners. EDI systems have been around since the early 1970s. Although EDI systems are considered B2B systems, EDI documents may contain personally identifiable data. For that reason, EDI may come under the auspices of privacy legislations of the countries of the trading partners.

There are two major sets of EDI standards. ANSI X.12 (X1.2) is used mostly in North America. EDIFACT is the international standard sponsored by the United Nations and is predominant in all areas outside of North America. For years, the two standards caused some problems in the worldwide transborder exchange of data.

Internet

The rapid expansion of the internet has intensified the threat to personal privacy and added to the transborder data flow problems. The use of the Internet in business to consumer (B2C) transactions poses particular problems in terms of privacy protection. In the online world, personal data can be collected from individuals or consumers in a way which is outside their knowledge or beyond their control. As a result, the concept of 'trust' has impacted peoples' use of B2C commerce, as consumers are wary of providing too much information to unknown recipients.

The more overt data collection occurs when the consumer provides personal information in the course of a web interaction. This may be in the form of name and address, email address, credit card and other payment details, personal preferences, etc. In transactions to buy goods or services over the Internet, the data transfer is usually incidental to the primary purpose. Browsing activity can also generate data when an individual merely visits a web site. When just browsing, the consumer may be viewing or downloading information and has not ordered any goods or services. However, in each of these cases, the data transfer is likely to be transborder. This means that in the context of online interactions, there is a need to bring privacy protection issues to the consumer's attention at the earliest possible stage in the web site interaction.

In the on-line world, the nature of B2C interactions is such that there is many times no pre-existing relationship between the business and consumer; the web browsing may be random, with many visits being first time visits. The exception is where the consumer has an established relationship with the business, such as the consumer has a history of ordering goods from a particular online business or the consumer has specifically applied for credit. The business and consumer will also be removed from each other in terms of distance, time and geographical location. Despite this separation, the technical features of the Internet are designed to facilitate data transfers. The disclosure of personal data is made possible through web browsing software, such as 'cookies,' software that identifies the network and machine used to access the web and the URLs of previously visited sites, caching, spyware, bots, and internet indexes.

TRANSBORDER DATA FLOWS - IMPACTS ON MNEs

As countries continue to join the parade in developing regulations regarding TBDFs, the impacts on MNEs have been substantial over the years. For MNEs, the changing political landscape of the global community with regards to TBDFs has meant that technical, systems, communications, and local and national laws all have an impact on the IS environment. These problems are not restricted to countries with existing national legislation on TBDFs. In the future, the greater problem and equally the greater opportunity lie with those nations which currently have no TBDF legislation, but may enact it. If a nation has existing TBDF legislation, an MNE can hire local attorneys or dispatch its contingent of attorneys. It is the unknown, those nations which currently have no TBDF legislation, that poses the greatest problems to the IS function of a MNE. Luckily, most TBDF legislation is closely aligned with or takes it roots from the EU data protection directive.

Some of the concerns and impacts that TBDF legislation has had on MNEs over the years are discussed in the following paragraphs.

Lack of Uniformity in TBDF Legislation

TBDF legislation has not been uniform in North America and Europe despite the existence of several international conventions (Woody and Fleck, 1991). Since most of the new laws will mandate that transfers to other nations will only take place if these countries have "equivalent protection", the MNE must be aware of the laws of all nations in which the data were either collected, stored, or disseminated (Reidenberg, 1992).

Increased Statutory Duties

In order to operate data facilities located in Europe, the MNE must comply with significant duties in all aspects of data processing. As mandated in the 1995 EC Directive (95/46/EC) some of the statutory duties would include (Walczuch, Singh and Palmer, 1995):
- All data collected must meet stated quality standards;
- Advance notice must be given in most situations;
- Data subjects must be notified when the outcome of computerized processing is used against them;
- Data subjects must be notified in certain cases when data is transferred to third parties;
- Data subjects must be granted access to data; and
- Data must be prohibited from being processed if it fails to satisfy a series of preconditions.

Increased Liability for MNE IS Executives

The 1995 EC Directive (95/46/EC) places direct personal liability on the "controller of the data." The "controller of the data" is the person that takes personal responsibility of the data, not the business entity. In most instances, this person will be the top IS executive. This liability looms only larger when one considers that the "controller of the data" has increased statutory duties and that persons who are harmed will be able to obtain judicial and "dissuasive penalties." Given this increased liability, IS executives must be especially diligent as they go about designing and implementing systems (Boehmer and Palmer, 1993).

Duplication of IS Facilities

Some TBDF legislation has led to a need to duplicate facilities. For example, Sweden mandated that all processing of information relating to Swedish citizens must be conducted in Sweden (Data Communications, 1986). This legislation led to many companies having to create duplicate facilities in Sweden. For example, Xerox was forced to open a duplicate data processing system in Sweden, even though its London based IS facility was capable of handling all European related data.

Data Transfers Prohibitions

Under most countries' current statutes, if the country which the data are being transferred to lacks equivalent privacy protection, then the transfer may be barred. Several years ago, a German bank refused its Hong Kong branch's request for access to customer information concerning German citizens in fear that this transfer would violate the German Federal Data Protection Act (Choy and Boyd, 1992). Sony Germany's request to export German consumer information to the United States was denied (Ratcliffe and Waltz, 1992). In 1991 the French Data commission prevented the Italian automobile maker, Fiat, from electronically transferring personal records between France and Italy (Rothfeder, 1992).

CONCLUSIONS

Thanks to the OECD and EU, there is a worldwide trend towards privacy legislation that is impacting TBDFs. These two organizations have set the standard. The EU's efforts towards privacy issues initially resulted in restricting the movement of data across country borders. But as countries align their laws to these standards, the path for transborder data flows will be easier for companies. There are still many nations in the world that have no privacy laws, especially in Africa, Latin and South America, and Asia. The lack of data export laws might contribute to the digital divide on a worldwide level.

From a technical standpoint, the barriers are being removed. With few exceptions (for example, Tibet), countries are being connected to the Internet, thereby increasing the flow of transborder data. Fiber optic lines have been laid around South America and Africa, increasing the connectivity of countries in those continents. However, there is a long way to go in these areas. Poor countries continue to suffer from a lack of available technology to maintain or upgrade their telecommunications infrastructure. The lack of connectivity in these countries continues to restrict the ability of business partners to exchange data.

Cultural differences can severely inhibit the flow of data between companies. These cultural differences manifest themselves in languages and dialects, alphabets, and other differences, such as distance measure, temperature, dates, addresses, postal codes, and use of periods and commas in numbers. These barriers make it difficult to understand what is transmitted. Executives must be sensitive to these differences in their communications with other people in the world. These differences cause mistrust among people and, eventually can block effective business communications.

Political restrictions on the flow of information between countries still exist. These restrictions can prevent access to communications channels by individuals and can stop companies from sending or receiving business-related data. These same political constraints can also prevent individuals from receiving educational and entertainment information.

The biggest hurdles to transborder data flow seems to be legal. The disharmony of privacy and data protection laws among countries does not allow for the free flow of data. A wide gap has existed for many years between the EU and the U.S. concerning their respective privacy laws. As the data privacy laws of the many countries of the world are synchronized, there will be an even greater flow of data between companies of different countries. Until that happens, there will continue to be problems with the flow of data between the countries of the world.

Transborder data flow issues are more than just Internet issues; they are technical, cultural, political, and legal issues. The flow of data across boarders will continue to be a worldwide problem for many years to come. They impact a company's ability to effectively communicate with subsidiaries and operate on a global basis.

MINICASE

The European RailCard

Introduction
In the 1990s, many of the European railroads tried to find a business solution to rail passes by offering a plastic credit card-type rail pass. Some of the railroads started to offer a discount system for their plastic card rail pass holders. In one European country, the Railroad created a plastic rail pass. Holders of the rail pass were entitled to certain discounts when traveling on the train system. The rail pass soon became very popular especially with commuters and pensioners. The rail pass was not equipped with a magnetic strip or a chip. The rail pass had to be applied for in train stations, had to be renewed each year, and was produced by a private company.

The RailCard
In late 1995 the Railroad decided to cooperate with a European subsidiary of the AmericanBank, one of the largest internationally operating banks. The two companies signed an agreement to co-brand a "new" rail pass, called the RailCard. When the agreement was signed, it was one of the biggest co-branding agreements in Europe. The agreement provided for the issuing of the RailCard with a cash-free payment function. All RailCards were to also be VISA credit cards at no additional costs to the customer. The RailCard included the holder's photograph. The RailCards were produced in the United States in a data center run by AmericanBank.

Starting on July 1, 1996, the RailCards, with the credit card capability, were issued to anyone applying for a rail pass. Anytime a train passenger wanted to renew his/her rail pass or apply for a new RailCard after July 1, 1996, they were told that they had to accept the RailCard with the credit card functions even if they did not want a credit card at all. This led to numerous complaints and negative reports in the media.

It was widely believed in Europe that the Railroad had sold the data of its RailCard customers to a big US-based bank which was very likely to use these data in their direct marketing business. The local data protection supervisory authority criticized a number of points in the application form issued by the Railroad and AmericanBank, especially the fact that personal data on creditworthiness were collected from people who simply wanted to get on a train regularly.

After strong public protests by consumer groups and data protection authorities - the Railroad and AmericanBank had to renegotiate their co-branding agreement to extend it to the production of the old-style rail pass without the credit card function and to offer it to customers as an option. It was called the P-RailCard. In the first year, approximately 3 million RailCards were issued to European customers, and the vast majority of the cards were P-RailCards. However, AmericanBank continued to try and increase the sales of the combined RailCard with the credit card functions.

Administering Adequate Data Privacy

One European Data Protection Commissioner took on jurisdiction for the RailCard in early 2006. From the beginning in the discussions with the Railroad and AmericanBank, he made it clear that the Railroad, as the primary collector of the passengers' personal data, should not be allowed to outsource the issue of data protection in relation to the RailCard, especially since this outsourcing led to a massive trans-border data flow into a non-EU country, i.e. the USA. The Data Protection Commissioner successfully argued that no transborder data flow to the United States should take place unless the requirements of Articles 25 and 26 were met. Obviously the Railroad and AmericanBank were interested in finding a solution which would allow them to continue processing the RailCard in the United States.

The basic issue was if the processing of the RailCard data met the adequate protection requirement. It was found that AmericanBank did accept the European level of data protection. In one respect, AmericanBank even accepted a standard of protection higher than under the current European regulations. If the Railroad had continued to produce the cards themselves or to have them produced by a European company, customers would only have had a right to object to the use or sale of their data to third parties for any marketing purposes. European regulators insisted on a strict purpose limitation that applicants' data would only be used for producing the card.

One of the far-reaching provisions in the co-branding agreement is the acceptance by AmericanBank that-on-the-spot audits by European authorities will be allowed. In practice the European Data Protection Commissioner would very likely employ a consulting firm in the United States with auditing experience to carry out the audit on site. The European Data Protection Commissioner had already paid for an exploratory visit to the AmericanBank data center engaged in the production of the RailCards. The findings regarding data privacy were very encouraging.

Conclusion

Multinational corporations such as AmericanBank can and will play important standard-setting roles in the global market-place. It will take time until an adequate level of privacy protection has been ensured in all third countries importing personal data from Europe. In any case they should at least contain the same safeguards relative to the European data privacy standards.

Discussion Questions:

1. What was the major question relative to the minicase?
2. Discuss at least two ways that the AmericanBank could have satisfied European regulators?
3. Would there have been any data privacy issues if the processing location was owned by AmericanBank and located in an EU country?
4. What are the issues of spot audits by European authorities at U.S. based processing centers?

KEY TERMS

Bandwidth
Connectivity
Cultural barriers
Electronic data interchange (EDI)
European Union
Information and communications technology (ICT)
Internet
Internet hosts
Legal barriers

Multinational enterprise (MNEs)
Organization for Economic Co-operation and Development (OECD)
Personal data
Political barriers
Technical barriers
Transborder data flow (TBDF)

STUDY QUESTIONS

1. What are the main problems with transborder data flows in African countries? How can these problems be overcome?

2. Why are the data privacy laws of the United States less stringent than those of the European Union?

3. What are the main differences between the European Union's data privacy laws and those of the United States?

4. Research the privacy laws of a country not mentioned in this chapter. Are their laws the result of technical, cultural, political, or legal issues? How do they relate to the privacy laws of the European Union? Can data be sent from a European Union country to the country that you researched?

5. Some people have talked about certain countries as being "data havens." Research the concept of "data haven." Why would a country be called a "data haven"?

REFERENCES

Ajami, R.. "Transborder data flow: global issues of concern, values, and options ", in *Lundstedt, S.V. (Ed.), Telecommunications, Values, and the Public Interest*, Ablex Publishing Corporation, Norwood, NJ, 1990.

Boehmer, R. and Palmer, T. S. "The 1992 EC data protection proposal: an examination of its implications for US business and US privacy laws", *American Business Law Journal*, 31(2), 1993, pp. 265-31.

Buchholz, R. A. *Business Environment and Public Policy: Implications for Management and Strategy*, Prentice-Hall, Englewood Cliffs, NJ, 1992.

Chandran, R., Phatak, A. and Sambharya, R. "Transborder data flow: implications for multinational corporations", *Business Horizons*, November-December, 1987, pp. 74-82.

Choy, L. and Boyd, A. "Hong Kong: local bank caught in a crossfire of data protection battle", South China Morning Post, 30 November, 1992.

Cooke, J. "Hong Kong: warning over data legislation", South China Morning Post, 28 October, 1992.

Culnan, M. J. "How did they get my name: an exploratory investigation of consumer attitude toward secondary information use", *MIS Quarterly*, 17(3), 1993, pp. 341-61.

Data Communications, "Transborder data flow: an old problem remains unsolved ", Editorial, 13, April, 1986.

Directive 95/46/EC of The European Parliament and of The Council of 24 October 1995 on the protection of individuals with regard to the processing of personal data and on the free movement of such data. The European Parliament and The Council Of The European Union, 1995.

Ethnologue 15th Edition, Gordon, R. G. ed, SIL International, 2005.

Guynes, J. L., Guynes, S.C. and Thorn, R.G. "Conquering international boundaries that restrict the flow of data", *Information Strategy: The Executive's Journal*, 6(3), 1990, pp. 27-32.

Herold, R. *Privacy Smoke: Transborder Data Flow*, 2004.

Hofstede, G. *Culture's Consequences: International Differences in Work-related Values*, Sage Publications, Beverly Hills, CA. 1984

Hofstede, G. *Culture and Organizations: Software of the Mind*, McGraw-Hill Book Company, London, 1991.

Jarvenpaa, S. L. and Ives, B. "Organizing for global competition: the fit of information technology", *Decision Sciences*, 24(3), 1993, pp. 547-80.

Lee, M. (1994). "Information privacy legislation: the case of Hong Kong", Working Paper Series No. WP94/03, City Polytechnic of Hong Kong, Kowloon, Hong Kong.

Longworth, E. (2002). Transborder Data Flow: EU Directive and Implications for International Business, URL

Organization for Economic Co-operation and Development (OECD) (1980). Guidelines Governing the Protection of Privacy and Transborder Data Flow of Personal Data, OECD, Paris.

Oz, E. (1994). "Barriers to international data flow", Journal of Global Information Management, Vol. 2 No. 2, pp. 22-9.

Ragen, P. M. Safe Harbors or Free Frontiers? Privacy and Transborder Data Flows. *Journal of social Issues*, 59(2), 2003, pp. 263-383

Ratcliffe, M. and Waltz, M. "Easing data transfers across borders: European laws can present roadblocks", *Mac Week*, Vol. 2, November, 1992.

Reidenberg, J. R. "Colloquium: the privacy obstacle course: handling barriers to transnational financial services", *Fordham Law Review*, 137, May, 1992.

Sainty, K. Managing Compliance in the Global Space –Transborder Data Flow, 2005.

Sardinas, J. L. and Sawyer, S.M. "Transborder data flow regulation and multinational corporations", *Telecommunications*, November 1983, pp. 59-62.

Shackleton, V. J. and Ali, A. H. "Work-related values of managers: a test of the Hofstede model", *Journal of Cross-Cultural Psychology*, 21(1), 1992, pp. 109-18.

Stewart, B. "Global Rules for Privacy Across Borders", http://www.knowledge-basket.co.nz/privacy/media/globps.html, 2000, Accessed June 21. 2006

United Nations Centre on Transnational Corporations (UNCTC) Transnational Corporations and Transborder Data Flow: An Overview, UNCTC, 1981, Geneva.

Wallraff, Barbara "What Global Language?", *The Atlantic Monthly*, 286(5), pp. 52- 66, 2000.

Waples, E. and Norris, D. M. "Information systems and transborder data flow ", *Journal of Systems Management*, 43(1), 1992, p. 28.

Yue, S. Y. "Hong Kong: call for new body to oversee data protection", *South China Morning Post*, 16 November, 1992.

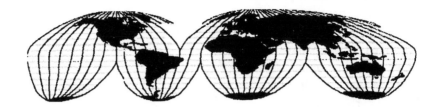

Global IT Supply Chain Strategy: Physical and Social Networks

Luca Iandoli
Pierluigi Rippa
Giuseppe Zollo
University of Naples Federico II, Italy

Barry Shore
University of New Hampshire, USA

CHAPTER SUMMARY

Few areas have had more influence on the competitive business environment than the internationalization of the supply chain. Effective management of these geographically dispersed supply chains promises shorter processing cycles, more flexible processing strategies, and lower costs to deliver goods and services. These benefits, however, can only be realized if several difficult problems can be addressed and solved. They include the establishment and management of effective global interorganizational alliances, the coordination of dispersed operations, and the organization of complex logistics operations. Information technology plays a major role in the effective solution of these problems. This chapter explores the trends in international supply chain management, the physical and social networks that facilitate the management of supply chain information systems, and the critical issues in developing a strategic IT plan.

INTRODUCTION

In the last decade of the 20th century, supply chain management (SCM) emerged as an important factor in the competitive strategy of the firm (Dyer, Cho, and Chu, 1998). Today, no firm can successfully compete without a carefully developed and effective SCM strategy (Garten, 1998) (Cho, 2006). The basic goal in supply chain management is to harmonize the flow of raw materials, component parts, finished goods or services from one end of the supply chain to the other. When successful, the right products or services are delivered to the right place at the right time, at the right price, and at the right quality level.

To achieve this goal several objectives must be met (Levary, 2000). They become important benchmarks in the supply chain management process.

- Reduce production or processing costs
- Shorten lead times
- Reduce in-process and finished inventory levels
- Improve product quality
- Lower transportation costs
- Improve supplier selection
- Reduce purchasing costs
- Raise customer service levels
- Improve cooperation between buyers and sellers.

Achieving these objectives is a challenge only a small percentage of firms has accomplished (Patterson et al., 2003). It is especially challenging because achieving them requires effective management from the beginning of the manufacturing or processing cycle through to the end-user (Handfield and Nichols, 1999). In the past, organizations could limit their focus to the management of their own internal primary activities; inbound logistics, operations, outbound logistics, marketing, and service. But the dramatic rise in the reliance on suppliers has changed this focus. The management of an enterprise is no longer restrained to its internal primary activities but extends to its suppliers' primary activities as well.

Management of any process requires information. While some firms may manage some of their business processes without appropriate information, meeting supply chain objectives in today's competitive environment without timely and accurate data is not recommended. Indeed, effective management requires evidence, and evidence is based upon information. But obtaining the right information at the right time is not always possible. This is especially true when information needs to be collected from suppliers in a geographically dispersed supply chain. Even if information is available from local and global sources it is still a challenge to use it effectively to identify problems and make decisions.

The objective of this chapter is to begin with a brief history of supply chain management, to identify the basic problems associated with managing a supply chain, to explore current trends, and to examine the physical and social networks that are at the center of contemporary supply chain systems. The chapter concludes with the issues that must be addressed when developing a strategic IT plan.

STRATEGIC SIGNIFICANCE OF SCM IN THE PAST AND PRESENT

Until the last two decades the use of external suppliers was limited for at least three reasons.
- Strategic focus on internal activities
- Geographical constraints
- Competitive Relationships with Suppliers.

Supplier strategy was limited in the past. The primary institutional customer in the supply chain, which in this chapter is called the focal firm, used as few external suppliers as possible because it feared losing control over its production or service processes. It preferred to invest and improve upon its own in-house capabilities. Rather than outsource, it engaged in process development and redesign in purchasing, manufacturing, distribution, and marketing. Since costs were not significantly different between in-house business processes and external sources, there was also little financial incentive to use suppliers.

Geographic scope also placed limits on the use of suppliers. The selection of trading partners was often limited to the focal firm's immediate region or country. This geographical focus avoided many problems that distance, language, culture, and logistics introduce (Ein-Dor and Segev, 1992). Above all, geographical preference 'seemed' to ensure better predictability and control over quality, delivery, and even costs.

Relationships and trust between focal firms and their suppliers also constrained the use of suppliers. The prevalent paradigm was one of competition. Buyers wanted lower costs and high quality, while suppliers demanded higher prices and often fell short on quality. Buyers, because they usually wielded the power in relationships, insisted on keeping their suppliers "on their toes." Neither wanted to collaborate too closely nor to share production, cost or quality data. Neither party had much trust in the other. Adversarial relationships between the two were the norm; strategic partnerships were rare.

Within this traditional framework, the role of SCM was of far less strategic significance than it is today. Buyers kept their distance from sellers and each supplier planned and controlled its own internal or primary activities. They maintained their own practices that often included very different and incompatible information systems. Some suppliers, in fact, had only very basic information systems or none at all. Furthermore, the goals of suppliers were often in conflict with the goals of their customers. Focal firms, for example, emphasized the need to minimize inventory and preferred a 'Just in Time' (JIT) strategy in which suppliers would provide appropriate and often small quantities at just the right time to meet assembly schedules or to meet customer delivery schedules. The supplier, on the other hand, preferred to produce in larger economic lot sizes with less frequent shipments and to deliver within flexible target dates. Further the supplier preferred not to spend much time communicating or sharing data with the focal firm. In the traditional framework this conflict often went unresolved.

Within the context of the trading environment just described, the role of information systems in the supply chain was bounded and somewhat simplified when compared to its role today. Little information was exchanged between trading partners, and the emphasis of the focal firm's IT strategy was, at best, to develop information systems capable of synchronizing its own internal enterprise operations.

Today SCM is a critical component of the firm's business strategy. Management has no choice but to rethink the strategic role of outsourcing, expand its supplier network throughout the globe, and engage in relationships with its suppliers.

STRATEGIC ISSUES

Supply chain decisions are both strategic and operational. Strategic decisions are those that deal with intermediate and long-term planning issues. They generally involve a time horizon longer than one year and are tied to corporate strategy. Operational decisions are short term and focus on the planning and control of day-to-day activities. They guide the production and manufacture of goods, the quality of goods and services, the storage of goods, and the transportation of goods to customers.

There are six major strategic problems that need to be addressed in SCM (Walker and Alber, 1999):

1. What to outsource
2. Where to outsource
3. Where to locate inventory in the supply chain and how much to store
4. Which transportation mode to use
5. How to transfer cash
6. How to support SCM with IT.

The first problem is to determine which components, subassemblies, finished products, or services to outsource. In this step, the process of delivering a product or service is decomposed into independent activities, and decisions are made to retain these activities within the firm or consider them as candidates for outsourcing. For example, the manufacture of a desktop computer includes the computer tower, keyboard, monitor, mouse, connecting cables, and a speaker system. Suppose all of these units are outsourced. In this situation, the only 'manufacturing' done by the focal firm, would be the assembly and test of the units before they are shipped to the consumer.

Once it has been determined to outsource, the next step, is to determine if a regional or global search for a supplier is appropriate. Can suppliers come from any corner of the globe, or must they be located regionally to facilitate coordination and logistics?

Closely related to the first two issues is the inventory decision. Inventories can exist at every stage in the supply chain as either raw material, semi-finished or finished goods. The computer company, for example, must determine how many computer towers, keyboards and monitors to stock at their assembly facility. One strategy is not to stock anything but to rely on Just-in-Time (JIT) strategies where shipments from suppliers arrive just in time for assembly. The concern with this strategy, however, is that as the geographic dispersion of suppliers increases, the tendency is to incur higher in-process (pipeline) inventories. While this ensures a buffer between suppliers and the focal firm, it also raises inventory-carrying costs.

The transportation mode decision is closely linked to the inventory strategy. As faster and more costly modes are chosen, the need for large in-process inventories decreases. Keyboards and monitors, for example, can be flown in at a moments notice. Since transportation can account for as much as 30 percent of logistics costs, choosing a transportation mode is an important strategy decision.

The next decision must address the mechanism to transfer cash among trading partners. As the geographic distance increases, and as legal, currency and accounting systems are spanned, this process becomes more complex.

Finally, decisions must be made about the information system used to link suppliers together. This includes hardware and software platforms as well as the extent to which the information will be shared among partners.

While each of these problems needs to be addressed, this chapter focuses on the strategic role that information technology must take in the development of a supply chain system. Furthermore, it addresses the challenges of developing an enterprise-wide system that weaves its partners into a synchronized flow of products and services for the benefit of the end-consumer.

SHARING DATA

The need to share data is underscored by an inherent structural problem that occurs when independent or separate stages in the supply chain must work together. This structural problem has been called the Bullwhip Effect. Unless it is addressed it will destabilize the ordering processes throughout the supply chain.

Lee et al. (1997) state that there are five fundamental reasons why the bullwhip effect occurs: (Disney and Towill, 2000) (Forrester, 1961)

- Non-zero lead-times
- Demand amplification
- Promotional effect
- Rationing and gaming
- Order batching.

Consider the situation in which customers purchase items from a retailer. When the retailer's stock runs low, it places an order with a distributor. The distributor then ships the order to the retailer and it is delivered at some future point in time (non-zero lead time). When the distributor's stock is low it places an order with a manufacturer and the manufacturer, in turn, replenishes its stock by placing orders with its suppliers. When customer demand data is not shared with every stage in the supply chain, the structure of this network is such that uncertainty in demand and local autonomy will lead to increasing variability in orders up the supply chain. In other words, small variations in customer orders will lead to large variations in orders at the manufacturer or supplier level. This is called demand amplification. Generally speaking, stages farther upstream (suppliers) experience more distorted and amplified order patterns than those downstream (retailers). The only way to reduce this bullwhip effect is to share retail customer demand with all stages in the supply chain.

The promotion effect occurs when products are sold at reduced prices to stimulate demand. Assuming an elastic demand, this creates a temporary increase in orders as customers "stock up." When the price returns to its previous level, demand slumps, creating a perceived need for further discounting in order to stimulate demand (Disney and Towill, 2003). This phenomenon adds to the structural problems inherent in the supply chain and leads to even higher levels of demand amplification.

When shortages or missed deliveries occur at any stage in the supply chain, the natural tendency is for the firm to protect itself in the future by increasing the size of the next order sent to its own suppliers (Houlihan, 1987). In addition, it may also permanently raise its safety stocks to provide a better cushion in the event that this problem should be repeated in the future.

Order batching refers to the practice of withholding the release of many small orders in favor of releasing a larger order at a later time (Burbidge, 1991). The logic behind this action is to minimize the set-up or fixed costs associated with placing orders. Fixed costs are those costs that do not vary with the quantity ordered. When larger, but more infrequent orders are placed, the fixed costs are spread over this larger quantity and incurred less frequently. Again, order batching has the consequence of increasing the bullwhip effect because it introduces greater variability into the order system.

Does information sharing really help relieve the bullwhip effect and improve the performance of the supply chain? Lee and Wang (2001) report that in a study of 100 manufacturers and 100 retailers in the food and consumer products industry, those who shared more information reported higher profits. In general, this and other studies have shown that information sharing can have a significant effect on supply chain performance. The Lee and Wang study further suggests that these improvements go right to the bottom line of the profit and loss statement.

TRENDS

Modern SCM has been influenced by several trends (Handfield and Nichols, 1999) (Lee and Wang, 2001).

- Outsourcing
- Globalization
- Information technology
- Inter-organizational alliances.

Outsourcing

Outsourcing occurs when a firm purchases goods or services from suppliers, some of which may have traditionally been supplied in-house. Two categories of outsourcing can occur. In the first, called internal outsourcing, a supplier is chosen from within the same corporation but from a separate division. In the second, called external outsourcing, an independent supplier is chosen. Each category may carry with it a significantly different ability for the customer to exercise control over its supplier, an important issue when developing and implementing IT supply chain systems.

The growth of outsourcing in the past decade has been so high that it has not only been at the forefront of corporate strategies but it has also been at the forefront of political strategies, as jobs are lost to overseas companies. Today, the average industrial firm spends more than half of every dollar on purchased products, and this share has been growing as more firms focus on their core competencies and outsource nearly everything else. Suppliers now provide research and development, marketing, manufacturing, information systems, and human resource services. But outsourcing is not limited to manufactured components or software development. Hospitals outsource the reading of X-rays, and accounting firms outsource the preparation of tax forms.

Not only is outsourcing increasing in scale but it is also increasing in scope. Rather than limited to commodity items (nuts and bolts) and conventional processes (sales order entry) that do little to differentiate the firm's product or service, outsourcing now extends to strategic or critical items (LCD monitors) and processes (call centers) that may be considered instrumental in establishing the firm's brand identity. An example of outsourcing a strategic process is the design, development and operation of a corporate web site. Many firms have chosen to outsource these activities when confronted with staff shortages, uncertain outcomes, unpredictable in-house schedules, and high costs. Choosing which components, sub-assemblies, products or services to outsource can be a difficult decision and has received considerable attention in the literature (Fisher, 1997) (Lacity, Willcocks and Feeny, 1996).

Globalization

In just the last decade, geographic limitations on outsourcing have all but disappeared. Focal firms now search all continents to find the most appropriate supplier. The software industry provides an excellent example of this trend. In the 1980's many firms turned to software houses in India for development, conversion, and maintenance of their systems. In the period from 1981 to 1994, software outsourcing to this country grew at the rate of 40 percent per year (Heeks, 1996). While India had the field to itself in the 1980's, suppliers now exist in China, Hungary, Ireland, Israel, Mexico, the Philippines, and Singapore. Choosing a software development supplier today means searching the world. In 2005 almost eighty percent of all firms expected to increase their outsourcing activities. Indeed, the trend in outsourcing continues.

Magretta (1998) provides insight into the direction of global outsourcing in an interview with the CEO of Li and Fung, Victor Fung. The company, located in Hong Kong, is one of the world's largest trading companies and relies upon thousands of suppliers around the globe to manufacture and assemble clothes and other consumer goods. Fung describes the sequence of steps that occur after a European retailer places an order for 10,000 garments. Yarn for the garment is purchased in Korea. It is woven and dyed in Taiwan. Zippers are ordered from a plant in China, and assembly of the garment takes place in Thailand. But assembly is scheduled across five Thai factories to meet the customer's need for quick response. Using this complex web of suppliers, Li and Fung can deliver sweaters to European stores in five weeks from receipt of order. This helps the retailer who can now release orders much closer to the market, thereby minimizing the risks that are often taken when orders are released long before goods arrive to be sold to customers.

The practices described in the Li and Fung article underscore the benefits of outsourcing and worldwide trading. When companies dissect the value chain and search the world for suppliers, both the manufacturer and customer reap the benefits.

Information Technology

Because the complexity of supply networks has increased, the role of IT has changed (Lee and Wang, 2001). There is no other way to integrate this web of suppliers with the focal firm. There is no other way to deal with a diverse set of suppliers that range from contract manufacturers, subassembly plants, factories, distribution centers, wholesalers, retailers, carriers, freight forwarders, customs brokers, to international procurement organizations. The consequence of this added complexity is that IT is now considered a strategic resource for the organization.

The problem is that each player in this complex web can be expected to maintain its own island of automation. The challenge is that all of these islands need to be connected, integrated, and synchronized. It is a challenge so great that many companies fail. Nonetheless, there are many examples of companies that have succeeded.

Hormel Foods Corporation, a multinational manufacturer and marketer of consumer-branded meat and food products, uses supply chain software to integrate its suppliers and optimize its transportation strategy including inbound, outbound and inter-company movements. They link all their carriers to a central logistics-planning center, and have the ability to receive, sort, explore, prioritize loads, and enhance communication with carriers, all via the Internet.

After implementing supply chain software, Motorola Information Systems Group reduced inventory by one-third, eliminated 50% of its warehouse space and cut its order cycle time from six days to one. Hyundai Motor's overseas distributors now receive spare parts almost 10 days faster than before they adopted SCM software from GE Information Services.

Pfizer, a global drug company, developed a process for demand planning across the globe that was instrumental in synchronizing their worldwide supply chain. Through access to timely global information they were able to improve their competitive position.

In these examples, the problem of synchronizing dispersed operations would be impossible without a carefully developed information systems strategy.

Interorganizational Alliances

One view of customer-supplier relationships is that the focal firm should take whatever steps are necessary to reduce supplier bargaining power and thereby improve its own position in the process of obtaining the best quality at the best price. Firms that take this view would be expected to invest little time or resources in supplier relationships. For them, sharing data and synchronizing operations is far less important than maintaining pressure on cost and delivery. This traditional view is often referred to as the arm's-length model of supplier management. It emphasizes independence and competition. Supplier relationships are characterized by:

- Short-term contracts
- Frequent rebidding
- Low levels of information sharing
- Low levels of relation-specific investments
- Low levels of trust.

In contrast to the arm's-length model is the partner model. Often attributed to the strategy followed by Japanese firms, this model suggests a close working relationship between the focal firm and its suppliers. Studies of firms whose supplier relationships can be placed in this category suggest that more information is shared among partners, interdependent tasks are better coordinated, and investments are made in relationship-specific technology. Furthermore, trust not suspicion characterizes the nature of the supplier-customer relationship (Kumar, 1996). The partner model is characterized by longer term contracts, integrated key process, and a commitment to cooperative relationships compared to the more traditional approach which reflects an adversarial stance, reactive suppliers and an emphasis on cost reduction (Macbeth, 1994; Burnes and New, 1996; Roberts and Mackay, 1998).

The downside in the partner model is that these relationships take time to develop and can be costly to establish and maintain. But of considerable concern is that these relationship 'investments' may make it difficult to terminate the relationship and switch vendors. In Porter's terminology, this model may reduce the bargaining power of the focal firm (Porter and Millar, 1985). What some firms have discovered, however, is that when this model is followed, the *overall value chain* is more effective as suppliers become full partners and work collaboratively to improve product design and manufacturing processes. Accordingly, the strategic view of SCM is to optimize the entire supply chain rather than focus on a more narrow set of objectives related to a single supplier.

Dyer, Cho and Chu (1998) studied three U.S. automotive firms, two Japanese automotive firms, and three Korean automotive firms. What they found was that the arm's-length model prevailed in the U.S. What was interesting, however, was that, while the U.S. firms believed they were following the partner model, the data suggested they were taking an arms-length approach. Apparently, perceptions and reality differed. In Korea, the partner model prevailed. Automotive companies in that country demanded a high degree of supplier loyalty but at the same time offered them long-term collaborative relationships. The Japanese automakers used both models. Some of their suppliers were placed in the arm's-length category while those they classified as strategic suppliers, were placed in the partnership category.

Which model is recommended? Both are appropriate. To optimize supply chain strategy, suppliers must be segmented into two categories. Strategic partners are those who provide inputs that are central to the maintenance of the brand name. The focal firm must maintain high levels of communication with these suppliers, exchange personnel, campaign for relation-specific investments, and make every effort to ensure that they engage in continuous improvement of their business processes.

How do these categories impact IT? The partner model would be expected to lead to an IT strategy emphasizing the development of an interorganizational IT relationship and facilitating connectivity, integration, and synchronization. An arm's-length model, by contrast, would be expected to lead to a strategy that places far less emphasis on interorganizational relationships and interorganizational information flows.

MANAGING PHYSICAL AND SOCIAL NETWORKS IN GLOBAL SUPPLY CHAIN

These trends including outsourcing, globalization, information technology, and interorganizational alliances have all contributed to the complexities of managing a supply chain. To reflect this complex environment, the supply chain is represented here as a social and physical network. Physical networks include the set of hard data connections linking all partners. Social networks include the cultural and social ties related to the increasing number of partnerships as well as long-term, collaborative interorganizational relationships. In a complex system such as global supply chain, network flows are not linear nor are they static. Rather, they are distributed among multi-actors, and occur in a dynamically changing physical and social environment.

PHYSICAL NETWORKS

Information systems can be classified as physical networks. They include nodes that represent users. In a supply chain, the nodes represent the focal firm and its suppliers. An example of a supplier network is shown in Figure 1.

The design and development of a network to facilitate information flows between these nodes must meet several criteria. It must have perceived value beyond its cost of operation, it must be relatively easy to use, it must be secure from malicious activity, it must be scalable to meet increasing volume, and it must be internally and externally adaptable to meet changing needs. Of critical importance, however, is that these nodes must be capable of communicating with each other. Otherwise data sharing would be impossible. This can be accomplished by using compatible software at each node or by using 'middleware' to communicate (translate) between dissimilar and incompatible software systems at each node. The ability to share data through common communication has traditionally been a problem, but it can be solved using one of the following technologies.
- Electronic Data Interchange (EDI)
- E-Commerce
- Enterprise Resource Planning (ERP)
- Supply Chain Management (SCM) software.

Electronic Data Interchange (EDI)

Electronic Data Interchange (EDI) a middleware solution to connect users, emerged in the late 1960s and was adopted by airlines, automobile manufacturers, and shipping companies. It was widely accepted as the standard for sharing data between focal firms and their suppliers. Ordering was usually the first process automated followed by billing and invoicing. A wide range of industries adopted this standard including shipping, retail, grocery, apparel manufacturing, textiles, warehousing, aerospace, chemicals, construction, automotive, financial, electrical and electronics, utilities, health care, petroleum pharmaceutical, metal, paper, entertainment, and higher education (Bower, King, Konsynski, 1990).

With EDI, data is transmitted between nodes in a specific and structured format and can be entered directly into the recipient's information system without any human intervention. Accordingly, EDI can be defined as the electronic exchange of business documents from one organization's computer to another organization's computer in standard format.

EDI standards are generic and therefore not dependent upon any specific hardware, software, communications system or processing environment. It does, however, require that users format their data according to these standards; and have access to communications media that can send the data between parties. Because EDI standards are generic, many commercial EDI software packages have been developed.

There are four main components of an EDI application. First is standards. They define the format of the transaction and govern the rules by which data are exchanged. The second is the business application that generates the paperwork to be sent over the EDI network. Examples of these applications

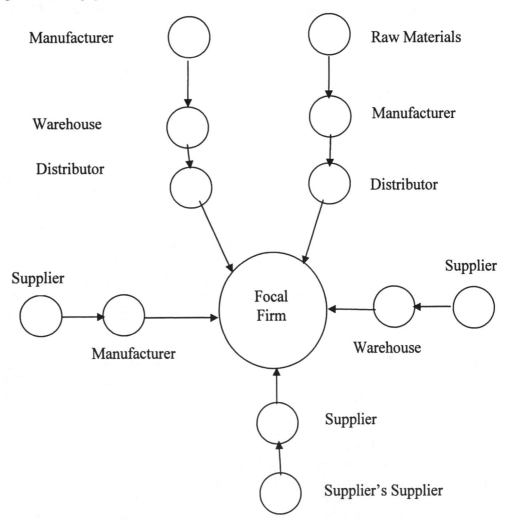

Figure 1. Supplier Network

include a procurement system, production-planning system, logistics system, financial accounting system, and order management system. The third component is the EDI gateway, whose function is to convert application data into a standard EDI format for sending and receiving messages to and from trading partners. The last component is the communication network that transmits the EDI document electronically to its destination.

Many companies using EDI rely on an independent provider called a Value Added Network or VAN to process and forward data to its destination. These organizations manage the flow between EDI sites charging users according to the volume of data sent through the network.

Traditional EDI has several shortcomings. Implementation and maintenance costs are high, hereby limiting the widespread use this technology. The user must acquire appropriate hardware to run the software. EDI software must be installed on user machines, and each user must be connected to the focal firm using direct point-to-point telecommunications technology or utilize the services of a VAN. Due to these shortcomings, many suppliers, especially smaller firms, have been unwilling to invest in this technology (Cho, 2006). As a result, many have not been EDI capable. The problem, then, is that falling short of 100% compliance affects the focal firm's ability to achieve the full benefit from an electronic network strategy. These problems notwithstanding, EDI has proved to be very successful in the past as one of the first technologies used to link nodes in a network (Jones and Beatty, 1997).

E-Commerce

The central concept behind E-commerce is the use of the Internet and browser technology to support business-to-business and business to consumer transactions. Because the Internet it is available throughout the world, can connect business users, and is easy to use, E-commerce is an important component in the effort to achieve network integration.

Many of the problems associated with traditional EDI including its high cost, inflexibility, and complexity of implementation, have been overcome by XML. This e-commerce technology relies on familiar and secure browser software technology, operates within a Windows or Windows NT environment on low cost personal computers, and utilizes the Internet to connect users and transfer data. While larger companies with high volumes of data are still using EDI technology, others, especially smaller companies, now favor XML-based e-commerce.

XML, or eXtensible Markup Language, is an extension of HTML, Hypertext Markup Language. HTML is a relatively simple and user-friendly language used to create web pages such as those found on Amazon or eBay. The problem with HTML, however, is that it is rigidly defined, and cannot support all enterprise data types. Only a predefined and limited set of 'tags' or program instructions can be used. XML is much more flexible and allows an organization to create its own markup language with emphasis on the business processes and specific tasks that the organization needs to automate. A simple example of an XML document designed to process an invoice is shown in Figure 2.

Program processing instructions in XML, as in HTML, are written as tags. These tags are identified by opening and closing brackets, <TAG>, and are traditionally written in capital letters. For example, the first tag in Figure 2 identifies that this XML program includes INVOICE data. A Tag must also have a closing tag in which the opening tag is repeated but preceded by a forward slash </INVOICE>. Closing tags are used at the end of each line or section. The tag </INVOICE> marks the end of the XML program. This XML document has several sections within the program. The first includes the name and address of the customer, the second includes the total amount of the order, and the third and subsequent sections include the details associated with each item in the order. If twenty different items were ordered, then the document would include twenty <ITEM> sections. Here only two items have been ordered. The purpose of including this sample program is not to teach XML but to illustrate that this language is flexible enough to allow the user to define application-specific tags such as <BILLING PARTY> and <ADDRESS> and that the language is sufficiently straight-forward and simple.

XML is a language that has been specifically designed to facilitate computer-to-computer exchange of data. Consider the data captured in the XML program shown in Figure 2. If needed the data could be rendered into HTML and displayed in a business-to-business web-shopping scenario where the customer enters the purchasing data. The data collected using the XML document can also be sent to the back-office where it will be used to update accounting and inventory systems. This illustrates how the output of one system can be used as the input to another system and thereby provide a simple means through which applications can be integrated (Morganthal, 2006). Nonetheless, EDI and XML are simple middleware solutions to the more complex challenge of complete interoperability across all business applications in the supply chain (Yang and Papazoglou, 2000).

A complementary technology to XML is the e-commerce portal. These portals, managed by the focal firm or an independent third party, provide access to business or consumer content through a web-based interface. This means that users can access this content using standard browsers and view the data in a familiar format.

The use of portals is growing rapidly. Companies often begin with an internal corporate portal that provides employees and business users with a personalized view of information on the corporate intranet. An e-supply chain portal is an Internet site used to connect the nodes in a supply chain network. It is capable of communicating with other nodes using either XML or EDI and as such provides a means for the focal firm to work with suppliers regardless of which technology they are using.

```
<INVOICE>
    <BILLING PARTY>
        <ACCOUNT NUMBER> B14327 </ACCOUNT NUMBER>
        <NAME> L.L. Bean </NAME>
        <ADDRESS> 17 WINGATE RD. </ADDRESS>
        <CITY> Freeport </CITY>
        <STATE> ME </STATE>
        <ZIP> 04033 </ZIP>
        <COUNTRY> USA </COUNTRY>
    </BILLING PARTY>

    <TOTAL AMOUNT> 8300.00 </TOTAL AMOUNT>

    <DETAILS>
        <ITEM>
            <DESCRIPTION> Blue Stripe Chambray Sport Shirt </DESCRIPTION>
            <SKU> 45729 <SKU>
            <QUANTITY> 400 </QUANTITY>
            <PRICE> 11.50 </PRICE>
        </ITEM>

        <ITEM>
            <DESCRIPTION> Khaki Tropic-Weight Shorts </DESCRIPTION>
            <SKU> 48701 <SKU>
            <QUANTITY> 200 </QUANTITY>
            <PRICE> 18.50 </PRICE>
        </ITEM>

    </DETAILS>

</INVOICE>
```
Figure 2. Example of XML Program to Process a Supplier's Bill.

With the convenience of browser technology, the relative simplicity of XML, the low costs associated with Internet communication, and the convenience of third party e-supply chain portals, the cost for suppliers to use this technology is significantly reduced. Now, with lower cost it is not unreasonable for focal firms to expect 100% supplier compliance at least for the basic order, billing and invoice tasks.

Enterprise Resource Planning

Enterprise Resource Planning (ERP) is a software system, usually purchased from a commercial software vendor that is built upon an enterprise-wide database. It centralizes and controls the process of data collection, storage, and access. The business objective of this centralized data environment is to provide widespread access to the firm's data. This is in marked contrast to older approaches where each department of the firm was likely to collect, store and process its own data thereby making it relatively impossible for others to search these independent databases. These older systems, for example, made it virtually impossible to track a customer's order through order processing, assembly, packaging, shipping, billing, and repairs. In its early stage the capabilities of ERP were limited to the internal primary activities of the firm. Even then, integration using this technology was a challenge. Many companies failed to reach their objectives.

Modern ERP systems are capable of extending their reach beyond the focal firm and can help synchronize data flows between the business units of the firm and those of its suppliers. Because effective interoperability between the software systems used by suppliers and the focal firm's ERP system is unlikely, transfer of data into the focal firm's computer systems must rely upon middleware such as EDI or XML.

ERP software is so complex that most organizations use commercial software. This software often supports specific industries and can be customized, to a limited extent, for each focal firm (O'Leary, 2000). Implementation, nonetheless, is complex. Most firms choose to implement one or a few modules at a time, each module focusing on a single functional area and capable of integration with subsequently installed modules. Examples of modules include finance, logistics, manufacturing, order fulfillment, human resources, and supply chain management.

Supply Chain Management Software

SCM software includes a combination of applications that span the stages in the supply chain from suppliers to customers. The following activities are supported.

- Sourcing. Evaluating, choosing and monitoring suppliers.
- Inbound Logistics. Managing the inventory received from suppliers. This includes receiving shipments, verifying them, transferring them to manufacturing facilities and authorizing supplier payments.
- Operations. Scheduling production, testing, packaging and preparation for delivery.
- Outbound Logistics. Coordinating the receipt of orders from customers, selecting carriers to deliver products to customers, and establish an invoicing system to bill customers and receive payments.
- Service. Creating a process for returned or defective goods and supporting customers who have problems or need more information about their purchased products.

In addition to these minimum requirements, many supply chain software packages also support order tracking, demand planning, transportation planning, warehousing planning, and inventory planning (Chopra and Meindl, 2001). But within each of these categories are many tasks. As a result, there is no clear agreement as to which ones should be incorporated in the software, or where supply chain management ends and manufacturing or Customer Relationship Management (CRM) begins. There is therefore considerable variability from one vendor's supply chain software system to another.

In a race to maintain competitive position in the ERP software industry, the scope of ERP modules has widened to include SCM modules. This extends the reach of ERP's internal focus to include many of the tasks needed to manage supply systems. Since ERP systems maintain a centralized and carefully controlled database environment, the addition of an SCM module has positioned ERP vendors to integrate both the internal and external environments of the firm. In one sense SCM has become a subset of ERP, although some might argue that ERP is a subset of SCM. Whatever the interpretation, the goal of these software systems is to provide a seamless software and database environment that supports the planning, synchronization and control of operational activities from suppliers to customers.

SOCIAL NETWORKS

While technical IT issues often dominate management's attention, modern supply chains require the development of social networks to support collaborative relationships among partners. Developing these networks must address both strategic and change-management issues.

Strategy Levels

There are three levels of strategy, all of them having implications to the social networks within which supply chains function. The first is organizational strategy. The primary focus here is on such issues as industry structure, competitive environment, and marketing mix. The next two levels address supply chain strategy and are conceived within the framework of organizational strategy. The second level addresses supplier selection and is concerned with the procedures to evaluate, select, and review suppliers. It focuses on the process of identifying strategic suppliers, and developing and maintaining such relationships. The third level concerns supply chain IT strategy.

New approaches to organizational strategy such as 'resource-based theory' and the 'relational view' while primarily focusing on organizational strategy can be very useful in developing supplier and IT strategy.

Change Management

Change management issues arise when focal firms and their suppliers bring very different working practices to the partnership. Negotiating these differences and establishing a relationship that supports the development and implementation of common technical platforms and appropriate levels of data sharing is challenging. What can't be ignored is what gets in the way. Indeed, a universal characteristic of humans, and the organizations within which they work, is that changes and compromise are always difficult to achieve. Change is almost always resisted regardless of the advantages that new methods and procedures bring to the participating organizations.

When people are expected to relate to others and work in ways that conflict with their basic corporate or cultural values, the success of a project can be jeopardized, just as much as if the problem were technical. When this occurs it may be helpful to ask if the methods and procedures imposed by a new application are compatible with the established working patterns of the supplier's management and workforce. If not, managers in the focal firm must be prepared to address the challenge that these cultural issues impose on new ways of working together. Research into the issues associated with national culture can help in understanding and addressing this problem.

Resources, Relationships and Networks

According to the 'resource based theory' (Barney, 1991; Conner, 1991), competitive advantage is related to firms' capability to acquire and develop rare and inimitable resources. Such resources have been classified as infrastructure, technical, financial, and human. The Resource-Based Theory (RBT) is in contrast to Porter's approach, which traces competitive advantage to structural aspects related to industry characteristics. By placing less emphasis on the role that structure plays in achieving competitive advantage, the RBT relates company success to issues of uniqueness, knowledge-sharing, exceptions, and costly-to-copy attributes.

A more recent perspective, the relational view, moves away from the juxtaposition between a structural vs. resource explanation of competitive advantage and assumes social networks and relational issues as more comprehensive and crucial competitive factors (Dyer and Singh, 1998). According to the relational view, an increasingly important unit of analysis for understanding competitive advantage is the relationships between firms, which is based on four potential sources:

- Relation specific asset
- Knowledge sharing routines
- Complementary resources and capabilities
- Effective governance.

These characteristics are present, although to a very different degree, in the networks created by both traditional and innovative firms. Sometimes these relationships are local. Industrial districts, firm clusters, Japanese keiretsu are examples of networks that nurture their competitive advantages through relational assets. In many cases, the competitiveness of these networks is strongly influenced by the close proximity of the business units in the network, despite the possibility that IT can be used to connect virtually any partner in the world. In other words, companies belonging to such local networks base a significant part of their competitive strategy on membership in a local business community and are less inclined to open their networks beyond local or regional borders. There is then evidence to suggest that a preference for membership in a local social and interorganizational network is an important factor in the ability of some firms to compete. The preference for this strong social network may suggest why it is difficult for firms to expand their networks globally in order to take advantage of price, quality, and even delivery advantages.

One example of this is found in Italy. Organizations in Italian industrial districts are having difficulty making the strategic shift from local to global supply networks. While there are many reasons, two that stand out are financial and cultural. Some success stories in Italy seem to show that medium-sized companies are managing the local-global dilemma by increasing their degree of integration and at the same time constructing supplier networks with a balanced mix of local and foreign suppliers. Increasingly the relationships are based on collaboration and trust and increasingly partnerships include suppliers in emerging countries.

The advantage of establishing trust-based, long term relationships is emphasized by the concept of embeddedness developed by Uzzi (1996). According to Uzzi an embedded network is a network in which "… the structure and quality of social ties among firms shape economic action by creating unique opportunities and access to those opportunities" (p. 675). Embeddedness is the capability of a social network to develop dense and strongly interconnected relationships among firms based on mutual trust, reputation, resources sharing and complementarities (Dyer and Singh, 1998).

Through a field study, Uzzi shows that the relationship between embeddedness and performance is problematic: if embeddedness is too weak or too strong firms experience lower performance, in the former case because they are unable to exploit relational assets, in the latter case because embeddedness may inhibit the inability to innovate. In short, the extent or degree of embeddedness cannot be too little or too much.

In the relational view, assuming embeddedness as a driver for firm performance, traditional views of supplier networks need to be reframed into a holistic view where social ties, relationships between firms, and embeddedness within a both local business community and global suppliers are considered with respect to the importance of knowledge flow and creation in supplier networks and organizational and business models for firms operating within supplier networks.

Another issue related to the social network is *the role of knowledge* in influencing performance and individual behavior. Soda et al. (2004) outline the effects on outcomes of enduring patterns of relationships and that "a past network with its accumulated relational experience becomes a kind of *network memory* that cannot be ignored as it may project a structural overhang over the present, much like a shadow of the past" (p. 893). Knowledge, then, can both be an advantage in the social network because it is necessary in achieving organizational objectives, or it can be a disadvantage because it represents the underlying foundation of experience upon which resistance-to-change is built.

Organizational and business models must now assume that the organizations within a supply chain network are increasingly characterized by blurred organizational borders and are increasingly dependent on external resources in the supply chain. In other words, some kind of resources can be said to belong to a firm with a certain degree of membership. Others are relation specific. The increasing fuzziness of organizational borders on one hand provide companies with higher organizational flexibility, on the other hand this fuzziness weakens control. Adaptation and rapidity are the result of loosely coupled organizational models characterized by low formalization and weak coordination. Companies are themselves networked organizations moving in a wider relational and knowledge network.

Change Management and the Role of Culture

To integrate organizations in the supply chain network, it is inevitable that some changes must be made. The degree of collaboration, including the extent of the information exchanged, must be negotiated. These negotiations and the changes that follow will be influenced by culture. Further, it is the weaving together of different cultures that will be most challenging.

There are two levels of culture; national culture and organizational culture. In general, national culture influences organizational culture. Hofstede (1980) defines national culture as a set of mental programs that control an individual's responses in a given context. Parsons and Shils (1951) define it as a shared characteristic of high-level social systems, while Erez and Earley, (1993) defined it as the shared values of a particular group of people. Organizational culture, on the other hand, influences the way people work, the way people are managed, and the way tasks are designed and even performed. Smircich (1983) defines it as the set of key values, guiding beliefs and understandings that are shared by members of an organization. Schein (1985) defines it as a pattern of basic assumptions that has worked well enough to be valid, and therefore to be taught to new members as the correct way to perceive, think, and feel about organizational problems.

Classifying national cultures and identifying those dimensions that differentiate cultural behavior is difficult and controversial. One major study, undertaken with the support of IBM and conducted by Hofstede (1980), provides a very useful framework. Utilizing data from 116,000 questionnaires administered in 40 countries, he found that national culture could be defined by four dimensions. He identified these dimensions as; power distance, uncertainty avoidance, individualism-collectivism, and masculinity-femininity. Other studies, such as Project Globe, have confirmed Hofstede view that these dimensions and others can be used to different behavior between cultures (Javidan and House, 2001).

Power Distance, according to Hofstede, is the degree of inequality among people, from relatively equal (small power distance) to extremely unequal (large power distance). Uncertainty Avoidance is the extent to which a society feels threatened by uncertain situations and avoids these situations by providing career stability, establishing formal rules, and not tolerating deviant ideas. Individualism-Collectivism contrasts a social fabric in which each individual takes care of himself or herself with a social fabric in which groups take care of the individual in exchange for his or her loyalty. Masculinity-Femininity reflects whether the dominant values are associated with the collection of money and things, which Hofstede classifies as masculine, as contrasted with values associated with the caring for others and the quality of life, which he classifies as feminine. Of these four dimensions, power distance and uncertainty avoidance are considered dominant in studying organizations within a particular culture (Hofstede, 1981).

Hofstede's work has been criticized in many ways. Some argue that his work implies that these 'common' cultural characteristics should be observable in all organizations within a specific culture. But we know this is certainly not the case, nor was it Hofstede's intention that this be implied. Organizations characterized by high power distance exist in low power distance cultures, and conversely organizations characterized by low power distance are found in high power distance countries. Clearly the range in any culture can be wide. Accordingly, Hofstede's model, and its use in this chapter, is intended to suggest general tendencies observable in a culture; variations are expected. Without the ability to make these generalizations, the development of a simple but useful conceptual framework of national culture would be limited.

Culture and Supply Chain Management

How does national and corporate culture affect SCM? The study cited earlier by Dyer, Cho and Chu provides some insight. It suggests that focal firms need to segment their suppliers according to the type of working relationship required, partner or arms-length. When the concept of cultural differences is introduced into this process it becomes clear that the decision is not simply a matter of choosing between the two. Indeed, the form of relationship desired may be difficult to achieve.

Consider the difference in supply chain relationships for American, Japanese and Korean automakers that Dyer, Cho and Chu found. American manufactures primarily followed the arm's-length model. The cultural characteristics that describe Americans are high individualism and low uncertainty avoidance (they ranked first in individualism and 43rd in uncertainty avoidance). It would therefore be expected that relationship distances between these focal firms and its suppliers would be high (high individualism) and that frequent bidding and supplier changes would be expected (low uncertainty avoidance). This is exactly what the Dyer, Cho and Chu study found. The opposite would be expected for Korean manufacturers. They ranked 43rd in individualism and 17th in uncertainty avoidance. It would therefore be expected that they would have few suppliers, that these suppliers would be integrated into their planning processes (low individualism), and that they would maintain a reliable and long-term relationship with them (high uncertainty avoidance). Again this is what the study found. While the study suggests that suppliers must be segmented, culture may play a dominant role in what can be expected.

Cultural influences are not limited to the nature of relationships that can be expected between focal firms and their suppliers. They can extend to the details of the data sharing process itself. In high power distance cultures, for example, it is not unusual for workers to be given very little authority and responsibility in the execution of a task. When an automated information system requires these workers to be responsible for entering job progress and quality control data into an automated system, a longer learning and training cycle should be expected before these workers are comfortable with added responsibilities.

STRATEGIC IT PLANS

The success of an international supply chain information system depends upon its strategic plan. As in any strategic plan, senior management must lead the effort. In large organizations the chief information officer (CIO) plays a critical role.

While the topic of strategic planning has been addressed elsewhere in the management literature, there are several issues that must be addressed when developing an IT plan for SCM. They include:

- Number of levels in the supply chain linked through IT
- Depth of integration
- Relationship-specific investments expected from suppliers
- Supplier contract
- Impact from resistance-to-change and cultural differences
- Choice between in-house and commercial software
- Implementation Strategy

Number of Levels in the Supply Chain Linked through IT
Because supply chains can extend to several levels, the IT planning process must establish the number of supplier levels that need to be integrated into the corporate IT system. Should integration stop with the first tier of suppliers, or should their suppliers also be included as part of the system? When warehouses, distributors and manufacturers are involved, should all of them be included? Where should integration stop?

Depth of Integration Desired
Once the number of levels is established, the plan must address the depth of integration. Will it be limited to the exchange of trading documents such as orders, invoices, statements, shipping and customs documents? Or, will integration extend to the management and control of the supplier's activities and provide the focal firm with access to production schedules, shop floor information, inventory levels, and shipping schedules (Barrett, 1986-87; Barrett and Konsynski, 1982).

With increasing frequency, the depth of integration is increasing. A good example is vendor managed inventories (VMI). Facilitated by the changes in technology and interorganizational alliances, VMI is having a profound impact on the retailing industry. Retail VMI involves a sophisticated information loop that aggregates each store's sales from Point-of-Sales (POS) terminals in order to drive product replenishment schedules. In these systems, suppliers access sales data and these data are automatically integrated into the supplier's enterprise systems and reflected in its master production scheduling, inventory and shipping schedules.

Wal-Mart is frequently used as an example of aggressive information sharing and integration strategies. For example, to manage on-the-shelf inventory levels, Wal-Mart permits Proctor and Gamble (P&G), one of its suppliers, to access aggregate point-of-sales data. Using this data and demand forecasts, P&G assumes the responsibility for maintaining appropriate stock on the shelves of Wal-Mart's retail stores. This vendor-managed inventory system (VMI) provides the timely data to help P&G become more responsive to the sales and marketing of its products while at the same time relieving Wal-Mart of inventory management and control. In addition, the sharing of demand data with its suppliers reduces the bullwhip effect. But access to data goes even deeper and allows P&G to access product supply, logistics, finance and accounting data (Handfield and Nichols, 1999).

It can be argued that the reason Wal-Mart has achieved this level of data integration is that it has a dominant position in the retail industry and that P&G is under pressure to comply with Wal-Mart to protect its access to retail markets. Indeed, other focal firms may have considerably less leverage. They may be smaller in size, may wield considerably less power, may not dominate their market, may use suppliers who have many channels through which its goods and services can be sold, and may use suppliers who are less willing to share data and make relationship specific investments. For them, the desired degree of integration may not be attainable.

Relationship-Specific Investments Expected from Suppliers

IT strategy is closely tied to the willingness of suppliers to make relationship-specific IT investments. These investments can be measured in terms of building relationships, becoming familiar with software systems, and training users to collect and process data to accommodate the focal firm's needs. If the supplier is internal to the corporation, an enterprise resource planning system can be implemented across the entire corporation. The 'common systems,' used by many Fortune 500 companies have the distinct advantage that they solve the interoperability issue. Using the same software systems with similar database structures makes it easier to develop the kind of applications that can be used to manage and control the linkages between the focal firm and its internal suppliers. But, when suppliers are external to the corporation, a strategy must evolve that addresses the extent to which they can be expected to make these investments. For example, it is not unreasonable, today, to expect that suppliers agree to use XML based systems.

Supplier Contract

Because the nature of the relationship to suppliers is so complex, and because strategic partnerships are complicated by issues of trust, culture and uncertainty, careful consideration must be given to the contents of the contract. To whatever extent is possible, the contract should not only address the traditional issues of cost, quality and delivery (Taylor at al., 1999), but also the more contemporary issues of relationships and data sharing. An expanded, but not exhaustive, list might include:

- Length of the contract
- Pricing
- Frequency of orders
- Quantity commitment and capacity available to fill orders
- Flexibility
- Lead time
- Quality
- Returns
- Technology for Data Sharing
    o EDI
    o XML
    o e-Commerce Portal

- Depth of data sharing
    - o Transaction data
    - o Tactical data
    - o Strategic data
- Processes for data sharing
    - o Order transmission
    - o Order tracking
    - o Inventory
    - o Manufacturing planning
    - o Logistics
- Relationship specific investments
    - o Training
    - o Software.

While some issues like pricing, quality and lead times may be more concrete and relatively straightforward to address, other issues like training or depth of data sharing deserve as much attention if not more in the contract. Problems should be anticipated and procedures articulated to resolve conflicts and negotiate differences as they arise.

Lee and Wang (2000) raise the important point that in addition to these issues it is important to ensure that the incentives of partners are aligned with the focal firm otherwise the commitment to share timely information may not be realized. An additional concern that also needs to be addressed in the contract is the ability to respect the confidentiality of shared information. Effective contracts can only be reached when information sharing is part of a mutual desire to coordinate and plan the activities of a Supply Chain (Capaldo et al., 2005a; 2005b).

The Impact from Resistance-to-Change and Cultural Differences

In most outsourcing decisions, especially those that cross national boundaries, the focal firm must be prepared to address the consequences of resistance-to-change and cultural differences. If ignored, these issues can seriously impair the transfer of technology, its implementation schedule, and its successful use.

The implementation of new software applications or the change in work practices often required when suppliers are first integrated into a network is not a neutral process. Compliance may be difficult and may lead to disappointing results. For example, the nature of the relationship expected, arm's-length or partner, may prove to be unrealistic. While many U.S. companies would insist that they follow the partner model of supplier relationships, Dyer, Cho and Chu found that U.S. automobile-supplier relationships followed the arm's-length model. It would be unreasonable to expect, then, that establishing a partnership relationship in the U.S. would be the same as establishing one in Japan or Korea.

Cultural factors also affect work practices. Existing practices may not be compatible with the methods required by a new software system. For example, integrated supply chain systems will fail unless accurate and timely data is entered into shared databases. Consider the differences in the work practices between Chinese and U.S. employees. The U.S. firm routinely requires employees to directly interact with information technology to update job progress, quantity, quality, and logistics data. In China, a high power distance country, it may be more difficult to collect and process this data in real time. IT strategy, therefore, needs to be sensitive to these problems and address the ways in which these differences can be accommodated and disappointments minimized.

Commercial Software

Choosing SCM software can be very challenging. Since it may not be clear which tasks need to be included in the design of a system, and since each vendor's package is different, drawing a comparison between offerings is difficult and at a minimum requires that the advantages and disadvantages of one be traded for the advantages and disadvantages of another.

There is a second major problem when commercial software is used. Left on its own, a company would naturally develop business processes, supply chain practices, and supply chain information systems to support its own needs. There is the possibility, of course, that left on its own these systems may not be very good. But if done well, these internally developed systems would support all of the business processes, both internal and external to the organization and reflect the tasks and work methods that the company best feels is appropriate for their success in the marketplace.

Commercial software, however, is very different. It is developed by an independent organization that has studied the supply chain process across many industries and across many firms. Furthermore, it has incorporated what it feels are the 'best practices' into the software. The problem, as one would predict, is that these 'best practices' seldom mirror the way in which one particular firm does its business.

The focal firm is then left with the choice of developing its own supply chain software, a very costly undertaking, or changing its practices to accommodate the commercial software. Most companies choose to change their practices. Not that that commercially developed software is inflexible. Most of these packages permit some customization. But customization increases the cost and complexity of the software implementation process.

Implementation Strategy

SCM systems are ambitious undertakings. Failure is not uncommon and is costly. Usually failure occurs during implementation when technical, business process and end-user activities converge.

To minimize the risk of a large-scale failure few firms choose to implement an entire software system at once. Instead, they install a limited number of tasks, respond to the problems that occur, and then systematically unroll the software for other tasks. Implementation, where possible, is undertaken one task or module at a time.

When following this implementation strategy, it is possible to run the old application in parallel with the new software. In this way outputs can be compared, and if discrepancies occur, the new application can be corrected. If the new application fails altogether, the old one is still available.

Another implementation strategy is called the 'big bang.' Here the new application is installed and at the same time the old one taken off-line. All changes are made at once. The advantage here is that only one application is running after the cutoff date, but the disadvantage is that any failure in the new application leaves the company with no backup.

CONCLUSIONS

Four trends at the turn of this century have had a profound effect on the way in which business is conducted and managed. Outsourcing has made the firm leaner, more focused on its core competencies, and critically reliant on its suppliers. Worldwide trading has greatly increased the range of possible suppliers. Information technology and electronic commerce has provided the means by which focal firms and their dispersed supply partners can integrate their information systems to meet ambitious schedules that deliver products and services where and when they are needed. Inter-organizational alliances have created a new paradigm that is changing the way firms relate; a change that would have been unheard of not more than a decade ago.

At the very center of these dramatic changes is the information technology that connects, integrates and synchronizes the far-flung operations of the modern organization. While we know that the objective of a supply chain management system is to support the management integration and control of the supply chain, it is still an elusive goal for many organizations. The technology is available, but implementation must depend upon effective social as well as physical networks. Success still depends upon the willingness of people and organizations throughout the world to accommodate changing business paradigms.

MINICASE

CAL South America

Introduction

CAL is a South American holding company that is wholly owned by its central government. They provide purchasing services for government owned companies and are located in Florida; the purpose of which is to be centrally and conveniently located to work with thousands of its suppliers.

This South American country has a very strong centrally controlled government. Many industries, including most basic industries, are owned by the state. While the government is planning to move from a centrally controlled economy to one that is market driven, current practices are more similar to economies that are centrally controlled.

Basic industries that the government owns and operates include steel, aluminum, mining, forestry and construction. These industries maintain their own management structures, set their own production plans, and operate their own businesses. There is however, one exception.

The state recognized long ago that many of the inputs required by these plants were purchased in the same geographic regions of the world and in some cases different plants used common or near-common inputs. The state concluded that it would be in the best interest of containing production costs to integrate the purchasing for all state owned companies and to coordinate shipping from several regions of the world to a central location in their country.

CAL emerged from the concept of centralized purchasing. Its charter is to provide a "total logistics service package" to its customers. Headquarters were established in the US with other offices in Holland, Japan and Venezuela. CAL's role is to coordinate purchasing and shipping activities between their client companies and 1,300 suppliers located throughout the world. Of these 1,300 suppliers, fifty can be classified as strategic while the remainder provide non-strategic products and services.

Purchasing Process

Purchase orders originate in one of the State owned companies and follow several steps:
- Order received by fax
- Original order also sent by mail to CAL headquarters in the U.S.
- Three potential suppliers identified (This is a state requirement).
- Requests for quotations sent to suppliers.
- Quotations received and evaluated in the U.S.
- Quotations sent by fax or e-mail to its clients in South America.
- Clients approve one quotation and return approval via fax or e-mail. All orders over $10,000 require three signatures including the buyer at the clients firm, finance manager, and general manager.
- Purchase order sent to supplier via e-mail or fax.
- Goods sent to U.S. facility where they are consolidated and shipped to clients.

Management Objectives

The current methods and procedures used to manage the supply chain system were developed to ensure effective execution of orders. Due to these safeguards, CAL has often been criticized for incurring delays in executing orders and delivering them to its customers. Some have complained about the delays while a purchase order awaits the appropriate signatures. Sometimes these delays exceed the quotation's expiration date and CAL must begin the bid process again. But the tradeoff for these delays is considered reasonable by management and provides them with the control they need to ensure effective execution of orders. By consolidating all purchasing into one agency they are able to obtain quantity discounts and to consolidate shipments from each region, thereby saving shipping charges. The savings, according to management, outweigh the disadvantages and delays inherent in the system.

Information Technology

Information technology at the US facility includes two major software systems. The first is a commercial package, initially installed in 1989-1990, with several upgrades since. It supports the purchasing process from the requisition of goods to receipt of goods. It involves requisition entry, quotation processing, vendor selection, purchase order creation, and purchase order verification. The second application is a financial management system that includes general ledger, accounts payable, accounts receivable, payroll, fixed assets inventory, and purchasing modules. These two information systems are not integrated nor are the systems integrated with CAL's clients. It is necessary, for example, to enter purchasing data manually, when an order from a client is received.

Optical fiber links are used between the U.S., The Netherlands, and Caracas, while digital microwave is used between headquarters, where most of its clients central purchasing offices are located. Dial up lines are used to connect the purchasing facility in Japan.

Louis Sandoval, managing director at CAL, has had the opportunity to observe the dramatic changes occurring in supply chain management in the U.S. In a memo to his boss back home he wrote.

Victor:

The changes are dramatic if not revolutionary. I see companies integrating their supply chains using the latest in computer and telecommunication technologies. They send their orders directly into their supplier's databases using XML, and can access these databases to see how their orders are coming and exactly when they will be delivered. One company I visited last week even has their suppliers print their own bar codes on products so the receiving process is completely automated. What really surprises me is that many of these companies have better working relationships with their suppliers. They don't seem as competitive as we are. They meet frequently and cooperate more.

I am worried that our systems are so far outdated that we will never be able to compete once we open ourselves to sell our aluminum and forestry products on the worldwide market. We need to act now before the world leaves us behind.

Two weeks later his boss replied.

Louis,

I agree with you on some of your points, but don't forget we have the advantage of batching our shipments and saving transportation dollars. This is one advantage we can't afford to loose.

Do we really need to look into our supplier's processes? I can't imagine this would help us very much. We already keep large inventories to prepare us for any problems with their shipments. If they deliver a day or two earlier or we know exactly when they deliver, I don't think this will make any difference. Don't forget we're located half the world away from some of them. We need to keep large buffer inventories just in case.

As for the working relationships that your friends have with their suppliers, I don't buy it. If we don't treat them aggressively and demand the best deal possible, how can we give our customers the best deal? We have to keep the bargaining power on our side. After all, we are big customers to many of our suppliers.

Persistent Problems

In general there is very little momentum toward changing current purchasing practices. Meanwhile the staff is kept very busy with meeting the needs of its clients. Just last week they solved a crisis of major proportions. One of the aluminum plants that produce aluminum sheets ran out of steel belting. When the sheets are made they are stacked together and rolled. The belting, wrapped around the roll, holds the roll from unraveling. The US purchasing office was notified only hours before the plant ran out of belting. The urgency of the problem was clear. If the plant did not receive belting within 48 hours, it would have to shut down. Shutdown and start-up costs are very high. The US office responded to this emergency by finding a supplier with stock on-hand. They then charted a Boeing 747 to pick up the belting and deliver it to its client. While the costs associated with this solution were very high they were lower than those associated with shutting the plant down.

Discussion Questions

1. Describe the current purchasing system used by CAL.
2. How does management justify current methods and procedures?
3. How do you think the move toward a more competitive market will affect CAL? What worldwide trends in supply chain management will they be forced to address?
4. What type of relationships do they have with their vendors? What other types of relationships are possible? Why might they be difficult to achieve?
5. Develop a strategic supply chain plan for CAL.
6. What problems would you anticipate in carrying out this plan?
7. How would you address these problems?

KEY TERMS

Arm's-length Model
External Suppliers
Enterprise Resource Planning
Focal Firm
Internal Suppliers
Interorganizational Alliance
Logistics
Outsourcing
Portal
Partnership Model
Primary Activities
Relationship-Specific Investment
Supply Chain Management
Synchronization
Transportation Mode
Value Added Network (VAN)
Value Chain
Vendor-Managed Inventories
XML

STUDY QUESTIONS

1. Explain the objectives of supply chain management?

2. Why do you think few firms have met their supply chain objectives?

3. What factors do you think explain why firms are extending their reach and outsourcing throughout the world?

4. Do you think outsourcing will increase in the future? Search the Internet for three references that will help you answer this question.

5. How does outsourcing affect supply chain management?

6. What is the difference between the arm's-length model of interorganizational alliance and the partner model? Which is preferred? Why might some firms find it difficult to implement one of these models?

7. Compare and contrast EDI and XML.

8. How does Information Technology help the firm to manage its supply chain?

9. Describe the different types of data that you think might be useful in managing a supply chain for a manufacturing company.

10. What is the Bullwhip effect and what can be done to alleviate this problem?

11. Explain how special promotions or sales affect the bullwhip effect.

12. After attending many trade shows, the Biltmore company, a manufacturer of cable winding machines used in the electronics industry, was convinced that it would be in its best interest to implement a much more effective supply chain system for its suppliers in the U.S. and Europe. Two years ago they started on the project but they have reached a dead end. Their objective is to integrate data from their suppliers' order, scheduling, inventory, quality control, billing and logistics systems into their own ERP system. Many problems have interfered with their progress to build this new network. Two months ago they were told by one supplier in France that it is having second thoughts on providing access to its data. This supplier is concerned that access will erode its bargaining power when the contract comes up for renewal in the future. Another supplier in China will only share ordering and billing data. How would you proceed?

13. You have been hired by a manufacturer of athletic shoes whose customers are some of the largest retailers in the country. While they assemble the shoes in their Miami plant, all of the component parts such as bottoms, uppers, and laces are purchased from suppliers in Asia. Their competitive advantage has been cost, and they have been able to provide a quality athletic shoe to retailers at a very competitive price. Growth has been extremely rapid. You have been asked to provide them with an IT supply chain strategy to take them into the next stage of growth. At present, communication with suppliers is by telephone or fax. Both the manufacturer and its Asian suppliers use very simple information technology. How would you suggest proceeding? Do you think EDI or XML technologies would help? Explain

REFERENCES

Barrett, S. S. and Konsynski, B. "Inter-organizational Information Sharing Systems," *MIS Quarterly*, 6(2), pp. 74-98. 1982.

Barrett, S. S. "Strategic Alternatives and Inter-organizational System Implementations: An Overview," *Journal of Management Information Systems,* 3(3), Winter 1986-1987. pp. 5-16.

Bower, M, J. King and Konsynski, B. Singapore TradeNet: A Tale of One City, Harvard Business School (9-191-009). 1990.

Burbidge J. L., "Period batch control (PBC) with GT – the way forward from MRP", *Proceedings of BPCIS Annual Conference, Birmingham,* 1991.

Burnes B., New S., "Understanding supply chain improvement", *European Journal of Purchasing and Supply Management*, 2(1), 1996, pp. 21-30.

Capaldo G., Raffa L., and Rippa P., "Information flows intensity, enabled by ICT, in buyer supplier relationships: an evaluation tool," in *Proceedings of XIV IPSERA Conference*, Archamps, France, March, 2005a.

Capaldo G., Raffa L., and Rippa P., "Information flows evaluation enhancing buyer-supplier relationships performance: the case of an e-supply chain portal," *EurOMA Conference*, Budapest, Hungary, June, 2005b.

Cho, V. "Factors in the Adoption of Third-Party B2B Portals in the Textile Industry," *Journal of Computer Information Systems*, Spring, 2006, pp. pp. 18-31

Chopra, S. and Meindl, P. *Supply Chain Management: Strategy, Planning, and Operations.* New Jersey: Prentice Hall. 2001.

Conner K. R., "A historical comparison of resource-based theory and five schools of thought within industrial organization economics: Do we have a new theory of the firms?", *Journal of Management,* 17, 1991, pp 121-154.

Disney S. M., and Towill D. R., "The effect of VMI on the bullwhip effect", *Proceedings of International Conference on Production Research*, Prague, 30 July-2 August, 2000.

Disney S. M., and Towill D. R., "Vendor-managed inventory and bullwhip reduction I na two-level supply chain", *International Journal of Operations & Production Management*, 23(4), 2003, pp. 625-651.

Dyer, J. H., and Singh, H. The relational view: cooperative strategy and sources of interorganizational competitive advantage", *Academy of Management Review,* 23(4), 1998, pp. 660-679.

Dyer, J. H., Co, D. S. and Chu W. "Strategic Supplier Segmentation: The Next "Best Practice" in Supply Chain Management," *California Management Review*, 40(2), Winter 1998, pp. 57-77.

Ein-Dor, P. and Segev, E. "End User Computing: A Cross Cultural Study," *International Information Systems*, 1(1), January 1992, pp. 124-137.

Erez, M. and Earley, P. C. *Culture, Self-identity, and Work.* New York: Oxford University Press. 1993.

Fisher, M. L. "What is the Right Supply Chain for Your Product," *Harvard Business Review*, March-April, 1997, pp. 105-116.

Forrester, J. *Industrial Dynamics*, MIT Press, Cambridge, MA, 1961.

Garten J. E. "Why the global economy is here to stay," *Business Week*, 23, 1998, pp. 21.

Handfield, R. B., and Nichols, E. L. Jr. *Supply Chain Management*, Prentice Hall, 1999.

Hartman, A., Sifonis, J. and Kador, J. *net ready – Strategies for Success in the E-conomy*, McGraw-Hill, New York, 2000.

Heeks, R., Global Software Outsourcing to India by Multinational Corporations in *Global Information Technology and Systems Management*, Palvia, Palvia, and Roche, Ivy League Publishing, pp. 364-392.

Hofstede, G. "Motivation, Leadership, and Organization: Do American Theories Apply Abroad?," *Organizational Dynamics,* Summer 1980.

Hofstede, G. " Culture and Organizations," *International Studies of Management and Organizations,* X(4), 1981, pp. 15-41.

Houlihan J. B., "International supply chain management", *International Journal of Physical Distribution and Materials Management*, 17(2), 1987, pp. 51-66.

Javidan M, House R. "Cultural Acumen for the Global Manager: Lessons from Project Globe," *Organizational Dynamics*, 299(4), 2001, pp. 289-305.

Jones, M. C. and Beatty, R. C. "EDI Benefits and Compatibility: An Empirical Comparison of End User and EDI Manager Perspectives," *Journal of Computer Information Systems,* Fall 1999, pp. 51-54.

Kumar, N. "The Power of Trust in Manufacturer-Retailer Relationships," *Harvard Business Review,* November-December 1996, pp. 92-106.

Lacity, M. C., Willcocks, L. P. and Feeny, D. F. "The Value of Selective IT Sourcing," *Sloan Management Review,* 7(3), Spring, 1996.

Lee, H. L., and Whang, S. "Information sharing in a supply chain". *International Journal of Manufacturing Technology and Management,* 1(1), 1997, pp. 79-93.

Lee, H. L.and Whang, S. "E-Business and Supply Chain Integration," *Stanford Global Supply Chain Management Forum,* SGSCMF-W2-2001, 2001.

Levary R. R. "Better supply chains through information technology", *Industrial Management,* 42 (3), 2000, pp. 24-30.

Macbeth D. K., "The role of purchasing in a partnering relationship", *European Journal of Purchasing and Supply Management,* 1(1), 1994, pp. 19-25.

Magretta, J. "Fast, Global , and Entrepreneurial: Supply Chain Management, Hong Kong Style" *Harvard Business Review,* September-October 1998, 103-114.

Morganthal, J. P. Portable Data/Portable Code: XML & Java Technologies, http://java.sun.com, 2006, pp1-7.

O'Leary, D. E. *Enterprise Resource Planning Systems.* Cambridge, UK: Cambridge University Press. 2000.

OECD, www.oecd.org, 2 March 2005. 1998.

Parsons, T. and Shils, E. A. *Toward a General Theory of Action.* Cambridge, MA: Harvard University Press. 1951.

Patterson K. A., Curtis M. G., and Corsi T. M. "Adopting new technologies for supply chain management", *Transportation Research Part E,* 39, 2003, pp. 95-121.

Porter M. E. and Millar V. E. "How information Gives You Competitive Advantage," *Harvard Business Review,* July-August 1985, pp. 149-161.

Roberts B., and Mackay, M. "IT supporting supplier relationships: the role of electronic commerce", *European Journal of Purchasing & Supply Management,* 4, 1998, pp. 175-184.

Schein, E. H. *Organizational Culture and Leadership.* Jossey-Bass, San Francisco, 1985.

Smircich, L. "Concepts of Culture and Organizational Analysis," *Administrative Science Quarterly,* (28), 1983, pp. 339-358.

Soda, G., Usai, A., and Zaheer, A. "Network memory: the influence of past and current networks on performance", *Academy of Management Journal,* 47(6), 2004, pp. 893-906.

Taylor, S., Ganeshar, R., and Magazine, M., *Quantitative Models for Supply Chain Management,* Dordrecht, Holand: Kluwer Academic Publishers, 1999.

Uzzi, B. "The sources and consequences of embeddedness for the economic performance of organizations", *American Sociological Review,* 61, 1996, pp. 674-698.

Walker, W. T., and Alber, K. L. "Understanding Supply Chain Management," *APICS Online Edition,* January, 1999, 99(1).

Yang, J. and Papazoglou, M. P. "Interoperation Support for Electronic Business," *Communications of the ACM,* 41(26), 2000, pp. 39-47.

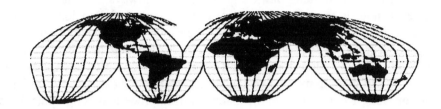

Cultural Asymmetries and the Challenge of Global Enterprise Integration

Barry Shore
University of New Hampshire, USA

CHAPTER SUMMARY

In a flatter and more competitive world, organizations, their customers, and their suppliers span the globe. While this distributed organizational environment may be necessary to improve the efficiency with which goods and services are produced and delivered it is not sufficient. Once distributed, the challenge is then to integrate these 'independent' units to facilitate efficient response from one end of the supply chain to the other. A critical component of an integration strategy is information. But bringing together and using information from many sources presents its own challenges. One factor, often difficult to address in a concrete way, is that social systems and work practices be can be very different throughout the world, and since enterprise integration imposes a structure on these social systems and work practices, geographically dispersed business units are often confronted with collaborative challenges that are difficult to accommodate. This chapter will consider these social or 'cultural' influences. It will conclude with several concrete suggestions that could help manage the process of globalization.

INTRODUCTION

In the struggle to maintain a competitive position, many organizations have been forced to compete globally, outsource to a global network of suppliers, and distribute to a globally dispersed customer base. It is only in this way that they can hope to deliver the right products to the right customers, at the right time and at the right price.

While pressures to globalize have been with us for over a decade, we are now witnessing the globalization of industry on a scale never before imagined. Limiting themselves to their core competencies, organizations have become flatter and more geographically dispersed. They are, as a result, more challenging to manage because these far-flung operations must be integrated to ensure that products and services are delivered on-time, to the the right place, and at the right price to its customers. Perhaps the central ingredient in integrating these operations is information technology.

But the challenge of managing global organizations has not been neglected (Bartlett and Ghoshal (1989) (Ein-Dor, Segev and Orgad, 1993) (Roche, 1992). Several factors including language, time zones, currencies, laws, and culture have always presented a challenge (Shore, 1996). The difference now is that there has been a significant shift. No longer can it be assumed that operations throughout the world can be left on their own, as many had been in the twentieth century, with varying degrees of control from headquarters (Cheung and Burn, 1994) (Magretta, 1998) (Harzing, 2000). Organizations today are different. The competitive environment now demands more effective control of operations. It is no longer acceptable, for example, to design fashion clothing in New York or Hong Kong, schedule the manufacturing process at geographically dispersed suppliers throughout Asia, and wait eight months for the finished goods to arrive in stores. At Zara, an international chain with headquarters in Spain, the time from design to delivery on store shelves has been reduced to weeks!

Information and telecommunication technologies are at the center of any strategy to link the dispersed global organization and maintain the efficiencies need to compete in global markets. Recent develops such as Radio Frequency Identity Tags (RFID), promise to reduce the cost of tracking products and parts and provide even more data in the struggle to coordinate dispersed operation (Bose and Pal, 2005). But technology is not enough. Management must be willing and capable of sharing value chain data from inbound logistics, operations, outbound logistics, and marketing (Lee and Whang, 2000). Without this capacity to share it is impossible to integrate.

Data sharing is a complex social and technical phenomenon. At a minimum it means common technical platforms. A common platform, in simple terms, is a system that permits users in one organization to electronically share information with users in another organization. Its goal is to facilitate access to data and to support inter and intra organizational decision-making. Using a common platform, for example, headquarters in Chicago can work collaboratively with a supplier in Malaysia and once a master production schedule has been established they can monitor the production schedule in the Malaysian manufacturing plant to ensure that shipments from this plant to an assembly plant in Hong Kong will include the correct quantity, colors and sizes. Furthermore, monitoring can ensure on-time deliveries.

Data sharing has also been shown to minimize the bullwhip effect where demand variations are amplified up the supply chain (Lee, Padmanbhan and Whang, 2004). Lin, Huang and Lin (2002) show that as the level of detail shared with other business units increases the lower is total cost, and the 'deeper' the information shared the shorter is the order cycle time. This suggests that the ability to share data is becoming essential if operational challenges such as overcoming the bullwhip effect, and realizing economies-of-scale and competitive advantage are achieved in today's worldwide market.

It is not enough, however, to implement effective information links. While a proven headquarters' information strategy is a necessary condition for success, it is not necessarily sufficient. This is not to suggest, however, that all organizations face these problems. Many efforts to integrate applications with disbursed business units experience about the same degree of success or failure, as do integration strategies at domestic business units. But problems, often beyond the scope of those experienced at home, can plague overseas integration projects.

In one Fortune 500 organization studied by the author, the full range of outcomes occurred, from total success to total failure. To integrate essential corporate functions, headquarters established a "common systems" group whose purpose it was to integrate common sales, financial, and manufacturing applications throughout the world. But several years after this project was initiated only one-third of the worldwide sites were successfully using these applications. Another third was still having problems with implementation, while the last third had yet to begin.

Technical factors certainly contribute to these problems: a business unit may lack experience with information technology; management may be technically out-of-date; technical support may be unavailable; and the telecommunications infrastructure may be inadequate. But technical factors alone cannot fully explain why problems occur when linkages that support data sharing are attempted between suppliers and customers. What needs to be considered is that headquarters, suppliers, and customers may exist in very different national cultures and that different preferences work practices,

IS practices and data sharing may exist within these cultures. Linkages, which attempt to integrate these geographically dispersed organizations, may therefore be subject to cultural as well as technical challenges.

Culture manifests itself in many ways, and many of them may not be obvious to headquarters' management. Culture may influence the way people work, the way they follow procedures, their inclination to take individual initiative, their response to hierarchical control, their willingness to share data not only with those in their own organization but with those in other organizations, and their willingness to accept technology (Parboteeah et al., 2005). When linking organizations and expecting the information system to integrate the far-flung operations of the enterprise, it is these social/cultural dimensions that may have as much if not more influence on enterprise integration as does hardware, software, or telecommunications. As such, culture becomes one of the variables that needs to be considered in the management process. But it is often difficult for management to attribute these problems to cultural differences, because culture is seldom adequately understood.

This chapter focuses on the cultural component of the integration and data sharing challenge. It explores the way in which national culture influences the IS culture and data sharing activities within an organization and why the differences between culture may lead to implementation problems of enterprise integration strategies. This is done in several steps. It begins by briefly exploring the issues associated with national culture. Next, the role of organizational culture is addressed, and finally the focus is placed on information systems culture. A hierarchy of cultural influences is suggested from national to organizational, and then to information systems. One level affects the next.

The chapter concludes with several suggestions that, if followed, can help managers cope with the added complexities that naturally occur as information systems are use to integrate the extended enterprise.

NATIONAL CULTURE

Hofstede (1980) defines culture as a set of mental programs that control an individual's responses in a given context. Parsons and Shils (1951) define it as a shared characteristic of a high-level social system, while Erez and Earley, (1993) defined it as the shared values of a particular group of people.

The influence of national culture on human behavior begins during childhood and is reinforced throughout life (Lachman, 1983; Triandis, 1995). More important to the practice of management is that national culture not only influences our responses in social situations, but as Hofstede concluded in his research, it also shapes our behavior in organizations.

Classifying cultures and identifying those dimensions that differentiate cultural behavior is difficult and controversial. One major study, undertaken with the support of IBM and conducted by Hofstede (1980), provides a very useful framework. Utilizing data from 116,000 questionnaires administered in 40 countries he found that national culture can be defined through four dimensions. He identified these four dimensions as: power distance, uncertainty avoidance, individualism-collectivism, and masculinity-femininity.

Power Distance is the degree of inequality among people, from relatively equal (small power distance) to extremely unequal (large power distance). Uncertainty Avoidance is the extent to which a society feels threatened by uncertain situations and avoids these situations by providing career stability, establishing formal rules, and not tolerating deviant ideas. Individualism-Collectivism contrasts a social fabric in which each individual takes care of himself or herself with a social fabric in which groups take care of the individual in exchange for his or her loyalty. Masculinity-Femininity reflects whether the dominant values are associated with the collection of money and things, which Hofstede classifies as masculine, as contrasted with values associated with the caring for others and the quality of life, which he classifies as feminine. Of these four dimensions, power distance and uncertainty avoidance are considered dominant in studying organizations within a particular culture (Hofstede, 1981).

Hofstede (1980) also describes four classifications of culture measured by combinations of power distance and uncertainty avoidance. These classifications, depicted later in Figure 2, represent regions or quadrants into which organizations within a specific culture can be placed. The first quadrant, called the *family* by Hofstede, is characterized by cultures displaying a high degree of centralization (high power distance) combined with a lower level of formalization (low uncertainty avoidance). The second quadrant, called the *market*, includes cultures that are neither centralized (low power distance) nor formalized (low uncertainty avoidance). The third quadrant, called the *machine*, is characterized by a high degree of formalization (low uncertainty avoidance) and decentralized power (low power distance). The fourth quadrant, called the *pyramid*, is both centralized (high power distance) and formal (high uncertainty avoidance). Several of the countries studied are listed in Table 1 together with the quadrant to which they belong.

MARKET	MACHINE	PYRAMID	FAMILY
Denmark	Finland	France	Hong Kong
Sweden	Switzerland	Japan	Singapore
Ireland	Germany	Mexico	India
New Zealand	Israel	Greece	Philippines
USA	Argentina	Arab Countries	West Africa
Great Britain	Costa Rica	Korea	Malaysia

Table 1. Examples of Countries that can be grouped in Hofstede's Quadrants.

Erez and Earley (1993) explain why Hofstede's model has been widely used to study organizations: they contend that it is not only 'approachable,' but is sufficiently clear and parsimonious to lend itself to empirical tests. Studies that have used this model as a framework includes papers by Kedia and Bhagat (1988), who use it to develop a conceptual model of technology transfer, and Shore and Venkatachalam (1995), who use it to develop a conceptual model of systems analysis and design. However, Hofstede's model has been criticized in at least two areas: one, the model is based on and specific to a single organization (IBM) and hence raises the question of generalizability; and two, the four dimensions used in the study are insufficient by themselves to study all aspects of culture. Addressing the first criticism, Erez and Earley (1993) argue that national culture reflects an individual's core values and beliefs, and it is these values that dominate corporate or organizational culture. They maintain that organizations can, at best, exert influence over an individual's peripheral values and beliefs. Using this argument it is reasonable to suggest that the Hofstede model can be generalized to all organizations throughout the world, not just IBM. To address the second criticism, Hofstede (1991) subsequently introduced a fifth dimension, namely long-term vs. short-term orientation.

Hofstede has also been criticized because his work suggests to some that these 'common' cultural characteristics should be observable in all organizations within a specific culture. But this is certainly not the case, nor was it Hofstede's intention that this be the case. Organizations characterized by high power distance exist in low power distance cultures, and conversely organizations characterized by low power distance are found in high power distance countries. Clearly the range in any culture can be wide.

A more recent study, Project GLOBE, compared 18,000 middle managers from 62 countries (Javidan and House, 2001). Again, culture was linked to behavior in organizations. Nine critical cultural dimensions were identified: performance orientation, future orientation, assertiveness, uncertainty avoidance, power distance, collectivism, family collectivism, gender differentiation, and humane treatment. Five of these dimensions are similar to those identified in the Hofstede study. Both studies, criticism aside, suggest that there is some validity in attributing management differences to variation in national culture.

Accordingly, the use of cultural models used in this chapter is intended to suggest general tendencies observable in a culture; variations are expected. Without the ability to make these generalizations, the development of a simple but useful conceptual framework would be limited.

ORGANIZATIONAL CULTURE

Organizational culture can be defined in many ways. Smircich (1983) defines it as the set of key values, guiding beliefs, and understandings that are shared by members of an organization. Schein (1985) defines it as a pattern of basic assumptions that has worked well enough to be valid, and therefore to be taught to new members as the correct way to perceive, think, and feel about organizational problems.

Organizational culture can also be expressed in many ways. Deal and Kennedy (1982) suggest that the manifestation of organizational culture can be placed into four categories, each one can be peeled off like the layers of an onion, until the core values are exposed. They include: (1) symbols, or the words or objects that carry a specific meaning within the organization; (2) heroes, or the persons highly prized as models of behavior; (3) rituals, or the collective activities that are socially essential in an organization; (4) and core values.

Hofstede, Neuijen, Ohayv and Sanders (1990) contend that there is no consensus about the definition of organizational culture. Most authors, they assert, will agree that it is: (1) holistic, (2) historically determined, (3) related to anthropological concepts, (4) socially constructed, (5) soft, and (6) difficult to change. To clarify its definition and introduce empirical evidence to a field dominated by what he criticizes as "in-depth case studies," Hofstede et al. studied ten organizations in Denmark and the Netherlands. They concluded that organizational values are partly determined by nationality, industry, and task. Furthermore, they concluded that while the popular literature insists that shared values represent the core of organizational culture, their factor analysis suggests that the way values affect ordinary members of an organization is expressed through practices. Practices represent what "is" in contrast to values that represent what "should be." Accordingly, an example of a value, in the context of an IS group, might be widespread participation, including end-users, in systems development. Another example would be the inclusion of a functional manger on all major IS development teams.

While Hofstede et al. contend that organizational culture is determined by both national culture and practices; others place more emphasis on national culture alone. Erez and Early (1993) argue that organizations do not possess cultures of their own, but are formed as a result of societal cultures. Triandis (1995) suggests that organizations may have a weak effect on an individual's peripheral values, but have no long-lasting effect on core or deep-seated values. Corporate culture may therefore only affect an individual's peripheral values while leaving core values, those learned early in life, intact (Erez and Earley, 1993).

In summary, organizational culture can be defined as a set of shared values, basic assumptions, and practices in an organization. It evolves historically and is difficult to change. While it is generally agreed upon that national culture affects core values established early in life, the influence of organizations may be limited to peripheral values.

INFORMATION CULTURE

The culture within an IS environment can be defined as the set of 'values' and 'practices' shared by those members of an organization involved in information activities including MIS professionals, managers and end-users. Examples of practices in a specific organization might include:

- Exclusive use of Windows environment.
- Limits on outsourcing IS functions.
- Extensive end-user involvement during systems analysis and design.
- Commitment to prototyping methodologies in systems development.
- Minimal support for end-user computing.
- Requirement for IS staff approval for all PC purchases.
- Open access by approved vendors to production scheduling databases.
- Restrictions on internet access.
- Minimizing access for certain departments to centrally maintained databases.
- Sharing only billing and invoice data with customers.

IS culture establishes boundaries for information technology and the use of this information to manage organizations. It determines which practices are acceptable and which are not; which technologies are acceptable, which are not; and which software is acceptable and which is not. Culture influences the process of developing and designing applications and even dictates how we use them (Shore and Venkatachalam, 1995).

Copper (1994) confirmed that IS culture plays a strong role in the IS function of organizations. He found that an IS culture may resist changes in technology that realign status, power, and working habits, especially when they violate some of the group's shared values. IS culture, he contends, may be more or less compatible with certain information technologies and to the degree to which it is less compatible, consequences may occur which include resistance to change, implementation failure, or disappointing results. In another study Davenport et al. (1992) concluded that IS and the information made available from these systems is often used politically, sometimes contrary to the best interests of the organization. This suggests that information sharing has a strong political overtone and as such can be influenced by national, organizational and information systems culture.

Research therefore concludes that an IS culture does exist and may have profound consequences on the ability of the IS function to deliver results. Indeed the increasing drive toward outsourcing IS activities may be influenced, in part, by the perception that the IS culture within an organization becomes incompatible with corporate goals and objectives, and since culture is difficult to change, an apparent attractive option for many organizations is to eliminate much of the IS organization and use outside vendors.

In building a model of IS culture, Cooper uses the competing values framework developed by Quinn and Rohrbaugh (1985). This framework emphasizes the competing tensions and conflicts inherent in groups. They suggested that two major conflicts include: (1) the need for *order* versus the need to remain *flexible*, and (2) the focus on either the demands of the *internal* social and technical systems of the organization versus a focus on the *external* world beyond the boundaries of the organization. When combinations of these conflicts are considered, four cultural archetypes can be defined: *survival*, *productivity*, *stability*, and *human relations*. The *survival* archetype is characterized by an organization that is flexible and external. Its leaders can adapt to a changing environment and are willing to take risks in the search for opportunities. The *productivity* archetype is characterized by an organization that prefers order and is responsive to its external environment. These organizations are very efficient, and nearly all decisions are driven by rational-economic considerations. The *stability* archetype is characterized by the need for order and internal focus. In these organizations there is a high degree of formalization, and leaders tend to be cautious, emphasizing technical issues. Flexibility and an internal focus characterize the *human relations* archetype. Emphasis is on informal roles rather than a formal structure, and maintenance of the organization is a primary goal.

Cooper's model is summarized in Figure 1. He associated several practices with each of the archetypes. The survival archetypes include such practices as scanning the external environment for project opportunities and inter-organizational linking. The productivity archetype is compatible with applications that facilitate organizational planning, directing and goal setting. Stability archetypes are more likely to emphasize applications that stress measurement and control such as accounting systems, cost-variance reporting, budgeting, and other record keeping applications. Human relations archetypes are compatible with systems that reinforce the social values of its members and provide interpersonal communication and cooperation such as teleconferencing, electronic mail, and group decision support.

Focus on
Flexibility

Human Relations

Computer Aided Instructing
Interpersonal Communicating
Conferencing
Group Decision Support

Survival

Environmental Scanning for Problem
Opportunities
Interorganizational Linking
Doubt and Argument Promoting

Focus on
Internal
Organization

Stability

Internal Monitoring
Internal Controlling
Record Keeping
Optimizing

Focus on
External
Organizational
Environment

Productivity

Modeling
Forecasting
Sensitivity Analyzing

Focus on Order

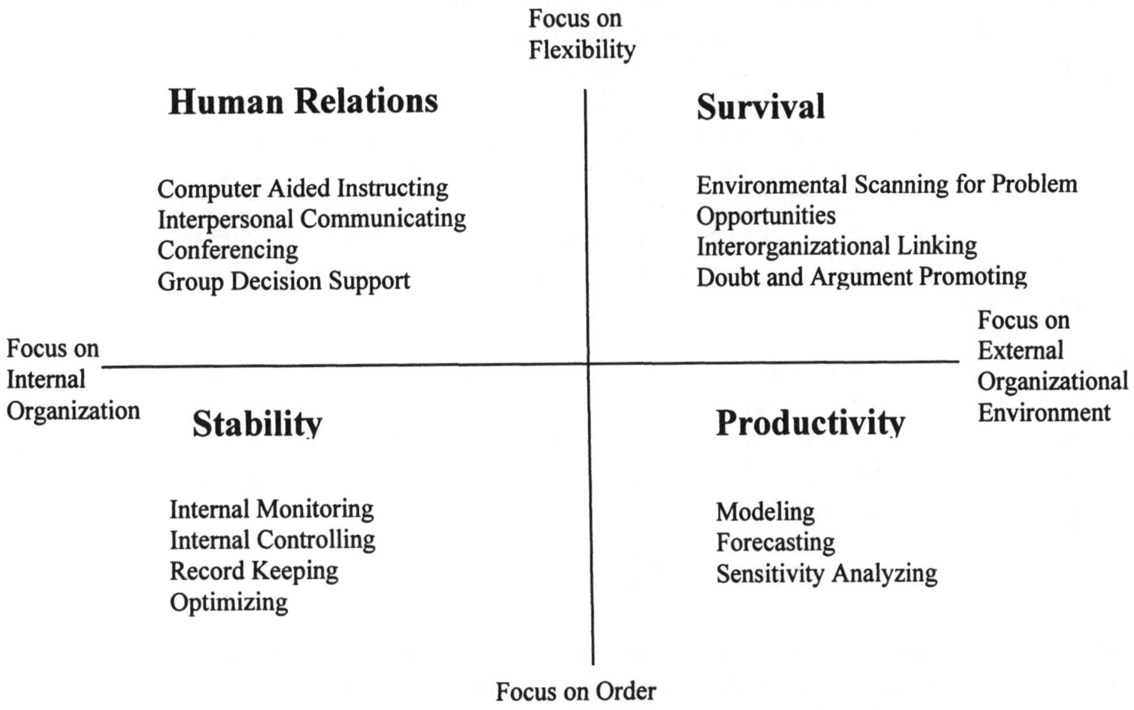

Figure 1. Organizational Practices Related to Cultural Archetypes (Adapted from Cooper, 1994)

This framework has major implications for the ability of the firm to establish common platforms and share data with its business units, suppliers and customers. For example, the Survival archetype, with its focus on survival and flexibility, is more likely to accommodate the demand by headquarters to collaborate on common platforms and share data. Accomplishing the same goals would be more challenging with the Stability archetype.

In summary, the culture of IS is an important variable in understanding the IS strategy within an organization and the type of practices which the organization follows. It also begins to suggest that establishing common platforms and sharing data from suppliers to customers can be a challenge.

INFLUENCE OF NATIONAL CULTURE ON IS CULTURE

To establish a link between national culture and IS culture, it would be useful to determine the extent to which Hofstede's model of national culture can be mapped onto the competing values model as it is applied to IS culture by Cooper. If successful, the competing values model could be used as the basis for an IS culture framework that takes into consideration national culture. Such a mapping, however, is difficult because there is no direct relationship between Hofstede's dimensions of power distance and uncertainty avoidance and the archetypes of IS organizational culture including stability, productivity, survival, and human relations. To some extent, it could be argued that stability archetypes can be expected to occur more frequently in the machine and pyramid quadrants since a stable organization would be expected to be high in uncertainty avoidance. But even organizations in the family quadrant would need to maintain stable organizations in order to protect their "family" structures. Productivity archetypes may be expected to occur more frequently in the machine quadrant, since they emphasize the improvement of efficiency and the reduction of uncertainty. Survival archetypes may be expected to occur more frequently in the market quadrant, since the willingness to take risks is an important component of this archetype. Finally, human relations archetypes might be expected to occur more frequently in the market and family quadrants since formal structures are not emphasized and teamwork is common.

There are at least three problems with this attempt to map culture onto archetypes. First, as suggested by the discussion about the stability archetype, more than one archetype is likely to exist in each quadrant. Second, the characteristics of each archetype may vary from quadrant to quadrant. For example, in the market quadrant the human relations archetype may emphasize informal structures, widespread participation from end-users, team approaches, and the reliance on group enhancing technology such as E-mail and decision support systems. But in the family quadrant, human relations may imply strong top-down management emphasizing the maintenance of the corporate family at all costs. The third criticism is that, unlike Hofstede's study, there is no empirical evidence to suggest the feasibility of such a link.

To summarize, national culture can be traced to IS culture, but when Hofstede's national culture model is mapped onto the competing values IS culture model, the results do not suggest a clear association between national culture and organizational archetypes. Rather than use the competing values model, it seems more appropriate to apply Hofstede's work on national and organizational culture directly to IS culture, but still preserve Cooper's approach in which IS practices are identified and placed in quadrants.

IDENTIFICATION OF IS PRACTICES

While one could hypothesize as to which practice would be most common in each of the Hofstede quadrants, the methodology used in this chapter was to scan the research literature on Global IS and place practices, reported in these studies, into the quadrant representing the country in which the study was undertaken. The result of the process is a model, summarized in Figure 2, that begins to build a sense of the prevailing IS culture associated with each quadrant.

The *market quadrant* includes cultures that are neither centralized nor formalized. Companies placed in this quadrant are likely, as Cooper has suggested, to scan the environment for project opportunities. Mouakket, Sillence, and Fretwell-Dowling (1994) found evidence of end-user participation during the development process in the United Kingdom. Wetherbe, Vitalari and Milner (1994) observed the use of groups or teams in North America. Nelson, Weiss and Yamazaki (1992) reported connectivity and widespread access in the U.S. Wetherbe, Vitalari and Milner (1994) found a reliance on distributed processing in North America, and innovation in the U.S. was suggested by Couger (1990).

The *machine quadrant*, which includes cultures that are not centralized but highly formalized, is compatible with practices more likely to improve existing IS operations rather than initiate innovation or reengineering. This was the conclusion reached by Schwarzer (1995) in a study of German firms. Both Schwarzer and Ein-Dor and Segev (1992) also suggest the difficult process of balancing distributed and centralized architectures in organizations in Germany and Israel. This struggle can be related to the conflict between low power distance, suggesting the acceptance of distributed architectures, and high uncertainty avoidance, suggesting a preference for centralized data to minimize risks of unauthorized access and fraud.

The *family quadrant* is characterized by a high degree of centralization but low formalization. A study by Sicar and Rao (1986) suggests IS organizations in Singapore are highly centralized. Limited end-user involvement was found in Hong Kong by Burn et al. (1993). Sicar and Rao (1986) also found limited use of networking and distributed processing in Singapore, with similar conclusions drawn by Goodman and Green (1992) for the Middle East. Lack of equality among team members was found in East Africa by Odedra-Straub (1993).

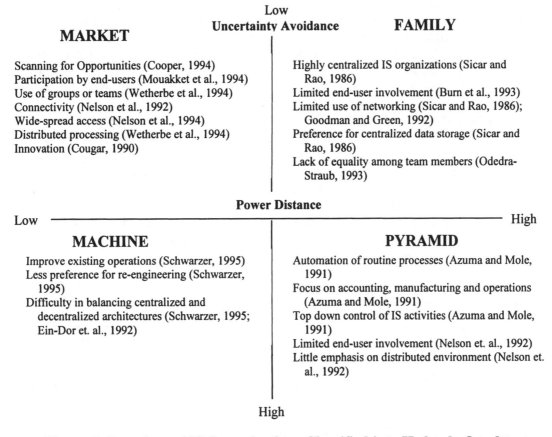

Figure 2. Practices of IS Organizations Classified into Hofstede Quadrants

The *pyramid quadrant* is characterized by high centralization and high formalization. Azuma and Mole (1991) in the study of Japanese firms found an emphasis on the automation of routine processes in manufacturing, accounting, and operations. They also found an emphasis on top-down control of IS activities. Nelson, Weiss, and Yamazaki (1992), also studying firms in Japan, found limited end-user involvement and a preference for centralized architectures.

In summary, the IS practices identified in many studies can be reasonably mapped into the Hofstede quadrants. This new framework then begins to suggest specific practices that differentiate IS cultures found in organizations throughout the world.

Of particular interest here is enterprise integration, and the framework suggests: data sharing, participation by users, widespread access to data and a collaborative environment for data sharing, may not be widespread beyond the market quadrant. One conclusion, then, is that enterprise integration beyond this quadrant presents its own challenges.

INTERACTION OF HEADQUARTERS, DISPERSED BUSINESS UNITS, AND SUPPLIERS' IS CULTURES

While national culture has been shown to influence IS culture, other factors contribute (Hofstede et al., 1990). They may include the competitive environment, business strategy and structure, and the portfolio of IS tasks. The competitive environment may not be perceived in the same way throughout the extended enterprise. Headquarters may perceive competition as much more intense than its subsidiaries. Suppliers may feel competitive pressures and be more willing to collaborate on price, quality and data sharing. Or suppliers, due to the demand for their products and services, may be unwilling to work with customers.

Business strategy and structure also play an important role in the interaction between the organizations. Global MNCs, because they are highly centralized and treat the world as one market, may require more compliance from their subsidiaries and therefore have less flexible IS cultures. Multi-domestic MNCs, because they see the world as many markets, may have more flexible IS cultures and may demand less in the way of compliance from their subsidiaries and suppliers (Harzing, 2000).

The portfolio of tasks is also a factor in establishing IS culture. For example, an organization that uses simple record-keeping and reporting applications may have developed a very different IS culture than one that uses a broader range of applications from transaction processing to executive support systems. Indeed, as the applications move up the information hierarchy from transaction processing to management information systems, decision support systems and finally executive support systems, cultural impact shifts. The role of national culture, organizational culture, and IS culture can be expected to increase as applications respond to environments which become less and less structured. Figure 3 summarizes the way in which these factors influence the development of IS cultures in both the headquarters and supplier organizations.

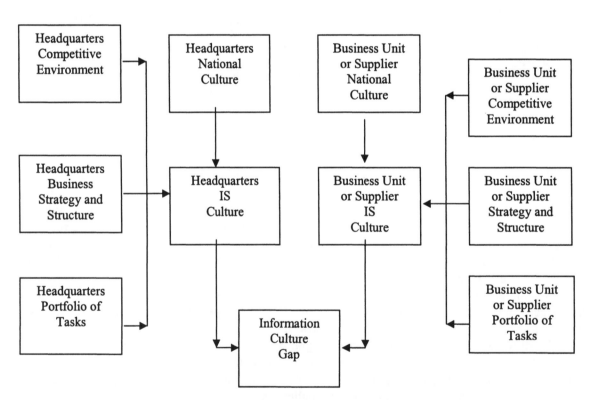

Figure 3. Factors that Influence Organizational Culture Gap

Meyer (1993) suggests that a cultural gap occurs when behavioral asymmetries exist between international work groups. Accordingly, the term *IS culture gap* can be used to refer to the asymmetries between headquarters and subsidiary or supplier IS cultures.

When common or shared information systems are attempted and the IS linkages between headquarters and other business units are attempted, challenges can be expected to surface. The presence of this gap may be expressed by headquarters IS personnel in indirect ways. They may complain that the foreign subsidiary or supplier is: too busy to accommodate data sharing; is unwilling to take ownership of the applications necessary to accommodate data sharing; doesn't understand the importance of the sharing process; is staffed with people who are 'stuck in their ways'; and does not see the big picture. IS management at the subsidiary or supplier location, on the other hand, may complain that headquarters is : asking too much; doesn't understand that their problems are different; and can't see things from their point-of-view. Often this unproductive cycle occurs with little progress in resolving the real issues that need to be addressed if data sharing and enterprise integration are to move forward.

It is undoubtedly difficult to operationalize the concept of a culture gap and measure its magnitude. Kedia and Bhagat (1988), addressing this issue, suggest that the greatest problems can be expected when applications are transferred between developed and developing countries. Perhaps it is reasonable to suggest that the IS culture gap may increase as the difference between power distance and uncertainty avoidance scores between headquarters, foreign subsidiaries and suppliers increase.

The framework established in Figure 2 can be used to evaluate the gap. Consider, for example, a multinational company with headquarters in the United States but with an extensive supply chain network across the globe, a significant protion of which is in China. Further assume that this company is in a very competitive market and, in order to maintain its competitive position, must integrate its own operations with those of its suppliers.

The United States is in the Market quadrant whose practices are characterized by user participation, teamwork, connectivity, widespread acess and innovation. The extent of the integration planned by this company would be expected to reflect these practices.

Now consider the suppliers in China. In the Family quadrant, the practices of companies within this culture include top down control, limited user involvement and little emphasis on a distributed environment.

Several conficts can be expected to occur as headquarters attempts to link the United States operations with the Chinese suppliers through information technology. For example, Chinese suppliers may be unwilling to share production and shipping data. There may also be more restrictions on the freedom given users in China to initiate data entry and update databases when changes to the schedule occur. Consider also that U.S. participants may expect to take more responsibility for the system, prefer wide access to data, and expect their views on the application to be taken into consideration. For all of these reasons an IS culture gap can be expected to develop.

Attempts may be made to resolve the conflicts associated with this gap. Headquarters may try to influence and change the culture by negotiating with suppliers or even requiring that certain access be permitted or procedures followed. They may even choose to ignore the gap and hope that the supplier will eventually adjust to the demands imposed by the application. Perhaps the supplier may even make changes in its own culture in an effort to close the gap.

Because, as Hofstede contends, culture changes slowly, the gap may close slowly, if at all. Furthermore, the efforts to close this gap will succeed or fail to the extent that core values are respected and left intact. When core values of power distance, uncertainty avoidance, individualism-collectivism, and masculinity-femininity are threatened, conflict between headquarters and suppliers may be extremely difficult to resolve.

IMPLICATIONS FOR MANAGEMENT

Several implications can be drawn from this framework and are summarized in Table 2. National culture is a powerful force and affects IS culture and IS practices in organizations. An IS group in a British organization, for example, can be expected to be influenced by British culture, while an IS group in France can be expected to be influenced by French culture.

When national culture, IS culture and IS practices at headquarters differ from the culture and practices at subsidiary or supplier operations, an IS gap is likely to occur. The wider the gap, the more difficult it may be to establish effective linkages between organizations.

IS gaps, however, are easy to neglect. It is easier to blame problems on: technical issues, inadequacy of telecommunications systems, unsatisfactory user training, uncooperative subsidiary and supplier organizations, and the absence of persons at the distant business unit who might 'champion' the need to integrate business flows.

---

1. Integration in flatter and geoghraphically dispersed organizational structure demands thoughtful integration in a competitive world-wide economy.

2. National culture can exert a strong influence over IS culture, IS practices and the willingness to share data across the extended enterprise.

3. Power distance and avoidance of risk are dimensions of national culture that can be expected to influence IS practices

4. When national culture, IS culture and IS practices at the headquarters operation differ from the culture and practices of other business units and suppliers, an IS gap occurs, and the establishment of effective IS linkages can become difficult.

5. IS gaps are easy to neglect. It is easier to blame problems on: technical issues, local infrastructure problems, uncooperative suppliers, and the absence of persons at the suppliers facility who might 'champion' the IS application.

6. Headquarters must address cultural issues with the intent of exploring potential sources of conflict. They must ask how cultural dimensions such as power distance and uncertainty avoidance might affect reliability of data, involvement of staff, willingness to share data, and authority to use data for decision-making purposes.

7. Answers to these and other culturally related questions must be asked and the temptation to focus solely on the technical issues resisted.

8. The insight gained from these answers must be used to develop a cultural/technical IS strategy for establishing improved data sharing strategies.

9. IS culture throughout the extended enterprise changes slowly. The strategic plan must take this fact into consideration.

10. There can be many benefits to a cultural/technical IS plan: conflict between business units reduced; implementation of integrative IT strategies faster and more effective; IS costs lower, more responsive extended enterprise, higher customer satisfatction, and increased profits.

Table 2. Implications for Management

Management must be cautious when placing emphasis on technical hurdles or 'unsophisticated' users. They must remain sensitive to cultural issues and consider them early in the planning process. For example, they might ask how a supplier in a high power distance country might react to the expectation that production scheduling and quality control data be shared. If the headquarters operation is in a low power distance culture and the supplier is in a high power distance culture, establishing a collaborative working relationship that requires the timely exchange of accurate data may be a challenge

Answers to these and other culturally sensitive questions must be studied carefully, and the conclusions used to develop a cultural/technical strategy for improving the chances of a successful IS linkage. In most cases this plan must acknowledge that culture changes slowly, and incremental change rather than abrupt change may be more successful.

There can be many benefits associated with a carefully crafted cultural/technical plan. By focusing on these differences and developing strategies to resolve them, headquarters management has the opportunity to: limit conflict, decrease implementation time, reduce costs, improve transfer success, and minimize disappointing results.

CONCLUSIONS

The purpose of this chapter has been to link the role of national culture to the challenges that managers must address when integrating a global network of subsidiaries or strategic suppliers. While many studies have addressed the role of national and organization culture on IS organizations, the influence of national culture on the extended enterprise, across many countries and cultures, has been largely ignored. Given the extended reach of an organization including its subsidiaries, suppliers, and customers, it seems appropriate to add culture to the evolving theory of global enterprise integration.

This chapter has suggested that the identification of IS practices associated with organizations in a specific culture embodies the values and beliefs of its national culture. Furthermore, by grouping these practices into one of four Hofstede quadrants it then becomes possible to predict the nature of the IS culture gap that may be expected, when national cultures are crossed.

While the quadrants into which these practices were grouped were limited to two cultural dimensions, including power distance and uncertainty avoidance, the goal was to keep the conceptual framework as simple as possible, but at the same time robust enough to provide insight. This is primarily a framework that suggests general directions. There will always be examples of integration projects that extend across cultures but experience few problems, and there will be examples of failed projects within the same national culture. However, the object of the conceptual framework developed here is not to explain the full range of possible outcomes but to: provide insight; promote consideration of culture early in the collaborative process; anticipate conflict; and improve the likelihood of a successful integration strategy.

MINICASE

Healthcare International Limited

Bill Horan had just returned from another trip visiting suppliers in China, Malaysia, the Philippines, Ireland and Spain. As he sat in his London office, he pondered over the frustrations he had encountered. The progress from the supplier in Ireland was not hitting any major snags. Spain was reasonably on schedule. The suppliers in Malaysia and the Philippines were having their problems, but the Chinese, in particular, were just not getting it. He made a note to himself to push harder on China.

Healthcare International Limited manufactures and distributes health care products worldwide. They sell through distributors in over 40 countries and carry a product line that includes shampoos, deodorants, cosmetics, and health care products such as vitamins and health-care aids. Eighty percent of the manufacturing is outsourced to overseas suppliers.

Three years ago Horan was hired to integrate strategic suppliers, reduce manufacturing costs in the supply chain, and improve the time between order placement and delivery. Until he arrived, the company had basically left its suppliers alone. As long as they delivered within a reasonable time frame and contained the costs, headquarters was pleased. But increasing pressure from competitors demanded that they integrate these operations and begin steps to make the supply chain more efficient. Headquarters wanted better ordering systems, better production scheduling systems, better inventory recordkeeping systems, better quality control systems, and better logistics systems.

Working with suppliers to improve their operations had proven difficult. Many did not have adequate information systems and when they did, they were reluctant to share anything beyond billing and invoice data. Horan wanted more. He wanted to monitor their production processes, their shipping schedules and even their orders for raw materials. He wanted integration from suppliers to customers. And he wanted to have this information accessible over the Internet.

As he confirmed on his recent trip, each site has its own problems.

In the China, supervisors were reluctant to use a simple inventory system and did not feel empowered to keep jobs moving if something got in the way. Traditionally they expected their supervisors to investigate the source of a problem when one occurred or when a schedule began to slip. While he was at the plant, one supervisor fell a day behind schedule because an ingredient was missing; the supervisor was waiting for the manager of production to solve the problem. Actually the ingredient had just arrived and the problem could have been solved had the supervisor simply checked the incoming order database in the new information system. Using that information he could have then expedited the ingredient through incoming inspection. It should have taken about fifteen minutes to do this! Horan had the sense that managers at this plant just didn't want things to change. What was puzzling, however, was that the managers all seemed willing to take the chance with a new system. They just couldn't make it work.

In Malaysia, the futility of a recently installed system became apparent. While visiting the site, Horan notice that when a worker accessed the screen to view the in-process schedule he found that the database was inconsistent with the actual progress of the jobs on the production floor. Curious, Horan then started checking other orders. The more he checked the system, the more he found bad data. The managing director wasn't too alarmed, when Horan confronted him. The director said they were doing the best they could.

In Korea, the problems were somewhat the same. Individual initiative was seldom shown. Workers relied on their supervisors for everything, and expecting them to take responsibility for data entry and use the information systems became a major hurdle. But of even more concern was the fact that many of the Korean managers were very reluctant to change. They were comfortable with their old ways and seemed unwilling to make the change that the new initiative to share data would require.

Pondering the events of the last two weeks, Horan got up from his desk and went to see his boss, Joan Williamson. After describing his frustrations with the Chinese plant, Williamson said she wasn't surprised. " Poor data quality from our suppliers has plagued us for a long time. It seems to be a deep rooted problem," she continued. "We're just paying the price for the absence of an established business culture in that plant. Maybe we should think of working with our suppliers to hire or train people who can work either of these systems and then get data to us that we need to integrate or extended systems." "Bill," she continued, "I think the only way is to push through these problems. We need to be able to access accurate and timely data on the internet or our effort to integrate these suppliers is in real trouble."

Discussion Questions
1. Summarize the problems faced by Horan.
2. Do you think that cultural differences are responsible for some of the problems faced by Horan? Explain.
3. Describe the practices that you think would describe the differences between headquarters IS culture in the UK and the IS cultures in China and Ireland.

4. Which components of the culture gap do you think have influenced the integration of IT between these suppliers?
5. Do you think that Horan and Williamson have recognized that part of their problem can be attributed to cultural differences? If not, why?
6. What would you advise Horan to do?

KEY TERMS
Common System
Competing Values Framework
Culture Gap
Enterprise Integration
Family Quadrant
Individualism- Collectivism
Information Culture
Machine Quadrant
Masculinity-Femininity
Market Quadrant
National Culture
Organization Culture
Power Distance
Pyramid Quadrant
Uncertainty Avoidance

STUDY QUESTIONS

1. Information systems are primarily technical systems that address logical ways of achieving concrete business objectives. As a result, a headquarters operation need not concern itself with the local environment of its overseas business units, suppliers and customers. As long as computer applications have been designed effectively, and a detailed implementation schedule has been followed, the headquarters operation should expect the cooperation and integration from all componets of the extended enterprise from suppliers to customers. Write an essay that comments on this statement.

2. An electronics firm in Denmark is about to establish a strategic relationship with a supplier in Mexico. The purpose of this relationship to is to outsource the final assembly of several of its major products. They expect the Mexican subsidiary to share production scheduling, manufacturing, logistics, sales, and billing data over the Internet with their headquarters in Denmark. With this common system, headquarters will be able to access data easily from the Mexican plant and keep on top of schedules and shipments. The project manager in Demark said that the better the integration between these companies the shorter will be the period from customer orders to customer delivery. Write a one page email that explains the importance of data sharing to Mexican managers.

3. In addition to the practices described in Figure 2, what other practices would you expect to find in these quadrants? Use Hofstede's definition of power distance and uncertainly avoidance and his quadrant model to help you.

4. What are the influences on IS culture and under what conditions would it be possible to change the IS culture of a supplier in another country to assure greater cooperation for the exchange of business data?

5. The media, including movies and Internet technologies, has had a remarkable effect on homogenizing the world into one marketplace. The widespread acceptance of movies, music, and products such as those produced by Dell, Gillette and Coke all suggest a convergence of culture. Do you think that the issue of cultural differences will disappear by the middle of this century, and that this will make it easier to integrate suppliers from around the world?

6. The last decade has witnessed countless examples of cultural intolerance and violence. Some suggest that this is inevitable when deep-rooted differences exist. Does this suggest, as Hofstede has stated, that culture changes slowly, and that the complexities when transferring technology into distant lands will be with us well into this new century?

7. Common airline reservation systems are successfully used throughout the world. There are few, if any, problems associated with integrating applications whether the reservation system is in Beijing, Boston or Bangalore. Why do you think a multinational company with subsidiaries on all continents might find it more difficult to implement common manufacturing planning and control systems than an airline would in implementing a reservation system?

REFERENCES

Azuma, M. and Mole, D. "Software Management Practices and Metrics in the European Community and Japan: Some Results of a Survey," *Journal of Systems Software,* 26(1), July 1994, pp. 5-18.

Bartlett, C.A. and Ghoshal, S. *Managing Across Borders: The Transnational Solution.* Boston, MA: Harvard Business School Press. 1989.

Bose, I. and R. Pal "Auto-ID: Managing Anything, Anywhere, Anytime in the Supply Chain," *Communications of the ACM,* 48(8), August, 2005, pp.100-106.

Burn, J., Saxena, K. B. C., Ma, L. and Cheung, H. K. "Critical Issues of IS Management in Hong Kong: A Cultural Comparison," *Journal of Global Information Management,* 1(4), Fall 1993, pp. 28-37.

Cheung, H. K. and Burn, J. M. "Distributing Global Information Systems Resources in Multinational Companies-A Contingency Model," *Journal of Global Information Management,* 2(3), Summer 1994, pp. 14-27.

Cooper, R. B. "The Inertial Impact of Culture on IT Implementation," *Information and Management,* 27, 1994, pp. 17-31.

Couger, D. J. "Ensuring Creative Approaches in Information Systems Design," *Managerial and Decision Economics,* 11. 1990.

Davenport, T. H., Eccles, R. G. and Prusak, L. "Information Politics," *Sloan Management Review,* Fall 1992, pp. 53-65.

Deal, T. E. and Kennedy, A. A. *Corporate Cultures.* Reading, MA: Addison-Wesley. 1982.

Ein-Dor, P., Segev, E. and Orgad, M. "The Effect of National Culture on IS: Implications for International Information Systems," *Journal of Global Information Management,* 1(1), Winter 1993, pp. 33-44.

Ein-Dor, P. and Segev, E. "End User Computing: A Cross Cultural Study," *International Information Systems,* 1(1), January, 1992, 124-137.

Erez, M. and Earley, P. C. *Culture, Self-identity, and Work.* New York: Oxford University Press. 1993.

Goodman, S. E. and Green, J. D. "Computing in the Middle East," *Communications of the ACM*, 35(8), pp. 21-25.

Harzing, Anne-Wil "An Empirical Analysis and Extension of the Bartlett and Ghoshal Typology of Multinational Companies," *Journal of International Business Studies*, 31(1), 2000, pp101-120.

Hofstede, G. "Motivation, Leadership, and Organization: Do American Theories Apply Abroad? ," Organizational Dynamics, Summer, 1980.

Hofstede, G. "Culture and Organizations," *International Studies of Management and Organizations*, X(4), 1981, pp. 15-41.

Hofstede, G., Neuijen, B., Ohayv, D. and Sanders, G. „Measuring Organizational Cultures: A Qualitative and Quantitative Study Across Twenty Cases," *Administrative Science Quarterly*, 35, 1990, pp. 286-316.

Hofstede, G. *Culture and Organizations: Software of the Mind*. London: McGraw-Hill. 1991.

Ives, B. and Jarvenpaa, S. L. "Applications of Global Information Technology: Key Issues for Management," . *MIS Quarterly*, March 1991, pp. 33-49.

Kedia, B. L. and Bhagat, R. S. "Cultural Constraints on Transfer of Technology Across Nations: Implications for Research in International and Comparative Management," *Academy of Management Review,* 13(4), 1988, pp. 559-571.

Javidan M., House R. J. "Cultural Acumen for the Global Manager: Lessons from Project Globe," *Organizational Dynamics*, 299(4), 2001, pp. 289-305.

Lachman, R. "Modernity Change of Core and Peripheral Values of Factory Workers," *Human Relations*, 36, 1983, pp. 563-80.

Lee, H. L. and S. Whang "Information Sharing in a Supply Chain," *International Journal of Technology Management*, 20(3/4), 2000, pp. 373-387.

Lee, H. L., Padmanabhan, V. and S. Whang "Information Distortion in a Supply Chain: The Bullwhip Effect," *Management Science*, 50(12), 2005, pp. 1875-1886.

Lin, F., Sheng-hsiu H. and Sheng-cheng, L. "Effects of Information Sharing on Supply Chain Performance in Electronic Commerce," *IEEE Transactions on Engineering Management,* 49(3), August, 2002, pp. 258-268.

Magretta, Joan. "Fast, Global, and Entrepreneurial: Supply Chain Management, Hong Kong Stryle, " *Harvard Business Review*, September-October 1998, pp. 103- 114.

Meyer, Heinz-Dieter. "The Cultural Gap in Long-term International Work Groups: A German-American Case Study," *European Management Journal*. (11)1, 1993, pp. 93-101.

Mouakket, S., Sillence, J. A. A. and Fretwell-Dowling, F .A. "Information Requirements Determination in the Software Industry: A Case Study," European Journal of Information Systems, 3(2), April 1994, pp. 101-111.

Nelson, R. R., Weiss, I. R. and Yamazaki, K. "Information Resource Management within Multinational Corporations," *International Information Systems*, 1(4), October 1992, pp. 56-83.

Odedra-Straub, M. "Critical Factors Affecting Success of CBIS: Cases from Africa," *Journal of Global Information Management*, 1(3), Summer 1993, pp. 16-31.

Parboteeah, D. V., Parboteeah, K. P., Cullen, J. B. and C. Basu, C. " Perceived Usefulness of Information Technology: A Cross-National Model," *Journal of Global Information Technology Management,* 8(4), 2005, pp. 29-48.

Parsons, T. and Shils, E. A. *Toward a General Theory of Action*. Cambridge, MA: Harvard University Press. 1951.

Quinn, R. E and Rohrbaugh, J. "A Spatial Model of Effectiveness Criteria: Towards a Competing Values Approach to Organizational Analysis," *Management Science*, 29(3), 1983, pp. 363-377.

Roche, E. M. *Managing Information Technology in Multinational Corporations*. New York: Macmillan. 1992.

Schein, E. H. *Organizational Culture and Leadership*. Jossey-Bass, San Francisco. 1985.

Schwarzer, B. "Organizing Global IS Management to Meet Competitive Challenges Experiences from the Pharmaceutical Industry," *Journal of Global Information Management*, 3(1), 1995, pp. 5-16.

Shore, B. "Using Information Technology to Coordinate Transnational Service Operations: A Case Study in the European Union," *Journal of Global Information Management*, 4(2), Spring 1996, pp. 5-14.

Shore, B. and Venkatachalam, V. "The Role of National Culture in Systems Analysis and Design," *Journal of Global Information Management.* 3(3). 1995.

Sicar, S. and Rao, K.V. "Information Resource Management in Singapore: The State of the Art.," *Information and Management,* 11, 1986, pp. 181-187.

Smircich, L. "Concepts of Culture and Organizational Analysis," *Administrative Science Quarterly,* (28), 1982, pp. 339-358.

Triandis, H. C. Culture: Theoretical and Methodological Issues. in M.D. Dunnette and L. Hough, Eds., *Handbook of Industrial and Organizational Psychology*, 2nd ed., Vol. 4, Consulting Psychologists Press, Palo Alto, CA. 1995.

Wetherbe, J.C., Vitalari, N.P. and Milner, A. „Key Trends in Systems Development in Europe and North America, " *Journal of Global Information Management*, 2(2), Spring 1994, pp. 5-20.

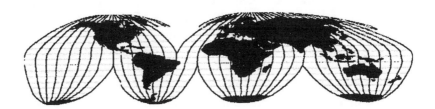

15

Information Systems for Multinational Enterprises: A Grounded Theory of Their Design and Implementation

Hans Lehmann
University of Auckland, New Zealand

Brent Gallupe
Queen's University, Kingston, Ontario, Canada

CHAPTER SUMMARY

Information systems for multinational companies (MNCs), referred to as international information systems (IIS), have been a problem area for many years, yet have failed to attract more than token attention from the academic information systems research community. This study applies a grounded theory method to establish a first theoretical framework dealing with the structure of IIS and the dynamics of their development and implementation. The substantive theory is based on extensive, long-term work with three MNCs and covers four key areas: (a) The dealings between the actors concerned with an IIS take place in a Force-Field; (b) The Force-Field is reflected in a generic two-dimensional architecture of an IIS, which always has a 'Core' of systems used by all (or many) of the regions and 'Local' systems, different at every regional site; (c) The balance of functionality between the 'Core' and the 'Local' parts of an IIS follows the degree to which the operations of the MNC require synchronous access to data and processing within the IIS; and (d) The interactions of IT and users in the Force-Field follow a cyclical, self-reinforcing dialectic such that an enforced consensus process is required in order to boost acceptance and to limit the probability that continuing rejection leads to catastrophic failure. The limitations of the theory are discussed and directions for future research are given.

INTRODUCTION AND RESEARCH QUESTION

Two trends have dominated the world of business during the last three decades: globalization and information technology. Yet the obvious fusion of these two pivotal driving forces, the application of information technology throughout global operations, is still largely misunderstood by practitioners and has long been widely ignored by academics. As a result, international information systems (IIS) projects over the last twenty years have often been less than successful. The consulting firm KPMG Peat Marwick, in an in-depth survey of 80 European MNCs, found that by 1994 less than 10% of European firms had completed IIS development projects satisfactorily. Most of the evidence for these failures is now contained as the (often historical) international cases in anthologies and monographs on large information systems failure, i.e. Glass (1992 and 1998), Flowers (1996), Yourdon (1997), and Collins and Kirsch (1999).

Research into why these applications are so difficult and how they could be mastered should be of high priority, but is not. Over the last thirty years the ProQuest database of academic periodicals lists 82,314 papers with "information systems" as a keyword. Of those, 309 articles have to do with information systems in international settings, representing less than half of one percent of published IS research. In addition, nearly 40% of these papers deal with instances and issues of domestic information technology, but in a country other than the author's (Gallupe and Tan, 1999) – a category that Palvia (1998) expressly excludes from the realm of global information technology research.

This dearth of research has left the field devoid of a firm theoretical base from which to provide the 'relevance,' which, given the history of large scale failure and dysfunction of IIS, is critically needed. The meager theoretical backdrop, in turn, means that the objectives of the research needed to be quite fundamental. They are expressed in two research questions:

What factors, structures and processes influence the effectiveness of an IIS?

How do such factors interact with each other?

In the following sections an overview of the literature on IIS and related themes is given, followed by a description of the key points in the substantive theories developed from the case analyses. A discussion of the theory in light of other knowledge in this and related fields together with some suggestions for further research concludes the paper.

INTERNATIONAL INFORMATION SYSTEMS IN THE LITERATURE

The term 'International Information System' was coined by Buss (1982) and proved to be a better fit than the notion of 'common systems' created by Keen (1982). Lehmann (1994) differentiates them from other types of distributed or systems by defining an IIS as:

Distributed information systems that are implemented at various sites within one enterprise to support similar business activities in highly diverse environments, commonly found across country boundaries.

In-depth coverage of the literature is available in more detail elsewhere: Hamelink (1984) covers the early research; Sethi and Olson (1993) give a very exhaustive overview; Lehmann (1996, 1997, 1998, and 2000) and Gallupe and Tan (1999) bring it more up-to-date. Most reviews tend to agree that past research into IIS is sparse, sporadic and diffuse. It also is largely confined to academic treatments of the subject, with very little evidence of applied research, even in the practitioner literature. The work of Collins and Kirsch (1999) is a recent exception. Part of the early research focused on external factors for an IIS (e.g. the framework developed by King and Sethi in 1993, updated in 1999; and the 'organizing' framework of Alavi and Young (1992). Other researchers, pre-eminently Butler Cox (1991), Kosynski and Karimi (1996), Sankar et al. (1993) and Ives and Jarvenpaa (1991, 1992 and 1994) contributed to the confirmation that IIS should align with global business strategy (usually defined in terms of Bartlett and Ghoshal, 1989). Only in the last few years have researchers begun to direct their attention to the design and development of an IIS, such as

King and Sethi (1993), Deans and Jurison (1994), Tractinsky (1995), Applegate et al (1996), Van den berg and Mantelaers (1999) and King and Sethi (1999). Where this research was concerned with frameworks for IISs, it focused on the structure and architecture of IISs. Examples are Gibson (1994), Burns and Cheung (1996), Targowski (1996), Grover and Segars (1996) and Peppard (1999). Others focused on the role of an information technology infrastructure: Weill (1992, 1993), Weill et al (1994, 1995), Broadbent and Weill (1997). Table 1 gives an overview of the topic areas covered by the research literature over the last three decades.

The table clearly reflects the early pre-occupation with technical issues and especially with cross-border information exchange legislation. Alignment of an IIS strategy with the multi-facetted policies at the business level of MNCs was the other dominant research focus, together with some musings on the challenges of managing information technology across MNCs. With the exception of discussions and research into technology aspects (such as infrastructure standards and internet-related issues) of IISs, virtually no serious research is reported about the issues surrounding the application of information technology in multinational settings, its analysis, design, and development processes. Implementation issues were covered from a cross-cultural perspective more than from a system's development and/or project management perspective.

Layer >> Perspective	Technology	Applications	Implementation & Social Issues	Management Issues	Governmental Issues
Scope and objectives	MEDIUM		MEDIUM	MEDIUM	MEDIUM
Business processes model			MEDIUM		
Information systems (design) model				LIGHT	
Technology model	INTENSIVE	MEDIUM		LIGHT	INTENSIVE

Table 1. Research Coverage of the International Information Systems Domain: Indications of LIGHT, MEDIUM OR INTENSIVE coverage of the topic in the literature (Source: Lehmann (1997))

RESEARCH METHOD

The method deemed most conducive to answering the research questions was Grounded Theory (Glaser and Strauss, 1967; Glaser 1978)[a]. It was adopted here for three reasons.

- First, an IIS is an 'ecology' (Davenport, 1997, Davenport and Prusak, 1997) of information technology and organizational elements. Its research thus requires a mix of positivist and interpretivist approaches for dealing with the technology parts and the organizational aspects respectively. Grounded Theory, as a "general" and "paradigmatically neutral" methodology (Glaser 1998, 2001) is therefore particularly appropriate here;

- Second, Grounded Theory, by definition, incorporates the complexities of the organizational context into an understanding of the phenomenon (Orlikowski, 1993; Martin and Turner, 1986; Pettigrew, 1990). This capability of dealing with the often complex information technology issues encountered by multinational enterprises is of particular importance here;

- Lastly, Grounded Theory is a "theory discovery methodology" (Martin and Turner, 1986, p. 141) and therefore the method of choice when there is no overarching theory for the research in hand (Denzin and Lincoln, 1994).

The methodology of Grounded Theory is comparative, requiring a steady iteration of analyzing data, generating concepts, and identifying new data. After each set of data gathering, a process of "theoretical sampling" determined where to go for the next stream of data. In this research project, the data was gathered from three very different, but mutually complementing case studies of international firms.

The first case, an agribusiness marketing co-operative (CO-OP), was a large-scale effort that was not successful. The other two, also, were different: the second case, a shipping company (SHIPPER), is one of solid success, albeit in a smaller firm, with restricted means; the third case, a freight forwarder (FREIGHTER), complements the first two, a large firm with a very successful, global and strategic IIS presence. All three companies were kept anonymous.

Fieldwork with the first case started in late 1996. The project then spanned five years of interviews, adding new cases, and carrying out periodic, targeted, updates. Data analysis, conceptualization and theory building progressed in parallel with data collection, following the Grounded Theory principle of "constant comparative analysis" (Glaser and Strauss, 1967, p7).

The primary data gathering comprised some 300 hours of interviews with executives, key management staff, and operations personnel, many of whom were interviewed more than once. The interviewees split equally into business and information technology people and just under two thirds of them were located in the 'regions' (as opposed to head offices) of the MNCs involved. The interviews were free-form, unstructured discussions, lasted on average about two hours and were tape-recorded. Their content followed the Grounded Theory logic of category saturation. Interview transcripts, together with observation transcripts filled more than 2400 pages. These field data were further complemented by 3,300 pages of internal material from the case organizations, such as meeting memos, internal reports, strategy documents and other data and information - contained in 280 additional document sets. Data acquisition took place in 19 locations in Australasia, North America, the UK, and continental Europe.

Grounded Theory was originally designed for conceptualizing the processes underlying human-to-human relationships, where individual interviews and observation were the main tools of data acquisition. This is too narrow a context for investigating how multinational firms use information technology. The method had to be extended to deal with technology and organizational issues in the form of case studies. This was achieved with the introduction of a two-tier coding structure. First, individual interviews, observations and other data were treated as single "texts". (Note: In the interpretivist sense this is defined as a "collection of symbols expressing layers of meaning" (Miles and Huberman, 1994, p8)). Appropriately grouped together, they then became the elements of another, larger text, the case (hi)story itself. The data first coded into primary categories (such as people, places, events, and other concrete phenomena) and then conceptualized into theoretical categories (such as causal/correlational linkages, hypothesized motivational and/or management processes). Coding as well as acquiring new data occurred at both levels of "text," single and composite. The enquiry case thus followed an analysis protocol (in Yin's, 1989, terms) of multiple cases with analyses both *within* each case (first) and (later on) *between* cases, where the unit of analysis was multi-level "text."

As concepts and relations solidified, a nascent 'theory' was postulated – only to be re-constructed, enhanced, and restated anew after each case. New data was obtained via theoretical sampling, where the weaknesses, inconsistencies and fuzziness of the theoretical constructs so far determined what the nature of the next "slices of data" (Glaser and Strauss, 1967, p 24) terminology for the individual items collated by the researcher) within the case in hand should be, or what qualities were required from the next case.

After three case studies, a set of main theoretical constructs had emerged that were deemed sufficiently consistent, informative and comprehensive to allow their consolidation into a first 'substantive theory of international information systems'. This "densification" process (Glaser and Strauss 1967, p.190) involved reducing the very large amount of concepts and constructs accumulated so far in order to produce a resultant theory that satisfies traditional parsimony requirements.

It is a notorious difficulty for Grounded Theory projects to distill all the data and analysis materials into a book chapter. For this reason, in the following sections only the end result of the work, the major elements of theory itself, will be discussed and reference to the cases will only be given where this adds to the understanding of the theory.

The Force Field

The first case was chosen because it provided the opportunity to study the development of an IIS right from its early stages. The project's ultimate demise has its roots in a misinterpretation of the firm's global strategy and disregard for its strong business culture. To understand both, a brief overview of the background is given in the following paragraphs.

The Co-op's Strategic Migration: The Austral-Asian Food Co-Op (CO-OP) was founded in the 1960s as a producer association and encompassed nearly all of the Austral-Asian commercial farming industry. In the late 1970s, the country where the CO-OP sold some 80% of its output market joined the European Union and drastically reduced its non-EU imports. This threatened the very existence of the majority of Austral-Asian farmers and the CO-OP needed to take dramatic action. It sent out its best executives into all corners of the world with just one mission: to sell as much product as they could, by whichever means they saw fit. This they did with spectacular results. By the end of the 1980s the CO-OP had transformed itself from a "sleepy antipodean farmers club" into a very successful international operator. It went on from strengths to strengths and by the end of the century, with revenue of over USD 7 billion, the CO-OP ranked 8th in the world in its industry.

This history left two legacies. One is a strong tradition of regional autonomy and the other is management's equally strong pride in their business professionalism and success. It was the latter that made the regional executives forego some of their autonomy, when a new Chief Executive Officer in the early 1990s introduced global brands and pushed for the unified marketing strategies to support them. In the terms of Bartlett and Ghoshal (1982), the CO-OP had started out with a Global strategy of strong central control and moved to an equally pronounced multinational stance (strong local autonomy) in the quest for developing new markets. The CEO's declared intent was to move the CO-OP to a transnational strategy of balanced central/local control.

The Chief Information Officer (CIO) took this as an opportunity to establish a global information technology strategy. The apparent need for this was that after a decade of regional autonomy the regions all had established substantial, but disparate information technology set-ups - and were managing them with variable success. The CIO, however, misinterpreted the CEO's thrust for a transnational strategy as one of returning to a Global strategy of dominating central control. Using the potpourri of IT installations as an excuse, he unilaterally initiated a project – the Food Information System and Technology (FIST) - to impose one global system, based on standard technology. Regional and local management revolted strongly against this unsolicited assault on their well-earned autonomy, especially when they could see no business use for FIST. Six years of acrimonious political infighting ensued, which eventually ended in the abandonment of the project.

The Interaction of Factors: Nearly immediately from its inception, FIST was afflicted by a strong undercurrent of adversarial interaction among the players at two levels:

- Antagonism over territorial issues between the headquarters and regional management;
- Conflict between the (regional) business users and the IT people over the functional content of the proposed IIS.

While the 'territorial' conflict between the new CEO and the regions central control over global marketing strategies was eventually resolved towards a team-oriented global collaboration, the IT/business controversy remained unsolved. Figure 1 shows the Force-Field and the interaction of the factors acting upon it.

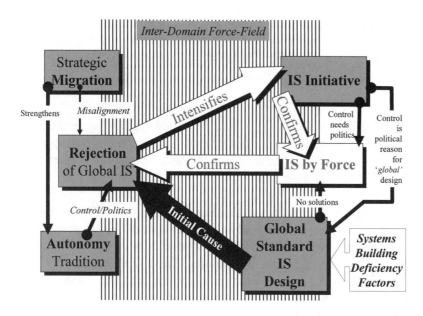

Figure 1. The Force Field between Business and IT People

The individual boxes in the figure represent some of the factors conceptualized from the case, the 'theoretical categories' in Grounded Theory terminology. The linking arrows explain their interaction. FIST was an *IS Initiative*, conceived by the CIO in isolation, with very little business input from the outset and designed by head-office IT people with little international business experience, mediocre systems building skills and limited conceptualization capacity (the *Systems Building Deficiency* factors). As a result, the proposed IIS lacked most operational functionality and the economic case for it was not credible. Because it was counter-aligned to the CO-OP's global business strategy (anchored in the CO-OP's *Strategic* Migration) and ran roughshod over their *Local Autonomy* the regional business people strongly (and correctly) suspected that all this was just window-dressing for re-instating central control. For this reason they roundly rejected the IIS outright. Their case was made easier because it was clearly unworkable. In response, the IT people, suffering from a continued inability to create functionality useful to the regions, found themselves increasingly isolated from the business and therefore ever less able to convince the regions with any rational argument.

The project subsequently degenerated into a series of ever more acrimonious political moves (named *IS by Force*) and countermoves. The CO-OP case shows six cycles of this dialectical interchange and this cyclical nature of the response to an IIS was later on confirmed by the other two cases.

The conflict-laden nature of the interchanges led to the concept of an ever-present socio-dynamic 'Force Field' (in the sense of Lewin, 1952) that governs the interaction between the business and IT domains. In multinational companies, an intersecting second dimension of conflict potential between Centre/Head-Office and Regions/Subsidiaries complicates the structure of the Force Field further. These 'territorial' forces between head-office and regional/local management overlay the 'functional' tensions between business users and IT people. Although not explicitly observed in the CO-OP case, it may be assumed that potential 'territorial' dynamics would also exist in the IT domain. Figure 2 demonstrates the Force Field structure of an IIS.

A Two-Dimensional Generic Architecture Model for IIS

What had made the CO-OP's IIS proposal so overtly unworkable was the unquestioning use of an architecture paradigm of one, globally standardized information system and technology platform. This should have come as no surprise. By the late 1990s, the CO-OP's global operations covered a broad diversity. Their operations differed in at least five dimensions. They would either be (1) *sales* or *manufacturing*, selling (2) *three product types* in (3) *sophisticated* or *developing* countries/markets, working out of (4) *large* or *small* local offices using (5) *computerized* or (predominantly) *manual* administration methods. Depending on how much correlation is allowed between dimensions 4 and 5, this could result in between 24 and 48 (i.e.2x3x2x2x[2]) orthogonal business process profiles[b] with significantly different operations – and clearly impossible to support with a one-size-fits-all IIS.

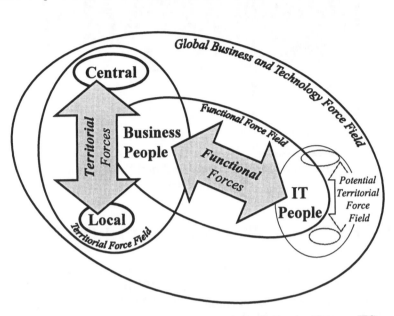

Figure 2. The Force Field Dimensions Surrounding an IIS

The fallacy of such a paradigm has first been highlighted by Buss as early as 1982. However, it was not until 1996 that Lehmann postulated a generic topology for IIS. He conjectured that every IIS consists firstly of a 'core' of systems, compulsory for all users. Secondly, there are 'local' systems to provide functionality specific to just one (or a group of) regional subsidiaries. Such a two-dimensional architecture model (depicted in Figure 3) is flexible enough to accommodate any form of global business strategy.

The usefulness of such a model was corroborated by the fact that, after all the regions had refused the one-dimensional architecture, the CIO conceded that only some systems needed to be a global standard and that others could be local.

While this structural concession should have now allowed a more rational discussion between the IT people and regional business users, the CO-OP soon found that deciding what should be the common, globally standard functionality proved an insurmountable hurdle. The IT people resorted – once again - to a unilateral initiative for solving this problem, this time to a 'Business Process Re-Engineering' program. Carried out at the CO-OP's head-office with limited regional input, the regions were nevertheless expected to change their operations to tie in with the future system. Regional management's protests met with the CIO's intransigence. This lack of rational dialogue then ignited a protracted period of acrimonious political infighting, which, in the end, was lost by the IT people when FIST was terminated without replacement. A mechanism that can ensure the initiation and continuation of rational dialogue about what should be a global standard and what should remain under unfettered regional control is clearly needed, if such a decision is not to be left to the vagaries of 'turf' warfare between the regions and head-office.

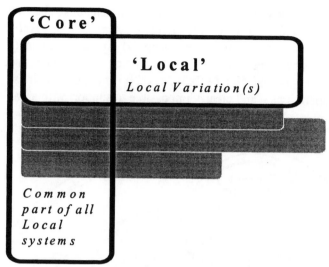

Figure 3. A Generic Architecture Model for International Information Systems (modified after Lehmann, 1996)

BALANCING THE ARCHITECTURE: SYNCHRONICITY

It was, however, not until the second case that the key to defining the content of the common, 'core' functionality was discovered. A Danish Shipping Group (SHIPPER) was selected through the first process of theoretical sampling as a juxtaposition to the CO-OP. SHIPPER, although only one tenth of CO-OP's size, had a very successful IIS with a 'core' of clearly defined and centrally run IIS, which were compulsory for all local and regional offices. As an international shipping firm, SHIPPER relies on the effective management of a common operating resource, i.e. the shipping fleet. Standardized access to a group of tightly integrated, common information systems, closely managed at the center, is essential for this. Several (local) users need to be able to interpret, discuss and manipulate information at the same time across the globe, a requirement termed *"synchronicity."* Table 2 demonstrates this.

Transactions	Systems/Data & Information	Interaction required between:
Journey Quotation	Operations Schedule, Cost Modeling	Centre, Originator, (Receiver), (Ships)
Cargo Enquiries	Manifests; Operations Schedule	Centre, Originator, (Ships)
Originating and Terminating Voyages	Manifests; Customs and other Regulatory Agency Documentation	Originator, (Customs), (Regulators)
Supplying ("Bunkering") Ships	Cost & Management Accounts, Budgets	Ships, Receiver, Centre

Note: Centre is the central operations department at SHIPPER's head office in Copenhagen; Originator is the SHIPPER's representative at the origin of the proposed journey; Receiver is the SHIPPER's representative at the receiving/terminating end of the proposed journey. Optional actors are in parentheses.

Table 2. Examples of the Synchronous and Interactive Nature of Key Transactions in SHIPPER's Business Operations

The central stewardship of the information systems and databases meant that users could rely implicitly on the accuracy and integrity of the data/information they used. This *synchronicity* requirement defined unequivocally what data and functionality was required in the suite of 'core' information systems. Furthermore, because the IT support thus provided was a critical instrumental necessity for their business operations, its functionality was largely undisputed. Similarly, any further, 'local', systems developments were put into the accountability of local management; all that was required was that they interfaced to the 'core' systems without any problems. The investment would come out of the regional profit center, implicitly assuring at once a clear focus on operational necessity and stringent economical justification for 'local' systems.

An analysis of the global/local business processes showed that the CO-OP, on the other hand, hardly had any need for such *synchronicity* of business transactions. In the absence of a common management object and task, the interaction between their business units was nearly always 'asynchronous,' i.e. did not require same-time/same-data transactions. With the possible exception of some aspects of the annual planning effort (determining the optimal allocation of product quotas) there was no need at all for any globally standard functionality, certainly not for day-to-day business operations. This absence of operational reasons for a global standard IIS was what made regional management suspect that this was all part of a covert ingression into their autonomy, which they resisted vigorously.

If the CO-OP had used the concept of *'synchronicity'* in both the design and the development of their IIS, the damaging political conflict would have been avoided and the success chances for FIST would have significantly improved. However, whereas removing the decision about 'core' and 'local' may ameliorate the politics; the existence of the Force Field, on the other hand, implies that political conflict is always latent and needs to be dealt with. While SHIPPER had added the important perspective of a successful IIS to complement the failure that characterized the CO-OP case, the firm's smallness and the narrowness of its business made it difficult to assess what factors would increase or defuse the strength of such political conflict. A further case was needed, partly similar and partly in contrast to the first two: It needed to be a successful IIS installation, but this time in a firm closer in size to the CO-OP. A large international Freight Forwarding Group (FREIGHTER), headquartered in Switzerland, fitted these requirements.

The Response Cycle

The Force Field between business and IT as well as between the center and the regions shapes a distinct pattern of dialectic interactions between them. The cyclical nature of the users' response to a – proposed or existing – IIS was one key finding from the cases. Equally important was the discovery that *rejection* (of the IIS by users) has a set of determinants that are not just the logical inverse of the factors that foster *acceptance*, but are different and independent.

The relationships between the factors involved in the dialectic dynamics are represented as "cause-effect-loops" [c] introduced by Weick (1979, p65-88). The full response cycle consists of the interactions between seven core factors. It contains a number of independent loops, connected by common factors. Figure 4 shows this diagram.

The *Acceptance* cycle begins with the functionality (Factor 1 in the diagram) of the IIS design. The higher the Functional Quality, the higher the chance of Acceptance (2) of the IIS by the business people. The higher the Acceptance, the more it deepens the IT/Business Integration (3), which in turn facilitates higher Functional Quality (1) of future enhancements. Thus the cycle enters another round.

The *Rejection* cycles also begin with Functional Quality (1). The stronger the rejection (4), the more increased is the isolation (5) of the IT people. This has a further negative effect on Functional Quality (1). At some stage, usually after several such 'content' rejections, the deepened isolation (5) leads to an increasing propensity to engage in antagonistic 'win/lose politics' (6) to 'force' acceptance of the IIS. The more antagonistic these political actions are, however, the stronger the rejection (4) from the intended users. This starts another turn of the rejection cycle.

Both cycles are of the type that Weick (1979, p76) calls "negative loops"[d]. They have an even number (e.g. 0,2,4...) of arrows with negative signs on them, which means that there is either no counteracting force or none that isn't neutralized by another (an odd number of minus signs would leave always at least one factor moving against the 'spiral'). Once a change has occurred in a negative loop, it will keep recurring until either *"the system is destroyed or...some dramatic change occurs"* (Weick, 1979. p72).

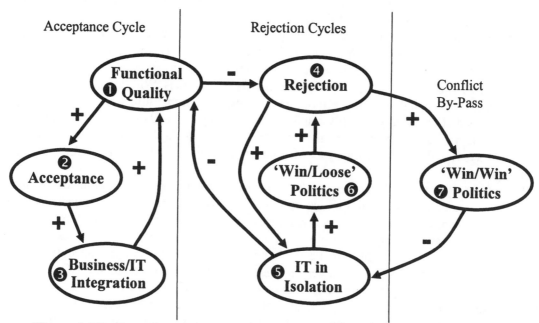

Figure 4. The Interaction of the Factors Determining Users' Response to an IIS

The cases bear this out: the *Acceptance* cycle is one of continuous self-reinforcement, i.e. with an 'even' number of (zero) minus signs. It was first observed in the SHIPPER case, where the 'synchronicity' of interactions between the main actors was the catalyst for high Functional Quality and a resulting strong IT/business integration. FREIGHTER, who had been in this virtuous circle for longer and with more resources, had by then reached a level of deep integration that does not just engender acceptance but has lead to a 'strategic unity' of IT and Business. For FREIGHTER, their IIS were the core competence from which flows the ongoing development of new strategic products and services.

The CO-OP, on the other hand, experienced the other 'negative loop', the *Rejection* cycles, with an equal number of minus interactions. As a consequence, several fruitless attempts to deliver acceptable Functional Quality led to ever deepening rejection. Trying to force the IIS onto users by executive decree started a vicious cycle of one round of acrimonious 'win/loose' politics after another until eventually the IT people 'lost' and FIST was terminated.

FREIGHTER, however, owed the high level of acceptance of its IISs not only to superior functional quality. They had also put in place organizational structures and management processes that were designed to counteract the Force-Field potentials for 'content' as well as 'political' conflict and rejection. Their project organization assures the broadest possible base of central and local knowledge and has an escalating conciliation procedure if consensus over system functionality cannot be reached the first time around - a procedure that explicitly introduces the 'win/win' sort of politics to deflect and defuse the destructive 'win/loose' infighting that paralyzed the CO-OP's IIS project. This *Conflict By-Pass* loop begins with rejection (4), which is, however, channeled into compulsory 'win/win politics' of re-analysis and/or conciliation (7). This forced co-operation between IS and business inhibits or reverses IT Isolation (5), which lifts the quality of the IIS's functionality (1), and lowers the potential for user rejection (4). This deviation-counteracting loop, with an odd number (three) of minus-type interactions, is the mechanism that can slow, stop or reverse the spiraling out of control of a cyclical interaction. With the inclusion of this *Conflict By-Pass* the whole system now has an odd number of 'negative' interactions. Like the single-loop variant, the multiple-loop system in this constellation, too, becomes self-regulating and self-stabilizing (Weick, 1979, p74).

DISCUSSION: A SUBSTANTIVE THEORY OF IIS

In the following paragraphs the gist of the theory is discussed in the light of related research and its relevance for the field.

The Force Field

Bringing about organizational change often meets with resistance. In the general field of human behavior, Lewin (1938 and 1952) modeled such social interactions as the interplay of 'forces' in a 'field,' using physical science notations of vectors and topology. Whereas his original vision of a 'general field theory' of human behavior has, in the main, not been followed by social science, the basic model has been used extensively to describe and analyze social change. Business research areas include strategic management (Thomas, 1985, Strebel and Valikangas, 1994, Ajimal, 1985), marketing (e.g. Hurt, 1998), human resources management (Elsass and Veiga, 1994), organizational development (Brager and Holloway, 1992) and management accounting (Grundy, 1997). In the information systems field 'Force Field Analysis' is used in the main as a project management technique in systems engineering (see, Nicholas, 1989 and 1990) or suggested as a catalyst to foster design creativity (Couger et al., 1989). Although the concept is very well established in organizational theory, Force Fields have not been featured very often in information systems research, and hardly, if at all, in international information systems theory. Their inclusion into the theory is warranted for two reasons:

1. The issues of territorial conflict (referred to as 'turf battles', 'fiefdoms' in the practitioner literature) are well known to international business theorists, and the functional conflict between technology providers and business users is a well established phenomenon in information systems and organizational research. However, conceptualizing a Force Field as the overarching framework to accommodate the interplay of both conflict areas in MNCs is a new contribution to the literature;

2. As a consequence of its ubiquity, the two interleaved Force Fields then become the very base for the architecture and response dynamics elements of the theory.

The Two-Dimensional Model of IIS Architecture

IIS for MNCs who carry out the same type of business in various locations around the globe are likely to have one set of functions that are the same for everybody – and therefore better administered centrally – and another set that is administered locally. This near truism, however, does not seem to be part of the "tribal knowledge" of practitioners involved with IIS, as the CO-OP's case illustrates. Neither is it an accepted theme in academic IS research – first mentioned twenty years ago (Buss, 1982; Keen, 1982) with little, if any, progress since (Ives and Jarvenpaa, 1991). Periodic research since has focused on a connection between the structure of international systems and the structure of the international firms which use them (King and Sethi, 1993 and 1999). With the exception of Roche (1992) however, this research did not address the issue of a generic architecture for IISs, but concentrated on establishing direct, one-to-one relationships between Bartlett and Ghoshal's (1989) global business strategies and IIS architectures. Table 3 contains an overview of the main architectures corresponding to MNC business strategies.

It seems that just as the '*international*' business strategy is an intermediary stage, so are the corresponding global information technology configurations. If these replicated/inter-organizational/ intellectually-synergized structures are regarded as embryonic 'integrated' architectures, then the previous research identified just three general architectures, namely:

- Centralized;

Bartlett and Ghoshal (1989)	Butler Cox (1991)	Kosynski and Karimi (1993)	Sankar et al (1993)	Jarvenpaa and Ives (1994)
Global	Centralized	Centralization	Centralized	Headquarters-driven
Multinational	Autonomous	Decentralization	Decentralized	Independent
International	Replicated	Inter-organizational	(undefined)	Intellectual Synergy
Transnational	Integrated	Integrated	Integrated	Integrated

Table 3. Proposed Linkages between Global Business Strategy and IIS Architecture

- Decentralized (including autonomous and independent); and
- Integrated.

The two-dimensional architecture proposed by the theory developed from the current research, however, replaces all three structural models with one generic architecture that can transform into either, as will be shown below. This brings three distinct advances: Because of its parsimony, clarity and simplicity, it is theoretically 'purer' than a framework of multiple, divergent architecture models; because it allows the IIS structure to change incrementally and entirely in step with business strategy evolution it is more useful for the practitioner; lastly, being just one, very flexible, structure avoids the discontinuity and disruption of fundamental architecture change every time a significant business strategy change happens.

For these reasons, including the generic IIS architecture into the substantive theory was warranted.

Synchronicity

It is one thing to establish the generic need for common systems, but quite another to define their functionality. Butler Cox (1991) found in a broadly based survey that for 90% of European IIS developers reaching agreement on the 'common' user requirements was the major hurdle for IIS development. In the absence of a 'rational' method, the determination was often left to political warfare, often of the territorial kind. Using the concept of *Synchronicity* to determine real-time, same-data, dispersed-location processes ameliorates or even avoids conflict altogether because it provides an objective yardstick for those business processes in need of common systems and delineates precisely where, and which, 'core' system needs to be compulsory for all users in all global sites.

Applying the synchronicity theorem to the IT architectures in the cases demonstrates the superior flexibility of the two-dimensional model. Figure 5 shows how the generic IIS architecture can be seamlessly adapted to varying business strategies.

The architectures for the three cases would be profiled as follows:

- An appropriate IIS for the CO-OP would have a very thin 'core' consisting of some production and logistics planning systems, which is all the 'synchronicity' needed in their business. Most other systems activity would be 'local,' governed by the autonomous regions;
- SHIPPER's IIS shows the opposite characteristics: a large 'core' of systems supporting the management of the common resource, with very thin layers of 'local' systems, mainly direct links to other transport providers and/or regulatory bodies such as Customs and Excise.
- The actual 'core' in FREIGHTER's IIS architecture is formed by the systems that are mission-critical and/or strategic because they form the foundations for further, strategic systems. The 'local' components support the 'in-sourcing' strategy of the deepest possible electronic linkage with customers.

As IIS designers take advantage of the Internet and as information technology architectures become more web-centric, there will be more, and more complex, options for functional architectures and technology configurations. This commensurately increases the importance of a rational, i.e. not political, and simple, framework for decision making based on the *Synchronicity* in the businesses linked by an IIS.

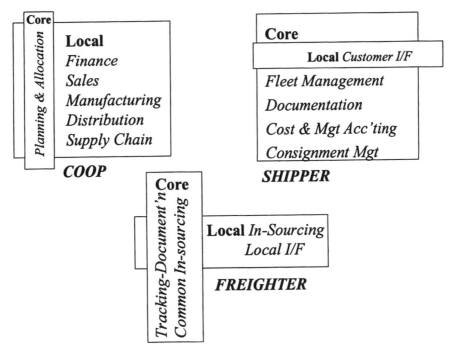

Figure 5. The Two-Dimensional Architecture Models of the IIS in the Three Cases.

The Response Cycle

Two of the cornerstones of the Response Cycle are Business/IT Integration and IT Isolation. They can be considered as two, somewhat opposite, manifestations of the concept of User-Participation, which includes also User Involvement and User Attitude (in the sense of Barki and Hartwick, 1994). On this topic there is a large body of literature[e] confirming that, in general, increased engagement of users in the information systems generating process is often positively correlated with higher 'system success.' This is borne out by the three cases.

The overall Response Cycle is a multiple-loop system, consisting of three single-loop cycles. Acceptance and Rejection are both self-reinforcing. Acceptance fosters IT integration and thus increases the usefulness of the IIS with every round in a 'virtuous circle.' Rejection, on the other hand, increases the isolation of IT, fosters antagonistic politics both of which only strengthen rejection with every round of this 'vicious circle.' It is only with the addition of a compulsory 'Conflict By-Pass' loop that the cause-and-effect system becomes able to regulate itself. In Force Field terms the *Conflict By-Pass* is an equilibrium inducing force (Lewin, 1952, p202).

The response cycle's importance for the substantive theory stems from three factors:

1. The clear definition of multi-directional vectors linking *user acceptance, business/IT integration* and *functional quality* of the IIS is a critical new discovery; while past information systems research has concentrated on relationships between paired elements of these phenomena, the multi-loop cycle puts a more comprehensive constellation of factors into one coherent theory;

2. IT Isolation, long known among practitioners as a serious risk element in information systems endeavors, is the key element in the logic of the *rejection cycle*. It firmly links both functional quality and 'win/loose politics' to the strength of rejection or acceptance. This is also new to the information systems research literature;

3. Participative organization has been regarded mainly as a critical success factor for the functional correctness of design projects. This study has shown that there is an equal, if not higher importance on its conflict avoidance role in implementation projects. In IIS, with their history of less than successful systems endeavors, earlier recognition of this role could have possibly avoided some of the more disastrous failures.

Furthermore, in the CO-OP case the Rejection cycles inflicted damage on the organization that went well beyond the narrow context of the information systems concerned. For that reason, the Conflict By-Pass is an important risk-reducing element in a design and implementation environment that is as highly charged with politics as multinational companies and as complex in its functionality as the information systems that support them.

Quality of the Theory

There is a plethora of opinion regarding what the criteria of a good theory should be. Having used a method they developed, it seems logical to use Glaser and Strauss' definition of the qualities of a good theory. They state (Glaser and Strauss, 1967, p4-5) that in addition to the traditional canons of good science, i.e. clarity, parsimony and logical coherence, a grounded theory should "work" in explaining phenomena in a way that facilitates understanding of "what goes on in a story." It should also "integrate" well into other bodies of research in the field of investigation. In the following paragraphs, the theory is assessed against each of these criteria.

Quality Criteria	Comment
Clarity	The theory elements are widely understood and used in the information systems field. Their relationships are expressed in terms of causality, both mono-directional but some multi-directional. However, some of the major constructs are only very broadly defined. While this does not affect the constructs' 'convergent' and 'discriminant' validity (in terms of Bacharach, 1989), future research needs to aim at maximizing concept clarity of a small set of constructs at a time.
Parsimony	This can be expressed as the ratio of the number of 'initial' theory elements to their sum total in the final form. Redundant categories were removed from the theory at a ration of 10:1 (from 193 to 18) and the interim theoretical construct was 'densified' at a ration of 4:1, from 127 theorems, theses and postulates to 34 in the final, substantive theory. These seem satisfactory.
Logical Coherence	The individual theorems[f] are largely logically independent but complement one another. Where applicable, they are also syllogistically sound, i.e. concluding theorems are supported by sufficient presuppositions.
'Workability'	Glaser and Strauss (1967) suggest to test if a theory 'works' by re-telling the story in the words and concepts of the theory and then to see whether this adds to the story. This was carried out a number of times[g] during theory development. As a mid-range theory, however, it only 'works' within the confines of its substantive scope and future research is needed to extend this.
'Integration'	As shown in the previous section, the theory fits well into a number of established frameworks, predominantly from the social sciences, but also from information systems research.

Table 4. Assessment of the Substantive Theory Against Some Qualities of a "Good Grounded Theory" (after Glaser and Strauss, 1967)

Good 'quality' in terms of these criteria, however, can also be an apparent weakness. The fit, particularly with some established 'canons' of information systems research, may be seemingly too good and the theory statements may be considered 'obvious.' or just 'common sense.' But as Weick

(1989, p526) points out, this obviousness often is "a clue to significance as well as a clue to triviality." An example is the two-dimensional nature of the generic IIS architecture. This may be an 'obvious truism,' but failing to state this architecture paradigm clearly, unambiguously and neglecting to spell out its implications has dire consequences for the practical resolution – or otherwise - of this issue. The high rank of the 'core/local' dilemma as a failure factor for IIS strongly demonstrates the significance such seemingly trivial, axiomatic theorems can have.

CONCLUSION

The most positive aspects of applying Grounded Theory to the case data in this chapter are that the method combines scientific rigor with built in relevance. As a result, the substantive theory developed in this research has substantial ramifications for practitioners working with IIS.

In the first instance, acknowledging the *Force Field* and the inter-dependencies of territorial and functional conflict potentials will assist the practitioner in identifying and assessing the degree and direction of resistance from central and regional management and from business and IT people respectively. This preparatory analysis will allow the early identification of areas of latent conflict and their damage potential, which can then be addressed before they erupt.

Similarly, an explicit acceptance of the two-dimensional *IIS architecture* would avoid the fallacious assumption of a globally standard system as the default IIS solution. Subsequent assessment of the *Synchronicity* requirements of the global operations enable rational identification of the application areas that are candidates for 'core' systems – from which the 'local' application systems and technology architecture can then be defined by complement. For example, such an assessment would have identified the asynchronous nature of the CO-OP's operations from the outset. This, in turn, would have clearly indicated that there was no need for a globally standardized information systems and technology, which would have avoided the damaging and ultimately catastrophic failure experienced there.

The 'core/local' IIS architecture furthermore allows the parallel design, acquisition and implementation of the various IIS elements. 'Core' elements would be assembled by a centrally managed team while each of the 'local' teams would implement their information technology independently and entirely to their own timetable, in parallel with everybody else. This simultaneity should ameliorate the time squeeze conundrum (technology becomes obsolete before it can be implemented globally) that more mature transnational companies, such as FREIGHTER, experience.

Setting up a consensus building project/program organization, as FREIGHTER did, is an effective answer to conflict management. These broadly based development teams for the design, acquisition and implementation of an IIS with specific emphasis on making/taking leadership positions have two benefits:

- Having the 'best' business experts in the team provides the vehicle for obtaining the most up-to-date knowledge - reinforcing the *Functional Quality* to *Business/IT-Integration* to *Acceptance* loop;
- It is a forum for settling differences, thus forestalling damaging conflict; escalation right up to executive board level assures closure in the resolution of persistent conflicts.

A further, overarching benefit for the practitioner is that the activities suggested by the theory lend themselves to be formulated as a step-by-step methodology.

For academic research, the substantive theory provides a rich framework. Many parts of the theory, however, are still in an 'approximate' state, to use Weick's (1995b) term. They point to several future research projects, concerned with refining concepts, constructs and their relationships as well as further adapting and improving the very methodology used. Two research topics stand out:

- Research to solidify the theses surrounding the *Synchronicity* theorem; the three cases in this study are somewhat polarized with respect to the synchronicity of their business processes. The CO-OP's operations were found to be mostly asynchronous, but both following cases had a relatively high degree of synchronicity due to some extent to the similar nature of their businesses: they both provide a physical service, which forms the backbone of their international operations. More MNC cases from more diverse businesses need to be studied;

- The *Response Cycle* theorems should be investigated further in a more organizational change management context as well as in a technology integration context to improve their fit with other, related theories in these fields.

The usefulness of the substantive theory discovered from this research should thus be taken as no more than a lead to begin work on its improvement – in the spirit of Glaser and Strauss (1967, p.28): "A theory's only replacement is a better theory."

ENDNOTES

[a] Grounded Theory is now an accepted research method in business and information systems research (the first applications of the method go back nearly twenty years with Turner, 1983, and Martin and Turner, 1986). The method exists in two variations, one following the approach and philosophy outlined by Glaser and Strauss (1967). Strauss (1987) developed a variation for use by students and geared to smaller, human-relations oriented research undertakings. Strauss and Corbin (1990 and 1994) then further procedurized the method. This was, however, roundly condemned and refuted by Glaser (1994) as too narrow, too prescriptive and too full of preconceived ideas, all of which would lead to nothing more than conceptual descriptions, but not generate theory. This research project used (and adapted) the original (Glaser and Strauss, 1967) method.

[b] This is even before any operations in 'mixed mode' are considered; 'orthogonal' profiles only have one manifestation of each dimension, e.g. either Sales or Manufacturing, but not both; this, of course, is never the case in reality. Only systems like SAP would have the width of functionality to cover (some of!) this diversity – and they had taken decades and 5-figure man-years of development effort.

[c] The technique is directional (rather than solely correlational), i.e. factors are linked with uni-directional arrows to indicate that a change in the factor at the blunt end of the arrow affects a change in the factor at the arrow's sharp end. Two types of effect are recognized: a change in the *same* direction, i.e. "the more of A, the *more* of B" or "the less of A, the *less* of B"; this is labelled with a 'plus' (+) sign. A minus (-) sign signals that the change will move into the *opposite* direction, so that "the more of A, the *less* of B" or the "less of A, the *more* of B" (*ibid.* p71). Such "causal networks" are considered particularly useful because they "respect [the] complexity" of cyclical interactions where causation is not unilateral and where cause and effect can be interchangeable (Miles and Huberman, 1994 p153).

[d] This is an adaptation of previous psychological research that used similar concepts, such as Maruyama's (1968) 'morphogenesis' or 'deviation-amplifying' loops, Bateson's (1972, p109) 'regenerative loops' and Wender's (1968) 'vicious circles'.

[e] While earlier studies, such as Hirschheim's in 1985, look at user participation as a univariate concept, later studies have found that it is a multi-facetted phenomenon (Barki and Hartwick, 1994, confirmed by Hunton and Beeler, 1997, and Hwang and Thorn, 1999). McKeen et al., (1994) furthermore discovered complex interactions between determining and conditioning variables: The configuration of 'participation' variables (which include User Influence and User-Developer Communication) and their effect on 'User Satisfaction' was found to be influenced by the complexity of the (business) task and/or the complexity of the system itself.

[f] The theory has been expressed in natural language, which in itself is more redundant than, say, mathematical notation. Future research should investigate the extent to which it would be possible to densify the theory further by expressing it in terms of qualitative mathematics (following Forbus, 1997) or by using formal logic notation.

[g] The cyclical model of Reaction/Rejection was developed by re-telling the CO-OP case. The 'Response Cycles', describing the stakeholder dynamics was further enhanced by re-telling both of the other cases with respect to this particular aspect. Similarly, the cycle-breaking influence of the Conflict-By-Pass Cycle on the Acceptance/Rejection loops was discovered in the FREIGHTER case but validated – and refined - by re-telling the stories and assessing what-if scenarios in all three cases.

MINICASE

Establishing a Multinational Presence

After receiving a degree in industrial engineering, Rui started his career with a one-year internship at the headquarters of EspanGen, a Spanish multinational corporation (MNC). After his internship was completed, he returned to Portugal where he worked at VinoPick, a family owned company that produced automated machinery for the wine makers. VinoPick imported many of its parts from the Spanish MNC, EspanGen. Over the course of the next five years, his relationship with the top managers of the Spanish EspanGen improved because of the close business relationship. When serious managerial problems occurred at EspanGen, the Portuguese company bought the Spanish importer and appointed Rui as CEO of the newly acquired subsidiary.

At first, Rui, the new CEO of EspanGen, concentrated on building up state-of-the-art practices in his subsidiary to better fulfill the supply chain tasks assigned by the Portuguese headquarters (basically, manufacturing, communication, distribution, and product adaptation). After about 1 year, Rui, with the approval of his Portuguese boss, relocated the subsidiary from Madrid to a location several hundred kilometers closer to Portugal. The aim of this move was to cut costs, speed the supply chain, and create more space for a planned increase in business activity. However, European Union agricultural reform caused cutbacks in demand for wine making machinery, which virtually stopped EspanGen's growth. In addition, the move was rejected by many of EspanGen's workers. As a result of these two events, the staff at EspanGen decreased from about 70 to 35.

Backed by the VinoPick CEO and several directors of EspanGen, Rui started looking for new business opportunities in Spain. As a result he succeeded in out-competing the Spanish service subsidiary of another Portugal MNC that produces a complementary range of wine making equipment. The Spanish service subsidiary of the other Portuguese MNC was closed down and the business was taken on by Rui and his subsidiary. In this take-over process, Rui demonstrated a well-functioning sales and maintenance organization. VinoPick gave credibility and support to the negotiations with the other Portugal supplier.

After taking on this new business, EspanGen almost doubled in size and gained critical mass for new entrepreneurial activities. This time, the stagnation of the Portugal market as well as the dominant position of the EspanGen on its home market led to a shift in strategy towards increasing the company presence within the Spanish market. Although Rui and the VinoPick CEO had reached a general consensus that the Spanish market should increase in importance within the MNC, the VinoPick CEO and several of the family member owners appeared unwilling to support this local strategy. Rui lobbied for this move and started to change internal practices at his subsidiary to better exploit the Spanish market. Thus, he decided to hire Spanish speaking product managers for every important product to improve the adaptation of products and services as well as the development of new products for the Spanish market. These measures were rather successful, and the Spanish subsidiary's competencies in product development expanded. Moreover, this led to the introduction of a similar product manager structure at the Portuguese headquarters. Some of the family member owners were not happy with these changes.

Another example of how Rui developed internal practices to better serve the Spanish market and triggered changes at HQ is related to market communication. Initially, the Portuguese CEO of VinoPick was not enthusiastic about Rui developing a separate product catalogue for the Spanish market. However, Rui's increased reputation, close personal relationships to one of directors, (a director who once was expatriated for a year to the Spanish subsidiary), and an integrated supply chain together were supporting the development of high-trust relationships. As a result of the increasing success in Spain and with the full backing of Rui, EspanGen developed a new local Spanish catalogue project. The new catalogue turned out to be a great success, and the Portuguese headquarters decided to adopt the idea and develop its own catalogue for the Portugal market to achieve comparable sales gains.

Despite his increasing reputation and influence in the strategic development process at VinoPick's headquarters, Rui was never interested in a career at the Portuguese headquarters for several reasons. One was that the Portuguese MNC offered only a few top management positions to non-family members. Furthermore, Rui could easily satisfy his entrepreneurial orientation by the many challenging tasks he encountered in developing EspanGen's mandate. Rui recently got VinoPick's CEO's approval to move the subsidiary again to a more spacious location, thus building the foundation for future growth and subsidiary upgrading.

Discussion Questions:

1. Describe the ongoing relationship of the Portuguese company and its Spanish subsidiary. How has it changed over the years?

2. Using Bartlett and Ghoshal's framework, what type of MNC is the Portuguese company?

3. What were some of the obstacles faced by Rui as he took over the Spanish subsidiary? How could he have overcome them?

Adapted from: Dörrenbächer, Christoph and Geppert, Mike, "Micro-Political Aspects of Mandate Development and Learning in Local Subsidiaries of Multinational Corporations," discussion paper, SP III 2005-202, October 2005, Social Science Research Center Berlin. Available at: http://skylla.wz-berlin.de/pdf/2005/iii05-202.pdf

KEY TERMS

Acceptance Cycle
Global Company
Global Business Strategy
Grounded Theory
International Business Strategy
International Information System (IIS)
Multinational Business Strategy
Multinational Company (MNC)
Response Cycle
Transnational Business Strategy

STUDY QUESTIONS

1. What is meant by the 'Acceptance Cycle'? Describe a situation that you have been a part of in which you have seen the acceptance cycle in action.

2. What is meant by the 'Rejection Cycle'? Describe a situation that you have been a part of in which you have seen the rejection cycle in action.

3. As a manager, how do you handle situations that result in the acceptance or rejection cycle being used by users?

4. Are IISs appropriate for all four of Bartlett and Ghoshal's business strategies? Is any one strategy better for use in an IIS?

5. What extent do organizational politics play in the implementation of IISs?

REFERENCES

Ajimal, K. S. "Force Field Analysis - A Framework for Strategic Thinking," *Long Range Planning*. 18(5), 1985, pp. 55-60.

Alavi, M., and Young, G. "Information Technologies in International Enterprise: An Organising Framework, in Palvia, S., Palvia, P., and Zigli, R. (eds.), *The Global Issues of Information Technology Management*, Idea Group Publishing, Harrisburg, PA, pp. 495-516. 1992b.

Applegate, L. M., McFarlan, F. W., and McKenney, J. L. *Corporate Information Systems Management, Text and Cases*. Chapter 12; 4th edition. Irwin, Chicago, pp. 684-691. 1996.

Barki, H., and Hartwick, J. "Measuring user participation, user involvement and user attitude," *MIS Quarterly*, 18(1), 1994, pp. 59-82.

Bartlett, C. A., and Ghoshal, S. *Managing Across Borders: The Transnational Solution*. Boston. Harvard Business School Press, ch 2-5. 1989.

Brager, G., and Holloway, S. "Assessing prospects for organizational change: The uses of force field analysis. Administration in Social Work," 16(3,4), 1992, pp. 15-28.

Broadbent, M., and Weill, P. "Management by maxim: how business and IT managers can create IT infrastructures," *Sloan Management Review*, 38(3), 1997, pp. 77-92.

Burns, J. M., and Cheung, H. K., Information Systems resource Structure and Management in Multinational Organizations, in Palvia, P. C., Palvia, S. C., Roche, E. M., (Editors) 1996, , *Global Information Technology and Systems Management - Key issues and Trends*, Ivy League Publishing, Ltd, pp. 293-324. 1996.

Buss, M. D. J. "Managing International Information Systems," *Harvard Business Review*, Sep/Oct 60(5), 1982, pp. 153-162.

Butler Cox plc. "Globalisation: The Information Technology Challenge," *Amdahl Executive Institute Research Report*, London, ch 3, 5, and 6. 1991.

Byrd, T A., and Marshall, T E. "Relating information technology investment to organizational performance: A causal model analysis," *Omega*. 25(1), 1997, pp. 43-56.

Collins, R. W., and Kirsch, L., *Crossing Boundaries: The Deployment of Global IT Solutions. Practice-Driven Research in IT Management Series™*, Cincinnati, OH. 1999.

Couger, J. D., Higgins, L. F., and McIntyre, S. C. "(Un)structured creativity in information systems organizations," *MIS Quarterly*. 17(4), 1993 , pp. 375-397.

Davenport, T. "The Bigger Picture." *CIO*. 10(15), pp. 88-96; Framingham, MA. 1997.

Davenport, T., and Prusak, L. *Information ecology: mastering the information and knowledge environment* Oxford University Press, New York, NY. 1997.

Deans, P. C., and Jurison, J. *Information Technology in a Global Business Environment – Readings and Cases*. Boyd and Fraser, New York, NY, ch. 5-7. 1996.

DiMaggio, P. J. "Comments on 'What Theory is *Not*'," *Administrative Science Quarterly*, 40, 1995, pp. 391-397.

Elsass, P. M., and Veiga, J. F. "Acculturation in acquired organizations: A force-field perspective," *Human Relations*. 47(4), 1994, pp. 431-453.

Flowers, S. *Software Failure: Management Failure*. John Wiley & Sons, New York, NY, ch 3, 4-8, 9. 1996.

Gallupe, R. B., and Tan, F. B., "A research manifesto for global information management." *Journal of Global Information Management*, 7(3), 1999, pp. 5-18

Gibson, R. Information Technology Planning and Architectures for Networked Global Organizations: in Palvia, P. C., Palvia, S. C., Roche E. M., Eds., 1996: *Global information technology and systems management.* Ivy League Publishing, Nashua, New Hampshire, pp. 276-292. 1994.

Glaser, B. G. *Theoretical Sensitivity.* Sociology Press, Mill Valley. 1978.

Glaser, B. G. *Emergence vs. Forcing: Basics of grounded theory analysis.* Sociology Press, Mill Valley, ch 1, 2, 5, 8, 11. 1992.

Glaser, B. G., and Strauss, A. L. *The discovery of grounded theory.* Aldine Publishing Company, Hawthorne, New York. 1967.

Glass, R. L. *The Universal Elixir and Other Computing Projects Which Failed.* Computing Trends, Bloomington, IN, ch 5, 6 ,9. 1992.

Glass, R. L. *Software Runaways.* Prentice Hall PTR, Upper Saddler River, NJ, ch3. 1998.

Gregory, F. "Cause, effect, efficiency and soft systems models," *Journal of the Operational Research Society.* 44(4), 1993, pp. 333-344.

Grover, V., and Segars, A H. "The relationship between organizational characteristics and information system structure: An international survey," *International Journal of Information Management,* 16(1,) 1996, pp. 9-25.

Grundy, T. "Management accounting for strategic performance," *Management Accounting-London.* 75(11), 1997, pp. 63-64.

Hamelink, C. J. *Transnational data flows in the information age.* Lund, Sweden: Student-litteratur AB, ch 4. 1984.

Hunton, J. E., and Beeler, J. D. "Effects of user participation in systems development: A longitudinal field experiment," *MIS Quarterly,* 21(4), 1997, pp. 359-388.

Hurt, F. "Implementing great new ideas through the use of force-field analysis," *Direct Marketing,* 61(1), 1998, pp. 54-56.

Hwang, M. I., and Thorn, R. G. "The effect of user engagement on system success: A meta-analytical integration of research findings," *Information Management.* 35(4), 1999, pp. 229-236.

Ives, B., and Jarvenpaa, S. L. "Applications of Global Information Technology: Key Issues for Management," *MIS Quarterly,* March 1991, pp. 33-49.

Ives, B., and Jarvenpaa, S. L. MSAS Cargo International: Global Freight Management. In T. Jelass, C. Ciborra (Eds.) *Strategic Information Systems: A European Perspective.* John Wiley and Sons, New York, pp. 230-259. 1994.

Ives, B; and Jarvenpaa, S.L. "Air Products and Chemicals, Inc: Planning for Global Information Systems," *International Information Systems* April, 1992, pp. 78-99.

Jarvenpaa, S.L., and Ives, B. "Organizational Fit and Flexibility: IT Design Principles for a Globally Competing Firm," *Research in Strategic Management and Information Technology,* 1, 1994, pp. 8-39.

Keen, P. G. W., Bronsema, G. S. and Auboff, S. "Implementing Common Systems: One Organisation's Experience," *Systems, Objectives and Solutions,* (2), 1982, pp. 125-142.

King, W. R., and Sethi, V. "Developing Transnational Information Systems: A Case Study," *OMEGA International Journal of Management Science,* 21, 1, 1993, pp. 53-59.

King, W. R., and Sethi, V. "An empirical assessment of the organization of transnational information systems," *Journal of Management Information Systems* 15(4), 1999, pp. 7-28.

KPMG Peat Marwick. Pan-European Business Systems. London. *KPMG Management Consulting - Research Report.* Brussels. 1994.

Lehmann, H. P. "Between Heterarchies and Serendipity - Exploring the Development of International Information Systems," *Proceedings of the Second European Conference on Information Systems,* Breukelen, Netherlands, 1994, pp. 463-485.

Lehmann, H. P. 'Towards a common architecture paradigm for the global application of information systems'. In Glasson, B.C., Vogel, D.R., Bots, P.W. and Nunamaker, J.F. (Editors) '*Information Systems and Technology in the International Office of the Future*', Chapman and Hall, London, 1996, pp. 199-218. 1996

Lehmann, H. P. "A Definition of Research Focus for International Information Systems," *Proceedings of the Thirtieth Annual Hawaii International Conference on Systems Sciences*, Maui, Hawaii, January, 1997.

Lehmann, H. P. "The Design of Information Systems for the International Firm: What are the Critical Issues?" *Proceedings of the Inaugural Conference of the Australia-New Zealand International Business Academy.* Gray, S. J., Nichols, S. (Eds). Melbourne, November 1998.

Lehmann, H. P. "The Fatal Politics of Multinational Information Systems: A Case Study," *Journal of Information Technology Cases & Applications,* 2(3), 2000, pp. 40-64.

Lehmann, H. P. "An Object Oriented Architecture Model for International Information Systems? An Exploratory Study," *Journal of Global Information Management,* 11(3), 2003, pp. 1-18.

Lewin, K. *The conceptual representation and the measurement of psychological forces.* 1(4) of the series: Contributions to Psychological Theory. Duke University Press, Durham, North Carolina, ch 5, 7-9. 1938.

Lewin, K. *Field theory in social science: selected theoretical papers.* (D Cartwright, Ed.) Tavistock, London, United Kingdom, ch 5, 8. 1952.

Lindsley, D. H., Brass, D. J., and Thomas, J. B. "Efficacy-performance spirals: A multilevel perspective," *Academy of Management Review.* 20(3), 1995, pp. 645-678.

Martin, P. Y. and B. A. Turner "Grounded Theory and Organizational Research," *The Journal of Applied Behavioral Science,* 22(2), 1986, pp. 141-157.

Miles, M. B., and Huberman, A. M. *Qualitative data analysis: an expanded sourcebook.* 2nd Ed. Sage Publications. Thousand Oaks, ch 1, 3-5, 7. 1994.

Montazemi, A. R. and Chan, L. "An Analysis of the Structure of Expert Knowledge," *European Journal of Operational Research.* 45(2,3), 1990, pp. 275-292.

Nicholas, J. M. "Successful Project Management: A Force-Field Analysis," *Journal of Systems Management.* 40(1), 1989, p24-30,36.

Nicholas, J. M. *Managing Business and Engineering Projects: Concepts and Implementation* 1st Edition. Prentice Hall Inc, London, ch 3. 1990.

Orlikowski, W. J. "CASE tools as organizational change: Investigating incremental and radical changes in systems development," *MIS Quarterly,* Sept, 1993, pp. 309-337

Palvia, P. C. "Global Information Technology Research: Past Present and Future," *Journal of Global Information Technology Management,* Vol.1, No.2, 1998, 12-32.

Peppard, J. "Information management in the global enterprise: An organizing framework," *European Journal of Information Systems,* 8(2), 1999, pp. 77-94.

Pettigrew, A. M. "Longitudinal Field Research on Change: Theory and Practice," *Organization Science,* Vol. 1, No. 3, 1990, pp. 267-292.

Roche, E. M., Managing Systems Development in Multinational Corporations: Practical lessons from 7 Case Studies. In Palvia, S., Palvia, P., and Zigli, R. (eds.), *The Global Issues of Information Technology Management,* Idea Group Publishing, Harrisburg, PA, pp. 630-354. 1992a.

Sankar, C., Apte, U. and Palvia, P. Global Information Architectures: Alternatives and Trade-offs. *International Journal of Information Management,* 13, pp. 84-93.

Sethi, V. and Olson, J. E. 1993 An integrating framework for information technology issues in a transnational environment. In *Global Issues in Information Technology,* Idea Publishers, Harrisburg, pp. 227-253.

Strauss, A. L. *Qualitative Analysis for Social Scientists.* Cambridge University Press, ch2-5. 1987.

Strebel, P., and Valikangas, L. "Organizational change processes in a force field," *International Review of Strategic Management,* 5, 1994, pp. 233-262.

Targowski, A. S., *Global Information Infrastructure – The Birth, Vision and Architecture,* Idea Group Publishing, London, UK, ch1,4. 1996.

Thomas, J. "Force Field Analysis: A New Way to Evaluate Your Strategy," *Long Range Planning,* 18(6), 1985, pp. 54-59.

Tractinsky, N. and Jarvenpaa, S. L. "Information systems design decisions in a global versus domestic context," *MIS Quarterly,* 19(4), 1995, pp. 507-534.

Van den Berg, W., and Mantelaers, P., "Information systems across organisational and national boundaries: an analysis of development problems," *Journal of Global Information Technology Management ,* 2(2), 1999, pp. 32-65.

Weick, K. E., 1989. Theory construction as disciplined imagination. *Academy of Management Review,* 14(4), pp. 516-531.

Weick, K. E.,. "What Theory is Not, Theorizing Is," *Administrative Science Quarterly,* 40, 1995, pp. 385-390.

Weick, K. E., 'Theory'. Entry in Nicholson, N., (Editor) and Schuler, R., Van de Ven, A. (Advisory Ed's.) *The Blackwell Encyclopedic Dictionary of Organizational Behavior.* Oxford : Blackwell Business, Cambridge, MA, pp. 563-565, 1995b.

Weick, K. E., *The social psychology of organising.* Reading, Management, Addison Wesley, ch 3-5, 1979.

Weill, P. The Role and Value of information Technology Infrastructure: Some Empirical Observations. *Working Paper No. 8, University of Melbourne.* Melbourne, July 1992.

Weill, P. The role and value of information technology infrastructure: some empirical observations. In: Banker, R., Kauffman, R. and Mahmood, M.A., (Editors). *Strategic Information Technology Management: Perspectives on Organizational Growth and Competitive Advantage.* Idea Group Publishing, Middleton, PA, pp. 188-210. 1993.

Weill, P., Broadbent, M., Butler, C., and Soh, C. "Firm-wide Information Technology Infrastructure investment and services," *Proceedings of the 16th International Conference on Information Systems,* Amsterdam, 1995, pp. 181-202.

Weill, P., Broadbent, M. and St.Clair, D. Information technology value and the role of information technology infrastructure investments. In: *Strategic Alignment,* Luftman, J. (Ed), Oxford University Press, Oxford, pp. 55-83. 1994.

Yourdon, E. *Death March: The Complete Software Developer's Guide to Surviving Mission Impossible Projects.* Prentice Hall PTR, Upper Saddler River, NJ, ch 5. 1997.

Yin, R. K. *Case Study Research: Design and Methods.* Sage Publications, Newbury Park. 1989.

Section 4

Global IS Development and Outsourcing

The development of a global information system (GIS) is a complex and challenging task. GISs cross national boundaries, cultures, time zones, and established patterns of organizational behavior. What works in one situation may not work in another. What works in one country may be totally inappropriate in another country. In addition, the concept of outsourcing, or hiring a vendor to manage or operate information system functions, is becoming commonplace. India has become an outsourcing power because of a skilled workforce and low wages. Other countries are vying to get a piece of the outsourcing pie. The section presents six chapters on GIS development and outsourcing.

Chapter 16 presents a contextual analysis of GIS development strategies. Nine strategies are identified and discussed in the chapter. A framework for GIS development strategies is presented. Three cases are presented to illustrate the concepts. Chapter 17 discusses best practices for GIS development. Five tactics for implementing the transnational model are presented. The authors present critical success factors for global information systems and strategies for GIS development. Chapter 18 kicks off the discussion of outsourcing by discussing dynamics of control modes in offshored information systems development projects. Culture plays a major role in managing offshore contracts and the authors discuss culture and control modes. An integrative framework for control strategies is presented. In Chapter 19, the author develops a sourcing framework and emerging knowledge requirements for offshoring. The author traces the evolution, the difficulties and risks, and the future of outsourcing and offshoring. A framework for making the outsourcing/offshoring choice is presented. Chapter 20 presents critical factors for managing offshore contracts. The final chapter in this section, Chapter 21, presents critical factors for countries and companies for outsourcing.

16

Global Information Systems Development Strategies: A Contextual Analysis[1]

Prashant C. Palvia
The University of North Carolina at Greensboro, USA

Murad Akmanligil
Fedex, USA

CHAPTER SUMMARY

Developing global information systems (GIS[2]) is a formidable task. Multinational companies operate in regions that are thousands of miles, many time zones, and many cultures away from the headquarters. Organizing the activities and aligning the tasks and mindsets of people that are so far apart and to actually change the way business is conducted through the use of new information systems is a major challenge. The global dimension presents even a bigger challenge. This chapter discusses alternative global IS development strategies that may be used and the factors that impact the selection of these strategies. The viability of these strategies and the accompanying factors is demonstrated through the approaches used to develop information systems in a large transportation company.

INTRODUCTION

Information technology (IT) and its impact continue to grow at whirlwind speed throughout the globe. Cheaper and faster computers and communication devices are introduced to the market every day. Nevertheless, the cost of building information systems (IS) still remains significantly high.

---

[1] This chapter is an updated version of: Akmanligil, M, and Palvia, P.C. "Strategies for Global Information Systems Development: A Critical Analysis" in Prashant Palvia, Shailendra Palvia, and Edward Roche, eds, Global Information Technology and Electronic Commerce, Marietta, GA: Ivy League Publishing. 2002, pp. 161-177. An updated version of the chapter was published as an article in *Information and Management* (Akmanligil and Palvia 2004).

[2] The term GIS, as used in this chapter, should not be confused with the more common usage of the term meaning Geographic Information Systems.

Companies spend millions of dollars in IT to automate their processes, to improve decision making, and to gain strategic advantage. In spite of that, large numbers of information systems projects are either excessively over budget, months or years behind schedule, of poor quality, or simply fail to adequately satisfy users' requirements (Doherty and King, 2001). According to the 2004 Standish Group survey reported by Softwaremag.com (2004), while project success rates have improved over a decade, most of the challenged projects had a cost overrun of 20% and the average project cost overrun was found to be 43%. According to the report, the U.S. project waste was found to be $55 billion in 2004, made up of $38 billion in lost dollar value and $17 billion in cost overruns. These are staggering figures. Management frustration with IT costs, backlog of new system requests, and establishing standards on infrastructure are forcing IT managers to seek alternative solutions to in-house development. Outsourcing and purchasing packaged software are frequently being selected as alternative solutions to these problems.

A new and major factor complicating the issue of IS development and its success is the globalization of companies. Today, the trend towards globalization is phenomenal, to the extent that some industries such as electronics, computer, and pharmaceutical are considered predominantly global. In order to successfully compete in these industries, companies have to exploit the advantages of globalization. Globalization brings forth the necessity and challenge of coordinating the activities of the company on a worldwide basis, mostly accomplished through information technology. However, globalization drastically increases the complexity of the development process by introducing many new variables and unknowns. As Karimi and Konsynski (1991) note, variations in business environments, availability of resources, and technological and regulatory environments are faced by the IS organization as soon as a system crosses national boundaries.

A global information system (GIS[2]) is used across one or more national borders (Burn and Cheung, 1996). The IS executive has many system development strategies to choose from in satisfying global information requirements. In addition to the known domestic challenge of choosing in-house development, outsourcing, or package software adoption, a global system presents additional challenges. Questions such as how to get support from subsidiaries for the system; how and who should go about gathering the information requirements from subsidiaries (or even whether to gather requirements from subsidiaries); who should build the system (if it is to be built in-house); how to exploit existing design and code from similar domestic applications; what code should be common and what should be local; how many versions of the code to support, etc., pose a wide variety of difficult choices. The choices are not clear-cut and require a careful consideration of a host of factors.

The next section identifies and discusses various global IS development strategies. A model is then presented to capture the factors that need to be considered in the selection of a strategy. An in-depth discussion of the model variables is provided. In the next section, four case studies are described that detail the various development strategies used in GIS projects. Finally, the last section provides a discussion of the findings and their implications.

GLOBAL INFORMATION SYSTEM DEVELOPMENT STRATEGIES

As information technology and software processes improve, firms find themselves faced with more options to solve their information requirement needs. Existing literature acknowledges that information systems development is a complex activity. This complexity is magnified by the continuous changes in user requirements due to changing organizational needs in changing external competitive environments (Benbya and McKelvey, 2006). Nelson, Richmond, and Seidmann (1996) state that a major problem facing the firm is to identify the acquisition/development strategy that will maximize the net present value of software acquisition, subject to organizational considerations (e.g., corporate policy and resource availability). While many system development strategies are available to choose from, it also makes the choice decision very difficult. We discuss alternatives available both in the domestic and global contexts.

In the domestic context, insourced development, package acquisition, and outsourcing are the primary development strategies available to companies. Additional alternatives are available to global companies. In the literature, eight GIS development strategies are noted (Ives and Jarvenpaa, 1991; Janz et al., 2002). We added another. The nine strategies are:

1. Development with a multinational design team (MDT)
2. Parallel development (PD)
3. Central development (CD)
4. Core vs. local development (CL)
5. Best-in-firm software adoption (BIF)
6. Outsourced custom development (OC)
7. Unmodified packaged software acquisition (UP)
8. Modified packaged software acquisition (MP)
9. Joint development with vendor (JDV)

Each category can be categorized across several dimensions. These are:

- Development approach: Build the application or buy a package
- Number of countries involved in the development: domestic or international development
- Degree of outsourcing: internal development or use of vendors
- Degree of customization: core and local components

1) Development with a Multinational Design Team (MDT): With this strategy, a design team that is comprised of systems and user personnel from multiple international sites of the company is formed. The team members gather at one location generally for months to work on the design of the system. It is argued that the participation of the involved parties not only allows the creation of a design that meets the requirements of all the regions of the company but also increases the likelihood of the acceptance of the software and the likelihood of adhering to international standards. However, the cost of this strategy is reported to be high. The right team leader and the right team composition are important for the success of the project completed with this strategy. According to Janz et al. (2002), the team leader should be multi-culturally aware and serve at least as a benevolent dictator.

2) Parallel Development (PD): Janz et al. (2002) describe this strategy as one where the requirements gathering and the construction of the systems are done locally and where these systems are connected through bridges. In order to achieve timely IS development and to increase the chances of successful implementation, the systems must be developed locally (with some preplanning) and then integrated with other systems. Some companies use a variation of this strategy: representatives of teams at different locations, after gathering local requirements, come together at a central side and try to resolve the differences and determine a common structure. At another extreme, the project is broken into multiple components and different components are designed and built at different locations. Coordination and consistency among these systems are provided through common development methodologies, shared software engineering tools, electronic mail, and consistent definitions of data.

3) Central Development (CD): With this approach the system is developed at one site (predominantly at the headquarters) and is installed at the subsidiaries. The advantages of this strategy is lower costs (compared to development with a Multinational Design Team and Parallel Development) due to economies of scale, the enforcement of standard operating procedures throughout the company, and better communications among the parties that are involved in the development of the system. The disadvantages are potential for resistance to the software at the subsidiaries, unsatisfied requirements of some regions, and diminished buy-in from uninvolved regions (Cash et al., 1992).

4) Core vs. Local Development (CL): Collins and Kirsch (1999) in their study of five global IS projects observe that "project team structures were typically complex, reflecting the need for centralized effort to create a common global solution, while at the same time understanding and accommodating local needs." Lehmann (2002) also proposed a two-dimensional topology as an architectural model for international information systems. The topology would consist of a "common core" and "local variations", linked together by an "interface". In this approach, local IT departments tailor the components created by the headquarters (and/or some regions) to fit their needs; we call this: Core versus Local Development. While minimizing local conflicts, this strategy tends to increase coordination and control requirements.

5) Best-in-Firm Software Adoption (BIF)*:* In an earlier article, this strategy was observed to be the most common in software acquisition by Ives and Jarvenpaa (1991). Janz et al. (2002) describe the basic philosophy behind this approach as searching throughout the company for the global application which best fits the best experience of every unit, i.e., the proven one, and then modify into a single, common system to be implemented globally. But the roll-out of the software to the regions is typically gradual. Some modifications are necessary due to differences in requirements and technological resources among regions. Sometimes, it may be necessary to provide each region with its own version of the software. This, however, will create duplication of effort and drastically increase the cost of maintenance in the long run. Janz et al. (2002) recommend changing the organization and its processes to fit the software rather than creating multiple versions of the same software.

6) Outsourced Custom Development (OC)*:* Outsourcing has become a popular strategy in software development. Some companies are now engaged in global (offshore) outsourcing (King 2005b). This strategy is chosen for various reasons: to implement and enforce global standards, to reduce cycle time in system development, to reduce costs, to gain access to state-of-the-art technological expertise, to shift focus to more strategic systems etc. (Harland et al., 2005). Opponents of outsourcing argue that loss of control and flexibility, loss of qualified IS staff, and loss of competitive advantage in information management are major risks that outsourcing involves (Rao et al., 1996). With this strategy, the system is developed or acquired by an external company (i.e., the service provider.) The service provider can choose to implement one or more of the other development strategies listed in this section.

7) Unmodified Packaged Software Acquisition (UP): Many companies are purchasing packaged software rather than developing it themselves. This strategy provides a working system to the organization right from the start. The packages are generally parameter driven and can be configured extensively (Emmerson, 1998). With unmodified packaged software, generally, vendors are able to provide better support and future modifications are guaranteed to be compatible with the application. However, the package may not fully meet the requirements and the firm may have to modify its processes to accommodate the software. Enterprise Resource Planning (ERP) systems are examples of packaged software which are gaining popularity among European and American companies. Although corporate expenditures for ERP were 530 billion in 2004 and have been growing at about 150% per year in recent years, many firms have had difficulties with implementation (King 2005a). According to him, two important measures that proved highly predictive of ERP implementation project success were the "arduousness of the consultant-client relationship" and the degree of "shared understanding.

8) Modified Packaged Software Acquisition (MP*):* The "vanilla" (i.e., not modified) package does not always meet the requirements of all regions of a company even if it is a parameter driven system. In these cases, the software needs to be modified to fit the needs of the company. For example, the ERP packages can be modified extensively. However, best practice in package implementation (Janz et al., 2002) recommends minimal modification to the package and that additional functionality not found in the package should be built independently and interfaced with the package. Ragowsky and

Stern (1995) also suggested minimal modification to the package due to the high development and maintenance costs in maintaining the integration of customizations, when the vendor continually upgrades the packaged software.

9) Joint Development with Vendors (JDV): This approach is also called a "strategic partnership" with the vendor. The strategy is different from just hiring 'contractors' to help code or deploy the system; it involves heavy and committed participation of vendors in one or more of the phases. In most cases, the vendor provides guidance or shares the responsibility of the success of the system. As in outsourcing, some of the reasons for involving vendors are: access to new technology, access to project management skills, and the desire to jump-start the project. As a variant, when the package acquisition approach is chosen, the package vendors could be asked to help in any modification. Generally in the JDV approach, the host company desires to take over the development or maintenance in the long term and wishes to internalize the skills brought in by the consultants.

A GUIDING FRAMEWORK FOR GIS DEVELOPMENT STRATEGIES

The framework in Figure 1 postulates the various factors that need to be examined in the selection of a GIS development strategy. Both the strategy and its success are dependent on these factors. Based on the review of IS development, IS outsourcing, and global IS literature, the following factors are identified as impacting the selection of a GIS development strategy: organizational characteristics, desired system characteristics, differences among subsidiaries, and IS department characteristics. These factors are discussed below.

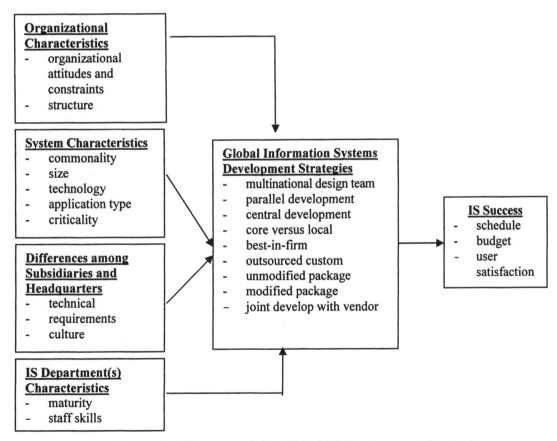

Figure 1. A Framework for Global IS Development Strategies

Organizational Characteristics

Organizational characteristics considered important in relation to the software development strategies are: organizational attitudes and constraints (Nelson, Richmond, and Seidmann 1996), and organization structure. A certain acquisition strategy may be preferred over others due to corporate policy or general organizational and management attitudes. For example, a corporation due to its polycentric disposition could choose to implement a policy that urges the subsidiaries or regions of the company to come up with their own solutions to their information requirements rather than depending on the headquarters. In another situation, management frustration over IT costs and response time or difficulties faced in installing global standards on infrastructure would be important factors that affect software acquisition decisions in favor of outsourcing (McFarlan 1996) or packaged software.

The organization structure could also impact the GIS development strategy. According to Ghoshal and Nohria (1993), there are four types of structures/environments: (1) international environment where forces for both local responsiveness and global integration are weak, and the focus is on transferring and adapting parent company knowledge in foreign subsidiaries; (2) global environment where forces for global integration are strong but forces for local responsiveness are weak; and the structures are more centralized in strategic and operational decisions; (3) multinational environment where forces for local responsiveness are strong but forces for global integration are weak; and the organization is managed as a portfolio of decentralized multinational entities; and (4) transnational environment where forces for both global integration and local responsiveness are strong, and adaptation to all environmental situations utilizing knowledge and two way information flows is the key.

As an example, in a multinational company where the subsidiaries act mostly as domestic companies, the cost of systems development using multinational design teams will be considerably higher than in a transnational company. This is because there is normally very little coordination among subsidiaries and greater differences in business processes in a multinational structure. According to Cash et al. (1992), as firms adopt different organization structures, they need different levels of international IT support and coordination. They argue that for "central development", the organization should have "established patterns of technology transfer, strong functional control over their subsidiaries, and some homogeneity in their manufacturing, accounting, and distribution practices." Therefore, centralized development is less likely to be used in a multinational structure. Galbraith (1980) stated that there was a relationship between the type, quantity and interrelatedness of the types of information and the organizational structure needed to process it. He concluded that three factors influence the amount of information to be processed: (1) the degree of uncertainty concerning task requirements, (2) the number of elements necessary for decision making; and (3) the degree of interrelatedness among the elements.

System Characteristics

The characteristics of the desired system play an important role in selection of the development strategy. Some key characteristics are: commonality, size, technology, type, and criticality. Commonality is the extent to which a particular type of software is used by other companies. There is empirical evidence that common applications are more likely to be outsourced or bought as a package rather than being custom built. Relative size of the project (compared to other projects in the company) is one of the factors that affect the risk of the project (McFarlan, 1996). As the size of the project gets larger in terms of its cost, staffing levels, duration, or the number of departments that are affected by it, the coordination costs and the risk of the project increase. Outsourcing the development of the system could reduce this risk. Collaboration and exchange among subsidiaries and headquarters can be used to reduce the risk that arises from the size of the project. In developing a large system, subsidiaries can ask for help from other subsidiaries or headquarters; however on the negative side, the coordination and control costs would rise.

New technology, in general, increases the risk of the project and outsourcing projects that require new technology should be considered seriously since a technically skilled outsourcer can alleviate this risk (Nelson, Richmond, and Seidmann, 1996). The risks of dealing with new technology can also be alleviated by collaboration among regions that do not have the expertise and those that have it. Therefore access to new resources and technical expertise is often among the reasons for outsourcing (Lacity and Hirschheim, 1993). Application type is another system characteristic that affects development strategy selection. While many transactional systems have fairly well understood requirements and can be outsourced or purchased as packages, systems with low structure (such as decision support applications) are poor candidates for outsourcing and package solutions. Since "highly structured" tasks have defined and fixed outputs, they are not subject to frequent change. Therefore, they are considerably easier to outsource. Finally, system criticality can also affect the choice of the development strategy. An information system is critical if it directly helps the company build or maintain its core competencies or is central to implementing a key strategy of the firm. For the acquisition of critical systems, using multinational design team strategy might be more effective, as it can help ensure management commitment in various countries. Furthermore, insourced development would be preferred over outsourced development to increase control over the system.

Differences among Subsidiaries and Headquarters

Foreign subsidiaries and headquarters may have significant differences in technology, information requirements, and culture. Technology variations include stark differences in the availability and quality of both hardware and software. These may force a firm to use different vendor products in different subsidiaries. Such variations can force the implementation of multiple versions of the system that run on different platforms or necessitate the involvement of an external company with technical expertise in bridging such platforms. The differences across subsidiaries are major obstacles in integrating communication networks, hardware, and disparate systems software for global applications.

Variations among subsidiaries can be overwhelming. Even seemingly minor requirement differences among subsidiaries can necessitate major local tailoring. DiNardo (1996) pointed out that the parameter driven software they used in Asia was significantly challenged in terms of accommodating the national/regional differences. In order to prevent system development failures and to increase global ownership and smoother implementation, Palvia and Lee (1996) recommend worldwide elicitation of requirements. One of the fallacies in global IS development pointed out by Lehmann (2002) is the belief that the application is serving merely geographically separate yet identical businesses.

It is crucial that cultural differences among subsidiaries and headquarters be considered in making acquisition strategy decisions. Shore (2002) recommends the inclusion of national culture in any research that attempts to create linkages between headquarters and subsidiaries. Hofstede in his seminal book (1980) identified four different dimensions of culture: power distance, uncertainty avoidance, masculinity, and individualism. As an example, organizations in less risk-taking cultures (i.e., high uncertainty avoidance) may find some of the development strategies more risk-prone than what they are accustomed to. Culture manifests itself in many ways, and organizations need to be aware of its many nuances and subtle expressions. It can affect the way workers relate among themselves, their superiors, and subordinates. Shore also alluded to the organizational culture and information culture. These are sets of shared values and practices in an organization. According to Robey and Rodriquez-Diaz (1989), organizational culture plays a more determining role than national culture. However, organizational culture may itself be influenced by national culture by way of core values established early in life.

IS Department Characteristics

The maturity of the IS departments and the difference in skills of the staff in IS departments within the organization also have a bearing on the development strategy. The specific technical capabilities of the IS department to build the needed system will directly influence whether the system will be built internally or not. Its maturity and experience in developing global information systems also have an important role in acquisition decisions (Meadows, 1996; Cash et al., 1992.) An IS department facing problems in establishing and enforcing global standards could choose to circumvent these problems by outsourcing (McFarlan, 1996).

Skill set differences between headquarters' and subsidiaries' IS staff is another concern (Shore, 2002). Lack of technical skills necessary for the development of the proposed system or lack of experience with large projects at the subsidiary or the region could influence the level of collaboration among regions and headquarters. Depending on the organizational policies and structure, lack of technical skills in regions could prevent the use of the parallel development approach and favor outsourcing or it could mandate extensive knowledge and resource sharing with the headquarters and other regions. On the other hand, headquarters' lack of knowledge of subsidiaries' business practices and cultures could mandate a cross-border solution (Palvia and Lee, 1996).

System Success

The choice of an appropriate development strategy would greatly determine the success of the project. However, the choice is dependent on many factors and the relationships are complex. Furthermore, the definition of success itself is elusive which makes evaluation of the strategy difficult. Delone and McLean (2003; 1992) studied the concept of "information system success" and concluded that IS success is a multidimensional construct whose dimensions are system quality, information quality, use, user satisfaction, individual impact, and organizational impact. These dimensions are interrelated. For research and evaluation, they recommend that the choice of a success variable should be "a function of the objective of the study, the organizational context, the aspect of the information system addressed by the study, the independent variables under investigation, the research method, and the levels of analysis." In the IS literature, user satisfaction as a success measure has received considerable attention

Not directly accounted for in the above IS success construct are two key aspects of development success: cost and project duration. The fact is that many projects today cost more than they were budgeted for and last longer than planned. Ewusi-Mensah (1997) argues that most information systems cannot be considered successful along these two dimensions.

CASES - GLOBAL INFORMATION SYSTEMS

Four cases are presented below to illustrate some of the GIS development strategies described above. The cases also discuss the factors influencing the choice of strategies and the success of the strategies. As Yin (1994) points out, the case study method is a distinctive form of empirical inquiry and is adequate for all types of investigation: exploratory, descriptive, and explanatory. These cases are actual projects from a major transportation company based in the U.S. The identity of the company and the people interviewed are concealed due to their request.

The Major Transportation Company (MTC) is a large company headquartered in the United States. This multinational company organized itself into five regions; each region being responsible for its own profits and losses. MTC, a highly customer oriented company, is trying to establish itself as a major player in the global network economy by leveraging information technology. The relatively large IT department of the company is largely centralized and the great majority of employees reside in the U.S. There are some additional IT personnel in the regions who are responsible for support, maintenance, and new development in their areas.

Recently, MTC started to implement an executive initiative to move its systems from mainframe platforms to client/server architecture. On the server side, UNIX, C/C++, Sybase/Oracle and on the client side, Windows, Java, and Visual Basic are becoming company standards. The majority of MTC's applications are custom built in-house; however, the company has been experimenting with packaged software and domestic as well as global outsourcing.

Case 1: Global Clearance (GC) System

With growing international operations, MTC created several country-specific domestic systems to handle customs clearance operations. However, not all clearance-related processes were available from any single system. The clearance systems were not integrated with related functional systems such as International Credit/Collections, Duty/Tax charges, and Sort Operations. This situation, compounded with the fact that some processes were not automated and some were outsourced, made maintaining control of data very difficult at best. There was a need for a single system that enabled conducting all clearance related processes. Therefore, a project called Global Clearance was initiated. Global Clearance was to be one of the first custom built global systems in the company. The proposed system was expected to reduce costs by "eliminating manual processes and paperwork, managing dispute processing, increasing productivity, and reusing detailed customer information."

There was considerable commonality in the existing clearance systems. A major objective of this project was eliminating this redundancy by creating a set of core components, which could be re-used in every country. It was expected that this strategy would reduce the development, maintenance, and support costs in addition to reducing the cycle time for delivering new clearance systems. The objective was stated in the project plan as "to develop a new and improved industry standard for conducting global trade." Also, the system was planned to provide a single point of access to clearance related information and to automate Import Clearance in the major countries that the company operates. The project plan defined the scope as follows:

"The scope of Global Clearance system extends from the point at which information and/or goods enter the country of importation through to completion and archiving of the associated financial transaction and encompasses all systems and data required for clearance."

The system was to be implemented at every site that has more than 500 shipments per day; the estimated break-even-point. As of September 1996, 31 sites in 15 countries met this criterion. The project actually originated from another project which started in Europe and was called Europe Clearance. The requirements for Europe Clearance were gathered by a team that consisted of U.K. IS personnel and user representatives from several European countries. The user interface development for Europe Clearance was carried out in Brussels using a fourth generation language (4GL) tool called Uniface. U.K. was responsible for building the back end. After about a year, it was decided that the headquarters' IT department could help U.K. in developing the system and a project called "International Broker Clearance system" was merged with Europe Clearance to become the Global Clearance system.

During the mid-1990s, corporate headquarters, before the start of Europe Clearance, had mandated that new developed or bought systems would have multi-tiered software architectures. The application development manager of the project describes their efforts in identifying a development strategy that would alleviate the difficulties faced due to lack of expertise in this new technology:

"I think we were looking at (outsourcing) to begin with to see how much of anything can be outsourced. And we always thought the broker piece was the central piece and the sooner we knew about it, (the sooner we could plan for it)... Before we really got going very far, we started looking at broker packages... It is hard to imagine today since things have changed so much but we didn't find any client server broker packages and we didn't find any people that were interested in working with us to build one. I think we had one company that said in the future they might like to have one. It was pretty lean."

Given this situation, the system had to be built in house. Since almost all of the clearance systems built before GC were not three tiered, the GC team could not use much code from these systems. Some faxing software from another system called Japan Broker was used with modifications and another system was studied to get business rules and ideas.

The decision to involve the headquarters in the development of Europe Clearance was made to expedite the development process since U.K. determined that the system could not be completed by the deadline. One explanation of U.K.'s delay was an unrealistic schedule given the resources that were available. The IT departments in the regions were much smaller than that of the headquarters. Unanticipated problems with new technology and "scope creeps" also seemed to have contributed to the delay. Headquarters could help as they had built at least functionally similar systems. Furthermore, some parts of a system called Japan Broker could be reused. One of the designers described how the joint development strategy would be implemented:

> *"Each site was going to take pieces of analysis and design and take it all the way through [the development life cycle]. The United Kingdom was going to do the user interface side since they recently had the necessary training."*

This idea clearly is division of work among countries according to SDLC phases. At the same time, the headquarters asked an external company to do an audit of several existing systems, including the clearance operations. This audit included recommendations for changes to the existing clearance systems. These enhancement recommendations were incorporated into the requirements of the Global Clearance System.

Later into the project, the division of labor was changed. Headquarters IS department was asked to build *core and common* components and U.K. to build the *local* pieces. U.K. representative of the project defined core components as those that are "must have" and needed in almost all countries; common components are nice to have and shared by some countries; and local components as specific to a country. According to the project manager, 90% of the code was expected to be core and common and 10% to be local. A decision was made that regional IT groups will develop, install, and maintain the necessary local components and local connectivity. The core and common pieces built by headquarters would be scalable and reusable and the regions would be free to select the components they need and tailor them to their own needs.

A few months later, the development strategy was changed once again to give headquarters the responsibility of building the entire system. Analysis, design, and coding were carried out *centrally*, only at the Headquarters. The system was unit and assembly tested at the Headquarters, user acceptance and volume tested in the U.K. Training was conducted internally in the U.K.

During these strategy changes, the U.K. and headquarters' IT departments periodically communicated with each other and visited each other's sites in attempts to coordinate their efforts. The U.K. personnel were able to install the hardware for the system in the U.K. and do a "proof-of-concept" to determine whether the proposed technology would be able to support the business. However, U.K. concentrated most of their efforts on the hardware since they had a separate budget for it. The differences in priorities (e.g., hardware versus software), politics, limited resources available to U.K., and the different ways the two groups conducted analysis and design seem to have contributed to the shift of the development strategy from parallel development to core-local to central development.

At this point, the development of the system was stopped. Only the first phase of the development, out of the planned eleven, was finished. The partially finished system is being used at one location in the United Kingdom. That location uses Global Clearance in conjunction with their existing system to carry out clearance tasks. These two systems do not interface with each other.

There are multiple reasons for discontinuing Global Clearance System. The first phase of the system was internally funded and a proposal for the remaining ten phases was to be presented to the Board of Directors (BOD) after the first phase was complete. However, the delays in both Europe Clearance and GC and the increase in requested funding due to the broadened scope reduced the systems' chances of getting BOD approval. Furthermore, the development manager indicated that one of the reasons the GC project was discontinued is that IT executive management started saying that the regions know their needs better than the headquarters does and "are fully capable of writing their own local applications."

Case 2: Global Accounts Receivable (GAR)

One of the major reasons MTC started to look at the possibility of a new accounts receivable (AR) system was that the largest AR system seemed to be reaching its limits in terms of handling the company's transaction volumes. This system was handling the receivables by U.S. payers and was about 14 years old. As expected from a custom built in-house system, it was patched many times and was losing its flexibility to handle code changes.

Another reason MTC wanted a new AR system was to have the ability to have a global financial picture of the company as well as customers. There were many AR systems in the company (e.g., one for domestic, one for international, one for air freight, one for non-transportation, etc.) and these systems did not necessarily interface with each other. This situation made preparing financial documents and balancing different accounts very cumbersome if not impossible. It was hoped that an integrated and re-engineered system would help the company reduce revenue leakage, day's outstanding sales, and bad debt; increase controls on all revenue (such as from duty and taxes); and increase productivity.

During the summer of 1995, with re-engineering in mind, MTC asked a consulting company to conduct an analysis of the U.S. AR system. The consulting company determined that (1) MTC had high transaction processing costs due to high number of customers receiving EDI invoicing but not using EDI remittance; (2) inefficient and outdated procedures resulted in duplicate handling of customer inquiries, costly research, and low employee morale; and (3) the system that handles U.S. payers (which is the largest AR system) needed to be replaced due to its inability to support the growth rate of the transactions and inflexibility. Furthermore, two AR systems that handled about 90% of the transactions were more than 10 years old and were not Y2K compatible. A small system did not have source code available and was also not Y2K compatible. Thus, in general, it was a good time for a global AR system.

A decision was made to examine the accounts receivable software packages existing in the market to determine how much they meet the requirements of MTC. The strong emphasis on package solution was due to several reasons. First, it was determined that a new AR system was needed soon and extending the existing system would be very costly. Second, the existing systems were not Y2K compatible and there was not too much time before the year 2000 arrived. Third, there was an impression, at least outside of the accounting and revenue operations community, that accounts receivable is mostly the same from one company to the next. And finally, there was a directive from the upper management that package solutions should be considered before custom building systems.

Several Request for Proposals (RFP) were sent to vendors, three of which responded. Consistent with the new organizational guidelines, a client server based open system was being sought. A team was formed to evaluate the selected packages. Functional and architectural aspects, supported interfaces, global support by the vendor during and after installation were analyzed. On the architectural side, databases, client and server environments, development/reporting tools, deployment modularity, security, and fail-over capability of the packages were investigated. On the business side, cash applications, credit and collections, accounting, and global functionality were studied. Packages were graded by the team members along these dimensions and the results were submitted to the executive managers who also did their own grading. The tentatively selected package scored about 80 percent by the team members and 87 percent by the executive managers; whereas the company policy was that a package should satisfy 80 percent of the overall requirements to be acceptable. In addition to evaluation, the vendors were asked to make presentations of their software.

After a potential package was selected, a pilot implementation was conducted. The objective was to test the performance of the package, both online and batch. Due to the nature of the business at MTC (i.e., very high volume of transactions with small dollar amounts), performance was a critical issue. It was a requirement that the system have the capacity to handle the growing transaction volumes. Some team members also visited a company in the U.K. and in New York to observe real life implementations of the package. A high-level enhancement requirement document was prepared to bridge the gap between the capabilities of the package and the requirements of MTC. The vendor agreed to implement these enhancements as standard package upgrades.

After the selection was made, a project team that consisted of members from MTC, the vendor that built the package (ARC – AR Company), and another consulting company (CC – Consulting Company) was formed. The team's objective was to detail requirements for enhancements to the base product and to "build the business model" for first the U.S. and then the other regions. Building the business model consisted of determining the parameters of the system, the products/services to include in the system, etc. It was a complicated process due to the highly parameterized nature of the package. A development team was also formed to help interface the package with existing systems and to help customize the package through report generation tools and hooks to external executables.

According to the U.S. Revenue Operations representative of the team, it was determined that the *core* functionality of the system would be modeled at the headquarters and the regions would be responsible for doing *local* tailoring. However, the company had problems "in pulling all the requirements and the organizations together in the international community." The representative of International Air Freight operations underlines some of the difficulties of global development:

> "The main problem in working with the regions is (the decision of) when to bring them in. If it is too soon, they complain that we are wasting their time. If it is too late, they complain that we have already decided what we are going to do so why ask them now. (Due to their limited resources,) they have difficulty in providing dedicated support for the project."

Currently, GAR has been implemented in the U.S. and it is being used for air freight and special non-transportation receivables. The implementation in other regions was stopped and the package did not replace the two existing major receivable systems. One of the primary reasons for not being able to replace these two systems is that not all the enhancements to the package were developed. The most commonly voiced explanation for this discrepancy in the realization of the enhancements was that the required enhancements were relatively large and the vendor had limited resources, and the enhancements were not necessarily requested or wanted by other customers of the vendor. So the development and especially the maintenance of those enhancements would be very costly to them. In addition, the managing director of IT stressed another reason for the outcome:

> "During the evaluation of packages we did not demand international representation. It was voluntary for regions to participate and we informed them about the progress but that is not enough."

Case 3: Logistics and Warehousing System (LWS)

Logistics and Warehousing System (LWS) is an information system to support the warehousing needs of the customers of MTC. MTC provides not only warehouses for its customers but also call centers to handle end customers' orders. End customers can choose carriers other than MTC. LWS supports the order entry and inventory accounting processes. The system also allows batch order entry through EDI. LWS runs on two Tandem machines in production and another Tandem machine is used for development; all machines are located in the U.S. The system is batch oriented; even the orders entered on-line are accumulated and processed as batches. The front-end of LWS is written in SCOBOL (screen COBOL) and the back end is written in COBOL85. A relational database, NSQL, is used.

The motivation for LWS was primarily strategic. It was expected that expansion into supply chain management would increase revenues due to the new line of business as well as increase the volume of existing transportation by attracting new customers with a "one-stop-shop" solution for their logistics needs. Thus, supporting electronic commerce was a key part of this initiative. According to the managing director of IT:

"(LWS is) the first attempt of MTC to expand beyond transportation to get into supply chain initiatives."

The origin of the need for a warehousing system goes back to mid 1980s. Then, a system was custom built internally to support warehousing of spare parts for a single customer. As more customers and more requirements were included in the system, it was decided that a package solution, called LWS, would better satisfy these requirements. In 1988, licenses to LWS were bought. Modifications were made to LWS by the vendor in order to satisfy MTC's requirements. In 1990, LWS went out of business; therefore, the source code of the system was acquired and was modified internally. In 1995, it became apparent that LWS could no longer support the business needs and thus, a major upgrade or a new system was needed.

In 1996, some maintenance activities were outsourced to an Offshore Outsoucing Company (OOC), based in Bangalore, India. The most important reason LWS was outsourced, according to the managing director of IT, was that "there was a certain amount of attempt to change what we are doing as a business." In order to enable the change, a new system to replace LWS was being sought. The people that needed to adapt to the change were going to be put to work on the new system. In order to free these resources, LWS was outsourced.

OOC was founded in 1992 and has offices in the U.S., Europe, South East Asia and Japan. The company offers solutions on a wide platform of technologies such as Tandem, mainframe, client server, Internet, object-oriented platforms, etc. OOC has a strong focus on quality; currently it is ISO 9001 and CMM level 4 certified. OOC keeps its costs down by employing a model called Coordinated Off-shore Onsite where majority of the work is carried out off-shore. This model is applied to the maintenance of LWS. A dedicated facility was created in India by OOC for MTC outsourcing tasks only. The network in India used by the OOC group is within the MTC firewall. Two communication lines between the two sites are established to facilitate data and voice transfer. Also, an Internet-based e-mail is used for communication among the project members.

Since the first outsourcing task in 1996, more and more maintenance has gone to OOC. Currently, on site OOC and MTC employees conduct requirements gathering, analysis and design activities. Offshore OOC employees conduct detailed design, coding, and unit testing. Then, back in the U.S., assembly and user acceptance tests are conducted. Both on-site and off-shore facilities share the responsibility of production support; critical and time-sensitive problems are fixed on-site and others, including those that take longer, are fixed in India.

Currently, LWS is in maintenance mode. The changes to the system mostly stem from customer requests and are implemented using an approach similar to the waterfall model. Customers communicate their requests for system enhancements or problems by calling the Help Desk. Help Desk tries to resolve the customer's issues; however, if it cannot, it gets in touch with the BAA (Business Application Advisors) team. Each BAA member is assigned to work with a specific set of customers. Based on the analysis of customer's request, a work request is entered into a system. A board, called Change Management Board (CMB), comprised of managers and the IT managing director evaluates and prioritizes the work requests. Work requests are either rejected or approved for analysis. After approval, cost benefit analysis is conducted and results are presented to CMB. MTC could ask the customer to pay if the enhancement is costly or MTC could choose to finance the work itself. When a work request is authorized, a deadline is also determined.

After the Change Management Board's approval of the change, a request is sent to the software configuration group to check out the code. The work is coordinated with the offshore OOC site. Further analysis, design, assembly and user acceptance testing are done in the U.S.; detailed design, coding, and unit testing are done in India. Fixes and enhancements are loaded to production once a month.

The managing director of IT speaks highly of the outsourcing company. However, he says "there are some cultural differences that have to be kept in mind when dealing with (an offshore outsourcing company). If anything, they have a tendency not to question things." He recommends that staff which interacts with the offshore service provider needs to be educated on cultural differences. He also warns that if you have a weakness in your processes, offshore development magnifies it. However, offshore outsourcing, with a company like OOC, makes maintaining costs and quality achievable. It also provides easy access to skills that are very difficult to find in the U.S.

Case 4: Operations Service Level System (OSL)

Operations Service Level System (OSL) is a system that provides near real time information on the service performance (e.g., timely delivery) of each shipped package. This information enables the analysis of MTC's service to its customers. It also helps identify systematic problems in operations. The system not only provides drill-down capabilities from the corporate level to the individual scan of a package but also provides extensive Intranet based reporting capabilities, such as reporting by date, by product, by type of failure, by route, by customer account number, etc. The system is intended to replace its counterpart on the mainframe. The company has established a service quality index based on different types of service failures and all MTC employees' bonuses are affected by this index.

There were several motivations for the project. The leader of business team of the project summarizes the major motivations as follows:

> *"The idea with this project is that anyone who needs service level information should come to us now. Since the old system could not accommodate all requests from the different departments of the company, some had their own systems. The new system is supposed to be the single point of source for all service level information. Some departments needed information, they needed a query based system and the old system did not have this capability. Using it was difficult too. They had to deal with Focus program tapes and not everybody could do that. Now, anybody can use this new system."*

Some requests could not be satisfied by the old system, e.g., determining the source of service failure at locations that were not either the origin or the destination of shipment and the ability to analyze service levels by customer account. Existing mainframe system did not provide these capabilities due to the changes in the business and changes in the target users. Also the system being 15 years old was reaching its limit of growth and flexibility. The team leader stated that they wanted a system which made it easy to add new products and features as the company was adding and deleting products very frequently. Furthermore, there was a corporate initiative that required moving systems from the mainframe to a client server environment.

Purchasing packaged software for OSL was never seriously considered due to the unique nature of the company's business rules and data. The OSL itself was part of another project, called Service Squared which began in 1995. The main objective of Service Squared was to provide an enhanced version of the mainframe service-level program. Service Squared consisted of two parts: the scan processor and OSL. Scan processor was for gathering raw shipment data and contained the logic to determine the success or failure of a service. Both parts were completely outsourced to a single company. This decision to outsource was based on the fact that there were corporate guidelines for new systems to be client-server based and the company did not have enough experience in building a system with such high performance. However, the outsourcing effort was not very successful. The managing director explains:

> *"The system was developed in a remote location to MTC. We are in a dynamic environment and we need to develop them on site. Dynamics of MTC change rapidly. This group was detached from MTC and stayed isolated... If you cannot work with them face to face, the project can lose focus and not stay current with the business demand. I am not saying that*

you cannot develop systems offsite but you need to make sure that a lot of people are moving back and forth. We need MTC people "living" with the service provider company. In every outsourced project that I am aware of which is about half a dozen, the ones that were successful worked with MTC on-site."

The managing director added that the service provider had problems due to its rapid growth. One of the specific problems encountered was that the two components of the system (the scan processor and OSL) were designed and built to be highly integrated which reduced flexibility. Another reason for redesign was performance related technical problems due to the hardware platform. The project leader of OSL also argues that MTC was not ready to take over the system from the vendor since tremendous amount of training would be required. She added that technical requirements were not well defined due to MTC's inexperience with client server and object-oriented technology and due to inadequate requirements gathering on the vendor's side.

In December 1997, the systems were redesigned and the components decoupled from each other. Also, the project scope got bigger considerably to re-engineer the way the shipment information is processed. This new project, called Collection, is "a collection of infrastructure projects that support down-line shipment management applications." Collection is aimed to be the only source of shipment information for the entire corporation.

The redesign of the system and other phases of development were conducted centrally at one of the sites of MTC in the U.S. Some of the requirements were gathered from the existing mainframe system through code diving. In addition, a central committee, located at another site in the U.S., was formed to gather requirements as well. This committee consisted of representatives from many departments including operations, sales, legal, and international. The international business representative coordinated with the subject matter experts from the various regions. During the development process, this committee and the development team worked very closely. The designs of the screens were presented to users for their approval and user acceptance tests were conducted after development. A prototype of the system was built and benchmarked for performance since performance was a major concern and was one of the shortcomings of the outsourced system. Further, tests parallel to the existing mainframe system were conducted to ensure appropriate data handling.

The development of OSL is complete and it was in "soft-rollout" since June 1999. During soft-rollout, the system is to be used for training. It was expected to be fully rolled out and completely replace the existing mainframe system by September 1999.

DISCUSSION

There are thirty two salient findings from these case studies (Akmanligil and Palvia, 2004), as shown in Table 1; each finding is also numbered in this section. Some of these findings may be considered tentative and will benefit from further verification in future research.

Packaged Software

Purchasing packaged software was one of the first development strategy examined in all projects. Cost effectiveness, achieved through economies of scale by the vendor, is the major underlying reason for acquiring them (1). There was a consensus that packaged software is cheaper than all other alternatives and maintenance costs are perceived to be less with them (2). They are also faster to implement (especially when unmodified) (3).

The commonality of the requirements across the organization seemed to be a prerequisite for packaged software (4). Nevertheless, it is practically impossible to find packages that meet all of the requirements of a company. To be successful in using a packaged software strategy, change and expectation management often becomes crucial.

Another option is to ask the vendor to modify the software. However, this generally involves high cost (5). The existence of enhancements not incorporated in the standard product would also decrease the level of support provided by the vendor and require additional contract maintenance (6).

1	Cost effectiveness is the major reason for acquiring packaged software.
2	Packaged software is cheaper than other alternatives and maintenance costs are less.
3	Packaged software is faster to implement.
4	The commonality of requirements across the organization is a prerequisite for packaged software.
5	The cost of modifying packaged software is high.
6	Enhancements not incorporated in the standard package decrease the level of support provided by the vendor and require additional contract maintenance
7	Management frustration with the IT department is one reason for outsourcing
8	The rise in outsourcing is fueled by its increasing popularity in the business world
9	Outsourcing is chosen if there is no internal access to required skills in new technologies
10	Frequently changes in requirements and services cause major problems with outsourcing
11	Parallel development is selected when the region starting the project does not have adequate resources to complete it
12	Co-development or parallel development is difficult when there is lack of accountability.
13	Co-development is complicated by cultural differences.
14	Differences in time and development methodologies add difficulties to co-development.
15	Core vs. local development is able to clearly separate the responsibilities of the various regions.
16	Core vs. local development leads to less coupling and expedited development.
17	The difference in development methodologies among regions require loose coupling.
18	The core of the system is much larger than the local parts.
19	Determining what is core what is local is difficult.
20	Some regions do not have resources for local tailoring.
21	Central development is done when the regions do not have adequate resources themselves.
22	Requirements have to be relatively uniform across the regions for central development.
23	Central development leads in face-to-face communication, improved team effectiveness and increased collaboration among the team members.
24	The involvement of the vendor increases the probability of success and expedites its implementation
25	Joint development with the vendor provides access to resources not available internally.
26	Joint development with the vendor faces difficulties in the assignment of accountability.
27	Joint development with the vendor is costly.
28	High cost and unavailability of regional resources are major obstacles to utilizing the multinational design team.
29	It is difficult to find packaged software for large-scale multi-country global projects.
30	Best in firm application is difficult to find for complex and large-scale global systems.
31	Global organizations may need multiple strategies for system development.
32	Global organizations may have to dynamically readjust the development strategy.

Table 1. Findings in Global IS Development

Outsourcing

When packaged software is not an option, custom building is the only choice, involving a software vendors or in-house effort. Increasing management frustration with the IT department provides one reason for the rise of outsourcing (7). Another explanation of the increase in outsourcing is its increasing popularity in the business world (8).

OSL management chose outsourcing over internal development because they did not have access to required skills in new technologies (9). In cases where system development is outsourced but maintenance is not, it is crucial that the customer understands the design and code developed by the vendor.

Requirements gathering and preparing the outsourcing agreement are important challenges. The system developed by a vendor does not generally allow easy addition and deletion of services and does not have the performance required to support large transaction volumes. Since MTC frequently added, changed, and deleted services, both of these drawbacks were major problems with outsourcing (10).

Parallel Development

Parallel development strategy is often selected because the region that starts the project does not have enough resources to complete it (11). One of the major reasons that a co-development attempt is fruitless is lack of accountability (12). According to the technical lead of one of the projects:

> "... You really need to have one person that would be the sponsor and the delegator... We had our own little teams and there wasn't one person running both teams, saying "you guys are going to do this and you guys are going to do this...""

Problems of accountability were exacerbated when complete responsibility of developing the system was taken from the U.K. team and the reasons given were not convincing. The resentment not only created a negative working environment but also the U.K. to shift their priority to other tasks. Further complicating the communications issue were cultural differences (13). It was suggested that the differences in time and development methodologies contributed to the frustration (14).

Core *versus* Local Development

After parallel development, GCS management decided to implement a Core versus Local strategy. The team manager argued that it separated the responsibilities of the regions more distinctly and clearly (15). Less coupling was later expected to expedite development, since there would be less need for communication (16). This was expected to decrease cost of coordination. The difference in development methodologies was another reason that loose coupling was welcomed (17).

The managers also considered using core versus local strategy. The core part of the system was expected to be much larger than the local parts (18). However, determining what is core what is local is not always easy (19) and sometimes regions do not have resources for local tailoring (20).

Central Development

MTC had a history of developing systems centrally, because regions did not have adequate resources to build systems (21). Also some requirements were relatively uniform across the international regions; thus, this strategy was appropriate (22). The preferred strategy of some project members was single site development because they believed that face-to-face communication improved the effectiveness of the team and increased collaboration among team members (23).

Joint Development with Vendor

Some systems used Joint Development with Vendor Strategy. GAR is a package solution and management of the project involved the package vendor to increase the probability of success and to expedite its implementation (24). It allowed access to additional resources not available internally (25). Since the vendor knew the product very well, it could help smooth the transition to the new system by providing product expertise, training users and developers, and helping develop custom reports and software exits.

Joint development with vendors was found to be relatively challenging due to difficulties in the assignment of accountability (26). Large amount of time was wasted in determining whether the defects in production software were caused by vendors or the host company. Another disadvantage of this strategy is its cost (27).

Multinational Design Team (MDT), Unmodified Packaged software Acquisition (UP), and Best-in-firm Software Adoption (BIF)

Cost and availability of regional resources were major obstacles to utilize the MDT strategy (28). Getting resources away from their daily jobs for an extended period of time is a challenge and a cause for high turnover. Based on the projects, it is unlikely that packaged software would be available or can be used, as is, for large-scale multi-country global projects (29).

None of the cases had systems in place that would meet the needs of the entire worldwide operations. In some cases, a BIF application provided the starting point for a global application. Even when processes were similar, there were still major differences. Thus it appears that BIF is not a viable strategy for the development of complex and large-scale global systems (30).

Some Overall Observations

Depending on its complexity, global organizations may need multiple strategies for system development (31). Different strategies may be suitable for different phases of the life cycle of the same project. Also strategy selection is not necessarily a single static decision made at a single point in time. Organizations may need to continually reevaluate their resources and problems, and may have to dynamically readjust the development strategy (32).

CONCLUSIONS

Classifying global system development projects as simply larger versions of their domestic counterparts is an oversimplification. They are huge and complex, involving issues from technical to behavioral. Their degree of difficulty seems to multiply with size. Delays and budget overruns are commonplace. Nine strategies for developing GIS were identified in the chapter. These strategies represent major ways of conducting development and distributing work between internal and external organizational entities. We are certain that variations and extensions to these strategies are possible and practiced in global firms.

A guiding framework was developed representing the underlying factors that may affect the choice of a strategy. The framework provided the backdrop for four qualitative studies that provided contextual results about development strategies used in global organizations. Thirty two findings were explicated from the case studies. Overall, no single strategy stands out as the dominant approach for global system development. Instead, different strategies are used by organizations in various combinations throughout the development cycle. Various factors need to be considered in strategy selection and one size does not fit all. The findings of the chapter should be useful to practicing global IS managers in three areas: the types of system development strategies that are available, the contextual factors that need to be considered, and the selection of appropriate strategies.

MINICASE

The GAA-IAP System

Get Away Airlines (GAA) is a global airline company based in USA and is a major player. The company employs around 90,000 people and its revenues exceed 17 billion dollars. GAA has structured its operations into four regions: Atlantic, South Pacific, North Pacific, and Latin America. Most of the company's processes are standardized and are created and controlled by the headquarters.

The Information Systems Division of the company provides IT services to internal customers. Systems development is carried out at four sites in the United States. Each country has its own systems support employees that help maintain local computer and communications equipment. All global information systems of the company are in English and have no local customizations.

The International Accounting Project (IAP) was an important systems project, it's mission being "to establish new international business processes with supporting automation in all on-line countries, regional accounting centers, and the world headquarters." The project will cover 28 countries, and will reorganize, reengineer, and automate financial reporting, accounts payable, accounts receivable, and invoicing processes. The regional accounting centers are created by this project as part of the reorganizing efforts. Originally, a separate copy of the system was going to be implemented in each country. However, the reengineering team, composed of international as well as domestic users, decided to create regional accounting clusters to improve control over the company's accounting data. These accounting centers, also called clusters, will be under the control of the Finance division as opposed to the International division. Finally, another objective of the project was to automate the accounting processes.

The system is the company's first global system that has local modifications. Existing global systems support the operations of the company that are standard in nature such as reservations, flight scheduling, aircraft maintenance scheduling, and check-in. In addition to reengineering, reorganizing, and automating of accounting processes, the IAP's scope includes (1) the installation of the hardware and software in the clusters and 28 countries; (2) developing the training materials and training the users and support personnel on the system and its processes; (3) loading data and verifying the data base; (4) interfacing the clusters with the World Headquarters accounting systems; and (5) making modifications to the system for local requirements.

The business community at GAA was an enthusiastic driver of the system. The initial request for the system was made by the administration/accounting managers of each country. In an annual meeting of administration managers, they made a "plea for automation." The required system was expected to not only have a very quick payback but also to provide much better control while increasing access to it. Improved productivity and reduced personnel costs were expected due to the reengineering and automation of systems. Through improved controls over corporate data, it was expected that cash flow for payables and receivables would improve. The largest percentage of return on investment was expected to come from "sales audits," which is the verification of the fare, taxes, commissions, etc.

One of the development strategies of IAP was package acquisition. The IS project manager says that purchasing packaged software was their first development strategy choice and they did not even seriously consider other alternatives. GAA's accounting processes are mostly common and the trick was to find a generic accounting package one could use internationally and could do some of the unique things that an airline needs.

Furthermore, with a package implementation, it was believed that the implementation could be much faster and much cheaper than custom building the system. They also expected that implementation might cause the business to change to adapt to the software. The project manager warned that with packaged software, you are somewhat at the mercy of the vendor for upgrades and support.

GAA chose to have a "partnership" agreement with the vendor. The vendor would provide consultants for implementation of the system. The inclusion of consultants, in addition to the vendor being partly responsible for success, was expected to expedite implementation due to the experience of the vendor in multi-country implementations and expertise in the software package. Another way GAA planned to increase the stake of the vendor was through a marketing agreement with the vendor for jointly marketing their software to other airlines. With this agreement, GAA also intended to gain some power in convincing the vendor to add some airline-specific functionality to the package if needed.

The project had functional and technical teams, in addition to a project board that was made up of the Vice Presidents of the sponsor departments (Finance, International, and IS). The functional (GL, AP, and AR) teams are responsible for designing the business model. At any time, the project employed 10-12 employees from different countries. This Multinational Design Team was also involved in requirements gathering for the package selection, package evaluation, and country implementations. The international team members came to the US for extended times. GAA provided them with furnished apartments, cars, and a meal allowance. From time to time, they came to the U.S. for specific tasks such as attending a system demonstration or reviewing a specification. On occasion, demonstrations were conducted overseas.

After the team was built, the vendor provided a 21-day, concentrated training to the team members on the three functional components of the package. GAA project team was responsible for providing training to its end users not only on the system but also on the business processes affected by the system.

A major objective of the project team was to build a "Gold Tape" which required business systems review, functional design, business modeling, and system building. Gold Tape constitutes about 80% of the overall solution and is the core of the system applicable in all countries. It includes: chart of accounts, standard reports, and screen changes. After a preliminary gold tape was built, a pilot implementation was conducted in London to test both system functionality and the implementation steps. London was chosen as the pilot site because it was also a cluster; language would not be a problem; and it was relatively close to the Headquarters. Implementation in other sites started after the pilot implementation was complete. The project team had four sub-teams responsible for local implementations so that four to five countries could be implemented at the same time. Every sub-team had a representative from each functional area.

In order to be able to limit the local customizations to the estimated 20%, the team accepted only the requests that were due to local government requirements and those without which the site could not function. Other requests were discouraged due to resource constraints and in order to keep focus. Some examples of the local customizations for a country are government required reporting, reporting required for taxing authorities, value added tax (VAT), format of the checks for local banks, Electronic Funds Transfer format, credit card settlement, and electronic bank statements for bank reconciliations. The biggest difference between local requirements and the gold tape is that some countries required an alternate chart of accounts. Local accounting in countries like Belgium, Argentina, and Italy is such that they cannot use the company chart of accounts for government reporting, so the project team had to use local chart of accounts.

Discussion Questions
1. Identify and discuss the various strategies that were used by GAA for system development.

2. What was the prevailing organizational structure at GAA before the implementation of IAP? What challenges it posed for IAP implementation and how was it itself affected by IAP implementation?
3. Evaluate the effectiveness of the "joint development with vendor" strategy in the context of GAA.
4. What approach was used by GAA in the worldwide implementation of GAA? Investigate other approaches that may exist and evaluate their applicability in the present context.

Condensed from: Akmanligil, Murad. Strategies for Global Information Systems Development: A Critical Analysis. Doctoral Dissertation, The University of Memphis, 2000. The identity of the company and the system are disguised.

KEY TERMS
Best-in-firm software adoption (BIF)
Central development (CD)
Core vs. local development (CL)
Core Competence
Joint development with vendor (JDV)
Modified packaged software acquisition (MP)
Outsourced custom development (OC)
Unmodified packaged software acquisition (UP)

STUDY QUESTIONS
1. What are the major GIS development strategies? Briefly describe three of them.

2. Why is GIS development strategy important to the corporation?

3. What are the different factors that impact the selection of a development strategy?

4. Discuss the impact of project size on development strategy.

5. Investigate the global IS development strategy in a firm in your area using the factors described in this chapter. Are the chapter findings supported in your investigation?

6. What is the impact of GIS development strategy on system development success?

7. What are the factors that influenced the success of the GAR system? Discuss what you would do differently to increase the success of the system.

REFERENCES
Akmanligil, M., and Palvia, P. "Strategies for Global Information Systems Development," *Information and Management*, 42(1), December 2004, pp. 45-59.
Benbya, H. and McKelvey, B. "Toward a Complexity Theory of Information Systems Development," *Information Technology and People*, 19(1), 2006, pg. 12-35

Burn, J. M., and Cheung, H. K. "Information Systems Resources Structure and Management in Multinational Organizations." In Prashant Palvia, Shailendra Palvia, and Edward Roche, eds, *Global Information Technology and Systems Management: Key Issues and Trends.* Nashua: Ivy League Publishing, 1996, pp. 239-322.

Cash, J. F., McFarlan, W., McKenney, J. *Corporate Information Systems Management: The issues facing senior executives.* 1992, 3rd ed. Homewood, IL: Irwin.

Collins, R. W., Kirsch, L. *Crossing Boundaries: The deployment of Global IT Solutions.* Pinnaflex Educational Resources, Inc., 1999.

DeLone, W. H. and McLean, E. R. "The DeLone and McLean Model of Information Systems Success: A Ten Year Update," *Journal of Management Information Systems*, 19(4), Spring 2003, pp.9-30.

Delone, W., and McLean, E. "Information system success: The quest for dependent variable." *Information Systems Research*," 1992, 3(1), pp. 60-95.

DiNardo, G. "Regional banking and credit card processing at Citibank Consumer Banking and its global implications," In Prashant Palvia, Shailendra Palvia, and Edward Roche, eds, *Global Information Technology and Systems Management: Key Issues and Trends.* Nashua: Ivy League Publishing, 1996, pp. 577-591.

Doherty, N. F., and King, M. "An investigation of the factors affecting the successful treatment of organizational issues in systems development projects," *European Journal of Information Systems.* Dec 2001. 10(3), pp. 3-50.

Emmerson, A. "BT and Pinacl start stacking the odds," *Communications International*, 1998, 25(1), pp. 22-23.

Ewusi-Mensah, K. "Critical issues in abandoned IS development Projects," *Communications of the ACM*, September 1997, 40(9), pp. 74-80. .

Galbraith, J. R. "Organization Design: An Information Processing View," in Litterer, J.A. (Ed.), *Organizations: Structure and Behaviour*, 1980, 3rd ed., John Wiley & Sons, New York, NY, pp. 530-48.

Ghoshal, S., and Nohria, N. 1993. "Horses for courses: Organizational forms for multinational corporations," *Sloan Management Review*, 1993, 34(2), pp. 23-35.

Harland, C., Knight, L., Lamming, R., and Walker, H. "Outsourcing: Assessing the risks and benefits for organizations, sectors and nations," *International Journal of Operations and Production Management.* 2005, 25(9), pp. 831-850.

Hofstede, G. *Culture's consequences: International differences in work-related values.* CA: Sage, 1980.

Ives, B., and Jarvenpaa, S. "Applications of global information technology: Key issues for management," *MIS Quarterly*, 15(1), 1991, pp. 33-49.

Janz, B. D., Vitalari, N. P., and Wetherbe, J. C. "Emerging best practices in global systems development," in Prashant Palvia, Shailendra Palvia, and Edward Roche, eds, *Global Information Technology and Electronic Commerce*, Marietta, GA: Ivy League Publishing. 2002, pp. 332-355.

Karimi, J., and Konsynski, B. "Globalization and information management strategies," *Journal of Management Information Systems*, 7(4), Spring 1991, pp. 7-26.

King, W. R . "Ensuring ERP Implementation Success," *Information Systems Management*, Summer 2005a, 22(3); pg. 83-84

King, W. R. "Outsourcing and Offshoring: The New IS Paradigm?," *Journal of Global Information Technology Management*, April 2005b, 8(2), pp. 1-4.

Lacity M, and Hirschheim R. *Outsourcing - Myths, Metaphors and Realities*, John Wiley, 1993.

Lehmann, H. "The Design of Information Systems for the International Firm: A Grounded Theory of Some Critical Issues," in Prashant Palvia, Shailendra Palvia, and Edward Roche, eds, *Global Information Technology and Electronic Commerce*, Marietta, GA: Ivy League Publishing. 2002, pp. 370-392.

McFarlan, W. 1996. "Issues in global outsourcing." In Prashant Palvia, Shailendra Palvia, and Edward Roche, eds, *Global Information Technology and Systems Management: Key Issues and Trends.* Nashua: Ivy League Publishing. 1996, pp. 352-364.

Meadows, C. J. "Globalizing software development." *Journal of Global Information Management,* 1996, 4(1).

Nelson, P., Richmond, W., and Seidmann, A.. "Two dimensions of software acquisition," *Communications of the ACM,* 39, 7, 1996, pp. 29-35.

Palvia, S., and Lee, K.. 1996. "Developing and implementing global IS: Lessons from Seagate Technology," in Prashant Palvia, Shailendra Palvia, and Edward Roche, eds, *Global Information Technology and Systems Management: Key Issues and Trends.* Nashua: Ivy League Publishing, 1996, pp. 559-576.

Ragowsky, A., and Stern, M. "How to select application software?," *Journal of Systems Management,* 46(5), Sept-Oct 1995, pp 50-54.

Rao, H. R., Nam, K, and Chaudhury, A. "Information systems outsourcing," *Communications of the ACM,* 39(7), 1996, pp. 27-28.

Robey, D., and Rodriquez-Diaz, A."The organizational and cultural context of systems implementation: Case experience from Latin America," *Information and Management,* 17, 1989, pp. 229-239.

Shore, B. "Cultural Asymmetries between Headquarters and Foreign Subsidiaries and their Consequence on the Integrative Role of Information Technology," in Prashant Palvia, Shailendra Palvia, and Edward Roche, eds, *Global Information Technology and Electronic Commerce,* Marietta, GA: Ivy League Publishing. 2002, pp. 161-177.

Softwaremag.com. *Standish: Project Success Rates Improved Over 10 Years.* Jan 15, 2004.

Yin, R. K. *Case Study Research: Design and Methods,* Second Edition. Sage Publications, Inc. Applied Social Research Methods Series, 1994.

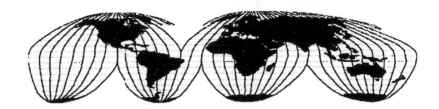

Global Information Systems Development: Best Practices[1]

Brian D. Janz
The University of Memphis, USA

Nicholas P. Vitalari
Energant, Inc., USA

James C.Wetherbe
Texas Tech University, USA

CHAPTER SUMMARY

With companies employing global structures to gain competitive advantages and ensure profitability, globalization of business is accelerating at a phenomenal rate. The primary objectives of this chapter are to explore the implications for companies "going global" and to identify the information technology (IT) infrastructure required to support global operations. The chapter draws upon previous work on global management and the role of IT in global enterprise. Five operational tactics, accompanied by case examples, for implementing the predominant IT strategy are also presented. The chapter concludes with an extensive look at five strategies for successful global applications development, and the ever-changing role information systems (IS) and global strategies play in that context.

INTRODUCTION

Global business is accelerating at a phenomenal rate. Since 1950, world trade has proliferated over 700%, while world GDP has grown 400%. Rarely a week goes by where the balance of trade between the major countries of the world (frequently, the U.S.A. and China) is not a news item. Exports are key to that growth, with most countries emphasizing exports and the balance of trade as a means and measure of economic growth and national vitality. When domestic markets may be saturated or limited, global markets often offer opportunities for profits and competitive advantage.

Companies are employing global structures to gain competitive advantages and ensure profitability. Some of the realized or expected economic benefits of globalization include:

---

[1] Much of this chapter is an outgrowth of previous research as discussed in Janz, Vitalari, and Wetherbe (2002).

- Economies of scale due to expanded markets for standardized products;
- Ability to locate value chain activities in locations offering strategic advantages, e.g., low cost labor, skilled workers, financial markets, physical infrastructure, customer proximity; and
- Diversification of demand in multiple markets stabilizing overall firm performance in the face of economic fluctuations in individual markets.

In this chapter, we explore the implications of companies "going global" and particularly the implications of accelerating improvements in information technology (IT), including the IT infrastructure required to support global operations. Using Bartlett and Ghoshal's model (1989) as the foundation, we examine four globalization structures employed by companies and Konsynski and Karimi's (1993) four approaches for aligning global structures with information management strategies. A discussion of the impact of companies' globalization on their industries and the ramifications for IT follows. The focus of the next section is the evolving IT strategy, examining five tactics for implementing the transnational strategy supported by case examples. Five strategies for success in global applications development follow. The chapter concludes with a look at the changing role of IT in future globalization efforts.

GOING GLOBAL: COMPETING IN THE INTERNATIONAL MARKETPLACE

What does the often-used phrase *going global* really mean and why is it of interest from an information technology perspective? From a company perspective, going global means operating as a single, unified company worldwide, balancing resources across the entire organization to implement a structure to compete with other firms, and maximizing total customer value. Operating as a global company entails different structures due to local, regional, national and worldwide economic, political, and social conditions. These structures in turn determine a firm's management control systems, operations, and sales. Ultimately they affect the development, deployment, and maintenance of information systems and the related IT infrastructure.

The role of IT in a globally operating company is a force for dissolving boundaries – reducing time and distance, bridging cultural and language barriers, effectively and efficiently addressing differences in governmental and regulatory policy, and responding to a diverse customer set from around the world. IT enables an organization to operate as if time and distance did not exist. The Internet for example, blurs the boundaries of time and space and is an example of global infrastructure that greatly enhances the transport, storage, and retrieval of information and ultimately serves as the conduit of electronic commerce. In reality, IT is an essential component for enabling firms to globalize and is critical to their success. Furthermore, IT is pivotal to the operation of the global marketplace itself. For example, shipping ports and airports can now provide in-bound ships and aircraft with customs clearances and other services based on digital manifestos that are accessible online, while the ship or aircraft are in route. Future technologies will continue to evolve and further support new and more streamlined forms of global trading and transaction processing.

Pressures Driving Localization

The global competitive landscape is also defined by many local factors. While many managers realize that local cultures and circumstances play a role in global competition, few realize the subtleties. For example, many managers realize the difference between doing business in Singapore versus France, but fail to recognize the importance from a global standpoint of conducting business in the Midwest region versus the Southwest region of the United States. Cultural and local subtleties exist within presumably homogeneous cultures. The astute global firm incorporates such features into their strategies. The following factors are some of the pressures driving localization:

- Local languages
- Local cultures
- Local business practices
- Local taste
- Local competitors
- Proximity to local customer
- National and regional protectionism
- Regulations and tariffs
- Labor unions
- Transportation
- Quality of local labor.

Evaluating these pressures is most useful from the perspective of a particular industry by creating an industry overlay for the above list. For example, create an overlay using the consumer products industry, for example, the classic soap consumer industry. Which localization pressures from the list above would be pertinent? The first might be local competitors, with transportation second, then local taste. If a company is going to manufacture soap, local labor, proximity to the customer, labor unions, local business practices, cultures, and language all become important. The machine tools industry is another interesting example. Both Japan and Taiwan have been very successful bringing machine tools into North America. Regulations and tariffs on machine tools, for instance, are much less critical than they would be for the insurance or consumer products industries. The same is true for local taste, e.g., a paper mill is a paper mill, a bulldozer is a bulldozer, etc. Thus, acting local is different depending on the industry and there are important ramifications from an information technology standpoint.

Status of Globalization

The status of globalization in different parts of the world depends on the indigenous situation in each area, e.g., the general business climate, IT infrastructure, market characteristics, boundaries, or obstacles. In North America for example, micro-economies (i.e., the economic conditions and factors of a particular region such as the Midwest, the Research Triangle of North Carolina, the Silicon Valley of California) are dominating the landscape of economic activity. In Europe, strong ethnic identities are a major factor requiring consideration during globalization. The evolving infrastructures in India, Latin America, and China impact companies' globalization efforts in those regions. In all of these and other similar areas of the world, *leapfrog computing* – rejecting proven, approaches that have evolved over time (e.g., circuit-switched land-based analog telecommunication infrastructures; centralized, mainframe topologies, etc.) and instead employing state-of-the art computing platforms and practices (e.g., packet-switched, wireless, digital telecommunications, web-based computing, etc.) provides its own set of challenges to companies with more traditional approaches. These factors are all pertinent to determining the best global structure to use when entering a new region or market, or when evaluating whether a certain approach is working or not working effectively.

GLOBAL STRUCTURES MODEL

In 1989, Christopher Bartlett and Sumantra Ghoshal formulated a powerful framework to view global organizational structures based on observations in the marketplace. The model postulates that global firms move from a traditional, divisional organization based on a domestic model of business, to a more elaborate and globally compatible organizational structure as they gain experience and success in global markets. They argued that, in general, a global firm can be characterized into four strategic structures: 1) multinational, 2) global, 3) international, and 4) transnational (see Figure 1).

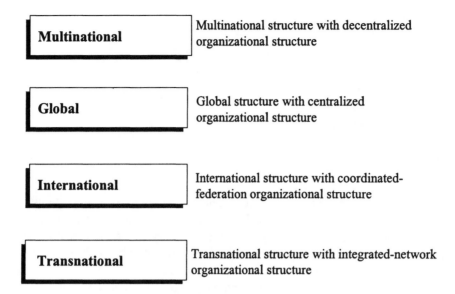

Figure 1: Global Business Structures Model

Multinational Structure with Decentralized Organizational Structure

In the globalization process, companies employing this structure have a headquarters base and operating units in various countries or markets. This structure might also be described as the classic, domestically controlled model that is really just an extension of a divisionalized organization. There is little difference whether the company is headquartered in the U.K., Germany, or China – the respective domestic business units tend to control their portion of the global operation. Organizationally, there are fairly loose controls with strategic decisions made remotely. Inward flowing arrows could represent the lines of communication from the remote business units to headquarters indicating that the remote sites funnel large quantities of information into headquarters. Strong financial reporting flow is a primary characteristic of the multinational structure. In fact, that is how control is exercised. Redundancy is a primary disadvantage because each site is performing its own activities. From an IT perspective, local autonomy creates difficulty for dissolving cross-functional boundaries, or developing compatible technology platforms that can be easily integrated.

Global Structure with Centralized Organizational Structure

Used frequently by those firms that ventured early into going global, this structure involves a centralized organization with a global management perspective. The global structure involves a strong headquarters base and operating units in various countries or markets. The global structure presumes that headquarters knows best what is useful and valuable at distributed sites and that headquarters knows what is happening remotely across many boundaries – e.g., different cultures or methods of operating – since all communication is outward from headquarters where all strategic decisions are made. This structure is difficult to maintain and keep stable. Unilateral information flow (from the headquarters location to the remote sites) allows little room for remote input. Thus site differences and local advantages are ignored operationally and, as a result, the information systems that are developed and used often do not incorporate the business requirements of the remote locations.

International Structure with Coordinated-Federation Organizational Structure

The international structure is a more contemporary approach that combines an international management perspective with an organization of coordinated federations, i.e., local units that have a federated relationship with each other. Assets and responsibilities are decentralized to the federations.

Formal control systems exist, but the federations are more likely to work together for the good of their common customers with headquarters supporting and encouraging such an approach. However, with assets and responsibilities decentralized, coordination and sharing of information or information systems between units are difficult.

Transnational Structure with Coordinated-Federation Organizational Structure

The transnational structure is the most contemporary approach and has the most promise for the future. With this structure, management has an international perspective in which the organization structure is a web-like, integrated network. Headquarters is highly involved in the complexities of both coordination activities across locations and the overall strategic decision processes. Capabilities, resources, and decision making are distributed to the remote sites where the resources are needed and the decisions are made. There are heavy flows of materials, people, information, and technology. Consequently, internal labor and resource markets develop, high coordination costs are incurred, and an absolute dependence on information systems and technology is created.

Bartlett and Ghoshal's framework is germane to our analysis for several reasons. First, the framework illustrates that as firms become more sophisticated, the organizational model they most closely resemble may evolve. For example, a firm may move to a more loosely-coupled, market-coordinated structure with hopes of being more responsive to global markets. This evolution reflects the need for more diversity in global operations and more flexible responsiveness to local market demands. Fortunately, advances in information technologies provide the capacity to handle greater diversity in operations through integrated systems, collaboration technologies (email, workflow management, etc.), intranets and extranets, and supply chain management systems. Given these technology developments, a growing number of researchers in organization theory and the global structure of firms have argued that information technology affects the structure of the firm (see Miles and Snow, 1994; Venkatesh and Vitalari, 1992; and Ives and Jarvenpaa, 1991). King and Sethi (2001) have extended this notion by conducting empirical research that suggests that the transnational strategy will be reflected in the design of an organization's information systems.

Second, as firms move to the international and transnational models, the control model changes by becoming more decentralized, permitting more local autonomy and local decision rights, but with the attendant costs of increased complexity and the need for increased coordination systems. For example, Lai (2001) has found that the key concerns of technical and non-technical managers of international information systems (IIS) center around the complexity of technology infrastructure issues as opposed to more general management or planning issues.

Third, although the transnational form is the most globally sophisticated, all forms are found at work today and have varying levels of success. Furthermore, since the firm structure varies, particularly around control and coordination, it is likely that the underlying information systems strategies and infrastructure will vary according to each of the four structures.

Jarvenpaa and Ives (1993) examined empirically whether or not information technology structures varied according to Bartlett and Ghoshal's categories and found some support. Alavi and Young (1992) have also postulated similar relationships between firm structure and information technology use. We would argue that, although the empirical data may be only suggestive at this point, as networks and information technology become pervasive throughout the world, the IT infrastructure will allow firms greater flexibility to operate in a manner best suited to their industry, customers, and global strategy.

ALIGNING GLOBAL STRUCTURES AND INFORMATION STRATEGIES

In 1993, Benn Konsynski and Jahangir Karimi took Bartlett and Ghoshal's framework and explored its implications for information systems. Konsynski and Karimi analyzed each of the four structures and proposed four different coordination strategies and the likely IS structure (see Table 1). Since that time, other researchers have also extended the research in this area (e.g., King and Sethi, 2001).

In the first example, the multinational strategy, Konsynski and Karimi contended that socialization is the key coordination control strategy to making this global structure work, i.e., people in the organization must believe this will work to overcome all the other issues working against it. And the correct IS structure is one of decentralization: stand-alone databases and processes, with information funneled back to the headquarters.

In the second example – a business structure characterized by a global centralized federation – centralizing corporate databases and encouraging the use of centrally managed development methodologies, implementation strategies, and support processes are key to achieving the necessary coordination and control. Evidence of this strategy translates to strong central control, and having the authority to mandate common systems. In fact, some research supports this approach as the best way to start going global, and then move into the other dimensions gradually.

Business Structure	Coordination/ Control Strategy	IS structure
Multinational/ decentralized federation	Socialization	Decentralization: Stand-alone Databases and Processes
Global centralized federation	Centralization	Centralization: centralized databases and processes
International and interorganizational / coordinated federation	Formalization	IOS: linked databases and processes
Transnational/ integrated network	Co-opting	Integrated architecture: shared databases and processes

Table 1. Alignment of Global and Information Management Strategies (Source: Adapted from Konsynski and Karimi (1993))

Linking the databases and processes of interorganizational systems (IOS) is the third IS structure, facilitated through formalizing the interaction between organizational units – the federations. Coordination and control is done primarily through formal means, usually from headquarters. Since this is a mixed model, linking together independent systems is probably the best approach from an IS development standpoint.

Finally, an integrated IS architecture with shared databases and processes is essential to aligning the global structures and informational strategies in the transnational model. The approach for accomplishing it is through co-opting and forming alliances.

From an information systems development perspective, the coordination and control strategy is critical to success. For an IS developer in a multinational, decentralized federation, for example, the only way coordination can occur is through socialization of management. That is, individual managers in the various countries or units have to have some sort of common, global vision. Otherwise, for example, if the developer goes to France to create a global system, the people there may be totally uncooperative because they see no need for what is being developed.

To facilitate globalization efforts, IS personnel must identify the coordination and control approaches in their organizations, and then determine how best to leverage them to accomplish having the various organization units share data and information, build common systems, etc. Often, there may be multiple approaches, e.g., some parts of the firm may be highly socialized and believe in the global process, others may be using the formal strategy, while still others are co-opting. The challenge is to find common concerns, common interests, or common values and form alliances accordingly.

For the purpose of this chapter, Konsynski and Karimi's analysis suggests that we should observe different IS strategies and systems in the global marketplace across firms. Both Bartlett and Ghoshal's framework and Konsynski and Karimi's analyses suggest that in the long run, most firms will progress to the transnational model. The move to the transnational model is consistent with broader trends in organization structure and design discussed by Miles and Snow (1994), Drucker (1988), Vitalari (1992), and Lipnak and Stamps (1994), which emphasize the emerging network-orientation of organizational structures.

In the next section, we examine five tactics that characterize the move to the transnational organizational model among global corporations. The five tactics represent the linking of information technology capabilities with business process innovations that enable the more loosely coupled organizational structure indicative of the transnational structure.

IMPLEMENTING THE TRANSNATIONAL MODEL

Figure 2 combines the pressures for localization, the pressures for globalization, and the four structure models, and illustrates the move to the transnational model. The transnational structure is effective when the pressures to globalize and localize are high because a company can maintain global economies and be locally responsive at the same time. Yet, it is also important to note that despite the movement toward the transnational model, some firms may find it useful to operate under other structures.

For example, if the pressures for globalization are medium (low was not used on the global scale because our research revealed there were no industries with a low need to globalize) and pressures for localization are low the multinational structure applies. The global structure works best where there is high pressure for globalization and low pressure for localization (homogeneous products). Where localization is high and the pressures for globalization are medium, the international model seems to fit best. Given the increasing pressures to globalize and localize simultaneously, the transnational model is evolving as the desired structure for companies and IT.

FIVE TACTICS FOR IMPLEMENTING THE TRANSNATIONAL MODEL

Companies have used the five tactics presented in Table 2 to facilitate the implementation of the transnational model. Since these five tactics are most easily understood in the context of the experience of actual companies, the following applicable examples are offered.

Mass Customization

In his book, *Future Perfect* (1987), Stan Davis proposes the idea of product and service customization for an individual on a mass basis as being the ultimate end point of the information age. Since then, similar themes, e.g., Joe Pine's "Segment of One Marketing" (1993) have been offered. Currently, the most common examples of mass customization are found on the Internet and in the telecommunications, mass media, and consumer products industries, where some products and services are tailored for each consumer on the basis of unique needs (see Figure 3). When the concept of mass customization is applied in the global context, the firm looks at local requirements and attempt to customize products to meet those needs.

For example, Amazon.com, the pioneer in Internet-based book selling, recommends individually customized reading recommendations to customers based on past purchase histories. The apparel industry is now finding companies enter the electronic commerce marketplace offering clothes with "the perfect fit" and virtual runway models when online customers enter their body measurements. In the publishing industry, selective binding, wherein specialized advertising inserts

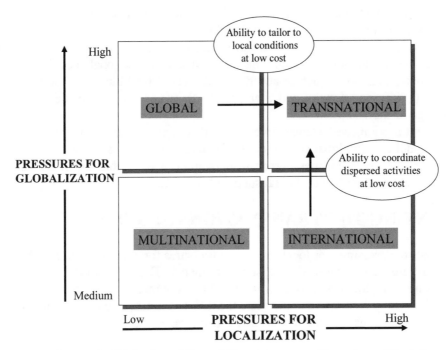

Figure 2: Global and Local Pressures vs. Structure Models

1	Mass Customization(synergies through global research and development)
2	Global Supply Chain Management
3	Global Business Intelligence and Information Resource Management
4	Global Customer Service
5	Global Alliances

Table 2. Five Transnational Implementation Tactics

or regional stories are inserted into the mass publication, is commonplace. Selective binding allows almost all national and international media firms to combine unique content of interest to local settings with common or reusable content that has mass appeal. Publications such as Time, USA Today, The Wall Street Journal, and U.S. News and World Report, selectively bind inserts, advertisements, and stories to fit regional needs. USA Today for instance, performs selective binding on a centralized basis for the most part. Then, using satellite-broadcasting technology sends different versions of the newspaper all over the U.S.A., appealing to local readership, cultural tastes, micro-economies, and other regional factors. Selective binding technology is also seen in the creation of mail order catalogs based on the examination of regional and individual consumer regional conditions. Time-Warner envisions using customer profiles, proprietary customer data warehouses, and regional information to develop customized television programming to the individual cable television consumer. With the advent of telephone caller-ID technologies, the capability to further refine the service that accompanies these products is expected to progress rapidly. For example, by knowing the origin of the phone call through caller-ID, region-specific pay-per-view programming can be ordered over the telephone and can then be delivered directly to the television without the need for human intervention.

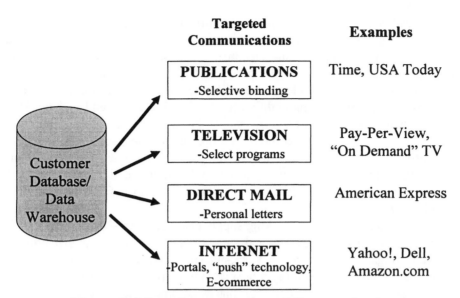

Figure 3: Mass Customization of Communications

The common denominator in the mass communication strategy is the use of market information drawn from multiple sources that indicate mass, regional and individual trends, preferences, and buying behavior. This information is collected by global firms in massive data warehouses, is analyzed, and is then employed to form custom responses to individual and regional market needs around the world.

Table 3 provides an example of the extremes that mass customization can take, as represented by Yahoo!, Inc. This Internet portal, developed by two Stanford graduate students in 1994, is the most visited website on the Internet today. The global network of Yahoo! websites received 3.4 billion page views per day on average (as of October 2005). Through a highly customizable website (My.Yahoo), visitors can specify the type of news headlines they are interested in viewing (world, business, science, etc.), the sports teams they are interested in following, the weather of specific cities they would like to track, the performance of personal investments they have made, the weight they have lost, to the television shows they watch. In addition, with associated popular websites like Yahoo! Mail and Yahoo! Groups, Yahoo! is well positioned to achieve their mission of being "the most essential global Internet service for consumers and businesses[2]."

TACTIC	MASS CUSTOMIZATION
CASE EXAMPLE	Yahoo!, Inc.'s web offerings: My.Yahoo!, Yahoo! Mail, Yahoo! Groups, etc.
IT ENVIRONMENT	Global databases, real-time web content management, globally dispersed R&D teams
OBJECTIVES	To "be the most essential global Internet service for consumers and businesses"
COMMENTS	Customers have the ability to completely tailor the web content that is presented to them through the Yahoo! portal, including news, sports headlines and scores, health information, movie releases, personal financial portfolio tracking, and TV listings.

Table 3: Mass Customization

---

[2] http://docs.yahoo.com/info/values/ as of November 9, 2006.

Global Supply Chain Management

While mass communication seeks to meet customer requirements on a global basis, the global supply chain management strategy seeks to optimize manufacturing cycle times and costs across an organization's supply chain of suppliers and customers. Global sourcing and logistics attempts to obtain materials from vendors as close to the production site as possible and to establish global sourcing agreements with materials vendors who will guarantee material consistency and delivery schedules on a global basis. One growing addition to the global sourcing and logistics strategy is to create joint agreements to co-locate warehouse, manufacturing, and logistics facilities at optimized regional locations. Such ventures, which combine multiple companies, are feasible due to Internet-EDI over virtual private networks (VPNs), highly integrated enterprise resource planning (ERP) systems within organizations, as well as interorganizational systems such as extended ERP systems. Dell Computer Corp. is widely credited with possessing one of the most efficient and effective supply chains in the world today.

As discussed in Table 4, by tightly linking supply chain partners – especially suppliers – with their corporate systems, Dell has created a global supply chain system that is synchronized around product related events, e.g., customer orders, stock-out situations, invoices, shipments initiated or delivered, etc. With their global customer-direct business model (through either their direct telephone number or global websites), every time a customer places an order – where each order is a uniquely customized computer system or basket of systems and peripherals – the relevant order information is transmitted throughout the supply chain so that updates can be made to accounts receivable, quantities on hand, replenishment requirements from suppliers, shipping requirements to shippers, etc. As a result of this automated system, Dell has not only created an *effective* system (customers get exactly what they want, when and where they want it), but also an *efficient* system (Dell provides their products and services at the lowest cost possible). In addition, Dell enjoys a negative cash conversion – receiving payments on computers sold before they must pay for the raw materials required to manufacture the computers – giving them an added revenue stream in the form of interest earned on customers' payments.

TACTIC	GLOBAL SUPPLY CHAIN MANAGEMENT
CASE EXAMPLE	Dell, Inc.
IT ENVIRONMENT	Global databases, world-wide reach through its website and telephone system, integrated systems throughout the supply chain
OBJECTIVES	➢ JIT inventory and production through integrated systems and collocated business partners ➢ Economies of scale in all aspects of manufacturing, pricing, logistics, and supply chain management ➢ Customer direct model to both businesses and consumer ➢ Negative cash conversion cycle
COMMENTS	By tightly linking supply chain partners with their corporate systems, Dell has the capability to allow every customer to uniquely configure its computer systems (which are manufactured in locations around the world, depending on where the order originates from) and to ship directly to customers in a matter of days. What's more, Dell takes payment on computers sold before they must pay for the raw materials – in essence giving them an added revenue stream in the form of interest earned on customers' payments.

Table 4. Global Supply Chain Management

For all supply chain initiatives, it is an awareness of one's place in the supply chain that is critical to success as well as having end-to-end networking and application solutions (e.g., procurement systems, inventory systems, manufacturing systems, materials forecasting systems, etc.) that permit an instantaneous "push" of information to suppliers and customers upstream and downstream whenever supply chain transactions occur anywhere in the chain.

Global Business Intelligence and Information Resource Management

Maintaining the appropriate level of understanding of local and global conditions of the business prior to the advent of computer and communication technology was a daunting, almost impossible task. However, the ability to mount an effective campaign for global business intelligence is now within the reach of most companies. The proliferation of Internet service providers (ISPs), the related growth in the off-the-shelf software, e.g., Microsoft Windows, Internet Explorer or Foxfire, and collaboration software (e.g., Lotus Notes, etc.), de facto industry standards (e.g., the World Wide Web, HTML, XML, TCP/IP, etc.), and the promising potential of tracking and sensing technologies like radio-frequency identification (RFID), enables firms to establish, with relative ease, global intelligence networks with facilities for information collection, interchange, storage, and distribution inside their own company (e.g., intranets) and outside their companies (e.g., extranets). Perhaps the most notable example of the use of emerging technologies can be found within Wal-Mart and its suppliers (Table 5). In 2003, Wal-Mart told its 100 largest suppliers that they needed to have all product cases and pallets destined for Wal-Mart stores labeled with RFID tags by 2005. RFID's superior tracking capability (automatically without manually scanning) and information storage capacity potentially could replace the time-honored barcode (Janz, et al., 2005).

Along with the proliferation of network capabilities has been the concomitant rise in information resources available in local markets throughout the world. With the force of network externalities, the more sites created leads to more users and this in turn leads to more information resources at lower cost. Thus, as the worldwide digital infrastructure develops, the ability to conduct global intelligence cost-effectively and efficiently increases rapidly. For example, most global firms today maintain a collection of local databases assembled from internal and external sources. Many external providers offer customized data and actually develop specialized filters to transmit the information (another example of "push") into a firm's information systems. Often, firms attempt to

TACTIC	GLOBAL BUSINESS INTELLIGENCE AND INFORMATION RESOURCE MANAGEMENT
CASE EXAMPLE	Wal-Mart and its 100 largest suppliers
IT ENVIRONMENT	Global network with contract manufacturers and suppliers transmitting supply chain information and now tracking information provided by RFID tags on cartons and pallets of products
RESULTS	An interorganizational and global system that can track information up and down the supply chain including: ➢ Customer and product forecast data ➢ Order and payment data ➢ Real-time inventory location data and warehouse status
COMMENTS	Wal-Mart's size enabled it to mandate the use of RFID tags on its largest suppliers' products (at the carton and/or pallet level). Armed with this information, Wal-Mart now knows exactly how many cartons of products are in their warehouses, how much inventory is on trucks bound for their warehouses, and how much inventory is residing in supplier warehouses.

Table 5. Global Business Intelligence and Information Resource Management

gather local intelligence on economic indicators, customers, business performance, competitors, and market conditions to make appropriate modifications to business strategies. From an information technology standpoint, the real differentiation among global firms is seen in the degree of seamless integration between the global intelligence activity and internal information sources and decision processes supporting company operations.

Global Customer Service

Major advances in global customer service depend on effective use of information technology. Many global industrial manufacturers depend heavily on suppliers, which can provide a single global view of the customer. Global customer service is now a highly sought after competitive advantage. For example, a global manufacturer expects to know order status, delivery schedules, invoices, outstanding balances, and quantity of business on a global basis. The global manufacturer also expects consistent prices, consistent performance, and consistent quality. The service layer supporting global operations increasingly determines which suppliers are selected and which are avoided. At the basis of global customer operations are global customer databases and/or data warehouses, common customer codes, sales force automation, interorganizational systems and interconnected supplier systems with manufacturer's systems. Typically, these system elements are integrated through the implementation of a customer resource management (CRM) system.

The same trends and conditions apply to other sectors. For example, investment banking and global retail banking success depend on global customer service operations. Customers of all types depend on access to financial markets and resources anywhere, anytime. Similarly, the airline, hospitality, and telecommunications industries require global customer service operations. American Express Corporation, perhaps the preeminent global player in customer service, has offices with a full spectrum of financial and travel services all over the world. Table 6 illustrates some of the services offered by American Express. Although many travel companies and credit card consortia have copied American Express, it still stands out as best practice in global customer service.

TACTIC	GLOBAL CUSTOMER SERVICE
CASE EXAMPLE	American Express
IT ENVIRONMENT	Global network linked from local branches and local merchants to the customer database and medical or legal referrals database
RESULTS	Offers companies faced with the common needs of traveling consumers (e.g., airlines, hotels, car rental, credit card usage, etc.), these customer service solutions: ➢ World-wide access to funds ➢ "Global assist" Hotline ➢ Emergency credit card replacement ➢ 24-hour customer service
COMMENTS	At the height of their operations, American Express was spending about one billion dollars a year on computing because their entire business is the information business. They had an early vision of what travelers would need, implemented it, and deliver it via a global network to airport kiosks and local branches. If someone loses a card, they send the information over the network and reproduce it locally. For cash advances, they comply with the local requirements on branch or non-branch banking. Regardless of the local requirements, they honor every request made of them. That's global customer service!

Table 6. Global Customer Service

Global Alliances

Being able to develop global alliances is perhaps the most important tactic to achieving a transnational structure in that the previous four tactics often depend on the existence of a healthy network of allied organizations. As such, global alliances have become much more common in all industries, with industry participants looking for increased influence and economies of scale. By aligning and sharing key resources and assets, each company benefits in gaining access to new markets or by gaining new skills and competencies.

The airline industry offers several examples of global alliances and illustrates the necessity of information technology to deliver global business objectives. Almost all airlines have formed alliances to gain access to markets, provide new service levels to local customers, and encourage customer loyalty (examples include British Airways and U.S. Air, KLM and Northwest, and American Airlines and Quantas). As mentioned in the discussion on global sourcing, alliances provide an effective way to make use of resources without major investment and ownership. Table 7 illustrates perhaps one of the most unique alliance partnerships in that it is composed entirely of organizations that compete with each other. The International Airlines Technical Pool, or IATP, is an association of airlines from around the world that work together to share expensive aircraft parts, putting these expensive parts around the world to assist associate members wherever they might be and whenever they might need emergency aircraft maintenance (IATP Pionairs, 1995). The IATP story shows that significant benefits can accrue to organizations if they are willing to overcome market challenges, as well as differences of company politics and culture, and nature of origin. Most importantly, such alliances are only feasible due to information technology that can track collections of data about travel routes, fleet distribution, and the location of key aircraft parts.

TACTIC	GLOBAL ALLIANCES
CASE EXAMPLE	The International Airlines Technical Pool (IATP)
IT ENVIRONMENT	Global network connecting a world-wide association of airline and airline-related companies
RESULTS	➢ Coordination of maintenance schedules ➢ Sharing of technical expertise ➢ Pooling and distribution of high-cost aircraft replacement parts
COMMENTS:	In existence for over 50 years, the sheer magnitude of information related to aircraft parts, maintenance, and transfer pricing made IT a critical necessity since the 1960's. A classic, yet very uncommon example of otherwise ruthless competitors joining together for mutual benefit.

Table 7. Global Alliances

Global Tactics Evolution

In the prior paragraphs, we reviewed five implementation tactics as separate approaches. In reality, each of the tactics is utilized in combination. For example, a firm may use global information sources to customer understanding and then, in turn, use that information to establish and monitor a global customer services strategy. A global alliance may be used to take advantage of global sourcing abilities in the alliance. As firm sophistication rises with regard to global operations, one can expect the transnational firm to employ many of the tactics discussed, adding new ones as the global information technology infrastructure progresses.

In addition, a word about the role of virtual teams in systems development is warranted since they often result in any of the tactics described above. This should not come as a surprise; as organizations disperse their IT resources internationally, it is often necessary to bring these resources together in a virtual way (capitalizing on telecommunication's benefits of greatly reduced time and distance). Maintaining high levels of performance in teams that must span time, distance, and culture barriers is not easy. Maintaining adequate levels of trust in these contexts is critical but not easy either (Jarvenpaa and Leidner, 1999). Extra attention to the communication between team members is suggested, insuring that the communication is frequent and rich. Best practices indicate that high-performing virtual teams in international settings will adapt their communication patterns to fit the task at hand, and that it is still important to have occasional face-to-face interaction (Maznevski and Chudoba, 2000). These situational communication challenges are yet another set of issues for global IT managers to attend to.

CRITICAL SUCCESS FACTORS FOR GLOBAL INFORMATION SYSTEMS

From our research on several case studies, we have investigated a wide range of industries, observed both successes and failures, noted the resulting systems that were implemented, and the key factors attributing to success or failure of these globally operating companies. Some common denominators appear to be evident upon closer examination of the system implementation failures and of the successes. For example, a lack of standards and regional differences are two key reasons why implementations were unsuccessful. On the other hand, the companies tallied successes where standards were in place and adhered to, where regional differences were identified and incorporated, or where there was a high need for the system across business units.

In assessing the successes and failures of these case studies, technology issues are often not the overriding factor tipping the scale either way. Rather, it is the *soft side* – the management philosophy and strategy of the organization, the cultural climate, and the ability to build healthy alliances – that dictates success or failure. Some of these equally important issues are presented in Table 8.

Issue	Facets	Discussion
Sorting It Out	Cultural vs. Organizational vs. Personal boundaries	Companies had difficulty distinguishing between cultural, organizational and personal issues. Often, organizational issues were more divisive than cultural issues. Others indicated that personal barriers or personal problems created obstacles to building global systems.
Rates of Growth and Change in Markets and Regions	Status Market Position Capability	The different rates of growth and change in different markets and regions affect globalization strategies. A company may have different market positions in different regions with differing capabilities it can mobilize. Depending on what is happening in the markets, a company may be forced to operate in ways which it had not predicted.
Mandates and Leadership	Common communication, common frameworks, common goals, common practices.	The extent to which solutions can be mandated versus getting consensus. Contrary to what we might like to believe, research suggests that successes occur in organizations where strategies were mandated or implemented by a strong leader and team. Trying to get everyone to agree is not very expedient when a company is faced with extensive diversity, differences, and boundaries. Sometimes mandating a solution, while it does not ensure success, is the only feasible approach.

Table 8. Other Global Issues

STRATEGIES FOR GLOBAL APPLICATIONS DEVELOPMENT

Given the critical success and failure factors previously discussed, one of the most important factors associated with success is following the right systems development strategy. What is becoming clear as global organizations like General Motors, Yahoo!, Micron Technology, and Monsanto gain sophistication in IT management and gain experience with global IT outsourcing and off-shoring, is that companies must adopt an over-arching "super strategy" which calls for simultaneously standardizing while innovating. These two seemingly paradoxical efforts can coexist if companies identify best practices, optimal business processes, and best-in-class systems, and standardize on them throughout the global organization. This standardization effort decreases complexity and cost in fundamental systems and practices, and thus frees up time, resources, and capital for the organizations to identify local innovations. Many of these local innovations may ultimately prove to be globally attractive and thus will be internalized as part of the standardization process.

In addition to the "standardize and innovate" super strategy, several sub-strategies can help support global systems development. Based on the cited case studies, research, consulting experience, the five strategies appearing in Table 9 offer suggestions for developing global applications. Note that there is no one best strategy. Rather, there are strategies that can be adopted in a mix and match manner.

1	Mandate use of best-in-firm application system
2	Use commercial off-the-shelf software packages
3	Cross-boundary development teams
4	Parallel development
5	Utilizing Software Components for Systems Development

Table 9. Five Sub-Strategies for Global Applications Development

Sub-Strategy #1: Mandate Use of Best-in-Firm Application Systems

The basic philosophy behind this strategy is to support the overall standardization effort. To execute this sub-strategy, the firm's IT and end-user organizations search throughout the firm for the global application which best fits the business experience of every unit, i.e., the proven one, and then determine whether the common system can be modified into a single, common system that will be acceptable to all global units. The following questions must be asked:

- Can it be globally deployed?
- Does the current IT architecture support it?
- Is the right equipment available to support it (i.e., hardware, networks, etc.)?
- To what extent is the application consistent with best practice?
- What is available in the marketplace?
- Is it feasible to mandate common use as the deployment option?

In addition to the above criteria, it is important to note that the best-in-firm strategy is based on several important assumptions: 1) The software provides the best match to the business process it supports; 2) It is better to modify the business organizations or processes to conform to the best-in-firm model; and 3) The firm can overcome local cultural and behavioral barriers to garner the appropriate level of acceptance.

A variation on mandating the best-in-firm system is to transform the best-in-firm system with local modifications on an as needed basis. The same evaluation process identified above is used. Essentially, the common system is cloned, and limited, but agreed upon changes are made to the system according to local demands, and then a separate modified version is deployed locally. However, even if this strategy is managed correctly, the change and configuration management issues proliferate. In essence, the global firm ends up with a portfolio of many individual systems doing largely the same tasks, duplicating effort, and increasing the cost of maintenance in the long run. Thus, experience in the vast majority of successful cases has shown (and this is an important point) that if the best-in-firm strategy is chosen, *it is far better to alter the local organization to fit the standard system than to modify the standard system to fit local conditions.*

Sub-Strategy #2: Use of Commercial Off-the-Shelf (COTS) Packages

Conceptually, this strategy is similar to the first strategy in that it starts with a standard "something" rather than nothing – in this case using a commercially available software package – for ultimate global deployment and use. This approach was originally popular in Europe and has since gained almost complete acceptance in North America and elsewhere with packages offered by SAP, Baan, Oracle, and PeopleSoft and J.D. Edwards (both now part of Oracle). Many of these packages are referred to as enterprise resource planning (ERP) systems and provide integrated software solutions across the enterprise (e.g., general ledger, human resources, manufacturing, sales, etc.). Although these ERP systems can be extensively modified, best practice in package implementation recommends minimal modification to the package and that additionally required functionality not found in the package should be built independently and interfaced with the package. Often, this independent functionality "wraps" around the commercial package (i.e., cocoons), with application programming interfaces (APIs) or middleware to facilitate interaction with other packages and systems.

Mindlessly adopting a COTS strategy is not a panacea however. When implementing the COTS strategy, it is wise to consider the following additional implementation ideas:

- Use JAD (joint application development) methods to determine requirements and prototypes to validate requirements;
- Incorporate an overall problem-solving focus with the JAD methodology rather than just a "build the system" mentality;
- Limit the number of vendors to be examined;
- Do not attempt to achieve a perfect fit between software product and requirements (the 80-20 rule – satisfy 80% of the requirements in 20% of the time – often results in improved user satisfaction);
- Test all candidate packages and negotiate with vendor;
- Adopt a time box approach for project management where actual business results are tracked rather than just project milestones (see Wetherbe and Vitalari, 1994, for a description of the time box approach);
- Change the business process and organization to conform to the package; and
- Adopt and enforce architectural assumptions and standards implied in the package.

Sub-Strategy #3: Cross-Boundary/Cross-Functional Development Teams

When today's integrated systems span organizational and national boundaries, they also span national cultures. Consequently, the philosophy behind this sub-strategy is to obtain support for global applications through the appropriate leadership and the appropriate multi-cultural, multi-disciplinary team. The team leader is a key position. The leader should be multi-culturally aware, and serve at least as a benevolent dictator (dictator in the worst case). This strategy employs the following steps:

a) Identify and assemble the multicultural and multidisciplinary team;
b) Assure the team is composed of opinion leaders and has strong leadership;

c) Identify specific business problems the new system should address;
d) Use JAD + Prototype + Time box to develop the application;
e) Track the resolution of identified business problems in the project plan rather than simply tracking application-specific milestones;
f) Adopt a progressive rollout strategy and clone rollout teams;
g) Incorporate local talent to build the application.

Generally the core team is fairly small – eight to ten people. When the application building process commences, the team size increases and incorporates local talent as needed. In this way, the cross-boundary/cross-functional takes on a "virtual" flavor.

Research in this area included banks, a worldwide manufacturing company, headquartered in Sweden with divisions in the U.S.A. and the Far East, and a medical products firm headquartered in the U.S.A. with product development and manufacturing divisions in the U.S.A. and Europe. The manufacturing company, in particular, contended that once it moved to cross-boundary development teams, the application development process worked much more effectively. In fact, the company now uses cross-boundary development teams everywhere in the world. Recently, the manufacturer deployed a system in Louisiana/Alabama/Florida using a cross-cultural team for building the system. Medtronic, a world leader in cardiac pacing products and orthopedic implants, has used this strong leader, multi-cultural team approach very effectively.

Sub-Strategy #4: Parallel Development Teams for Innovation
This sub-strategy differs from the previous three because the underlying philosophy here, rather than standardizing across geographies, emphasizes innovating from an understanding of regional differences with steps established later to create a global system. Using parallel development teams for systems development is approached in this way:
a) Local or regional teams are formed;
b) Local teams examine local requirements for application and infrastructure requirements that are non-standard and that could result in unique innovations;
c) Separate systems are constructed for each location or region;
d) Applications interconnections are established via bridges (e.g., internal EDI, intranets, etc.);
e) Strong decoupling is maintained if innovations can not be standardized/replicated.

This sub-strategy relies on cooperation at the end to create the global system. Eventually, a multi-cultural, cross-boundary team develops from this approach. One variation observed had the local teams come together at a central site after developing their local requirements. At the central site they resolved differences building the system with a certain percentage of regional differences, but with a common structure. Care must be exercised with this approach since despite obtaining local input and having representation, the local representatives may encounter problems upon returning to their local units, perhaps being accused of selling out, omitting strong regional preferences, and not bringing back the system the region wants.

Sub-Strategy #5: Utilizing Software Components for Systems Development
The final sub-strategy is more of a systems development philosophy and as such, is a strategy that can be employed in any of the previous four systems development sub-strategies. In essence it entails utilizing object-oriented class libraries for a component-based "plug and play" systems development strategy. This approach makes heavy use of object-oriented (OO) technology, and approaches development following this methodology:
a) Cross-boundary development teams work to develop local and global requirements;
b) A version 1 object class architecture is established;
c) The need for high-level, reusable object-based components are assessed;
d) A search for pre-existing relevant commercial class libraries is conducted;

e) A fast-cycle development approach is used to develop class libraries;
f) The object class architecture refined and local and global class variation and standards established;
g) Integration and rollout are performed in concert with existing legacy architectures.

This development philosophy takes advantage of the fact that different object class libraries reflect the different local and global requirements and that there can be inheritance within the object structure. Once the common objects are identified, they can be combined into higher-level "components" and variations can be incorporated to reflect local requirements. The end result is a system that operates locally with global commonality. This philosophy can be used by either cross-functional development teams or parallel development teams, and the component-based nature of the philosophy lends itself to either maintaining and enhancing internally-developed systems or customizing COTS applications.

The popularity of the object-oriented paradigm can best be evidenced by the growth and popularity of development languages that utilize its principles. From the modest introduction of Smalltalk in the 1970's and 1980's (Kay, 1993), to the broad use of C++ in the 1990's, to the ubiquitous adoption of the Java and .NET platforms, system developers around the world are embracing OO's tenets (Armstrong, 2006).

CREATING A TRANSNATIONAL IT DEPARTMENT

The extensive consolidation around going global requires that both companies, and IT personnel re-think their role in the organization. The global movement demands a shift from passive (order takers) to proactive problem solvers (information sharers); from cost driven to business or customer value driven; from independent support to intimate partner. In the absence of a company-wide global business structure, research suggests that IT managers should create a prototype transnational IT department to effectively deliver and support IS in their organizations. The following four-step approach provides one proven method for success:

1. Conduct a skills inventory, identifying within organization "centers of competence";
2. Define technology management principles, models, and standards, seeking senior management endorsement when the timing is right;
3. Link up – expand the global network for information systems professionals and provide other mechanisms, e.g., meetings, electronic mailing lists, electronic forums/web logs (blogs), or collaboration systems for sharing and learning; and
4. Look for opportunities for rationalizing systems and data center operations regionally and globally to achieve the "standardize and innovate" super strategy introduced earlier.

CONCLUSIONS

In this chapter, we have examined a range of contemporary strategies employed by global corporations in the use of information technology. We have argued that the structure of the global firm differs substantially from strictly domestic firms and that this structure has an impact on the information technology strategies deployed. In addition, our observations of the global setting suggest that most firms with global objectives and operating models are moving over time to the transnational model. Interestingly, the transnational model more closely resembles some of the recent network-style organizational structures that are more team-based and flat in comparison to the classic, divisionalized structure.

We have noted that many of the firms observed in our research and work utilize several tactics to leverage information technology for global purposes. In many cases, these tactics are also consistent with recent reengineering plays to take advantage of process simplification and the power of shared databases. We argued that the actual process of systems delivery and implementation plays a significant role in the use of technology in global operations. "Soft" issues like teamwork, alliance building, and change management, traditionally an important issue in systems implementation, seem to play an even more important role in the successful implementation of global systems.

Finally, we have suggested that senior information executives in global firms begin to model their own IT organizations on the transnational model. We introduced an over-arching "standardize and innovate" IT strategy along with several sub-strategies to help support the IT organization as it evolves to the transnational model. By moving to the transnational model within the IT organization, IT managers and professionals will become familiar with the issues of network organizational design and operating in a highly distributed fashion.

As firms have entered the 21st century, it is becoming increasingly clear that technology is further blurring traditional boundaries and our sense of time and space. Perhaps in the long run, we will look back and consider the global firm an interesting anachronism for a point in time when human collaboration and organizational structures were limited more by local traditions than by technological capabilities.

MINICASE

Information Technology, Culture, and Learning at Federal Express

Introduction
By all accounts, the Federal Express Corporation, or "FedEx," is a global success story. In a little over 30 years, the company has grown from a start-up to an industry leader in the overnight package-delivery business. A case in point: for four hours every evening, the Memphis International Airport becomes the busiest airport in the world as FedEx airplanes land and take off every 45 seconds in an effort to successfully haul over 4 million packages every 24 hours. Today, FedEx employs more than 260,000 people, flies over 650 airplanes, and drives almost 70,000 vehicles as it provides unequaled service to 220 countries and territories worldwide. FedEx has achieved these impressive results through innovative applications of information technology (IT), and has found that long-term global success depends on placing a high priority on cultural issues.

Information Technology: A Corporate Priority
One way to judge the priority that an organization places on IT is to examine the IT budget. Now a $29-billion company, FedEx spends over $1 billion annually on information technology. Investing in IT appears to be money well spent. FedEx counts on information technology to boost growth and flatten costs. According to Fred Smith, the chairman, CEO, and founder of FedEx, "We're getting a higher payoff from information systems than from adding aircraft. It lets us save potentially hundreds of millions of dollars."

COSMOS: A Platform for IT Synergy
As FedEx's business volumes accelerated over time, the management and information systems the company had been using to control operations were becoming obsolete and unable to support the requirements of the company. FedEx realized that it needed to upgrade those systems or risk the possibility of compromising customer service. Using a "best practice" approach, FedEx executives looked outside the company to the computerized reservation systems the commercial airlines had in place to develop FedEx's automated transaction processing systems. That development group gave birth to COSMOS – Customer Oriented Services and Management Operating System.

COSMOS connects the physical handling of packages with information concerning each shipment – from the time the customer requests service to the package's delivery. FedEx employees often offer the following analogy that reflects the significance of the impact:

If passenger airlines had systems comparable to FedEx's, whenever you were traveling, your family, friends, or business associates would be able to sign onto the Internet and in real-time learn your exact location, as well as every step of your trip history. They would know whether you were in the air or on the ground, and how close you were to your destination. If you happened to be in a cab, they'd know its number as well as the cab's destination. And, with that information, they would be able to phone the taxi and speak with you directly.

Another benefit FedEx experienced from the COSMOS development effort had to do with second-order innovations – that is, COSMOS as an innovation in turn served as a catalyst for other innovations. For example, the following IT applications are just a few that can be traced back to COSMOS:

- SuperTracker, a computerized tracking system that customers can use to determine where any package or document is at any moment – from pickup through delivery.
- DADS, a digitally assisted dispatch system that communicates to couriers through computers in their vans. DADS provides quick courier response to dispatches and allows them to manage their time and routes efficiently and accurately.
- POWERSHIP, the software for customers' on-premise computers, which now process about one-third of all FedEx shipments. The POWERSHIP systems provide automated billing, allow customers direct access to their package information, and supply detailed information and shipping instructions for international shippers.
- FedEx.com, the highly successful global website where FedEx customers can track the status of their package shipments around the world. Since 1994, customers with service-related questions or issues find answers on FedEx.com rather than relying on customer service representatives. This "self-service" saves the company millions of dollars a year.

The POWERSHIP application mentioned above represents one of the industry's most effective uses of customer on-premise technology. As an inter-organizational information system, POWERSHIP allows FedEx to enhance the customer relationship through computer networking. The vast majority of the company's shipments today are made via POWERSHIP or via FedExShip electronic shipping systems. FedEx.com gives FedEx customers access to a great deal of useful information, including its POWER SHIP database.

Understanding Culture

Unfortunately, having a world-class IT infrastructure that spans the globe does not insure global success. For example, most organizations understand that the cultural environment profoundly affects global business. However, there is a potential chasm between *understanding* these implications and effectively *implementing* a strategy given the political and cultural implications. Over time, FedEx has found ways to conduct business effectively around the world.

One of the most important things an organization can do to effectively deal with foreign national cultures is to first have a good understanding of their own organizational culture. At FedEx, delivering every package "absolutely, positively" on time is the essence of their organizational culture. In addition to a macroculture, FedEx also has several "microcultures" that co-exist along with the macroculture. For example, the sense that FedEx is an industry-leading innovator in the use of IT is a microculture that permeates the entire FedEx's IT organization.

The pilots flying FedEx aircraft, the truckers driving FedEx Freight's over the road trucks, and the couriers that drive FedEx Ground vans to deliver packages to customers each have their own microculture that suggests that all packages will be delivered on time regardless of the situation.

FedEx not only tolerates these microcultures, but also encourages them as long as they are consistent with the overall quality and service maxims, which exist in the macroculture. Their stated strategy of "operate independently, compete collectively, manage collaboratively" draws attention to culture as well as the point that a strong, succinctly stated macroculture is essential to a company when it expands into overseas markets. FedEx learned that when it moved into Asia in 1991.

Bridging the International Culture Gap

FedEx has always recognized that their couriers are the people who have the most direct contact with FedEx customers. In Asia, however, people regard delivery personnel at a low level in the occupation hierarchy. As a result, human resources consultants back in the United States had set wage scales and job descriptions based on the earnings of Asian messengers. Consequently, FedEx found itself hiring unskilled and untrained workers – people at the lowest pay scale – to fill its courier slots. To an executive sitting in Memphis, this seemed a perfectly acceptable recruiting policy. To a customer in Hong Kong, it meant disaster. A courier dispatched to pick up three boxes, for example, would absolutely refuse to accept any more than three. In the United States, the FedEx courier was committed to 100 percent customer satisfaction. It looked like 100 percent customer satisfaction would be unattainable in Asia. FedEx had no choice but to fully understand the Asian culture and try to find areas where it and FedEx's corporate culture could be adapted to be consistent with the FedEx culture as well as world-wide customer expectations. As FedEx's senior vice president for Asia and Pacific Operations said, "It took us four years, and a lot of effort. We didn't want to impose American values in Asia, but we felt we had to keep to our core corporate philosophy. We tried to train the Hong Kong couriers to understand that service comes first, and we tried to train them to understand what FedEx means by service." Today, when Hong Kong couriers arrive at pickups, they courteously accept customer orders and react competently and intelligently to the unexpected. FedEx devoted a lot of time and attention – not to mention money – to hiring and training the couriers who would ultimately become assets to the company.

FedEx has spent time and effort in an attempt to find the balance between offending people (i.e., "You are trying to Americanize us") while helping them to understand that FedEx is a global company. FedEx has had countless group meetings with employees, and has sponsored many cultural training programs. FedEx has provided English language training at its expense and has given employees who complete the course a pay premium. FedEx's management development courses stress the cultures of the countries where their people work, and help managers understand that cultural differences matter from everyone's point of view. Overall, FedEx's strength has been its ability to learn and benefit from the challenging lessons of its early forays into foreign markets. The company redesigned its strategies in ways that complement each culture's preferences, and now it is enjoying successful growth in both Europe and Asia.

Conclusions

FedEx's use of IT is often mentioned as the dominant characteristic explaining their long-term business success. In actuality, the environment at FedEx is more complex than that. To be sure, IT is a top priority at FedEx and it has staked its future success on the ability of it to capitalize on innovative ways to use IT for competitive advantage. However, this point focuses on only one of FedEx's priorities. In addition to IT, FedEx has been and continues to be ever mindful of the confluence of organizational culture, the prevailing national cultures of its customers and worldwide locations, and the impact that this cultural amalgam has on global operations.

IT and culture are not mutually exclusive but rather tightly coupled. It is perhaps useful to think of IT and culture in the following terms:

- Culture is pervasive and constantly changing (albeit relatively slowly). Everything an organization does is affected by it. Ignoring it in business or academia constitutes ignoring a defining boundary condition or potentially confounding force. Learning how to leverage culture can and should be a core competency worth striving for.

- IT should be viewed as the facilitator for culture, learning, and ultimately organizational performance. For example, IT can serve to define culture (e.g., "we are a technology leader"), and can also serve as the common thread which binds otherwise disparate cultures together (e.g., "things are done differently in Asia, but they recognize the importance of IT just like we do here."). In terms of organizational learning, IT is critical in measuring and gathering performance information, assisting in the evaluation of the information, and ultimately disseminating findings (i.e., learning) throughout the organization.

Discussion Questions

1. As FedEx continues to grow in international markets (most notably the vast market represented by China), to what extent should FedEx management arm themselves with prior learning of their global forays versus making the assumption that each new market is unique and previous experiences may not apply?

2. What role should IT play in FedEx's continuing globalization? Should it be a key component to their corporate globalization strategy, or should it play a less visible (but yet still important) support role?

3. When penetrating global markets, how safe is it to assume that what worked in one part of the country, e.g., Hong Kong or Beijing, will apply in other parts of the country, e.g., Chongqing, Tianjin? Provide relevant examples from your home country to justify your position.

Source: This mini-case is an updated version of an article of the same name published earlier in the *Journal of Global Information Technology Management*, volume 1, issue 1, pp. 17-26.

KEY TERMS
Alliance
Caller-ID
Cocooning
Co-locate
Electronic Data Interchange (EDI)
Extranet
Groupware
HTML
IBM AS/400
Intranet
Joint Application Design (JAD)
Leapfrog computing
Legacy systems
Mass customization
NEXTStep
Supply chain management

TCP/IP
Time-boxing

STUDY QUESTIONS

1. Discuss the challenges and issues that systems developers must contend with in each of the strategies outlined in Konsynski and Karimi's alignment of global and information framework presented in the chapter. From a purely technological perspective, is there a strategy that is most desirable?

2. Mass customization was identified as one tactic that could help in implementing the Transnational Model. Identify an additional example of an organization that is capitalizing on mass customization and explain how they are achieving mass customization.

3. Global supply chain management was identified as one tactic that could help in implementing the Transnational Model. Identify an additional example of an organization that is capitalizing on supply chain management and explain how they are achieving benefits.

4. Customer service was identified as one tactic that could help in implementing the Transnational Model. Identify an additional example of an organization that is capitalizing on superior customer service and explain how they are achieving success with this tactic.

5. Developing global alliances was identified as one tactic that could help in implementing the Transnational Model. Identify an additional example of an organization that is capitalizing on their global alliances and explain how they are achieving mass success with this tactic.

6. The two components of the "standardize and innovate" super-strategy described in the text seem at first to be mutually exclusive. Describe how these two efforts can in fact be used in concert when developing a global IT strategy.

7. The five sub-strategies for global applications development have a lot in common. After reviewing these strategies, put yourself in the role of a global applications development manager and discuss the top three goals that you would concentrate on in developing global applications. In addition, justify why you chose these particular goals.

REFERENCES

Alavi, M. and Young, G. Information Technology In an International Enterprise An Organizing Framework, *Global Issues of Information Technology Management*, P. Salvia, S. Salvia, and R. Zigli, (eds.), Idea Group Publishing, 1992, pp. 495-56.

Armstrong, D. J. The Quarks of Object-Oriented Development, *Communications of the ACM*, February, 2006, pp. 123-128.

Bartlett, C. A. and Ghoshal, S. *Managing Across Borders: The Transnational Solution*, Harvard Business School Press, 1989.

Davis, S. *Future Perfect*, Addison-Wesley Publishing Company, 1987.

Drucker, P. The Information-Based Organization, *The Harvard Business Review*, January-February, 1988, pp. 45-53.

IATP Pionairs Association. *The IATP Story : The International Airlines Technical Pool and How It Came to Be*. Published by the IATP Pionairs Association, 1995.

Ives, B. and Jarvenpaa, S. Applications of Global Information Technology Issues for Management, *MIS Quarterly*, March 1991, pp. 33-49.

Janz, B. D., Pitts, M .G., and Otondo. R. F. "Back to the Future with RFID: Lessons Learned – Some Old, Some New, " *Communications of the AIS, 15(article 7),* January, 2005, 132-148.

Janz, B. D., Vitalari, N. P., and Wetherbe, J.C. "Emerging Best Practices in Global Systems Development," Palvia, P., Palvia, S., and Roche, E. (Eds.), *Global Information Technology and Systems Management,* Ivy League Publishing. 2002.

Jarvenpaa, S. and Ives, B. The Global Network Organization of the Future Information Management Opportunities and Challenges, *Journal of Management Information Systems*, 10(4), Spring 1994, pp. 25-27.

Jarvenpaa, S. and Ives, B. Organizing for Global Competition. The Fit of Information Technology, *Decision Sciences*, Vol. 24, No. 3, 1993, pp. 547-580.

Jarvenpaa, S. and Leidner, D. Communication and Trust in Global Virtual Teams, *Organization Science,* 10(6), 1999, pp. 791-815.

Kay, A. *The Early History of Smalltalk.* In Proceedings of 2nd ACM SIGPLAN History of Programming Languages Conference. ACM SIGPLAN Notices 28(3). Pp. 69-75. 1993

King, W.R. and Sethi, V. Patterns in the organization of transnational information systems. *Information and Management,* 38(4), 2001, pp. 201-215.

Konsynski, B. R. and Karimi, J. On the Design of Global Information Systems. In S. P. Bradley, J.A. Hausman, and R. L. Nolan (eds.) *Globalization, Technology, and Competition: The Fusion of Computers and Telecommunications in the 1990s*, Harvard Business School Press, 1993.

Lai, V.S. Issues of international information systems managements: A perspective of affiliates. *Information and Management,* 38(4), 2001, pp. 253-264.

Lipnak, J. and Stamps, J. *The Age of the Network Organizing Principles for the 21st Century*, Oliver Wright Publications, Inc., 1994.

Maznevski, M.L. and Chudoba, K.M. Bridging space over time: Global virtual team dynamics and effectiveness. *Organization Science,* 11(5), 2000, pp. 473-492.

Miles, R. and Snow, C. *Fit Failure and the Hall of Fame*, Simon and Schuster Inc., 1994.

Pine, B. J. *Mass Customization: The New Frontier in Business Competition*, Harvard Business School Press, 1993.

Venkatesh, A. and Vitalari, N. An Emerging Distributed Work Arrangement: An Investigation of Computer-based Supplemental Work at Home, *Management Science*, 38(12), December, 1992.

Vitalari, N. Exploring the Type-D Organization. Distributed Work Arrangement, Information Technology and Organizational Design, *Research Issues in Information Systems: An Agenda for the 1990's*, A. M. Jenkins et al. (Eds.), Wm. C. Brown Publishers, 1990.

Wetherbe, J. and Vitalari, N. *Systems Analysis and Design Best Practices*, West Publishing, 1994.

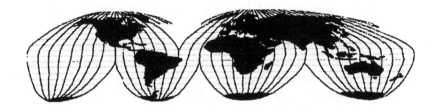

Dynamics of Control Modes in Offshored Information Systems Development Projects

Ravi S. Narayanaswamy
Rahul A. Gokhale
Varun Grover
Clemson University, USA

CHAPTER SUMMARY

In today's competitive arena, companies are increasingly exercising the option of IT outsourcing for realizing strategic and non-strategic business initiatives. One aspect of IT outsourcing is globalization of information systems development (ISD) activities. The reasons why companies offshore their ISD activities (reduced costs, abundant skills, etc) have been well documented. However, many recent studies report that the benefits intended from the offshoring arrangement are usually not realized, and more than 75% of projects are partial or outright failures. Conversely, the project management literature portrays control as an important factor that enhances project success. This chapter draws from the extensive ISD literature to develop a theoretically grounded framework to examine the dynamics of control in offshore context. We conduct an in-depth analysis of literature related to project management, organizational control and national culture. Our findings reveal that culture differences are important and must be considered when designing control strategies for offshored projects. Further exploration reveal other factors such as task characteristics, project characteristics, environment and people characteristics influence the control strategy. Managerial implications for the same are presented towards the end of the chapter.

INTRODUCTION

Ever since Kodak's landmark decision to outsource the bulk of its information technology (IT) functions in the late 1980s, IT outsourcing has been a widely publicized practice (Rottman and Lacity, 2006). Despite the recent softening in the technology sector, the world wide market for externally provided IT services continues to grow (NASSCOM, 2004). Two generic trends have been observed in IT outsourcing. First, the outsourcing of IT products and services has evolved from a solution to the problem of incompetent IT management to a key competence of IT management (Lacity and Willcocks, 2000). This trend captures evolution in the types of technological needs outsourced. Starting from an initial portfolio that comprised of procurement of "packaged services," desktop management services, and IT infrastructure services, we observe a distinct movement towards application services, and parts or whole of strategic information systems development initiatives ,Lacity and Willcocks, 2000). The other prominent trend in IT outsourcing has been the movement from onshore outsourcing to offshore outsourcing (a.k.a. offshoring). According to International Data Corporation (IDC), offshore IT services vendors will capture $29.4 billion in worldwide customer spending by 2010, with little sign of a market slowdown (IDC Report, 2006). The US software industry in particular has been a leader in this trend; outsourcing projects totaling billions of dollars have gone to countries like India, China, and the Philippines to reap gains from reduced labor costs and economies of scale (Takac, 1993). Consequently, offshore outsourcing is predicted to become one of the biggest trends for the next 10 years (Gurubaxani, 2003).

While offshoring trends make economic sense, it is naïve to assume that everything flows smoothly when offshoring and many of the initially proclaimed benefits of IS outsourcing are actually realized. For instance, in a study of 116 sourcing decisions assessing various outcomes, it was found that approximately two-thirds of the outcomes to be either failures or mixed-results (Lacity and Willcocks, 2000). In 2003, a survey of 219 offshoring clients revealed that more than half failed to realize the expected value from offshore outsourcing (NASSCOM, 2004). Accordingly, the vital question is how to foster success of offshored projects. The systems development literature posits a control strategy as an important factor for enhancing project success (Kirsch, 1996; 1997). In particular, control strategies have been found helpful for balancing the competing demands of scope, time, cost, quality, and stakeholder needs and expectations (Kirsch, 2004). Intense research has been done on exploring the factors influencing the control strategies. Factors such as project characteristics and task characteristics are found to influence the control strategies. However, most IS control research has been done in internal information systems development (ISD) context, where the client and vendor reside within same organization or at least same country. In offshore outsourcing the client (the organization outsourcing its services) and vendor (the organization offering services) are located in two different countries. They vary in their cultural values, beliefs, rituals, and management practices, among others. Further, practices used to manage in-house projects when extended to the context of offshoring, result in complete or partial failures (Palvia et al., 1996). Accordingly, it becomes imperative to study the factors affecting the control strategies in offshore context. The challenges posed by offshore outsourcing can be broadly placed into three categories: cultural factors, geographical distance, and infrastructure and security issues (Nicholson and Sahay, 2001). In this chapter we mainly focus on challenges posed by cultural factors and theoretically examine its impact on choice of control strategies. Further we include the findings from prior IS control research to develop an integrative framework for control strategies.

Cultural Heterogeneity
Consider the following vignettes:

❖ "Folks from some countries tend to be less aggressive than folks from the U.S. when you come up with deadlines; you have instances when the worker isn't saying anything, even though he thinks that the deadline is unreasonable"-Mukesh Mehta (2003), Vice-President, IT financial systems, MetLife.

❖ "Americans usually think "yes" means a person agrees with a statement or a question, while Indians will often use the word to confirm they understood what the speaker was saying, not that they necessarily agree"(Hayes, 2003, p.1).

❖ "US managers say they encounter employees from Indian firms who consider it rude to say "No" to a client, even when the client is making a flat out illogical request; The US company thinks that it has communicated adequately what it is looking for, and then three or four months later when they receive the work done, its nowhere near what they expected". - Frances Karamouzis (2003), Gartner analyst.

❖ "IT staffs take a while to get used to one another. Different cultures handle situations in different manners. For example, when Tufts and Wipro started working together, project leaders at Wipro didn't tell Tufts when a project was not going according to schedule because that's their culture" - Rick Shoup, VP and CIO, Tufts (Mateyaschuk, 1999, p.1).

These and similar comments concern questions regarding the influence of cultural factors and their associated impact on performance of Offshore Outsourced Information System Development projects (OOISD). Such comments and consequent project failures are not uncommon, especially in OOISD projects. One of the key issues in OOISD projects is that when organizations (vendor-client) from different cultures are involved it raises the issue of cultural differences that could impact the effectiveness of some management practices. What works well for US managers may not work as well in cross cultural situations. This is especially important given the risks associated with offshore outsourcing. These include scope creep, timely completion of the project, increased coordination costs, poor software quality, work flow communication, project methodologies, and budgeting (Krishna et al., 2004) that can all undermine the intended benefits of offshore outsourcing. These risks all represent management issues that may be caused or exacerbated by lack of harmonization of project processes and methodologies, and divergence of peoples' values and beliefs (Nicholson and Sahay, 2001). Given the geographical and cultural distance introduced by offshore outsourcing, it is imperative to consider how cultural differences impact successful management of ISD projects. In particular, when cross-cultural issues are likely to become an important factor, as they have in the management of international joint ventures (Brannen and Salk, 2000), it is vital to understand (and manage) them to ensure success in OOISD projects.

Control in Offshore Projects

Moving IT overseas can be complicated due to the following reasons:

❖ IT is an integral part of every business process, requiring communication and management (Takac, 1993).

❖ ISD is a complex, intensive, and dynamic activity that requires close cooperation and coordination among diverse stakeholders (Beath, 1987).

❖ The complex nature of IS outsourcing relationships makes them more susceptible to failure (Barthelemy, 2001).

Due to the nature of IT projects in general, and OOISD projects in particular, one important aspect of project performance is how the client exercises control over the vendor, which largely dictates the success of outsourcing (Clark et al., 1998). While attributes of control have been examined in the literature (for example, Kirsch, 1996, 1997, 2004), there has been little discussion of control in OOISD context. Given increased coordination costs and the separation between stakeholders in OOISD, control becomes important for organizations to achieve the desired outcomes (Henderson and Lee, 1992; Kirsch, 1997). Further, and as noted earlier, there are cases where concepts from in-house management of IT projects (including those of control), when extended to offshore outsourcing arrangements, cause failures. For instance, while in-house rationale might dictate extensive use of authority and evaluation, differences in the way people value and do their work in might call for other control strategies (unrelated to authority).

Taking note of the importance of these factors, this chapter relates to the impact of culture differences on choice of control modes in OOSD projects. To explore this issue we develop a theoretically grounded framework from the diverse literature of organizations control, project management and culture. We first present an overview of culture and its associated dimensions, followed by a brief overview of control. Based on these discussions, we present a conceptual framework illustrating the effect of culture on control modes. In addition we extend the framework by integrating the findings from prior IS control literature. We conclude with some implications of our framework for research and practice.

CULTURE

Importance of Culture

Conventional wisdom holds that national cultural differences will significantly impact cross-national business relationships. Prior literature in anthropology and management highlight the moderating effect of culture on organizational effectiveness (Hofstede, 1980; 1991), management practices (Jaegur, 1986; Newman and Nollen, 1996), and individual/team performance (Chow et al., 1991; Keil et al., 2000). While some scholars are ready to accept that national culture may influence the way people relate to each other, they are less convinced that it can really affect the organization systems and processes. The culture-free argument is that business relationship success is determined by organizational features such as size and technology. On the other hand, some scholars argue that societal context creates difference in ways organizations are structured in different countries. In effect, culturalists argue that culture creates norms which influence the individual behavior, and while organizational norms/structure direct individuals' ways of behavior; the national culture dictates the extent to which the individual will adhere to those norms. For instance, in the "non-culturalist" tradition, Myers and Tan (2002) argue for departure from the use of national models of culture as a tool to explain information systems phenomena. Their arguments center around the practice of associating a nation state with a culture, the heterogeneity of culture within nation states, the use of culture as a means to differentiate one individual/group from another as an outdated concept, and the notion of linking culturally influenced work values as not directly related to national culture. In the culturalist stream, scholars have empirically demonstrated how national cultures can significantly affect organizational processes (House et al., 1999). They argue that knowledge of cultural dimensions can go a long way in tempering management decision making that might otherwise be based on institutional or economic rationales.

In addition to these views, there also exists some practical evidence as to the impact cultures have on organizational processes, and performance. For example, emphasis on human relations was brought in by series of Hawthorne studies (1930s) held in United States; socio-technical emphasis was brought in by Tavistock studies of the coal mines in the United Kingdom (1930s). These approaches reflected different cultural assumptions regarding how to best accomplish the task, how best to establish relationship with employees/team members, and how to motivate employees (Hofstede, 1980; 1991).

In sum, there are arguments on both sides of whether national culture impacts organizational processes and performance. However, given anecdotal evidence in the context of offshore outsourcing that describes how cultural heterogeneity leads to communication and coordination issues and in turn performance, it would be naïve to ignore the role of culture or treat it as an academic fad. In fact, scholars who have indeed argued against the importance of culture in examining information systems phenomena have never stated that culture is not important, but rather that its direct or main effects are difficult to support (Ford et al., 2003). Thus a synthesis of the arguments presented in the literature helps in recognizing that culture might play a role in determining information systems phenomena at project level, but do so indirectly through mechanisms like communication, coordination, leadership style, and so forth. Put differently, the presence or absence of culture might affect how these variables influence performance. Culture thus can be seen as playing an indirect or moderating role in determining performance on OOISD projects. This does not suggest that other institutional factors are not important. However, we do suggest that the study of culture can provide a useful perspective on performance of OOISD projects.

Defining Culture and Its Dimensions

Culture has often been considered to be a nebulous construct that is difficult to define. Depending on the field of exploration, there are differing definitions of culture. All these definitions have certain themes in common: culture is learned, associated with values and behaviors that are shared by individuals and groups, and these values are passed along from one generation to the next.

The culture definitions and dimensions provided by Hofstede have been widely adopted in IS research (Ford et al., 2003). Among the many attempts to define the construct of culture, Hofstede's (1980) study is considered as one of the most important attempts to establish of impact of culture differences on management (Ford et al., 2003). The study was based on an employee opinion survey involving 116,000 IBM employees in 40 different countries who were asked about there preferences in terms of management style and work environment. Hofstede (1980, p.5) describes culture as "a collective programming of mind which distinguishes the members from one group or category of people from another." Culture is learned from the social environment, which causes cultural differences to exist both at the society level and the nation level (Ford et al., 2003; Hofstede, 1980). Based on the results Hofstede identified four value dimensions on which countries differed: power distance, uncertainty avoidance, individualism and collectivism, and masculinity/femininity.

Power distance: Power distance (PD) is "a measure of the interpersonal power or influence between a manager and sub-ordinate as perceived by the subordinate" (Hofstede, 1991, p.71). Broadly it indicates the extent to which a society accepts the unequal distribution of power in institutions and organizations. It refers to the extent to which inequality, often as in a hierarchy, is seen as significant, salient and real. It informs us about manager-subordinate's relations - autocratic versus paternalistic. In high PD societies such as India, Philippines, and Malaysia, superiors make decisions without consulting with subordinates and subordinates feel comfortable with this practice. The subordinates are apprehensive about disagreeing with their superiors because they are seen as correct just because of their position In low PD societies such as Ireland, Israel, and New Zealand, subordinates participate more in decision-making activities and prefer a consultative relationship with their superiors. Subordinates not complying with a directive will not hesitate to question their superior decisions or easily refuse to implement it.

Uncertainty avoidance: Uncertainty avoidance (UA) refers to a society's discomfort with uncertainty, preferring predictability and stability (Hofstede, 1980, 1991). It is the degree to which individuals feel threatened with unpredictability; they try to avoid unambiguous situations by establishing more formal rules and procedures. It informs us about the employee's willingness towards risk. People in countries scoring high on UA such as Belgium, Portugal, and Japan, would tend to seek ways such as developing a structured work environment to reduce/avoid uncertainty. On the other hand people in countries scoring low on UA such as Sweden, Jamaica and Singapore are more open to uncertainty.

Individualism/collectivism: The Individualism/collectivism (IC) dimension represents a continuum defining the preference of people to belong to a loosely versus a tightly knit social framework. It reflects the extent to which people prefer to take care of themselves and their immediate families, remaining independent from groups, organizations, and other collectivities (Hofstede, 1980). In cultures that rank high on IC (individualistic), such as United States, Australia and Canada, people are more self-oriented, and encourage autonomous work environment. In cultures that rank low on IC (high on collectivism), such as India, Japan and Columbia, people value groups norms and values. Individuals perceive groups as the main source of their identity.

Masculinity/Femininity: Masculinity/Femininity (MF) refers to degree to which people prefer values of success and competition to modesty and concern for others. In masculine countries, for example, Japan, Austria and Italy, people emphasis work goals, assertiveness and material success. In contrast, people in feminine society like Sweden, Norway, and Netherlands focus on quality of life goals, nurturing, and modesty (Hofstede, 1991). Some scholars argue that this dimension is highly correlated to gender roles and requires further development. For instance, males emphasize masculine values while females stress feminine values. Similarly some contend this dimension varies with age, i.e., masculinity is more common among young individuals while femininity is found more among older individuals (Ford et al., 2003). Due to its controversial nature, we do not include this dimension in our analysis.

Long term/Short term orientation: This dimension refers to people's consideration of the future, being comfortable with sacrificing now for long term benefit (long-term orientation) or more focused on immediate results (short-term orientation) (Bond, 1991). This dimension was developed by using a Chinese entrepreneurial survey because some argue that this dimension closely reflects the Confucian values (Ford et al., 2003). Further, given the newness of this dimension, it needs further development before it can be considered for conceptual testing. While informative, we do not include this dimension because of its cultural bias and subjectivity.

We summarize the cultural dimensions used in this chapter in Table 1. Table 2 shows how different countries fare along all of the dimensions proposed by Hofstede. We argue (later) that managers should consider the cultural differences while structuring a portfolio of control modes.

Dimension	Definition	Rank	Key Organization Characteristics
Power Distance	Indicates extent to which a society accepts the unequal distribution of power in institutions and organizations	High	❖ Vertical differentiation (more levels of hierarchy) ❖ Narrow span of control ❖ Centralized decision making ❖ Status and power as motivators ❖ Superiors will be venerated or obeyed as authorities
		Low	❖ Decentralized decision making ❖ Less delegation ❖ Informal relationships ❖ Coordination through personal communication
Uncertainty Avoidance	Refers to a society's discomfort with uncertainty, preferring predictability and stability	High	❖ Formalized work environment ❖ Strict and precise definition of roles and responsibilities ❖ Managers and employees will be risk aversive ❖ Stability and security motivates employees ❖ Greater specialization of skills
		Low	❖ Decentralized work environment ❖ Coordination through informal and personal communication ❖ Flexible in ways to carry out tasks ❖ Roles more emergent
Individualism /Collectivism	Reflects the extent to which people prefer to take care of themselves and their immediate families, remaining independent from groups, organizations, and other collectivities	High	❖ Individual initiative and effort ❖ Individual values more valued ❖ Status and power motivates achievement ❖ Autonomous work environment ❖ Independent decision making
		Low	❖ Preference for group decision-making process ❖ Consensus and cooperation ❖ Sense of belonging enhances motivation ❖ Rewards are based on the extent to which the individual adheres to groups' norms and values. ❖ Team effort

Table 1. Cultural Dimension and Key Organizational Characteristics (Source: Hofstede, 1980)

Country	Power distance		Individualism		Uncertainty Avoidance	
	Index	*Rank*	*Index*	*Rank*	*Index*	*Rank*
Argentina	49	35-6	46	22-3	86	10-15
Brazil	69	14	38	26-7	76	21-2
Hong Kong	68	15-16	25	37	112	1
India	77	10-11	48	21	40	45
Ireland	28	49	70	12	35	47-8
Israel	13	52	54	19	81	19
Jamaica	45	37	39	25	35	47-8
Mexico	81	5-6	30	32	82	18
Japan	*54*	*33*	*46*	*22-3*	*92*	*7*
Netherlands	38	40	80	4-5	53	35
Philippines	94	4	32	31	44	44
Pakistan	55	32	14	47-8	70	24-5
Thailand	64	21-3	20	39-41	64	30
United States	*40*	*38*	*91*	*1*	*46*	*43*

Table 2. Country Rankings of most Outsourced Countries (Source: Hofstede, 1991)

Summary of Discussion on Culture

Based on our discussion so far, scholars are divided as to the direct effects of cultural on organizational level processes and performance. However, collaboration between parties who are not co-located and culturally homogeneous creates new dynamics. In the digital age, there is no obviously dominant culture, and there maybe little incentive to create a negotiated culture (MacGregor et al., 2005). Intercultural factors are catching projects off guard and are the source of countless misunderstandings. There is convincing evidence of indirect but strong effects of culture on effectiveness of factors such as leadership, communication, and coordination (House et al., 1999; Palvia et al., 1996). Consequently, it is beneficial to consider the role of culture in offshore ISD projects.

Given the difference in value orientations of the countries, scholars often questioned whether American theories could be applied universally. In countries with high power distance, organizations would tend to have strong hierarchy systems evident in centralized decision-making structures. Employees respect and accept their superior's authority. The role of the manager is to monitor, coordinate and control the activities.

In countries with high uncertainty avoidance, organizations would tend to have more formalization evident in greater structured work environments. Further there would be greater specialization evident in the importance attached to technical competence in the role of staff and in defining jobs and functions. Project managers would avoid taking risks and would be strongly motivated by security and stability. The role of the manager would be more one of planning, organizing, coordinating, and controlling.

In countries with high collectivist orientation, employees would prefer for group versus individual decision-making. Team members would appreciate cooperation more than individual initiative and effort. The role of the manager in such cultures is to facilitate team effort and integration to facilitate a supportive atmosphere, and to create the necessary context or group culture.

CONTROL MODES AND MECHANISMS

General Background

As mentioned earlier, ISD projects involve complex and dynamic activities. Organizations face major challenge in managing these projects, which often exhibit low success rates. A major focus of research on this problem reveals that managing socio-political and motivational issues arising from interaction among diverse stakeholders including senior managers, team members and project managers is vital to project success (Kirsch, 2004). Hence, continued effort leading to better understanding of both social and motivational factors affecting the project's success is clearly warranted. In the past, studies in the project management arena have analyzed the relationship between project manager and team member(s) (Henderson and Lee, 1992), user and developer (Beath, 1987), vendor and client (Choudhury and Sabherwal, 2003). All these efforts have in common the idea that developing a collaborative process for seeking stakeholder cooperation and coordination is vital to facilitate project success.

Consistent with the above perspectives, we define control as an organization's attempt to motivate employees to behave in a manner consistent to attain organization goals (Flamholtz et al., 1985). Put differently, the problem of control is one of achieving cooperation and coordination among a diverse group of stakeholders who share only partially congruent objectives. Control thus forms a fundamental backdrop to the factors affecting project performance. This view helps us not only better understand the role of the IS project manager, but also elevates the control relationship between vendor and client as being central to enhance IS project performance in an outsourcing context (Choudhury and Sabherwal, 2003). The historical view of control reveals that the main objective of control is to regulate employees' activities in order to create patterns of interaction and provide feedback (Ouchi and Maguire, 1975). However given that an IS project is socially constructed and politically constituted (Mähring, 2002), it is important to understand the social factors influencing control relationship in the offshore context. This becomes more imperative when we assume that control is dynamic and accept that not all behaviors are amenable to traditional modes of control (Kirsch, 2004).

Control Modes

In ISD projects, the controller implements a variety of mechanisms in an attempt to increase the probability that the controllee behaves in ways that lead to the attainment of project goals. The combination of control modes used represents a portfolio of control. The control literature presents four modes of control grouped into formal control (outcome, behavior) and informal (clan, self) modes. Formal controls are performance evaluation strategies of an organization, where the controller observes the controllee's behavior or states the desired outcomes (Kirsch, 1997). Informal control modes are based on social or people strategies (Kirsch, 1997). Earlier studies have considered these control modes in different contexts and have found that managers use a combination of formal and informal control modes creating a portfolio of control modes (Choudhury and Sabherwal, 2003; Henderson and Lee, 1992; Kirsch, 1997). However, the factors affecting the managers choice of control modes is under explored. In particular, given the presence of differential culture in offshoring, it is logical to posit culture as a possible factor affecting the manager's choice of control modes.

Formal controls: For outcome control, the controller articulates the desired goals or outcomes and sets up performance targets (e.g., functional specifications and target implementation date) and rewards the controllee for meeting these goals (e.g., software testing by client personnel) (Kirsch, 1997). The use of mechanisms that specify desired outcomes help the controller measure the controllee's performance with respect to the specified outcome. Here the controller's focus is on the outcomes of the project and not on the process by which these outcomes are achieved (Choudhury and Sabherwal, 2003).

Behavior control is implemented when the controllee's behavior is known. The controller seeks to influence the process, or the means to goal achievement, by explicitly stating specific rules and procedures, observing the controllee's behaviors, and rewarding the controllee based on the extent to which they follow stated procedures (Choudhury and Sabherwal, 2003; Kirsch, 1996). Behavior control is implemented through either direct observation using information-gathering mechanisms, or information systems (e.g., weekly reports) or mechanisms that specify behaviors (e.g., development methodology), and allow the controller to evaluate behavior.

Informal controls: Clan control is used to create convergence in the values and beliefs between the controller and the controllee. Clan control operates through interpersonal dynamics of team members within a group (Kirsch, 1996). The success of clan control depends on the degree to which all members of the work group identify and enforce the same values (e.g., adopt similar problem-solving approaches) and commit to achieving group goals (Kirsch, 1997).

Self-control is a function of individual objectives and standards (Henderson and Lee, 1992). Some authors assert that self-control is implemented when the organization cannot adequately measure the behavioral performance (Henderson and Lee, 1992). The controller sets specific goals, objectives and standards such that individuals can work independently and monitor their progress. The rewards are based on how well the individuals (controllee) manage their work to meet the goals set by the controller (Kirsch and Cummings, 1996). This is based on the idea that self-managed individuals are intrinsically motivated to achieve their objectives which requires the work environment be structured to encourage the exercise of self-control.

Unlike internal ISD, in offshored projects, the controller (organization or individual implementing control modes) and the controllee (entity being controlled) are not located in the same countries. Accordingly, it is logical to assume that the factors affecting the choice to structure a portfolio of control modes vary between internal ISD and offshored ISD projects. Since cultural factors influencing individual/group beliefs are exogenous and difficult to modify, the cultural conditioning or "programming" of the individuals/groups in a specific country can largely determine the type of control modes used. Thus in OOISD projects it is important to consider culture as a factor influencing the manager's choice to structure portfolios of control modes.

EXAMINING CULTURE AND CONTROL INTER-RELATIONSHIP

The significance of the role of culture on control has emerged since the writings of Ouchi (1980). The argument made by Ouchi that culture under certain circumstances can provide a synergistic element to control systems and facilitate their operations. This notion was prominent in the discussion of *clan* form of control. In offshoring, where two countries with different cultural backgrounds are involved, we believe the role of culture in selection of control modes to be important. Prior literature on IS outsourcing emphasizes issues such as political and cultural implications of global outsourcing (Krishna et al., 2004; Nicholson and Sahay, 2001), the role of trust in outsourcing (Sabherwal, 1999) and transactional views of outsourcing (Aubert et al., 1996). However control issues have received very little attention in outsourcing (Choudhury and Sabherwal, 2003) and have not been addressed in OOISD context.

In OOISD projects, the controller and controllee are from distinct organization and cultural backgrounds. The controller is the individual representing the client organization and the controllee is the individual/team representing the vendor organization. Thus, the different cultural backgrounds of vendor and client may cause variation in their organizational norms and values. In addition, since the individual norms and values derive from deep-rooted differences in cultural background, education and working life (Hofstede, 1980), we argue that it constrains use of certain control modes.

In the global context, other differences exist among global locales, as well as geographic, time zone, and cultural differences. Difficulties arise because of these other differences, for example, communication barriers can be partially addressed with the addition of formal and informal mechanisms to ensure cooperation and coordination (Carmel, 1999). Cultural differences become pronounced when the involvement and participation of individuals from multiple locations increase. Aligning control mechanisms with the societal characteristics can help bridge these differences, as they engender learning about different cultures, improved relations, and ultimately project progress (Palvia et al., 1996). Some societies may prefer mechanistic ways to perform tasks while others may prefer an organic approach. For example, Belgium firms explicitly define procedures to perform tasks while Irish firms use the socialization approach (Hofstede, 1980). Hence, from a control perspective, outcome control suits Belgium employees and clan control is better for Irish employees. In outsourcing arrangements, it is important for the controller to adopt a negotiated culture perspective, which is, an attempt to understand and move towards the controllee's norms and values (Palvia et al., 1996). The following excerpts highlight the relationship between culture and control modes:

❖ A study by Walsham (2002) examining the impact of cultural differences on software development (India vs. Jamaica) found that cultural differences affected formulation of organizational patterns of mobilizing commitment to collective tasks. The author argues that nature of participation particular to these societies resulted in divergent patterns of management; more restrictive/authoritative by the Indian manager while more collegial/consultative by Jamaican's manager.

❖ Sewell and Wilkinson (2002), in their study investigating use of surveillance systems, found that using surveillance systems to monitor the production quality processes was acceptable in British firms but was resisted in Japanese firms.

❖ Weisinger and Trauth (2003), analyzing the impact of culture on IT management, reveal that when American IT firms tried to install software systems that were developed locally in Japan, there was great deal of inconsistency. This occurred because Japanese firms view IT as operational systems while North American firms view IT as strategic systems.

❖ Birnberg and Snodgrass (1988), in their study exploring the impact of culture on control systems, found that Japanese firms had informal control systems while U.S. firms had explicit formal control systems. Further it was found that U.S. workers preferred more explicit role definitions and evaluation criteria in the control systems. On the other hand Japanese workers did not have extensive formal evaluation criteria, but had more explicit performance recording and rewards in the control systems.

❖ Chow et al. (1991), in their study analyzing the effect of management controls and national culture on manufacturing performance, found that U.S. firms considered cooperation among workers less important than Singapore firms. Further it was found that high collectivist subjects performed better than the individualistic subjects when the rewards were group based.

CULTURAL DIMENSIONS AND CONTROL MODES

Individualism and Collectivism

The differences in individualism-collectivism have main and moderating effects on cooperation in groups, causing variations in the way individuals perform tasks (Chow et al., 1991). In high individualistic countries, employees prefer to be independent and self-reliant (Hofstede, 1991). The employees prefer to define objectives and define their own ways of achieving them. They tend to perform better when they are less monitored and given liberty to perform tasks (Chow et al., 1991). In individualistic cultures, personal goals have priority and attitudes, personal needs, rights, and contracts guide the team members' behaviosr. For example, U.S. workers (ID score: 98) desire well-defined objectives and do not want to be constantly monitored. Hence, in OOISD projects involving individualistic countries, controllers can increase performance by articulating the rules and required outcomes while allowing the controllee to manage the tasks on their own. This will be best accomplished through the use of outcome controls (where desired results are explicitly stated) and self control (where individuals are given autonomy to monitor their own progress towards stated goals).

On the other hand in high collectivist countries, employees feel more interdependent and tend to cooperate with groups (Hofstede, 1980). It is posited that members of collectivist societies view self-development occurring through harmony and reciprocity in interpersonal relations and contributing to the welfare of other group members (Chow et al., 1991). In collectivist societies, group goals have priority and social norms, obligations and duties guide team members' behaviors. For example, in India (ID score 48) team members prefer to obtain consensus of their subordinates and the project manager before implementing any decisions/changes (Krishna et al., 2004). Hence implementing control through a process of socialization and promoting interpersonal dynamics to create shared beliefs, will harmonize the values and beliefs among the team members.

Further, in collectivist countries, employees view their relationship with the employer in moral terms. They appreciate training and other learning opportunities indicating their dependence on the organization (Triandis et al., 1988). It was noted that Japanese (ID score: 46) managers were concerned about how well the team-members followed the desired procedures rather than merely the outcomes. Hence, we expect that using behavioral control, where the emphasis is on dependence and organizational procedures, will lead to increased project performance. Table 3 summarizes the above arguments.

Individualism	Preferred Control Modes	Implications
High	Outcome, Self	Structuring a portfolio of control modes with outcome and self controls as dominant control modes will foster team performance
Low	Behavior, Clan	Structuring a control portfolio with behavior and clan controls as dominant control modes will foster team performance.
Table 3. Relationship between Individualism/Collectivism and Control Modes		

Uncertainty Avoidance

Uncertainty avoidance (UA) expresses the society members' need for written or unwritten sets of rules to deal with ambiguity and complement the need for predictability (Hofstede, 1980). In strong uncertainty avoidance countries, employees have minimal tolerance towards deviant ideas and prefer to work in a structured environment (Hofstede, 1991). For instance, in Belgium (UA score: 94) employees prefer stringent rules to perform their work activities; a little deviation causes considerable problems. Further, they regularly consult the rule book for input on resolving issues (Hofstede, 1980). The team members are dependent on experts/superiors for answers and feel secure when the desired outcomes and behaviors are defined.

On the other hand, in weak UA countries, employees prefer rules only in situations of absolute necessity. They are more open to newness and change, and feel motivated towards developing basic ideas to full-scale implementation. For instance in American (UA score: 46), IT firm managers view timecards as anti-professional to their work culture and believe that effective accomplishment of the task or project is what really matters, not whether someone is at work at 8:00 am sharp. Hence in weak uncertainty avoidance countries instead of requiring employees to follow a set of procedures, providing autonomy will increase project performance. Table 4 summarizes the above arguments.

Uncertainty Avoidance	Preferred Control Modes	Implications
Strong	Outcome, Behavior	Structuring a portfolio with formal controls as dominant control modes will foster team performance.
Weak	Self	Structuring a portfolio with self control as dominant control mode will foster team performance.
Table 4. Relationship between Uncertainty Avoidance and Control Modes		

Power Distance

Power distance (PD) defines the individual's acceptance of authority. It can be further explained as the individual's preference in the type of *manager-subordinate* relationship (Hofstede, 1991). In countries with high PD scores, the relationship between the manager and the subordinates is more authoritative. Subordinates are less participative and do not contend the decisions of their managers (Ford et al., 2003; Hofstede, 1980; 1991). There is acceptance of a "broad and unquestioned authority" of the superior (Bond, 1991). Employees regard their superior as the most knowledgeable and perform well if they are told what to do (Chow et al., 1999). For example, British managers were astounded when their Indian (PD score: 77) vendor's employees failed to participate in the project discussions (Nicholson and Sahay, 2001). In another instance, Chinese subordinates (PD score: 68) felt that their opinions, information and questions are less important than those of their superiors and that they are relatively less knowledgeable and intelligent (Chow et al., 1999). Hence, in OOISD context, we expect that in projects involving countries with large PD scores that explicitly defining the required outcomes and closely monitoring the project progress will increase project performance.

In the countries with smaller PD scores, subordinates' dependence on mangers is limited and they prefer more consultative relationship (Hofstede, 1980; 1991). The subordinates feel more comfortable in debating/contradicting. The managers prefer using the bottom-up approach for decision-making. For instance, in an Irish (PD score: 28) IT firm when knowledge management was implemented using formal and structured rules, the employees were resistant to share information. However, they agreed to share information only when the system was implemented on informal socio-cultural norms. Hence, in OOISD projects involving countries with lower PD scores, the use of informal modes of control, which make the relationship less structured, will enhance project performance. Table 5 summarizes the relationship between power distance and control modes.

Power Distance	Preferred Control Modes	Implications
Large	Outcome, Behavior	Structuring a portfolio with outcome and behavior controls as dominant control modes will foster team performance.
Small	Clan, Self	Structuring a portfolio with self and clan controls as dominant control modes will foster team performance.
Table 5. Relationship between Power Distance and Control Modes		

The findings depicted in Table 6 are consistent with prior control literature which posits that managers use a combination of control modes. In the past, scholars have been limited in their explanation of why mangers use different combination of control. This is particularly true with respect to informal control modes. Accordingly, by including culture as a possible factor influencing the manager's choice to structure portfolio of control modes helps us elucidate the dynamic nature of control modes. At this point, it is important to consider the other factors affecting control strategies injunction with culture. Accordingly, we integrate our findings with those from extant literature and present an integrative framework for control strategies in the following section.

Culture Dimensions	Key Characteristics	Formal control modes		Informal control modes	
		Outcome	Behavior	Self	Clan
High Individualism	Prefer clearly defined goals, autonomy and value individual effort.	High	Low	High	Low
High Collectivism	Group values are appreciated. Prefer to work in cooperation and rely on guidance.	Low	High	Low	High
Strong Uncertainty avoidance	Strong orientation for written rules and goals. Prefer structured work environment and frequently seek guidance from superiors.	High	High	Low	Low
Weak Uncertainty avoidance	Value achievement though individual effort. Rules are preferred only in situations of absolute necessity.	Low	Low	High	Low
Large Power Distance	Respect and accept superior authority. Prefer to be told what to do.	High	High	Low	Low
Small Power Distance	Do not appreciate intervention from superiors. Prefer consultative approach and readily participate in decision-making	Low	Low	High	High

Note: The "high/low" in the table refers to the dominance of the control modes.

Table 6: Culture and Control Interrelationship

AN INTEGRATIVE FRAMEWORK FOR CONTROL STRATEGIES

The main thrust of this chapter is to analyze the impact of culture on control modes; however it is important to acknowledge the findings in prior control research. Most of the prior research has been in the context of internal software development, with the exception of Choudhury and Sabherwal (2003). Consequently, scholars have dominantly focused on project and task characteristics and have ignored factors like environmental characteristics. However, very little empirical evidence exists to extend these findings to offshore context. Accordingly, we draw from the management literature to develop an integrative framework for control strategy. The outsourcing literature suggests that success of outsourced projects depends on the relationship between client and vendor, the project, and the people involved (Lacity and Willcocks, 2000). In the IS control literature, studies have found that factors such as availability of pre-existing mechanisms, task characteristics (behavior observability, outcome measurability), and project related knowledge and skills, affect controllers' choice of control modes (Kirsch, 1996; 1997, Kirsch et al., 2002). The organizational control literature emphasizes the impact of factors like trust, team size, and turbulence on control strategy (Flamholtz et al., 1985). We merge the findings from these streams to develop an integrative framework (Figure 1).

Task Characteristics

Outcome Measurability: Outcome measurability refers to the ability to measure achieved results and has been associated with choice of outcome control across numerous empirical and conceptual works. The argument posed is that if the desired outcomes can be articulated and measured, controllers will increasingly choose to exercise outcome control (Kirsch, 1997). Outcome control reflects a more market like mechanism that allows one to examine progress of a project in a comparatively costless fashion. In the offshore context, it is expensive and also problematic to monitor whether the project team adhered to all departmental and organizational guidelines or practices of system development. However it may be relatively easy to assess if the project was completed on time, within budget, and whether the needed functionality has been incorporated. Similarly, it was found that the controller used existing control mechanisms (predefined standards and methodologies) when other forms of control can be exercised (Choudhury and Sabherwal, 2003). In addition, studies have demonstrated that controllers choose to prefer outcome control when outcome measurability is high. Given these arguments and the widespread support for the link between outcome measurability and outcome control we posit that outcome measurability will be associated with use of outcome control.

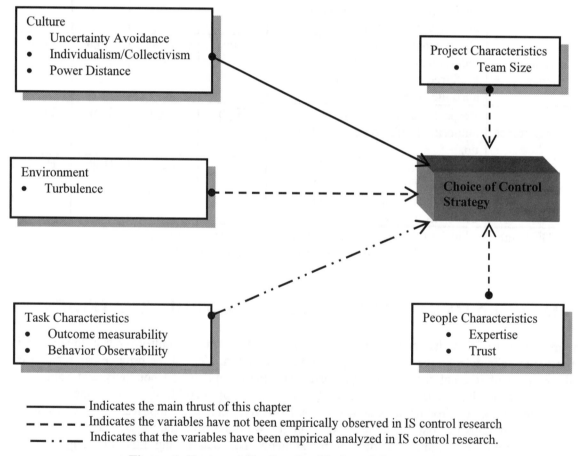

Figure 1. Factors Affecting the Choice of Control Strategy

Behavior Observability: Previous studies contend that when controllers have access to information that can be used to assess the controllee's behavior, they tend to use behavior control. Consistent support has been found for this argument (Kirsch, 1996; 1997). However, in an offshoring context, given the geographic distance, it becomes difficult to obtain information about the controllee's behavior. Nevertheless, developments in telecommunication technologies (video-conferencing) have facilitated access to the information. Accordingly, it is feasible to posit that high behavior observability will be associated with use of behavior control.

Environment Characteristics

Turbulence: Turbulance refers to stability in the environment. In prior IS control research, scholars have often explored the project level factors. Accordingly they ignore the environmental factors. While exploring control strategies in internal ISD, it is safe to assume social, political and technological environment to be constant. However, in offshoring it is not the case. The countries involved in the offshoring can vary in their social and political factors, technological advancements, and infrastructure. In particular, the technological capabilities of the vendor organization become important for fostering the quality of the software being developed. Specifically, technological competitiveness of the vendor is used as one of the criteria while selecting a vendor organization (IDC, 2006). Furthermore, given that one of the reasons why organizations outsource is to achieve competitiveness and stay abreast with technological developments, it is important for organizations to retain control without inhibiting innovativeness. For instance, the literature on transnational management and international joint venture (Barkema and Vermeulem, 1997) conveys that dynamic efficiency is important for organizations operating in turbulent environments. Such firms prefer to explore rather than exploit their competencies. In line with these arguments, it can be expected that firms operating under environmentally turbulent conditions need to make decisions rapidly and this should be reflected in the organizational form and structure. While the hierarchy (or bureaucracy) might ease the problem of decision making by centralizing all decision rights, it is invariably a slow responding structure since decisions at lower levels first need to be moved up the hierarchy, and down again which consumes time and resources. Too much time lag in turbulent environments on "making the decision" may imply lost advantage. To prevent this outcome, firms will attempt to decentralize the decision rights and put them in the hands of people who are both closest to the problem situation and knowledgeable about it. Accordingly, we posit that turbulence is important to be considered while designing control strategies. In particular, we expect high turbulence to be positively associated with choice of informal controls.

People Characteristics

Trust: The interrelationships between trust and control have been the subject for some recent research. In the past, control is often believed to be detrimental to trust because regulation implies a sense of mistrust (Das and Teng, 1998). In contrast, some scholars argue that proper control mechanisms may, in fact, increase trust (Sabherwal, 1999). Adopting a more contingent perspective, few others have argued that relationship between control and trust may not be the same across all situations (Das and Teng, 1998; 2001). They argued that formal control, that is, behavior control and output control, may undermine trust, because the employment of strict rules and objectives means that members do not have the autonomy to decide what works best. Informal control, that is self control and clan control, may foster trust by influencing people's behavior through creating shared goals and norms.

In outsourcing, relationship between the client and vendor is dynamic; hence factors like familiarity, vendor track record, and good-will will affect the way of monitoring (Choudhury and Sabherwal, 2003; Mähring, 2002; Sabherwal, 1999). For instance, when the controller (client) had less knowledge about the controllee, outcome control was used, but as the two sides learned from their interactions, they reassessed the alliance and made adjustments (less outcome and more clan control was used) (Choudhury and Sabherwal, 2003). These findings imply that the extent of influence will be affected by the level of expectancy (how confident are we in expecting others to act in a manner consistent with our objectives?). Therefore, it is logical to conclude that trust will affect the controller's choice to structure control modes. Specifically, trust in the agent on part of the principal will be associated with more informal modes of control while an absence of trust will be associated with a formal choice of control.

Expertise: Expertise refers to knowledge and experience about the transformation process. Expertise of agents, teams, staff, or units implies that they possess a repertoire of abilities and experiences. The project management literature suggests that units, individuals or teams that possess a repertoire of experience and skills are more likely to solve problems better than ones that do not enjoy the same privilege (Aladwani, 2002). Within the IS control literature it was found increased knowledge of the transformation process was associated with behavior control (Kirsch et al., 2002). This finding can be substantiated further using some prior research in the knowledge based view of the firm which argues possession of differential knowledge as the reason for vertical integration (Conner and Prahalad, 1996). In an outsourcing context, it was found that both client and the vendor's knowledge of the transformation process affected the choice of control mode (Choudhury and Sabherwal, 2003). For instance, when the controller had greater knowledge of the transformation process outcome control was used. This is because of the difficulty in implementing behavior control in an outsourcing context. On other hand, when the vendor/controllee had proven expertise, the controller used informal controls. This is again consistent with the knowledge based view of the firm. According to the knowledge based view of the firm, if the principal holds more knowledge about how a particular task is accomplished than does the agent and if this knowledge cannot be communicated without costs (or the unit or individual being directed), then vertical integration is more likely. Consequently if the agent or unit possesses more knowledge that the principal or if the principal cannot bring any unique and additional insights beyond those already possessed by the agent, then markets will be preferred. Based on these arguments, we posit that expertise will influence choice of control modes. However, unlike traditional ISD projects, in offshored projects the choice of control modes will depend on the level of expertise borne by the controller and controllee.

Project Characteristics

Team Size: Early work by Galbraith (1977) suggests that bigger team sizes will be associated with increased information processing and problems related to coordination that can adversely impact project outcomes. While bigger teams may be seen as sources of increased expertise since participants bring in and unite diverse abilities to the table, at least two arguments may be made for why this would result in counterproductive outcomes, and hence the need to exercise appropriate controls. The first line of argument is related to "free-riding" behavior while the second is related to cognitive limitations of individuals. Further as team sizes increase, the pressure for any one individual to free ride increases while the personal motivation to contribute diffuses (Aladwani, 2002). As a result individuals will attempt to shirk their part of the responsibility in achieving an outcome (Ouchi, 1980). On the contrary, in smaller teams shirking or free-riding may not present a serious problem, since the controller can always monitor and act accordingly to correct such shirking behaviors. In large teams however, there is only a limited span over which the controller can exercise control. This is so because as team sizes increase, so do the costs of monitoring and enforcing rules, regulations and the like. Given the geographic distance, monitoring costs maybe high in offshored projects. It implies that the controller may have to spend significant time looking over the controllee, and as a result divert attention from other activities that concomitantly demand attention. These arguments suggest that while the effectiveness of control may be limited, the controller will desire to exercise additional control by investing in vertical information systems, creating formalized procedures through rules, and regulations and functional groups that allow easier monitoring of overall project. Control studies in the management arena have examined the link between team size and span of control (Ouchi, 1980). Findings from these studies reveal that outcome control was positively associated with larger team sizes. In line with the prior literature, we posit that increasing team sizes will be positively associated with formal control modes. In particular, we suggest that outcome control can be used as the dominant control mode.

CONCLUSION

A major underlying argument of this chapter is that culture is an important factor to consider while developing control strategies in an OOISD context. The approach has been to combine three distinct streams of research, organizational control, project management and culture, to understand the effect of culture on control strategies.

While cultures, by definition, change slowly, the effect of cross culture issues on ISD projects have become increasingly important (Gosain et al., 2003; Krishna et al., 2004). The rapidity and intensity of globalization in the IT industry emphasizes the importance of acknowledging cross-cultural issues to ensure project success. One of the limitations of the existing control research is omission of cultural variables and circumstances, thus neglecting their effect on the control strategies. There is much systematic evidence suggesting that the pursuit of identical tasks or goals takes place in dissimilar ways from one national society to another (Ford et al., 2003). Understanding the dissimilar sets of core values which are thought to affect work motivation and propensity to favor one method of control over another, offer the potential of developing broad nationally specific solutions to problems of control strategies in OOISD projects.

A suggestion from the broader framework proposed is to design a control strategy that fits the offshore setting. This will enhance the effectiveness of control modes and thus increase the project performance in offshore context. Addressing the cross-cultural issues will lead to convergence of attitudes, values, and beliefs, helping organizations meet the challenges of working in multicultural teams. Also, creating a fit between the project characteristics, task characteristics, environment, culture, people characteristics and control modes will help managers successfully manage OOISD projects. With globalization becoming a prominent trend in the IT industry, it is increasingly important to gain insight into how control interventions can have the highest likelihood of success in light of cross-cultural issues. This framework offers a modest step in that direction, with the potential of leading to more effective project management practices.

MINICASE

Goras – Software Development in Cross Cultural Setting

Catastrophes like hurricanes and earthquakes are common in Caribbean islands like Jamaica. People residing in Jamaica rely on insurance companies for protection during the time of catastrophes. Alas, the capital base of general insurers in Jamaica is insufficient for high risk insurance coverage. Most of the Jamaican general insurance companies rely on worldwide reinsurers, who underwrite some of these high risks. However, as the catastrophes increased, the reinsurers started to demand better quality information on risks and levels of exposure.

In 1988, Hurricane Gilbert swept through Jamaica disrupting all the business activities on the island for a couple of months. Affected individuals and businesses were making claims for their losses. However, insurance companies were in an impasse for processing these claims as the computer records were completely destroyed. Abco, a Jamaican general insurance company faced a similar situation. Abco is part of a broader Jamaican conglomerate called Jagis. Abco was not able to process the claims as there were no records present in its batch system. As catastrophes continued to increase, reinsurers demanded better quality information from Abco on risks and levels of exposure. In response to these demands, the Chairman of Jagis group decided to leverage information technology to develop a state-of-art insurance system. The project objective was to develop an insurance system that will provide better quality service to its clients, and quality information to help reinsurers to better evaluate risk. GORAS, development of new insurance system was initiated in 1990. An external software consultant agency, GTEC, was hired to conduct requirement analysis and software development. GTEC recruited software experts from Indian software houses. During the requirement phase Jagis realized that Goras required inputs from insurance experts. Consequently, insurance experts from Jagis information technology team were involved in the GORAS project. The GTEC team was lead by a Senior Indian software expert, Raj, and the Jagis team was lead by its information technology manager, Robert. Both Robert and Raj were responsible for monitoring the project activities and delivering the project goals. Both the teams together estimated GORAS to be completed in a year's time frame. Raj employed an autocratic approach to manage the project. He believed that the project manager's role was walking around and seeing how people are progressing, coordinating and administering activities. Raj retained complete authority on making all projected related decisions. He was responsible for both technical and human issues. On the other hand, Robert used a consensual approach to manage the project. He believed that a problem can be efficiently solved by team effort and not by some sort of hierarchy.

In the initial stages of the project, all the team members showed enthusiasm and treated each other equally. Awards and incentives were offered for "most helpful member" and "project champion." While most team members were motivated with the pay plus bonus reward structure, some felt the deadlines were stringent and difficult to meet. In particular, the Jamaicans gave excuses for extending the deadlines. Conversely, Indian team members never argued or negotiated the deadlines. They worked extended work hours and, if necessary, on week-ends to meet the deadlines. Raj became critical about their more laid back attitude to deadlines, regarding their formal working hours as being all they were prepared to offer to the project. He felt that the Jamaicans were not trained in the project coordination activities.

Supervisor-subordinate relationship: The Indian team members believed in monitoring systems and willfully gave decision-making authority to Raj. They considered Raj to be superior in knowledge and followed his rules as if it was a law. The team members were comfortable with the hierarchy system, and cogently worked together to achieve the goals and objectives.

In contrast, the Jamaican team members did not believe in monitoring system, they felt it was rude for the boss to question about the project progress. They did not prefer their boss looking over their shoulders; their work attitude was "we will let you know if the job is done or not, if you are not satisfied with our work, fire us with redundancy pay and do not intervene in our job functions." Further, they were incapable of working together in a coordinated way.

As a result of these differential cultural attitudes, the Jamaicans refused to integrate themselves with the Indian team, as they did not believe in neither the hierarchy system nor the authoritative supervisor-subordinate relationship. Some thought that the Indians were comfortable using a hierarchy system because of their deep-rooted caste system where hierarchy and status were deemed important. Some Jamaican developers referred to Raj's approach as adult-child mentality and were reluctant to his school-room attitude. On the other hand, Raj felt the Jamaicans were too equal to make project monitoring and control effective.

Furthermore, as Indian developers assumed senior posts in the project, the Jamaican developers felt that Abco respected the Indian developers more than themselves, and hence were given more power. All these differences caused momentous delay in GORAS progress.

At the team level, the Indian developers mostly assumed the role of advice givers. This made the Jamaican developers feel inferior; some of them felt that the project was taken away from them. GORAS failed to meet the deadlines; the project faced significant delays and major project cost overruns. The system was finally completed after two years but failed to meet the end user expectations. Further, substantial inadequacies were found during the testing phase. On the management front, a new CEO was appointed to head GTEC, Raj was made the technical director and was no longer involved in organizational issues. GORAS was finally moved to Jagis group and GTEC continued to provide technical support. Five years later, the system was still not completed; it remained a promise rather than reality.

Discussion Questions:
1. What measures can be taken to negate the effect of cultural differences between the GTEC and Jagis development team?
2. What factors must be considered while deciding to offshore software development activities?
3. Do you agree that national culture affects the personality of project managers? Explain your answer.

Adapted from Walsham, G. "Cross-cultural software production and use: A structural analysis," MIS Quarterly 26(4), December 2002, pp 359-380.

KEY TERMS
Control
Control modes
Control mechanisms.
Control portfolio
Cultural heterogeneity
Cultural homogeneity
Culturalist
Culture
Dimensions of culture
Hawthorne study
ISD projects
Moderating effect/variable
Non-culturalist
Offshore outsourcing or offshoring
On shore outsourcing
OOISD
Outsourcee
Outsourcer
Outsourcing Portfolios of Control
Vendor - Client relationship

STUDY QUESTIONS
1. Explain the debate between the culturalists versus non culturalists on the practice of using national models of culture? Is there evidence to suggest that culture can influence the way organizations can be managed?

2. Define Hofstede's power distance, uncertainty avoidance, and individualism and collectivism as major dimensions of culture. Which countries are at the extreme points with respect to each dimension?

3. Define control modes? Distinguish between formal and informal controls.

4. What is Clan control? Why do you believe it would work well in cultures that are (a) highly collectivist, (b) weak on uncertainty avoidance and (c) have small power distance?

5. What is outcome control? Why do you believe it would work well in cultures that are (a) highly individualistic, (b) strong on uncertainty avoidance, and (c) have large power distance?

REFERENCES

Aladwani, A. M. "An integrated performance model of information systems projects," *Journal of Management Information Systems* 19(1), Sum 2002, pp. 185-210.

Aubert, B. A., Rivard, S., and Party, M. "A transaction cost approach to outsourcing behavior: Some empirical evidence.," *Information Management* 30(2) 1996, pp. 51-64.

Barkema, G. H., and Vermeulem, F. "What differences in the cultural backgrounds of partners are detrimental for international joint ventures?," *Journal of International Business Studies* 28(4), Winter 1997, pp. 845-865.

Barthelemy, J. "The hidden costs of IT outsourcing," *Sloan Management Review* 42(3), Spring 2001.

Beath, C. M. "Managing the user relationship in information systems development projects: A transaction governance approach," 8th International Conference of Information's Systems, 1987, pp. 415-427.

Birnberg, J. G., and Snodgrass, C. "Culture and Control - a Field-Study," *Accounting Organizations and Society* 13(5) 1988, pp 447-464.

Bond, M. H. *Beyond the Chinese face: Insights from psychology.* Oxford University Press, Hong Kong, 1991.

Brannen, J. V., and Salk, J. E. "Partnering across borders: Negotiating organizational culture in a German-Japan joint venture.," *Human Relations* 54(4) 2000, pp. 451-487.

Chow, C. W., Shields, M. D., and Wu, A. "The importance of national culture in the design of and preference for management controls for multi-national operations," *Accounting Organizations and Society* 24(5-6), Jul-Aug 1999, pp. 441-461.

Clark, T., Zmud, R. W., and McCray, G. "The outsourcing of information services: Transforming the nature of business in the information industry.," in: *Strategic Sourcing of Information Systems.*, Willcocks, P. L., and Lacity, M. C. (ed.), Wiley, NY, 1998.

Conner, K. R., and Prahalad, C. K. "A Resource-based Theory of the Firm: Knowledge Versus Opportunism," *Organization Science: A Journal of the Institute of Management Sciences* (7:5), September/October 1996, pp. 477-501.

Das, T. K., and Teng, B. S. "Between trust and control: Developing confidence in partner cooperation in alliances," *Academy of Management Review* 23(3), Jul 1998, pp. 491-512.

Das, T. K., and Teng, B. S. "Trust, control, and risk in strategic alliances: An integrated framework," *Organization Studies* 22(2) 2001, pp. 251-283.

Flamholtz, E. G., Das, T. K., and Tsui, A. S. "Toward an Integrative Framework of Organizational Control," *Accounting Organizations and Society* (10:1) 1985, pp 35-50.

Ford, P. D., Catherine, E. C., and Meister, B. D. "Information systems research and Hofstede's culture's consequences: An uneasy and incomplete partnership.," *IEEE Transactions on Engineering Management* 50(1), February 2003, pp. 8-25.

Galbraith, J. R. *Organization design* Addison-Wesley Pub. Co., Reading, Mass., 1977, pp. xvi, 426.

Gopal, A., Mukhopadhyay, T., and Krishnan, M.S. "The role of software processes and communication in offshore software development." *Communication of the. ACM* 45(4), April 2002, pp. 193-200.

Gurubaxani, V. "Value Networks and Offshore Outsourcing," CSC Archives, 2003.

Hayes, M. "Precious Connection Companies thinking about using offshore outsourcing need to consider more than just cost savings," Information Week, 2003.

Henderson, J. C., and Lee, S. "Managing I/S Design Teams - a Control Theories Perspective," *Management Science* (38:6), Jun 1992, pp 757-777.

Hofstede, G. *Culture's Consequences: International Differences in Work-Related Values.* Sage, Newbury Park, CA, 1980.

Hofstede, G. *Culture and Organizations: Software of the mind.* McGraw Hill, Cambridge, UK, 1991.

House, R., Hanges, P. J., Quntanilla, A., Dorfman, P. W., Dickson, M. W., and Javidan, M., *"Culture, Leadership, and Organizational Practices."* JAI Press, 1999.

IDC "Worldwide and U.S. Offshore IT Services 2006-2010 Forecast," 202411, International Data Corporation, pp. 55.

Jaegur, A.M. "Organization Development and National Culture: Where's the Fit?," *The Academy of Management Review* 11(1), January 1986, pp. 178-190.

Keil, M., Bernard, C. Y. T., Kwok-Kee, W., and Saarinen, T. "A cross cultural study on escalation of commitment behavior in software projects," *MIS Quarterly* 24(2) 2000, pp. 299-325.

Kirsch, L., and Cummings, L. L. "Contextual influences on self-control of IS professionals engaged in systems development," *Accounting, Management Information technology* 6(3) 1996a, pp. 191-219.

Kirsch, L. J. "The management of complex tasks in organizations: Controlling the systems development process," *Organization Science* 7(1), Jan-Feb 1996, pp. 1-21.

Kirsch, L. J. "Portfolios of Control Modes and IS Project Management," *Information Systems Research* 8(3) 1997, pp. 215-239.

Kirsch, L. J. "Deploying Common Systems Globally: The Dynamics of Control," *Information Systems Research* 15(4), December 2004, pp. 374–395.

Kirsch, L. J., and Beath, C. M. "The Enactments and Consequences of Token, Shared, and Compliant Participation in Information Systems Development," *Accounting, Management and Information Technology* 6(4) 1996b, pp. 221-254.

Kirsch, L. J., and Cummings, L. L. "Contextual Influences on Self Control of IS Professionals Engaged in Systems Development," *Accounting, Management and Information Technology* 6(3) 1996c, pp. 191-219.

Kirsch, L. J., Sambamurthy, V., Ko, D. G., and Purvis, R. L. "Controlling information systems development projects: The view from the client," *Management Science* 48(4), Apr 2002, pp. 484-498.

Krishna, S., Sahay, S., and Walsham, G. "Managing cross-cultural issues.," *Communications of the ACM* 47(4), April 2004, pp. 62-66.

Lacity, M. C., and Willcocks, L .P. "Survey of IT Outsourcing Experiences in US and UK Organizations. (Industry Trend or Event)," *Journal of Global Information Management* 8(2), June 2000.

MacGregor, E. H., and Kruchten, P. "Cultural patterns in software process mishaps: Incidents in Global Projects," *Human and Social factors of Software Engineering*), May 2005.

Mähring, M. "IT project governance: A process-oriented study of organizational control and executive involvement," in: *SSE/EFI Working Paper Series in Business Administration,* Stockholm, 2002.

Mateyaschuk, J. "Foreign Aid for IT - U.S. Companies seeking to Outsource their Critical Projects are increasingly turning to India.," Information Week, 1999.

NASSCOM ""Business in India: Quality,"", India, 2004.

Newman, K. L., and Nollen, S. D. " Culture and Congruence: The Fit between Management Practices and National Culture.," *Journal of International Business Studies*), September 1996, pp. 753-779.

Nicholson, B., and Sahay, S. "Some political and cultural issues in the globalization of software development: Case experience from Britain and India." *Information Organization* (11) 2001, pp. 25-43.

Ouchi, G. W., and Maguire, A. "Organizational Control: Two functions," *Administrative Science Quarterly* 20(4), December 1975, pp. 559-569.

Ouchi, W. G. "Markets, bureaucracies, and clans." *Administrative Science Quarterly* 25(1) 1980, pp. 129-141.

Palvia, P., Palvia, S., and Roche, E. *"Global Information Technology and Systems management: Key Issues and Trends"* Ivy League Publishing, 1996.

Rottman, J., and Lacity, M. ""Proven Practices for Effectively Offshoring IT Work,"" *Sloan Management Review* 47(3), Spring 2006, pp. 56-63.

Sabherwal, R. "The role of trust in managing outsourced IS development projects." *Communication of the ACM* 42(2) 1999, pp. 80-87.

Sewell, G., and Wilkinson, B. "Someone to watch over me: Surveillance, discipline and the just-in-time labor process," *Sociology* 26(2) 1992, p.p 271-289.

Takac, F. P. "Outsourcing technology." *Management Decision* 31(1), January 1993, pp. 26-38.

Triandis, H. C., Bontempo, R., Villareal, M. J., Asai, M., and Lucca, N. "Individualism and collectivism: Cross-cultural perspectives on self-ingroup relationships." *Journal of Personality and Social Psychology* (54), pp. 323-338 1988.

Walsham, G. "Cross-cultural software production and use: A structural analysis," *MIS Quarterly* 26(4), December 2002, pp. 359-380.

Weisinger, Y. J., and Trauth, E. "The importance of situating culture in cross-cultural IT management," *IEEE Transactions on Engineering Management* 50(1), February 2003, pp. 26-30.

Rottman, J., and Lacity, M. ""Proven Practices for Effectively Offshoring IT Work,"" *Sloan Management Review* 47(3), spring 2006, pp. 56-63.

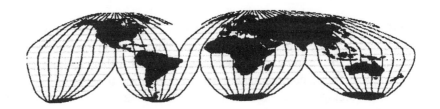

IS Offshoring: A Sourcing Framework and Emerging Knowledge Requirements

William R. King
University of Pittsburgh, USA

CHAPTER SUMMARY

The offshoring of information systems tasks has come to be a major feature of the international IS domain. This chapter introduces some basic concepts of offshoring, some reasons companies are offshoring, how offshoring has evolved, the costs and benefits of offshoring, difficulties and risks of offshoring, and the future of offshoring. It also provides a framework for analyzing IS offshoring and outsourcing decisions and discusses the emerging offshoring-related knowledge requirements for people working in the IS field. This chapter makes a case for IS professional who are knowledgeable in offshoring management by providing management and skill requirements and implications for IS/IT educational programs.

INTRODUCTION

The outsourcing and offshoring of information technology (IT) activities has become an important element of information systems (IS) management. IT activities, which were once performed almost exclusively in-house by most kinds of business firms, are now often outsourced to vendors who are specialists in some phase(s) of IS such as programming, help-desk operation, or data center operations. Increasingly, vendors are "moving up the value chain" to offer ever-more-sophisticated services.

Dealing with a myriad of such arrangements has become an important element of the IS manager's job. The knowledge and skill requirements for managing outsourcing and offshoring are quite different than were the requirements for effectively performing these activities in-house. It is these new managerial knowledge and skill requirements on which this chapter focuses.

Because IS is the third largest corporate expense category and about 50% of U.S. capital expenditures by business are in IS/IT, the potential for IS outsourcing is huge. So, the prevalence of offshoring and the demands for new skills and knowledge to manage it are likely to grow.

BASIC CONCEPTS

The term "Information Systems" (IS) is used in this chapter to refer both to the systems themselves and to the IS function in the organization. The term "Information Technology" (IT) is used to refer to the hardware, software, communications networks and other technological elements that the organization employs for its communications and information processing.

IS/IT outsourcing is the execution of IS/IT activities by a vendor firm who specializes in performing that activity and usually does so for many client firms. This enables the vendor to consolidate the work of many clients, thereby achieving cost and performance advantages due to specialization and economies of scale. Often, these activities have previously been performed in-house by the client firms.

The arrangements under which the outsourcing is done vary from a pure contractual relationship to various forms of partnerships, some involving cost- and benefit-sharing, to the creation of alliances or a subsidiary firm, often in a low-cost "developing" country.

Outsourcing may involve a single client and vendor or multiple vendors ("multi-sourcing"). When client and vendor form a partnership and/or share in the costs and benefits of the relationship, the relationship may be referred to as "co-sourcing."

Offshoring (or, offshore outsourcing) is outsourcing in which the client and vendor are in different countries. The term is typically applied even if no "shore" is actually crossed, such as when an activity is "offshored" from the US to Mexico or when a Western European company "offshores" to a firm in Eastern Europe.

An Association for Computing Machinery Report (Aspray et al., 2006) delineates six varieties of work related to IS that are often offshored: (1) programming, software testing, and software maintenance; (2) IT research and development; (3) high-end jobs such as software architecture, product design, project management, IT consulting, and business strategy; (4) physical product manufacturing, including semiconductors, computer components, computers, etc.; (5) business process outsourcing/IT Enabled Services, including insurance claim processing, medical billing, accounting, bookkeeping, medical transcription, digitization of engineering drawings, desktop publishing, and high-end IT enabled services such as financial analysis and reading of X-rays; and (6) call centers and telemarketing. Some of these are more relevant to IS management than are others.

Companies in developed nations most frequently offshore such work to firms in less-developed countries. India is the biggest vendor nation for IS-related work, but many other countries perform work for US firms including China, Malaysia, the Philippines, and South Africa (Economist, July 17, 2003 and November 20, 2003).

REASONS FOR OUTSOURCING AND OFFSHORING

The primary rationale for outsourcing is based on the antithetical concepts of "commodity" and "core competency." If an IS activity can be considered to be a commodity — something that is widely available and more or less the same in kind of quality from whomever it is purchased — it is argued that there is little justification for performing the activity internally. In such a case, a specialist vendor may normally be able to provide the service, perhaps at a higher level of quality, a lower level of cost, or both (Quinn and Hilmer, 1994).

The business enterprise, so the argument for outsourcing goes, should outsource "commodity" activities and focus its attention and energy on its "core competencies" — a notion that is intuitively appealing, but is often only imprecisely defined. In many enterprises, IS has historically been thought of as a service activity rather than a core competency; so it is often considered to be a prime candidate for outsourcing.

A number of studies have focused on the organization's motivation to engage in offshoring and/or outsourcing (Straub and Watson, 2001; Adler, 2003; Levina and Ross, 2003). The internal IS function is often viewed by senior managers to be costly, difficult to understand and peripheral to the firm's core business. As firms shifted in the 1990s to business strategies that focused on their core competencies rather than strategies for mediating risk through diversification as had previously been emphasized, attention was focused on IS and the role that IT played in the enterprise. Since IS was frequently judged to be "non-core," it became a prime candidate for outsourcing.

The most important reasons for IS outsourcing are its perceived non-core nature (Grover and Teng, 1993), the significant cost savings that may often be gained if IS activities were performed outside the firm (Loh and Venkatramen, 1992), the difficulty that firms have in assessing the business value contributed by IT and the lack of understanding of IT by top-level business executives (Lacity and Hirschheim, 1993).

As Larry Ellison, CEO of Oracle has said, "Why should every automaker, publisher or doctor's office have to be a tech company too, employing high-paid staff who spend all of their time fiddling around with computers?" (Jenkins, 2004).

The cost-savings motivation is an element of most offshoring arrangements and is usually fairly easy to demonstrate and to quantify. The other reasons for offshoring are less easy to demonstrate or quantify. For instance, many firms have been able to demonstrate the business value of IS activities. For those which have not done so and claim this inability as a reason for offshoring suggests that they may be rationalizing and unwilling to do the hard work of measuring business value. That, along with the desire of some business executives to rid themselves of activities that they don't understand, represent poor reasons for offshoring choices. For them, offshoring may be the "easy solution."

However, offshoring often carries with it problems and risks that are unanticipated. We shall explore these further in a later section.

THE EVOLUTION OF OUTSOURCING AND OFFSHORING

Outsourcing may be viewed as a natural step in the evolution of a business. In the early 20th century, auto companies made many of the parts for a car. Over the years, they subcontracted (outsourced) the manufacture of parts to others, each of whom could focus on producing only a few parts. Initially, this was done to achieve cost savings, but through their limited focus, parts providers often developed higher quality levels than the automakers, with their wide diversity of activities, could attain. Today, virtually every auto company outsources the production of parts, sub-assemblies, assemblies and major modules of autos.

Many of these outsourcing vendors are "offshore" in large part because of the lower costs that can be attained outside of home countries in the industrialized West. This exploitation of international cost differentials has been termed "global arbitrage" (Sawhney, 2002) as it is an extension of the classic economic arbitrage strategy.

IS is going through similar phases as manufacturing did previously. The outsourcing of IS began with the hiring of external consultants to aid in areas where companies did not have sufficient skills to accomplish the range of necessary applications and systems. As early as 1963, Electronic Data Systems (EDS) contracted with Blue Cross of Pennsylvania to handle its data processing. In 1989, Kodak outsourced most of its IT to IBM and two other vendors. This was a large, prominent and comprehensive outsourcing contract that involved the hiring of many of Kodak's IS personnel by IBM. From that point, outsourcing became very visible and has grown rapidly.

Computer activities, once done internally, are commonly outsourced to vendors who can achieve high efficiencies through combining the computing tasks of various clients on a limited set of hardware and software. Now, virtually any IS activity can be considered as a candidate for outsourcing and/or offshoring since specialized firms offer software packages of the most sophisticated varieties (e.g., Enterprise Resources Planning, or ERP) as well as operational services.

The cost factor has been, and remains, one of the most critical practical arguments put forward by U.S. companies for offshoring. Inexpensive labor as the primary motivation for offshore production for the electronics industry was empirically examined by Moxon (1975). The importance of production costs has also been suggested in information system studies (Ang and Straub, 1998; Wang, 2002). Clearly, advancements in communication and computer technologies in recent years have made this option ever more credible, and offshoring opportunities ever more feasible, particularly in the service domain.

Just as auto firms began outsourcing to achieve cost efficiencies only to find that quality, and eventually delivery time, also improved, some argue that the same scenario will be played out in offshoring IS. Already, some companies that have outsourced call-center operations to India report that customer satisfaction has increased. Overall, the quality gap with US call centers appears to be closing rapidly. A survey of software projects by the Center for eBusiness at Massachusetts Institute of Technology found that projects developed in India had only 10% more bugs than comparable U.S. projects (Ante, 2004). Many software development teams in India use Six Sigma approaches to quality management that are equivalent to those in use in world-class firms (McDougall, 2005). Given the abundance of skills at offshore sites as well as pressure on executives to drive down costs, there is little doubt that this trend will continue and even increase for some time (Overby, 2003) despite warnings and cautions (Thurm, 2004).

With the increase in the "export" of high-skilled, highly-paid jobs, the expectation for cost savings has also increased. However, if cost reduction is the primary goal, a very significant cost difference maybe necessary before an offshore venture can be considered worthwhile (Wang et al., 1997). Cost advantages on the order of 60-70% have been reported for some outsourced IT activities.

THE NATIONAL AND INTERNATIONAL COSTS AND BENEFITS OF OFFSHORING

There is no doubt that offshoring benefits client companies through cost savings and in other ways. It also benefits offshore vendors by creating revenues and high-quality jobs in their countries.

While there is a great deal of arguing and posturing among politicians about offshoring, economic theory and empirical evidence suggest that offshoring is a win-win proposition at the national level. While jobs are lost because of offshoring, temporarily hurting the individuals who filled them, the economic benefits to companies, to the economy, to workers in general and even to the displaced workers in the long-run (because if they are flexible, they often obtain higher-paying jobs than those that they lost) are clearly understood and primarily positive.

Even the lost jobs, which are the focus of most political debate, have a modest impact when viewed at the national level. The previously-noted ACM study found that while 2 to 3% of US technology jobs are moved overseas each year, the ongoing computing boom results in the creation of more jobs than are lost (Aspray et al., 2006). Moreover, the number of "replacement" jobs that can be calculated is clearly an underestimate, since IT continues to creep into every business and every job, defying the usual classifications of what is a "computer-based job."

As a result of offshoring, firms save costs; these funds can be redeployed elsewhere – into developing new products, doing more research and development or expanding existing businesses, for instance. This creates new, generally-higher-paying jobs than those which were lost. Even if firms return these savings to stockholders in the form of dividends or share buybacks, the individuals typically invest the funds in companies that they expect to grow and prosper, thus enabling them to do so (Simon, 1965).

These benefits are empirically confirmed by studies of national and international economics that suggest a diverse and positive impact on the home-nation economy due to outsourcing and the globalization of information technology (Levy, 1995; McLaren, 2000; Mann, 2003).

THE FUTURE OF IS OFFSHORING

The nature of potential outsourcing tasks continues to become more complex and sophisticated as do the skills available through offshore vendors. There is no shortage of computer skill and competency offshore. The Software Engineering Institute suggests that about 40% of the top-rated (Level 5) software companies are located in India (Milligan, 2004).

There are nuances to offshoring that makes it different from the traditional outsourcing phenomenon. Offshoring is expected to have greater impact on the demand side of IT services by creating new global markets and by adding new products and services through greater talent pools and innovation. However, as offshoring increases there will inevitably be a lessening availability of talent. McDougall (2005) suggests, "While Indian technical schools are churning out more than a half million programmers per year, that's barely enough to meet the growing demand for workers in indigenous services firms and the foreign multinationals that are tapping the country's IT workforce." China is expected to soon become the biggest market for Indian-made software. Oracle alone employs more than 5,000 developers in India, and IBM has plans to hire about 14,000 programmers there (McDougall, 2005).

As vendors' businesses have developed and prospered in India, it could reasonably be foreseen that personnel costs would increase, the availability of trained professionals would decrease and the overall cost advantages of offshoring would decrease. Could this perhaps mean that offshoring would become less desirable in the future than it has recently been?

These changes are now occurring. Labor costs are rising in both China and India and vendors in both countries, for the first time, have recently faced shortages of skilled employees. So, one might reasonably expect that the advantages of offshoring are shrinking, particularly in the area of cost savings.

However, this conclusion would be based on only part of the overall picture. The other relevant parts are the high and ever-increasing levels of sophistication of Indian vendors, their focus on improving quality and efficiency, and their "insurance policies" concerning the availability of talented professionals.

The level of sophistication of Indian vendors such as Wipro, Infosys Technologies, and Tata Consultancy, already high, is growing rapidly. Their goal is to move up the value-added ladder to offer even more sophisticated services. They know that so long as their primary advantage is cheap labor, they have a dim long-term future, so their attention has turned to doing ever-more-sophisticated tasks, to automating their processes and to improving quality and productivity. Indeed, recent evidence suggests that "reverse offshoring" is occurring. The sending of call center jobs back to the US by Indian vendors who no longer consider such low-level activities to be profitable (Kripalani, 2006).

Most large Indian vendor firms use Six Sigma approaches to quality management. They are focusing on improving the quality of their output and their processes. For instance, Wipro has extensively studied the "Toyota way" of continuous improvement - automation, process re-engineering, respect for employees, and the acceptance of change. All are non-traditional in the Indian culture, but all necessary to compete in the global environment. Wipro wishes to be the "Toyota of business services" and it is already well along the way to becoming the world's most efficient provider.

Vendors like Wipro, Infosys, Tata and Satyam Computer Services also ensure a continuing supply of engineers and technical people by reaching into India's "second-level" engineering schools to hire people before their last year of study and to provide job-related course material and teacher training for that last year. Students therefore become committed early, and on graduation, are well-versed in the ways of their employer, up-to-date on the latest relevant innovations and ready to undertake their jobs with less in-house training.

India's "first rank" engineering and technical schools enroll only thousands of students, while these second-level schools enroll tens of thousands who are nearly as good. Moreover, these schools are willing to mix practical job-focused training with theoretical studies for students who have already been hired by outsourcing vendors. Thus, these offshore vendors ensure themselves a continuing supply of top people to help them defeat the natural results of their success – the need for more people and limits on the availability of talent.

Anyone who expects that the natural processes of increasing salaries and limited availability of trained people will seriously influence the prevalence or advantages of IT offshoring is probably not aware how sophisticated these offshore vendors are, how much they have adopted the best management practices and how they are creatively insulating themselves against the inevitable decline in the supply of talented professionals.

The economic and business logic for offshoring suggests that the offshoring of IS activities will continue to expand. Similar outsourcing phenomena are likely to occur in other areas of business. Generally speaking, these changes will both follow and amplify the existing trends in manufacturing and in IS. For instance, various Human Resources (HR) activities are more frequently outsourced than are IS activities. This is interesting because the technological advantage of HR vendors is usually important to firms who outsource to them. The results and offshoring in a variety of business functional areas are a lessening of internal demand on the IS function and the shrinking of the internal functional departments as well as the internal IS department.

Thus, a strong case can be made that, unless the political system behaves irrationally, the offshore outsourcing trend in IS and IT is likely to continue. These future trends have been summed up by Overby (2003) in an article that incorporates comments by Doug Busch, Chief Information Officer (CIO) of Intel, Larry Pickett, CIO of Purdue Pharma, and Nancy Markle, President of the Society for Information Management. They suggest that in the near-term future, the following will occur:

1. IT jobs will be lost to offshore companies.
2. U.S. IT staffing levels will never return to their previous highs.
3. IT work that remains will be more important to the business.
4. Firms will continue to offshore application development, legacy maintenance, call center operations and the like.
5. U.S. companies will keep work that requires close contact with the business such as strategy development, business process improvement, and actual application of IT in the business.
6. IT will become a core competency and economic engine in emerging economies, and these emerging economies will complement the U.S. IT industry.
7. U.S. IT executives look beyond the possible short-term offshore savings to the long-term impact on the nation's ability to remain innovative.
8. The higher-level IT positions that remain will require new skills.
9. U.S. IT degree programs should move more toward broader business education.
10. The IT cohort of the future has to be a good technologist but also be a savvy businessperson, a hybrid and versatile person.
11. Issues of infrastructure, security, communication and project management are important to onshore jobs.
12. There is a need to protect intellectual capital, especially when IT is integrated in business processes.

DIFFICULTIES AND RISKS IN OFFSHORING

While cost savings is the primary motivation for offshoring, it actually often causes cost increases in the short run. This is due to disruptions in the client firm's activities during the transition to offshoring and the fact that displaced personnel are often absorbed into other operations of the client firm.

A major category of risk in offshoring is that of expected performance levels not being met. Thus, higher-than-expected costs, lower-than-expected service levels, client dissatisfaction or vendor shutdown caused by unexpected events are some of the basic risks. These are only partly ameliorated by having a fixed-price contract and specified service levels.

Other, longer-term performance risks include "price creep" and a low rate of vendor innovation. Price creep usually reflects the monopoly power that the vendor accrues after obtaining the contract, which many lead to shirking or opportunistic contract renegotiation. Clearly, the contract must provide an escape clause should these sorts of behaviors occur.

Organizations adopting offshoring typically make changes in task structures, processes and internal systems that involve many employees. The risk of losing valuable employees at such times is significant and steps should be taking to minimize these losses (Straub and Watson, 2001).

One of the most obvious risks in offshoring is that of information security. The potential client must be assured that such security is as carefully treated by the vendor as it is within the firm itself. Most top vendors devote significant effort and resources to ensuring that this is so. Indeed, some firms have found that a vendor's security practices and norms are superior to their own.

The trend toward characterizing and implementing offshoring arrangements as "partnerships" will undoubtedly continue as technology changes (Grover et al., 1996). Others suggest that the belief that suppliers can be strategic partners is usually wishful thinking (Lacity et al., 1995). Lacity et al. (2003) argue that "Once the contract is signed, buyer and seller incentives do not align, and power shifts to the supplier, which can lead to premium prices for additional work, reduced levels of attention from the supplier as time goes on, and an overall deterioration of the relationship into an us-versus-them mentality". Based on their experience, McFarlan and Nolan (1995) disagree because "Individual companies have very different IT situations and needs." Cullen et al. (2005) mention that outsourcing contracts are agreed to in concept but delivered in detail and that is the reason that they can break down.

King and Malhotra (2000) identified a number of generic risks associated with IT outsourcing as compared with performing IT activities within the firm. There is a growing awareness of the difficulties inherent in offshoring, pointing out that hidden structural, cultural, legal, and financial risks, and hidden costs are often overlooked.

Among those risks that have been identified, the long-term organizational risks of offshoring are potentially serious, but difficult to quantify. For instance, IT capability is frequently cited as a key for companies to lead their competitors and/or change their industry (Straub and Watson, 2001). From this viewpoint, offshoring may be shortsighted.

Also, engaging in offshoring may be a signal to customers, competitors, suppliers and employees that an irreversible change has occurred in the firm's outlook, vision, strategy and commitments. This may operate in the firm's strategic disadvantage.

Any of these risks can impact the client firm's market performance both to internal clients of IS services and external customers. So, they must be taken seriously and addressed as well as possible in the contract and in the creation of backup.

Among other major risks from offshoring identified by King and Malhotra (2000) is that of deskilling the organization in the relevant capabilities and supporting technologies. Over time, few organizations will be able to maintain skills that are practiced only through an external vendor. This means that the outsourcing decision is not a classic "make or buy" choice, since when a contract comes up for renewal, the client may no longer have the skills that are necessary to even consider the "make" option (King, 1994).

The counter argument to deskilling risk is that this does not apply if "commodity" activities are the only ones considered for outsourcing (Quinn and Hilmer, 1994; King, 2004). The problem with this argument is that the distinction between "commodity" and "core" activities is not simple. Quinn and Hilmer (1994) point out that much of the literature that views this distinction to be simple is tautological, since "core" is defined as "key or fundamental." IT is so integrated into all organizational processes that it is often difficult to make the "core versus commodity" distinction (Earl, 1996). Most IS functions/activities may have components that are core and others that are commodities (Barthelemy, 2003). There is evidence to suggest that some organizations have outsourced IT activities and later discovered that elements of the outsourced activities are part of their core competency (McLellan et al., 1995).

Among the other risks from offshoring are those of possible monopoly practices by the vendor and the threat of opportunism on the part of the vendor as the outsourcing firm becomes deskilled. Not only does an offshoring commitment put the vendor in a monopoly position regarding contract changes and contract renewal, but it offers the vendor the opportunity to learn critical business skills that the vendor could use to compete with the client at some future time. This threat of opportunism also extends to a reduction in the client's opportunity to influence critical decisions, such as the level of technology that will be applied to the outsourced activity as new technologies become available. Orlikowski and Robey (1991) suggest that technology shifts by the vendor may often reflect more of a focus on the vendor's goals than on the client's needs.

Another major risk factor that is specific to offshore outsourcing is the threat of major disruptions arising from political upheaval, war, or other unexpected events in an offshore host country. Businesses prefer to operate overseas in countries that are politically stable. However, because wages tend to be lower in less stable countries, organizations are often tempted to operate in relatively unstable environments.

The political stability risks associated with offshoring may be significant. For instance, Jeffery Campball, CIO of Burlington Northern-Santa Fe Railway was quoted in *Computerworld* as saying, "I have 40% of my applications, development and maintenance... in India. There are ongoing pressures about that region" (Vijayan, 2004). He is referring to the Pakistan-India conflict over Kashmir, which requires his firm to create backup centers outside the region, perform security checks on contractors and add resources to quality assurance and testing, all of which add to the costs of a venture that has the objective of reducing costs.

Related to this issue is the fact that disaster recovery sites are often shared and operate on a "first-come–first-served" basis. The presumption, like that of insurance, is that a disaster is unlikely to strike multiple companies and multiple locations simultaneously. However, with the enormous proliferation of vendor sites in Bangalore, India, this assumption may be faulty, thus requiring firms to operate their own backup sites elsewhere, a very expensive proposition which directly impacts both the economics of offshoring, and its associated risks (Twing, 2005).

A FRAMEWORK FOR MAKING THE OUTSOURCING/OFFSHORING CHOICE

A sourcing decision for any IT activity must be based on the answer to a key question: Is the activity that is being considered for a change in sourcing an element of an IT capability that might currently be, or have the potential to be, a core competence and/or a critical success factor for the organization?

This is a simply-stated, but complex, criterion involving two constructs, critical success factor (CSF) and core competence (CC), in both current and predicted temporal contexts. A CSF is something that is necessary, but not sufficient for success. A CC is a capability that is valuable, difficult to imitate, and difficult to substitute.

In applying this criterion, as suggested here, a group of executives should begin the sourcing decision process by taking an activity that is being considered for a sourcing decision, and make judgments concerning the degree to which it is, or may become, an organizational critical success factor as well as the degree to which it is, or may become, an organizational core competence.

Here, we provide a framework based on King (2001) that builds on such judgments by suggesting an appropriate "working option" as well as the sometimes unrecognized, inevitable consequences of selecting that option and the issues that are likely to arise if it is chosen. Thus, the framework requires managers to make specific key judgments and then directs them on a path of thinking that will enable them to fully explore the consequences of these judgments.

The framework provides guidance to managers, but it does not provide "answers." If the consequences and issues raised by using the framework make the working option undesirable, the framework can be used to consider other options as well. It is meant to stimulate thinking along paths that might otherwise go unexplored, and in so doing, provide the basis for a clearer and more comprehensive formulation of the sourcing decision. It makes use of many theoretical concepts and relationships and it has been developed in a series of real-world contexts by the author while working as a consultant.

An IT Sourcing Framework

Table 1 provides the framework for guiding executives in making an IT sourcing decision. It anticipates that an organization's relevant managers will develop an initial evaluation of the activity being considered for a change in sourcing in terms of two key constructs — Critical Success Factor (CSF) and Core Competence (CC) — at both a present and predicted future time. Then, the row of the table corresponding to that preliminary assessment should be entered.

The various columns of the table for the row that is designated by the preliminary judgment concerning CSF and CC in the two temporal contexts indicates a "working option" for a sourcing approach as well as a rationale for, and salient consequences of, choosing the option. This working option is the one that logically follows from the preliminary judgments that have been made concerning the activity's current and potential criticality and its current and potential core nature. The working option, its rationale and these consequences should be carefully analyzed, discussed and considered before a final sourcing decision is made.

When this approach has been used in practice, it has been done with a group of IS and non-IS executives meeting regularly. Typically, using the table as a guide, as a stimulant for discussion and as a preliminary source of issues, such a group develops a broader and deeper set of possible ramifications and consequences of their decision. Then, the group can do studies or convene other groups to consider these issues before arriving at an overall judgment on a best sourcing option.

Sometimes, this process has led to a re-evaluation of the initial judgment that was made in terms of CSFs and CCs, and therefore to the identification of a new working sourcing option. More typically, when the initial judgment has been rendered carefully, it leads to a rich set of issues and potential problems that can be useful both in selecting the best sourcing option and in pursuing its successful implementation.

To explain the framework of Table 1 in detail, we first develop a specification of the salient constructs — core competencies and critical success factors — and then specify the nature of the alternatives to outsourcing that various rows of the table suggest should be considered. Finally, we give a detailed exposition of each row of the table in order to explain its use.

Core Competencies

The notion of a core competency is fundamental to the resource-based view of the firm (Wernerfelt, 1984), but it is more widely discussed than it is understood (Quinn and Hilmer, 1994). Barthelemy and Adsit (2003) argue that core competencies are the resources and capabilities of the organization that are valuable, difficult to imitate and difficult to substitute. In particular, to qualify as a core competency, a strategic capability – one that is closely related to the strategy that the organization is pursuing– should do the following (King, 1994; 1995a; 1995b):

- Have evolved slowly through collective learning and information sharing;
- Be incapable of being readily enhanced through additional investment;
- Be synergistic with other capabilities;
- Not be readily duplicable by others;
- Not be readily transferable to others;
- Play a role in creating a competitive advantage.

Clearly, the conventional "CC" view of activity sourcing is that if an activity meets these criteria, it is a core competence and should not be outsourced. If it is a "commodity," loosely speaking, something that does not meet any, or most, of the core competency criteria, it may be considered for outsourcing (Quinn and Hilmer, 1994; Hancox and Hackney, 2000; Insinga, 2000; King, 2001).

If an IS Activity is Assessed to be a:	"Working" Option to be Considered	Rationale for Suggested Option	Implications (Actions Required)	Other Issues
Not currently or potentially a core competence or a CSF	• Outsource/ Offshore	• Why do it internally?	• Develop Contract Negotiations and Contract Management capability • Need to understand foreign culture • Need for baseline and benchmark measures • Need for vendor monitoring	• Loss of Control • Loss of Expertise • Create a competitor • Create a technological ceiling • Risk • Feasibility of developing a "partner" relationship
Currently a CSF & a Core Competence	• Insource	• Preserve capability • Continue to improve/ develop	• Invest • Cost-benefit and risk assessment • Integrate into strategic capabilities architecture	• Feasibility of improving through re-engineering, new incentives, or other "creative" options • Cost/benefit (C/B) assessment
Currently a Critical Success Factor & Not Currently Core Competence	• Use insourcing or any other option to develop	• Mandatory development	• Investment required	• Feasibility & C/B assessment • Risk of other-than-insourcing strategies • Viability of the business
Currently a Core Competence & a Potential CSF	• Internal markets	• Refine capability • Continue to improve/ develop • Develop necessary scale	• Develop internal markets infrastructure • Develop plan for transformation to internal markets	• Feasibility • Fit with culture • Fit with incentives
Potential Core Competence & a Potential CSF	• Strategic alliance (or) • Internal markets (or) • Monitor	• Secure complementary skills for development • Provide scale for development • Obtain further information	• Develop project management system • Develop internal markets infrastructure • Develop plan for transformation • Secure & develop sources of information and perform timely reassessment	• Impact on the internal culture • Risk • Potential for losses to exceed gains of expertise and information • Feasibility • Fit with culture and incentive system • Cost/benefit of waiting to decide

Table 1. Framework for IS Sourcing Decision Process (Adapted from King, 2001)

However, today's information technologies are so integrated into business processes that it may not be possible to clearly distinguish between what is core and what is not core (Earl, 1996). Also, most IS functions have some elements that belong to the core and some that do not (Barthelemy and Adsit, 2003). Thus, it may not be a simple exercise to separate core from non-core activities when deciding about the 'outsourcability' of any IS activity. As a result, various studies have suggested that at times organizations may tend to outsource broad IT activities, part of which may happen to be a core competency (McLellan et al., 1995; Hancox and Hackney, 2000).

Critical Success Factors (CSFs)

Loosely speaking, critical success factors (CSF) are those attributes that generally lead to success in a business. The notion is imprecise, but it has long been recognized that there are generally a relatively small number of activities that, if exhibited or performed well, will create the opportunity for success (Rockart, 1979). Conversely, organizations that do not possess these attributes or perform these functions well will often not be successful.

More precisely, CFSs are necessary, but not sufficient, for success in a particular business context. Success at a CSF, or a set of CSFs, enables an enterprise or unit to compete for the prize, but it does not guarantee that it will win it. Lack of success at CSF, or a set of CSFs, means that an organization is unlikely to be successful.

The CSF notion has been widely used in IS contexts, such as IS strategic planning (Pollalis and Grant, 1994; Bullen, 1995; Rockart and Earl, 1996). Here, it is applied in the context of IS sourcing.

Because CSFs may be identified at the industry, market, business, or organizational levels, in this framework, criteria that are based on the CSF notion offer the opportunity for the inclusion of external factors that transcend the internally-oriented resource-based view.

Core Competencies and CSFs

Although the notions of a core competency and a critical success factor emanate, respectively, from the resource-based and industrial economics views of business, they are not mutually exclusive in their application. First, although the former has an internal focus that the latter may not, they can coincide — e.g., a core competence may be a CSF. Indeed, this may be thought of as an important goal of management — i.e., to create core competencies that are, or can be, critical success factors. This relationship between the two criteria forms the basis for the initial phase of the process and the use of the framework.

Sourcing Options

The options that are dealt with in using Table 1 require some explanation. The broad alternatives that are considered are outsourcing, insourcing, strategic alliances and internal markets. Since each of these may have a range of possible forms, this set is sufficiently diverse to offer a rich basis for making a strategic sourcing choice.

Outsourcing/Offshoring

The business enterprise, so the current strategy wisdom says, should outsource "commodity" activities and focus its attention and energy on its "core competencies." In many enterprises, IS has historically been thought of as a service activity rather than a core competency; so it is often considered to be a prime candidate for outsourcing because of that and for all of the reasons given previously.

Insourcing

Insourcing, as the term is used here, simply means that the enterprise performs the function internally, thereby incurring all of the relevant fixed and administrative costs in addition to the variable costs of the activity. When IS is insourced, it is often handled on a "charge back" basis to the user organization with somewhat arbitrary transfer prices being applied (King, 1995b). In an era in which the reduction of investment and fixed-cost levels is a way of managerial life and in which employee benefits are viewed as very expensive, there is great appeal to the idea of trading the fixed and variable costs of conducting an activity internally and the contentiousness that is often associated with transfer pricing, for the presumably lower, fixed and readily predictable costs of a long-term outsourcing contract.

However, the choice of the insourcing option need not be associated with the status quo. The re-engineering of development processes should be considered in assessing this option as should the providing of new incentives to departments and groups to conduct their activities more productively.

For instance, firms need to create ways to perform higher-level IT activities that are better than those offered by vendors and that are difficult to imitate and cannot be readily duplicated outside the firm. Such activities will typically evolve through collective learning or creative design that creates, or plays on, a comparative advantage.

Several examples come to mind. First is the use of home-based call-center operators by JetBlue and other firms. When such "distributed call centers" replace traditional ones, the costs may be comparable to those offered by Indian call-center operators, particularly when communications and setup costs are factored in and risks are considered.

For instance, India faced a nuclear confrontation only a few years ago and while international communications with India is good, local communications and transportation infrastructures there are poor. Many firms have considered that the risks created by such considerations require them to have "back ups," often in the Philippines. This increases the cost and broadens the risk of offshored activities, since the Philippines has its own unique risks. When all of these costs are accounted for and risk factors are taken into account, the net advantage of offshoring may be significantly affected.

Home-based call-center operations are only one illustration. A better example is one that was suggested by the director of software testing of a major US transportation firm. After a try at offshoring that failed badly, this executive reasoned that it would be best if software were tested in the US cultural context in which it was to be primarily used rather than in the non-US national culture in which it was developed. But, how could this be done on a cost-effective basis? A possible solution is now being experimented with the testing of offshore-developed software in the US using IT students working part-time rather than full-time professionals to perform the tests.

This may provide lower-cost testing depending on exactly which setup is determined to be best; possibly even at a cost level that is lower than similar-quality testing can be offered by Indian vendors.

Of course, the level of needed redundancy using relative novices rather than professionals has to be worked out, but this creative idea has sound research on its side. There is ample evidence that, in some arenas, multiple novices can outperform expert professionals since they bring together multiple perspectives that often more directly relate to the "hands on" requirements for the use of the software.

Another possibility is the adoption of incentives, or a market-based approach. Basically, management just suggests the productivity/cost/quality level that must be reached if a particular activity is to be kept in-house and allows departments or groups to adapt their methods to try to achieve that goal. This is the equivalent of the "China price," which is often used as a target by retailers like Wal-Mart or assemblers like GM, in dealing with their suppliers.

Such an approach may, at first, seem harsh, but it reflects the realities of the present-day environment. In practice, usually an immediate improvement is expected together with a plan and timetable for achieving the goal.

Strategic Alliances

Strategic alliances are activities conducted jointly by two or more organizations. There are various formal/legal ways in which this may be done; for instance, through a joint venture. The primary basis for a strategic alliance is the ability of one "partner" to provide a capability, asset or service that complements those provided by the other partner, and the simultaneous inability, or lack of desire, of each enterprise to provide or develop the complementary capabilities on their own.

Strategic alliances, if well conceived, designed, and implemented can be classic "win-win" situations for both partners, because the joint activity can operate at a high level of effectiveness and efficiency because of the synergies among the complementary activities and capabilities of the participants. The parties to the alliance can also moderate their investment and risk versus that which would be required to perform the activity internally.

The potential problems associated with strategic alliances have to do with the difficulties in administering a complex activity involving participants from two or more cultures and the possibility that more information and knowledge will be taken away by the partner than will be gained.

Although many outsourcing ventures are often referred to as "alliances," true alliances involve the creation of a joint, focused activity rather than a vendor-client relationship such as is the norm in conventional IT outsourcing.

Internal Markets

Internal markets are organizational structures within which activities such as IS operate to provide services both within the enterprise and outside it (King, 1995b). By having a unit sell its services on the open market, it is expected that it will be forced to provide a competitive level of quality and price - something that is difficult to ensure when the unit is operating internally and providing services only internally on a noncompetitive basis.

The internal markets approach is a way of allowing external market forces to operate within the enterprise, so that a unit such as IS must effectively compete or go bankrupt, much as a business enterprise is forced to do (Ackoff, 1993; Halal, 1993).

One of the major appeals of this approach is that many of the arbitrary and subjective aspects of evaluating and rewarding an internal unit are avoided, because each is rewarded on the basis of the revenues and profits that it can generate. The unit need not suffer the derogatory opinions that managers often hold concerning the quality of in-house service providers. Managers who are unhappy with the price or service level that they are getting from an internal unit in an internal markets situation are free to look elsewhere for the service. Similarly, the service provider is not forced to agree to an arbitrary transfer price for services; rather, the unit can price at the market levels at which it can attract internal and external clients.

Using the Methodology to Support a Sourcing Decision

The framework for selecting an IS sourcing strategy is outlined in Table 1. The process that supports the framework is one in which a group of managers judgmentally makes a series of evaluations. The evaluations may be made on the basis of consensus judgment, analysis of data, or both. In implementations of the framework and process, it has been typical that the group discussions adjourn from time to time so that additional data may be collected and analyses performed. Thus, the framework supports and guides a judgmental decision-making process that involves five steps.

1. Identification and Preliminary Assessment of the Activity under Consideration

The first step of the process is performed to identify an IS activity that is at issue — e.g., one that is not performing adequately or one that has been proposed for outsourcing or offshoring — and to preliminarily assess the activity in terms of a key question: Is the activity, in and of itself, or in terms of the role that it plays in a broader organizational capability, a current or potential critical success factor and/or a current or potential core competence?

The preliminary assessment of an element is made in terms of the two criteria — CC and CSF — each at one of three levels: "not currently or potentially," "currently," or "not currently, but potentially." In other words, each element may be assessed to be either "not currently or potentially a core competence," "currently a core competence," or "not currently, but potentially, a core competence." It should also be assessed as being either "not currently or potentially a CSF," "currently a CSF," or "not currently, but potentially, a CSF."

Nine theoretical possibilities may result from this preliminary assessment. However, four of them are illogical or infeasible and are not considered in the framework.

In taking the resource-based view that is necessary for the core competence element of the preliminary assessment, the following questions should be addressed:

- Is the activity in question itself a strategic capability?
- If not, is it a component of an existing strategic capability?
- If not, is it likely to be required as a component of a future strategic capability?
- Is it, or should it be, a core competence?

As previously noted, these questions are not amenable to simple "yes or no" answers. In some instances, firms have taken the core competency criteria outlined earlier and used them as items in an overall core competency measure; for instance by associating seven-point scales with each criterion and having a variety of people rate the activity in terms of the criteria. Finally, they are either aggregated into an overall "score" or depicted as a profile of the mean and range of scores for each criterion.

The initial assessments of whether an activity is a current or potential CSF provides a broader industrial economics-based perspective on an activity's current and potential importance. The key questions in this phase are as follows. What have been the CSFs in this business/industry/market? What changes are likely in the array of CSFs for the foreseeable future? In many instances, these questions are more susceptible to "yes or no" answers than those that are used to address the CC concept, but there will invariably be extensive discussion needed in order to arrive at a consensus.

These questions motivate the participating executives to analyze the business and what is important for success, rather than to simply dismiss a "service" area such as IS on a casual historical basis as has so often been done in making outsourcing decisions.

These preliminary assessments will typically require considerable discussion and some data gathering and analysis. Once the preliminary assessment has been made, the relevant row of Table 1 is identified and the table comes directly into play.

2. Use the Framework to Identify Sourcing Option to be Initially Considered

Once a preliminary assessment has been made and used to identify a row in Table 1, the framework identifies a prime candidate, or "working" option, that is consistent with the assessment. For instance, if the assessment is that the activity is "currently a core competence and potentially a CSF," which corresponds to the fourth row of Table 1, the entry in the second column suggests that the initial focus should be on the "Internal Markets" working option.

3. Use the Framework to Guide the Development of a Rationale for the "Working" Sourcing Choice

The third step is to develop the initial statement of a rationale for the "working" sourcing choice. Very brief rationales that are meant to be suggestive are provided in the third column of the table. For instance, in column 3 of row 4 the rationale for the "Internal Markets" strategy suggests the need to refine the capacity and to continue to improve and develop it. The logic of this rationale is that the activity is clearly important to the organization because it is a core competence, and that it could become critical in the future, because it is a potential CSF. Thus, logic suggests that although it does not require mandated ("full speed ahead") development, it would be prudent to continue its evolutionary development in a cost-effective fashion. The internal markets approach is such a cost-effective approach since it leads to a new revenue stream and to new internal pricing that allows prudent investment and development.

If the suggested option brief and rationale makes sense to the group that is participating, they will often create a more elaborate and sophisticated statement of the rationale as a means of focusing their thinking and communicating to others.

4. Consider the Organizational Implications of the Working Sourcing Option

The fourth step in the process is to use the framework to suggest the *nearly-certain organizational implications* of the working strategy. These implications emanate from "lessons learned" in a variety of circumstances in which this sourcing strategy has been adopted. For instance, in row 4, the working sourcing option is "Internal Markets," and the fourth column of the table suggests the need to develop an internal markets infrastructure (King, 1995b). The organizational implications in this column are the direct and certain consequences of selecting this sourcing strategy. Others may be suggested by the group that are reflective of the client firm's unique situation.

5. Use the Framework to Suggest Other Issues that May Arise

The fifth step in implementing the framework is reflected in the fifth column of Table 1. For instance, if the fourth row is the one that has been entered, this column also identifies "lessons learned" from the choice of the Internal Markets strategy in various firms. The issues in this column are different from those in the previous one in that they represent possibilities that *may* ensue if this sourcing strategy is selected. In this case, the issues relate to the feasibility of the working strategy and its "fit" with the organization's existing culture and incentives.

Alternatively, if the first row is the one that has been entered, the fourth column suggests that the "outsource" option will create the need for the contract negotiation and management capability, the need for baseline and benchmark measures and measurement processes, and the need for vendor monitoring. The fifth column in this row identifies some issues that may need to be addressed, such as the possible loss of control, loss of expertise, risk, etc..

Summary of Using the Methodology

Table 1 thereby provides the basis for a five-step framework for identifying an option and for testing and exploring the implications of the preliminary assessment of an activity that is being considered for a new sourcing choice. At any phase of the process, it may be determined that the working option is inappropriate; in which case, another preliminary assessment should be made or another row of the table should be considered. When this occurs, there is great value in developing a statement, similar to that which represents the rationale for the working strategy. In the rare cases in which this has been done, such a statement — basically, one that argues why the initial working option is not the best one — is very useful to bringing a group to consensus and in communicating with others. Most often, the consideration of the various issues that are raised as the group proceeds across a row may serve to validate the working strategy to be both feasible and desirable.

IS/IT OFFSHORING MANAGEMENT AND SKILL REQUIREMENTS

Carmel and Agarwal (2002) describe how globally dispersed projects are more difficult to manage because of cultural differences, time zone differences, language skills differences, work-hour regulations, high employee turnover, visa difficulties, lack of domain knowledge at an offshore unit, and poor local telecommunications infrastructure.

As the offshoring trend accelerates, there will be a changing mix of IS job and educational opportunities, weighted with gains toward the "high end" in several areas of IS. There are several aspects of the changes that will be induced in IS practice that need to be recognized because many of the well-understood programming and systems analysis tasks will be offshored. This will extend well beyond "basic" tasks since offshore vendor firms are very capable and are moving up the value chain in terms of the tasks that they can take on.

This means that IT departments will change drastically in terms of the mix of tasks that they perform and skills that they require. Making decisions in the IS/IT offshoring environment will place new demands on IS management; it will reduce some existing demands and change others.

For instance, Table 1 suggests some new capabilities that will need to be developed or significantly enhanced, such as contract management and negotiation capabilities. Other functions, such as the development of non-critical software, will be eliminated. But, the development of mission-critical software will need to be retained by many organizations.

It is fairly easy to forecast that there will be significantly greater needs in a number of areas:

- Relationship and contract management
- Risk assessment and management
- Technology assessment and monitoring
- Systems implementation and integration
- Integrated business and IS planning
- Mission-critical systems development and testing
- Security
- IS personnel development.

Relationship and Contract Management

Effective relationship management has been frequently shown to be related to outsourcing success. Many firms who thought that they could offshore through a contract and then do little to monitor and manage the client-vendor relationship have been surprised with negative results from this style of outsourcing. In these instances, communications and coordination processes and their associated costs often were not given much attention. For success in IS offshoring, close attention must be paid to everything about the client-vendor relationship, from the criteria for selecting a vendor, to the details of the outsourcing contract, to the frequent monitoring of progress, to the level of control exerted over the vendor, to the level of trust that is developed in the client-vendor relationship. None of these things can be ignored or taken lightly since all have been shown to be critical success factors for effective outsourcing.

Risk Assessment and Management

Risk assessment and management will become a greater focus in vendor selection and in continuing relationship management. The risks that are involved in performing critical functions in third-world countries have not been fully recognized by most firms who have begun offshoring. Everything from political risk, to risks of natural disasters, to the risks associated with marginal infrastructures needs to be taken into account and monitored. After all, India almost became involved in a nuclear confrontation only a few years ago and while international communications from India have improved dramatically, local communications and transportation infrastructures are often marginal. This leads to greater risk, especially when unplanned activities must be performed. Often, this will be addressed using "backup" sites, but this involves a new layer of complexity in the overall management process.

Technology Assessment and Monitoring

In an outsourcing/offshoring environment, a technology and vendor assessment capability must be maintained, or developed by the outsourcing client, since the vendor's objectives with regard to technology are not always consistent with those of the client. In many situations, vendors wish to consolidate the work of many clients on their own legacy technology to achieve economies of scale and high returns. This may not always well serve specific clients, even if it meets their initial cost goals, since some clients might benefit greatly from greater accuracy, reduced cycle time or a greater security level than is initially offered by the vendor.

The monitoring of technological advances may, in fact, be performed outside the organization. But the CIO and other IS executives must be certain that they are aware of these developments, if only because it will enable them to anticipate technological changes that a vendor may be about to consider. The need to independently keep abreast of technology becomes apparent to every CIO shortly after he or she outsourced operational computing systems. The outer office is no longer filled with vendor salespeople because the outsourcing client is no longer a potential customer for entire categories of hardware and software. Only on recognizing that the outer office is no longer full, do many IS executives realize how much imported technological information they formally obtained from salespeople. Those "pests waiting for an appointment" (as one IS executive put it) suddenly are recognized for their value and the IS manager realizes that he/she must do something to replace those old sources of information concerning technology.

So, the client must independently assess evolving technology in order to maintain an awareness of potential service-level improvements that may become feasible through technological advances.

The client must continuously be aware of the offerings and capabilities of other offshore vendors as well. Even if a firm is involved in a long-term contract, this is necessary. It also illustrates why negotiations and the terms of the contract are so important. No client should allow themselves to be truly "locked into" a long-term contract in which the vendor can attempt to provide, on a continuing basis, service levels that are less than others routinely offer. Contracts must provide for the continuous benchmarking of service-levels against other providers.

Systems Implementation and Integration

Systems implementation and integration is another area in which competence must be maintained and enhanced by an IT department that is going out of the programming and systems development "business," (which will increasingly be the norm). Increasingly, software will be developed by vendors, purchased by clients and then customized and integrated with other internal systems. These implementation and integration processes may be aided by external consultants, but they often cannot be effectively done by outsiders; an internal capability that reflects a deep understanding of the business, its operations, goals and priorities, is required. This extends to the software testing arena since externally-developed software, which can be mission-critical for the client firm, must be thoroughly tested on an independent basis.

Even when external consultants are used in these roles, the goal of the client must be to have their own personnel learn the skills that are necessary to perform these tasks with increasingly lesser levels of outside help.

Integrated Business and IS Planning

Strategic IS Planning is the link between the business strategy and the mission, strategy, goals and architectures for IS in the organization. As such, this planning process requires in-depth understanding of the firm. It should (almost) never be outsourced or offshored.

IS strategic planning has been integrated into strategic business planning in many firms. This activity will need to be maintained as no firm can ignore the potential role of IT in its future business strategy. When outsourcing takes place, top managers tend to presume that IT's role in the business is lessened and they may give less attention to it. IT people must understand business strategy and IT's role in it (even when large segments of traditional IT have been outsourced) and keep these issues in the mix of those treated in strategic business planning.

Mission-Critical Systems Development and Testing

The development and testing of mission-critical software/systems must usually be retained in-house since this is where the essence of one's informational core competence resides. Most organizations have trade secrets and/or critical key processes embedded in their software and systems that they would not wish to be made available to outsiders. The testing of software is typically performed by the developer, but in the case of offshored development, clients often wish to perform their own post-delivery testing.

Security

Sharing critical processes and software with vendors may increase risk to some degree. Of course, most vendors apply elaborate security systems and procedures. Indeed, in some cases, consultants have found that vendor security is better than client security. Nonetheless, the ultimate responsibility for the security of data, especially customer data, is with the client, so the necessary skills must be available in-house to assure adequate security.

IS Personnel Development

IS employee development programs involving the IS jobs that are kept in-house as well as the "IS interface" jobs in the marketing, production, finance and other departments should also be retained in-house. Such programs may involve on-the-job training and/or job relations through IS and business functional job assignments. In that way, career progression plans can be developed involving the set of IS functions that are retained.

IS/IT EDUCATIONAL PROGRAM IMPLICATIONS

What does this changing mix of skill requirements imply about IS education and curricula?

First, outsourcing / offshoring must be treated as a major and central IS paradigm. It can no longer be thought of as an interesting appendage to basic IS. Second, the specific skills necessary for performing the activities that will remain in the IS portfolio – relationship and contract management, risk assessment and management, technology assessment and monitoring, systems implementation and integration, integrated business and IS planning, mission-critical systems development and testing, security, and IS personnel development must be given central a focus in IS education and curricula. These are typically not major foci of today's curricula.

This means that IS students will need to understand negotiation techniques, contract law, and change management, and develop the "softer" skills involved in partnering and developing trust between partners. Strategic issues such as understanding the sort of benefits that may be expected from various kinds of possible "strategic alliances" with vendors will become essential. Vendor selection, which has not been central to IS, will become of greater importance.

All of the concepts used in Table 1 – core competency, critical success factors, internal markets, etc. – must become familiar to IS students and professionals through revised curricula and training.

The focus for systems implementation and integration will need to shift from an internal orientation to one which addresses working in joint consultant-client teams. For instance, the typical ERP implementation project, in which joint teams work, often for several years, to customize and implement a vendor-supplied system to meet a firm's unique needs, is a good prototype for a process that will become increasingly common for various types of vendor-supplied systems. Thus, inter-firm implementation processes will need to be more fully developed and studied (Ko et al., 2005).

Even though integrated customer relationship management, enterprise resource planning, and supply chain management systems will increasingly become the core organizational enterprise systems, it will be many years before most firms have substantially converted to such systems, so the evaluation of vendor-supplied software, software testing, and the integration of software with legacy systems will be a continuing need.

Another critical need will be developing an understanding of relevant foreign cultures. For instance, the Indian culture is quite unique. Although the caste system has been officially outlawed, its vestiges remain strong. Even well-educated professionals usually have their spouse chosen for them by their families (often with a right of refusal on meeting). In many vendor nations, businesses and government agencies operate on the routine basis of bribery, hiring of relatives, unaccountability of relatives, and other-than-merit-based promotions. Of course, large Indian outsourcing vendors are much less traditional and more Westernized, but one need only look at the marriage system to recognize how much traditional cultural practices permeate all aspects and levels of Indian society.

Anyone who routinely deals with foreign vendors must recognize these and many other aspects of the national culture of the vendor in order to understand the proposals of, and responses given by, the employees of foreign vendors. Most of these areas involve skills that go well beyond the traditional domain of IS education. But, since overall IS success will be more and more dependent on them, IS education must adapt and change.

In some sense, IS is quite well suited to changing these ways since IS educators are not people who are used to teaching from the same yellowed notes each year. But, the changes that are now required are more substantial than those with which we are familiar. They involve more than just updating methods to deal with evolving technologies.

Most IS faculty are not themselves well versed in some of the required areas — contract law, for instance. Many have not traditionally focused on the "soft-side" skills that are involved in contract negotiation, contract management, and client-vendor relationship management. This means that there will need to be a period of "retraining" which might rival that which took place in the late 70s and early 80s when so many faculty who were not formally trained in IT availed themselves of the opportunity to develop skills in the new "hot" growth area of IS. Whether this needs to be done formally, as was done then, through joint teaching of IS courses with non-IS faculty who have these complementary skills, or in other ways, is not clear. But, it needs to be done.

MINICASE

Financial Services Firms Offshoring to India

Credit Suisse announced its plans to establish a Center of Excellence (COE) in Pune, India, to be operational by January 2007. With the growing global acceptance of India as a banking and financial services (BFS) outsourcing hub, more and more global financial services houses are joining the offshoring bandwagon. For the COE, Credit Suisse has partnered with Wipro for the necessary IT and basic operations support. State Street has partnered with Syntel.

Maturing To Complex Services
With the growing maturity of vendors, functions with increasing complexity are being offshored. Functions being offshored have graduated from the support functions, such as F&A support and voice based services, to complex functions including financial modeling, equity research support, and portfolio tracking. Research and analytics is an emerging service area that has picked up steam in the last two years. Global investment banks are getting their number crunching work done in India.

Players Active in India
Different models of offshoring are in vogue. While captive and the third party models are being traditionally followed, financial service companies are constantly experimenting with new models

---

and their innovations are likely to drive BPO sourcing as a whole. The latest to emerge is hybridization of sourcing models that calls for multi-locational sourcing as well as combination of captive, third party and joint venture sourcing models.

There are around 30 global financial service providers with captive setups in India. These include players like HSBC, AXA, Citigroup, Deutsche Bank and ABN Amro. Top tier investment banks including Goldman Sachs, Lehman Brothers and UBS also have captive centers in the country. Setting up of a captive center and the related infrastructure and manpower management involves significant financial outlay. Hence typically only the larger players aggressively follow the captive model.

For many others, offshoring volumes are currently not large enough to make captives viable. This springs opportunities for the third party service providers. There are more than 50 large and small third party players catering to the requirements of the BFS clients globally. Some of the big players in the country include Genpact, IBM Daksh, ICICI Onesource, WNS and Wipro BPO. There are some smaller niche service providers including Amba Research, Irevna and Copal Partners that have captured the high-end research and analytics work.

Cost the Predominant Driver

Cost savings is a significant driver of offshoring to India. Companies have been able to realize cost savings to the tune of 30- 50 percent. According to a study conducted by Nasscom, American BFS companies saved $6 billion in the last four years by offshoring to India. However, cost is not the only driver.

Other crucial factors driving offshoring to India include regulatory compliance requirements, large-scale availability of skilled personnel, English speaking capabilities and favorable cultural issues. Given the tremendous cost savings, other factors provide a support platform for offshoring. Over the years, these secondary drivers have become more compelling.

Going Forward

Going forward, global sourcing that follows a best- of-breed approach will find greater acceptability as firms adopt a multiple-model, multiple-vendor and multiple-location approach. Blended or hybrid models will be the preferred model for financial institutions.

With almost 50% of the world's biggest banks in terms of asset size offshoring to India, the country remains the most preferred offshoring destination. However, India faces stiff competition from emerging offshoring hubs in Asia Pacific and Eastern Europe. Despite such stiff competition, India will retain its dominant position at least for the next couple of years.

Discussion Questions

1. Why are banking and financial service firms establishing financial service centers in India?
2. What advantages does India have when it comes to offshoring?
3. Research and name some other industries (and specific companies in those industries) that are using offshoring for competitive advantage.
4. What type of capabilities do the financial services companies need to manage their offshoring operations and contracts?

Source: FinancialWire. Forest Hills: Dec 13, 2006. pg. 1 (http://proquest.umi.com/pqdweb?did= 1179160391&sid=2&Fmt=3&clientId=15105&RQT=309&VName=PQD)

KEY TERMS
Charge back
Commodity
Core competency
Co-sourcing
Critical success factor (CSF)
Global arbitrage
Internal markets
Multi-sourcing
Offshoring
Outsourcing
Six-sigma
Strategic alliance
Transfer prices

STUDY QUESTIONS

1. Explain the economic argument for why offshoring is a win-win proposition for client-firm countries and vendor-firm countries? Construct the best counter-argument that you can.

2. Give some examples of things that Indian vendor firms are doing to deal with rising salaries and the increasing scarcity of professionals. Do you think that these measures will be successful?

3. What sorts of things can be done to improve IS performance and control costs while retaining an IS activity in-house?

4. Explain what a "critical success factor" (CSF) is. Give some examples from business situations.

5. Explain what a "core competence" (CC) is. Give some examples from business situations.

6. Explain why and how the two concepts (CSF and CC) interact to determine the best sourcing choice.

7. What are some of the traditional IS functions and activities that are likely to be kept in-house in the age of offshoring? Which are likely to be offshored or outsourced?

8. Explain the economic argument for why offshoring is a win-win proposition for client-firm countries and vendor-firm countries? Construct the best counter-argument that you can.

9. Give some examples of things that Indian vendor firms are doing to deal with rising salaries and the increasing scarcity of professionals. Do you think that these measures will be successful?

10. What sorts of things can be done to improve IS performance and control costs while retaining an IS activity in-house?

11. Explain what a "critical success factor" (CSF) is. Give some examples from business situations.

12. Explain what a "core competence" (CC) is. Give some examples from business situations.

13. Explain why and how the two concepts (CSF and CC) interact to determine the best sourcing choice.

14. What are some of the traditional IS functions and activities that are likely to be kept in-house in the age of offshoring? Which are likely to be offshored or outsourced?

REFERENCES

Ackoff, R. L. "Corporate Perestroika: The Internal Markets Economy," in *Internal Markets: Bringing the Power of Free Enterprise INSIDE Your Organization,* W.E. Halal, A. Geranmayeh, and J. Pourdehnad (eds.), Wiley, New York, 1993.

Adler, P. S. "Making the HR Outsourcing Decision," *Sloan Management Review* (45), 2003, pp. 53-60.

Ang, S. and Straub D. "Production and Transaction Economies and IS Outsourcing: A Study of the U.S. Banking Industry," *MIS Quarterly,* 22(4), 1998, pp. 535-552.

Ante, S. "Commentary: Shifting Work Offshore? Outsourcer Beware," *BusinessWeek online,* March 2, 2004.

Aspray, W. Mayadas, F. and Vardi, M. Y. (Eds.) "Globalization and Offshoring of Software: A Report of the ACM Job Migration Task Force," Association for Computing Machinery, 2006, http://www.acm.org/globalizationreport

Barthelemy, J. "The Hidden Cost of IT Outsourcing," *MIT Sloan Management Review* 42(:3), 2003, pp. 60-60.

Barthelemy, J. and Adsit, D. "The Seven Deadly Sins of Outsourcing," *Academy of Management Executive* 17(2), 2003, pp. 87.

Bullen, C. V. "Reexamining Productivity CSFs: The Knowledge Worker Challenge," *Information Systems Management,* 12(3) 1995, pp. 13.

Carmel, E. and Agarwal, R. "The Maturation of Offshore Sourcing of Information Technology Work," *MIS Quarterly Executive* 1(2), June 2002, pp. 65-77.

Cullen, S., Seddon, P., and Willcocks, L. "Managing Outsourcing: The Life Cycle Imperative," *MIS Quarterly Executive,* 4(1), March 2005, pp. 229-246.

Earl, M., "Limits to IT Outsourcing," *Sloan Management Review* 37(3), Spring 1996.

The Economist, "The New Geography of the IT Industry," July 17, 2003.

The Economist, "It's Not Just India," November 20, 2003.

Grover, V., Cheon, M.J. and Teng, J. T. C. "The Effect of Service Quality and Partnership on the Outsourcing of Information Systems Functions," *Journal of Management Information Systems,* 12(4), 1996, pp. 89-116.

Grover, V. and Teng, J. T. C. "The Decision to Outsource Information Systems Functions," *Journal of Systems Management,* 44(11), 1993, pp. 34.

Halal, W. E. "The Transition from Hierarchy to ... What? Market Systems are the Paradigm of Information Age," in *Internal Markets: Bringing the Power of Free Enterprise INSIDE Your Organization,* W. E. Halal, A. Geranmayeh, and J. Pourdehnad (eds.), Wiley, New York, 1993.

Hancox, M. and Hackney, R. "IT Outsourcing: Frameworks for Conceptualizing Practice and Perception," *Information Systems Journal,* 10(3), 2000, pp. 217.

Insinga, R. C. "Linking Outsourcing to Business Strategy," *Academy of Management Executive* (14:4), 2000, pp. 58.

Jenkins, H. W, Jr. "Twilight of the Software Gods," *Wall Street Journal,* February 11, 2004, A19.

King, W.R. "Strategic Outsourcing Decisions," *Information Systems Management,* 11(4), Fall 1994, pp. 58-61.

King, W. R. "Developing a Sourcing Strategy for IS: A Behavioral Decision Process and Framework," *IEEE Transactions on Engineering Management,* 48(1), 2001, pp. 15.

King, W. R. "Creating a Strategic Capabilities Architecture," *Information Systems Management,* 12(1), 1995a, pp. 67.

King, W. R. "Creating Internal Markets" *Information Systems Management* 12(2), 1995b, pp. 61.

King, W. R. "Outsourcing and the Future of IT," *Information Systems Management* 21(4), Fall 2004.

King, W. R. and Malhotra, Y. "Developing a Framework for Analyzing IS Sourcing," *Information and Management* 37(6), September 2000, pp. 323-334.

Kripalani, M., "Call Center?; That's so 2004", *Business Week*, August 7, 2006, pp. 40-41.

Lacity, M. C. and Hirschheim, R. *Information Systems Outsourcing: Myths, Metaphors and Realities.* Wiley, Chichester, U.K, 1993.

Lacity, M. C., Willcocks, L. P., and Feeny, D. F. "IT Outsourcing: Maximize Flexibility and Control," *Harvard Business Review*, May-June 1995, pp. 84-93.

Lacity, M. C., Feeny, D. F. and Willcocks, L. P. "Transforming A Back-Office Function: Lessons from BAE Systems' Experience with an Enterprise Partnership," *MIS Quarterly Executive* 2(2), September 2003, pp. 86-103.

Levina, N. and Ross, J. "From the Vendor's Perspective: Exploring the Value Proposition in Information Technology Outsourcing," *MIS Quarterly* 27(3), September 2003, pp. 331-364.

Levy, D. "International Sourcing and Supply Chain Stability," *Journal of International Business Studies* 26(2), 1995, pp. 343-360.

Loh, L. and Venkatraman, N. "Determinants of Information Technology Outsourcing: a Cross-sectional Analysis," *Journal of Management Information Systems* 9(1), 1992, pp. 7.

Mann, C. "Globalization of IT Services and White Collar Jobs: The Next Wave of Productivity Growth," *International Economics Policy Briefs*, PB03-11, Washington: Institute for International Economics, December 2003, pp. 1-13.

McDougall, P. "First it Became a Hub for IT Services. Now, India Stands to Become a Major Force in the Software Industry, Too," *InformationWeek*, August 2005, pp. 34-39.

McFarlan, F. W., and Nolan, R. "How to Manage an IT Outsourcing Alliance," *Sloan Management Review*, Winter 1995, pp. 9-23.

McLaren, J. "Globalization" and Vertical Structure," *American Economic Review*, (90)5, 2000, pp. 1239-1254.

McLellan, K. L., Marcolin, B. L. and Beamish, P. W. "Financial and Strategic Motivations Behind IS Outsourcing," *Journal of Information Technology* (10), 1995, pp. 299-321.

Milligan, J. "Offshoring's Allure," *Banking Strategies*, (www.bai.org), January – February 2004.

Orlikowski, W. and Robey, D. "Information Technology and the Structuring of Organizations," *Information Systems Research* 2(2), 1991, pp. 143-169.

Overby, S. "The Future of Jobs and Innovation," *CIO Magazine*, December 15, 2003.

Pollalis, Y. and Grant, J. H. "Information Resources and Corporate Strategy Development," *Information Strategy: The Executive's Journal* 11(1), (1994), pp. 12.

Quinn, J. B. and Hilmer, F. G. "Strategic Outsourcing," *Sloan Management Review* 35(4), 1994, pp. 43-55.

Rockart, J. F. "Chief Executives Define their Own Data Needs," *Harvard Business Review* 57(2), 1979, pp. 81.

Rockart, J. F. and Earl, M. J. "Eight Imperatives for the New IT Organization," *Sloan Management Review* 38(1), 1996, pp. 43.

Sawhney, M. "What Lies Ahead: Rethinking the Global Corporation," Digital Frontier Conference, accessed at http://www.mohansawhney.com/Default.asp, 2002.

Simon, H. "The Long-Range Economic effects of Automation" in *The Shape of Automation for Men and Management*. Harper & Row, New York, 1965, pp. 1-25.

Straub, D. W. and Watson, R. "Transformational Issues in Researching IS and Net-Enabled Organizations," *Information Systems Research* 12(4), 2001, pp. 337-345.

Thurm, S. "Lesson in India: Not Every Job Translates Overseas," *The Wall Street Journal*, March 3, 2004.

Twing, D. "Could You or Your Outsourcer Handle a One-Two Disaster Punch?" *Network World*, www.networkworld.com/newsletters/asp/2005/0926out1.html, September 28, 2005.

Vijayan, J. "On-the-Job Hazards: Outsourcing," *Computerworld* 38(1), January 5, 2004, pp. 28-29.

Wang, E., T. Barron, and Seidmann, A. "Contracting Structures for Custom Software Development: The Impacts of Informational Rents and Uncertainty on Internal Development and Outsourcing," *Management Science* 43(12), 1997, pp. 1726-1744.

Wang, T. G. "Transaction Attributes and Software Outsourcing Success: An Empirical Investigation of Transaction Cost Theory," *Information Systems Journal* (12), 2002, pp. 153-181.

Wernerfelt, B. "A Resource-Based View of the Firm," *Strategic Management Journal* 5(2), 1984, pp. 171.

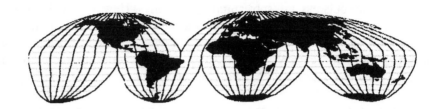

Critical Success Factors in Managing Offshore Software Outsourcing Relationships

Nilay V. Oza
Software Business Lab, Helsinki University of Technology, Finland

Shailendra C. Jain Palvia
Long Island University, USA

CHAPTER SUMMARY

This chapter presents the empirical investigation of offshore software outsourcing relationships between high maturity Indian software companies and their US and European clients. Comprehensive literature survey serves as the basis for the grounded case research methodology utilized for the contents of this chapter. We have identified critical success factors for effectively managing offshore software outsourcing relationships. The critical success factors common to both clients and vendors are: managing constant communication, having in place a structured process driven approach, doing appropriate resource allocations, and managing outsourcing projects' expectations. Additional critical success factors identified by clients are: spending time together by visits to each others' sites and making regular payments. Vendors also identified other factors as important -- cooperation, transparency, consistency, and proactive stance. Based on the emergent critical success factors, working solutions for identified challenges, testable propositions and a working model on managing offshore software outsourcing relationships are proposed.

INTRODUCTION AND LITERATURE REVIEW

The critical success factors in managing offshore outsourcing relationships described in this chapter are based on the empirical investigation into high maturity Indian software companies and their offshore clients. High maturity is referred to companies having CMM (Capability Maturity Model) certification level 4 or 5. The empirical investigation focused on motivators, difficulties, management issues and trust building in offshore software outsourcing relationships (for example, refer to Oza et al., 2006; Oza and Hall, 2005; Oza and Mäkelä, 2006). In this chapter, only results specific to relationship management are reported. Since 1988 (when Kodak outsourced all of its IT functions to IBM), global outsourcing – onshore and offshore – has gained increasing acceptance as a competitive business strategy. The main reasons include cheaper and more efficient information transfer and, in the case of offshore outsourcing, substantial cost savings. However, with more and more companies outsourcing their software operations offshore, issues associated with the establishment and management of outsourcing relationships have attracted research interest (Reifer, 2004; Lacity and Hirschheim, 1995). Particularly, how offshore software outsourcing relationships can be made successful (Stralkowski and Billon, 1998) is becoming a critical challenge. Despite this, there remains a lack of comprehensive research into the management of offshore outsourcing relationships. The following section presents the rationale for conducting empirical investigation into the relationship aspect of offshore software outsourcing.

Rationale for Investigating Relationships in Offshore Software Outsourcing

With the growing volume of offshore software outsourcing, failed outsourcing projects are also increasing. For example, Nam et al. (1996), in their investigation of 93 North American client companies found that 36 companies did not intend to continue their relationship with their respective vendors. King (2005) notes that JP Morgan decided to perform many software activities that it had previously outsourced and has not renewed its $5 billion contract with IBM. Ozanne (2000) found that 20-25% of all software outsourcing relationships fail within 2 years and 50% fail within 5 years. It is observed in the literature that the problems in the 'relationship' between clients and vendors are the underlying reason for most of the outsourcing failures (Palvia, 1995; Prakhe, 1999; Miles and Snow, 1992). In other words, a successful client–vendor relationship is a 'recipe' for success in the offshore software outsourcing. Kern and Willcocks (2000) in their UK-wide empirical investigation of seven outsourcing relationships found that outsourcing seemingly is only successful when relationships are effective and functioning.

Continuing failures in offshore software outsourcing not only indicate ineffective relationship management, but also substantive lack of research in this area. A number of difficulties have been reported in managing offshore relationships. Some of the difficulties are presented in Table 1 with their relevant literature examples.

Identified Difficulty	Example from the Literature
Cultural differences	Nicholson et al. (2000)
Incomplete contract	Brynjolfsson (1994)
Language differences	Krishna et al. (2004)
Loss of control	Currie (2000)
Loss of jobs	Herbsleb and Moitra (2001)
Transfer of work	Oza and Hall (2005)
Geographical distance	Lacity (2001)

Table 1. Difficulties in Managing Offshore Software Outsourcing Relationships

Table 1 will be revisited later in this chapter to compare our findings with the results in this Table. In the next section, we present critical success factors as reported in the literature.

Critical Success Factors in Managing Offshore Outsourcing Relationships

A relationship in software offshore outsourcing needs to be developed between two culturally diverse communities with less or no physical proximity. Physical proximity is referred to show the geographical distance between clients and vendors who operate from different countries in offshore software outsourcing. Physical distance and diversity in working styles and culture make the management of client – vendor relationships more complex. Therefore, relationship management becomes critical to the success of an offshore software outsourcing project.

Several studies have concentrated on the factors critical to successfully managing the relationship in offshore outsourcing. For example, Kern and Willcocks (2000) suggest that issues such as communication, exchange of information and cultural convergence are critical in managing client – vendor relationships. Brereton's (2004) study on software supply chain indicates that mutual respect and a willingness to share information transparently are critical for successful relationships. Stralkowski and Billon (1988) claim that the success of the relationship relies mainly on the level of customer satisfaction, achievement of expectation, and longevity of the venture. Kishore et al. (2003) claim that a mutual understanding between clients and vendors is critical for the success of outsourcing relationships and go on to suggest that mutual understanding between clients and vendors should be developed through adequate mechanisms for information sharing. Lacity (2002) suggests that the ability to commit to what was agreed, to fairly adapt to change, and to identify value-added services are critical to success. Nam et al. (1996) emphasise the technical competence of the vendor as critical in the relationship. Nystrom's (1997) findings indicate that understanding different cultures and developing cross-cultural communication skills are critical success factors in offshore outsourcing.

In addition, several studies indicate the role of trust in outsourcing relationships. For example, Stralkowski and Billon's (1988) focus on customer satisfaction, achievement of expectation and longevity of the venture, and Kishore et al.'s (2003) claim about mutual understanding echo the importance of trust. Moreover, other studies more directly suggest that trust is one of the most critical success factors in managing outsourcing relationships (e.g., Kern and Willcocks, 2000; Kishore et al., 2003; Sabherwal, 1999; Nam et al., 1996). However, the importance of trust is described at highly abstract levels by most studies in software outsourcing. Contradictorily, trust has received a great deal of detailed research attention in other disciplines such as management, economics and social science. Recognising the importance and need for detailed research on trust in software outsourcing, trust was investigated separately in this study. Oza et al. (2006) presents the full study on trust building in offshore software outsourcing relationships. The following table summarizes critical success factors identified in the literature review.

Critical factors identified in the literature review		
Communication	Cultural Convergence	Personal Relationship
Expectation Management	Longevity of Venture	Mutual Understanding
Transparency of Information Exchange	Flexibility	Commitment
Value Addition	Technical Competence	Trust building

Table 2. Critical Success Factors in Managing Offshore Software Outsourcing Relationships

Relating to the critical success factors presented in Table 2, the literature also reports a few models for managing offshore software outsourcing projects. However, coverage of relationship management is lacking. Some of the existing models are described in what follows.

Smith et al. (1996) propose a model from the resource, environmental, and project management perspectives of outsourcing. This model covers a wide range of issues such as resource requirements, factors that affect resources and the characteristics of software projects that affect resource requirements in offshore outsourcing. Kern and Willcocks (2000) propose an exploratory model of outsourcing relationships. Their model is based on an empirical investigation of twelve UK based companies. It focuses on behavioural, contractual and financial issues relevant to software outsourcing. It is observed that the models presented in the literature concentrate on specific issues such as outsourcing decision (Willcocks and Fitzgerald, 1993); types of contracts (Nam et al., 1996); feasibility of an offshore option (Ravichandran and Ahmed, 1993) and financial issues (Loh, 1994). However, none of these models concentrate explicitly on relationship management.

Carnegie Mellon University (CMU) has presented a model – eSCM (eSourcing Capability Model – Service Providers) which claims to cover 'all' sourcing issues (Hyder et al., 2004). At this stage, CMU has published eSCM for vendors (eSCM-SP) only. A similar model for clients (eSCM-CL) is currently under development. Although eSCM-SP addresses the needs of outsourcing partners, it is not tailored specifically to software outsourcing. The model seems more relevant to business process type of outsourcing (BPO). Although the e-SCM-SP attempts to cover all issues of outsourcing project, it does not cover low level details of specific areas of outsourcing such as relationship management. Moreover, the eSCM-SP concentrates primarily on evaluation of the vendors' capabilities. However, some explicit relationship practices are suggested in the eSCM-SP. Different models identified in this section are summarised in Table 3. The models identified in the literature are limited in terms of explicit emphasis on relationship management. The eSCM-SP focuses explicitly on relationship management but lacks details regarding software specific outsourcing.

Context of the model	The literature reference	Is relationship management covered? [Partly/Explicitly/Not covered]
Resource, environmental and project management perspectives of outsourcing	Smith et al. (1996)	Partly covered
Exploratory model of outsourcing behavioural, contractual and financial issues relevant to outsourcing	Kern and Willcocks (2000)	Partly covered
Outsourcing decision	Willcocks and Fitzgerald, 1993	Not covered
Types of contracts	Nam et al. 1996)	Not covered
Feasibility of an offshore option	Ravichandran and Ahmed, 1993)	Not covered
Financial issues	(Loh, 1994)	Not covered
eSCM-SP	Hyder et al. 2004	Explicitly covered

Table 3. Models Related to Managing Software Outsourcing

Later, in this chapter, an empirical model on managing offshore software outsourcing relationships is proposed. The following section presents the research methods used to conduct the proposed empirical study.

RESEARCH METHODOLOGY

This chapter is based on the empirical investigation into multiple case studies. The underlying methodology uses multiple case studies, to collect and organise the overall investigation and grounded theory principles, to analyse and the collected qualitative data. Grounded theory echoes the idea of developing theory from empirical data rather than testing an existing theory or hypothesis (Glaser and Strauss, 1967; Strauss and Corbin, 1998). This is particularly useful when the subject under investigation is relatively less researched or requires fresh perspective.

Qualitative data from eighteen vendor companies and six of their client companies were collected by using Patton's (1990) recommendations on qualitative interviewing. Interviews also included observations during the study visits. All interviews were audio recorded. They were transcribed for further analysis. Qualitative data was then analysed using coding techniques of grounded theory methodology. Coding techniques include open coding, axial coding and selective coding.

Open coding refers to the process of identifying the thoughts, ideas and meanings contained in the properties of the data (Strauss and Corbin, 1998). Axial coding is then used to group the coded themes in main themes and sub-themes. Particular themes are selected for further work based on a particular strategy. Then, as part of the selective coding, core themes that hold best and that are central to all other themes should emerge with high frequencies of mention (explicitly or implicitly) are identified. Subsequently, core themes are further enhanced by propositions. Propositions generated in this process are validated by comparing them with raw data. This process of integrating propositions and higher level themes develops into emergent model or a theory.

Core themes and propositions are presented in this chapter with the qualitative description. Empirical results are tied back with the literature and discussed qualitatively. Finally, a working model is also proposed. The research instrument was piloted with two case companies before using for the actual empirical investigation. Detailed research procedure is also reported in Oza et al. (2006). Research strategy for selecting empirical results is presented in the following subsection.

Strategy for Identifying Critical Success Factors

The main research questions and provisional insights are based on an exhaustive literature review in the area of offshore software outsourcing. Research questions were probed with the empirical data collected. The answers are in the form of themes that emerged from the empirical investigation. The strategy for selecting themes is as follows.

An emerging theme (from the literature review and empirical investigation was retained if it satisfied at least one of the following three criteria (in order):

Criterion 1: A theme identified by both groups - client and vendor.
Criterion 2: A theme not identified in criterion 1, but is identified in at least half of the total number of case studies in either the client group or the vendor group.
Criterion 3: A theme not identified in criterion 1 and criterion 2 but is overlapping with the theme identified in the literature.

EMPIRICAL RESULTS

This section presents an analysis of the qualitative data collected from eighteen high maturity Indian software companies and six of their offshore clients. We provide cross case analysis for client and vendor perceptions. Themes are first analyzed across cases in each group i.e. client and vendor. Then, themes are analyzed for their replication across both groups – client and vendor.

Research Question

Empirical results presented in this chapter relate to the following research question:

What are the critical success factors in managing offshore software outsourcing relationships?

To adequately answer this research question we collected information about how clients and vendors manage relationships with each other and what they perceive as important in managing their outsourcing relationships. We report detailed analysis of the collected data.

Vendors' Critical Success Factors

Figure 1 identifies seventeen critical success factors from the standpoint of vendors in managing their relationships with the clients. Figure 1 shows that adequate communication, a process driven approach and adequate resource allocation are the three most frequently cited critical factors in managing offshore outsourcing relationships. These themes are described below in detail.

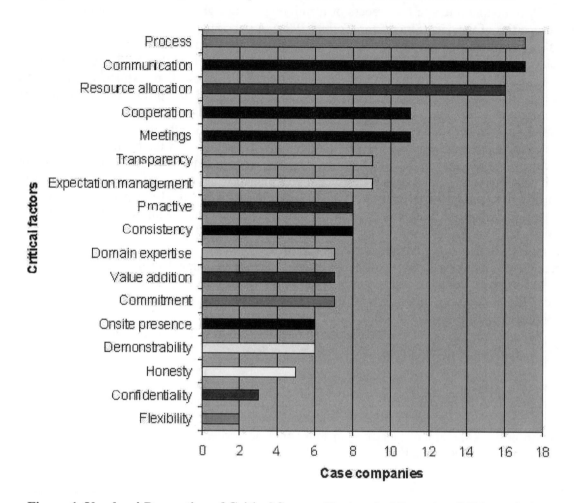

Figure 1. Vendors' Perception of Critical Success Factors in Managing Offshore Software Outsourcing Relationships with Clients

Process Driven Approach: Seventeen out of eighteen vendors identified establishing right processes as an important factor in managing relationships. One interviewee described how processes are useful:

'Processes are very important. Actually when things are going fine, nobody cares, frankly speaking. But my processes have accountability when things go wrong. Processes are very important to make sure that a certain level of quality is maintained. If processes are in place, there will be some accountability, some transparency into why it is going wrong'.

Some vendors also said that processes cannot be rigid. One interviewee said:
'Process is critical as it builds faith in the customer that ok they are going to use this process, they are going to follow it, regular feedback on the process and on the various aspects of what is happening at what stages should be delivered. I am not denying the importance of process but the fact that process should not be such that you can't be flexible, it is very important to be flexible and adapt to the client's requirements and no process can be 100% adaptive so I think while process is important to act as a guideline, it must be flexible to the client'.

Constant Communication: Maintaining constant communication with clients was another frequently identified critical success factor. Vendors identified various means of communication, including email, phone calls, conference calls, net meetings and video conferencing. One of the vendors said:

'Setup the communication matrix, who is going to be responsible for what, there are multiple channels of information flowing in, setup the communication channel very well, you must just use the telephone to say at least 'hi' initially, but keep it on, keep communicating more than required so that none of them have that anxiety about what is happening and what is not happening'.

In general, vendors reported that they had set up communication plans and ascertained periodically that they communicate constantly with the client to understand the business better, to let the client feel part of the project and to deliver information on project progress. Vendors also described a formal approach to maintaining communication. One vendor reported:

'Because communication is a key thing, we have various levels of communication that happens like direct contacts, face-to-face meetings, continuous telephonic meetings, where processes are established, how often to contact, what issues need to talk about, who is the person etc. We kind of formalize these things to ensure that we fill these gaps'.

Vendors reported on the use of various communication means to constantly update clients about the outsourced project.

Proper Resource Allocation: Figure 1 shows that 16 out of 18 vendors identified resource allocation as a critical success factor in managing offshore outsourcing relationships. Vendors said that how they allocate resources in terms of people, skill sets, time and processes for the outsourced project are important. Vendors varied in their ways of establishing resources across their offshore projects. Figure 1 shows that six vendors reported that their onsite presence (at the client site) is an important part of managing relationships. For example one vendor said:

'We have an account manager for each and every large client account. We allocate our resources according to project and business sides. From the project delivery side, we have project directors, project managers and every one who is facing the client side whether the designer, programmer or anyone, plays very core part in how we manage the entire relationship. From the business side, we have a client champion who mirrors the account manager, who makes sure that the entire account management is cohesive and there is a project plan that exists for every account from the business side as well as the execution side'.

Mutual Cooperation: Vendors consider mutual cooperation as critical in managing relationships. Vendors think that clients must be cooperative in terms of giving the right inputs when needed. Mutual cooperation is also considered critical in the sense that vendors embrace the premise that outsourcing relationships are mutually beneficial. They also think that both parties should consider outsourced work as a common project rather than being vendor's sole responsibility. One vendor said:

'I think, first of all, when a relationship gets established, and when it would work. It could get established and work if there is a win-win situation for both. And therefore there has to be an important contribution, which, each party in the relationship brings in. Obviously, what customer brings in is an opportunity for us to do business, create success, get more revenue and establish our good track record. So that is clearly the fundamental reason why we are here. And the customer should get good value for money. The customer has to get various things such as the combination of cost savings, quality, our experience, and our highly disciplined processes'.

Meetings: More than half of the vendors identified conducting regular meetings as a key factor. They also said that face-to-face meetings are the most effective means of communication. Regular meetings were reported to enhance transparency in the project and understanding of the project. Vendors perceived that regular meetings were helpful in making clients feel part of the project. Due to significant geographical distance between clients and vendors, frequent face-to-face meetings were not possible.

Maintaining Transparency: Figure 1 shows that half of the vendors identified transparency as one of the critical success factors. One vendor said:

> *'It is important to be transparent in all undertakings with the customer. It helps. And it means that whatever is happening here on the project, customers should be in a position to take a view of it'.*

Vendors highlighted the importance of transparency in their processes, demonstrating the progress of the project and communication.

Expectations Management: Figure 1 also shows that half of the vendors identified managing expectations as one of the critical success factors. Vendors consider this aspect as challenging and difficult. Vendors report that both clients and vendors should know what they will get from an outsourcing project and all expectations should be clearly specified and mutually agreed to. One vendor said:

> *'The fundamental of our relationship is that the expectation match has to be very high. Therefore what we can offer to the client, the manner in which we offer it, the manner in which we will expect to get paid for the work we offer, what the client should expect from us, how will that ramp up expectations, how that delivery will take place, we try to make all these absolutely clear. If expectations are managed well and are very clear, there is no tension in the relationship'.*

Other Critical Success Factors: Figure 1 also shows that vendors (8 out of 18) consider it important to be proactive in terms of delivering information, outcomes and services to clients. Eight out of 18, vendors identified that it is also important to be consistent in delivering successful outcomes to clients. One of the vendors said:

> *'I will say consistency in delivery is very important. If you commit something, the ability to deliver it and maintain that is extremely important. Consistent delivery helps building an effective relationship with the client'.*

Figure 1 also shows that nearly half, 7 out of 18, of the vendors identified value addition as an important factor. Vendors considered value addition in the sense that how they can create value for clients' project by delivering beyond the contracted deliverables of the outsourced project.

Other critical success factors are domain expertise, commitment, demonstrability, client visits (onsite presence), confidentiality, honesty and flexibility. Vendors commented that they have to be competent enough and have expertise in the area of work. A quarter of vendors commented that they should be able to effectively demonstrate their processes, offerings and project outcomes to the clients. One vendor said:

> *'There are many things a customer expects as a given. It is important that it needs to be highlighted to the customers because many US and UK customers still are not aware of the offshore outsourcing business model, and how it works and what are the key issues to be taken care of. There are learning curves for them. Therefore we as a vendor should be able to demonstrate our capabilities and results effectively to our clients'.*

A few vendors specifically commented on honesty as a critical success factor. Vendors reported that clients and vendors should be honest and straight in their approach. One vendor said:

'When you say certain things, follow it and make sure you can do it as stated. If you cannot, be straight, don't wait until the disaster happens; tell that person that you cannot do it and also tell them why you can not do it. One has to be very honest in your commitments with the client'.

Only a few vendors referred to the importance of confidentiality in managing relationships. However, the majority of vendors had internationally recognised BS7799 certification and other confidentiality measurements in place. BS7799 (now referred to as ISO17999) is an international standard that sets out the requirements of good practice for information security management. However, the majority of vendors did not explicitly specify confidentiality as a critical success factor in managing relationships.

Clients' Critical Success Factors

Figure 2 presents ten critical success factors identified by clients in managing their offshore outsourcing relationships.

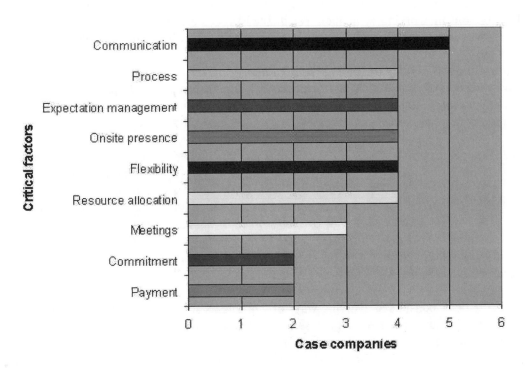

Figure 2. Clients' Perception of Critical Success Factors in Managing Offshore Software Outsourcing Relationships with Vendors

Constant Communication: Figure 2 shows that constant communication is the most widely (by 5 out of 6 clients) reported critical success factor in managing offshore outsourcing relationships with vendors. Clients reported the use of various primary means of communication with vendors – emails, conference calls, net-meetings and occasional telephone calls. One client said:

'The relationship is virtually exclusively on email, occasionally telephone calls, but not frequently. We have access to a joint server, sharing the actual work, in this case obviously the computer software. But the contact is exclusively by email'.

Another client reported that verbal communication with vendors was critical in building their relationship. He said:

'I guess the only strategy we have is that we have constant contacts with them (vendors), in other words, because they are so far away, if you don't have contact with them at least once a week, things seem to fall apart. So I guess that contact is the main strategy. We have verbal communication with them once a week where we meet them for about an hour, and we use net-meeting and conference calling for that. So we have whole group in Washington and Phoenix who sit down and talk for an hour with the folks in India to find out their progress. We also constantly deal with emails, probably in order of twenty or thirty a week where in between our weekly meetings, if there is any question from any side, or get an update like that'.

Vendor's Process and incorporating flexibility: Vendor processes and their flexibility came up as second most widely reported critical success factors. Client companies reported the use of a formal vendor initiated process that can also incorporate flexibility in dealing with the vendor. However, clients reported that they were not following any formal quality process in managing offshore outsourcing projects. One client identified that they are generally happy to follow their vendors' methodology or process if there is one. This is because this client perceived that the vendors might feel more comfortable in working with their established processes. According to clients a high maturity process was important. Clients also indicate that they tend to be more informal. One client said:

'I have set through whole day of 'boring' presentation of internal processes in some of the vendors we review. And from the client's perspective it is great because it helps us to see the way they deliver things but as far as the client is concerned it is probably not as important. It is important that they use formal processes'.

Expectations Management: In terms of expectation management, clients emphasised on articulating what is expected from outsourcing project and that it should be conveyed to vendor in detail.

'Knowing what you want very specifically and with great details, specifying all these and communicating it to the vendor are very important. I think the biggest problem is that people tend to think that something will get done or seems obvious that something will get done and they don't specify it, don't state it specifically and at the end they don't get that done and the problem with the vendor arises. So you should know what you really want to have get done and communicate that in detail'.

Onsite Presence: Clients considered evolving ways of working as suited to both of them rather than necessarily following a blueprint of some process especially when the project is relatively small. In regard to spending time together, clients identified onsite presence as critical. The majority of clients identified bringing some individuals from the vendors' side to their own site to understand the project. Clients also had visits to the vendors' site initially. In some cases, clients identified that throughout the life of the project there was someone from the vendor side at their site to work as a key contact person and to address their concerns. One client who appraised the management of the project as highly satisfactory, commented:

'Overall the way the project was managed was very good. They brought a person to our site who directly worked with my project manager. They had here an onsite manager, there were six people who worked directly with us and they had a team of many more in India working on the project'.

Proper Resource Allocation: Furthermore, resource allocation was considered to be a key issue. Clients reported how they allocated resources to manage relationship effectively. One client said:

'When we begin a project as I said, we have documents of what type of work exactly needs to be done so from those documents we can decide how many people are necessary and what sort of skill-sets those people have to have. The overall management structure is designed and then our management people go to the management in India to assign relevant people and resources for the project'.

Other Critical Success Factors for Clients: Three case companies particularly emphasized the importance of having regular meetings. As part of spending time together and constantly communicating with the vendor, clients undertook frequent meetings over the phone or internet. Meetings were also conducted across different management levels in two companies. Face-to-face meetings were relatively rare. In one case, client did not have any face-to-face meetings with the key person with whom he had been working for two years in the project.

Finally, clients of two case companies identified making regular payments to vendors and committing to what they have agreed in the project. One interviewee said:

"You need to have timeline of payment which the vendor will always want and that you know, those payments are made when the work is done. But that has to be periodically throughout the project".

OVERALL ANALYSIS

Now we provide analysis of critical success factors according to vendors only, clients only, and both. Factors that are embraced by only one of the partners in a relationship and not the other --point to potential areas of conflict and consequent deterioration in relationship. Such factors ought to be brought to the attention of both partners to facilitate appreciation of the needs and concerns of the other partner. Factors that are embraced by both vendors and clients need to be reinforced in both organizations throughout the relationship. Table 4 summarizes these factors.

Critical success factors reported by both - vendors and clients	Critical success factors reported by vendors only	Critical success factors reported by clients only
Communication	Cooperation	Spending time together
Process	Transparency	Payment
Resource allocations	Consistency	
Meetings	Proactive	
Flexibility	Domain expertise	
Onsite presence	Value addition	
Expectation management	Demonstrability	
Commitment	Honesty	
	Confidentiality	

Table 4. Overall Analysis of Critical Success Factors Reported by Vendors, Clients, and Both

Critical Success Factors Reported By Both Clients and Vendors: Table 4 shows that there are eight critical success factors common to both clients and vendors. Communication, process and resource allocation are the most widely acknowledged factors from both sides. Vendors identified the use of more verbal means of communication such as telephone calls whereas clients identified more use of email communication. Furthermore vendors ascribed to following a formal approach to communication by planning a communication matrix to consider issues such as when to communicate, how much to communicate and how often to communicate whereas clients indicated an informal approach.

In the context of process, the approaches of clients and vendors differ. Vendors generally were highly concerned about following CMM processes. However, clients considered process to be important but ignored its importance in the sense that they were content to know that vendors were following CMM processes. Clients did not consider implementing any formal processes within their own organisation. Clients talked about a flexible approach to managing offshore outsourcing relationships. Most clients considered flexibility essential in a process driven approach.

Both clients and vendors had similar views on resource allocation and meetings as critical success factors in managing relationships. However, resource allocation was considered a vendor's responsibility. Vendors also suggested the importance of establishing resources for clients to retain control and monitor an outsourced project. However, in one case, client had not even met the key individual of a vendor company with whom he worked for two years. However, the outsourcing project was considered successful.

However, most clients identified the onsite presence of individuals from the vendor company to be important. A few vendors also commented that an onsite presence as part of their resource allocation strategy. Onsite presence was considered important in the sense that the client can have one locally based contact point available for any issue of concern.

Most clients considered expectation management as an important factor. Half of the vendors also considered the importance of expectation management. Both clients and vendors specified that they should have a clear understanding of what is expected from each other and whether these expectations have been clearly communicated. The importance of expectation management is suggested when both communities say that it is difficult to manage expectations.

Critical Success Factors Reported By Vendors Only: Table 4 documents nine critical success factors identified by vendors. It is, however, not meant to convey the message that clients did not consider the factors identified by vendors.

Half of the vendors identified that both clients and vendors should proactive in exchanging the status of the project and other relevant information. They also should cooperate without fearing the loss of control or knowledge. Nonetheless, vendors emphasised on being transparent in all actions and processes relating to outsourced project. In addition, some of the critical success factors such as domain expertise, value addition and confidentiality were also only mentioned by vendors. For example, vendors considered that they should be able to add value to the outsourcing project by offering something additional to the contracted deliverables or by helping clients to improve their existing processes. However, clients did not identify this issue. This may lead to speculation whether vendors actually do add value and if they do, then to what extent. It might also be possible that the six clients investigated in this study might not have experienced added value in their outsourcing projects.

Vendors reported to have extended their efforts in assuring their clients on confidentiality by achieving international certifications of security standards and transparency in their operations. However clients did not comment on confidentiality. This may be possible because clients might be very satisfied with their vendors' security arrangements or clients may not have enough awareness on security issues in offshore software outsourcing.

Only vendors considered domain expertise as critical in building their relationships. The reason why clients might not have considered domain expertise as critical could be that they are not necessarily exposed to problems stemming from lack of domain expertise. However, clients mentioned an onsite vendor presence during the project. This may provide opportunities for vendors to understand the local domain for the relevant outsourcing project. Therefore it is difficult to speculate that the clients do not have knowledge of domain expertise issue as a critical success factor.

Critical Success Factors Reported By Clients Only: Table 4 shows that critical success factors such as spending time together and regular payments were only identified by clients. Half of the clients reported that the relationship builds as they spend time with the vendors and work together. However, vendors identified a formal approach to relationships. They emphasised more on following high maturity processes. However, vendors' perceptions such as maintaining an onsite presence at the client side, keeping constant communication and conducting regular meetings may suggest that they also value 'working together'.

Summary of Empirical Results

In this chapter critical success factors in managing offshore software outsourcing relationships were identified. It is evident from the analysis presented above that both clients and vendors have several commonalities in their perceptions on the critical success factors to manage their relationships. Constant communication between clients and vendors, process driven approach to work and efficient resource allocation emerged as crucial in managing relationships. Communication mainly involved undertaking regular meetings and exchanging information regularly with each other over phone and emails. Resource allocation was further evident in allocating vendor representative at client site. Such onsite presence was considered important by the clients as they wanted the vendor contact to be available locally. Furthermore managing 'hidden' expectations and being flexible to adjust to unpredicted changes were considered important. Since distance limits clients to conduct regular physical check over outsourced project in offshore outsourcing and vendors do not have any direct opportunity of verification on the inputs they receive for the project, commitment from both sides was also identified as critical in managing relationships.

Following on the similarities in perceptions of clients and vendors, a few emergent differences were also identified. For example, client views did not directly indicate the importance of cooperation, transparency, process driven approach and proactiveness. Vendors considered process driven approach as critical to managing their outsourcing project and subsequently deliver outsourced project successfully. Vendors' approach to managing relationships emerged as somewhat more formal than of clients. However, clients were happy to acknowledge that their vendors follow high maturity process driven approach.

The next section presents the relationship management model and proposes testable propositions derived from this study.

RELATIONSHIP MANAGEMENT MODEL

Managing relationships is at the core of managing software outsourcing contract. Therefore, discovering central factors to managing relationships is also important. Based on the empirical results, propositions and their discussion, a model for managing offshore software outsourcing relationships is presented in Figure 3. The purpose of the model is to contribute to the understanding of software outsourcing, particularly involving India. There are several definitions of 'model' across disciplines. In this study, the model is the end result of the qualitative data analysis conducted by following grounded theory methodology. Thus in this study 'model' is taken to mean a simplified representation of a phenomenon based on empirical research.

Figure 3 shows that communications, commitment, process and transparency most affect relationship management in offshore software outsourcing. Additionally, they may be influenced by other factors. For example, Figure 3 shows that communication comprises two other relating critical success factors including meetings and onsite presence. Similarly, process, transparency and commitment also relate to other factors identified in the study. Propositions identified in the discussion section also helped to decide four central factors and their related factors.

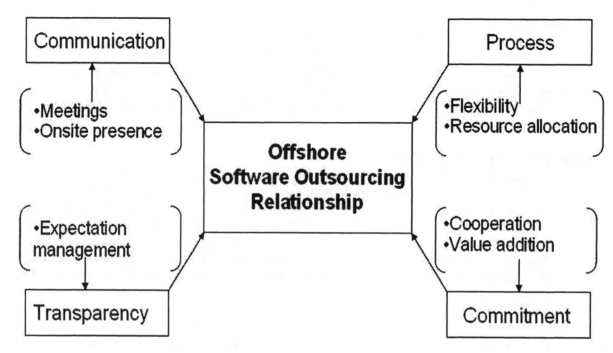

Figure 3. Managing Offshore Software Outsourcing Relationships

Figure 3 shows that the relationship may not be successful if the identified factors are not addressed effectively. For example, if communication is not efficient or commitment in the project is poor or process driven approach is not followed or actions of vendor are not transparent then the relationship will be negatively affected. However, effectively managed communication, process, transparency and good commitments from clients and vendors into the project is likely to foster successful client – vendor relationships.

Applicability of the Model
The scope of the proposed model spans across high maturity Indian software vendor companies and their US and European client companies. Although the investigation on which the model was based only covered high maturity India software companies and their clients, it still can be used by other (non-high maturity) software vendor companies and their clients. The scope of this model is questionable if clients are from countries other than USA or Europe and vendors are from India. This is because the approach to managing offshore software outsourcing relationships may differ in other regions.

No specific model for managing offshore software outsourcing projects is yet in use or has yet been presented in the literature except the eSCM-SP, which is still undergoing revisions. This model can well be used with eSCM-SP as it addresses only the relationship management part of the eSCM-SP and it complements what is currently offered by the eSCM-SP.

Limitations of the Model
The model has not been tested in real outsourcing relationships. Therefore, at this stage, the model may be limited in terms of commercial applicability. However, it has been developed on the basis of real empirical data and has gone through rigorous academic discussion. The other limitation of the model, as explored earlier, is that it may not be applicable in contexts other than the one studied in this investigation. However, the factors identified in the proposed model are highly abstract. Therefore, their applicability in other contexts cannot be completely ruled out. For example, issues

such as transparency, communication or process grow out of 'distance,' so the 'offshore' context may be more important than the country to which the software is outsourced. The proposed model does not present the complete process of managing outsourcing contract. For example, trust, being one of the most critical success factors is yet not seen in the above model. The reason is that the model is solely based on empirical data corresponding to the study question. This exclusion may also be attributed to the fact that it is quite likely that commitment may lead to trust. Despite these limitations, the model's exclusive focus on offshore relationship management between vendor and client is a significant contribution. However, the presented model's explicit focus on client-vendor relationship is considerable. Nonetheless, the detailed theorising of the model is under process.

		VENDORS			
		India		Countries other than India	
		High Maturity Companies	Low Maturity Companies	High Maturity Companies	Low Maturity Companies
CLIENTS	From USA and European countries	Focus of this study			
	Other Countries				

Table 4. Research Scope Framework

Table 4 documents the fact that the scope of this study is limited to outsourcing practices of Indian high maturity companies and their corresponding clients from the USA and Europe. In Table 4, all the cells except the 'focus of this study' are empty. This indicates that the similar empirical investigations may be replicated in other contexts. For example, investigation into relationship management of High Maturity Vendor Companies of China and their US and European clients may reveal other interesting results. Replications will also allow higher comparability and consensus building for management of outsourcing relationships at theoretical level. Based on the above model, we articulate four propositions.

PROPOSITIONS FOR OFFSHORE OUTSOURCING MANAGEMENT

Based on the strategy identified for selecting critical success factors for further discussion i.e. proposition and model building, the following emergent critical success factors came out as the core or central ones. In this section, testable propositions, centred on central critical success factors are proposed.

Critical success factors discussion		
Communication	Process	Resource allocation
Expectation management	Flexibility	Onsite presence
Meetings	Commitment	Transparency
Consistency	Value addition	

Table 5. Critical Success Factors to Be Considered for Further Discussion

Proposition One - Effective Communication - Client and vendor should build effective communication to successfully manage offshore outsourcing relationships.

The literature on relationships (such as the business literature and the social science literature) emphasises the importance of communication for successful relationships (e.g. Olkkonen et al., 2000). Similarly, in the investigation presented in this chapter, both clients and vendors rated communication as of great importance in managing their relationships, as has also been noted in the literature (Kern and Willcocks, 2000; Zhu et al., 2001). Managing communication effectively is not easy, particularly in the offshore context, where difficulties such as distance, time zone difference and cultural differences constrain effective communication. However, constant and fruitful communication was imperative to both clients and vendors in managing their relationships. Communication can at least be explored from two dimensions, oral and written.

Both oral and written communication were described as important. For example, in this study vendors raised the issue that knowing how much to communicate with an offshore client is important, in addition to what is communicated, whereas clients placed greater emphasis on managing written communication with the vendor. Krishna et al. (2004) also observed that Indian software vendors had to approach communication with U.S. and Japanese clients in very different ways. Krishna et al. (2004) says:

> 'U.S. client companies normally work with extensive written agreements and explicit documentation, reinforced with frequent and informal telephone and email contact. In contrast, Japanese clients tend to prefer verbal communication, more tacit and continuously negotiated agreements, and less frequent but more formal use of electronic media'.

Clients in this study are large US based clients. The difference found in this study further substantiates the observation made by Krishna et al. (2004) observation. Some literature (e.g. Olkkonen et al., 2000; Kern and Willcocks, 2000) emphasises that a communication plan is essential to outsourcing, and especially to offshore outsourcing (Parkhe, 1998).

Similarly, Paasivaara and Lassenius (2004) also note the importance of a communication plan in global software development projects. However, they explain that in their case studies, companies did not agree upon a formal communication plan or practices. Subsequently, it was found that team members did not know whom to contact and eventually it became difficult to advance the project. In this study, vendors emphasised having and following a formal communication plan from the beginning of their projects. They identified the full communication setup, including details such as whom to contact, when to contact and how often to contact. The reason why all vendors were found to follow a formal communication strategy may reflect their high maturity status and other international quality certifications such as PCMM and ISO 9001. However, clients in this study did not report having any communication strategy or plan and said that they were happy to follow vendors' plans. Clients however said they made sure they worked jointly with vendors and spent time together, which helped them in their efforts to build a relationship with the vendor.

Sufficient communication does not replace the need for clear and transparent communication. Vendors said they are proactive in communicating with clients if they find something 'wrong' in the project, even if it may create extra work or incur additional costs for them. This was further said to build confidence and trust in the vendor. However, it can be said that in addition to having a detailed communication plan, clients and vendors should follow the identified plan by actually communicating.

Proposition Two - Process Driven Approach - Client and vendor should adopt a software process approach (such as CMM), establish a resource allocation plan and communication processes to manage their relationships, with flexibility integrated into the processes.

Similar to the communication plan, it is also essential to determine and allocate resources for the outsourcing project. Efficient resource allocation makes the outsourcing process easier to follow and gives clients and vendors a clear idea about the time, manpower and money required to conduct the outsourcing project (Krishna et al., 2004; Kern and Willcocks, 2000; Zhu et al., 2001). In addition to communication, a process-driven approach was considered crucial for managing relationships. The process approach is also reflected in the design of a detailed communication plan and resource allocations. Moreover, all vendors in this study were high maturity companies and therefore the process approach may be of greater importance to them. However, processes must not be followed rigidly. In other words, designed processes should be flexible enough to accommodate any unpredicted circumstances. This is reflected in Jiang et al.'s, (2004) study on the relationship between software development process maturity and project performance. They assert (based on Weinberg, 1971 and Bailyn, 1984) that technical project performance can be improved if team members engage in higher levels of self-control as opposed to rigid organizational control. Jiang et al. (2004) highlight the flexibility issue in CMM by clarifying that *CMM provides 'what to do' but allows flexibility on the part of the team members in 'how to' accomplish their tasks*. Furthermore, Haag et al. (1997) studied process improvement in geographically distributed software engineering. They also found communication to be of significant importance and also suggested that project coordination should take flexibility and resource allocations into account.

This study also found that the client's approach to relationship management was more informal. For example, they did not follow any formal process such as CMM, whereas the vendor's approach was more formal. For example, communication was considered critical by most clients and vendors. However, clients did not report having any communication strategy or plan in place to communicate with their vendors. Clients only reported that they communicate regularly with their vendors but do not follow any formal guidelines, in contrast to the vendors' emphasis on following a formal communication plan. However, clients considered it important and helpful for their vendors to follow high maturity processes and standards such as ISO and CMM.

Proposition Three - Relationship Transparency - Client and vendor should maintain a transparent relationship and manage each others' expectations.

The other critical success factor observed in this study is transparency. The importance of transparency in the success of the business is evident in the literature. For example, Eggeft and Helm (2003), basing their argument on the interaction model of business relationships, claim that transparency in the relationship contributes to the overall success of a business relationship. In particular, they found that *transparency delivers value to the customer, increases customer satisfaction and ultimately leads to favourable behavioural intentions*. In this study, transparency means that clients and vendors are aware of each other's actions, of the project status and of all other information affecting the project. This is also consistent with Eggeft and Helm (2003) who defined relationship transparency as *an individual's subjective perception of being informed about the relevant actions and properties of the other party in the interaction*. Transparency may also increase if the vendor can efficiently demonstrate the actions taken at each stage. For example, a vendor might be regularly producing metrics to measure the quality of the results, but if he does not show the measurements and their results to the client, the transparency in the status of the project described by vendors will be weakened.

Transparency is also related to expectation management. It may be difficult to manage the 'hidden' expectations in the relationship. It was observed in this study that, proper documentation and determination of each action in the project will help to manage expectations better. In relation to this, better expectation management will be realised if the actions of clients and vendors are transparent. Transparency also relates to the honesty of clients and vendors. Although honesty may be used interchangeably with transparency, it is considered in this study in terms of communicating honestly and not being opportunistic in the relationship.

Proposition Four - Commitment - Clients and vendors should be committed to the outsourcing project as a shared project. Particularly, commitment may be realised by creating more value propositions, maintaining consistent delivery of successful results and mutually cooperating to make the project successful.

Commitment in the relationship is another important factor observed in the study. Commitment also relates to a few emergent critical success factors. Clients said that they should pay their vendors as agreed. This primarily signifies that the agreement or contract between clients and vendors should be properly drawn up and mutually agreed (e.g. Willcocks and Fitzgerald, 1993; Whang, 1992). In addition to payment, the addition of value to the outsourced project is important and takes place if the vendor can add offer more value propositions than anticipated by client. This may also relate to the vendor's domain expertise in a particular outsourcing project. However, throughout the project, consistency in the vendor's capabilities and deliverables and the client's cooperation in providing necessary inputs to the vendor were essential ingredients of commitment.

CRITICAL SUCCESS FACTORS REVISITED

During empirical investigation into difficulties and relationship management, clients and vendors expressed their perspectives on how they resolve some of these difficulties identified earlier. Table 6 also presents solutions for the emergent difficulties based on the empirical results emerged from the study. The literature evidence supporting each solution is also proposed. In this section, the difficulties in managing offshore outsourcing relationships, identified from the literature review, are related back to the relevant critical success factors emerged in the empirical study.

The first column in Table 6 presents the difficulties reported by clients and vendors in the empirical investigation. Corresponding critical success factors emerging from this study are presented in the second column. Based on the critical success factors, for each identified difficulty a resolving activity is proposed in column three. Column four provides literature support for the solution identified. The objective is to review the examples of proposed recommendations for each difficulty against the existing literature. Therefore, if there is 'none identified' in the last column, a resolving activity was not found in the literature. It does not mean that the literature has not addressed that particular difficulty.

In terms of resolving cultural differences, this study uncovered that vendors may give a cultural handbook to clients to assist in the development of cultural harmony in the relationship. Cultural training programs, particularly, for outsourcing managers also emerged as one of the solutions in resolving cultural differences. Krishna et al. (2004), in terms of culture, also found that challenges not only concern the need to adapt to different ways of working but to cultural norms of social behaviour, attitudes toward authority, and language. They, in addition to giving culture training as a solution to managing cultural difference, observed that in most cases, cultural training was perceived as one way learning process. It was argued that cultural training for both clients and vendors should be encouraged as it will develop well-informed understanding of the culture and business practices of both groups in offshore software outsourcing.

It also emerged in this study that expectation mismatch may be addressed by efficient contracting, documentation and clear and sufficient communication. The literature has also touched on these issues. For example, Whang (1992) argued that due to limited information, clients and vendors make decisions in their own interest, leaving each party vulnerable to the other's opportunistic behaviour. In this context, Koh et al. (1999) emphasised efficient documentation to avoid expectation mismatch which also emerged as one of the solutions in this study.

Table 6 shows that bi/multi-lingual managers may be used by clients and vendors in managing language differences in the project. However, it is considered a responsibility of the vendor to make such provision. Krishna et al. (2004) found differing viewpoints on multi-language provision in offshore software outsourcing. For example, they found that some Norwegian clients expressed a preference for Russian software vendor companies rather than Asian companies. One reason was that the Norwegian clients experienced that Russians learned the Norwegian language with relative ease compared with their Asian counterparts.

Emergent difficulty	Critical success factor identified in this study	Examples of resolving activity to manage the identified difficulty	Examples from the literature that support the proposed activity
Cultural differences	Communication [Spending time together, meetings]	Constantly communicate (formally and informally) in the project and when required work together to conduct the outsourcing project Culture training programs for outsourcing project managers A concise handbook which can help in understanding a company's corporate and societal cultural environment	None identified Krishna et al. (2004) None identified
Expectation mismatch	Transparency [expectation management]	Better contract management Documentation Clear and sufficient communication	Whang (1992) Koh et al. (1999) Lacity (2001)
Language	Process [resource allocation]	Bi-/multilingual managers	Krishna et al. (2004)
Loss of control	Transparency [demonstrability, honesty]	Using more than one vendor Transparency in vendor's processes Transparent and open access to client on outsourcing work	Currie (2000) Lacity (2001) Lacity (2001)
Loss of jobs	Commitment [cooperation, value addition]	More opportunity at client company Value added work	None identified Levina and Ross (2003)
Transfer of work	Process [resource allocation, onsite presence]	Better contractual agreements Mutual understanding and cooperation Efficient process to manage transfer of work Documentation	Lee et al. (2003) Kern and Willcocks (2001) Zhu et al. (2001) Koh et al. (1999)
Distance	Communication, Transparency	Using efficient communication links and tools Transparency building in the work More communication and regular meetings Regular visits by project personnel Retaining core knowledge in house	Lacity (2001) Kern and Willcocks (2000) Lacity (2001) Shaffer (2000) Lacity (2002)
Time zone differences	Process [resource allocation, onsite presence]	Process driven approach to alleviate time zone differences Onsite presence of vendor to give client a contact point in local time zone	None identified None identified

Table 6. Emergent Difficulties and Solutions - Offshore Software Outsourcing

Table 6 shows three recommendations for managing their client's perceived loss of control in offshore software outsourcing – using more than one vendor, transparency in the vendor's process and open access to outsourcing work being carried out at the vendor's site. It was found that Currie (2000) and Lacity (2001) have also addressed this issue. However, Currie (2000) argued that the overall knowledge of outsourcing vendors as a community is very limited. This signals caution in using more than one vendor for one project as it may create more overhead costs for the client. In other words, managing multiple vendors may be more difficult as there are still several challenges in successfully managing relationship with one vendor in offshore project.

Another difficulty, perceived loss of jobs, is also difficult to manage in offshore outsourcing. If client employees fear losing their jobs to Indian vendors, they may not be motivated to actively cooperate in transferring outsourcing work to vendors. Table 6 shows that one resolution to manage this difficulty is joint effort by clients and vendors to create more opportunities on the client's side. Of course, the literature has focused heavily on job losses on the client's side (e.g. McLaughlin, 2003; Bhagwati et al., 2004) in offshore outsourcing but there is lack of focus on resolving it (Drezner, 2004).

CONCLUSIONS

In this chapter critical success factors in managing offshore software outsourcing relationships were identified. Subsequently, a provisional relationship management model was presented. The literature review into software outsourcing helped to identify the main research question. Grounded case research strategy was then used to conduct the empirical investigation. Subsequently, a provisional relationship management model was presented followed by four value propositions.

Empirical results suggest that both clients and vendors have several commonalities in their perceptions on the critical success factors to managing their relationships. Communication between clients and vendors, process driven approach to work and efficient resource allocation to the project emerged as crucial in managing relationships. Communication mainly involved undertaking regular meetings and exchanging information regularly with each other over phone and emails. Resource allocation was further evident in allocating vendor representative at client site. Such onsite presence was considered important to clients as main point of vendor contact available locally. Furthermore managing 'hidden' expectations and being flexible to adjust to unpredicted changes were considered important. 'Geographical Distance' limited clients to conduct regular physical check over outsourced project in offshore outsourcing. Similarly, vendors did not have any direct opportunity of verification on the inputs they receive for the project. Therefore, commitment from both sides was also identified as critical in managing relationships.

Following on the similarities in perceptions of clients and vendors, a few emergent differences were also identified. For example, client views did not directly indicate the importance of cooperation, transparency, process driven approach and proactiveness. Vendors considered process driven approach as critical to managing their outsourcing project and subsequently deliver outsourced project successfully. Vendors' approach to managing relationships emerged as somewhat more formal than of clients. However, clients were happy to acknowledge that their vendors follow high maturity process driven approach.

Finally, communication, process driven approach, transparency and commitment emerged as the most central critical success factors in managing offshore software outsourcing relationships. Relating to that, meetings, onsite presence, flexibility, resource allocation, expectation management, cooperation and value addition also emerged as important factors in managing relationships. Their relationship to the central critical success factors emerged in the identified propositions in the study.

MINICASE

A Global Insurance Company Keeps Their Promise of Unsurpassed Customer Service

As insurance options broaden and products grow more complex, customers seek superior and personalized service more than ever. To maintain a competitive edge, insurance companies are focusing on enhancing their customer service. This leading global insurance provider was looking for a customer resource management (CRM) solution that would give a unified customer view, driving an efficient customer service.

Single System for Homogenous Processes
Various companies under this insurance provider's umbrella had their own business systems. These disparate systems led to fragmented information. Separate silos of customer data, insurance policies, claims, activities and correspondence made it difficult for the staff to gain a complete picture of each customer's situation. Lack of knowledge of customers affected timely decision making. There was no single system to track and manage customer calls either that led to limited visibility into the volume and type of customer phone calls. Operational bottlenecks translated to inconsistent customer service across the company's five commercial insurance business lines.

The staff spent considerable time tracking and managing customer service issues rather than focusing on business development. Lack of homogenous processes across the enterprise led to unproductive staff and inefficient operations.

Focus on Customer Retention
With increased competition and better informed customers, this global insurance company realized the need to focus on customer retention, growth and acquisition. This could be achieved by controlling and integrating all customer touch points across the enterprise with the right CRM application that would help the company improve their quality of customer interaction, target offerings and utilize cross selling opportunities.

The proposed system would be a single platform that would provide complete, real-time enterprise view of customer data accessed by business users like the company's employees, call center representatives, agents and brokers.

Standardizing on Siebel Technology
Tata Consultancy Services' (TCS') CRM practice specializes in providing services by identifying customer service standards and optimizing the client's infrastructure and processes to help the client enterprise meet their objectives. A comprehensive CRM solution was implemented that provided call tracking feature, automation of claims induction process and better account management capabilities.

Siebel was used as the enabling technology. Systems requiring online updates were integrated with TIBCO while Siebel EIM connected other internal systems. Siebel Sales Force was integrated with Microsoft Outlook using Siebel PIMsync. Use of web based solution and Siebel workflow processes digitized the entire claims management process. Claims could be received and reviewed electronically. Uniform and easy-to-use interface allowed easy access and modification of data across all systems in the enterprise. Call center operations using Computer Telephony Integration enabled features like routing calls to smallest queue and automated answering. Electronic storage, indexing and retrieval of claim related documents were implemented by Document Management.

Incoming and Outgoing emails were fully integrated into Siebel using eMail response feature. Electronic alerts could be sent to the company's staff who could proactively contact customers if they did not receive the customer's supporting claims documentation within 48 hours from the time of initial inquiry. A customized feature developed by TCS' CRM consultants ensured that all service requests were resolved and there were no misdirected tickets.

Multiple Business Support, Consistent Customer Service
All five commercial insurance lines were standardized on Siebel technology suite, providing an enterprise-wide view of customer service levels. The customer service center resolved 80% of calls. Processes became efficient, staff more productive and customers more satisfied with consistent service. The implemented CRM solution enabled the company to increase the rate of call resolutions. Claims induction was completed in 30 seconds, a significant reduction in time from 3 days as was the situation before. With a centralized system, the company had access to better talent, knowledge and analytics that translated to enhanced services. Optimized support processes with a single system led to cost efficiencies as well. Complete access to data benefited the corporate sales team with significant improvement in account and lead management processes.

With an integrated system, this insurance service provider was able to serve customers better, more accurately target marketing to specific groups of customers and more intelligently up-sell and cross-sell additional products and services across all channels.

The benefits accrued from the integration exercise have led the insurance company to plan a portal solution that would enable self-service and ability to create new tickets via Siebel portal integration. Maximum calls will be resolved on first interaction either on phone, fax, email or web. New businesses will be brought within the purview of Customer Service Center to get economies of scale and scope.

Discussion Questions:
1. Which function was outsourced by the insurance company?
2. What was the rationale behind initiating outsourcing activity (by the insurance company)?
3. How the vendor company i.e. TCS resolved the insurance company's problem?
4. What benefits were achieved by the insurance company from outsourced activity?

Used with permission of Tata Consultancy Services.

KEY TERMS
Axial Coding
Client
Coding
Grounded Theory
High Maturity
Offshore
Open Coding
Partners / Parties
Selective Coding
Software outsourcing
Vendor

STUDY QUESTIONS

1. What are the main reasons for growth of offshore software outsourcing?

2. Why is it important for clients and vendors to effectively manage relationships?

3. What difficulties clients and vendors may face in managing their relationships?

4. Which models have been proposed relating to management of offshore outsourcing relationships in the in the literature?

5. Which critical success factors emerged as the most central in the empirical investigation of this study? How were only some of the critical success factors determined to be the most central ones?

REFERENCES

Bailyn, L. Autonomy in the Industrial R&D Lab. *MIT Press.* Cambridge, MA. 1984.

Brereton, P. February, "The software customer/supplier relationship," *Communications of the ACM.* 47(2). 2004, pp. 77-81

Brynjolfsson, E. "Information Assets, Technology, and Organization," *Management Science.* 40(12), 1994, pp. 1645-1662.

Currie, W. "The supply-side of IT outsourcing: the trend towards mergers, acquisitions and joint ventures," *International Journal of Physical Distribution & Logistics Management*, 38(4), 2000, pp. 238-254.

Eggeft, A. and Helm, S. "Exploring the impact of relationship transparency on business relationships: A cross-sectional study among purchasing managers in Germany," *Industrial*

Marketing Management, 32 (3), 2003, pp. l01-108

Foote, D. September "Recipe for offshore outsourcing failure: Ignore organization, people issues," *ABA Banking Journal.* 96(9), 2004, pp. 56-59.

Glaser, B. and Strauss, A. *The Discovery of Grounded Theory.* London: Weidenfield & Nicolson. 1967.

Haag, Z., Foley, R. and Newman, J. "Software process improvement in geographically distributed software engineering: An initial evaluation," *New Frontiers of Information Technology: from the 23rd EUROMICRO Conference '97,* 1997, pp. 134

Herbsleb, J. and Moitra, D.. "Global Software Development," *IEEE Software.* March/April 2001, pp.16-20.

Hyder, E. B., Heston, K. M. and Paulk, M. C. *The eSCM-SP v2 - Model overview.* Technical Report number CMU-ISRI-04-113. Informatoin Technology Services Qualification Center, CMU. 2004.

Jiang, J. J., Kleinb, G., Hwangc, G., Huangc, J. and Hungc, S. "An exploration of the relationship between software development process maturity and project performance," *Information and Management,* 41, 2004, pp. 279-288.

Kern, T. and Willcocks, L. "Exploring information technology outsourcing relationships: theory and practice," *Journal of Strategic Information Systems.* 9, 2000, pp. 321-350.

King, W. "Outsourcing becomes more complex - IT Strategy and Innovation," *Information Systems Management Journal,* Spring 2005, pp. 89-90.

Kishore, R., Rao, H. R., Nam , K., Rajagopalan, S. and Chaudhury, A. "A relationship perspective on IT outsourcing," *Communications of the ACM.* 46(12), December, 2003, pp. 87-92.

Koh, C., Tay, C. and Ang, S. Managing vendor-client expectations in it outsourcing: a psychological contract perspective. *Proceedings of the Twentieth International Conference on Information Systems.* Charlotte, NC. 1999, pp. 512-518

Krishna, S., Sahay, S. and Walsham, G. "Managing cross-cultural issues in global software outsourcing," *Communications of the ACM*. 47(4). April 2004, pp. 62-66.

Lacity, M. "Lessons in Global Information Technology Sourcing," *IEEE Computer*. 35(8), 2002, pp. 26-33.

Lacity, M., Hirschheim, R. *Information Systems Outsourcing - Myths, Metaphors and Realities*. Wiley. 1995.

Levina, N., and Ross, J. W. "From the Vendor's Perspective: Exploring the Value Proposition in IT Outsourcing," *MIS Quarterly*. 27(3), 2003, pp. 331-364.

Loh, L. "An organizational-economic blueprint for information technology outsourcing," *Proceedings of the International Conference on Information Systems*. Vancouver, BC, Canada, 1994, pp. 73-89.

Miles, R., Snow, C. "Causes of Failure in Network Organizations," *California Management Review*, 1992, pp. 53-72.

Nam, K., Chaudhury, A., Raghav Rao, and H., Rajagopalan, S. "A Two-Level Investigation of Information Systems Outsourcing," *Communications of ACM*. 39(7), July 1996, pp. 36-44.

Nicholson, B., Sahay, S. and Krishna, S. "Work practices and local improvisations with global software teams: A case study of a UK subsidiary in India," *Proceedings of the IFIP Working Group 9.4 Conference on Information Flows - Local Improvisations and Work Practices*. Cape Town. May 2000.

Nystrom, H. E. "Managing cultural differences for engineers," *IEEE - Frontiers in education conference*, 1997, pp. 812-814.

Olkkonen, R., Tikkanen, H. and Alajoutsijärvi, K. "The role of communication in business relationships and networks," *Management Decision*, 38 (6), 2000, pp. 403-409.

Oza, N., Hall, T., Rainer, A. and Grey., S. "Role of trust in software outsourcing relationships.," *Journal of Information and Software Technology*. 48, May 2006, pp. 345-354.

Oza, N. and Hall, T. "Difficulties in managing offshore software outsourcing relationships: An empirical analysis," *Journal of information technology cases and applications research (JITCA), Special issue on Global Software Outsourcing, 7(3),* November 2005.

Oza, N. and Mäkelä M. "The culture-based challenges in offshore software outsourcing," *International Association for Management of Technology (IAMOT) 2006*. Beijing: China. [http://www.iamot.org/conference/viewabstract.php?id=1677&cf=10]

Ozannne, M. R. Barometer of Global Outsourcing-The Millennium Outlook. *Dun & Bradstreet*. February 2000.

Paasivaara, M. and Lassenius, C. "Collaboration practices in global inter-organizational software development projects," *Software Process: Improvement and Practice: Special Issue on Global Software Development: Growing Opportunities, Ongoing Challenges*. 8 (4), September 2004, pp. 183-199.

Palvia, P. "Case Study: A dialectic view of information systems outsourcing: Pros and Cons.," *Information and Management*. 29, 1995, pp. 265-275.

Parkhe, A. "Building trust in International Alliances," *Journal of World Business*. 33(4), Winter 1998, pp. 417-437.

Patton, M. Q. *Qualitative education and research methods*. Sage Publications. 1990.

Ravichandran, R. and Ahmed, N. U. "Offshore systems development, "Information *and Management*, 24(1). January 1993, pp. 33-40.

Reifer, D. J. "Seven hot outsourcing practices," *IEEE Software*. January/February 2004. , pp. 14-16.

Sabherwal, R. 1999. The role of Trust in Outsourced IS Development Projects. *Communications of the ACM*. 42(2), pp. 80-86

Shaffer, F. A. "Outsourcing: A managerial competency for the 21st century," *Nursing Administrative Quarterly*. 25 (1), 2000, pp. 84-88.

Smith, M., Mitra, S. and Narasimhan, S. "Offshore outsourcing of software development and maintenance: A framework for issues," *Information and Management*. 31, 1996, pp. 165-175.

Stralkowski, C. and Billon, S.A. "Partnering: a strategic approach to productivity improvement," *National Productivity Review*. 7(2), 1988, pp. 145-151.

Strauss, A. and Corbin, J. *Basics of Qualitative Research: Techniques and Procedures for Developing Grounded Theory*. Sage publications. 1998.

Weinberg, G. The Psychology of Computer Programming, *Van Nostrand Reinhold*, New York, NY, 1971.

Whang, S. March "Contracting for software development," *Management Science*. 38 (3), 1992, pp. 307-324.

Willcocks, L. and Fitzgerald, G. "Market as opportunity? Case studies in outsourcing. information technology and services," *The journal of strategic information systems*, 2, 1993, pp. 223-242.

Yin, R. *Case study research: Design and methods*. 2nd ed. Beverly Hills, CA: Sage Publishing. 2003.

Zhu, Z., Hsu, K. and Lillie, J. "Outsourcing – a strategic move: the process and the ingredients for success," *Management Outsourcing*. 39 (5/6). 2001, pp. 373-378.

21

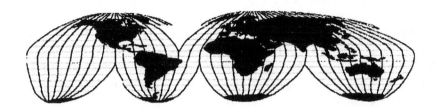

Global Outsourcing of IT and IT Enabled Services: A Relationship Framework and a Two Stage Model for Selecting a Vendor

Shailendra C. Jain Palvia
Long Island University

CHAPTER SUMMARY

Information systems outsourcing has become an accepted practice and a strategic choice for many firms in the Western world. The global market for outsourcing of Information Technology (IT) functions took off in the late 1980s. Since the beginning of the new millennium, the global market for IT as well as IT enabled services (ITES) has been growing steadily. The functions being outsourced have increased in scope and magnitude as well as climbed the value chain ladder. IT functions include IS analysis, IS design, IS development, IS implementation, and the management of entire data centers. IT enabled services, also called business process outsourcing, include functions like call centers, accounting, payroll, employee benefits, tax preparation, radiology analysis, films and cartoons production, healthcare, medical tourism, and research and development. Outsourcing locations can be onshore, nearshore, offshore or farshore. This chapter provides a relationship framework for global sourcing arrangements, subsidiary, joint venture, or outsourcing, for accomplishing IT and IT enabled services in the context of on-shoring as well as off-shoring. We also articulate and describe a two-stage model for selecting a vendor country and a vendor company.

GLOBAL MARKET FOR OUTSOURCING: PAST, PRESENT, AND FUTURE

Outsourcing, especially offshoring, exemplifies the essence of true globalization, with services being provided where they can be most efficiently and cost effectively produced and delivered where they are most needed and valued. With the boom in globalization, both IT outsourcing and business process outsourcing (BPO) have reached new heights and continue to climb.

In 1989, outsourcing was approximately a $4 billion business (Lacity et al., 1996). In 2000, outsourcing of IT functions reached $56 billion per year (Casale, 2001) and by 2005 it was approximately a $160 billion industry in the United States alone (Vijayan, 2002). It has been reported that the IT work that is outsourced offshore has reduced corporate IT expenses by 20% to 50% (Hoffman, 2003). According to the Global Insight report, by 2008, IT offshoring will account for roughly $125 billion in additional US GDP annually, a $9 billion jump in US exports and a net increase of 317,000 jobs; and the amount is expected to increase to $250 billion by 2015.

What about the market for IT Enabled Services (ITES) or Business Process Outsourcing (BPO)? Gartner Dataquest (2003) estimates the global market for BPO would reach $131 billion in 2004, $131 billion in 2007, growing at a compounded annual growth rate of 9.5%. IDC estimated that the global BPO market was expected to grow to $1.2 trillion in 2006 from $300 billion in 2004 (Minevich et al., 2005). They expect about 25% of US spending on application development, integration, and management services to go to offshore providers.

Over the years, India has become the primary destination for offshore outsourcing of IT as well as ITES and BPO. AT Kearney ranks India highest in an index of country attractiveness for offshore outsourcing of IT among 11 countries. India scored 7.3 (out of 10), with 3.4 in cost (out of 4), 1.6 in environment (out of 3), and 2.3 in people (out of 3). Canada is #2 with a score of 6.2. Philippines, Ireland, Australia, and China have been respectively ranked as 5, 7, 8 and 11. The remaining six countries that were ranked are: Brazil, Mexico, Hungary, the Czech Republic, and Russia.

The notion that global outsourcing reduces employment and hurts economies of countries such as the U.S. and U.K. may be a myth. Outsourcing activities directly benefit the US economy. McKinsey & Co. (2003) report cost savings of approximately $ 0.58 for every dollar spent on outsourcing jobs to India. Furthermore, American jobs outsourced to China and elsewhere have generated demand for other products made in the US, and created jobs in other sectors as well. Other benefits include the fact that many foreign firms outsource back to the United States. Some have labeled this phenomenon as "reverse outsourcing" or "backsourcing." For example, many Japanese automobile manufacturers have created substantial employment and income in the US by outsourcing production to the U.S. Atkinson (2004) reports that the United States gained more from this type of outsourcing than it lost over the 1996 – 2001 period. Thus outsourcing can be viewed as a form of international trade benefiting the U.S., or as a means by which globally competitive firms become more efficient and viable over the long run (Marshall 2003). Recent developments suggest that IT outsourcing by U.S. firms may itself create new IT related jobs here in the United States (Gross 2005). As one CEO of a Midwestern US company put it, "We can compete and create new jobs, but not without outsourcing" (Engardio, 2006).

BENEFITS AND RISKS OF OUTSOURCING

The benefits of outsourcing can be summarized as follows (Saji, 2006):
- Cost Reduction - This applies mainly to offshore IT outsourcing owing to labor arbitrage, economies of scale and specialization (Clemons and Hitt, 1997)
- Quality - This is a result of Service Providers' IT capability, achieved through the integration of their human skills, IT infrastructure, reputation, etc. (Bharadwaj, 2000)
- Leveraging Time Zones - Work can be performed continuously 24x7, passing across different time zones of the globe
- Higher capacity on demand
- Access to advanced technologies (Lee et al., 2003)
- Opportunity to transform an organization through partnerships (Linder, 2004)
- Emergence and maturation of process management standards such as Software Engineering Institute's (SEI) Capability Maturity Model (CMM), Capability Maturity Model Integration (CMMI); and ISO 9000. (For details of CMM, visit http://www.sei.cmu.edu/cmmi/).

However, the promising side of the IT outsourcing opportunity comes at a cost. IT outsourcing partnerships carry innate risk elements as evidenced by reported failures of such engagements in the recent past (Prewitt, 2004; Andersen, 2002). The sourcing of a function from outside a firm's boundaries also results in the loss of:

- Control
- Flexibility
- Qualified personnel
- Competitive advantage in Information Communications and Technology (ICT).

Outsourcing contracts carry risk owing to limited understanding about the future and bounded rationality of humans to analyze the past and the present. Therefore it is essential to understand the process involved in IT outsourcing decisions, the risk factors at each phase of the decision process and measurement and management of the same at the time of contracting. Previous research has focused on identifying the variables involved in the outsourcing decision process at various levels and also the strategic risk dimensions involved in the process with a client focus (Ge et al., 2004; Gottfredson et al., 2005; Palvia, 2004; Graf and Mudami, 2005).

WHAT FUNCTIONS CAN BE OUTSOURCED?

Information Technology (IT)
IT functions were the first to be outsourced onshore or offshore. IT functions that can be selectively outsourced are: IS development, IS maintenance, and IS operation. Some organizations have outsourced the entire IT function, including all of the company's computers and data centers, PC maintenance and support, and the acquisition and maintenance of the IT infrastructure (hardware, systems software, and telecommunications networks).

Accounting
The global market for outsourcing finance and accounting (FA) functions is expected to grow at a 9.6% compounded annual growth rate, and top $47.6 billion in 2008 (IDC, 2004). The IDC report presents the worldwide and US finance and accounting (FA) business process outsourcing (BPO) market forecast and analysis by major region and distinct FA sub-processes, such as transaction management, finance, general accounting, treasury and risk management, and tax management, that make up the FA function. Spending on outsourcing of the transaction management function is expected to grow the fastest, at 9.8%, over the next five years. The author has personal experience with small accounting firms in the New York and New Jersey area exploring offshoring accounting functions for their clients to a firm near Bangalore, India during 2006. An accounting firm in the US allowed the Indian start-up firm to download its accounting files from a website and then within 2 weeks received accounting reports uploaded on the same website by the Indian firm.

Human Resources
In a 2003 survey by the Society for Human Resource Management, HR professionals were asked if they outsource any HR functions and why do they outsource. The reasons cited for outsourcing included: saving money, focus on strategy and core business, improving compliance, improving accuracy, lack of experience in house, and taking advantage of technological advances. Functions that were outsourced included: 401 (k) administration, employee assistance/counseling, retirement planning help, pension administration, temporary staffing, background checks, training and management development programs, executive development and coaching, health care benefits administration, employee benefit administration, payroll, risk management, executive staffing, employee relocation, Human Resources Information Systems selection/training/implementation, recruitment, executive compensation and incentive plans, policy writing, administration of compensation/incentive plans, and wage and salary administration.

Research and Development

AMR Research conducted a survey in 2003 and found that 50% of R&D groups in the auto, high-tech, aerospace and defense industries had no interest in outsourcing IT support; but 12% said they were outsourcing IT projects related to R&D. Companies in the technology sector exhibited the least interest, just 4% said they do any outsourcing of this function. Even when companies do, for outsourcing functions that require sharing proprietary or extremely sensitive data, they generally look within the United States, or at a company that melds both onshore and offshore services. The U.S. medical device and diagnostics industry was estimated to have outsourced more than $300 million in R&D in 2003. This figure has been growing at a consistent rate for a number of years, and continues to accelerate.

Companies choose R& D outsourcing to reduce costs, minimize business risks, and hasten market entry of products. The cost reduction may result from improved organizational effectiveness, shorter product development cycles, greater access to high technology, or restructured and improved use of resources. Outsourcing often leads to enhanced effectiveness by permitting the company to focus on core competencies and lessen its demands on tangible resources.

An innovative application of offshore outsourcing was made by the author in the conduct of a recent research study. Data needed to be collected from India with a three months deadline. While the time frame was short and the contract was for a relatively small amount, the research team was able to find an Indian vendor with offices in New York. The vendor exceeded expectations in three areas: the quality of the data was excellent, more data was delivered than was requested, and they finished ahead of schedule.

Customer Relationship Management and Call Centers

Outsourcing means that client companies do not have to invest heavily in customer relationship management services and infrastructures with expensive in-house IT and service departments. Companies are generally skeptical and concerned about entrusting their most important asset - their customers - to a third party. The outsourced call center can administer technology and human resource functions, increasing customer satisfaction and retention at a lower cost. A good barometer for measuring the success of an outsourcing agreement is the seamlessness of the line between the client and the customer relationship manager. The customer (of the client) should not be able to distinguish between the two. Additionally, the vendor should not offer a one-size-fits-all package. Its infrastructure should reflect the profile of the customer, not the reverse. For example, insurance agencies are requiring the outsourced call center staff to be flexible in their ability to switch from placing an outbound call to suddenly being available to receive an inbound call and handle both with aplomb. In the past, clients typically had divided the two functions, using one outsourcing group for inbound and another for outbound calls.

Tax Preparation

Spending on outsourcing of tax return preparation is expected to grow by 9.3% per year over the next five years while spending on general accounting functions is expected to grow 8.3% per year (IDC, 2004). The largest outsourcing companies claim that thousands of returns were processed during the 2003 tax season and hundreds of thousands for the 2004 season. CPA firms claim that it is increasingly difficult to find qualified part-time staff during tax season, and that there are significant cost savings from outsourcing. Besides cost savings, other benefits include: (a) Improved turnaround time and increased productivity, because the return comes back in less than 48 hours; (b) Reduced tax preparation workload frees up a CPA firm's professional staff to find ways of offering their clients new value-added services; and (c) Tax outsourcing can serve as a catalyst for business transformation, enabling a firm to outsource other accounting functions, such as bookkeeping.

According to Mintz (2004), there are several ethical concerns in regard to offshoring of tax documents. Four rules in the AICPA Code of Professional Conduct are of particular relevance to tax outsourcing: Rule 102, Integrity and Objectivity; Rule 201, General Standards; Rule 202, Compliance with Standards; and Rule 301, Confidential Client Information (*AICPA Professional Standards Volume II*; AICPA, New York, 2003).

Radiology Analysis and Medical Tourism

Teleradiology is a growing healthcare business niche that helps ease the shortage of radiologists and increasing work loads. Providing radiological services around the clock has become a serious problem for many hospitals. On-call radiologists, who once were contacted at home perhaps once a night to read an X-ray or MRI, now find themselves dealing with four or five calls and getting little or no sleep and having to report to work the next morning.

Technology that once produced only fuzzy images now permits Internet transmission of crystal-clear radiological scans, so more and more hospitals and radiology practices are contracting with so-called nighthawks - radiologists who do not mind covering night shifts in the United States because where they are across the globe in Israel, Australia or Switzerland, it is daytime.

NightHawk Radiology Services out of Coeur d'Alene, Idaho, established in 1994, coined the term "Nighthawk" because that was the nickname for pilots who flew night missions. Today, NightHawk Radiology provides overnight radiology services for hospitals and radiologist practices in 46 states. There are issues of credentialing, licensing, accuracy of the readings, liability, and public perception. Most of these concerns have already been answered. They maintain strict requirements that all teleradiologists be US trained, licensed, and board certified. The new nighthawk radiologist is one that relocates his or her own job overseas, but still holds a license to practice medicine in each US state where contract clients are located and also is individually credentialed by each hospital for which the work is done. The technology has moved from more primitive e-mail delivery, to having a private Web server, to sending scans via the Internet to radiologists in Australia, Israel, India or Italy.

The United States has no jurisdiction outside its borders, so there are questions about what could happen if a teleradiologist in Australia, for example, were sued for malpractice. At this time, it appears that the hospital would be liable but the radiologist is under no obligation to come to the United States for trial.

According to Lancaster (2004), Howard Staab learned that he suffered from a life-threatening heart condition and would have to undergo surgery at a cost of up to $200,000, an impossible sum for the 53-year-old carpenter from Durham, N.C., who had no health insurance. So he outsourced his surgery and post-surgery care to India. Staab flew in September, 2004 about 7,500 miles to the Indian capital of New Delhi, where doctors at the Escorts Heart Institute & Research Centre - a sleek aluminum-colored building across the street from a bicycle-rickshaw stand - replaced his balky heart valve with one harvested from a pig. Total bill: about $10,000, including roundtrip airfare and a side trip to the Taj Mahal. Staab is one of a growing number (running into more than a million) of people known as "medical tourists" who are traveling to India, Thailand, and other third word countries in search of First World health care at affordable costs. McKinsey & Co. estimated that India's medical tourist industry could yield up to $2.2 billion in annual revenues by 2012.

Taken as a whole, India's health care system is hardly a model, with barely four doctors for every 10,000 people, compared with 27 in the United States, according to the World Bank. Health care accounts for just 5.1 percent of India's gross domestic product, against 14 percent in the United States. On the other hand, India offers a growing number of private "centers of excellence" where the quality of care is as good as or better than that of big-city hospitals in the United States or Europe. So asserts Naresh Trehan, a self-assured cardiovascular surgeon who runs Escorts and performed the operation on Staab. Trehan said, for example, that the death rate for coronary bypass patients at Escorts is .8 percent. By contrast, the 1999 death rate for the same procedure at New York-Presbyterian Hospital, where former president Bill Clinton recently underwent bypass surgery, was 2.35 percent, according to a 2002 study by the New York State Health Department.

Many patients in the US and Western Europe have found their treatment solutions in Thailand, spurring a trend in 'medical tourism' to that country (Medical Tourism in Thailand, 2007). The Thai medical profession is probably one of the most advanced in the region. Successive governments have invested in ensuring the education and training Thai doctors receive is parallel to that offered elsewhere in the region. Many doctors undertake specialist training abroad, particularly the United States and Europe and are at least equally as well qualified as physicians in the west. Thailand's hospitals and clinics are world class. Huge investments have been made in equipment and management standards are so high that hospitals achieve ISO 9001 accreditation. Thailand's medical solutions do not rest at major surgery or treatments. A variety of cosmetic surgery options are available, as is cosmetic dentistry (laser teeth whitening, etc.), and laser sight correction (LASIK, etc.). Thailand is also a very popular choice for people requiring sex reassignment surgery.

Film and Cartoon Production

Digital animation has become essential from Hollywood to Bollywood (India's film industry is nicknamed as Bollywood). The king of animation is Walt Disney Studios. Now India could become an outsourcing hub for animation cartoons, with Jaddoworks.com leading the way.

India is coming of age in the animation field and is emerging as a new destination for the international animation and special effects industry. According to an independent trade survey, the Indian animation industry, which is now pegged at $550 million, is expected to grow at 30% annually in the next couple of years and reach a level of $15 billion by 2010. Some notable companies in India are: Pentamedia Graphics, Jadoo Works, CD India, UTV Toons, Moving Picture Company, Heart Entertainment Ltd., Color Chips, and Toonz Animation. Pentamedia has unveiled *Sindbad: Beyond the Veils of the Mists*, the first full-length Indian animated 3D film using the technique of "motion capture." The film was completed in a record time of 18 months instead of the usual two years and more, and the total cost of the film was about $14 million. The average cost of such productions anywhere else in the world is around $40 million.

WHERE CAN A FUNCTION BE OUTSOURCED?

The following description of outsourcing locations is from the perspective of the U.S. The sourcing arrangement can be either onshore or offshore. Within the offshore category, there are three sub-categories: nearshore, middleshore, and farshore. These terms are described below.

Onshore

Onshore simply means outsourcing within the boundaries of one's own country. This was the first era of outsourcing, starting with Kodak outsourcing its entire IT functions in 1988 to IBM. Recent outsourcing contracts mirror that growth of the outsourcing strategy: Sabre outsourcing to EDS, DuPont outsourcing to Computer Science Corporation (CSC) and Andersen Consulting, Xerox outsourcing to EDS – all for billions of dollars. A very large business process outsourcing deal was when Nortel Networks outsourced its Human Resources and Procurement functions to PriceWaterhouse Coopers in a $630 million (5 years) agreement in 2002.

Nearshore

From the vantage point of the US, Canada and Mexico form the nearshore countries. A huge advantage is that the North American Free Trade Act (NAFTA) has created a large trading alliance between the US and Canada and Mexico. This trade zone allows the free flow of people, goods and services between the three nations and establishes a compatible legal framework for protection of property in all three nations.

Outsourcing to Canada is probably the least risky proposition. It is the most familiar place to outsource IT services. The dominance of the US market is seen in the fact that Canada's top two outsourcing software services exporters - IBM and EDS - are both US firms. Canada's dependence on the US market is further highlighted by the fact that 84% of all information and communications technology products and services are exported to the US Canada has the same time zones as the US, its major cities are located near US major cities, English is the primary language (except for French in Quebec province) in Canada, and its culture and business practices are similar to the U.S.

The Mexican Information Technology software outsourcing sector is a $30 million industry. Although the industry is small, Mexico has unique advantages for nearshore software outsourcing. The chief among them is the proximity to the US market, NAFTA, low-cost qualified personnel, and access to the Latin American market. The advantages of Mexico's proximity to the U.S. is that not only is it easy to access Mexico from almost anywhere in the continental U.S., but many Mexican and American firms already have extensive experience working together. This familiarity breeds similar business cultures and allows for US firms to be comfortable in outsourcing key software processes to Mexican firms. Another big advantage for Mexico is NAFTA. NAFTA allows the free flow of goods and services between Mexico, Canada and the U.S. and protects intellectual property rights. Mexico is an ideal point for accessing the vast Latin American market due to similar language, culture and knowledge of that market by Mexican firms. The disadvantages can be summed up in Mexico's lack of experience, lack of English speaking skills, and lack of expertise. Mexico itself has a serious marketing problem in that the country is not seen as a prime location for outsourcing software development work. Mexican software services industry has not done a good job of talking up its strengths and capabilities. Americans tend to view Mexico as a Third World country, which is technically the case. Less appreciated is Mexico's rank as the 11th-biggest economy in the world. With an important economy so close to the US, Mexico can become a player in the global market for IT outsourcing services.

Middleshore

The middleshore category can be construed as countries in West Europe, who have similar culture and similar economic status. Countries in this category include Ireland, the Czech Republic, Hungary, and Belarus. The value of the outsourcing market in Ireland passed $234 million in 2003. By 2007, it was estimated to be $357 million (Ulfelder, 2003). According to Uldelfer (2003), both Ireland and Northern Ireland are relatively close to the U.S., and their language, infrastructure, and inhabitants' culture and work ethic are all familiar and comfortable to the American eye. Irish vendors have generally focused on the aggregation and implementation of packaged software applications, rather than on development and maintenance. Both Northern Ireland and Ireland are a six-hour plane ride from the East Coast of the U.S., and there is plenty of overlap in the business days of U.S. and Irish workers. That makes it possible to pick up the phone and make a call when necessary. Salaries in Ireland are between 50% and 75% of contractor rates in the U.S. Irish IT salaries are about midway between those in the US and those in India.

Farshore

Among farshore countries, India clearly leads the way. Other farshore players are China, Russia, Philippines, Taiwan, Malaysia, and Pakistan.

India is regarded as having invented the modern offshore outsourcing industry. In 2003, India exported about $9.875 billion a year in software and IT services, with expected growth rates of over 28% annually. Indian software companies initially concentrated their efforts by providing low level design, coding, testing, maintenance and support services for the export market. Although, Indian companies have moved up the value chain into areas such as systems integration, network and infrastructure management and system planning and design work, they do not have the name recognition that US based consulting firms do. US companies estimate projected savings of 50% to 70% by doing projects in India. All top-tier Indian vendors are certified at Capability Maturity Model (CMM) Level 5, the highest level of the CMM designed by Carnegie Mellon University. India has provided software solutions to many Fortune 500 companies. Citibank, Morgan Stanley, Wal-Mart,

AT&T, General Electric, Reebok, General Motors, Sony, Boeing, Coca-Cola, Pepsi, Swissair, United Airlines, Philips, General Electric, IBM, Reebok, Lucas, British Aerospace, General Motors, and Sears are some of the companies that have outsourced to Indian vendors. Studies by several think tank companies, including Gartner and Forrester Research, have concluded that India is likely to remain the number one destination for outsourcing of IT functions and ITES. Pearl, the Peterborough (U.K.) based closed fund group, signed a £486 million (12 years) deal with Diligenta, a subsidiary of Tata Consultancy Services based in India on April 25, 2006.

Business process outsourcing is the fastest-growing sector in India's IT industry, which include functions like filing US tax returns, handling billing questions, and telemarketing at call centers. Besides English, Indian call centers offer services in Spanish, French and German. The combination of large supply of high quality low cost labor, high quality software processes, and the scale to handle all types of work has allowed the Indian software industry to become a global software powerhouse. However, Indian firms now face the threat of lower cost software developers from other far shore nations such as Romania, China, and Russia. The next step for the Indian software firms are too move up the value chain and provide total solutions for their clients. Namely, the Indian firms are now concentrating on providing IT and business consulting services to their global clients, going head to head against global giants such as Accenture and EDS. The Indian companies will have to make a large investment in hiring, training, and retraining their employees to compete in a global market. They will also have to expand overseas and establish subsidiaries in the US and Europe.

In BPO delivery, India is being increasingly challenged by the Philippines. The Philippines Government plans to develop and promote the country as a hub in the delivery of customer contact centre, medical transcription, animation, BPO and shared financial services. China is also challenging India, offering lower billing rates but only limited language capabilities. Offshore BPO today accounts for only two percent of total business process service delivery contract value worldwide and is expected to rise to six percent of the total by 2008.

After emerging as the world's hottest manufacturing hub, China is joining English-speaking countries as a key destination for outsourced service jobs The Chinese IT outsource software services sector is a $1.5 billion market (2003) with an annual growth rate of 30%. The sector can be characterized as being in the same position as India was 12 years ago, with a large supply of low cost workers and a huge internal market in which to base a outsource services sector. The Chinese software services industry would like to follow the same development path that Indian firms took. However, due to a lack of entrepreneurial, managerial, and technical skills, Chinese companies lag far behind larger, more established companies in India and the Philippines. Furthermore, there is a large demand for IT solutions from China's big domestic market, meaning that their foray into outsourcing market will be further delayed. China's software services market suffers from numerous problems: software piracy, little experience in developing and maintaining complex software, lack of expertise in project management, lack of proficiency in English, lack of quality standards and processes (only one Chinese company, Neusoft Co., has achieved CMM level 5), and an authoritarian political regime.

China's software services industry's main international success has been in obtaining software outsourcing contracts from Japan. The industry recently has begun to develop, relationships with Indian software outsourcing firms which have set up software centers in China. The Chinese industry would like to see the Indian companies outsource their cheaper work to China. The business would support the development of management and technical capabilities of the Chinese software industry, while allowing India to focus on higher value-added activities.

Russia is a promising new entrant in the field of outsourcing for software services. It has many promising natural resources, including, a large well-educated low-cost workforce of scientists and engineers. Although, Russia does not have any dominant software firms, the Russian outsource software services sector has grown to $200 million (2003) annually with a 50% annual growth rate. However, there are obstacles to the continued growth of the market in Russia. These obstacles include immature marketing, poor sales and project management skills, a scarcity of employees with English-language skills, a decrepit telecommunications infrastructure, and a shortage of qualified managers.

A FRAMEWORK FOR GLOBAL OUTSOURCING RELATIONSHIPS

Outsourcing relationships can be classified as captive, outsource, and joint venture. The pros and cons of these options are captured in Table 1.

	Pros	Cons
CAPTIVE (Subsidiary)	Retain full control Retain unit cost savings	Slower to set up Reduced benefits Higher financial risk Management headache
JOINT VENTURE	Fast Share additional client revenues Share financial risk	Long term partnership means possible control problems Share unit cost savings Confusing strategy message
THIRD PARTY SERVICE PROVIDER	Faster to implement Realize maximum economies of scale Incur limited financial and geopolitical risk Can tap specialized management	Long term commitment (average contract is more than five years) Incur cost of managing (governance) Reduced cost savings

Table 1. Pros and Cons of Outsourcing Relationships (Source: Ton Heijmen, Senior Adviser, Offshoring/Outsourcing, The Conference Board, 2005)

The above framework can be augmented to reflect the ability of a company to outsource onshore and offshore, as shown in Figure 1. There are six options for outsourcing. If GE America was considering outsourcing some of its work, its six options are presented in the Figure 1.

	Vendor Location (vis-à-vis Client Location)	
	Onshore	**Offshore**
Insourcing	GE subsidiary in America	GE subsidiary in India
Outsourcing	IBM America	Infosys India
Joint Venture	Joint venture with IBM America	Joint venture with Infosys India

Figure 1. Relationship Framework for Outsourcing Options

More nuances of global outsourcing arrangements exist. For example, GE may outsource its IT functions to IBM America, which in turn can outsource to IBM India or to Infosys. Furthermore, Infosys India can outsource some of its work to Infosys subsidiary in China, where labor pool is available at even lower cost than India.

The following discussion is in the context of offshore sourcing arrangements and much is based on the Conference Board Report (2005). If there is an expectation of rapid growth - from 0 to 200 employees within a short period (1-3 years) - then offshore *insourcing* might make sense. A few managers at home can't manage hundreds from afar very effectively. In many key offshoring destinations, the process of setting up a subsidiary operation is well established, so there is little risk of making blunders. Advisers experienced in specific regions can assemble a plan, identify a location within the selected country, help you incorporate, find suitable real estate, set up the office technology, handle legal matters, and even help recruit staff. Some companies choose the offshore subsidiary route because the supply market is not sufficiently mature. Companies in the financial and insurance industry do so because they are in highly regulated industries and need greater control over their processes. A growing number of companies are offshoring both high volume business processes and higher-value work through offshore subsidiary operations. A company may also be banking on the possibility that its subsidiary operation could eventually offer services to compatriot companies, increasing its value as a separate company that could someday be sold off or taken public.[1] As a subsidiary, unless you are (or promise to be) an employer of choice in the local market, you might experience employee retention problems. After investing in training people, you would lose them, because of the huge turnover problem in countries like India and China, thus always being in the expensive position of having to train anew.

Concerns about data privacy and security (especially financial and human resources data) are also prompting more companies to use the captive or joint venture structure. Region-specific advisers can perform due diligence on *alliance/joint venture partners*. Technology companies focusing on intensive R&D or intellectual property development will frequently turn to the captive or joint venture model. It is important to be an attractive employer that offers career opportunities if you want to pursue offshoring through the captive or joint venture route.

Today, more IT is handled by *third-party providers* than any other option, in part, because the information technology offshoring market is mature. A third-party vendor makes sense for offshoring those processes for which a deep labor pool exists (notably finance and administration), when you want to test the waters, or if you don't necessarily anticipate rapid growth or increase in scale. Some third-party providers offer multi-client service locations, in which one location services the outsourcing needs of a number of clients, providing full capabilities, scale, and expertise cost effectively. Other providers operate specialty locations, each handling a different discipline for clients, such as customer relationship management, business intelligence, or payment systems.

Another way of selecting the most appropriate offshore sourcing arrangement is to define the organizational benefits you are seeking through outsourcing or offshoring, which will govern the optimal allocation of technology ownership.

- Are you seeking to *arbitrage* cost via a low-cost location, while keeping the process centralized? In the *lift-and-shift* approach, you would ideally maintain ownership of the key technologies (core applications, middleware, and enabling technology), or else use the provider's. (For call center operations, the provider's technology is typically used.) Either way, this approach requires considerable coordination for tech-related projects and yields limited efficiencies. The typical savings rate is between 20 percent and 30 percent.

- Are you looking for *cost effectiveness*, along with *process improvement* (including greater standardization)? The *enhancement* approach generally uses the company's own core applications and the provider's middleware and enabling technology, which, for technical projects, necessitates considerable coordination between the two parties. Your choice of software solutions is a key determinant of success. Savings of between 30 percent and 40 percent are the norm.

- Do you want *integrated solutions*, *leading-edge tools*, and an *extended enterprise?* This is a new way of doing things that creates new sources of value creation. In a *transformation* model, the provider takes over completely to reengineer processes, using its own technologies. This approach requires less coordination between you and the provider. Savings rates of between 40

---

[1] As mentioned previously, this was the case with GE's decision to sell its captive behemoth GECIS in November 2004. With four centers and 12,000 employees in India, GECIS was the largest business process outsourcing operation in India held by a Western company. See "In India's Outsourcing Boom, GE Played a Starring Role," *Wall Street Journal*, March 23, 2005; and "GE Plans to Sell Call-Center Unit Based in India," *Wall Street Journal*, September 17, 2004.

percent and 50 percent are typical, the result of the reduced need for interaction with the provider and newfound process efficiencies.

STAGE ONE: A MODEL FOR CHOOSING A VENDOR COUNTRY

Organizations must first define the scope of their prospective offshoring initiative: the location or geography, the process or function (e.g., finance and accounting), the sub-process (accounts receivable), and the business units that will participate.

One of the first matters to consider for off-shoring is the nearshore/middleshore/farshore decision. The advantages to *nearshoring* are cultural similarities, geographic proximity, and a closer time zone. *Middleshoring* offers somewhat lower costs, quicker time to market, and cultural proximity. *Far-shoring* IT and ITES offers the advantages of significant cost arbitrage, acceptable quality standards, and access to the vast resources of a developed, populous marketplace that enables economies of scale. Two other related options to be considered are multi-shoring and right-shoring. *Multishoring*, as the name implies, provides not only a hedge against risk, but also the opportunity to accelerate the development of new processes and products by dividing work among locations. Spreading one's application portfolio globally avoids excessive dependency on a particular region to deal with the issues of sovereign risk. Force majore, natural disasters, sabotage, etc., are all real issues, which require a more nuanced global sourcing strategy. *Rightshoring* refers to allocating work strategically between locations near, middle, and far: for example, shifting simple customer inquiries to offshore call centers while keeping complex inquiries on the caller's shore.

Using a top-down approach, the first decision should be in terms of choosing onshore, near shore, middle shore, far shore or a combination of these approaches. The next step should be to drill down to countries, to cities, and then to companies.

Figure 2 is a conceptual model to choose a country for outsourcing. Once the client company has decided the region of the world - nearshore, middleshore, farshore - the conceptual model would help in selecting the appropriate country or countries in case of a multi-shoring strategy. This model suggests focusing on factors like political system, ICT infrastructure, regulatory regime, workforce quality and quantity, judicial and legal system, and language/culture. Ultimately, these factors will distil into issues of costs, quality, and speed for both short and long term for getting work done in another country.

Economic Conditions
Cost advantage in terms of labor arbitrage is the often cited reason for offshoring IT and ITES to countries like India, China, Philippines, Russia, etc. But client companies must stay away from taking a static picture on this factor. A leading US HR outsourcing firm noted that its costs had risen in India by nearly 10 percent from 2002 to 2003. With rising demand, call center companies are looking to new shores, such as Davao in the Philippines, and cities in the Baltic states, whose workers provide a closer cultural match for Europeans than Asian workers. Executives must also factor into their calculations general inflation in candidate destination countries. Most outsourcing/offshoring contracts will include provisions for cost increases based on general inflation, using a CPI-type adjustment. The explosion of labor costs in India at a double-digit rate has created pressure for much work originally sent to India to now be redirected to other lower-cost venues - China and the Philippines today, and perhaps Vietnam tomorrow. Tata Consultancy Services (TCS) of India, for example, has dramatically increased its presence in China to take advantage of lower costs.

Political System
The political system may vary across countries of the world ranging from democratic capitalism (US) to democratic socialism (India) to autocratic (Singapore) to monarchy (Saudi Arabia and Jordan) to communist (China and Cuba). All things being equal, perhaps client and vendor countries would like

to have homogeneous or near homogeneous political systems to forge sourcing alliances. For such alliances to occur between countries of different political systems, other factors become more important. Regardless of the political system, political stability may be of higher concern. For example, the US and India have much in common in terms of political system. However, we see alliances between US and China also.

Political insurgency, terrorism, and war are not only disruptive to normal commercial and economic activity, but may endanger the safety of employees at captive or joint venture operations. Insurgents and terrorists may view Western companies and personnel as attractive targets; employees or contractors, especially executive-level ones, could be the victims of kidnapping or death threats. Political militants are not the only ones to commit such attacks; organized criminals engage in these tactics as well.

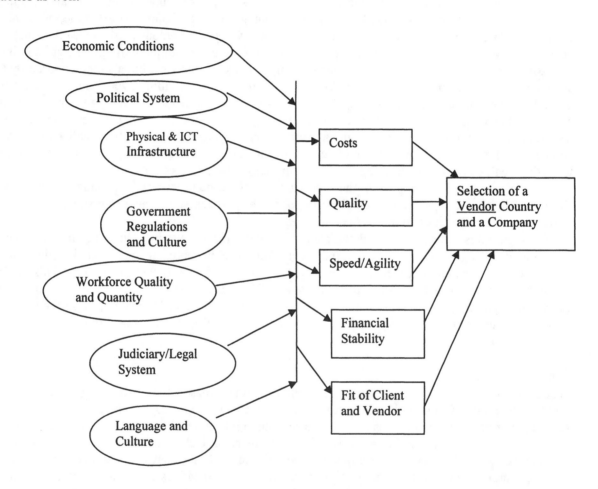

Figure 2. Two Stage Model for Choosing Vendor Country and Company

Physical and Information Telecommunications and Technology Infrastructure

Bad road conditions, traffic congestion, and unreliable air and maritime transport may cause delays, making it difficult for employees to get to work or for supplies to arrive in time. In China, air and water pollution from unbridled industrialization (with no environmental regulation) are not only deteriorating the quality of life, but are also threatening public health and future economic growth. In offshoring hubs like Bangalore, officials recognize the importance of addressing infrastructure problems that have been exacerbated by the boom. For example, executives from U.S. companies

Dell and IBM and India's Wipro and Infosys met with the recently elected chief minister of Karnataka state in August of 2004 to discuss infrastructure problems affecting Bangalore: electricity shortages, inadequate public transport, and traffic congestion, as well as the need for an airport upgrade.

According to 2001 data (see Figure 3), the top ten nations of the world in the descending sequence of compounded annual growth rate in ICT spending over the 8 years period 1993-2001 are: U.S., Japan, Germany, U.K., France, China (PRC), Italy, Canada, Brazil, and Australia. For global communications and collaboration over the Internet, it is crucial that the vendor countries have high levels of ICT infrastructures. One question that crops up is -- given the tremendous ICT spending gap between India and the US, how are they still able to engage in the largest amounts of outsourcing contracts and alliances. Part of the answer may be a better match on other criteria and also the fact that a better measure of ICT spending in this context is Internet penetration rate and Internet accessibility – which can be achieved by Internet accessibility through Internet cafes, libraries and other central locations within villages, towns, and cities.

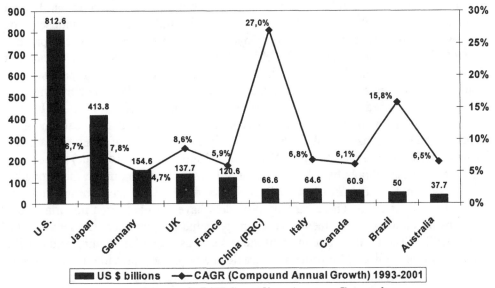

Figure 3. ICT Spending Among Countries

Whether it is poor maintenance, capacity shortfalls, or an inability to keep pace with accelerating demand, infrastructure problems can mean routine delays or major business interruptions. Most of the leading service providers have their own power supplies, but the thousands of smaller operators depend on the energy grid. Apart from its other attractive features, India's huge success as an offshore destination is in part due to the government's proven commitment to developing infrastructure, most notably, its major investment in telecommunications. By dramatically reducing the cost of overseas phone calls in the 1990s, the government enabled the country's now-booming offshoring services industry. Recently, cost of a telephone call from U.S. has gone down to as low as 7 cents a minute (e.g., Reliance India overseas phone service).

Government Regulations and Culture

Policies and regulations regarding tax incentives, foreign direct investment, repatriation of earnings, import duty, export duty, value added taxes could be different in different countries. From a client's perspective, fewer restrictions and more relaxed these regulations are, the more attractive the country is. One way to examine is the current and projected future tax environment. A ruling in India in early 2004, for example, arguably would have required a foreign entity to pay taxes to India on revenues that were generated by an off-shoring activity that produced income for that foreign entity. Subsequently, India modified the ruling in a way that Indian law firms believe eliminates this potential tax. Nonetheless, it is unclear how these rulings will actually be applied.

Due diligence is necessary to ensure the character of foreign suppliers and prospective partners—and not just in less-developed countries. In much of the former Soviet Union, for example, many politically connected businesses are fronts for protection rackets run by ex-KGB operatives. Bribery is not uncommon. Bureaucracy and red tape in India and China can become frustrating. However, there is improvement in this area with the increasing computerization of government operations since the year 2000. Electronic government is ushering in a new era of less corruption, increased transparency, revenue growth and cost reductions in government operations.

Workforce Quality and Quantity

This factor can be a key determinant in choosing a vendor country. Since India and China are the two top most destinations for global outsourcing of IT and ITES, a comparison of the two countries on this factor follows.

India has many prestigious technical universities, including the distinctive Indian Institutes of Technology. India produces 75,000 IT graduates annually. The Indian software industry boasts a large supply of over 415,000 IT professionals employed by export-only software companies, with approximately 68,000 new entrants into the IT field each year. Although wages for Indian software engineers is low compared to their Western counterparts, Indian engineers are well paid compared to Chinese and Philippine engineers. The average Indian IT programmers salary is approximately USD $6,400 annually with advanced software engineers earning over $20,000. One of India's core strengths is its education system, both at the University level and through its technical schools and IT training companies. The Indian Institute of Technology (IIT) is a collection of seven elite engineering institutes (Chennai, Delhi, Guwahati, Kanpur, Kharagpur, Mumbai, and Roorkee) which graduate India's best engineers. These schools have been compared to MIT. Building up on the strength of the Indian educational system, training institutes, such as NIIT and APTECH, have sprung up to provide software training throughout India. These training providers have fulfilled three important functions for the Indian software industry. First, they have given potential programmers the facilities to learn and practice their skills. Second, the training institutions serve as bases for training and certification of foreign software firms such as Microsoft and Oracle. Finally, they provide a direct avenue for cheap labor on software related contracts such as consulting and setting up IT systems.

The Chinese software industry boasts a large supply of 400,000 IT professionals, with approximately 50,000 new entrants into the IT field each year. However, the supply of highly qualified computer and software graduates remains limited. Most Chinese universities do not teach software engineering, so software engineers are sought from Computer Science and Math departments. Most Chinese programmers are proficient in low-level coding and maintenance of existing programs. The Chinese IT industry's biggest labor problem is a real shortage of high-level systems architects, systems designers and project managers. University engineering programs continue to emphasize traditional engineering fields rather than computer science. As a result, Chinese programmers lack technical capabilities required for systematic analysis and design of software. The average Chinese IT programmers salary is approximately USD $5,850 annually. With the growth of the domestic IT market, there has been growing demand for skilled labor. It is expected that as the software services industry matures, Chinese programmer will upgrade their skills to move up the skills value-chain and wages will increase. There is huge demand inside China for skilled service workers to meet the needs of both the country's own economy and of thousands of multinationals. Chinese officials aim to give this burgeoning industry a push, by forging partnerships with multinationals to train information technology engineers. For example, IBM has contracts to train 100,000 software specialists in various Chinese cities over three years.

Judicial and Legal System

In case of legal disputes and wrangling, stable legal system is needed in the vendor country. From the standpoint of US and UK, India is a primary desired destination. India's legal and judicial system is based on that of the United Kingdom, as they ruled over India for over 200 years. India's stable legal infrastructure benefits potential client companies and helps to free them from having to learn idiosyncrasies of a different legal system. Since no treaty exists between the United States and India to grant full faith and credit to the other nation's legal decisions, it's unlikely that an Indian court would recognize and enforce a judicial decision rendered in the United States by a US court. You would have to retry the decision in an Indian court if you wanted it enforced in India. Much of the discussion that follows below in this section is derived from Conference Board Report, 2005.

After the founding of the People's Republic of China in 1949, four Constitutions have been formulated successively in 1954, 1975, 1978 and 1982 (The Constitution and Legal System, 2006). The present Constitution includes four chapters in addition to the Preamble: "General Principles," "The Fundamental Rights and Duties of Citizens," "The Structure of the State, and "The National Flag, the National Emblem and the Capital," totaling 138 articles. Revisions and amendments to some articles of the Constitution were made and adopted by the National People's Congress in 1988, 1993 and 1999. The Constitution guarantees the basic rights and interests of citizens, including the right to vote and stand for election; freedom of speech, of the press, of assembly, of association, of procession and of demonstration; freedom of religious belief; the inviolability of the freedom of the person, the personal dignity and the residences; freedom and privacy of correspondence; the right to criticize and make suggestions to any state organ or functionary and exercise supervision; the right to work and rest and the right to material assistance from the state and society when they are old, ill or disabled; and the right to receive education and freedom to engage in scientific research, literary and artistic creation and other cultural pursuits. China's legal system includes laws of seven categories: the Constitution and related laws, civil and commercial laws, administrative laws, economic laws, social laws, criminal laws, and litigation and non-litigation procedural laws. Since 1979, legal system building in China has developed rapidly and in an all round way. By the end of 2001, more than 400 laws and legal decisions had been made by the NPC and its Standing Committee, about 1,000 administrative laws and regulations made by the State Council, and more than 10,000 local laws and regulations made by local people's congresses, covering political, economic and social fields. A comparatively complete legal system is now basically in place in China.

Data Protection: Because most offshore locations lack "safe harbor" legal status, companies that offshore or are considering doing so are concerned about protecting sensitive data[2]. How can they be sure that suppliers and local employees will not misuse or steal such sensitive data as employee data about Social Security numbers or medical information, customer financial information, or other proprietary company information? Privacy protection and data security have become hot-button issues, not as a result of any documented violations thus far, but as examples critics cite of the potential dangers of offshoring. Nonetheless, whether real or perceived, given the worldwide rise in identity theft, it behooves companies and third-party providers to implement safeguards. In general, business leaders should take into account the possibility of bugging, wiretapping, and other forms of electronic surveillance and commercial espionage. They should also investigate whether a prospective vendor subcontracts out work, to ascertain how many eyes and ears are privy to proprietary information. This is especially important with the rise of cyber crimes such as "phishing"; most of the

---

[2] "Safe harbor" principles compel commercial entities to protect customers' privacy by requiring them to inform customers how and why their information is being collected and to whom it is disseminated. They must also ensure that their data is used for legitimate purposes only, stipulate the protections taken to keep the information secure, and provide recourse for individuals. These principles were promulgated by the US Commerce Department in 2000 in response to the 1998 Eurin response to the 1998 European Union (EU) Directive on Data Protection.

criminals involved in these activities originate from Russia and Eastern Europe.[3] In the United States, federal statutes such as the Health Insurance Portability and Accountability Act of 1996 (HIPAA)[4] and Gramm-Leach-Bliley,[5] and state regulations such as California's Financial Information Privacy Act, require companies to maintain strict controls over how confidential information is handled. These laws also delineate the actions that must be taken in the event that data security is breached through outsourcing or off-shoring activities.

Key destination countries are taking positive steps to fortify security and neutralize fears that could obstruct the flow of offshore outsourcing, even though there is no evidence that identity theft and credit card fraud are any more of a threat in these countries than in the United States. At many work sites, workers must pass through elaborate screening systems before they can enter the building. Once inside, employees at many companies must log on to access systems and data, creating an electronic trail that can be used to monitor their activities. Many firms put their most sensitive data on home-country servers and strictly control access. Call centers and captive operations are also installing the latest systems to guard data and record and monitor workers' phone conversations. Some offshore operations have gone so far as to remove printers, hard drives, e-mail software, and CD-ROM drives from computer terminals, making it impossible for employees to copy, print, or store data. MphasiS, a leading IT and BPO service provider, has accelerated its ability to bar access to computers and phones after an employee resigns or is fired from three days just one year ago to three minutes today.[6]

Privacy and data protection are much more sensitive issues in the European Union than in the United States. The EU's comprehensive privacy legislation—the 1998 Directive on Data Protection—requires that for transfers of personal data to non-EU countries, those countries must provide an "adequate" level of privacy protection. This puts the onus of protection on the home-country company, not the third-party provider. EU law also regulates where data can be stored and what types of data can flow across national borders. Since such regulations don't exist in most offshoring destination countries, new members of the EU have become attractive offshoring destinations for Western European companies.

Intellectual Property Protection: Current and would-be offshorers are also worried about the safety of intellectual property. This is not merely a matter of what the local law states, but, practically speaking, of whether the court system overseas is willing and able to handle your case. In the less-developed countries, judicial systems are often so overloaded that they have little room to deal with commercial cases brought by foreigners. For that reason, the best protection isn't through after-the-fact legal enforcement, but preventively, through carefully crafted contracts and judicious practical choices. In China and East Asia, as well as in Russia, piracy is rampant in software and digital media such as CDs and DVDs, including movies, music, and business software. According to the

---

[3] Phishing involves sending e-mails that appear to come from credible (and major) vendors (often banks) and directing recipients to fake sites that lure them into giving out their account numbers or other sensitive information. In 2004, the value of the theft alone from phishing—not of any associated impacts—was estimated at more than $1 billion. See Lea Goldman, "Cybercon," *Forbes*, October 4, 2004.

[4] HIPAA requires improved efficiency in healthcare delivery by standardizing electronic data interchange, as well as the protection of confidentiality and security of health data through the setting and enforcement of standards.

[5] The Gramm-Leach-Bliley Financial Services Modernization Act of 1999 repealed the Glass-Steagall Act, opening up competition among banks, securities companies, and insurance companies by allowing investment and commercial banks to consolidate. Gramm-Leach-Bliley also governs the disclosure of privacy policy to customers and requires financial services firms to allow customers to opt out of private customer information-sharing agreements between their banks and third parties.

[6] Peter Engardino, Josey Puliyenthuruthel, and Manjeet Kripalani, "Fortress India?" *BusinessWeek*, August 16, 2004.

International Intellectual Property Alliance (IIPA), which tracks trade losses due to copyright piracy and estimated levels of piracy, total losses worldwide of US trade dollars alone amounted to more than $13 billion in 2003. The Asia-Pacific region accounted for $5.2 billion of that, and among individual countries, China and Russia were the most egregious violators, at $2.9 billion and $1.4 billion, respectively.[7]

Breaches can occur in many ways. A manufacturer under contract might take proprietary information and use it for its own operations, or employees might act as internal "moles," stealing data or intellectual capital when they leave at night. Piracy results in more than just lost sales; software firms lose licensing revenues and legitimate buyers who do pay licensing fees, and whose operating costs are therefore higher, are at a competitive disadvantage. Investment banks, which have a considerable presence in India and other leading offshore locations, are particularly concerned about the misuse of information for insider trading purposes.

Nonetheless, because intellectual property and patent theft is a key concern of clients, providers recognize the need, as with data and privacy, for good controls, hiring responsible and ethical staff, and overseeing them properly. Patent protection is not a priority in the court systems of most offshore destination countries. American executives should bear in mind that the US patent system is among the worlds most liberal in terms of granting and enforcing patents (particularly in the areas of software and business processes). In this respect, for example, American companies should not assume that Indian courts, for example, would enforce US patents.

According to Shaw Pittman's Zahler, although India's legal system is a common law system, based on English law, businesses cannot count on legal protection after the fact. India's judicial system is bogged down, under funded, encumbered by bureaucracy, and the courts struggle to cope with criminal cases, making it unlikely that a foreign entity would gain the court's time for a commercial case. Therefore, it is best to think proactively and create a framework by which your company's rights will be protected. He prescribes two components to help form this protective shield: make systematically sound practical choices in how you establish and manage operations, and draft a legal contract that explicitly states terms and conditions.

Language and Culture

The greatest and oft cited reason for India's attractiveness as destination country for outsourcing of IT and ITES is that nearly all educated people are proficient in the English language. India produces over 2 million English-speaking graduates annually. This

A country's culture is derived from a number of factors including the religious values it embraces, its heritage of role models, the political philosophy it practices, and its social customs. The influence of national culture on human behavior begins during childhood and is reinforced throughout life. National culture not only influences our responses in social situations, but also it shapes our behavior in organizations. Hofstede's classical study identified four dimensions as determining national culture: Power Distance, Uncertainty Avoidance, Masculinity-Femininity, and Individualism-Collectivism. Subsequently, he added a fifth dimension Short Term-Long term orientation.

For India, *Individualism* rank stands at 48. For US, Individualism ranks highest at 91 and is a significant factor in the life of US citizens. India has *Power Distance* as the highest with a ranking of 77 compared to a world average of 56.5. This Power Distance score for India indicates a high level of inequality within the society. This condition is not necessarily subverted upon the population, but rather accepted by the population as a cultural norm. For the United States, Power Distance is at 40. This is indicative of a greater equality between societal levels, including government, organizations, and even within families. This orientation reinforces a cooperative interaction across power levels.

---

[7] Compiled by Thomas E. Cavanagh, senior research associate in global corporate citizenship at The Conference Board, from revised 2003 IIPA data released in 2004.

India's *Long Term Orientation* (LTO) rank is 61, with the world average at 48. A higher LTO score can be indicative of a culture that is perseverant and parsimonious. The LTO is the lowest dimension for the US at 29. This low LTO ranking reflects a freedom in the culture from long-term traditional commitments, which allows greater flexibility and the freedom to react quickly to new opportunities. India has *Masculinity* ranking at 56, with the world average just slightly lower at 51. The higher the country ranks in this Dimension, the greater the gap between **values** of men and women. It may also generate a more competitive and assertive female population, although still less than the male population. For US, this ranking is at 62. This indicates the country experiences a higher degree of gender differentiation of roles. The male dominates a significant portion of the society and power structure. This situation generates a female population that becomes more assertive and competitive, with women shifting toward the male role model and away from their female role. India's lowest ranking dimension is *Uncertainty Avoidance* (UAI) at 40, compared to the world average of 65. On the lower end of this ranking, the culture may be more open to unstructured ideas and situations. The population may have fewer rules and regulations with which to attempt control of every unknown and unexpected event or situation, as is the case in high Uncertainty Avoidance countries. The UAI for the US is 46. Table 2 summarizes a comparison of US, India, and China on these cultural dimensions.

Country	Cultural Cluster	Power Distance	Individual- ism	Uncertainty Avoidance	Masculinity	Long-Term Orientation
United States	Anglo	40	91	46	62	29
China	Far Eastern	80	20	44	54	118
India	South Asian	77	48	40	56	61

Table 2. Culture Dimensions and Their Values of the United States and China (Source: Hofstede's Dimension of Culture Scales, 2006)

STAGE TWO: MODEL FOR CHOOSING A VENDOR COMPANY

The first stage of our model above shows distilling the above seven factors into more tangible factors of cost, quality, and speed/agility of doing business in a country in the short term as well as in the long term. Furthermore, these three factors along with company-specific factors would apply while choosing a company within the country.

Fit between Client Needs and Potential Vendor Capabilities
For selecting a vendor, an important factor is determining the fit with the vendor. The following questions need to be addresses.

What IT or ITES function is to be outsourced? Is it call center, tax preparation, IS development, accounting functions, or human resource function? Once a niche is defined, then it is relatively easy to identify 10-20 companies within a country. How do you decide what to outsource and what not to outsource? One guideline many companies follow: if the work is strategic, keep it in-house. When United Technologies decided to offshore IT work, its chief information officer sent all help desk, network, desktop, midrange, mainframe, and web-hosting work overseas. He assigned 80% of the application development and support function to an Indian vendor, keeping 20% on the home shore. He also retained IT leadership, project management, and business analysis in-house. Training in American accent and American culture may be sufficient for basic retail order taking and customer service, but many companies (Dell and Gateway included among them) do not send their business customers to offshore call centers. The level of communication necessary for business customers is generally higher and more nuanced. Firms should also include as many business units as possible in the effort, to maximize scale and opportunity. They need to think cross-functionally to maximize the value of subsequent reengineering. Once the functions to be outsourced are decided, the next step is to determine which companies in the country have a track record of providing quality services in these functions. Such information can be obtained from web sites (e.g., www.nasscom.org for India, Guru.com), electronic marketplaces, published sources and consultants.

What is the level of compatibility of the client company's ICT Infrastructure with that of the vendor? Just as this issue is important at the national level in the first stage, it becomes important again at the second stage. Issues that need to be addressed include compatibility of computer platforms, e-mail facilities, EDI infrastructure, and teamwork/collaboration. Visits by the client personnel to vendor sites will allow the client to assess the adequacy of the physical and ICT infrastructure of the vendor as well as of the city where the vendor is located.

What is the level of cultural compatibility between the client and the vendor? This issue becomes moot if the client establishes its own subsidiary in the offshore country. However, in case of a joint venture or outsourcing, compatibility of organizational cultures cannot be ignored. This issue is discussed at length by Barry Shore in another chapter of this book under the theme of "cultural asymmetries between headquarters and foreign Subsidiaries". A very good way to check on the cultural compatibility is to make visits to vendor sites and have interviews with vendor's personnel in their offshore location and if applicable in their onshore locations. It is not uncommon for the vendors to have business offices in the host country. For example, all major vendors from India, China and Russia maintain offices in the US

Financial/Cost Considerations

Financial criteria are justifiably considered as the major driving force in an outsourcing decision. However the financial consideration, in itself, brings additional complexities into an outsourcing relationship. Because clients use financial benefits as the major driving force, IT vendors often promise IT delivery services on a slim or no-margin profit that often leads to potential conflicts with the client company. At the same time, costs of IT services are very difficult to estimate because IT is not homogeneous; it is comprised of many activities and services that evolve over time (Kern et al., 2002). Furthermore, clients should be wary of not only the current costs but also of future costs and any built-in escalation clauses.

Speed/Agility of the Vendor

One of the major reasons cited for outsourcing is the significant reduction in the time to create products (whether physical or digital) and also the speed with which the ICT infrastructure can react to and respond to changing business requirements. For this reason, it is important to evaluate carefully the ICT infrastructure, the human resources, the references, the financial stability, and the cultural compatibility of the vendor company. It may also help to examine the past performance of the vendor in projects conducted with other clients.

Quality Considerations

The quality of software can be defined as "the extent to which the product satisfies its specifications." ISO 9000 certifications became the first major way of outsourcing vendors showing commitment to quality. In the second stage, the Capability Maturity Model (CMM) developed by the Software Engineering Institute at Carnegie Mellon University has become a worldwide standard and has provided an objective basis for measuring progress and quality in software engineering and for comparing service providers. This makes software development process more transparent to clients and helps them explore service providers in offshore destinations. CMM levels range from 1 (lowest) to 5 representing the best software development practices. India now has far more SEI CMM Level 5 companies than any other country in the world. The new third stage is driven by the desire to institute processes, metrics and a framework for improvement in all areas including those sales, billing and collection, people management and after sales support. This is characterized by companies aligning their internal practices with the People CMM framework and by the use of the Six Sigma methodology for reducing variation and assuring "end-to-end" quality in all company operations.

Capability Maturity Model Integration (CMMI) is a suite of products used for process improvement. The old CMM model was retired by the Software Engineering Institute of CMU. The primary features of CMMI are (Wikipedia in December, 2006):

- supports process integration and product improvement
- enables the integration of multiple disciplines into one process-improvement framework that helps to eliminate inconsistencies and reduces duplication.
- provides a framework for introducing new disciplines as needs arise and therefore reduces the cost of implementing model-based improvement.
- is designed to build on legacy process improvement efforts and investments.

The People Capability Maturity Model (People CMM or simply PCMM) is a framework that helps organizations successfully address their critical people issues. Based on the best current practices in fields such as human resources, knowledge management, and organizational development, PCMM guides organizations in improving their processes for managing and developing their workforces. Since its release in 1995, thousands of copies of the People CMM have been distributed, and it is used worldwide by organizations, small and large. PCMM consists of five maturity levels that establish successive foundations for continuously improving individual competencies, developing effective teams, motivating improved performance, and shaping the workforce the organization needs to accomplish its future business plans (Source: CMU SEI website for CMMI).

Figure 3 depicts attractiveness of the vendor companies in various countries based on the dimensions of cost and quality. As a note of caution, the standing of the countries on cost-quality considerations may change over the years, but as of yet they have not changed substantially.

SUMMARY AND CONCLUSIONS

The above analysis reinforces the argument that for any client company in US considering offshore outsourcing, it ought to decide on the region and the country first and then follow it by choosing an appropriate vendor in that country based on a sound analysis of a fit between the needs of the client and the competencies of the vendor. Besides the objective analysis for choosing a region of the world, common knowledge must not be ignored. As examples indicate below, several countries and regions are known for their strengths:

- Philippines, which boasts English as a main language, a cultural proximity to America, and a US-based legal system, is a good choice for call centers.
- Dalian, on China's northeastern coast, has become an offshoring haven for Japanese companies, with its strong cultural ties to Japan, thousands of software engineers, two dozen universities and technical institutes, and low costs.
- Ukraine has many IT workers with strong math and sciences backgrounds that make them suitable for R&D or innovative programming work.
- Certain cities, especially in India, have become specialty hubs: Bangalore, known as a high-tech center, is favored for finance and accounting processes, while Chennai, home to a number of universities, is favored for accounting processes.

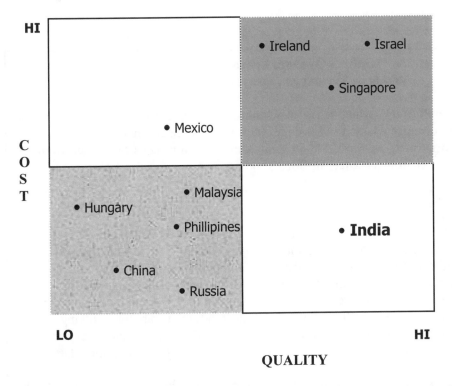

Exhibit 4. Country Attractiveness Based on Cost and Quality (© 2001 Jupiter Media Metrix, Inc.)

In the increasingly flattening world, it is predicted that 3.4 million American domestic jobs will be outsourced to foreign firms by the year 2015. Moreover, since IT tasks are outsourced to low wage rate countries, some feel that American wages and standards of living will eventually be lowered (Atkinson 2004). To make matters worse, approximately half of the jobs off-shored from the US within the next decade are likely to involve higher paying white collar jobs (Atkinson 2004, The Economist 2004). Apart from job losses, many believe that outsourcing is an undesirable side effect of globalization and should be actively discouraged. Opponents also point out the potential strategic vulnerability – the loss of control, the hidden costs, the transfer of proprietary information - may create long-term problems for the firm that attempts to use foreign outsourcing as a "cure-all" to reduce costs and improve performance.

Ultimately, we live in an exciting and changing world. We all have to start admonishing the old accepted order of South-North Divide or Global Economic Divide between nations of the world, thinking of ourselves as world citizens, and be willing and happy to share the resources of the earth for a better world.

MINICASE

Online: Offshore Learning
Students Turning to India for Tutors

It's pitch-dark and a chilly rain is tapping at the windows as Samuel Gozo sits down at the computer for an 8 p.m. chemistry lesson in his cozy Rahway home. More than 7,000 miles away in Agra, India, the sun is rising as Gozo's tutor, Anil Kumar Mathur, does the same. Moments later, Mathur's voice echoes from a speaker in Gozo's room.

"Hello Sam, how are you?"

Sam, a 15-year-old sophomore at Rahway High School in New Jersey, is one of the thousands of US students turning to online tutors overseas, driven by a desire for affordable, quality instructions and concerns about test scores and a competitive college admissions market. The demand has been met by an emerging industry of offshore e-tutoring firms that have used technology and an abundance of highly educated, low-wage workers in Asia to compete directly with traditional tutoring companies. It's just the latest trend in a rapidly evolving global marketplace that has already seen the outsourcing of accounting functions, laboratory science, airline ticketing and many other knowledge-based services to India, the Philippines, Israel and elsewhere.

"Normally you would think something like tutoring should be very local, but with the internet and technology, things like this can be done at a fraction of the cost of doing it in the United States," said Rakesh Sambharya, a professor of management and international business at the Rutgers Business School in Camden, NJ.

Whether e-tutors from different time zones can be as effective as face-to-face tutors is still being debated by educators, and the trend has sparked controversy. Last week, New York City education officials suspended a contract with a Texas-based company, Socratic Learning Inc., for failing to disclose it was using tutors based in India who were not subjected to the city's fingerprint and background checks. The company claims the tutor had FBI background checks, and that the city's system requires Social Security numbers, which the Indian tutors don't have.

But those who use or sell the online services say they can be as effective, more convenient and less costly than traditional tutors. For the Gozos, the price offered by the India-based firm TutorVista was a deciding factor-$100 per month for unlimited sessions. Sam takes one-hour sessions about a dozen times a month-less than $10 a lesson and much less than the $25 or more per hour charged by American online tutoring services like e-tutor.com or the $100-an-hour fee that face-to-face instructors can charge.

"Where I work, the parents send their kids to summer classes, which can cost an arm and a leg." said Gabrielle Gozo, who works in the fashion industry. "I can't afford an arm and a leg."

Krishnan Ganesh, founder and chairman of TutorVista, said he wants to change the "paradigm" of education so that tutors become part of every family budget. "There is very little personalized education available in America, because it is too expensive and the education system is not ahead on technology," said Ganesh, whose service offers 24-hour tutoring in subjects ranging from Geometry to Grammar. TutorVista has joined other offshore tutoring companies, as well as online tutors in America, to tap into the federal dollars provided for failing schools under the *2002 No Child Left Behind Act*. If schools don't meet testing requirements for three years, they must offer students tutoring or other academic help through what is called supplemental education service providers.

It's a growing area," said Judy Alu, New Jersey's federal tutoring coordinator. She said tutoring services with an online component make up more than half of the 160 companies approved by the state for students in about 300 struggling schools. India is especially fertile ground for tutors because of the country's advanced education system in math and sciences, the prevalence of English and a lower wage scale, experts say.

"The average income per person in India is about $650 a year." said Robert Kennedy, director of the William Davidson Institute and a professor of business and administration at the University of Michigan. "In India you can hire well-educated people with master's and Ph.D.s for $400 or $500 a month."

Many Indian tutors are trained to speak with an American accent and are exposed to U.S. teaching methods and culture. Last week in Rahway, Sam's tutor Mathur, a 54-year-old former teacher and business owner with a master's degree in chemistry, kept the teenager's attention for the entire hour, writing formulas on a whiteboard, asking questions and offering friendly encouragement.

"It's a new experience, because you don't have the student in front of you," Mathur said. "You have to make it as interactive as you can. If you don't, they can walk away, and you won't know it."

Sam said that when he first started using the service, he struggled with his instructor's accent, but he quickly adapted and it never kept him from understanding the lessons. "Chemistry class has become a lot clearer and easier to me," he said.

Critics say the potential for misunderstanding is one reason to be wary of online tutoring. "The best tutoring is when you're working with someone one-on-one or in a group, where a tutor can recognize whether a student is understanding something or not," said Lynn Giese, interim president of the National Tutoring Association based in Columbus, Ohio.

"With the Internet, you don't get that physical connection," said Giese, who represents about 5,000 tutors and educators in the industry, many of whom earn between $20 to $25 hourly.

Kaplan, one of the most popular tutoring companies in the United States, charges $2,799 for 20 hours of one-on-one academic instruction in a student's home. "The strength of that environment comes when the tutor is able to build a rapport with the student and they can gauge the student's motivation and understanding based on nonverbal cues," said Annette Riffle, general manager of the Kaplan Premier Private Tutoring division.

Saji Philip, a founder of Growing Stars, a California-based online tutoring company that has a center in India, said his service is more convenient and affordable than traditional one-on-one services. "If you want a personal touch, your parents have to take you to a tutoring center," said Phillip, a native of India who now lives in Princeton. "This is better for the parent and student; there's no running back and forth, no transportation costs."

Sanya Bhambhani, an eighth-grader at Voorhees Middle School, takes tutoring classes in math and SAT preparation with Growing Stars. Both of her tutors have postdoctoral degrees. "I'm getting straight A's in math, and I have to thank my tutor for that," Sanya said.

Sanya's father, Raju Bhambani, said he looked up Growing Stars after reading about the service in "The World is Flat," Thomas L. Friedman's best-selling book about trends in the global marketplace. At the time, Bhambani was driving his daughter to a tutor more than an hour away from home for $75-an-hour lessons. Growing Stars charges $25 an hour. "This is a huge difference for us," the father said. "The private tutor we found on our own was a very good teacher, but the distance killed us, and the price killed us."

Source: Star-Ledger Staff Ana M. Alaya (Reference: New Jersey, Page 19 and 22; October 29, 2006)

Discussion Questions:
1. What are some of the advantages of outsourcing to India?
2. How has outsourcing impacted the Indian way of life?
3. How has the Indian education system aided the ability of the country to capture offshore contracts?
4. How has outsourcing impacted the Indian education system?

KEY WORDS

Bollywood
Business Process Outsourcing (BPO)
Call Centers
Capability Maturity Model (CMM)
Individualism-Collectivism
ISO certification
IT enabled services
Joint Venture
Long Term Orientation
Masculinity-Femininity
Medical Tourism
Middle Shore
Offshore in-sourcing
Offshore outsourcing
On-shoring
Off-shoring
Power Distance
Teleradiology
Third Party Service Provider
Uncertainty Avoidance

STUDY QUESTIONS

1. Find out the latest information about the number of qualified engineering and IT graduates in India, China and Russia. Based on this information, make a prediction about trends in global outsourcing of IT and ITES.

2. Are the legal concerns in offshoring significantly different from those surrounding domestic outsourcing in the areas of data and privacy protection, intellectual property and patent protection, methods of dispute resolution, and venues for litigation or arbitration? Please discuss in the context of India, China, and the U.S.

3. Since India's legal system is a common law system, based on English law, businesses should be able to count on legal protection after the fact. Why or why not? Please comment.

REFERENCES

Andersen E., Hostile IS Outsourcing: The Story of Manufact, *Norwegian School of Management*, NSM-2002-034-CA-EN, August 2002

Atkinson, R. D. (2004). "Understanding the Offshoring Challenge". Progressive Policy Institute. Policy Report. www.ppionline.org

Bahli, Bouchaib, "Towards a Capability Maturity Model (CMM) for the management of outsourcing information services," Proceedings of the AMCIS'04 conference, New York, NY, August, 2004.

Bharadwaj A. S., A Resource-Based Perspective on Information Technology Capability and Firm Performance: An Empirical Investigation, *MIS Quarterly*, 24(1), pp. 169-196, 2000

Clemons E. K. and Hitt L. M., Strategic Sourcing for Services: Assessing the Balance between Outsourcing and Insourcing, Operations and Information Management Working Paper, 97-06-01, Wharton School of the University of Pennsylvania, 1997

Casale, F. (2001) The IT Index, The Outsourcing Institute.

Conference Board Report, "Beyond Costs: Financial and Operational Risks," 2005.

Engardio, P. (2006) "Why outsourcing to India is a good idea". Business Week, January 25. http://www.rediff.com/money/2006/jan/25bpo.htm.

Gartner Dataquest (2003), BPO Market to Grow to $173 Billion in 2007, Gartner Dataquest Report.

Ge L., Konana P., and Tanriverdi H, Global Sourcing and Value Chain Unbundling, Dept. of MSIS, The University of Texas at Austin, 2004

Gottfredson M., Puryear R., and Philips S., Strategic Sourcing from Periphery to the Core, *Harvard Business Review*, 83(2), p132-139, 2005

Graf M. and Mudambi S. M., The outsourcing of IT enabled business processes: a conceptual model of the location decision, Journal of international management, 11, pp. 253-268, 2005.

Gross, G. (2005). Study: Offshore Outsourcing Creates Jobs". Info-world, November 2. http://www.infoworld.com/article/05/11/02/HNoffshorejobs_1.html?source=rss&url=http://www.infoworld.com/article/05/11/02/HNoffshorejobs_1.html

Hoffman, T. (2003, January 27) Big Outsourcing Shift predicted for IT jobs, Computerworld, 37, 4.2.

"Hofstede's Dimension of Culture Scales," http://spectrum.troy.edu/~vorism/hofstede.htm accessed on February 21, 2007, 2006

Lacity, M. C., Willcocks, L. P., and Feeny, D. F. (1996) The Value of Selective IT Sourcing, Sloan Management Review, 37(3), pages 13-25.

Lancaster, John, "Medical tourists to India," Washington Post, October 21, 2004.

Lee J., Huynh M. Q., Kwok R. C., and Pi S., IT Outsourcing Past, Present and Future, *Communications of the ACM*, 46(5), pp. 84-89, 2003.

Linder J. C., Transformational Outsourcing, *MIT Sloan Management Review*, 45(2), pp. 52-58, 2004

McKinsey & Company, Inc. (2003), "Offshoring: Is It a Win-Win Game?" McKinsey Global Institute. August. San Francisco.

Marshall, J. (2003). "'Offshoring' Drive for Savings Accelerates". *Financial Executive*, 19(6). September, pp. 52-55.

"Medical Tourism in Thailand," http://www.discoverythailand.com/medical.asp accessed on February 21, 2007, March 2007

Minevich, M., Going global Ventures Inc., Richter, F-J. Global Outsourcing Report 2005. HORASIS, March 2005.

Mintz, Steven, " The Ethical Dilemmas of Outsourcing," The CPA Journal, March, 2004.

Palvia, Shailendra, "Global Outsourcing of IT and IT Enabled Services: Impact on US and Global Economy," JITCA, 5(3), 2003.

Prewitt E., Filing for Divorce, *CIO Magazine*, February 2001

Radkevitch Uladzimir, Heck Eric van, and Koppius Otto, "Leveraging Offshore IT Outsourcing by SMEs through Online Marketplaces", Journal of IT Case and Application Research (JITCAR), 8(3), 2006, pages 40-57.

Saji, Matthew, "Understanding Risk in IT Outsourcing: A Fuzzy Framework," Journal of IT Case and Application Research (JITCAR), 8(3), 2006, pp. 27-39.

"The Constitution and Legal System," http://www.china.org.cn/english/features/38127.htm accessed on February 21, 2007, 2006

Ulfelder, Steve, "Comfort and Convenience at a Higher Cost: Ireland", Computerworld, September 15, 2003.

Vijayan, J. (2002). The Outsourcing Boom. Computerworld (Online).

Section 5

E-Commerce and E-Government

By harnessing the power of the Internet, e-commerce has fundamentally changed the way business is conducted around the world. E-commerce has the ability to make businesses of all sizes, large or small, global. Time and distance are no longer barriers to serving clients. The impact on performance of firms and industries and competitiveness is achieved through increased information flows and knowledge transfer. On the same theme, e-government allows government services and information to be available at anytime and from anywhere, thus meeting the needs of the citizens more efficiently and effectively.

This section has four chapters. Chapter 22 provides an understanding of the business-to-consumer (B2C) e-commerce diffusion and the underlying infrastructural factors in six important economies of the world: USA, Germany, and the emerging BRIC countries, i.e., Brazil, Russia, India and China. Chapter 23 discusses various facets of e-commerce at the organizational level and offers strategies and issues requiring careful consideration at the firm level. Chapter 24 appraises the changes in the industrial organizations that are propelled by the advances in information technology and electronic commerce. A major conclusion is that the dichotomous partitioning of the economic agents into firm and outsiders may no longer be valid since the organizational boundaries are becoming blurred. Chapter 25, the last chapter in the book, addresses e-government, where government agencies use information technology and particularly the Internet to support its operations, engage citizens, and provide services. The chapter discusses benefits and challenges for e-government as well as offers several frameworks for its successful implementation.

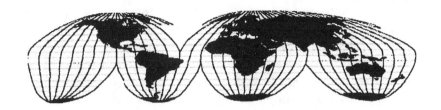

Global E-Commerce: Domain, Business Models, Framework, Barriers, and Future Trends

Shailendra C. Jain Palvia
Long Island University USA

Vijay Vemuri
University of Bahrain, Kingdom of Bahrain

CHAPTER SUMMARY

In a little over a decade, the Internet has been transformed from a messaging system to a vast information source to a comprehensive commercial platform. The impact of the Internet has been profound in almost all aspects of human endeavor. Internet and global private networks provide the necessary IT infrastructure to conduct e-commerce globally. The nucleus of electronic commerce can be a business, a government organization, or a non-governmental organization. Four types of electronic commerce are elaborated -- B2B, B2C, B2G, and NGO2C. A framework is presented to aid in comprehending and addressing global electronic commerce issues. This framework articulates and describes several barriers -- cultural, administrative, geographical, and economic-- to global e-commerce and the four phases of Customer Service Life Cycle -- requirements, acquisition, ownership, and retirement/upgrade. Next, some critical factors for success of global e-commerce are presented, followed by some future trends for e-commerce.

INTRODUCTION AND STATISTICS

In the wake of the cold war between the US and the USSR in the 1960s, Advanced Research Projects Agency NETwork (ARPANET), funded by the U.S. government, created a network of a few computers to share and save sensitive and security related information. The modern Internet evolved in the late 1980s to facilitate efficient e-mail communication and data sharing among geographically dispersed computers. Within a span of less than two decades, the Internet has changed from novelty to being an essential part of individuals, organizations and governments. In 1990s, the Internet became popular for its usability for instant messaging, bulletin boards, and message threading. During this period, the World Wide Web (WWW) became a treasure of human knowledge -- ranging from architecture, astronomy, and biology to telemedicine, video-conferencing, and zoology -- accessible from anywhere by anybody at anytime. The Internet has exploded exponentially, empowering world citizens and confirming Metcalf's law. Lately, e-commerce has been also expanding at a fast pace.

Internet Statistics

According to the Wall Street Journal Online (May 24, 2006), the number of adults who are online in the US has increased from 163 million in 2004 to an estimated 172 million in 2005, and to over 205 million by March 2006. Approximately 77% of Americans are now online, up from 57% in 2000, and only 9% back in 1995. The same article reported that 37% of people online are 50 and above, and 52% of online users are women. Growth in Internet access is not limited to the US; the worldwide growth has seen over 1 billion people having access to Internet by March 31, 2006. More than half of this population resided in 30 countries, with the remaining spread over 160 countries (Table 1). The number of Internet users by language is shown in Table 2. Between 2004 and 2006, the number of English users dropped from 35% to 30%. Internet use in other countries, such as China and Russia, continues to increase at a fast pace.

#	Country or Region	Penetration (% Population)	Internet Users Latest Data	Population (2006 Est.)	Source and Date of Latest Data
1	New Zealand	76.3 %	3,200,000	4,195,729	ITU - Sept/05
2	Iceland	75.9 %	225,600	297,072	ITU - Sept/05
3	Sweden	74.9 %	6,800,000	9,076,757	ITU - Oct/05
4	Falkland Islands	70.4 %	1,900	2,699	CIA - Dec/02
5	Denmark	69.4 %	3,762,500	5,425,373	ITU - Sept/05
6	Hong Kong	69.2 %	4,878,713	7,054,867	Nielsen//NR Feb./05
7	United States	68.6 %	205,326,680	299,093,237	Nielsen//NR Jan/06
8	Australia	68.4 %	14,189,557	20,750,052	Nielsen//NR Jan/06
9	Canada	67.9 %	21,900,000	32,251,238	eTForecasts Dec/05
10	Norway	67.8 %	3,140,000	4,632,911	C.I.Almanac Mar/05
11	Singapore	67.2 %	2,421,800	3,601,745	ITU - Oct/05
12	Japan	67.2 %	86,300,000	128,389,000	eTForecasts Dec/05
13	Korea (South)	67.0 %	33,900,000	50,633,265	eTForecasts Dec/05
14	Greenland	66.5 %	38,000	57,185	ITU - Oct/05
15	Switzerland	66.0 %	4,944,438	7,488,533	Nielsen//NR Jan/06
16	Netherlands	65.9 %	10,806,328	16,386,216	Nielsen//NR Jun/04
17	Faroe Islands	64.5 %	32,000	49,598	ITU - Dec/05
18	United Kingdom	62.9 %	37,800,000	60,139,274	ITU - Oct/05
19	Finland	62.5 %	3,286,000	5,260,970	ITU - Sept/05
20	Bermuda	60.7 %	39,000	64,211	ITU - Oct/05
21	Taiwan	60.3 %	13,800,000	22,896,488	CIA Mar/05
22	Germany	59.0 %	48,721,997	82,515,988	Nielsen//NR Jan/06
23	Luxembourg	58.9 %	270,800	459,393	ITU - Sept/05
24	Portugal	58.0 %	6,090,000	10,501,051	C.I.Almanac Mar/05
25	Austria	56.8 %	4,650,000	8,188,806	C.I.Almanac Mar/05
26	Liechtenstein	56.7 %	20,000	35,276	CIA - Dec/02
27	Guernsey & Alder	56.5 %	36,000	63,683	ITU - Oct/05
28	Barbados	56.2 %	150,000	266,731	ITU - Sept/05
29	Ireland	50.7 %	2,060,000	4,065,631	C.I.Almanac Mar./05
30	Estonia	50.0 %	670,000	1,339,157	ITU - Sept/05
TOP 30 in Penetration		66.2 %	519,461,313	785,179,437	IWS - Mar/06
Rest of the World		8.8 %	503,401,994	5,714,517,623	IWS - Mar/06
World Total Users		15.7 %	1,022,863,307	6,499,697,060	IWS - Mar/06

NOTES: (1) Only countries with a penetration rate higher than 50% qualify for this list; Malta was removed from the list until its statistics are verified. (2) Data from this site may be cited, giving due credit and establishing an active link back to Internet World Stats. ©Copyright 2006, Miniwatts Marketing Group. All rights reserved.

Table 1. Top 30 Countries with the Highest Internet Penetration Rate as of March 31, 2006

Language	Number of Internet Users (Millions)	Percentage of Worldwide Users
English	313	30
Chinese	132	13
Japanese	86	9
Spanish	81	8
German	57	6
French	41	4
Korean	34	3
Portuguese	33	3
Italian	29	3
Russian	24	2
Totals	830	81

Table 2. Number of Internet Users by Language

Websites and Internet Protocol

A website is a distinct location on the Internet, identified by an IP address that returns a web page in response to an HTTP request. A web site consists of all interlinked web pages. Netcraft's (http://www.netcraft.com) January 2007 survey revealed that there are at least 106,875,138 web sites, an increase of 1.63 million from last month's survey. Leading the growth is Microsoft, which added more than 650K hostnames on its Windows Live Spaces blog service, while Go Daddy (+165K) and Google (+105K) also had growth of more than 100,000 sites in one month. The largest growth of 3.3 million websites was recorded in March of 2003. Assuming approximately 10 web pages per website, the world has more than 1 billion web pages. However, there is no central website registry system to allow an accurate count of the number of websites in the world. It should be noted that there are significant differences in the estimates of this number from different sources.

What is the limit to growth of websites and web pages? The only real limit is the number of individual Internet Protocol (IP) addresses available in the public domain to be assigned to websites. Internet Protocol version 4 (IPv4) is an addressing scheme that uses a 32-bits string of numbers organized into four sets of numbers organized from 0 to 255 and supports 4,294,967,296 addresses. There are over 6.5 billion people in the world. This addressing scheme has worked well so far, but is inadequate for the future. A new version of the IP addressing scheme being developed is called Internet Protocol version 6 (IPv6). It contains 128-bit addresses (2 to the power of 128) translating to over 340 undecillion (1 undecillion = 10^{36}). With the potential for almost every electronic device on the earth's surface to be networked together in the future, this kind of increased scalability and connectivity will be a necessity rather than a mere luxury. IPv6 addresses are normally written as eight groups of four hexadecimal digits usually followed by a slash and the prefix length.

Global Electronic Commerce Statistics

Global electronic commerce is the buying and selling of products, services, and information worldwide via private computer networks and mainly the Internet. Approximately 90% of the revenues in e-commerce are generated through business to business (B2B) transactions. B2B e-commerce preceded the Internet; B2B transactions were done through private networks prior to the Internet. The reengineering of the procurement process has simplified, automated, speeded up and reduced costs of B2B transactions. Commerce One is a leading provider of e-commerce solutions with over 550 customers, including Boeing, Deutsche Telekom, and General Motors, in over 150 e-marketplaces and mega-exchanges. Commerce One operates the world's largest B2B community called Global Trading Web (GTW). GTW connects several independently operated B2B portals, each designed to serve a specific region or industry. A portal is a cyber-door, or customizable gateway, into a company's web site. Using open platform and eXtensible Markup Language (XML), Commerce One enables any company to buy and sell products to the buyers directly. As reported in Turban et al. (2006), estimates of the size of the B2B online market vary.

- eMarketer (2003) and International Data Corporation (IDC) (2004) estimated the worldwide B2B transaction volume at $1.4 trillion in 2003 and $2.4 trillion in 2004.
- Mehrotra (2001) reports forecasts of $7 to $10 trillion by 2008 for global B2B transactions.
- Chemicals, computer electronics, utilities, agriculture, shipping and warehousing, motor vehicles, petrochemicals, paper and office products, and food are leading items in B2B.
- According to eMarketer (2003), the dollar value of B2B commerce comprises at least 85% of the total transaction value of e-commerce.

The projected B2B growth in Asia-Pacific, Western Europe, and Latin America are even more dramatic. Not only has B2B e-commerce struck roots in India, sites like www.Indiamarkets.com launched in December 1999 are providing relevant infomediary type services to small and medium size enterprises (SMEs) across over 140 product categories.

On the B2C (Business to Consumer) front, according to the Census Bureau (2006):

- The estimate of U.S. retail B2C e-commerce sales for the first quarter of 2006 was $25.2 billion, an increase of 7.0 percent (±3.5%) from the fourth quarter of 2005.
- Total retail sales for the first quarter of 2006 were estimated at $976.1 billion, an increase of 3.2 percent (±0.3%) from the fourth quarter of 2005.
- The first quarter 2006 e-commerce estimate increased 25.4 percent (±5.9%) from the first quarter of 2005 while total retail sales increased 8.1 percent (±0.5%) in the same period.
- E-commerce sales in the first quarter of 2006 accounted for 2.6 percent of total sales.

According to www.comscore.com and www.clickz.com/showpage.htm, e-commerce growth was spurred by Christmas holiday season sales in 2006. For example:

- The holiday shopping season, November 1 through December 31, brought in $24.6 billion, up 26 percent from $19.6 billion in 2005.
- Each of six days in November and December topped $600 million in sales.
- The highest sales of the holiday season occurred on December 13 with a total $666.9 million.
- The week before Thanksgiving, sales were 30% over the corresponding week in 2005.
- Season's weeks four through six were measured at 26% over the same period in 2005.
- Online sales in the final three weeks of the season were 31% over the year before.
- Christmas week (the week ending 12-24-2006) was 45% over the same period in 2005.

B2B and B2C sales continue to rise as businesses and consumers realize the ease of doing business using e-commerce and the Internet.

DOMAIN OF GLOBAL ELECTRONIC COMMERCE

Global e-commerce can be centered around businesses (for-profit private sector organizations), governments (not-for-profit public sector organizations), or non-government organizations (not-for-profit private organizations). Under the first category, Business to Business (B2B) utilize mostly extranets developed to build alliances with suppliers and customers; business to customer (B2C) utilize the public domain Internet; and business to government (B2G) that generally utilizes the Internet (or extranet sometimes) to allow businesses to sell products and services to governments. Under the second category, we have Government to Citizen (G2C), Government to Business (G2B), and one government to another government or one government agency to another government agency (G2G). This category is also given the name e-Government. For the third category of non-government not-for-profit organization (NGO), we can have NGO2C, NGO2B, NGO2G. Of course, we can think about more combinations like Business to Employees (B2E), Citizen to Government (C2G) and Consumer to Consumer (C2C). In what follows, details of B2B, B2C, B2G, and NGO2C are provided.

Business to Business (B2B)

The traditional methods of mail, phone, fax and courier services are slow, expensive, and error-prone for a company to conduct business with its suppliers, customers, distributors and other value chain partners. B2B is a fast growing segment of e-commerce. B2B began in the 1980s, when a few businesses, including some mass merchandisers, began to restructure their procurement processes by linking with their suppliers through private computer networks. These networks, utilized electronic data interchanges, or EDIs, which were expensive and closed to outsiders. The globally cost effective access to the Internet has now made it an attractive medium for B2B transactions. B2B has a tremendous track record and potential in improving operational efficiencies and integrating supply chains. In the global context, B2B can be either intra-organizational (i.e., between the headquarters office and foreign subsidiaries or among foreign manufacturing plants, warehouses, marketing/sales offices) or inter-organizational (i.e., between different organizations across national borders worldwide). B2B normally operates through extranets and enables companies to extend boundaries of the organization to reach suppliers, business partners, consultants, and customers. Extranets enable organizations to streamline their operations, achieve just-in-time supplier relationships, improve customer service, reduce operating costs, and increase revenues.

B2B storefronts enable the partners to check and track existing orders, handle order returns, process adjustments, handle service requests, and facilitate field service scheduling. In addition to reducing the cost of selling, storefronts enable the business to concentrate on channel relationships and selling strategies. In many industries (automotive, electronics, energy, food, chemical, construction), B2B exchange sites have emerged to allow manufacturers, wholesalers, retailers, and end consumers to buy, sell, and barter over the web. For example, an automobile exchange site (www.covisint.com, www.cliqexpress.com, or www.autovia.com) can give an automobile manufacturer access to hundreds of suppliers, each competing for its business, potentially leading to lower prices and/or better services. In the global context, Asian countries have also entered the B2B fray. China's www.alibaba.com since starting in 1999 has grown into a trade portal connecting small buyers and sellers of products. By 2004, it had over 4.8 million registered traders in over 150 countries. It is currently the world's largest online import-export marketplace connecting buyers and sellers for products and services (McFarland, 2001).

In a *sell-side e-marketplace*, a seller can be a manufacturer selling to a wholesaler, to a retailer, or to an individual business. Intel, Cisco, and Dell are examples of such sellers. The seller can also be a distributor selling to a wholesaler, to retailers, or to individual businesses. Three major pricing methods utilized in this type of marketplace are: selling from electronic catalogs, selling via forward auctions (as GM does with its old equipment), and one-to-one selling by a negotiated contract. In a *buy-side e-marketplace*, generally, a corporate-based acquisition site uses reverse auctions, negotiations, group purchasing, or other e-procurement method. Large buyers, like GM, open their own e-marketplaces. Public exchanges connect many buyers and sellers utilizing many approaches for price announcements, negotiations, and contract executions. Thomas Register for America (www.thomasnet.com), an information portal, publishes a directory of millions of manufacturing companies. In 1998, it teamed up with GE to create the TPN Register (now embedded in www.gxs.com), a portal that facilitates business transactions for maintenance, repair, and operation transactions.

Business to Consumer (B2C)

Online retailers signified the first imprints of structural changes in business due to e-commerce. The first wave of online retailers received enthusiastic response and instant recognition. For certain products (like books, computers), brick-and-mortar retailers may become extinct and may be replaced by click-and-portal retailers. A substantial proportion of computer software, books, videos, and DVDs is now being sold by online merchants including Amazon.com, CDNow.com, and Buy.com. Today, it is hard to find a bookseller without an online sales outlet. An Internet-based presence has become the norm rather than an exception. The excitement over e-commerce is evident from the incredible market capitalization of the electronic retailers (increasingly being termed e-tailers). For example, Amazon.com with a total loss of more than $1.2 billion loss since its inception in 1995, commanded a market capitalization of $5.3 billion on February 2, 2001, rivaling well-established industrial giants.

According to The Internet Retailer Top 500 Guide to Retail Web Sites, total B2C e-commerce sales reached $109.4 billion, 25% higher than 2004's $87.5 billion, which was 25% more than 2003's $70 billion. The industry was on track to achieve total sales of about $136 billion in 2006, which would be a 25% increase over 2005's sales. Here are the highlights from The Internet Retailer (2006):

- In 2005, the top 500 retailers recorded an estimated 523.9 million separate sales at an average ticket value of $118. By comparison, in 2004 the top 400 retail web sites had an estimated 401.5 million individual sales with an average ticket of $107.

- The 11 major categories - apparel/accessories, books/CDs/DVDs, computers/electronics, flowers/gifts, food/drug, health/beauty, housewares/home furnishings, mass merchant/ department store, office supplies, specialty/non-apparel and sporting goods - each generated more than $1 billion in their retailing segments.

- In 2005 the mass merchant and department store category's online sales totaled $18.3 billion; followed by computers and electronics with $17.7 billion; office supplies with $10.3 billion; apparel and accessories with $7.1 billion; and books, CDs and DVDs with $2.5 billion.

- Spending in the hardware and home improvement category increased 46.4% from $482 million in 2004 to $705.6 million in 2005. The top merchant in the hardware and home improvement category was The Home Depot Inc., with 2005 estimated sales of $279.7 million, followed by Lowe's Cos. Inc. with estimated web sales of $148.8 million. The Top 500 Guide reveals that today hardware and home improvement is the web's fastest growing sales category, increasing at an annual rate of about 50%.

- Online office supplies sales for the same merchants ranked in both the Top 400 Guide and Top 500 Guide grew 60% from $6.4 billion in 2004 to $10.3 billion in 2005. The field was led by Office Depot Inc. and Staples Inc., each with 2005 web sales of $3.8 billion, and OfficeMax Inc., with e-commerce sales of $2.6 billion.

- Other online retail categories with fast-growing annual sales from 2004 to 2005 include: apparel and accessories, up 42% to $6.3 billion; books, CDs and DVDs, up 36% to $2.3 billion; mass merchandise, which increased 26.8% to $18.3 billion; food and drug, up 26% to $1.8 billion; and toys and hobbies, up 24% to $705 million.

- Sporting goods merchants also posted a good year, growing their combined annual web sales in 2005 24% to $1.2 billion from 2004's $998 million. Sporting goods was followed by: flowers and gifts, up 20.3% to $1.1 billion; jewelry, up 19.7% to $515.6 million; computers/electronics, up 16.1% to $16.6 billion; specialty/non-apparel, up 12.2% to $1.9 billion; and health and beauty, up 11.3% to $1.7 billion.

- With 2005 e-commerce sales of $8.5 billion, an increase of 22.7% over 2004's $6.9 billion, Amazon.com is the top retailer in the mass merchandizing category, with market share of 12.3%. Other major retailers are beginning to close the gap. In 2005, 14 companies generated more than $1 billion in annual web sales, compared with just 10 in 2004. Some of these are: Office Depot Inc., $3.8 billion; Staples Inc., $3.8 billion; Dell Inc., $3.78 billion; HP, $2.8 billion; OfficeMax Inc., $2.6 billion; Sears, $2.2 billion; CDW Corp., $1.8 billion; SonyStyle.com, $1.6 billion; and Newegg.com, $1.3 billion.

Business to Government (B2G)

B2G is a rapidly growing sector of e-commerce and improves efficiency when businesses deal with federal, state and local governments. Increased access and reduction of paperwork can be achieved through customizing B2B technologies to suit interactions with governments. In addition, many portals are emerging to streamline government procurement processes and sale of surplus resources of the government. Two key areas in this domain are: e-procurement and auctioning of government surpluses.

Governments buy large amounts of MROs (Maintenance, Repair, and Operations) and other materials directly from suppliers. In many cases, RFQs (Request for Quotations) and tendering are mandated by law. These were accomplished manually in the past, but there is an increasing implementation of systems using the Internet infrastructure. An example of G2B procurement in Hong Kong is available on www.info.gov.hk. In the United States, many federal government agencies are increasingly using e-procurement.

- The U.S. Government practices group purchasing to avail of quantity discounts from suppliers. The eFast service of www.gsa.gov conducts reverse auctions for aggregate orders. Government hospitals and public schools actively participate in group purchasing to reduce costs.
- Many government agencies auction equipment surpluses, ranging from vehicles to foreclosed real estate. The auctions can be carried out online from government auction sites such as www.auctionrp.com, or www.governmentauctions.org, or from third party sites such as www.eBay.com, www.bid4assets.com, or www.governmentauctions.org.
- Businesses can now file their income taxes electronically in over 100 countries including Thailand, Finland, and the US. In several countries, including the US, businesses file quarterly reports electronically. Businesses can also pay their sales taxes and value added taxes electronically.

FedBid.com (www.FedBic.com) is the first web-based market for B2G transactions. This site is used by many public sector organizations to purchase hundreds of millions of dollars worth of commodities. This easy access to public sector markets levels the competitive playing field for businesses of all sizes. At this site, a government purchaser can shop with government purchase cards, much like a consumer with his/her credit card. In addition, the site facilitates reverse auctions where the sellers compete to supply the government's procurement needs at the lowest cost. Reverse auctions are Request for Quotes with one buyer (the government) and many sellers. The buyer (government agency) purchases from the lowest bidder.

Non-Governmental Organization (NGO) to Citizens (NGO2C)

Democratic party presidential candidate for the 2004 presidential campaign Dr. Howard Dean revolutionized communications and appeals for donations using electronic means. Presidential candidates started using the Internet to establish their own websites since the 2000 Presidential campaign in the US. Most political organizations have established their own websites and several creative electronic tools to start people's movements on national, regional, and local public policy issues. NGOs include republican party, democratic party, ImpeachBush.org, International committee of Red Cross http://www.icrc.org/ (it is hosted in seven languages – English, French, Spanish, Arabic, Chinese, Russian, and Portuguese), American Red Cross http://www.redcross.org/, Earthquake India, Earthquake Pakistan Charitable organizations, Tsunami Indonesia, India Charitable Organizations, Katrina USA Charitable Organizations, and Political Action Organizations like www.MoveOn.org.

BUSINESS MODELS FOR GLOBAL ELECTRONIC COMMERCE

The Internet marketing channel is in cyberspace and eliminates the costs of acquisition and maintenance of physical space for the traditional marketing channels. Cyberspace based businesses can be accessed at electronic speed 24x7, if bottlenecks in the cyberspace infrastructure (power failure, lack of access to the Internet, etc.) can be eliminated or kept to a minimum. Physical space based businesses can be accessed only at human speed with many bottlenecks in the infrastructure (traffic jams, parking problems, walking around for shopping, standing in line for checkout and payment, etc.).

Broad Business Models: Traditional, Internet, and Hybrid Retailers

This is a very broad classification of how companies can sell their products and services in the Internet age to other companies or to consumers (B2B and B2C). They can sell exclusively through the traditional brick-and-mortar channels (supermarkets, malls, retail stores), or exclusively through Internet based click-and-portal channel (pure play e-tailers) or through both channels. Pure play e-tailers include www.amazon.com (selling books and CDs and lots of other products), www.dell.com (selling personal computers in many configurations), www.layoyo.com (selling DVD, VCD, music CD). Hybrid retailers, called click-and-mortar, are essentially traditional brick-and-mortar retailers with a transactional website. Examples include department stores such as Macy's (www.macys.com) or Sears (www.sears.com) as well as discount stores like Wal-Mart (www.walmart.com). Brick-and-mortar only businesses are increasingly becoming a minority, with only a small percentage of businesses having no online presence. Many experts predict that the ultimate winners in many market segments will be the companies that are able to leverage the best of both worlds using the click-and-mortar approach. How do these channels compare against each other?

Robert Kuttner, in Business Week, May 11, 1998, said, "The Internet is a nearly perfect market because information is instantaneous and buyers can compare the offerings of sellers worldwide. The result is fierce price competition, dwindling product differentiation, and vanishing brand loyalty." In a study by Brynjolfsson and Smith (2000); 8,500 price observations were made to analyze price levels, price adjustments and price dispersion for 20 titles of books and CDs (homogeneous products) sold by 4 internet only, 4 conventional only, 4 Internet-hybrid, and 4 conventional-hybrid retailers over a period of 15 months (during 1998-99). Conventional retailers were selected from geographically dispersed locations: CA, GA, MD, MA, OR, and VA. Salient results were as follows:

1. Prices for books and CDs sold on the Internet averaged 9-16% less than the identical items sold via conventional channels. The mean price for books was $2.16 less and $2.58 less for CDs when purchased over the Internet.
2. Internet retailers changed prices in smaller increments than conventional retailers. The smallest observed price change on the Internet was $0.01 while the smallest observed price change by a conventional retailer was $0.35.
3. There were substantial and systematic differences in prices across retailers on the Internet. Prices posted on the Internet differed by an average of 33% for books and 25% for CDs. At the same time, retailers with the lowest prices did not receive the most sales.

Specific B2C Business Models and Classification Criteria

Popular textbooks on IT and e-commerce identify Internet based business models as Virtual Storefront (Amazon.com, Dell.com), Information Broker (Insweb.com, Realtor.com), Transaction Broker (Expedia.com, Travelocity.com), Online Marketplace (eBay.com, Priceline.com), Content Provider (WSJ.com, MSNBC.com), Online Service Provider (Monster.com, Salesforce.com), Virtual Community (Motocross.com, Friendster.com), and Portal -- Horizontal or Vertical (Yahoo.com, MSN.com). It should be noted that almost all of these business models can be characterized in terms of the classification criteria described below: Product Type, Search Online or Offline, Sell Online or Offline, Negotiate Online or not, Pay Online or Offline.

Product Type: Selling a physical product versus selling a digital product has significant implications on the business model deployed. If a vendor is selling a physical product, it has to have a global supply chain that delivers purchased products to the customers undamaged and efficiently. Such a vendor needs also to provide for return of such products. Dell or Gateway computers who sell PCs to its customers fall into this category. Sony or Kodak selling digital cameras also fall into this category. Software, music, photographs, videos, information (newspapers and journals) have become digital products over the years and avoid the Global Supply Chain challenges.

Search Online or Offline - Sell Online or Offline: How does a potential customer go about searching for products or services (the flip side for manufacturers and service providers is how they go about advertising and promoting their products and services) and how does one buy these products or services (the flip side is what selling channels are used by manufacturers and service providers)? Table 3 provides a simple framework for the options.

Offline and Online Options for Searching for and Buying a Product or Service		Buy/Sell a product or service?	
		Offline	Online
Search for a product or service?	Offline	**Option 1**	**Option 2**
	Online	**Option 3**	**Option 4**

Table 3. Offline and Online Scenarios for Search and Sell

- **Option 1** is the traditional selling. Search for a product or service is based on looking at newspaper and magazine ads or listening to TV and radio ads or searching for product and service by actually visiting a retail store. The selling (selecting, ordering, and paying) in this case occurs at the physical store.
- **Option 2** implies searching for a product or service offline, but selling (buying) online. This would happen for the case of selling (buying) electronics gadgets like a camera, DVD player or music. One would search in offline media or channels and actually buy from an online retailer.
- **Option 3** might be used for buying a car. One would visit several websites (based on search engine results) and decide on a particular manufacturer and model of a car. Armed with information about the best price for this car, one would visit a few car dealers before finalizing the deal and buying the car at the dealership.
- **Option 4** is 100% e-commerce, where one searches online only and buys/sells online.

It should be noted that some businesses do not sell their products or services directly to online customers. They only provide product, pricing, and availability information to individuals and businesses. Examples include www.Edmunds.com, www.Insweb.com, and www.Realtor.com.

Negotiate Online: Most Internet-based storefronts do not allow for online price negotiation. However, eBay and even the auction segment of Amazon precisely allow online price negotiation. Such business models have numerous challenges which have been documented in the literature.

Pay Online or Offline: In the beginning of e-commerce, customers were hesitant to give their credit card information on the Internet. They would order the product or service online, but pay for it offline by credit card or check or even cash. Now that confidence and trust in the Internet's security features have increased substantially, buyers in the U.S. invariably type their credit card information to make the payment. However, in countries other than the U.S., customers still prefer offline payment to online payment.

FRAMEWORK FOR GLOBAL ELECTRONIC COMMERCE

Table 4 presents a framework to come to grips with the myriad of issues that need to be tackled in the context of global e-commerce. We essentially combine the concepts of "Barriers to Global e-commerce" and "Customer Service Life Cycle (CSLC)" as follows. While conducting global e-commerce or building a website for global e-commerce, one has to ask the question – have we addressed cultural barriers for the requirements phase of the CSLC? When one incorporates the solutions for the barriers to global e-commerce in all phases of the CSLC, we can call it the Global Customer Service Life Cycle – GCSLC.

Based on our experience in teaching courses and also in the real world, we also indicate in the framework which barriers are critical in which phase. The following two sections describe the barriers to global e-commerce and the details of the CSLC.

		Barriers to Global E-commerce			
		Cultural	Administrative / Legal	Geographic	Economic/Regulatory
Customer Service Life Cycle	**Requirements**	Critical			
	Acquisition	Critical	Critical	Critical	Critical
	Ownership		Critical		
	Upgrade/Retirement		Critical		

Table 4. Framework for Global E-commerce

BARRIERS TO GLOBAL E-COMMERCE

Ghemawat (2001) collapsed the barriers to e-commerce into four classes known by the CAGE acronym - cultural, administrative/legal, geographic, and economic/regulatory.

Cultural
The oft cited cultural artifacts of power distance, uncertainty avoidance, individualism-collectivism, and masculinity-femininity are a good starting point for understanding this barrier. These cultural artifacts have already been described elsewhere in the book and are also included in the glossary of terms. Language is a major component of the cultural barrier (American English versus other languages). Spelling differences should be taken into account to show respect for diversity (American versus British spelling). Information formatting differences also abound around the world – date formatting (MM/DD/YY versus DD/MM/YY versus YY/MM/DD), time formatting (9:50 PM versus 21:50 hours), calendar design, starting with Monday (Sunday is a holiday in Christian countries), or Saturday (Friday is a holiday in Islamic countries). Measurement standards also differ – only two countries have stuck to the Imperial system as opposed to the internationally accepted metric system. Meaning of colors is different in different parts of the world. Postal codes differ – 5 digits (US) versus 6 characters (Canada) versus no postal codes in some countries.

Administrative (Legal)
A Country's legal and regulatory restrictions have substantial impact on the initiation and continuation of e-commerce with other countries. National governments have been working together under the auspices of international and regional organizations like the United Nations, World Trade Organization (WTO), and Asia-Pacific Economic Cooperation to come up with uniform legal standards, pricing regulations, customs, imports-export restrictions, tax issues, and product specification regulations. The United Nations Commission on International Trade Law has attempted to reduce differences in international law governing e-commerce. The Model Law created by this commission has been adopted in some form in numerous countries including Australia, Canada, Hong Kong, Singapore, and some American states.

When a copyrighted work on a computer in one country is accessed in another, which country's copyright laws should be applied? Privacy protection standards are stricter in Europe than the US. Which standards should apply when sharing information created in one country and accessed in another? Governments must determine whether an e-business that maintains a website is subject to the laws of all countries from which the site can be accessed. For example, in May 2000, the destructive ILOVEYOU virus was spread via e-mail to computer systems around the world. Although the virus led to billions of dollars in damage globally, the suspected Philippine citizen could not be prosecuted for lack of applicable laws in his home country. Globally adopted laws must address cybercrimes, such as copyright infringement, cybersquatting, cyber terrorism, violation of privacy rights, etc.

- Per recommendation of the American Bar Association (www.abanet.org), there is a need to form a "global online standards commission" to mediate and govern Internet and e-commerce related disputes among countries.
- The World Intellectual Property Organization (www.wipo.int) set up by United Nations primarily deals with cybersquatting disputes.
- The Organization of Economic Cooperation and Development (www.oecd.com), a forum for its 29 member countries, suggests increasing the scope of its jurisdiction to include collecting data related to computer-related security breaches and supervising the creation of national policies on digital certificates.

After three years of research, the Council of Europe (www.coe.int), composed of 41 countries (with additional representatives from Canada, Japan, South Africa and the U.S.), released in 2000 a draft of the world's first international treaty relating to cyber crime (Deitel et al., 2000, page 343). The treaty mandates that all signatories will establish laws prohibiting unauthorized access of computers, interception of computer data, and exchange/possession of equipment used in hacking. Yet some issues continue to differ by nation. For instance, it is illegal to use a foreign language to advertise in France. And in terms of e-mail marketing restrictions, the United States is very lenient, while the European Union has banned spam by its citizens.

Geographical
As far as communication, information dissemination, and transaction activities are concerned, geographical distance has essentially become a non-issue. Time zone differences across the globe must be taken into account for synchronous and asynchronous communications. It must be recognized that Internet infrastructural differences across countries (digital divide) like bandwidth requirements may pose an impediment to uninterrupted and speedy realization of e-commerce activities. When it comes to the delivery of products, one has to be concerned about the state of the global supply chain for forward and backward (returned goods) movement of products. Transportation infrastructure within and between countries would be a major factor in effective implementation of global e-commerce. However, there is a silver lining here, too. For services like banking, insurance, and investments, global supply chain infrastructure would not be a concern. Also, many erstwhile physical products have become digital products during the short Internet age, including software, music, greeting cards, photographs, video clips, and audio clips.

Economic/Regulatory
These issues include government tariffs, customs, and taxation. Generally, regulatory agencies have tried to apply the principles of traditional commerce to e-commerce with substantial success. However, exceptions exist. For example, software shipped as physical product in a box would be subject to duties and tariffs when it arrives in a country, whereas the same software downloaded online relies on self-reporting and voluntary payment of tax by the purchaser, a rare occurrence.

When deciding on a market, factors such as the number of people online, Internet usage growth rates, per capita income, existing competitors in the product or service arena of a country, host government's restrictions on imports and other factors must be considered. Two useful sites for learning about foreign markets are www.glreach.com and www.idiominc.com. Note that smaller, less obvious markets are sometimes better choices for marketing specific products. For example, Russia is predicted to be a strong emerging market for golf supplies (Deitel et al., 2000, page 345). Even though, geographical location of a websites' host should be logically immaterial, some governments require it to be registered and hosted in their own countries.

According to Cyber Dialogue, Inc., approximately 88% of the $53 billion dollars spent online in 2000 in the US was paid with credit cards (Crocket, 2000). Contrast that with Europe – only approximately 30% of Europeans have credit cards, and many feel uncomfortable revealing credit card numbers over the telephone or Internet (Mullen, 2000). Credit cards are rare in developing countries, because of infrastructure and trust issues. Cash on delivery (COD) is likely to be a more feasible option in Europe. According to Mullen (2000), DirectDebit™ is likely to be available throughout Europe. DirectDebit enables electronic debits from a European customer's bank accounts to be sent to merchant's bank accounts for a small fee. Few Indians have credit cards, and e-shopping sites avoid credit cards because the country does not have good verification systems. One Bangalore-based site, www.fabmart.com came up with its own currency called "Fabmoney," sold in Internet cafes (Pearl, 2001). Given India's low labor costs, delivery companies pick up cash at one location and deliver the gift to another location for about $1 to avoid the credit-card problem.

The relative ease with which e-Businesses can buy and sell internationally is a major advantage, but it makes violation of import and export laws much simpler. Selling and distributing animals, plants, products made from endangered species, arms and explosives, toy guns, Viagra, weapons of any kind, pornographic material, items related to the Nazi era, certain software, and certain nuclear technology are prohibited to be exported or imported by certain countries (Tapper, 2000). E-businesses should also investigate international tax laws as they apply to Internet sales. In many countries, including all members of the European Union, a value-added tax (VAT) is also added to all goods sold to consumers. Companies like www.mycustoms.com and www.worldtariff.com help in computing international taxes and other fees for global businesses.

A primary barrier to global e-commerce is electronic payment systems. To be successful globally, EC firms must have flexible payment systems that match the prevailing norms of different countries and regions. Although credit cards are used routinely in the US, many European and Asian customers prefer to pay for online transactions with offline payments. For example, French consumers prefer to pay with a check, Swiss expect an invoice by mail, Germans commonly pay upon delivery, and Swedes are accustomed to paying by debit cards. Pricing is another economic issue. The issues are – how to implement differential pricing for consumers in different countries, what currency to use for pricing, and what currency to use for payment. This has been experienced by the author as Managing Director of the Center for Global Outsourcing; delegates from the US have generally paid by credit card; European delegates have preferred to pay by bank transfer; some of the Indian delegates would pay about 20% in advance by credit card and the remainder by cash at the time of registering for the conference.

CUSTOMER SERVICE LIFE CYCLE

The Customer Service Life Cycle (CSLC) can be broken down into four broad phases: Requirements, Acquisition, Ownership, and Retirement. A potential customer may be browsing for a product in general or searching for a specific product/service. The CSLC helps a customer differentiate the various stages he/she goes through in acquiring a product/service from a firm. The basis for the differentiation is improved customer service, and other advantages for a firm. In acquiring a product or service, a customer has to go through significant investment of time and effort. According to Ives and Mason (1990), in the *requirements* phase, the customer realizes he/she needs a product or service and then begins to focus in on specific attributes. During *acquisition,* the customer orders, pays for, and acquires, the product. In the next major phase *ownership*, the customer has the product/service and must deal with issues of training, repair, maintenance and so on. The final phase is *retirement*, where the customer is beginning to think about buying again, upgrading, or disposing of the item. Exhibit 1 describes pictorially the four phases of CSLC. Table 5 breaks these four phases into 13 sub-phases. Some sub-phases may be absent, combined, or named somewhat differently for any particular business. For an innovative product, one for which there are no competitors, the *requirements* phase may be the most challenging to overcome. According to Ives and Mason (1990), "before you can sell the product, you will have to educate the potential customers about its capabilities. However, for a

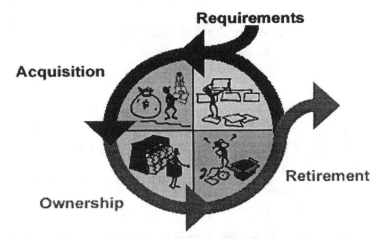

Exhibit-1: Four Major Phases of Customer Service Life Cycle (Source Ives and Mason, 1990)

Requirements

1. Establish Requirements	Establish a need for the product
2. Specify	Determine the products attributes

Acquisition

3. Select Source	Determine where to obtain the product
4. Order	Order the product from a supplier
5. Authorize and Pay For	Transfer funds or extend credit
6. Acquire	Take possession of the product
7. Test and Accept	Ensure that the product meets specifications

Ownership

8. Integrate	Add to an existing inventory
9. Monitor	Control access and use of the product
10. Upgrade	Upgrade the product if conditions change
11. Maintain	Repair the product as necessary

Retirement

12. Transfer or Dispose	Move, return, or dispose of product
13. Account For	Monitor expenses related to the product

Table 5. Thirteen Sub-phases of the Customer Service Life Cycle

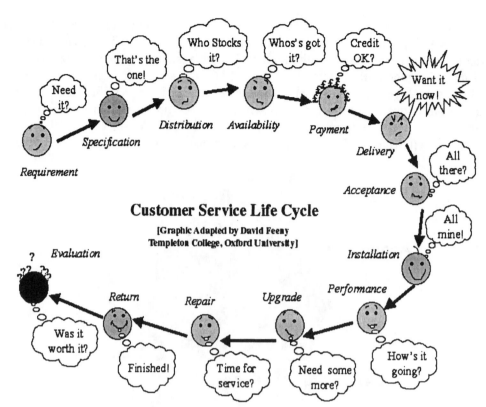

Exhibit-2: Customer Perspectives Highlighted for the CSLC (Source: DesSantos, 2006)

product such as software, upgrade will likely be a critical process, particularly for sophisticated users. Novices, on the other hand, may have problems in the 'integrate' stage, as they learn to use the new product." The CSLC model has proven useful in e-commerce contexts as well as traditional contexts (Cenfetelli and Benbasat, 2002).

Exhibit 2 shows customer perspectives highlighted for the CSLC. It uses expressions on color coded faces to draw attention to the importance of focusing on the customer perspective. According to DesSantos (2006), "What I was trying to capture through the faces was the importance of targeting CRLC services at stages which the customer finds a real hassle - I am astonished at how often businesses are creating services which 'fit' the model but create no value/result because the customer does not experience any felt need to improve the stage targeted." Organizations have to devise their marketing, promotional, pricing, product, and place strategies to maximize their effectiveness in the thirteen sub-phases. Here we elaborate the role of advertising in the Internet Age for the Requirements/Acquisitions phases.

An Example of Customer Service Life Cycle Management

The following is an illustration of how the concept of CSLC applies to the website designs of three global automotive companies, Honda, BMW, and Ford. This example is adapted from a student project done for an MBA class during the summer of 2006. IT provides the necessary tools and infrastructure for Honda, BMW, and Ford to serve their customers by assisting them to identify the right products, manage purchased products, and become repeat customers. These companies have all benefited in the following ways from Customer Service Life Cycle Management:

- Give every employee a 360-degree view of the customer
- Use customer data to optimize business processes and improve decision-making on both a tactical and strategic level

- Maintain accuracy of customer data to maximize value
- Increase revenue during post-sales interactions with customers throughout the lifetime of the relationship
- Leverage customer data to improve customer satisfaction, retention, loyalty and longevity

Requirements Phase: Focusing on the requirements phase, site navigation on BMW's sites is mainly static, company-centric, and incapable of creating a personal connection with customers. Honda's "Find Answers" search applications and Fords "Virtual Showroom," in contrast, are dynamic, responsive to customer needs and suited for engaging customers in a dialogue. Visitors control the website. Forcing potential customers down a navigation path prescribed by the seller inevitably leads to high abandonment rates and dissatisfaction. From a marketing perspective, Honda's "Find Answers" search and Ford's "Virtual Showroom" represent alignment between understanding and fulfilling visitor information needs with corporate marketing objectives. Honda and Ford are able to understand and dynamically respond to a visitor's unique needs in a manner that encourages him/her to continue the buying process.

Acquisitions Phase: Fewer than 10% of new cars today are built to order; most automakers build and equip cars in standard configurations that are often based on outdated sales information. Building cars based on Internet orders is something that virtually everybody is working on, but Ford and Honda get credit for being first to implement such systems. This is a major differentiator and a valuable marketing tool for both firms. Increasingly, sales will be made over the Internet as e-commerce reshapes the industry. Ford hopes it can use the Internet to reinvent the automobile industry it helped to create decades ago. Even though the selling process isn't fully automated, BMW's "have it in your driveway within 10 days" concept is innovative and serves as a source of competitive advantage for the firm.

Ownership Phase: During the ownership phase of the CSLC, BMW, Honda, and Ford use similar web-based tools giving the customer everything he/she needs to know about owning, driving, and caring for the vehicle. With these exclusive owners' web sites, one can personalize the ownership experience and obtain valuable information, accessories and services tailored to the car owned. Honda's Owner Link however is a more versatile, feature packed innovative application. Available at any time from the comfort of one's home or office, Honda's superior Owner Link gives additional access to personalized service records, and tips for caring for Honda. One can even manage the OnStar account online. Owner Link is the source for Customer Relations contact information and details about car care benefits.

Retirement Phase: At the retirement phase of the CSLC, all three companies have the same goal in mind. They each want to maintain customer loyalty and ensure that once the customer decides to move from one vehicle to the next they stay with their brand. Ford and BMW use a similar technique in that they attempt to collect a large amount of information through a customer-centric website. Based on the data collected and preferences of the customer, e-mail and personalized promotions are delivered to the customer. Honda has a similar idea in mind; however they use an innovative Enterprise Management System, which is able to pinpoint exactly what customers are looking for based on a thorough analysis of survey data collected from customers.

While the Internet is just beginning to change the auto industry and its selling process, it has already had a profound effect on the way companies create strategic and innovative applications that are a source of competitive advantage for the firm. Ford, Honda, and BMW have, in particular, shown that they use the internet in a strategic way to enhance their business and the effectiveness to acquire and retain customers through each phase of the CSLC. Additionally, each auto company, across three different countries and cultures, has shown that they use the same fundamentals in the CSLC, with some techniques that are similar and some that are different.

Advertising in the Requirements/Acquisition Phases

Recent advertising statistics from DoubleClick.com (2006) show that online advertising spending and the share of online advertising as a percentage of total advertising spending is steadily increasing -- 3.1% in 2001 to 5.7% expected in 2008 - and expected to grow further. Furthermore, the composition of advertising dollars among the Internet, print media, TV and radio is also gradually shifting in favor Internet advertising. Table 6 shows the gradual shift in the composition between the years 2000 and 2004.

	2000	**2004**
U.S. spending of advertising	$185 billion	$197 billion
Share of Internet advertising	2.3%	3.6%
Share of Newspaper	6.7%	6.1%
Share of Magazine	10.0%	10.0%
Share of Radio and TV	30.1%	31.2%
Share of Other	50.9%	48.1%

Table 6. U.S. Spending on Advertising

The Internet as an advertising medium is very different from magazines, radio, and TV where the written or unwritten rules are known to all. Since e-commerce is steadily taking off on a global basis, advertisers have been inventing a set of rules that are very different from those in the print or the broadcast media. Table 7 captures the fundamental differences between Internet-based advertising and traditional advertising. We describe some of the distinguishing criteria; others are self-explanatory.

Advertising versus Contents: Increasingly, contents of editorial and news items determine advertisements rather than advertisements and editorials being independent. Sometimes the contents of the editorial and news items are determined by the sponsors of the underlying advertisements. An examples is El Cholo restaurant (restaurants are rank ordered based on the size of the displays on their Internet sites) being recommended by the Mexican Restaurants section for the LosAngeles.com site. Amazon.com has been found to recommend books from publishers who paid for the favor. Many news websites provide hyperlinks (advertisements) to one or more books from Amazon.com or Barnesandnoble.com related to the topic of the news item. Advertising is becoming more context-based rather than independent. Often when the product is referred to in the text of the article the hyperlink takes the readers to the company's website where they can purchase the product or read more praises of it. When Internet users search on a search engine like Google or Yahoo, the resulting hyperlink to a website may not be as objective as they would like to believe. Some sponsored links will show up on the top. With this type of online advertising, it gives a whole new meaning to the phrase "Buyer Beware."

Payments Tied to Performance: Advertisement payments tied to performance is becoming one of the most popular types of advertising on the WWW. In this form of advertising, an advertiser pays only when the advertisement produces a result. An online store will generally pay only when a web surfer views its ad, clicks on its ad (click-through), provides information abut himself/herself as a potential customer (customer lead rate), or actually makes a purchase. Service enterprises such as travel agents, car dealers, and banks will often pay for the referral or pay when the customer actually requests the services offered.

Criterion	Traditional Advertising	Internet-based Advertising
Advertising versus Contents	Advertising driving contents	Contents are increasingly driving advertising
Payments Tied to Performance	Advertising payments are <u>not</u> tied to actual advertising effectiveness	Advertising payments are increasingly being tied to advertising effectiveness
Value Velocity versus Visual Virtuosity	Preference for upscale image	Preference for relevant information fast
Measurement of Advertisement Effectiveness	No or little information on exposure. Based on sample data.	Complete information on surfer activities on a server. Also surfer profile collected by usual methods.
Use of Search Engines	None or Limited	Extensive, based on keywords and Boolean expressions
Linking Websites	No hyperlinks	A network of hyperlinks
Timing of viewing	View when broadcast or printed	View on demand
Control over Exposure Time	Exposure time determined by advertiser with the exception of print medium	Exposure time determined by web surfer
Interactive or not?	Advertising is non-interactive	Can be interactive by including chats with experts
Focus on Target	Limited target advertising	Many ways to promote target advertising including e-mail campaigns

Table 7: Comparison of Internet Based and Traditional Advertising

Value Velocity versus Visual Virtuosity: Value velocity is the notion that it is better to have a fast site with minimal necessary features than visual virtuosity (flash presentations or fancy graphics), a slow site that has lots of bells and whistles. It is a good practice to minimize photographs and elegant colorful images to avoid unnecessary downloading time. It may sometimes be hard to imagine, but most people in the world still use dial up Internet connections. Due to this, sites which are flashy and graphical will take far too long to load, if they even load at all. Most visitors will leave a site if it is not finished loading and ready to browse within 30 seconds or less. Most websites allow for text to appear before images appear (allowing for image borders to appear along with the text) to maintain the interest of the surfer viewer. Such gulag-style design standards are anathema to retailers who have spent years cultivating upscale images (Kaufman, 1999). Once the desired website has loaded, velocity of navigation enhances shopping interest and motivation. Web retailers like Amazon.com observe the "3-click rule" meaning that a shopper can get to the product he/she wants within three clicks of a mouse. In addition to simplifying access to desired products with three clicks, purchasing the selected products can be simplified with few clicks. Amazon pioneered the use of 1-click ordering; a customer with an account with Amazon can complete an order with a single click of the mouse.

Measurement of Advertising Effectiveness: Making decisions about advertising medium and form is undoubtedly based on advertising effectiveness. For print media, the Audit Bureau of Circulation, among others, verifies circulation. Viewer reach and advertising effectiveness of television programs are measured by AC Nielsen ratings, which are also used for establishing advertisement rates. The measurement of effectiveness of Internet advertising is new and requires modifying traditional measurement techniques. There are basically two approaches for measuring Internet advertising effectiveness. With Internet website server log, every user of WWW leaves an electronic trail of visits made to different websites. The trail of visitors can be logged, stored and analyzed. Server-based measurement provides a footprint of everything every visitor does on a website. It tells how they got there, how long they stayed, how many pages they viewed, their operating system and browser, number of clicks, time of visit, where visited from, how much bandwidth they used, and what page they exited on or if they made a purchase. Although it seems that the Internet log solves the measurement problem, the process is imperfect. For security reasons, many websites utilize a proxy server to connect the clients to the real server. A proxy server intercepts and evaluates client's requests for a particular service and decides which to pass on to the real server and which to drop. To speed up processing information requests, proxy caches are used. Some client requests are satisfied by the information stored in the proxy caches and therefore these requests never reach the real server. Widespread use of proxy caches is making server-based measurements difficult if not impossible. Due to inexpensive collection of visitor information and their journey through the site with clicks, server based log analysis remains a useful measurement tool. The data generated is anonymous giving little information about the demographics of the user. To alleviate this, Internet surfer based measurement is accomplished by observing consumers' surfing habits. In the U.S., surfer-based measurement avoids measurement of international traffic by utilizing a panel of American users. Relevant Knowledge (relevantknowledge.com) has 10,000 members and their web surfing habits are sent to the company. Media Metrix (mediametrix.com) on the other hand, uses a panel of 30,000 members and their web usage is stored on the user's computer and automatically mailed to the company every month. In 2000, Nielsen Media Research started Nielsen//NetRatings (nielson-netratings.com) with 110,000 panelists to measure Internet audience habits in real time.

Use of Search Engine: Search engines are the vertical portals that lead 8 to 9 out of every 10 web visitors to a specific web site. About 50% of a typical web surfer's time is spent in searching and about 25% of web surfers give up in frustration not able to find what they are looking for. Not finding needed information is not due to lack of available information, but, rather paradoxically, due to abundance of information. Each webpage is a potential target of a search engine's search. In the late 1990s and early 2000s, there were about 12 main search engines. Now the list has consolidated to four main search engines – Google, Yahoo, Ask, and MSN - and several other lesser search engines. Registering with multiple search engines and submitting keywords and information geared towards the ranking strategy of each search engine will improve the chances of a website being found. Most search engines with their bots, crawlers, and spiders take a proactive stance and crawl through the HTML code of websites looking for keywords (especially repetition of keywords) or other search-engine ranking criteria. Search engine ranking is important to bring new visitors to a site. Most web surfers do not look beyond the top ten ranked sites. Two primary search engine strategies are:

- **Registering with search engines to have website spidered.** Spidering means a search engine sending an automated piece of software (spider) to visit your site to index all of the content. Then, the search engine's algorithm goes through the contents, determines the key words, and indexes the website's URL with these key terms. This is how websites end up in the Organic Search Section of the search results page. This section is generally surrounded by sponsored links. No one knows for sure what algorithms are used to make a site relevant for a term or key word, but it depends on few factors. First, a site looking for good organic search position should have meta tags in the HTML code which include all the key terms which are relevant to the mission and contents of the website. For example if you sell mailboxes, the meta tags should include every possible spelling and phrase you think a customer would type in the search engine's box to find your website. Second, your site should not just be pictures and snippets of text. There should be unique, keyword rich text, on every page which relates to exactly what that page is about. The third factor is to have as many other websites as possible establish hyperlinks to your website.

- **Being a sponsor with search engines.** This requires upfront payment to the search engine company so that your website will show up in the sponsored results area based on certain keywords search; almost always the placement is based on the reimbursement scheme. For example, in Google an advertiser can set up an account and bid on a specific key term which is relevant to its website's products and services. The advertiser can, within Google, monitor how many impressions the site has received (times the ad was shown) and how many clicks those impressions generated. The advertiser only pays for the clicks. The ads appear in the sponsored links section of the search page. The place in which the ad appears depends on relevance and how high the bid was. If another advertiser bids more and is more relevant they will be listed higher in the rankings.

When advertising with a sponsored search, there are three main search companies which sell their results to the smaller search companies. The major companies, known as the *Tier One Search Engines* are Google Adwords, Yahoo Search Marketing, and MSN Adcenter. *Tier Two Search Engines* include Lycos, Excite, AltaVista, Ask.com, and AOL Search. These search engines may have their own sponsored search programs set up; however, they buy most of their ads from the partner programs of the Tier One search engines. There are also *meta-search engines* which aggregate results from a variety of search engines. Two examples are metawcrawler.com and framesearch.net. As a point of interest, the results of the top 3 search terms by search volume in the following categories (for four weeks ending November 28, 2006) are shown in parenthesis: IT and Internet (PayPal, white pages, people search); Automotive Manufacturers (Toyota, Honda, Nissan); Movies (Imdb, Netflix, Movies); Internet Advertising (free samples, work from home, free stuff); Food and Beverage Brands and Manufacturers (Pizza hut, Starbucks, McDonalds); Pharmaceutical and Medical Products (lexapro, cymbalta, depression); Blogs and Personal Websites (Xanga, Myspace, Yahoo 360); Broadcast Media (CNN, MSNBC, Fox News); Travel Destinations (Mapquest, maps, driving directions) (www.hitwise.com).

Linking Websites: Many electronic retailers and service providers offer incentives if you put their ads on your websites. Take the example of Amazon.com, if your website offers book reviews, you could enroll in Amazon.com's affiliate program. Through this program, Amazon issues your site a unique ID which is placed in the hyperlink to Amazon.com and uses this to record if your website referred sales to Amazon. Amazon then in turn will pay 10% of the resulting sale price to you as a referrer. So if you run a well known and respected book review site or even blog, this arrangement could turn a significant profit while also helping Amazon.com. Link sharing sites may also form alliances and have links on each site pointing to the other. Generally, link sharing does not take place between competing sites but complementing sites, thus allows each site to focus just on its core competency while still offering their customers one stop shopping.

CRITICAL SUCCESS FACTORS FOR GLOBAL ELECTRONIC COMMERCE

Critical success factors are things that must go right to ensure success. When looking at global e-commerce, there are several critical success factors that will help to ensure success. Eleven of these critical success factors are discussed here. They are presented so readers can understand some of the issues for successful global e-commerce.

Be Strategic
Identify a starting point and plan a globalization strategy for the business. In terms of a starting point, it can be a static website design, global business strategy, Internet only business model, B2B only, etc. Plan how you will move from this starting point to your ultimate objective. The strategic

objective can be different for different companies. Consider the global e-commerce framework discussed in this chapter and have a plan for overcoming the barriers for e-commerce for each phase of CSLC.

Complement High Touch with High Tech

While deploying high tech to promote efficiency, the fundamental of human touch must not be forgotten. For example, language translators bring tremendous efficiency, but the machine translations from one language to another have been found to be only abut 60% accurate (Dubie 2003). That is why many companies use native language in-country human translators to review and revise the results from machine translation. One slight mistranslation or one out of place graphic may cause havoc.

Clarify, Document, and Explain Rules and Policies

Pricing, privacy policies, return policies, shipping restrictions, custom duties, taxation, delivery charges, contact information etc. should be well documented and placed on the website for the customer's review and affirmation, if necessary. To help protect against foreign litigation, identify where the company is located and the jurisdiction of all contract or sales disputes.

Offer Services that Reduce Barriers

It is not feasible to offer prices and payments in all currencies, so link to a currency exchange service (e.g., www.xe.com) for the customer's convenience. In B2B commerce, be prepared to integrate the e-commerce transaction with the accounting/financial internal information system of the buyer. Offering language translators on your website for languages beyond the primary languages in the world may alleviate language barriers and keep customers glued to the website.

Think Global Customers and Global Suppliers

This applies to B2B e-commerce. If Dell computer sells its PCs to businesses, it should think about companies like General Motors (GM) who have a global presence. Selling its PCs and related services to GM in several or all countries would be to the advantage of Dell. GM should be treated as a global single customer and provided several benefits, like quantity discount, best possible service package, and attractive computer upgrade options. In the same vein, having a reliable, trustworthy global single supplier like Dell is to the advantage of GM also.

Think Customer Service Life Cycle

Understanding the purpose of a web surfer's visit to your website is the first step in serving the surfer (current or potential customer) in the best possible manner. As explained earlier, CSLC has four broad phases – Requirements, Acquisition, Ownership, and Retirement. Website design should cater to the needs of the surfer in all these phases. Most websites try to determine if the surfer already has signed up on the website or not. Based on that information alone, it can be determined that the CSLC phase is Requirements, Acquisition, Ownership, or Retirement. While Ives and Mason (1990) articulate CSLC phases and Ghemawat (2001) articulates the CAGE framework (as described earlier), in this chapter we have integrated the two frameworks to suggest that global barriers should be considered in the design of a website to cater to the customers in each phase of CSLC.

Foster Trusting Relationships with Customers

This is a challenge given the lack of face to face contact in an e-commerce environment. Add to this the challenges of differences illustrated by our global e-commerce framework, and it follows that building trust may be a formidable challenge. Three measures that can help in building trust include: (1) having a physical presence in as many countries as possible, even if it is a one person office; (2)

being accessible when a current or potential customer wants to contact by you e-mail, phone, or fax; and (3) being above board and prompt in all financial transactions.

Simplify and Expedite Transaction Process

Hyperlinks can bring a customer to an e-commerce site with a few mouse clicks and also can take him/her away from the site as easily. The web is creating shoppers with short attention spans. If the ordering process is complex and involves prolonged navigation through the web site, the shopper may be lured away from the transaction. For example, PayPal's initial sign-up process required users to click through seven screens – the company discovered that with each new screen, 25% of the users dropped off (Gomes, 2001). That would result in only 17% of the original potential customers remaining. In the international context, it would be disastrous to have to go through seven web pages in India, for example, where Internet connections are shaky (Pearl, 2001). The use of the '3-click rule' and 1-click ordering, as practiced by Amazon.com, are some of the more successful and effective design features. Also, in the context of global e-commerce, culturally attractive icons must be used.

Get Yourself Found Often and on the Top

Eighty percent of the time, web surfers rely on search engines to find what they are looking for. Furthermore, almost 90% do not look beyond the first 10 sites found by a search engine. Thirty percent of web surfers give up their search in frustration. Clearly, it is critical for an online business' success that it is found by potential customers. So, it is important not only to register with several search engines, but also to understand and utilize search engines' algorithms so that your website shows up among the top ten. One way is to be part of a web wheel; a grouping of similar websites that agree to cross-reference each other for the greater good of the virtual community (Huff and Wade, 2000).

Prepare for M-Commerce

Mobile Commerce is generally understood to involve an electronic transaction via the use of a mobile phone. In some instances, it has been predicted that the mobile phone could actually replace the credit or debit card. In Europe, especially in Finland, accessing the Internet and corresponding via e-mail on the mobile phone is pervasive. Doing e-commerce transactions over the mobile phone in Europe and Japan has also become popular. In the United States, the use of mobile phone to access the web is growing rapidly. A number of mobile phone companies are offering wireless Internet access for laptops and hand-held devices in public places like airports, hotels, and stores. For users, the mobile phone offers convenience, immediacy and personalization for consumer transactions. The number and variety of goods and services available to wireless subscribers is skyrocketing. From the seller/supplier point of view, m-commerce allows enterprises to expand their market reach, provide better service and reduced costs. Examples of m-commerce services in popular use today include mobile parking meter payments and the purchase of ring tones for telephones. Such services are known as 'micropayments'; transactions with an average value of under $10. While m-commerce applications can also include the purchase of various high value items, growth in the near future is expected to come from compelling digital content and services, most of which is expected to be valued at under $10. Other m-commerce services include financial applications such as m-banking. This service enables users to check their bank account details and pay bills. Such services have been especially popular in the Philippines, where the conventional banking system is arguably not as well developed as other regions of the world. In many developing countries, particularly in rural areas, access to financial services is limited, resulting in a large percentage of the population operating on a cash only basis and outside of the formal banking system. However, the proliferation of mobile services in these countries has created a unique platform to provide financial services over the mobile network. In light of the growing size of international and national banking remittances, there is a great opportunity to capitalize on the benefits of such a system. According to Jupiter Research (August

2004), global m-commerce revenues are projected to be $88 billion by 2009. According to IDC and Jupiter Media Metrix), the US revenue for m-commerce is expected to be $58.4 billion in 2007.

Customize Product/Service Optimally for Customers Worldwide
Customers around the world differ in tastes, preferences, and may be bound by certain country based regulations, such as cars must have a steering wheel on the right hand side in India. Company websites should provide the capabilities to design and deliver customized products and services. Customization is important to flourish and stay in business.

FUTURE TRENDS

What is next in the world of e-commerce? In this section, we provide a glimpse into the future.

1. Young job hunters are starting to make a video clip part of their job application, sometimes even posting them on sites like Google Inc.'s YouTube and Google Video. Jobster.com, a web site for job seekers, is exploring the possibility of enabling users to add short video clips to online member profiles. (Athavaley, 2006)

2. The underlines in articles such as FoxNews.com are not for emphasis -- they are clues that those words were doubling as advertisements. When readers moved their cursors over the underlined words, a pop-up advertisement would appear, obscuring some of the text of the article. That marks a departure from a long-observed tradition in the print medium of keeping editorial content separate from advertising. (Kesomodel and Angwin, 2006).

3. Just as Microsoft Corporation is about to roll out the latest version of its cash-cow Office applications, Google Inc. is increasing its efforts to win away some of the customers Microsoft is targeting. Google's latest move is a plan to bundle its existing word-processing and spreadsheet offerings under the name Google Docs and Spreadsheets and more tightly weave them together. The services are available free, but offer more-limited functions than Microsoft's word processor and spreadsheet programs. (Delaney and Guth, 2006).

4. It makes some of us nervous that Google and other Web companies are building huge collections of data about our surfing habits. There are several ways of surfing anonymously; the most common involves going "stealth." The idea is to surf as you normally would, but mask the information that could be used to discern your identity. This means cloaking your Internet protocol address -- a unique number identifying a computer on the Web. That way, companies can't tell your PC searched on "avoiding taxes." (Kesmodel 2006).

5. Major Internet companies are moving to better meet the needs of the hundreds of thousands of blind people who regularly browse the Web. Blind Internet users generally use software that reads a description of a site's features aloud, sometimes in conjunction with some hardware that displays portions of the site in Braille. But navigating increasingly feature-heavy Web sites, whose messy and complex programming can be difficult for the software to translate, poses many problems. Internet companies are now launching new - and tidying up old - services for easier use by the blind. Google Inc. will launch Google Accessible Search, a search tool that ranks results based on the simplicity of the site's page layout. Pages with a large number of headings and lack extraneous images and text, two factors that make the page easier to read with a screen reader, will rank higher, saving blind Internet users the time of navigating to results their software won't be able to "read" (Vascellaro 2006).

6. The blogosphere contains an estimated 41 million blogs, and the number has been doubling every six months. How one should sort through all that content to find useful information is an increasingly vexing question. InterActiveCorp's Ask.com unveiled a new blog search engine based on information that users subscribe to through its popular Bloglines service. The new tool allows consumers to conduct keyword searches across 1.5 billion blog postings and more than 2.5 million so-called feeds, which is syndicated content from Web sites that is sent

to subscribers. Ask.com's new blog search, which is available through blogsearch.ask.com and also through Bloglines.com, aims to let consumers sift through mountains of material by creating its index from member subscriptions, which includes content from mainstream media sites like MSNBC Entertainment, popular blogs like Instapundit.com, and niche sites like CrazyAuntPurl.com, a blog on knitting. The new blog search engine Sphere.com hopes to attract mainstream users by displaying media such as photos and podcasts along with its search results. At the same time, blog sites like Feedster Inc. and Technorati Inc. are rethinking how they search blogs, in some cases trying to make the process more closely resemble a standard Web search by developing new ways to calculate relevancy and new tools for helping users sort the content themselves. (Vascellaro – Blogs, 2006).

7. Web search engines rely on complex algorithms and tens of thousands of computer servers to provide the best results. Some of the biggest search companies are turning to real live humans to boost their offerings. In December, 2005, Yahoo Inc. introduced an ad-supported service called Answers that allows regular consumers to answer questions posed by other Yahoo users. In May 2006, Microsoft Corp. disclosed plans to be release a similar service called Windows Live QnA. To query Yahoo's Web-based service, available at answers.yahoo.com, a user enters a question and is then able to view a list of answers as other users enter them. Consumers can also search through past questions and answers and forward them to friends. The companies believe that the user-submitted answers will improve the quality of their search services, tapping knowledge and opinions not easily accessed otherwise, though they acknowledge that some users may submit wrong or misleading responses. Yahoo and Microsoft both hope that over time the services will help increase their shares of the multibillion-dollar search market. Yahoo says its search-market share in Taiwan rose significantly from the end of 2004 to the end of 2005 in part as a result of an answers service it released there in 2004. (Delaney 2006).

CONCLUSIONS AND SUMMARY

This chapter focused on the emergence and evolution of Internet since the late 1980s. Internet has brought a revolution in the way we communicate with one another, access information, ask questions, get answers, learn about products and services, and even conduct global transactions. The chapter provided Internet and e-commerce statistics to highlight the exponential explosion of Internet and to create awareness of Global Digital Divide. The scope of e-commerce encompasses two-way transactions between businesses, customers (citizens), government, and non-governmental not-for-profit organizations. In terms of classifications for business models, the broad classification is: Traditional, Internet-based, and Hybrid. The chapter also provided a classification framework for B2C e-commerce business models and also for B2B business models. The next section articulated a framework to help in addressing global e-commerce challenges. The framework was elaborated by describing the four primary barriers to global e-commerce: cultural, administrative (legal), geographic and economic (regulatory); and then the four phases of Customer Service Life Cycle. Towards the end of the chapter, factors critical to the success of global e-commerce were described, along with some future trends for e-commerce.

MINICASE

Breaking Barriers for Global Electronic Commerce

Pierre Lang Europe

Pierre Lang Europe (pierrelang.com) sells designer jewelry throughout Western Europe. Its traditional business model was to sell earrings, pendants, necklaces, and other jewelry through the firm's 5500 sales representatives. When the company decided to expand into Eastern Europe, it decided to change its business model along with the underlying information systems and the business processes.

Pierre Lang knew it was losing business because it was unable to keep track of customers and it did not have direct contact with them. If sales representatives left the company for any reason, they would take their customers with them. The company wanted more than one time sales from its customers - it wanted lasting customer relationships that provided customer support for any concerns and that resulted in repeat sales.

Like many companies expanding globally, Pierre Lang also anticipated that this expansion could double its revenue and order volume. The company needed better information about its finances, improved control of its order process, and a system that could handle the multiple legal and language requirements of doing business in many different countries.

Pierre Lang selected mySAP after evaluating several competing solutions. Installation began in July, 2003, early rollout projects were in place by November, and financial and controlling capabilities were live in all company locations in January 2004.

Today, Pierre Lang uses country specific versions of mySAP to handle invoicing, tax, language, and fiscal issues. France, for example, has unique requirements for tracking the import and export of gold and silver -- they had to deal with all the tax issues which vary from country to country, since there are no homogeneous tax systems in Europe.

Pierre Lang expects to increase the accuracy of its information and eliminate the need for manual transfers of tax data to develop reports. Executives also anticipate decreased inventory costs through improved material disposition as well as better information about sales efforts and costs that will lead to improved forecasting and planning.

Northwest Airlines-Ion Global

Ion Global has worked with Northwest Airlines - the world's fifth largest airline - since 1998. Ion Global built the company's first Asian language web sites covering 6 languages and 14 countries, based on English language templates provided by Northwest.

- In 2001, a user-friendly two-stage CMS was devised for Asian-based marketing managers to publish English, Chinese, Korean and Thai content to a server-farm in Minneapolis.
- In 2002, a translation repository was developed to enable Northwest to flexibly manage the content translation/publishing for its online services.
- In 2003, an n-stage multi-lingual content approval mechanism was created- the first of its kind in the world - to help the airline work more effectively with its partners across time zones, and to speed its time to market for promotional offers.
- In 2003 Northwest refreshed its brand, necessitating a major overhaul of everything that had been done until then, and Ion Global rolled out a dedicated travel agents' web site.

Tourism Australia-Ion Global

Tourism Australia is the Australian statutory authority responsible for increasing tourism to and within Australia. While much of its effort is spent building consumer led demand, B2C marketing to global corporate clients - whereby companies send groups of employees overseas as an incentive or for team building - is a growing segment. Tourism Australia approached Ion Global to provide e-mail marketing services including design, tracking, copywriting, translations and database management. Ion Global provided Tourism Australia with a branded version of its *tntmail* e-mail marketing platform for database management, campaign management and multi-lingual WYSIWYG editing of B2C, B2B and media e-mail campaigns. Continuous monitoring of the success of the campaigns enables Tourism Australia to increase the relevance of each issue of its newsletters in Korean, Thai, Simplified Chinese, Traditional Chinese and English, and ultimately attract more visitors to Australia.

Source: Ion Global website accessed on January 7, 2007

Discussion Questions
1. Why did Pierre Lang Europe change its business model when it decided to enter the East Europe market?
2. What features of mySAP did Pierre Lang implement to be successful in East Europe?
3. How did Ion Global help Tourism-Australia?
4. What language related features were implemented on Northwest Airline's website by Ion Global?

KEY TERMS
1-Click Ordering
3-Click rule
ARPANET
B2B
B2C
B2G
CAGE (barriers to global e-commerce)
Customer Service Life Cycle (CLSC)
Digital Divide
e-Marketplaces
HTTP
Hybrid Retailers
Intellectual Property
Internet Penetration Rate
IPv4/IPv6
Meta-search engines
Micropayments
Maintenance, Repair, and Operations (MROs)
NGO2C
Portal
Reverse Auction
Spidering

STUDY QUESTIONS

1. Critique the assumption: "Technology is the answer to all business problems."

2. The movie Field of Dreams' maxim, "if you build it, they will come," may not be appropriate for developing a successful Internet retail business. Discuss what an entrepreneur may have to do to build an e-commerce site besides setting up a website?

3. In global e-commerce, history, customs, culture and habits play an important role. Humor often is an effective advertising technique to draw attention to a product or service. Give three examples where a humorous advertisement in one culture is considered off-limits or offensive in another culture.

4. "Worldwide E-Commerce: It's More Than A Web Site," quips a headline in Information Week on May 8, 2000. Discuss the issues to consider and how to resolve them in fulfilling retail sales to overseas customers.

5. Critique the assumption: "All of the industry leaders and gurus are on the e-business bandwagon; if it's good for GE, it must be good for us."

6. Select two once popular companies during the dot.com boom that are no longer in existence due to bankruptcy or business failure. Discuss what they should have done differently to survive or succeed.

7. The four phases and 13 sub-phases of Customer Service Life Cycle are named from customer perspective. What would you name them from merchant/seller perspective?

8. Visit as many websites of Fortune 500 companies as your time permits and track the proportion of companies that provide information in languages other than English. Also, note the importance of non-U.S. activities in overall operations of the firm. Write a short paragraph reflecting on your observations.

REFERENCES

Athavely, Anjali, "Posting Your Resume on the YouTube," Wall Street Journal, December 6, 2006.

Bingi. Prasad, "Societal Application of Information Technologies," Journal of Information Technology Case and Application Research, (8:4), 2006, pp. 1-5.

Brynjolfsson, Erik and Smith, Michael D., "Frictionless Commerce? A Comparison of Internet and Conventional Retailers," Management Science, (46:4), April 2000, pp. 563-585.

Bruce Clay, Inc. (2006) http://www.bruceclay.com/branding/web_email.htm accessed on February 4

Cenfetelli, Ronald T. and Benbasat Izak, "Measuring the e-Commerce Customer Service Life Cycle," Proceedings of the ECIS 2002 conference, June 6–8, 2002, Gdańsk, Poland, Pages 696-705.

Census Bureau (2006), Department of Commerce (http://www.census.gov/mrts/www/data/pdf/06Q1.pdf , accessed on July 19, 2006)

Crocket, R. (2000). No Plastic? No Problem, Business Week E.Biz, 23 October 2000:18.

Deitel, H.M., Deitel, P.J., and Steinbuhler, K. (2001). E-Business and e-Commerce for Managers. Prentice Hall.

Delaney, Kevin J., "Search Engines Find a Role for Humans," May 11, 2006.

Delaney, Kevin J. and Guth Robert A., "Google's Free Web Services Will Vie With Microsoft Office," The Wall Street Journal, October 11, 2006,

DesSantos, R. L. (2006) http://dossantos.cbpa.louisville.edu/courses/Imba/records/secure/ Internet-Strategy. Pp. 287 and accessed on January 31, 2007

Dewan, Rajiv, Jing, Bing, and Seidmann, Abraham, "Adoption of Internet-based Product Customization and Pricing Strategies," Journal of Management Information Systems (JMIS), (17:2), Fall 2000, pp. 9-28.

DoubleClick.com. (2006) accessed from (http://www.doubleclick.com/us/knowledge_central/ documents/RESEARCH/dc_decaderinonline_0504.pdf, on January 14, 2007

Dubie, D., "Going Global" *eBusinessIQ,* March 13, 2003, www.knowledgeiq.com/news/208-knowledgeiq_news.html (accessed April, 2004).

Einhorn, Bruce, "Search Engines Censured for Censorship.Authors: *Business Week Online;* 8/11/2006, pp. 9.

Ghemawat, P., "Distance Still Matters: The Hard Reality of Global Expansion," *Harvard Business Review,* September 2001, pp 137-147.

Goldman Sachs Group, "Glodman Sachs Reports on Worldwide B2B Commerce," Godman Sachs report, February 15, 2001.

Hong, Weiyin, Thong, James Y.L. and Tam Kar Yan, "The Effect of Information Format and shopping Task on Consumers' Online Shopping Behavior: A Cognitive Fit Perspective," JMIS, (21:3), Winter 2004-05.

Internet Retailer (2006), Top 500 Guide to Retail Web Sites
   http://www.internetretailer.com/article.asp?id=18747.

Ives, B. and Mason, R., (1990) "Can Information Technology Revitalize Your Customer Service?" Academy of Management Executive (4:4), pp. 52-69.

Kaufman, Leslie (1999). Playing Catch-Up at the On-Line Mall, *The New York Times*, February 21, 1999.

Kesmodel, David, "It's Easy to Complain About Web Privacy, A Lot Harder to Act," The Wall Street Journal, September 13, 2006.

Kesmodel, David and Angwin, Julia, "E-Commerce Is It News...or Is It an Ad?," The Wall Street Journal, November 27, 2006.

Lagon, O. (2000). Culturally Correct Site Design, *Webtechiques*, September 2000:51.

McFarland, Sofia (2001). B2B Squeezed, The Wall Street Journal, 02-12-01, R28.

Mehrotra, P., "Dotcoms Back with a Bang," Cyberzest.com, March 2001.

Mullen, T. (2000). Service Aids Selling to Europeans, *Internet Week* 17 July, 2000: 13.

Pearl, Daniel (2001). Lost in the Translation. *The Wall Street Journal*, 02-12-01, R12.

Sang-Pilhan, J. and Shavitt S., "Individualism-Collectivism in Persuasive Appeals," Journal of Experimental Social Psychology, ISSN 0022-1031, (30:4), 1994, pp 326-350.

Tapper, S. (2000). Is Globalization Right for You? *Webtechniques*, September 2000:26.

The Net Effect (2007), http://www.the-net-effect.com/articles/multiculture.html. Accessed on 1-21-07

Turban, Efraim, King, David, Viehland, Dennis, and Lee, Jae, *Electronic Commerce: A Managerial Perspective,* Pearson/Prentice Hall, 2006.

Vascellaro Jessica E., "Web Sites Improve Service for Blind People," The Wall Street Journal, July 20, 2006.

Vascellaro, Jessica E., "New Tools for Searching Blogs," The Wall Street Journal, June 01, 2006.

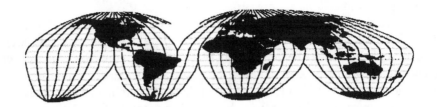

Diffusion of E-Commerce
in Several Economic Regions of the World

Prashant Palvia
Praveen Pinjani
The University of North Carolina at Greensboro, USA

CHAPTER SUMMARY

E-commerce is one of the most visible examples of the way in which Information and Communication Technologies (ICT) can contribute to economic growth. It helps countries improve trade efficiency and facilitates the integration of developing countries into the global economy. Electronic commerce has fundamentally changed the way business is conducted around the world. The importance of e-commerce adoption and the associated socio-economic impact on various countries has been widely acknowledged. There is evidence that countries that are at the forefront of the e-commerce revolution have benefited immensely. The commercialization of the Internet and World Wide Web (WWW) has driven electronic commerce to become one of the most important mechanisms for facilitating the sharing of business information between organizations, consumers, and business partners. The objective of this chapter is to understand B2C e-commerce diffusion and the underlying infrastructural factors in six important economies of the world: USA, Germany, and the emerging BRIC countries, i.e., Brazil, Russia, India and China. The chapter explores the current status of e-commerce in these countries, current initiatives underway and future trends that can lead to sustained national and economic growth.

INTRODUCTION

The growth, integration, and diffusion of information technology and communications are changing our society and economy. Today, computers and electronic devices increasingly communicate and interact directly with other devices over a variety of networks, such as the Internet. They are able to foster innovation and improve productivity. They can reduce transaction costs and make available in mere seconds a rich store of global knowledge (Ecommerce and Development Report, 2004). ICT and globalization have combined to create a fundamentally new economic and social landscape with borderless states. The impact of ICT on the performance of firms and industries and competitiveness is achieved through increased information flows, resulting in knowledge transfer as well as an improved organization.

Electronic commerce or simply E-commerce is one of the most visible examples of the way in which ICT can contribute to economic growth. E-commerce helps countries improve trade efficiencies and facilitates the integration of developing countries into the global economy. The importance of e-commerce adoption and the associated socio-economic impact in various countries has been widely acknowledged (Ngai and Wat, 2002). There is evidence that countries that are at the forefront of e-commerce adoption have benefited immensely from being the early adopters of such technologies. The commercialization of the Internet and World Wide Web (WWW) has driven electronic commerce to become one of the most important mechanisms for facilitating the sharing of business information between organizations, consumers, and business partners. It is estimated that by the year 2010, US e-commerce sales will reach $329 billion, growing at approximately 15% compound annual growth rate (Forrester Research, 2005). In the area of business-to-consumer (B2C) e-commerce, estimates of total online retail sales for 2002 were $43.5 billion for the United States, $28.3 billion for the European Union, $15 billion for the Asia-Oceania region, $2.3 billion for Latin America and as little as $4 million for Africa (UNCTAD Development and Globalization Report, 2004)

The objective of this chapter is to understand and analyze e-commerce diffusion and the underlying infrastructural factors in six countries of the world: Brazil, China, Germany, India, Russia and USA. These countries were selected as they represent some of the most powerful economic regions of the world. Besides USA and Germany, Brazil, Russia, India and China are collectively referred to as the BRIC countries. It is widely recognized that the BRIC countries are rapidly emerging as the strongest economies of the world. The chapter explores not only the current status of e-commerce in these countries but also current initiatives underway and future trends that can lead to national and economic growth.

E-COMMERCE AND NATIONAL INFRASTRUCTURE

Electronic commerce is a catchall term that embraces a complex amalgam of technologies, infrastructures, processes, and products which enable sales and related processes over electronic networks. It brings together whole industries and narrow applications, producers and users, information exchange and economic activity into a global marketplace called the Internet. There is no universal definition of electronic commerce because the Internet marketplace and its participants are so numerous and their intricate relationships are evolving so rapidly (Ngai and Wat, 2002). A broad definition offered by Turban et al. (2004) states that electronic commerce describes the process of buying, selling, transferring, or exchanging products, services, and/or information via computer networks. Its main components are business-to-business (B2B) and business-to-consumer (B2C) applications. In this chapter, we focus on B2C e-commerce.

Electronic commerce as it has evolved today requires several components. In a framework proposed by Turban et al. (2004), there are three layered functionalities needed for e-commerce. The bottom one is for the technology infrastructure that includes common business services, messaging and information distribution, multimedia content and network publishing, network facilities, and interfacing. The middle functionality includes support services such as logistics, payments, content, and security. The top functionality has applications such as direct marketing, e-government, auctions, e-purchasing, online banking, etc.

The infrastructure itself can be viewed as having several components. The *technological infrastructure* is needed to create an Internet marketplace. Numerous technologies are required, e.g., telecommunication systems including cable, satellite, or other Internet backbone; Internet service providers (ISPs) to connect market participants to that backbone; and end-user devices such as PCs, TVs, and mobile telephones. The *process infrastructure* is needed to connect the Internet marketplace to the traditional marketplace. This infrastructure makes payment over the Internet possible (through credit, debit, or Smart cards, or through online currencies). It also makes possible the distribution and delivery of these products. The *infrastructure of protocols, laws, and regulations* affects the conduct of business engaged in electronic commerce, as well as the relationships between businesses, consumers, and government. Examples include technical communications and interconnectivity standards; the legality and modality of digital signatures, certification, and encryption; and disclosure, privacy, and content regulations.

In his seminal article, Zwass (1996) proposed a framework capturing many of the elements discussed above. It comprises of seven levels grouped into three general layers. The three layers are: e-commerce infrastructure (including physical, network, and hypermedia functionalities), e-commerce services (including secure messaging and enabling services), and products and structures (including products, systems, electronic markets, and hierarchies).

One of the best ways to understand global electronic commerce is to consider the elements of its infrastructure, its impact on the traditional marketplace, and the continuum of ways in which electronic commerce is manifested. This approach shows clearly how electronic commerce is intricately woven into the fabric of domestic economic activity and international trade. Electronic commerce and its related activities over the Internet can be the engines that improve domestic economic well-being through liberalization of domestic services, more rapid integration into globalization of production, and leap-frogging of available technology. This approach to studying e-commerce diffusion comes from a holistic evaluation of a country or region's infrastructural preparedness to engage in Internet and e-commerce activities (Okoli and Mbarika 2003). In that light, Wolcott, et al. (2001) presented the Global Diffusion of the Internet (GDI) framework to investigate the spread of the Internet into countries around the world. The GDI framework has six dimensions: connectivity infrastructure, geographical dispersion, organizational infrastructure, pervasiveness, sectoral absorption, and sophistication of use.

The GDI framework examines the Internet in general, rather than focusing specifically on electronic commerce. Therefore, it is helpful to further delineate the components of infrastructure identified in the above frameworks, and enhance it with additional elements specific to e-commerce diffusion at the country level. An enhanced model was proposed by Travica (2002) that integrated the various aspects of physical, cultural, economic and legal infrastructure that are necessary to support successful diffusion. This model will be described next and will serve as the basis for assessing the e-commerce readiness of the six countries mentioned earlier.

AN E-COMMERCE ADOPTION MODEL

The model of business-to-consumer (B2C) e-commerce diffusion presented by Travica (2002) is shown in Figure 1. The model reflects the conditions for developing e-commerce in the countries that were early entrants, such as the United States and Western European countries. Travica signified the origins of the model in correspondence with the generic trade cycles proposed by Whiteley (1999). It was observed that e-commerce in developed countries has replicated this cycle with some modifications with regard to time, technological conditions for completing electronic trading, dimension of economic evolution, cultural conditions, and division of delivery into transportation and delivery.

The model has six layers. The *transportation layer* at the bottom of the pyramid concerns basic infrastructure to move goods (e.g., roads, air, railroad, etc.). B2C commerce expands the marketplace and therefore necessitates more frequent transportation with less regular spatial and temporal patterns. Consequently, the transportation infrastructure in the country adopting e-commerce needs to be supportive of these changes. In addition, the safety of the routes requirement needs to be satisfied.

The *delivery layer* builds on transportation and needs to be reliable, efficient and supportive of the same changes that e-commerce imposes on transportation. Since e-commerce can open up the global marketplace to customers and bring even the most remote customer to this marketplace, crucial is the capability of the delivery infrastructure to support significant fluctuations in geographical delivery patterns. The impact of increased pressure on a global supply chain with increase in e-commerce requires a competitive delivery service which becomes indispensable in order fulfillment.

The *telecommunication layer* refers to the pervasive, modern, secure, and affordable telecommunication channels that are the key to e-commerce, because the marketplace is created through telecommunications and information systems. Social processes that have coincided with these conditions are deregulation and privatization.

A *software industry* capable of supporting standard e-commerce applications is needed for e-commerce. Minimally, a domestic software industry needs to be capable of adopting software imports and maintaining them. For e-commerce to be successful, a country needs the personnel and computer equipment (hardware and software) to build and maintain Internet applications. In addition, in many developing countries, technical experts from the West are preferred for maintaining computer systems; such dependency may hinder the development of necessary expertise among nationals (Okoli and Mbarika, 2003).

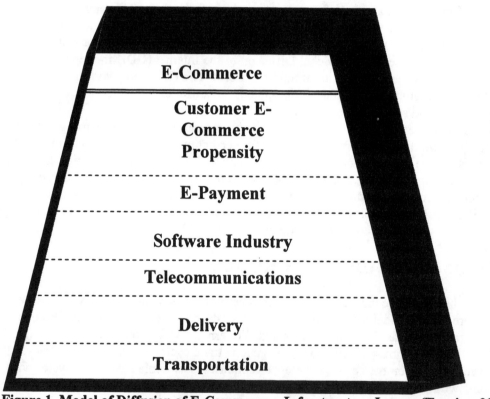

Figure 1. Model of Diffusion of E-Commerce – Infrastructure Layers (Travica, 2002)

E-payment is a necessary link in the trade cycle of e-commerce and so an indispensable infrastructure layer. E-payment involves three players – the buyer, the seller, and the financial institution. The buyer must be willing to make remote payment, the creditor (financial institution) must allow for safe transactions, and the seller should provide various remote options for payment. Credit card payments have become the *de facto* standard for e-commerce implementation because they can be electronically transmitted and verified. Other options also exist, for example: PayPal, pre-paid cards and direct bank transfers.

People's beliefs and values, ingrained by their cultural context, significantly affect their thinking and perspective, and hence their approach to using technology (Straub et al., 2002). A *cultural layer* at the top of the pyramid captures these issues. One of the aspects of e-commerce that is most taken for granted is the consumer behavior associated with shopping online and making purchases based on the information obtained from a website (Okoli and Mbarika, 2003). In general, trust issues loom large in the context of e-commerce. In the developed countries of the West, e-commerce took off rapidly because consumers were already used to making purchases from non-traditional remote mediums, like catalog marketing. They were accustomed to making a trust decision based on the information presented and ordering items that the merchant would deliver after several days. Furthermore, the existence of standardized goods and services that relieve the customers of the need to inspect these in person, ferments a culture of trust between the vendors and the customers. Table 1 portrays the diffusion conditions required under each infrastructure layer of e-commerce.

Infrastructure Layer	Diffusion Condition
Transportation	• Diverse safe means • Functionally catering to delivery needs
Delivery	• Dependable post service • Alternative delivery service • Absolute building addressing • Broader reach • Increased volumes • Irregular pattern
Telecommunications	• Broad availability of telephone and internet access • Faster and secure internet lines • Deregulation and privatization • Affordable internet access
Software Industry	• Support to diverse foreign and own software products for e-commerce
E-Payment	• Capabilities for and adoption of non-cash payments • Credit card culture • Secure telecommunications • Software industry support • Customer trust in financial institutions
Customer E-Commerce Propensity	• Remote ordering, payment and customer support • Standard quality assurance • Adoption of email communication

Table 1. Infrastructural conditions for E-Commerce

METHODOLOGY

In this chapter, Travica's model of e-commerce diffusion has been used to assess the diffusion of e-commerce in six countries: Brazil, China, India, Germany, Russia, and the United States of America (USA). These countries were selected as they represent some of the most powerful economic regions of the world. USA and Germany represent the strata of countries which are highly developed economically and boast high rates of e-commerce adoption. Currently, Brazil, Russia, India and China are collectively referred to as the BRIC countries. The BRIC countries are rapidly emerging as the strongest economies of the world. India and China have huge middle classes which have the ability to engage in many e-commerce activities. Russia and Brazil show promise in terms of their economic development but are faced with many obstacles in effective e-commerce adoption.

In most of the earlier studies of this type, a major weakness has been the inadequacy and availability of good statistical data. Some of the most serious problems cited in the literature have been the availability of good data from a single source that conveys a shared and common meaning (Ein-Dor et. al., 2004). To overcome this weakness, we utilized data from single sources wherever possible, like E-Commerce and Development Reports 2001, 2002, 2003, & 2004, World Fact Book 2004, and Forrester and Gartner Research Reports. Data was gathered and analyzed for the various infrastructure layers of the six selected countries.

In order to place the country results in perspective, Table 2 provides some important characteristics of the six countries including population, number of PCs, phone land lines, cell phones, and Internet users. Table 2 provides a clear indication of the technology infrastructure, penetration, and usage in each country. Table 3, on the other hand, provides the number of telephone lines, which is a rough surrogate measure of efficiency in technology deployment.

Country	Popu-lation (millions in 2005)	Cell phone users (millions in 2005)	Cell phone users per 100	Main telephone lines (millions in 2005)	Main tele-phone lines/ 100	Internet Users millions in 2005	Internet Users per 100	Personal Computers – PCs (millions in 2004)	PCs per 100
Brazil	184.28	86.21	46.78	42.38	23.00	25.90	14.05	19.35	10.71
China	1,313.97	393.43	29.94	350.43	26.67	111.00	8.45	52.99	4.08
Germany	82.52	79.20	95.98	55.05	66.71	48.72	59.05	40.00	48.48
India	1,095.35	76.00	6.94	48.84	4.46	50.60	4.62	13.03	1.21
Russia	142.89	120.00	83.98	40.10	28.06	23.70	16.59	19.01	13.18
USA	298.44	201.65	67.57	177.95	59.62	205.33	68.80	223.81	76.21

Table 2. Technology Penetration in Six Countries (Sources: CIA fact book, http://www.teleco.com.br/en/en_estatis.asp, http://www.internetworldstats.com/top20.htm, http://www.itu.int/ITU-D/ict/statistics/, http://64.233.187.104, http://www.itu.int/ITU-D/ict/publications/wti2004-05/index.html)

Country	Main Telephone Lines (millions in 2000)	Number of Employees (in 2000)	Lines per employee (in 2000)
Brazil	30.93	196,707	157.22
China	144.83	912,711	158.68
Germany	50.22	239,006	210.12
India	32.44	516,745	62.77
Russia	32.07	427,828	74.96
USA	192.51	1,118,221	172.16

Table 3. Efficiency in Technology Deployment (Source: http://humandevelopment.bu.edu/dev_indicators)

COUNTRY SPECIFIC STUDIES

Brazil

Brazil is the largest country in South America – it shares boundaries with all other Latin American countries except Chile and Ecuador. It is the most economically developed country in South America and has diplomatic and trading relations with almost every country in the world. It is among the ten largest economies in the world, ranking at the ninth position, and stands fifth in terms of population and territorial size (Wikipedia, Brazil).

Since the beginning of the 1990s, Brazilian markets for goods and services have become increasingly liberalized. Tariff and non-tariff barriers have been lowered. Inflation rates declined from three digits in 1993 to one in 2000, as a result of the Plan Real, a macroeconomic stabilization plan. Restrictions on foreign direct investment that existed in sectors like banking, public services and mining have been relaxed (Tigre, 2001).

There is relatively little agreement on the data available about the size of the e-commerce market in Latin America. In 2000, online retailing in Latin America reached US$ 263 million according to the IDC, and US $580 million according to The Boston Consulting Group (BCG). As per BCG, Brazil continues to be the largest online market in Latin America, accounting for US $300 million in revenues and just over half of the entire market. The Mexican and Argentinean markets, however, have grown out of their nascent stages and in 2006 have 17 million and 10 million Internet users, respectively (internetworldstats.com). Brazil has even a higher number of Internet users, at 26 million. It represents more than 50% of the Latin American online market, with more people online than any other country in the region. However, the huge income disparities and the technological divide mean that e-commerce has not permeated into the masses and is restricted to a small percentage of the population. Much of the online revenues come from the B2B sector.

Brazil had 184 million inhabitants in 2005. More than 80 percent of its population is living in cities, ten of which have more than one million inhabitants. The population is predominantly young, with 30 percent of the population under 15 years of age, and 49 percent aged 24 or younger. These factors may play a positive role in Internet diffusion.

In terms of wealth and income distribution, Brazil ranks third in the Americas in GDP value. However, in per capita terms, Brazil falls behind the top five wealthiest countries in Latin America. Also, it presents one of the most skewed income distributions in the Americas. While the share of income of the richest 20 percent of the population was 63.8 percent, the poorest 20 percent earned only 2.5 percent (International Telecommunication Union, 2001).

As per The World Factbook (2006), as per 2005 estimates, the GDP of Brazil is at 1.556 trillion USD and per capita GDP stands at 8400 USD. As elsewhere in the Americas, the Brazilian sector of distribution of employment shows an increasing role of the services sector. About 50 percent of the labor force works in services, 14 percent in industry and about 20 percent in agriculture. The industrial sector produces a wide range of products for the domestic market and for export, including consumer goods, intermediate goods, and capital goods.

The six infrastructure layers for Brazil are described below and summarized in Table 4. Each layer is given a (subjective) rating by the authors on a 1-5 scale, where 5 represents the most positive rating, 3 an average rating, and 1 the most negative rating.

Transportation: The transport system in Brazil is heavily dependent on roads. While other modes received little investment in the past four decades, government attention was directed to integrate the country through roads. This policy is often referred to as a driving force behind the development of the automobile industry. However, since the 1980s the investment in roads faded, as stabilization policies became a priority. The concentration of the population in cities will facilitate the delivery of goods ordered online, and in part compensate for the vast distances that separate Brazil's many urban centers.

To move non-perishable cargo over long distances, rail is the second most important transportation mode in Brazil. Brazil's long coastline and vast waterways have not been fully exploited for transportation purposes. However, there is increasing investment into this sector and it is expected that low cost of water transportation will enhance its importance.

Delivery: The postal service in Brazil is efficient but slower as compared to some of the postal services in developed countries. The express door-to-door service in Brazil is called SEDEX and operates from most of the main post offices. SEDEX is available at all Brazilian post offices. The service provides reliable 1-2 day delivery. Brazil lacks in this aspect, although the post office department is upgrading its system and providing online tracking of shipments, but the efficiency and reliability of the system cannot be compared to systems in developed countries.

<u>Telecommunications:</u> Liberalization of the public telecommunication markets in Brazil has not only enabled new players to enter the market, but has also encouraged the development of new ways of buying and selling. New carriers are bypassing the established landline method of connecting calls between telecommunication carriers in major cities and are increasingly using cellular services

Since 1998, when the Brazilian telecommunications infrastructure was privatized and the market re-regulated, telecom services have become one of the most attractive sectors for investments. ANATEL estimates that the total investment in telecom infrastructure reached US$ 9 billion in 2000, of which 77% was in fixed mainlines and 23% in mobile lines. As a consequence, the availability of telecom services has increased dramatically in a wide range of services. In the last four years, fixed line teledensity doubled while cellular subscribers quintupled. In per capita terms, Brazil is now on track with the Latin American average, both in fixed line and cellular phones. With 42.38 million main phone lines in use, and 25.90 million Internet users (World Factbook, 2006), Brazil is on its way to establish a strong telecommunication infrastructure required for e-commerce diffusion.

Infrastructure Layer	Diffusion Conditions in Brazil	Evaluation on 1-5 scale
Transportation	• 60% of cargo by roads • 95% of passenger circulation through roads • 250 billion USD worth flow of commerce • 3083 runways (2003 estimate) • Privatization of rail networks • 18235 miles of rail networks	4
Delivery	• 1-2 day delivery through SEDEX • Inefficient and unreliable postal system	2
Telecommunications	• Privatization and Liberalization • Changing pattern of ownership and sourcing of financing • High competition and low prices • 11.5/1000 subscribers in cable data dispersion	4
Software Industry	• Low computer diffusion • Advanced domestic industry • Government support through SOFTEX	3
E-Payment	• High percentage of online transactions • Increased use of credit cards	4
Consumer E-Commerce Propensity	• 200% growth levels in internet users • Only 10% of penetration level • Primarily service sector commerce • Strong government support	3

Table 4. E-Commerce Diffusion in Brazil

<u>Software Industry</u>: Since the early 1970s, Brazil has developed capabilities both in production and use of information technologies. Prior to liberalization in the early 1990s, Brazil had a larger and more technologically advanced domestic IT industry, which produced a wide range of systems, peripherals and even components. Despite setbacks, the country is one of the few developing countries with extensive technology capabilities in both hardware and software design and manufacturing. There are 800,000 computers with permanent Internet connections (hosts). These figures indicate that computer diffusion is high as compared to the country's level of development. However, other per capita indicators, such as computer diffusion – 36 PCs per 1,000 persons – fall behind other Latin American countries.

The Brazilian Software Export Program (SOFTEX 2000) was created in 1993 as a joint venture between the National Technology R&D Council of the Brazilian Ministry of Science and Technology and the United Nations Development Program (UNDP). A survey by the Brazilian software association (Abas) reports that Brazil's information technology market, which includes programming, equipment, telecommunications systems and data management, was worth US$ 11 billion in 2004 (Brazzilmag.com, 2005). The large Brazilian market offers opportunities for start-ups to target niche markets at home, as government programs actively support local entrepreneurs through export assistance and incubator programs. According to Dedrick et al. (2001), the fact that Brazil had a domestically-owned computer industry before liberalization meant that many professionals gained experience in financing, launching and managing their own companies.

<u>E-Payment</u>: The Government of Brazil and the Brazilian banks are proud to point out that they are the largest online banks outside the US. Sixty five percent of all transactions are online and major banks offer advanced e-banking services and m-banking services. The use of credit cards in Brazil has been growing at a fast pace since the early 1990s. Two factors were key driving forces to the boom – the liberalization of credit card use by Brazilians traveling in foreign countries, and the stabilization of the national currency, which improved the acceptance of credit cards by the retail sector. Brazilian consumers are now the largest users of credit cards in Latin America, and the country ranks eighth worldwide, with about 30 million cards issued and over one billion transactions per year. In 2000, overall purchases by credit cards reached US$ 26.5 billion, equivalent to 7% of total private domestic consumption in Brazil.

<u>Consumer E-Commerce Propensity</u>: As elsewhere in the Americas, the diffusion of e-commerce in Brazil has increased rapidly in the last two years. With approximately 25.9 million Internet users, Brazil has witnessed more than 200% growth in the five year period from 2000 to 2005. The striking figure is that while this is only 10% penetration level into the country, it represents almost 50% of the total online community in South America. An alternative way of evaluating Internet diffusion is the number of hosts in the country. This is more reliable information than the number of users, since it is based on registered domains rather than estimates. As per the World Factbook (2006), there are 4.39 million registered hosts with the .br domain.

Business-to-business is widely recognized as the most important sector for e-commerce. Firms are more likely to buy through the Internet than individuals since they traditionally shop at a distance using communications means such as telephone and fax. Excluding government transactions, approximately 90% of all e-commerce by value is conducted between businesses. Large enterprises have used Internet technologies to develop networks between their business operations.

The popularity of consumer-to-consumer auctions has surged dramatically, making it the largest category in the Latin American market, reaching US$ 192 million several years ago (Tigre, 2001). Their success can be attributed, in part, to the massive marketing campaigns and the fact that they do not require an elaborate delivery and payment infrastructure. The second largest market is computer hardware and software, accounting for US$ 72 million in sales. Financial services follow, generating US$ 61.5 million - a reflection of the aggressive moves by financial institutions; and books-music-video is the fourth-largest category, at US$ 59 million, representing a staggering 800% growth rate.

Support from the government in promoting e-commerce should also be accounted for in understanding the consumer's e-commerce propensity. The government continues to pursue its interests in e-commerce by offering tax reforms to reduce the burden for investing in e-commerce ventures. It has also formulated an e-government action plan to focus on increasing the access of information, offering government services online, and to implement an advanced telecommunications infrastructure.

In summary, Brazil's transportation, telecommunications, and e-payment systems are fairly good. However, its physical delivery systems are lacking. The software industry is not as advanced as the developed nations and the consumers' willingness to engage in e-commerce is limited and not pervasive.

China

China is geographically a vast country in Eastern Asia and has the highest population in the world (over 1.3 billion people) with a 0.59 percent population growth rate. China's real term GDP is 8.859 trillion USD, which has seen a significant annual increase of 9.9% over the last decade. The per capita GDP is 6800 USD with 53% contributed by industry, 32% by services and approximately 15% by agriculture. The country's economy has grown on an average about 8% per year for the last 2 decades. This growth has created huge demand for products, services and knowledge that has further fueled the economy and led to the growth if ICT and e-commerce.

For a country that is as vast, over-populated, regionally different, has multiple languages, and wide disparities in infrastructure, all this alloyed with complex and variable government controls, the conditions for diffusion of e-commerce have been improving surprisingly rapidly. The Chinese e-commerce market can be considered potentially one of the largest in the world, even though currently it is in the early stages of development. Even so, in 2000 there were close to 9 million computers connected to the Internet in China (CNNIC, 2001) and the number of users exceeded 111 million as per 2005 estimates (World Factbook, 2006). All of this growth occurred since 1996, and China is now considered one of the top five nations in terms of Internet use, and some experts predict that China is making strides towards having the second largest population of web surfers in the world. Clearly, this is a vast potential market which has yet to be tapped and exploited. Table 5 summarizes China's e-commerce infrastructural layers.

<u>Transportation</u>: Transportation and distribution in China are still not advanced. China boasts of the largest rail network in Asia, employing 2.2 million and operating over 43,435 miles of rail network. The complete rail system is under the monopoly of China's Ministry of Railways. The cost and speed of rail transport remains low and the quality is below standard when compared to western rail systems. In addition, China has 869,672 miles of highways and has 507 airports. The local government is also focusing on improving the water ways by developing and modernizing major ports for movement of goods to and from mainland China.

<u>Delivery</u>: The China Postal Bureau (CPB), remain the dominant monopoly in the Chinese Postal market and has 236 delivery centers linking more than 2300 cities and counties. The bureau offers most of the package and letter delivery services both offline and online. The presence of the international courier companies is there but they have to rely on local delivery companies to reach door-to-door. This has some effect on quality and reliability considerations being faced by international companies.

Infrastructure Layer	Diffusion Conditions in China	Evaluation on 1-5 scale
Transportation	• Largest Rail network in Asia • Monopolistic market • Mostly undeveloped transportation industry	2
Delivery	• Government controlled postal services • High presence of local delivery companies	3
Telecommunications	• Concentrated in urban areas • 40-50% penetration level in urban areas • High availability and growth in wireless sector	4
Software Industry	• Growth rate of greater then 20% • Major International outsourcing player • High rate of piracy in software market	4
E-Payment	• Lack of e-payment infrastructure • Advanced IT infrastructure • Low penetration of credit cards	2
Consumer E-Commerce Propensity	• Cautious and conservative consumers • 7.3 % diffusion rate • Potential for m-commerce • Strong government support	3

Table 5. E-Commerce Diffusion in China

<u>Telecommunications</u>: There have been wide disparities in the availability of telecom services throughout China. Many rural areas still do not have basic telephone services, whereas major cities and urban areas have access to broadband and digital communication media.

China has been rapidly building up its telecommunications infrastructure since the late 1980s. On average, more than 10 million telephone lines were added to China's telecom network each year in the last decade. Total telephone lines in China reached 180 million in 2001 and 311 million in 2004. While China's telephone penetration rate was only 0.3 per 100 capita in 1980, it rose to 26.67 in the year 2004. Many big cities and economically developed areas such as Beijing, Shanghai, and Guangdong have seen telephone penetration rates of 40-50%. The remote rural areas often lag behind with single-digit penetration rates.

China's wireless phone network has experienced an even higher growth rate than its landline network since the first TACS cellular phone system was installed in 1987. In July of 2001, China's 120.6 million mobile phone users made it the largest mobile communications market in the world, surpassing the 120.1 million users in the United States. Wireless phone users in China reached 145.2 million by the end of 2001 and 334 million by 2004.

<u>Software Industry</u>: China has identified its IT industry sector as the most significant driving force for economic growth since the 1980s, as well as for sustainable economic growth in the future. This is a consensus among government policy makers, industry executives, and academic researchers in China.

China's computer market is about USD 50 billion. The software component is registering annual sales of over USD 5 billion. The software industry has developed rapidly in recent years with an average annual growth of 30% in sales and 7 times growth in software export for the past five years. The software industry has already become a strategic industry for national economy and social development. China's high tech sector and potential for outsourcing ventures from developed countries is scheduled to grow by about 20% over the next few years and will be appropriate for the country's ecommerce diffusion conditions.

There are many small weak companies in China that compete on cost alone. Most firms are not at high levels of process maturity. Many of the largest firms are doing either systems integration, or a combination of products and systems integration. There is also activity in software that is embedded in consumer products and appliances. However, the software market is still fledging, extremely fragmented and suffers from high rate of piracy. The market is mainly made up of system software, application software, supporting software, and a small percentage of platform software and middleware.

E-Payment: The main form of settling transactions in China is still the traditional use of cash. There is no robust e-payment infrastructure. The Chinese consumers lack trust in advanced forms of transactional media like credit cards, online banking etc., although the banking/insurance sector has one of the most advanced IT infrastructures among the various sectors. This strong IT presence is aiding the diffusion of e-commerce within the banking and insurance sector. All of the large state banks have set up their own websites that are able to support online transactions and payments

Given the well-established IT infrastructure in the banking/insurance sector, significant e-commerce activities are expected to take place. The banking/insurance sector is traditionally regarded as a highly secure business with reliable and credibility. This should alleviate customers' concerns about conducting B2C transactions with banks and insurance companies. Still the absence of cross-bank and regional settlement services, security and the need for a standard protocol make e-payment difficult in China. In addition, procedures for obtaining credit cards or debit cards are very complex, rigid and more or less out of common Chinese's reach.

Customer E-Commerce Propensity: In general, Chinese consumers are more cautious and conservative than consumers in developed countries. Still, China continues to experience an expansion of its e-commerce industry. This is true both for B2C and for B2B sectors. China's B2C sector was forecasted to cross USD 1 billion by 2005. According to the World Factbook (2006), more than 111 million Chinese are using Internet, showing a staggering 317% growth between 2000 and 2005. China represents 31% of the Internet users and dominates in whole of Asia. In spite of this huge number, it still represents only 8.4% of the Chinese population. Some of this can be attributed to the intense digital divide between urban and rural areas in China.

The Chinese government is keen to promote the growth of the Internet for business in China and is planning to infuse substantial amount of investment in the coming years.

Mobile services are being increasingly utilized in China. Mobile subscribers have nearly doubled each year. About 35% of China's banking and insurance firms have already had mobile content or services available, which is much higher than the average of 21% among global banking and insurance firms. With the increase in the use of SMS and mobile technologies, m-commerce has a huge potential in China.

In summary, China's infrastructure was extremely poor before the 1980s compared to other nations. Significant expansion occurred in the past two decades, which makes China one of the largest technology infrastructures in the world. However, China's huge population drags the per capita share of almost every statistic of infrastructure to a very low level, close to that of most developing countries. Thus, there is great need and potential for its infrastructure to expand further.

Germany

Germany is located in the middle of Europe with a population of 82 million, which is the second largest in Europe. The German age distribution is somewhat lop-sided for the aged with 18% of the population over 65 years of age. This trend is expected to continue as the fertility rate is steadily declining. Being the third most technologically powerful economy, according to World Factbook

(2006), Germany reported a GDP of 2.5 trillion USD. This is equal to per capita GDP of 30,400 USD. Approximately, 70% of the GDP is contributed by the services sector, 28% by industry and only 1% by agriculture. The long term inflation rate has remained low, averaging 1.6% since 1994.

Germany has the third largest industry in the world and the largest in Europe. It exhibits somewhat contrasting forces for the growth of e-commerce (Table 6). On one hand, 82 million highly educated people squeezed into a comparatively small land create an enormous demand for adopting new technologies in order to increase ease and comfort of life; yet a nation which traditionally has had relatively high government regulatory levels, restricts certain amenities and general comforts that are widely practiced and accepted in numerous industrialized nations. Although, Germany has a very sound infrastructure, advanced telecommunications facilities, and a very competitive software industry, Internet penetration has not progressed at an advanced pace. But seeds of change are visible in the past few years. Worldwide, Germany belongs to the top group of countries with a high-quality telecommunications infrastructure, as well as high penetration and usage levels.

Transportation: Germany has a 28,544 miles long railroad network which is of high importance especially for the transport of passengers. Very high speed trains or intercity express trains with speeds up to 240 km/h on high speed rail routes connect all bigger cities. Germany has a high quality road network of municipal, regional, state and federal roads amounting to a total of 143055 miles. Its superb national *Autobahn* system of very well planned and designed roads permitting high-speed movement of vehicles is almost legendary. Germany has around 550 airports and 17 ports which aid in the movement of goods and passengers in its territorial boundaries.

Delivery: Based on the strong transportation backbone, the German postal sector with such major firms as German Parcel, UPS and Deutsche Post AG can provide a one day guarantee or even faster for all postal deliveries. Package delivery systems are very important for many e-commerce firms in both B2C and B2B applications. Such package delivery firms may become important, even strategic

Infrastructure Layer	Diffusion Conditions in Germany	Evaluation on 1-5 scale
Transportation	• 550 Airports • 17 ports • Advanced Rail network • Developed Road network	5
Delivery	• 1-day guarantee services • Presence of International carriers	5
Telecommunications	• High competition and low prices • Largest ISDN connection • 6/100 household have DSL connection	5
Software Industry	• Marked by dominant International players • Low presence in world market • Low PC penetration rates	3
E-Payment	• Low use of credit card • High transaction costs	2
Consumer E-Commerce Propensity	• 56% of penetration level • Primarily service sector commerce • Complicated ordering system and payment methods hinder growth • Strong government support	4

Table 6. E-Commerce Diffusion in Germany

partners of these firms as it is the only economical way to deliver packages reliably and timely. In addition, the German mail is one of the fastest in the world, capable of sending letters and packages throughout Germany and most of Europe within a day. There is also the presence of private delivery and courier services like UPS, FedEx, and DANZAS.

Telecommunication: Since 1998, the telephone customer can choose among different carriers for each call by call or pre-selection. Telecommunication prices have been falling over the last few years due to heavy competition in this market. Fast and cheap Internet access is becoming more widely available. Prices for national long distance connections declined over 90% in the last three years. The regulatory authority and the private carriers are working hard to break down the *de facto* last monopoly of the German Telecom. On October 10, 2001 a German court ordered German Telecom to open the local phone networks for its competitors. The telephone penetration is at 54.57 million main phone lines and 71.3 million cell phone users. The conventional telephone network in Germany is still growing but mobile connections are growing much faster.

Germany has more ISDN connections than any other country in the world, with 23.9 per 100 household (Federal Statistics Office Germany, 2005). For high speed Internet access, not only analog telephone lines or ISDN connections are available but also high speed (e.g., over DSL) connections which are getting more and more popular. Germany was among the first countries where DSL was available. With 7.5 million DSL connections, twelve of 100 households had DSL access, more than in any other country in Europe (OECD Report, 2005). Besides digital telecommunication technologies, German households are wired by cable television and can access the Internet via cable.

Software Industry: Germany is one of the biggest and most important IT markets in the world, but dominated by US vendors. With the exception of MNCs like SAP and Software AG, German software industry does not play a major role in the software market. Germany's diffusion rate for PCs per thousand is the highest in comparison to other large countries in Europe but still behind the penetration rate of the Scandinavian countries.

E-Payment: Cash is the most popular way of paying for goods, but debit cards and credit cards are also widespread. The most common credit card in Germany is the EuroCard – a cooperation partner of MasterCard. However, due to high transaction costs of credit cards for merchants and restaurants and the fact that debit cards are widespread, most customers pay with debit cards. Due to the relatively low penetration of credit cards in Germany, in comparison to other European countries, online payment with a credit card is also low. This hinders faster development of e-commerce, especially when online shops do not provide additional payment methods.

E-Commerce Propensity: With over 48.7 million Internet users and 56% penetration of Internet, Germany has the highest percentage of Internet users in Europe. The Internet is used primarily for information access. As such, the most often used services are e-mail, search engines and news channel and services. But the B2C e-commerce use is growing. As per the emarketer.com Europe ecommerce report (2004), about 47.9 % of all Internet users have had experiences in buying online in 2003.

Barriers for most customers were complicated ordering processes or uncomfortable payment methods and choices. When a customer does not have a credit card or is unwilling to provide credit card information for security reasons, transactions are not possible if the credit card is the only mode of payment that is offered. The most often used payment method in Germany is sending an invoice which is used by over 60% of online customers. In contrast, credit card payment is used only by 30% of customers (NFO, 2001). Germany is ahead in the use of online banking. Thirty seven percent of all Internet users conducted online banking. No other country in Western Europe is using online banking as often; the average of all European countries was 17 % (Gruner und Jahr Electronic Media Service 2001).

The financial sector in Germany offers programs together with the government for start-ups; existing enterprises offer a large variety of readily available low interest loans; and there are many government grants. These financial resources available from private and public funds are very attractive features for newly founded firms and young entrepreneurs in the e-commerce world.

Previous studies by leading research companies have shown that Germany could become the leading European country in e-commerce. In our analysis too, we found that most of the infrastructure layers are in place for development of e-commerce in Germany. If issues pertaining to privacy and safety are successfully resolved, e-commerce activities in Germany could be on a significant upward trend.

India

India is the second most populated country with slightly over a billion people on a land mass approximately one third of the size of US, located in the south part of Asian continent. India is not typical of most developing countries in that it has a sophisticated administrative and political structure, a well equipped government sector, developed transport and communication infrastructure, and a large supply of educated manpower. In spite of its industrial base, India remains a largely rural country, with about 70% of the population living outside metropolitan areas. Approximately 60% of the work force is in the agricultural sector (World Factbook, 2006).

India's GDP is about 3.61 trillion USD. But striking is the USD 3300 per capita income which reflects the huge income disparities between urban and rural areas and the impact of population growth on economic development. The GDP distribution is: 51% from the services sector, 17% from industrial and around 20% percent from the agriculture. India has a sophisticated industrial base that places it among the top industrialized nations of the world. However this is not reflected in its foreign trade – as exports account for less then 1% of world exports. The New Industrial Policy (NIP), put in place in 1991, reflected a greater willingness to let market forces shape economic decisions. As a result, foreign direct investment rose from $162 million in 1990 to $5.3 billion in 2004 (UNCTAD World Investment Report, 2005).

Electronic commerce is today a vital part of India's trade facilitation policy. As of year 2000, there were 5 million Internet users, whereas in 2005 there were 50 million depicting a growth rate of more than 600% over the period 2000-2005. Further, there are about 500 licensed ISPs in the country while the e-commerce market size according to the IDC report is estimated to be USD 1.75 billion, including both business to business (B2B) and business to consumer (B2C) sectors. Table 7 summarizes India's infrastructural conditions.

Transportation: In the past, India has focused more on its rail and road development. As per the World Factbook 2004, there are about 2,058,179 miles of highways in India. Still a large amount of population that lives in small distant towns and villages and is not connected to major highways and lacks logistical connectivity, could hamper the e-commerce development from reaching the masses of the country. Railways have been well developed with 39,146 miles of tracks and with more than one third of it electrified. Air transport in India has seen quite a surge post the liberalization of this sector in 1991. India has a total of 333 airports but the network is limited to urban areas and is not capable of reaching the masses. Inland water transport is available in few areas, sometimes seasonally but is unorganized and unreliable.

Delivery: The delivery system in India is fairly reliable for traditional mail deliveries, considering the vast complexity in geographical distribution of the population and an old and unreliable addressing system. The government operated and controlled postal department is old and marked with slow delivery speed and unreliability, but it still manages to unify the vast geographic boundaries of the country. International and national courier services are in abundant but still suffer from reach and reliability. In the modern age, India needs to make substantial improvements to its transportation infrastructure as well as overhaul its delivery infrastructure. The delivery system would require major upgrading and enhancement in order to handle the increased volume brought on my e-commerce.

Infrastructure Layer	Diffusion Conditions in India	Evaluation on 1-5 scale
Transportation	• Reforms starting to show positive signs • Large rural population still not connected • Airways limited to urban areas	3
Delivery	• Slow and unreliable local postal system • Presence of major international players	3
Telecommunications	• Emergence of private market players • Increase in wireless penetration	4
Software Industry	• High growth rate of IT and ITES sector • Major outsourcing vendor • Availability of skilled workforce • Low penetration in local organizations	4
E-Payment	• High growth rate in financial card industry • More competitive environment • Positive outlook on using cards for online	3
Consumer E-Commerce Propensity	• Strong government support • Adoption of international standards in laws and reforms • Some cultural constraints	3

Table 7. E-Commerce Diffusion in India

Telecommunications: All civil and commercial telecommunications in India, except for radio and television broadcasting, fall within the purview of the Ministry of Information Technology and the Telegraph Act of 1885. As a result of this Act, the Government of India held a total monopoly on all types of communication until the late 1990s; this monopoly included voice and data transmissions, domestic and international, and local and long distance. Under the National Telecommunications Policy of 1994, the Indian government introduced measures that for the first time permitted the private sector to supplement the government's telecommunications services. Through a rather involved bidding process, licenses were issued to a private carrier in each of the country's 20 telecommunications circles.

As per the World Factbook (2006), there are 67.28 million of main lines in use depicting about 6% teledensity. The penetration of cellular mobile phone is expected to continue to increase. At present, there are about 69 million cell phone users. With decline in prices and increase in competition, this rate is expected to increase substantially in the coming years. This signals immense scope for m-commerce initiatives in India. Currently, Internet growth in India is limited by low PC penetration, which in turn, is inhibited by the high prices of computer hardware.

Software Industry: As per NASSCOM (National Association of Software and Service Companies) reports, the Indian IT-ITES (IT and IT enabled services) industry is broadly categorized into IT services and software, ITES-BPO and hardware segments. The industry continues to chart remarkable double-digit growth with industry aggregate revenue in 2004-05 at about USD 28 billion, and expected to grow to USD 57 billion by 2008. The export of IT and IT-enabled services is expected to grow between 30-35 per cent in 2005-06. Nasscom has projected exports to grow 27-30% in 2006-07 to USD 29-31 billion, while the overall industry is expected to grow 25-28% to USD 36-38 billion. According to Nasscom President, the industry will reach the targeted $USD 60 billion in exports by 2010. In order to reach that level, the growth rate needs to be 26.3% as opposed 34.6% growth achieved between 2000-06. While each segment has witnessed consistent year-to-year growth, the share of hardware, as a percentage of the total industry revenue, has declined from 28.6% in 1999-2000 to an estimated 21.3% in 2004-05.

Offshore outsourcing continues to gain momentum, turning into a mainstream phenomenon. Key drivers of growth include the growing adoption of IT outsourcing and the rapid expansion in the scale and breadth of ITES-BPO offerings by Indian vendors. Many foreign companies are setting up shops in India because of the availability of skilled labor and a well educated, English speaking and less expensive technical workforce. Indian vendors successfully executed the offshore delivery model to achieve sustained growth in service exports and established India as the most preferred destination for global sourcing of services.

Despite of these impressive figures, software penetration in Indian organizations is relatively low. Although India is regarded as the world's software giant and other countries have emulated India's example and success in software exports, the Indian software industry has neither generated significant employment in Indian companies nor has it contributed to major reengineering of business processes. Particularly, smaller organizations are not able to leverage the potential of software for productivity improvements.

E-Payment: In India, retailing as it is known in USA, is emerging in recent years with a splurge of shopping malls. Also on the rise is the use of the credit card which until now had not evenly penetrated into the transaction market. There is a huge divide or disparity in credit card usage and acceptance between urban and rural areas.

The banking scenario has changed rapidly since the 1990s. The decade of 90s has witnessed a sea of change in the way banking is done in India. Technology has made tremendous impact in banking. 'Anywhere banking' and 'Anytime banking' have become reality. The financial sector now operates in a more competitive environment than before and mediates relatively large volume of international financial flows. In the wake of financial deregulation and global financial integration, the biggest challenge before the regulators is of avoiding instability in the financial system.

The year 2003 was bountiful for financial cards in India. As a result of the thriving economy, there was an increase in disposable income and a rise in consumer expenditure. As a result, financial cards witnessed robust growth. Specifically, in 2003, the number of financial cards in circulation increased by nearly 49% over 2002. In terms of transaction value, growth was 95% over the previous year. Consumers in India were not only more open to the possibility of owning a financial card but were also not averse to using the card for payment. Financial cards are still perceived as a status symbol contributing to their healthy performance.

Customer E-Commerce Propensity: In India, even though there is lot of exposure through media to international ways of life, consumers follow local market practices to a large extent. These practices are influenced by the diversity of languages, religion, and social customs within the country.

E-commerce transactions in India were expected to grow from USD 28 million in 1998-99 to USD 255.3 million in 2001, and to between USD 5.7 billion and USD 13.4 billion in the year 2008. Clearly, e-commerce was at a nascent stage in the early years. However, recently it seemed to have picked up steam. According to research conducted by Internet & Online Association of India, the e-commerce volume grew to USD 121 million in 2004-2005 and is expected to grow to 489 million by 2006-2007, an estimated 300%+ growth. India is expected to log the highest compounded annual growth rate (CAGR) of 83.7 percent among Asia-Pacific countries in e-commerce revenues between 2003-08, even exceeding the growth rate displayed by neighboring China in the five-year period, according to research firm IDC (Hindu Business Line 2004). As for demographic profiles, 25% of regular shoppers are in the 18-25 age group, 46% in the 26-35 age group and 18% in the 36-45 age group. Eighty five percent are males and 15% are females.

The Government of India has been pioneering in their approach to implement laws and reforms to boost the use of Internet and develop infrastructure for development of ICT in the country. Some of the formidable policies affecting the development of ICT infrastructure in the country have been The National Telecommunications Policy (1994), Inclusion in WTO (1995), The Telecom Regulatory Authority of India Act (1997), IT Action Plan (1998), New Internet Policy (1998), New Telecom Policy (1999), Information Technology Act (2000), The Communication Convergence Bill (2000), and several more.

These laws and reforms will help Indian companies and individuals to conduct business within the country as well as globally and compete with developed nations. These laws will further instill trust and ensure safeguards in Internet transactions. While the B2B transactions account for 90% of the total e-commerce in India, B2C transactions need to gear up to international standards by providing adequate infrastructure. In spite of progress made in recent years, B2C transactions continue to be hampered by cultural constraints as Indians in general tend to favor face-to-face contact in their shopping behavior.

Russia

Russia is potentially an attractive market for ICT services with its 150 million people, a technically sophisticated and inexpensive workforce, and abundant supply of natural resources. Despite this, limited purchasing power, a low penetration of computers and internet access, and a poor transportation and communication infrastructure, cause significant challenges for e-commerce development in this country.

Economic downturns, political turmoil, and a lack of sufficient foreign investment dominated Russia's attention in the 1990s, leaving little room for ICT development, as reflected in the nation's sixty-first rank in overall Readiness for the Networked World. The country's vast territories, poor-quality telephone lines especially in rural areas, and an inefficient legislative base, also make the process of national ICT development complex and challenging. Nonetheless, Russia's high literacy rate with strong academic and scientific base, in conjunction with sufficient foreign investment, could contribute to long-term economic activity and the evolution of the IT and telecommunications sectors. A decade after the implosion of the centrally planned Soviet Union in December 1991, Russia is still struggling to establish a modern market economy, modernize its industrial base, and maintain strong economic growth. The period 1992-98 was marked by a poor business climate, deterioration in already threadbare living standards, and failure to institute modern market reforms. Conditions improved markedly in 1999-2002, with annual output growing by an average 6% and with progress in structural reforms. Yet serious problems persist. Russia remains heavily dependent on export of commodities, particularly oil, natural gas, metals, and timber, which account for over 80% of exports, leaving the country vulnerable to swings in world prices.

As per the 2006 World Factbook, Russia has a GDP of USD 1.58 trillion and a per capita income of 11,100 USD. Services sector contributes almost 60 percent of this GDP and the remaining is contributed by industry at 35% and agriculture around 5%. The country is suffering from immense income disparities as more then 25% of the population is below poverty line and a growing economy is hampered by an 11% inflation rate.

Although the differences between Russia and most developing countries are profound in geopolitical status, culture, education levels, and natural endowments, Russia shares a salient problem with many emerging economies: shortage of hardware, software and adequate infrastructure. Despite the challenges, the potential for development of e-commerce in Russia is significant due to a number of factors. The most important is the availability of goods not only in developed regions but also rural and underdeveloped regions of the country. The infrastructural factors are discussed below and summarized in Table 8.

Infrastructure Layer	Diffusion Conditions in Russia	Evaluation on 1-5 scale
Transportation	• Well developed transportation system • Railways is prime mode of transportation • Well connected waterways system	5
Delivery	• Government controlled • Unreliable and poor service	2
Telecommunications	• Monopoly conditions • Increase in wireless penetration • High speed internet availability is low	3
Software Industry	• High PC market sales growth • Software is fastest growing industry • Abundance of skilled workforce	4
E-Payment	• Low credit card penetration • Adoption of creative methods for online transactions	3
Consumer E-Commerce Propensity	• Low internet penetration hinders growth • Low levels of trust • Computer hardware dominant shopping category	2

Table 8. E-Commerce Diffusion in Russia

Transportation: Russia's status of an economic power in the early decades has much to do with the existing infrastructure in the country. It is a country which has seen much development and is vastly endowed with developed and concrete infrastructure to build its e-commerce activities upon. Russia has a well developed transportation system with 33083 miles of highways and 54037 miles of railways. Railways are the prime mode of transportation due to difficult terrain. It also has 2609 airports and boasts of a well connected waterways system with 33 operational ports.

Delivery: Russian Post is the government controlled and operated postal service in Russia. Russia has 40,000 post offices. All of them sell stamps and envelopes and can process domestic and international letters and cards. Larger post offices offer more service, including domestic and international parcel post, telephone calls, domestic and international express letters, Internet service and currency exchange. The post can take some time to be delivered in Russia as the service is unreliable and poor.

Telecommunications: Until 1993, the Russian telecommunication network was fully controlled by the Russian Ministry of Communications. Local network operators were privatized so that each of the 85 regions had one provider. Rostelecom is still a strong monopoly in the long distance and international phone service market, and the waiting list for phones is extremely long at about 5 years. Most of the local phone providers are only partially privatized under the umbrella of the state holding company, Svyazinvest. The popularity and development of mobile services have increased rapidly due to the poor quality and long waiting periods for obtaining a fixed line. As per the World Factbook report (2006), there are around 39.61 million main phone lines in use and around 74.42 million mobile phone users in Russia. In 2002, the industry was reorganized and seven new interregional companies were formed, but their market capitalization is small by international standards.

Dial-up connection is the most common way of accessing the Internet in Russia. The broadband access is rather expensive, ranging from $40/month (IDSN, 64 K/s, 1 GB monthly data transfer) to $300/month (dedicated line, 64-128 K/s, unlimited transfer) with a set-up fee of $200 to 300, plus hidden charges that are common for local providers. Thus, only corporate clients can enjoy the privilege of broadband. There are about 6 million Internet users in Russia, mainly residing in the urban developed regions. Only 2% of the population has broadband access. Satellite communication is in relative high demand because of the country's expansive territory and poor conditions of its landline networks.

Software Industry: The Russian software industry dates back to the 1950s. The Soviet government controlled the software industry, which dealt mainly with military and industrial applications. Unfortunately, things worsened during the 1970s. The crisis persisted until the beginning of the 1990s and the introduction of the market economy. The computer market in Russia grew quickly until 1998, when Russia suffered the worst financial crisis of the post-Soviet era. Since then the national currency, the ruble, has been devaluated five times, and the prices of imports have skyrocketed. The computer industry suffered severely because of its dependency on the Western market. Despite the setbacks, Russia demonstrates one of the best growth rates in computer sales, and the market is still unsaturated. There are approximately only five computers for every 100 people (compared to 62 computers for every 100 people in the US).

Brunswick Warburg, a Russian investment company, estimated that the Russian software market grossed $560–$580 million in 1999 and is estimated to be $831 million in 2005. Although this represented only 0.1 percent of the national GDP, the software market is very efficient and one of the fastest growing industries. Currently, 50,000 to 80,000 people work in the programming industry. Domestic Internet markets have grown 9% to more than $4 billion and will grow 2-3 times by 2005. Russia's great advantage is its abundance of highly skilled technical workers, which is the basis for the creation of a major offshore software development industry.

E-Payment: Low credit card penetration (according to the American Trading Chamber statistics, only 5.3% of Russian population are debit or credit card holders), low solvency level (this problem however is less critical for Internet retailers than for on-ground ones) and overall insecurities about the Russian reality are the main constraints for online retail industry development.

Russian retailers have to be really creative to make their business succeed. There are several ways that payments are accepted by online shops. The majority of e-shops offer more than one way of making payments. Ninety five percent of online shops accept cash (the customer can either physically come to a pick-up location to pay and pick up the order, or pay the company's courier or the Russian State Post Service upon delivery). Half of the shops are working on cash on delivery scheme. Other means of payment are money orders through Sberbank and new digital money payments systems like CyberPlat or Assist.

Consumer E-commerce Propensity: Despite the underdevelopment of and pessimistic perspectives toward business-to business activity, revenues from the business-to-consumer Russian Internet segment are predicted to grow significantly over the next several years. The B2C activity in Russia increased nine times during the period from October 1999 until January 2000. In 2004, E-commerce retail sales were estimated at $660 million (20 % of all Russian etrade), according to the National Association of E-Commerce Participants (Nauet, 2004). However, the attractiveness of new revenue opportunities and new ways of reaching new customers is limited by low Internet penetration, undeveloped payment systems and delivery problems.

A growing tendency in Russian e-retail activity is online malls. One of the first online malls to open was www.torg.ru. Russian analysts believe in the high potential of this type of the e-commerce activity. Similar to the US market, computer hardware is the dominant online shopping category in Russia. A majority of online shops offer computer goods either exclusively or with other shopping categories to their customers. Other popular items are books, CDs, video tapes, flowers, and gifts. Because of payment problems, time constraints and the low level of vacation activity, travel services have not become a popular online sales category. Travel agencies are primarily using the Internet to communicate information to potential consumers, to give a better idea of trips and hotels, and to persuade consumers to visit their brick-and-mortar facilities. Companies are also finding innovative ways to retain and maintain the trust of online customers. For example, Ozon, an online bookstore, has managed to engender trust by offering cash back if the unreliable postal system is not able to deliver on time.

Despite economic and political turmoil, the Russian Internet is alive and growing rapidly. Though the Internet penetration is relatively low and will not reach critical mass in coming years, there is opportunity and hope that the Internet users, whose demographic is skewed toward being young and educated, will be able to put Russia on the e-commerce map of the world.

USA

The United States of America (USA) is the world's third largest country in population (behind China and India), with about 300 million people. It is the world's wealthiest country in terms of Gross Domestic Product, at USD 12.36 trillion as of early 2006. The US GDP per capita is about 41,800 USD which is 1.5 times that of the OECD country average. It has had significantly lower unemployment and inflation than did the average of OECD countries, at around 6% and 2.3% respectively. The service sector contributes 78% to GDP, industry 20%, and agriculture 1%. It has a less egalitarian income distribution, with significantly more of its wealth held by the wealthiest people. This "digital divide" has created a large technology gap between the affluent and the less affluent population. However, this divide is being narrowed by significant government funding for technology in schools, widespread availability of affordable Internet access in American homes and the downward trend in personal computer prices.

The US is regarded as the economic and commercial epicenter of the world. Throughout history, the US has set the benchmark for the establishment of new modes of conducting commerce, and the implementation of innovative business models. Currently, the US is said to have "the most wired population on earth" and "the best country to initiate e-commerce" (Forrester Research, 2005). The Internet and e-commerce have become integrated into most citizens' daily lives as they have grown to depend on it for many forms of information, communication and commerce. Nevertheless, several concerns have limited the Internet's diffusion to date. Most significantly, the US economy's recent downturn slowed the adoption of e-commerce. Online consumer spending growth fell short of projections. The death of many dotcoms caused skepticism on the part of investors and consumers. Furthermore, the lack of common protocols and platforms caused B2B exchanges and marketplaces to fall far short of achieving widespread implementation. These barriers are compounded by the US's laggard position in the wireless communication sector.

Although the US has recently been in the midst of a slowdown, history has proven its ability to rebound strongly. Although the current economic picture does not appear favorable in the short term, all indications are that long-term growth will occur which will present a favorable environment for e-commerce. With such an impressive economy, there is little doubt that US is and will continue to be at the leading edge of e-commerce. Table 9 lists its infrastructural conditions.

Transportation : Boasting as one of the best developed networks of expressways and freeways, the US has around 3.98 million miles of highways. These highways form the backbone of this wide country spanning from the east coast to the west coast. The US department of transportation serves the country by ensuring a fast, safe, efficient, and accessible transportation system that meets vital national interests and enhances the quality of life of the American people, today and well into the future.

Infrastructure Layer	Diffusion Conditions in USA	Evaluation on 1-5 scale
Transportation	• Well developed transportation system • Developed network of freeways and expressways • Well connected air network	5
Delivery	• Highly connected • Reliable and efficient services	5
Telecommunications	• High penetration • Growth rate high towards high speed • Lagging in cellular telephony	4
Software Industry	• Presence of dominant players • One of the largest consumers of IT and ITES	5
E-Payment	• High credit card penetration • Concerns for privacy and security	4
Consumer E-Commerce Propensity	• Positive attitude • Adequate infrastructure • Strong government & Industry support	5

Table 9. E-Commerce Diffusion in USA

With 14,893 airports, the air network also serves in the movement of people and goods. Also adding to the infrastructure are the 22 ports and 141,647 miles of rail network. Though railways is not the primary mode of transportation for people, who prefer roads and airways, the rail network helps in movement of good from industries to wholesale hubs and distribution centers. The development of the transport infrastructure, especially for freight, is a key factor in the evolution of the e-commerce sector.

Delivery: Based on the strong transportation backbones, the US transport sector with such major firms as the Unites States Post Office (USPS), UPS, Fedex, and DHL can provide a one day guarantee or even faster for all deliveries. The postal system is very reliable and accurate, and provides efficient services even in remote areas. On a daily basis, the postal service delivers more that 670 million messages and billions of dollars in financial transactions to eight million businesses and 250 million Americans.

Telecommunications: The US has traditionally had a strong lead in the field of telecommunication as seen in the areas of telegraphy, telephony, radio, television, satellite communications, digital communications, and fiber optics. Indeed, perhaps cellular telephony is the only area of communications technology where the US has lagged behind some other industrial nations. In the area of wired communications, the US has led the shift towards packet switched networks, which have become the key element in the telecommunications infrastructure enabling e-commerce.

As per the world Factbook, in the year 2006 there were about 268 million main phone lines in use in the US and around 194 million mobile phone users. The advanced telecommunications services market has grown steadily, and investment in infrastructure for advanced telecommunications has remained strong in spite of slowing investment trends. The US has long had a convention of flat rate local telephony service. This might have been an important enabler of B2C electronic commerce because Internet users on dial-up service do not incur high telephony charges while searching on-line for product specifications and pricing.

The National Cable and Telecommunications Association (NCTA) estimates that 27% of homes with personal computers and those with access to Cable TV are now using cable Internet service. Digital Subscriber Line (DSL) is expanding slower than cable broadband. DSL growth rate was 36% and had 2.7 million subscribers in the first half of 2003. With investments made in broadband access infrastructure to increase quality and availability, the US is positioned well for future growth in the use of the Internet as a tool for conducting e-commerce.

<u>Software Industry</u>: The US has long been a leader in the area of computing technology, from the mainframe strengths of IBM and the minicomputer strengths of Digital Equipment Corporation, to the world of personal computers dominated by the Intel/Microsoft nexus and Apple Computer.

During the late 1970s and early 1980s, the US established itself as one of the world's leading users of the first generation B2B systems relying on Electronic Data Interchange (EDI) protocols (ANSI/X12 standard). These enabled automation of payments and integration of business transactions across organizational borders, especially in the retail, computer and car industries. Intel Corporation has grown into the world's leading supplier of microprocessors and assorted chip sets. Microsoft has become the world's largest and most powerful software company, dominating the market in PC operating systems and leveraging that advantage in a wide array of applications and utilities. The invention of the Ethernet transmission protocol during the late 1970's by Xerox Corporation started a whole new industry in computer networking, that has produced companies like 3COM and Cisco, as well as drawn active participation by hardware manufacturers such as Lucent, Alcatel, Nortel, NTT, and others. Furthermore, in the last few years, Google has emerged as a software giant.

<u>E-Payment</u>: The credit card is the most important payment mechanism in B2C commerce, and is a key factor enabling such commerce. The credit card was invented in the US by Diners Club and has expanded into a global service infrastructure. It is the most widely used medium in e-commerce transactions today. The US has been pioneer in the use and diffusion of this form of payment. In addition, other forms of payment mechanisms like Paypal, debit cards, smart cards, etc. are also prevalent in the country. In spite of a mature market and the credit card as payment mechanism, there still remain a few risks related to consumer privacy concerns and criminal activity. These involve financial stealing by way of credit card theft and identity theft. These concerns obviously impede the growth of e-commerce in the US.

<u>Consumer E-commerce Propensity</u>: With a few caveats, US consumers seem willing to use e-commerce. According to a Forrester report (2005), online retail sales in US will grow from $172 billion in 2005 to $329 billion in 2010. As per the UNCTAD Development and Globalization Report (2004), North American share of e-commerce sales is at about 58.2%. These data suggest positive consumer attitudes towards e-commerce. Language is not a barrier in the US; most web sites use English as a first language. It is easy to search for product information, availability, and prices online. B2C e-commerce for physical products is conceptually just an extension of catalog-based mail-order. The US shoppers have had more than a century of experience with mail-order based entirely on the postal system, and nearly a half century of experience with mail-order using the telephone for order-entry. With around 115 million Internet hosts and around 159 million Internet users, e-commerce is well poised for tremendous growth over the coming years.

Globally, the US has been the quickest to develop and adopt new e-commerce business models. Many facts corroborate this leading position: the US' overall societal tendencies towards collaboration and community, the nature of its consumers to engage in liberal credit card spending, limited fear of risks inherent in e-commerce, its established role as a leader in the IT industry, and a superior telecommunications infrastructure. The US has the world's most substantial infrastructure for e-commerce, the highest penetration of this infrastructure into the population, and the highest measured rates of e-commerce transactions.

Recent statements by the Department of Commerce emphasize that the US Government sees the importance of e-commerce and IT to our society and to US business. The government characterizes the online dynamic that is occurring as "a transformation of America's economy and society". It cites that the IT sector has accounted for nearly one third of the US economic growth in recent years and has helped spark an increase in US productivity and global competitiveness.

DISCUSSION

In contrast with the weak performance of several key developed and developing economies and the difficulties experienced by the IT sector, Internet use and particularly electronic commerce have continued to grow at a fast pace over the past few years. The number of Internet users worldwide was expected to reach 1.02 billion by the end of 2006. A whopping growth rate of 146% has been witnessed in the worldwide Internet users in the last 5 years, but at the same time alarming is the 13% penetration rate worldwide. While the developing countries, predominantly in Asia, accounted for almost one third of new Internet users worldwide, their Internet penetration rates remain very low.

Jupiter Research (Jupiter Media, 2006) predicts that by 2010, US online retail spending will reach somewhere around 144 billion USD. According to UNCTAD development and globalization report (2004), the e-commerce market is estimated to be around USD 12.87 trillion by end of 2006. Projections are that while the United States and North America currently dominate the majority of online transactions, that will shift in the coming years as Asia and European nations become more active. As evident from country specific case studies, governments of developing countries are providing the required impetus in terms of infrastructure development for the growth of e-commerce and Internet in their respective countries.

In addition to Internet diffusion, there are traditional infrastructural needs for e-commerce and these may lead to interesting patterns of e-commerce development in developed and under-developed nations. Distribution and delivery systems round out the set of service infrastructures that are key components to developing e-commerce. Speed is one of the most important manifestations of electronic commerce. Overnight delivery, just-in-time processing, 24x7 operations all are examples of how much faster and more precisely timed economic activities are in the e-commerce world. Therefore a country with inefficient distribution and delivery systems and without multi-modal transport for international participation will be left behind in e-commerce. Russia is an example. Russia has a vast amount of intellectual workforce and consumer propensity towards internet and e-commerce is favorable. Still, Russia has not witnessed and is not at par with other countries in terms of e-commerce diffusion. The main reasons cited are the prevalent infrastructure problems. Moreover, there is a very important link between the effectiveness of the distribution and delivery systems and the incentives for the private sector to innovate and invest in new technologies related to the Internet.

The government and the private enterprise need to work synergistically in their efforts for reforms and policies toward developing the infrastructure within the country and the development of ICT and e-commerce. Developing countries can look at the examples and models deployed by the advanced nations. A "best practice" example is the flat rate telephone system that has made a huge contribution in the development of e-commerce in the United States. The policy makers should also recognize and exploit key synergies and interrelationships between telecommunications, financial sector, and transportation sector for the development of e-commerce. Liberalization efforts and private ownership need also be targeted if the benefits of e-commerce are to be fully reaped.

CONCLUSION

In this chapter, we have provided an overview of the global diffusion of Internet and e-commerce in several important countries of the world. Also examined were various infrastructure factors that have shaped and continue to shape the diffusion dynamic of e-commerce. Despite possible limitations of the data due to secondary sources and covering different time periods, it is evident that the diffusion pattern of e-commerce is a function of economic, political, cultural and infrastructural factors. Since these factors vary widely across the world, diffusion patterns of e-commerce also vary widely. Newly industrialized countries and developing countries may examine the diffusion factors and successes of developed countries, and implement similar reforms and introduce similar policies.

Low levels of income, income disparities, authoritarian government, unfavorable consumer propensity toward e-commerce, socio-cultural environment, and absence of adequate transportation, delivery and financial systems are some factors that are incompatible with Internet development and have hampered the rapid diffusion of e-commerce in various parts of the world. Concentrated effort is required on part of policy makers in government, private enterprise, as well as international agencies in extending and developing e-commerce to all parts of the globe.

MINICASE

E-Commerce Development in Japan

Background
E-commerce in Japan has lagged behind the United States. Various trials and errors have been made since its beginning. Development varies from industry to industry and depends on consumer purchasing behavior to a particular good or service. To close the gap, the Japanese government took a major leap forward by passing the IT Basic Bill. This eased regulations on the Internet, set up rules to expand electronic commerce and made Internet access more affordable. The newly enacted law calls for an "e-government," utilizing IT for online national and local government services, available around the clock. Now, e-commerce became one of the priority policies in Japan. Civil organizations and governmental agencies are promoting construction of e-commerce infrastructure. In addition, the Japanese government is proposing campaigns on basic IT strategies to further advance the IT facilities. Efforts include building an ultra high-speed Internet network with constant Internet access, instituting rules on electronic commerce, realizing an e-government and developing high quality human resources.

The government is actively promoting the use of IT through the creation of a broadband network infrastructure, e-commerce promotion and the protection of private information through secure networks. For example, during 1996 to 2000, the government allocated about US$1 billion for 200 projects to boost the Japanese e-commerce market. A new division known as ECOM (Electronic Commerce Promotion Council of Japan) was established, whose main objective is to develop policy for all areas of e-commerce. With the recent increase in security and privacy issues, the Japanese government has stepped up its effort in safeguarding consumer protection and security.

New Forms of E-Commerce in Japan
Mobile Commerce: Compared to the users in the United States, incredibly high number of the Japanese users access Internet through their mobile devices. There are over 20 million people online in Japan, of which 4 million (or 20%) people use their mobile phones. This makes Japan the current world's leader in mobile commerce (m-commerce). The emergence of i-mode service from NTT DoCoMo and the multimedia services from 3G systems have made m-commerce a major success in Japan. The fastest and most popular segment of the telecom industry, "i-mode", which is a digital packet based mobile phone with Internet access, is a popular alternative from regular personal computer access. Due to the product's success, DoCoMo incorporated "i-mode" as a standard feature in all its mobile phones.

Japan's m-commerce has been greatly stimulated by the availability of wireless data transmission technology. The always 'on connection' creates a convenient and reasonable charge for data sent and received rather than the amount of time spent online. Japan has low wired home connection due to limited housing sizes and high cost of living standards. With Japanese spending numerous hours on public transportation, mobile communication devices such as cellular phones and pagers are very popular. With tiny cellular handsets, users can also send/receive e-mail messages and develop their own home pages. Small electronic devices and gadgets, ranging from car navigation systems to palm-held devices to toys, like Sony's PSP or Nintendo's DS, are very popular in Japan.

Entertainment is the biggest application in the m-commerce market. Digital content for mobile phones, such as ringers, ringer music tones, and screen pictures have been a major commodity in m-commerce. In November 2004, a new service "Music Tone Full" was introduced. Music and interactive games are gaining popularity due to the advantage of ubiquity and flexibility of availability. Another market demand exists in the reservation of goods and services especially travel Industry and event management (tickets reservation), with approximately 8.5% and 30%, respectively, of the transaction ordered/placed by mobile Internet devices. Included are non-Internet transactions, rendering them inherently compatible with telephone transactions. The urgent nature of this business makes it suitable for transactions by mobile terminals, which are always carried by the customers.

<u>A New Platform – Convenience Stores</u>: In Japan, the convenience stores (known as *konbini*) plays a major role in the e-commerce field. These ubiquitous convenience stores set up kiosks on which customers can shop online and then receive the merchandise at the store. One of the more popular is known as 7dream.com, established by 7-Eleven Japan. Since 2000, Seven - Eleven have established joint ventures with companies to provide services such as travel, music, mobile telephones, computers, peripherals, software, books, flowers, information on auto dealers and driving schools, entertainment, and some miscellaneous services.

Customers purchase goods from home or in store multimedia kiosk. For example, the three million customers of Japan's largest virtual mall, *Rakuten Ichiba,* can pick up and pay for purchases at Seven-Eleven stores. Customers are also able to download music from the Internet into mini-discs. Payment and delivery for goods and services can be made at the stores (using cash or credit), or over the web using credit cards. Convenience stores are also able to capitalize on delivery problems. With many consumers working long hours, rather than have their goods delivered to an empty house or waiting at home for them all day, consumers can have purchases delivered to the nearest Seven – Eleven store for pick up at a time of their choosing.

Japanese subscribers mainly used the Internet for information collection, communication (e -mail), and shopping. Online purchase of goods does not seem to be a priority and can be partly explained by problems such as difficulty of ascertaining the quality of goods, expensive communication, privacy, payment security, and insufficient trust in web merchants. Another barrier is the low usage rate of credit cards. Japan is very much a cash society and to do transaction via credit card online is not considered safe. Many Japanese consumers prefer to transact primarily by postal and bank transfers. Seven-Eleven also began selling books on the Internet in collaboration with Softbank. For this service, consumers have at least three payment/delivery options: payment and book delivery at Seven-Eleven outlets, door-to-door delivery service utilizing a C.O.D. or online credit card payment. The majority of the customer opted for the first option. Some of the more successful B2C companies are: *Yamato Transport* (a delivery company with its own online mall where delivery people can take payment from customers for any store in the mall), *Yamadaya* (an online site selling Japanese noodles with affiliation with noodle vendors), and *Rakuten Ichiba* (one of the most successful online mall with over 4000 online shops).

Some Observations

E-commerce in Japan is taking a different form from the United States. B2C e-commerce is conducted increasingly via wireless devices and less via PCs. It relies less on credit card payment and more on mechanisms such as billing by wireless service providers, and cash payment to convenience stores and delivery companies.

The growth potential for Japanese B2C e-commerce is vast. It was estimated that in 2004 Internet transactions should surpass ¥5.6 trillion (about $50 billion: METI, et al., 2005). Indeed, the foundations of this expansion are already evident. The number of subscribers to NTT DoCoMo's Internet-capable cellular phones (i-mode) rose from zero in mid-1999 to 7 million a year later, and over 45 million in 2005. A few video game companies are designing programs that operate upon the Internet facilities.

Convenience stores are transforming into outlets where consumers can order, receive, and authorize payments through automated teller machines (ATMs).

Japan seems to have discovered the Internet's potential as an e-commerce platform relatively late but it has restructured what it has adapted to fit into the Japanese culture.

Discussion Questions

1. Describe the development of e-commerce in Japan using the model of diffusion presented in the chapter.
2. Does the model of diffusion and the various layers of infrastructure apply to Japan? Are some layers more important than others? Are there other layers or factors which have played a key role in Japan?
3. What strategies the government or business may apply to address the "consumer's e-commerce propensity"?

Adapted From: Vairappan, C., Cata, T., and Sakaguchi, T. "E-Commerce Development in Japan" *Proceedings of The 7th Annual Global Information Technology Management Association World Conference*, June 11-13, 2006, Orlando, Florida, USA

KEY TERMS

BRIC countries
Business Process Reengineering (BPR)
Business-To-Business (B2B)
Chief Information Officer (CIO)
CMM (Capability Maturity Model)
Data Security
Delphi method
E-commerce (EC or Electronic commerce)
Electronic Data Interchange (EDI)
GIGO (Garbage In Garbage Out)
Information architecture
Privacy
Sarbanes-Oxley Act of 2002
Society for Information Management (SIM)

STUDY QUESTIONS

1. Describe the model of diffusion of e-commerce and its various layers. In your view, what layers are more important than others? Are there other factors which influence e-commerce diffusion in a country?

2. Select an advanced country (not included in this chapter) and conduct research into its various e-commerce infrastructural layers. How do your findings compare with those reported in the chapter?

3. Select an under-developed country (not included in this chapter) and conduct research into its various e-commerce infrastructural layers. How do your findings compare with those reported in the chapter?

4. Select a former Soviet Union country (not included in this chapter). Suppose you are the chief technology advisor to the President of the country. What recommendations you would make to the President to significantly enhance e-commerce in the country within five years? Justify your recommendations.

5. Select a poor African country. Suppose you are the chief technology advisor to the President of the country. What recommendations you would make to the President to significantly enhance e-commerce in the country within five years? Justify your recommendations.

REFERENCES

Boston Consulting Group (BCG) report, "Online Retailing in Latin America: Beyond theStorefront." 2001. Brazzilmag.com, http://www.brazzilmag.com/content/view/4784/, 2005.

CNNIC, Semi-Annual China Internet Report, 2001

Dedrick, Jason, Kraemer, Kenneth L., Palacios, Juan J., Tigre, Paulo Bastos and Botelho, Antonio. "Economic Liberalization and the Computer Industry: Comparing Outcomes in Brazil and Mexico". *World Development*, 29(7), pp.1199-1214. 2001.

E-Commerce and Development Report prepared by UNCTAD Secretariat for United Nations Conference on Trade and Development, 2004 http://r0.unctad.org/ecommerce/ecommerce_en/edr04_en.htm

Ein-Dor, Philip, Myers, Michael, and Raman, K.S., IT industry development and the Knowledge Economy: A four country study, *Journal of Global Information Management*, 12(4), 2004, pp. 23. emarketer.com Western Europe Report, http://www.emarketer.com/Reports/All/West_eur_b2c_jul04.aspx, 2004.

Federal Statistics Office Germany, http://www.destatis.de/basis/e/evs/budtab2.htm, 2005.

Forrester Research, US Ecommerce 2005-2010, http://www.forrester.com/Research/Document/Excerpt/0,7211,37626,00.html

Gruner und Jahr Electronic Media Service, 2001, *Online-Monitor Welle 7*. Hamburg Hindu Business Line, http://www.thehindubusinessline.com/2004/08/04/stories/2004 080400260300.htm internetworldstats.com, Internet Usage Statistics for the Americas., 2004.

Jupiter Media, http://www.jupitermedia.com/corporate/releases/06.02.06-newjupresearch.html,

NASSCOM Reports, 2005. http://www.nasscom.org/artdisplay.asp?cat_id=794, 2006.

Nauet, http://www.buyusainfo.net/docs/x_2489973.pdf, 2004.

NFO Infratest, *Monitoring Informationswirtschaft*. 3. Faktenbericht 2001. Munich.

Ngai, E. W. T., and Wat, F. K. T. A literature review and classification of electronic commerce research, *Information and Management*, 39(5), 2002, pp. 415-429

OECD Report, http://www.oecd.org/document/39/0,2340,en_2649_34223_36459431_1_1_1_1,00.html, 2005.

Okoli, C., and Mbarika, V.A.W., A Framework for Assessing E-Commerce in Sub-Saharan Africa, *Journal of Global Information Technology Management*, (6:3), 2003, pp. 44.

Straub, D.W., Loch, K.D., Evaristo, R., and Srite, M., Toward a theory based definition of Culture, *Journal of Global Information Management*, 10(1), 2002, pp. 13-23.

Tigre, P.B., "Globalization and Electronic Commerce: Growth and Impacts on Brazil" Globalization and E-commerce project of the *Center for Research on Information Technology and Organizations* (CRITO) at the University of California, Irvine, June 2001, http://www.crito.uci.edu

Travica, Bob, Diffusion of Electronic Commerce in Developing countries: The case of Costa Rica, *Journal of Global Information Technology Management*, 5(1), 2002, pp.4.

Turban, E., King D., Lee, J., and Viehland, D. *Electronic Commerce: A Managerial Perspective.* Pearson Prentice Hall, 2004, Upper Saddle River, NJ 07458.

UNCTAD Development and Globalization Report prepared by UNCTAD Secretariat for United Nations Conference on Trade and Development, 2004. http://www.unctad.org/en/docs/gdscsir20041_en.pdf

UNCTAD World Investment Report prepared for United Nations Conference on Trade and Development, 2005. http://www.unctad.org/Templates/webflyer.asp?docid=6087&intItemID=3489&lang=1&mode=downloads

Whiteley, D. Internet Commerce- Hot Cakes and Dead Ducks. In Sudweeks F., and Celia T. Rom (Eds), *Doing Business on the Internet: Opportunities on the Internet*, pp. 9-20, Springer: London, 1999.

The World fact Book (2006) CIA http://www.cia.gov/cia/publications/factbook/index.html

Wolcott, P., Press, L., McHenry, W., Goodman, S. E., and Foster, W. A framework for assessing the global diffusion of the Internet, *Journal of the Association for Information Systems,* (2:6), 2001.

Wikipedia, Brazil (http://en.wikipedia.org/wiki/Brazil)

Zwass, V., Electronic Commerce: Structure and Issues, *International Journal of Electronic Commerce*, 1(1), 1996, pp. 3-23.

24

Global Information Technology and the Rise of Global Corporate Alliances

Shailendra C. Jain Palvia
Long Island University, USA

Vijay K. Vemuri
University of Bahrain, Kingdom of Bahrain

CHAPTER SUMMARY

This chapter discusses the changes in the industrial organizations that are propelled by the advances in IT. A major conclusion is that the dichotomous partitioning of the economic agents into firm and outsiders may no longer be valid since the organizational boundaries are becoming blurred. Other major changes that are defining the new industrial organizations are the emergence of redesigned and realigned distribution channels, industry alliances among once competing firms, and a trend toward smaller firms. IT is pivotal in these changes in industrial structures and in creating agile organizations that can respond quickly to customers and markets. Technologies are needed to create closely integrated operations and meld disparate hardware and software platforms to work in unison, while keeping all or most of the existing computing infrastructure. Web services are the new technologies that will solve the hardware and software heterogeneity and incompatibilities that are prevalent in global operations. Recent advances in technologies and architectures to integrate information systems are outlined.

INTRODUCTION

Advances in information technology (IT) have transformed the organization, operation, and management of businesses. It is well documented that IT is instrumental in reducing layers of middle-level management, resulting in flatter organizational hierarchies, the use of matrix organizational structures to work on specific organizational goals and projects, the creation of virtual organizations, and in making geographic distance, for most purposes, irrelevant. Yet, the changes in the relations that are taking place between a firm and its competitors, partners, customers, and suppliers are not well understood. Ease of establishing interoperable information systems among organizations has triggered the avalanche of changes that are redefining the role of firms in an industry and among industries in a constantly shrinking world. The metamorphosis in the interactions among the firms has profound strategic implications for worldwide commerce.

In the last two decades, advances in Global Information Technology (IT), such as broadband networks, mobile communications, and the Internet have brought about profound changes in almost every aspect of human endeavor. The recent information revolution has fundamentally changed how we are informed, entertained, and educated, as well as how we communicate with each other and how we shop. The sweeping changes are not just limited to how individuals conduct themselves. During this period, the Internet has become an important medium to conduct commercial transactions. Further, it has become the adhesive that bonds together global value chain partners, enabling the value chains to function as though they are a single entity.

In this chapter we will focus not only on the momentous changes that are brought upon by the rapid growth in Internet penetration (despite continuing digital divide) and global electronic commerce, but also on how these technologies are transforming the function, scope, the environment, and structure of the industries within which the individual firms operate. These transformations are very slow and difficult to detect. However, from a strategic perspective, management has to be aware of, react to, and cope with these slow structural shifts that have far-reaching consequences.

ORGANIZATIONAL CHANGES DUE TO INFORMATION TECHNOLOGY

Organizational changes can be thought of as "within" firm changes. The within firm changes are more visible in the literature. The taxonomy of organizational change by Laudon and Laudon (2006) is a good framework for understanding the organizational changes that are taking place within a firm. The changes brought about by IT and the Internet can be categorized in four stages/phases: automation, rationalization, business process reengineering, and revolution (paradigm shift). Each successive phase of organizational change exposes a firm to higher levels of risk and also provides greater opportunities for greater rewards/returns.

- Automation is the first wave of organizational change in which IT applications running on faster and more accurate computers are substituted for older, repetitive, low-skill manual processes. This phase took place mainly during 1965-75 in the U.S. and accounted for productivity gains experienced in the later years. Automation is generally considered to be associated with low risks and low returns since none of the organizational processes are affected and old and well-understood processes are simply computerized.
- Rationalization of procedures follows automation in the enormity of organizational change. In this phase, the old standard operating processes are streamlined to remove inherent inefficiencies.
- Even further profound changes in organizations are affected through business process reengineering (BPR). A catch-phrase definition of BPR is "the fundamental rethinking and radical redesign of business processes." In this level of organizational change, business processes that were developed prior to availability of automation technologies are discarded or redesigned, and, in their place, new processes that exploit the unique capabilities of newer technologies are developed. Typically, BPR reorganizes workflows, reassigns tasks, and eliminates repetitive tasks and waste.
- An even more fundamental change in the nature of the business and the nature of the organization is effected by revolution (paradigm shift). In this form of organizational change, the nature and the conduct of the business itself may be revised as a result of the newly found capabilities of the information systems. For example, paradigm shift occurs when Jack Welsh of General Electric seeks and champions and brings about a new paperless corporate

environment by having all communications, forms, calendars, appointments, bulletin boards, message boards become electronic.

Advances in information technology (IT) have forever changed the organization, operation, and management of businesses. It is now almost axiomatic that IT has flattened organizational hierarchies by removing layers of management, especially mid-level management. A recent addition to the vocabulary of organizational structures is "virtual organization," which refers to a company and the loose coalition of members connected by IT and appears to outsiders as a single, unified organization. Matrix organization is another IT-propelled structure in which mostly temporary teams are formed to work on specific organizational goals or projects. Increasingly decentralized, collaborative and globally distributed work environments are all, to a large extent, made possible by advances in IT. Although the changes that are taking place within the firm are well documented, the fundamental changes in the role of the firm in an industry – its interactions with other firms within the industry — are more recent and not well understood.

In the next section, several evolving structural changes that are redefining the role of a firm and its strategic options are discussed. In the final section, we outline the IT changes that are making the interoperability of applications across the organizational boundaries effortless.

STRUCTURAL CHANGES IN ORGANIZATIONS DUE TO INFORMATION TECHNOLOGY

Before we expand on our discussion of structural changes that are taking place in industrial organizations globally, we will describe the well known Coase's theorem which can explain why these sweeping changes are possible and expected as a result of advances in information technology. Interpretations of this theorem, based on Farrell (1987) are:

- If a group of firms can deal among themselves costlessly (no transaction costs), it does not matter from the standpoint of efficiency which firm has the legal right.
- Yet another way to restate this famous result is that in economic transactions, efficiency will prevail as long as information among the transacting entities is perfect, cost of transactions is low, and negotiations are not too complicated or hindered.

The three causes for inefficiency in an economy: imperfect information, high transaction costs, and difficulties in negotiations are strongly affected by the recent advances in information technologies. Transaction costs consist of the costs of gathering information, evaluating available options, negotiating, contracting, and the change of legal ownership of the object. These costs increase with the complexity and uncertainty of the economic system. Many, including Malone, Yates, and Benjamin (1987), argue that IT can be used to reduce transaction costs in economic organizations. The reasoning is that information technology is capable of making more information available to decision makers, thus contributing to the reduction of uncertainty. To further understand the nature of transaction costs, these costs are divided into infrastructure costs and coordination costs categories. Infrastructure costs, as the name suggests, are the costs of establishing the capabilities to enable exchange information between economic agents. Coordination costs, on the other hand, are the costs of uncertainty and of imperfect information and opportunistic behavior of economic agents. Coordination can be internal and external: Internal coordination costs are the costs of coordinating activities within divisions, department, and other units of the firm, while external coordination costs are the costs of transactions with suppliers and other value chain partners. External coordination costs may include costs of searching for suppliers, negotiating contracts, bargaining, and transfer of funds. Figure 1 shows the components of transaction costs.

Malone, Yates, and Benjamin 1987 discuss three possible influences of IT on transactions:

1) Electronic Communication Effect: IT can increase the rate of processing of transactions and reduce the cost per transaction.

2) Electronic Brokerage Effect: IT, via the use of vertical portals and other means, can provide a better match for buyers' needs and sellers' offerings. A vertical portal is a gateway to information related to a particular industry, such as the automobile and health-care industries. It is a business to business community that brings together people interested in a particular industry. These vertical portals, in addition to the sharing of information, facilitate buying and selling of goods or services. Recent advances in open protocols, such as TCP/IP, browser-based transactions, and database and Web integration, make universal connectivity possible and transactions effortless.

3) Electronic Integration Effect: This effect is due to the integration of various processes within a firm or due to enterprise systems that enable integration of operations across the value chain. Enterprise systems such, as enterprise resource planning systems and supply chain management systems (on global scale), enable a firm to integrate its processes or operations and make just-in-time inventory management systems possible.

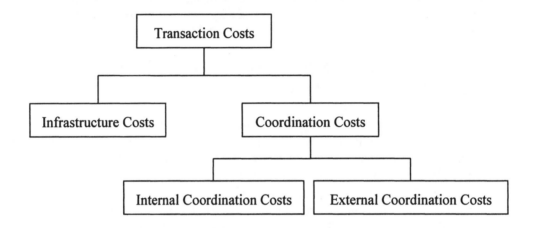

Figure 1. Components of Transaction Costs

To understand the impact of IT on transaction costs further, we can compare costs of day-to-day consumer to business transactions.

- A typical bank account balance inquiry through a telephone operator costs around $1 per inquiry compared to $.13 if the inquiry is made through self-serve Internet account access (Laudon, and Laudon 2006).
- The costs of tracking a package in the UPS system using the above alternatives are $2 and $.10 per package, respectively, (Brynjolfsson and Hitt, 2003).

To appreciate why advances in IT can result in structural changes in global industrial organizations (beyond reduction in transaction costs and coordination costs), we need to understand the role of prices and markets in aggregating, processing, and disseminating information among market participants. The concept that "markets mechanisms and price systems can solve the economic problems of society by making all the dispersed pieces of information that underlie decision making to coalesce," goes back to Hayek (1945). Markets can be viewed as information processing units. As such, the enormous improvements in IT capabilities have strong impact on the global market structure. It is naïve to expect that the structure of global industrial organizations that were created and evolved since the time of very low information processing capabilities will remain unchanged by the unprecedented information revolution.

The next four sub-sections discuss the profound changes that are taking place in distribution channels, organizational hierarchies, shifts in pricing mechanisms/systems, changes in the size and boundaries of the firm, vertical alliances along the supply chains, and horizontal alliances among the firms in the same industry worldwide.

Change #1: Realignment of Distribution Channels

The information and Internet revolution has improved quality, customer service, price, assortment of offering, and speed of delivery of almost every product and service. The World Wide Web provides a platform for a paradigm shift in how commerce will be conducted globally in the future. The easy accessibility of vast amounts of information on the Internet and the ability to effect transactions using ubiquitous tools such as a Web browser have fundamentally altered the channels of distribution of products and services. Researchers have predicted the demise of traditional marketing channels and foresee a direct channel in the flow of goods and services from manufacturers to consumers. Notably, Tapscott (1996) argues that "middleman functions between producers and consumers are being eliminated through digital networks" (p. 56). This process of elimination of middlemen due to direct online channels is termed disintermediation. Tapscott goes on to surmise that "[t]he age of electronic commerce might bring to an end the intermediate enterprise." (p. 436). Benjamin and Wigand (1995) analyzed the effect of electronic markets on the value chain of a company and conclude that "electronic markets lower coordination costs for producers and retailers, lower physical distribution costs, or eliminate retailers and wholesalers entirely, as consumers directly access manufacturers" (Roche 1996). The concept of disintermediation has gained considerable support in the popular media, trade journals, and industry magazines. Extensive evidence supports the dwindling role of middlemen in bringing buyers and sellers together and affecting the sale of goods and services.

However, the disintermediation hypothesis is based mostly on anecdotal evidence alone and not based on systematic analysis. In what follows, we analyze the role of, the functions provided by, and the efficacy of utilizing traditional middlemen. Then we discuss how electronic commerce and digital networks are being increasingly equipped to fulfill various functions provided by traditional middlemen more efficiently. With this understanding of efficiency gains, and traditional intermediary functions, we are able to make predictions of how marketing channels will evolve in the age of electronic commerce and about the product and industry characteristics that will most impact electronic commerce marketing channels.

Anecdotal Evidence Supporting Disintermediation: Considerable anecdotal evidence exists to support the disintermediation process. Reduction in sales of airline tickets, books, computers, music, and securities by traditional outlets are often cited as examples of fundamental sweeps that are bringing providers and consumers of products and services closer in the information age. Between 1991 and 2002, the number of travel agencies dropped by nearly 30 percent in the U.S. A predominant mode of airline travel booking is through Expedia, Orbitz, Travelocity, or other online travel agencies. Music distribution has also gone through a major shock. The sales of prerecorded music are down and the sales of digital music such as iTunes are up dramatically.

Traditional Intermediary Functions: Middlemen perform a variety of functions in facilitating transactions between ultimate buyers and sellers. The following list discusses some of these functions.

- **Communication, Coordination, and Exchange Costs:** Middlemen reduce the number of communications and exchanges needed in the delivery of goods and services. Here we will use wholesalers as an example of how the middlemen will reduce cost of communication and exchange. For exchange between four manufacturers and three retailers, without a wholesaler, 12 exchanges are required. With the incorporation of a wholesaler into the marketing chain, the number of exchanges is reduced to seven. In general, exchange between m manufacturers and n retailers, without the aid of wholesalers, requires m * n exchanges, while a single wholesaler will reduce the number of exchanges to m + n. The efficiency gains in transaction and communication costs are even higher if transactions with many consumers are considered.

- **Assortment of Products:** By carrying a variety of products, middlemen, especially retailers, make shopping convenient. By eliminating the need to visit many shops for comparisons, retailers reduce shopping time and enable consumers to purchase goods and services closely matching their preferences for attributes, quality, and price.

- **Warehousing and Distribution:** The movement of products from the manufacturer to the retailer consists of complex routing and storing decisions. Manufacturers are not well equipped to deal with the complexities of network routing and warehousing decisions to ship products to numerous consumers. Middlemen enable decentralization of complex network and warehousing problems into smaller, more manageable problems. They specialize in solving logistical complexities and relieve the manufacturer of these complexities. They contribute to the efficiency and cost reduction of the marketing chain by exploiting the favorable bulk rates offered by transporters of goods.

- **Financing and Risk Sharing:** The provision of goods and services involves many uncertainties, including demand uncertainties. Inclusion of middlemen partially relieves the manufacturer of many uncertainties. Most products are sold (in contrast to consignment) to middlemen by manufacturers. This ready market for the output relieves the manufacturer of tying up funds in inventories. The sale of output to middlemen provides indirect financing to the manufacturers. In some cases, middlemen provide funds for financing manufacturers' operations. As a part of the marketing chain, middlemen, at least partially, shield the manufacturers from the risk of manufacturing, marketing, and distribution functions. For example, the risk of less than expected product demand is, at least partially, absorbed by the wholesalers, retailers, and manufacturers.

- **Product Promotions:** For many products and services, sales promotion is a more effective tool in generating sales than advertising. The total expenditure on sales promotions in the U.S. was about $85 million in 1985, about twice the combined advertising budget of that year. In addition, increases in sales promotions outpace increases in advertising budgets. In trade promotions (push promotion), promotional efforts are directed at the marketing channel partners rather than the consumers (pull promotion). In the U.S., the typical trade promotion budget exceeds consumer promotion budget. In trade promotions, marketing intermediaries are an essential part of the promotional strategy. In highly competitive product markets characterized by proliferation of brands, marketing channel members provide an important service.

Selling products without the involvement of middlemen is not an entirely new phenomenon. To sell their products, many companies have experimented with vertical integration of marketing channels. Sherwin-Williams sells paint directly to consumers in about 2,000 retail outlets. Hart, Shaffner, Marx has about 200 retail outlets to sell its own clothing. Gap and other fashion clothing lines use direct retailing to reach consumers. Still, selling directly to consumers is not the predominant approach for selling products for manufacturers.

Emerging Intermediation Trends in e-Commerce: Despite the well-publicized evidence of disintermediation, electronic commerce does not eliminate the need for middlemen. E-commerce is transforming the marketing channels into new configurations best suited for capabilities of new information technology. A manifestation of the disintermediation process occurs when manufacturers or service providers utilize electronic commerce to sell products and services directly to the consumers. However, this anecdotal evidence cited earlier that supports the emergence of disintermediation does not present a complete story. Amazon.com is selling books on the Web without utilizing traditional retailing facilities. Yet, Amazon.com is really an online retailer of books, fulfilling an important function of the middlemen in transferring books from publishers to the readers. Online travel agents, Travelocity and Expedia, also provide centralized access to fares, schedules, and reservations much like traditional travel agents, but they exploit the unique features of electronic commerce. Palvia and Vemuri (2002) postulated trends in intermediations as: 1) the number of intermediaries will decrease across all industries; 2) the reduction of layers of intermediaries will take place more rapidly in the service industry than in the manufacturing industry; 3) the diminishing role of middlemen will depend on product and service characteristics – reputed brands will have an advantage in direct selling; and 4) newer forms of intermediaries will emerge (like priceline.com). Most of these assertions have been supported in the last 5 years.

Change #2 - Shift toward Smaller Firms and Emphasis on Core Competencies

Predicting the impact of IT on industrial organizations, in terms of form, contents, operations, structure, jobs, and culture has not been easy. Advances in IT have far-reaching effects on many aspects of business operations. The effect of these changes on industrial structure, in many cases, can be difficult to assess and ambiguous (Gurubaxani and Whang, 1991). In the previous sections, it is argued that the effect of IT is to clearly lower the coordination costs. It is further shown that there are two aspects of coordination costs: internal coordination costs affect the costs of controlling operations within a firm, while external coordination costs affect the costs of controlling operations outside the firm, such as coordinating activities with suppliers for just-in-time inventory control systems. Although improvements in IT have the effect of reducing both internal and external costs, the resulting implications differ. Lower internal coordination costs (especially agency costs) make it possible for a firm to internalize more operations. On the other hand, lowered external coordination costs (especially transaction costs) make it possible for the firm to concentrate on a few core competencies and delegate other less important operations to outside entities. These two forces have opposing effects on the firm size; lower internal coordination costs make firms larger whereas lower external coordination costs make firms smaller. Which of these effects prevails is an empirical question explored by Brynjolfsson, et al. (1994). This study finds that there is broad evidence to conclude that a decrease in the average size of a firm (as measured by number of employees and sales per firm) is antecedent to investment in IT. Further, these decreases in firm size lag by IT investments by two to three years.

Hitt (1999) finds a strong negative relationship between IT capital and the level of vertical integration and a weaker positive relationship between IT capital and the level of diversification. These findings also reinforce the earlier findings that IT has the effect of decreasing firm size. Lower external coordination costs make it rational for the firm to delegate or outsource some business processes to external entities. The firm size findings also have a bearing on the recent emphasis on core competencies to gain sustainable competitive advantage. The decoupling of business processes and delegating the processes that can be performed better by other entities can both be technologically challenging and risky. The potential benefit, however, is the ability to stay focused on the operations that provide competitive advantage. The recent advances in IT capabilities enable a firm to reduce the cost and risk of decoupling and outsourcing of business processes. Thus, IT capabilities provide justification for dropping some of the operations performed internally, resulting in streamlined business operations.

Corporate downsizing and outsourcing are two important forces that are also associated with reduction of firm sizes. Advances in IT are the main enablers of these two important business phenomena. Many claim that IT is the main cause of downsizing of white-collar employees and middle management. To reduce operating costs, increase flexibility, and improve responsiveness, most Fortune 1000 firms and others have downsized their operations. In the late 1980s more than five million white-collar jobs were eliminated. A model by Pinsonneault and Kraemer (2002) theorizes that IT facilitates work and structural changes that lead to organizational downsizing. Their study found that IT does facilitate organizational downsizing but did not cause it. A similar link between IT and global outsourcing is also postulated. Al-Qirim (2003) supports that IT is the main enabler in automating operations, seeking new opportunities, and enhancing a firm's strategic business positioning in local and international markets. However, many companies, especially small and medium size enterprises (SMEs), are not equipped to cope with rapidly changing aspects of IT due to their size, resources, and ability to take technological risks. In normal circumstances these companies would have been precluded from benefiting from the advances in IT. The proliferation of e-Commerce has further strained resources of these companies, preventing them from fully benefiting from advances in IT. One way out of this complex situation is to outsource the IT and e-commerce technology functions. As some companies began to benefit from outsourcing of business functions, many other companies have also realized that they can reduce costs, avail of specialized talent, and reduce task completion times without hiring more employees.

Change #3: Ever Changing Firm Boundaries

If you purchased an item recently from Target.com, you may not be aware that the transaction, including back-end operations and fulfillment functions, is performed by Amazon.com. In 1999, Toys "R" Us failed to deliver Christmas gifts on time to thousands of kids because its inventory and fulfillment capabilities could not meet the online demand for its products. Due to insufficient knowledge and expertise in the toy market, that year Amazon.com ended up with $35 million excess inventory. Toys "R" Us entered into a strategic alliance with Amazon to merge its knowledge and expertise in selling toys with Amazon's expertise in e-commerce. This alliance became very successful with 123 million visitors; this co-branded site became one of the most visited sites of that season, and has generated sales of $180 million in that season. In 2006 this strategic alliance ended due to Toys "R" Us's legal dispute over its exclusive arrangements to sell toys with Amazon.com. The conclusion from this episode should not be that strategic alliances will not work, but that strategic alliances can be very successful, and that establishing and dismantling these alliances need not disrupt normal business operations.

Global systems such as ERP (enterprise resource planning) and SCM (supply chain management) are becoming a way of organizational life. They link suppliers, manufacturing plants, distribution centers, retail outlets, and customers to achieve free flow of goods, services, information, and funds. Enterprise systems make it possible to share information within the firm and with other firms. The information is no longer localized and no additional effort and costs are needed to communicate this information to other units that need it. By symmetrically sharing accurate information, the company can improve its decision making and instantaneously react to any anticipated situations.

Enterprise systems have made it seamless and relatively simple to establish strategic alliances. The number of strategic alliances is increasing and, in the year 2000 alone, over 10,000 new corporate alliances were formed (Schifrin, 2001). Currently 65 percent of non-U.S. and 75 percent of U.S. companies have some form of strategic alliance and alliance formation has been growing at a rate of 25 percent since 1985 (Xie and Johnson, 2004).

Corporate groupings and strategic alliances are not new. In Japan, family owned industrial groups called *zaibatsu* were prevalent before World War II. *Zaibatsu*s as a whole were very focused and vertically integrated, with influence over many industries. After World War II, *zaibatsu*s evolved into keiretsu. These new corporate structures do not involve family ownership but are characterized by cross ownership and common directorships. The keiretsu systems are known for long-term close relationships that have features of both markets and hierarchies. The members develop their unique business focus with an implicit understanding that the other members will not compete (Ito and Rose, 2004). This system of alliances helped the member companies to develop trust, and tradition and to share knowledge, resources, and capabilities. These arrangements allow the member companies to focus on core competencies, yet benefit from economies of scope. In the western corporate world these long-term relationships and implicit contract motivated by trust and tradition are not common. To achieve these goals, western corporations mainly rely on ownership control and legal contracts. Holmstrom and Roberts (2003) observe that keiretsu-like mutually interlocking and long-lasting corporate arrangements are becoming prevalent in the U.S. auto industry. As the Toys "R" Us and Amazon.com relationship between the years 2000 and 2006 illustrates, it is probably too early to expect long-term relationships, such as *keiretsu*s, to be sustained in the U.S. However, what can be accomplished by the Japanese firms by trust and tradition can be accomplished in the U.S. through interlocking information systems. Furthermore, these relationships can be replaced or reversed without normally expected traumatic changes.

Change #4: Escalating Strategic Alliances

A recent article in a special issue on strategic alliance appeared in Forbes magazine with the caption "Good-bye Mergers and Acquisitions" (Schifrin, 2001). The author said that in a global market tied together by the Internet, corporate partnerships and alliances are proving a more productive way to keep companies growing. One of the fastest growing trends for business today is the increasing number of strategic alliances. They are sweeping through nearly every industry and are becoming an essential driver of growth. Both globalization of business operations and convergence of technologies and services (such as the combination of video broadcasting, data and voice communication into one platform) contribute towards the growth in the number of strategic alliances. Alliances range in scope from an informal business relationship based on a simple contract to a joint venture agreement in which, for legal and tax purposes, either a corporation or a partnership is set up to manage the alliance. These alliances enable a firm to maintain its individuality, while working with others toward a common goal. Other benefits include: achieving advantages of scale, scope, and speed, enhancing competitiveness in domestic and/or global markets, speeding up product development, and diversification, creating new businesses, and reducing costs.

Advances in information technology make it possible to have lasting and close alliances without ownership transfers. Mergers, especially horizontal mergers between competing firms, are subject to antitrust laws and considered anticompetitive by consumers. These horizontal mergers are viewed with suspicion by consumers and enforcement agencies as anticompetitive. However, most of the goals of mergers can be achieved simply by forming strategic alliances without arousing suspicions of collusion. Instead of creating an internal governance structure through mergers and acquisitions, firms can benefit from the synergies of unified efforts through strategic alliances while maintaining their present ownership structures.

Three airlines alliances, Star Alliance, Oneworld, and Skyteam, participate in extensive code sharing (flights operated by an airline are jointly marketed by others in the alliance), as well as have joint sales offices, maintenance and operational facilities, operational staff, and investments and purchases. (More details of airlines alliances are provided in the mini case at the end of the chapter.) In mid 2006, GM investors were encouraging a strategic alliance between GM, Nissan, and Renault. An important reason for this call is to bring the managerial capabilities of Mr. Carlos Ghosn (Nissan CEO) to the management of GM and consequently improve its profitability. Many of the benefits of the 1998 merger between Chrysler and Daimler-Benz involving a $38 billion stock transfer can also be achieved by the proposed alliance. Such alliances are flexible and reversible. The companies within the alliance continue to maintain their unique characteristics and individuality and retain the flexibility to reevaluate the viability of the alliance in the future.

Change #5: Competition among Supply Chains

Many believe that the ultimate core competency of an organization is its supply chain design, implementation and operation (Fine, 2003). In the past, success of a company depended on how well the company managed internally the quality of its operations, organization, and decision making. Still, the quality of the internal management of a company is no longer a guarantee for the firm's financial success. Instead, the competitive advantage is now derived from how well a firm works together with its business partners and how well it manages its supply chains. Prior to the information revolution, most departments within a firm were operated as independent functional silos. The integration of operations/logistics, marketing, research and development, finance and accounting has made it possible to improve processes and profitability. The shift in focus from improvements in management of a company to improvements in management of a supply chain follows the path of advances in capabilities of information technology. The focus has shifted from cross-functional integration to cross-enterprise integration. The competitive advantage gained by Dell Computer Corporation and Wal-Mart with their exemplary supply chain integration is well known in the business folklore. Because of the realization that an effective and efficient global SCM can provide competitive advantage, an additional dimension of this competitive advantage, namely organization of the SCM, became available. Many companies began to emphasize their operations of SCM as a source of competitive advantage. This emphasis on SCM has led many to believe that in the future competition will be between supply chains. Over 70% of the supply chain experts from the industry, consulting, and academia agreed that the future competition will be between supply chains (Rice, Jr. and Hoppe 2003).

In the previous five sub-sections we reviewed some of the important strategic shifts that are taking place. A significant link connecting the structural changes discussed is the ability of an organization to integrate its business processes with those of its business partners. The next sub-section discusses the connection between advances in information technologies and global business integration (globalization).

INFORMATION TECHNOLOGIES AND GLOBAL BUSINESS INTEGRATION

IT is a key driver and enabler of globalization (Palvia, Palvia and Whitworth 2002). IT is the critical element needed to cope with additional difficulties in planning, control, coordination and decision making facing multinational enterprises due to differences in language, currency, culture, national infrastructure, and availability of qualified IT personnel (Ives and Jarvenpaa, 1999). As outsourcing of manufacturing operations, software development, and other business functions is becoming an important business practice, every business executive must have an understanding of the link between global operations and IT. Additionally, free trade agreements, and economic and political unions among nations are making globalization of operations a possibility for all firms, not just large corporations. The additional difficulties facing global supply chains that span many countries are manageable due to the improved connectivity and global reach of the Internet. However, the impact of the Internet is not just limited to improved connectivity. The communication tools spawned from Internet technology and the widespread adoption of nonproprietary communication protocols by companies all over the world have made access to the customers, suppliers, employees, and other stakeholders less difficult.

The role of the Internet in facilitating communication and standardizing communication tools at a global scale is undeniable. However, the importance of the Internet technologies in resolving planning, control and decision making challenges in a global environment are often exaggerated. Despite the great importance of messaging and communication links between business partners, these links do not solve all of their communication and coordination problems. Integration of disparate information systems along many dimensions will contribute significantly towards the evolving structural changes in the conduct of businesses worldwide.

An important technical problem in managing global information systems remains the integration of business processes. Mere exchange of information is insufficient to achieve integration of business processes. IT, through its ability to provide integration of business processes within the enterprise and among the value-chain partners, is an important component of global corporate strategy. A model by Palvia (2002) recognizes the importance of integration of business processes and ranks it high among twenty variables that have most impact due to IT. Ives and Jarvenpaa (1999) also recognize the importance of integration of business processes as an important factor in achieving a firm's global business strategy. They argue that "Worldwide variations in hardware and software features, i.e., availability and quality, force firms to use different vendor products in different parts of the world - this causes major obstacles in integrating communication networks, hardware, and disparate systems software for global applications" (p. 36-37).

Viewing information system integration as an absolute characteristic of systems will obscure our understanding of the link between business strategy and information systems. Almost all businesses that can benefit from sharing dispersed data have already achieved this low level data integration. Now, when we think of information system integration, we strive to achieve application level integration. Application integration is a strategy to bind many information systems together. Application integration can take many forms: Internal application integration; external or enterprise application integration; and business-to-business (B2B) application integration. Each progression of these integration levels poses higher technical challenges and risks, but offers potential for higher rewards. The strategic advantages of integration are mainly derived from B2B application integration. The ability to form, maintain, and benefit from alliances, business networks and supply chain teams spanning vast geographic regions and ownership control will create new strategic opportunities.

Another dimension of classifying integration is based on different approaches of integration: Information oriented; business process oriented; and service oriented. In information oriented integration, the concern is simple sharing of information between applications. Typical information oriented integration frees data from applications through application programming interfaces. Business oriented integration provides a single logical model that spans many applications and data stores, creating a common business process that controls many business processes spanning inter- and intra-company information systems. Service-oriented integration provides yet higher levels of integration by permitting applications to share common business logic and methods. Service-oriented integration allows enterprises to share common application services as well as information. Service-oriented integration is especially important for global information systems. For supply chains in many countries to function cohesively and for networks of firms to coordinate their activities, at least business process oriented integration is needed.

Asking for the ability to closely integrate operations, meld disparate hardware and software platforms to work in unison and yet not replace all or most of the existing computing infrastructure is an astonishing demand. Web services are the new technologies that solve the hardware and software heterogeneity and incompatibilities that are prevalent in global operations. Advances in IT have created opportunities for value chain partners to act as a cohesive unit. Web services, with their open standards and loose coupling, reduce the cost of integration, and facilitate communication among systems across enterprises. They enable automation of complex and dynamic business processes. Advances in service-oriented architecture (SOA) have enhanced the capabilities of supply chain management solutions using eXtensible Markup Language (XML) and Web services. A SOA is essentially a collection of services that communicate with each other across organizational boundaries. The communication can be either simple data passing through, or two or more services coordinating some activity. The next sub-section outlines these important developments.

Specific Information Technologies and Architectures for Cross-Functional and Cross-Enterprise Integration Worldwide

The structural changes discussed above did not occur in a vacuum. Advances in information technology, the interoperability of information systems, and free exchange of data within and between enterprises are a catalyst for these structural changes. Without the smooth exchange of data, transition of processes and interface between applications, and accounting for large volume of transactions across the functional units of a firm and among firms, would be nearly impossible. The alignment of strategies among partners would have been impossible.

The rapid development in information technology during the 1980s made it difficult for a firm's information systems that supported the business to have a cohesive structure. The information systems developed during this period supported individual functional departments using the best software, hardware and protocols that were available at the time of their development. The main concern during this period was how well each unit or function of the firm operated. Subsequent emphasis on speed to market, customer service, and more efficient execution made it necessary to focus on the enterprise as a whole, not individual functional units. Combining data from different systems to make information flow across the enterprise became a major challenge. Figure 2 shows the components of global enterprise system that integrate key internal business processes of a firm. The bulleted text next to the functional unit shows a partial list of input and output data available in that functional unit. This enterprise system is supported by a suite of integrated software modules and central databases. The database system collects data from a functional unit and makes it immediately available to other functional units and to numerous applications that support a firm's operations. Accuracy, timeliness, and efficiency of the data is achieved by making the data available to all functional units as soon as the data are recognized by one unit.

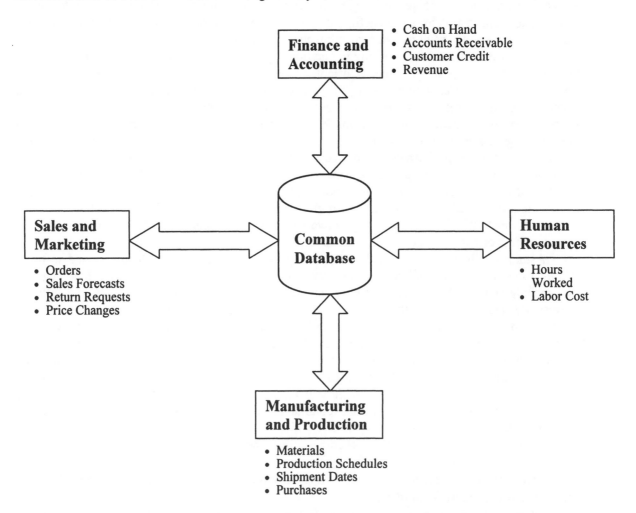

Figure 2. Global Enterprise Systems with Internal Focus

The success of cross-functional systems during 1985-1995 led to efforts after 1995 to integrate information systems across the enterprises. But the incompatibility among the systems of business partners around the world posed a major hurdle. Since the demand for interoperability is a new concept, many existing systems were not developed to interoperate with other systems even when using the same hardware and software platform and databases. These legacy systems were internally developed without much concern for standards, and, further, most of these systems did not exploit the capabilities of the Web. For the benefits of exchanging information to accrue, custom-built application program interfaces (API) have to be developed. A solution for exchanging information without throwing away existing legacy systems is enterprise application integration (EAI). EAI is the process of linking supply chain management (SCM), customer relationship management (CRM), partner relationship management and knowledge management environments. Although client/server architecture provided much flexibility -- interoperability and scalability in a networked environment was inadequate to handle large volumes of transactions in enterprise systems. Distributed object technology (DOT) was introduced as a solution to inadequacies of client/server architecture. DOT relies on middleware to provide integration, but middleware alternative to integration can be costly and difficult to develop and maintain. Web services provide an easy alternative to difficulties in integration of systems across enterprises. Figure 3 presents architecture for global enterprise systems that focuses on both internal and external information needs.

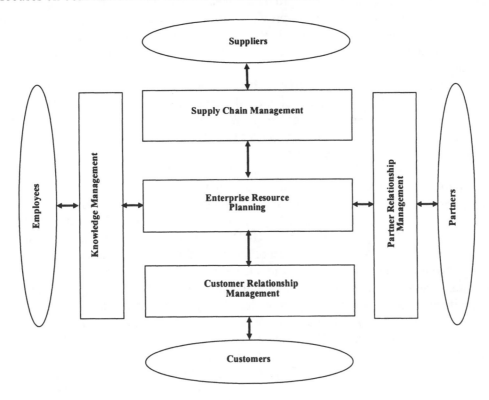

Figure 3. Global Enterprise Application Architecture with Internal and External Focus

XML is a text-based markup language specification from the World Wide Web Consortium (W3C). Unlike HTML, which uses tags for describing presentation and data, XML is strictly for the definition of portable structured data. It can be used as a language for defining data, such as markup grammars or vocabularies, and interchange formats and messaging protocols.

Web services are self-contained, modular applications that can be described, published, located, and invoked over a network, typically the World Wide Web. These software tools let application software in one organization communicate with other applications over a network using a specific set of standard protocols. These standards include XML-based technologies that enable distributed computing to support large-scale business transactions in an Internet environment. The Web services architecture describes three roles:

- service provider
- service requester
- service broker

and three basic operations:

- publish
- find
- bind.

A network component can play any or all of the three roles and three operations. Emerging technologies within Web services help promote interoperability between systems, including both legacy applications and applications that are yet to be developed.

SOAP (an abbreviation for Service-Oriented Architecture Protocol) is an XML-based protocol for the exchange of information in a decentralized, distributed environment. SOAP defines a messaging protocol between requestor and provider objects, such that the requesting objects can perform a remote method invocation on the providing objects in an object-oriented programming fashion. SOAP forms the basis for distributed object communication in most vendor implementations of SOA. SOAP is vendor-neutral, and independent of platform, object model, operating system, and programming languages.

Web Services Description Language (WSDL) is a document written in XML to describe the services a business offers and to provide a way for individuals and other businesses to access those services electronically. The document describes a Web service's capabilities as collections of communication endpoints capable of exchanging messages. It specifies the location of the service and the operations (or methods) the service exposes.

Universal Description, Discovery and Integration (UDDI) standard is an XML-based specification to publish and discover information about remote services. Remote services may include legacy systems wrapped using Distributed Object Technology, or specific software applications that deliver specific business functionality exposed by an organization through Internet protocols. The core component of the UDDI specification is the UDDI business registration module. This module consists of three major parts: "white pages" denoting the address, contact, and identifiers for the service offering; "yellow pages" for providing a categorization of the offered service according to standard taxonomies; and "green pages" for denoting technical information about the offered services. The UDDI specification also includes programmatic interfaces so that technical details about the offered services can be linked to WSDL descriptions, and service invocation can be accomplished by utilizing the SOAP protocol. Other UDDI programmatic interfaces allow for the localization, and selection of remote services on behalf of clients given specific search criteria.

Web Services Flow Language (WSFL) is an XML language for the description of Web services compositions. WSFL deals with two types of Web service compositions: the Flow Model, and the Global Model. The Flow Model is normally used to describe a business process. This is done by specifying the appropriate usage pattern of a collection of Web Services, in such a way that the resulting flow composition describes how to achieve a particular business goal. A Flow Model can be converted into a Web Service by wrapping it within a WSDL document.

Web Services Platform Alternatives for Implementing Information Systems that Integrate Across Enterprises

There are alternatives to Web integration platforms. Java 2 enterprise edition (J2EE) is a set of specifications and a platform developed by Sun Microsystems and widely adopted by many developers, including IBM, BEA Systems, Oracle, and HP. The main goal of J2EE is to produce a platform for building portable, scalable, secure, and robust enterprise-level applications. The .NET platform alternative is a broad framework that describes Microsoft's strategy for delivering software as services across the Web. .NET supports multiple development languages, including VB.Net and C#. It is an integrated development model that provides built-in support for building and debugging Web Services. .NET offers integration through BizTalk Server and Microsoft Message Queue. Both of these platforms are mature technologies with extensive adoption and support.

SUMMARY AND CONCLUSIONS

The rapid growth in electronic commerce and advances in IT are transforming the function, scope, and structure of the industries within which the individual firm operates. Broadly, we can classify the impact of information technology on the operations of the firm at two levels: organizational changes that are happening within the firm; and changes that are taking place outside the firm that are shaping the entire industrial organizations. Factors that are causing structural changes include: role of intermediaries in distribution channels; increasing shift towards smaller size firms' focus on core competence and global outsourcing; ever changing firm boundaries; escalating strategic alliances; shift towards competition among strategic alliances; and increasing role of information technologies towards global business integration. Distribution channels are being reshaped and realigned to utilize the capabilities of new technologies. Global outsourcing, both onshore and offshore, is becoming part of overall business strategies of multinational corporations. Firm boundaries that were once clearly demarcated are becoming blurred. The technological ability to create interlocking information systems quickly and inexpensively is enabling firms to form strategic alliances and blend operational activities for competitive advantage. The nature of the competition in an industry itself is shifting. Competition among firms is gradually shifting towards competition among network of firms and competition among supply chains. Key information technologies contributing to global business integration are: XML, SOAP, WSDL, UDDI, DOT, and WSFL. WSFL enables a multitude of web services that have sprung over the last 10 years. Web services have become the main enabler of global business integration and global strategic alliances. Web services are the new technologies that will solve the hardware and software heterogeneity and incompatibilities that are prevalent in global operations.

MINICASE

Northwest Airlines and KLM Alliance: The Role of DOTJ and DOT

In general, collaboration among competing firms is frowned upon by consumers, economists, and policy-makers. The fear is that the coordination of activities by competing firms may ultimately lead to price fixing, bid rigging, the market allocation schemes, and increased prices and illegal overcharges. In the U.S., the Antitrust Division of the Department of Justice (DOJ) enforces antitrust laws. But in recent years, the Department of Transportation (DOT) has been granting airlines immunity from antitrust prohibitions. In 1993 Northwest Airlines and KLM requested DOT to grant antitrust exemption and proposed the coordination of operations, pricing, marketing, including yield management, scheduling, utilization, seat inventories, gates, ground support, reservations, and advertising. Normally such intense coordination is tantamount to a horizontal merger and requires approval from DOJ. The DOT granted the exemption claiming that this alliance is between smaller airlines, and that infusion of capital into ailing Northwest airlines would make air transportation more competitive in the future, and the alliance would be beneficial to consumers. In the following years, alliances among many larger airlines were also given immunity by DOT. DOT's rationale is that competition in the air transportation industry will be between alliances of airlines – not among individual airlines.

History of Cooperation between Airlines
Travelers choose single-carrier service since connections will be smoother, baggage service more dependable, and check-in faster and more convenient. Travel between smaller locations requires several transfers, and it is very unlikely that a single airline connects the two locations. This problem is more pronounced in international travel. The problems are alleviated using Codeshare

agreements, whereby one carrier markets service and places its code on another carrier's flights. These code sharing agreements between larger airlines and smaller commuter airlines or between larger airlines specializing international travel and those specializing in domestic travel have provided significant convenience to travelers for several years. Associated services of code sharing such as common gates at the airports and combined frequent-flier programs improved traveler satisfaction. Over time these arrangements evolved from mere schedule coordination to tighter integration involving shared aircraft, ground support, reservations, and marketing programs. These Codeshare arrangements of non-overlapping routes expanded into those for overlapping routes by 1999.

The proposed alliance between American Airlines and British Airways has been controversial because of concerns about the alliance's potential anticompetitive effects. By 2005, the structure of competition in the airlines is no longer between competing airlines, but it is between competing alliances. Normally, alliances among firms serving the same markets are thought to be anticompetitive resulting in higher prices, but these alliances have also created value to travelers. Some benefits of airlines alliances are: more available flights; easier connections between carriers; more fare options; unified check-in for all carriers; consistent quality standards across carriers; and one reservation network for all members. Three strategic alliances, Star Alliance, Oneworld and Skyteam Alliance, dominate the aviation industry: As of April 2006, these three alliances account for over 63% of worldwide passenger miles. Table 1 shows the composition of major airlines within each alliance and their corresponding market share.

	Star Alliance	**Oneworld**	**Skyteam Alliance**
Passengers	425 million	242.6 million	372.9 million
Number of airlines (as of January 1, 2007)	18	8	9
Market Share (in 2005)	23.6%	13.5%	20.7%
Larger airlines	Air Canada Air New Zealand Asiana Airlines LOT Polish Airlines Lufthansa SAS Singapore Airlines TAP Air Portugal Thai Airways International United US Airways	Aer Lingus American Airlines British Airways Cathay Pacific Finnair Iberia LAN Qantas	Aeroflot Aeroméxico Air France-KLM Alitalia Continental Czech Airlines Delta Korean Air Northwest

Table 1: Characteristics of Airlines Alliances

Airlines in the same alliance need to communicate information and share a common information system with alliance members. Enterprise information systems provide a common platform for the alliance members to share information and to compete as one unit. Preliminary evidence indicates that these alliances are beneficial to the travelers, as well (Brueckner 2001).

Discussion Questions:

1. Discuss the effect of airlines alliances on convenience and airfares of customers traveling between small towns in domestic markets and in international markets.

2. Briefly list the difficulties in routing luggage between routes that span two or more airlines in an alliance. What information needs to transferred or jointly accessible between different airlines in an alliance?

3. What is the effect of airlines alliances on competition? Is the airlines industry peculiar to encourage alliances of airlines, or would we expect these alliances to spread into other services? Name one other service or group of services that are conducive to formation of industry alliances.

4. In the world without enterprise systems, interoperable systems and services, and open standards, tight coupling of alliance members may not be possible. List the difficulties that travelers would encounter if the technologies mentioned above did not exist.

KEY TERMS

Business Process Oriented Integration
Business Process Reengineering (BPR)
Coase's Theorem
Electronic Brokerage
Electronic Communication
Electronic Integration
Information Oriented Integration
Keiretsu
Paradigm Shift
Service Oriented Integration
SOA (Service Oriented Architecture)
SOAP (Service Oriented Architecture Protocol)
Transaction Costs
UDDI (Universal Description, Discovery and Integration)
Web Services
WSDL (Web Services Description Language)
WSFL (Web Services Flow Language)
XML (eXtensible Markup Language)

STUDY QUESTIONS

1. Some suggest that electronic commerce, rather than eliminating intermediaries, is creating more intermediaries. The term "hyperintermediation" is coined to describe this phenomenon. List and explain all potential entities that may receive payments when you complete OneClick™ transaction at Amazon.com.

2. Information asymmetry is a term used to describe the situation in which economic agents possess varying degrees of information regarding an object, event, or circumstance. For example, quality of a used car is known to the seller, but a potential buyer may not be aware of it. Information asymmetries result in inefficient resource allocations. Discuss how information systems can mitigate the inefficiencies caused by information asymmetries.

3. Biotechnology companies rely heavily on alliances with pharmaceutical companies to finance their research and development expenditures, and pharmaceutical firms rely heavily on alliances to supplement their internal research and development. Discuss why these alliances are not anticompetitive.

4. In the late 1920's Ford Motor Corporation owned and operated a rubber plantation in Brazil called Fordlândia. Discuss why such a high-level of vertical integration in automobile industry is not evident in the 21ˢᵗ century.

5. Give two examples of changes in distribution channels, one in which the number of participants in the channel has shrunk and the other in which the number has increased. In the last ten years, in general, which one of these two changes is more predominant?

6. List and discuss the benefits of airline alliances to travelers. Evaluate which of these benefits critically depend on interoperable information systems. Discuss if these gains due to efficient combined operations would have been possible twenty five years ago. Discuss if industry alliances in other industries can be beneficial to consumers.

REFERENCES

Al-Qirim, A. Y. "The strategic outsourcing decision of IT and eCommerce: The case of small businesses in New Zealand," *Journal of Information Technology Cases and Applications,* 5, 2003, pp. 32-56.

Benjamin, R., and Wigand, R. "Electronic Markets and Virtual Value Chains on the Information Superhighway," *Sloan Management Review*, 36, 1995, pp. 62-72.

Brueckner, J. K. Airlines Alliances Benefit Consumers, Institute of Government and Policy Affairs, University of Illinois, 14, 2001, pp. 1-4.

Brynjolfsson, E., and Lorin, H. M. *Beyond Computation—Information Technology, Organizational Transformation, and Business Performance, in Inventing the Organizations of the 21st Century* by Thomas W. Malone, Robert Laubacher and Michael S. Scott Morton (eds) The MIT Press. 2003.

Brynjolfsson, E., Malone, T. W., Gurubaxani, V., and Kambil, A. "Does Information Technology Lead to Smaller Firms?," *Management Science*, 4(12), 1994, pp. 1628-1644.

Brynjolfsson, E., and Smith, M. D. "Frictionless Commerce? A Comparison of Internet and Conventional Retailers," *Management Science*, 46(4), 2000, pp. 563-582.

Byrd, T. A. "Information technology: Core competencies, and sustained competitive advantage," *Information Resources Management Journal,* 14, 2001, pp. 27-36.

Cordella, A. "Does Information Technology Always Lead to Lower Transaction Costs?," *The 9ᵗʰ European Conference on Information Systems*, Bled, Slovenia, June 27-29, 2001.

Cordella, A. and Simon, K. A. "The Impact of Information Technology on Transaction and Coordination Cost," *Conference on Information Systems Research in Scandinavia (IRIS 20),* Oslo, Norway, August 9-12, 1997.

Farrell, J. "Information and the Coase Theorem," *Economic Perspectives*, 1, 1987, pp. 113-129.

Fine, C. Clockspeed-based Strategies for Supply Chain Design, in Malone, T.W., Laubacher, R., and Scott Morton, M.S. (eds) *Inventing the Organizations of the 21st Century*, The MIT Press, 2003.

Gurubaxani, V., and Whang, S. "The Impact of Information Systems on Organizations and Markets," *Communications of the ACM,* 34, 1991, pp. 59-73.

Hayek, F. A. "The Use of Knowledge in Society," *American Economic Review*, 35(4), 1945, pp. 519-530.

Hitt, L. M. "Information Technology and Firm Boundaries: Evidence from Panel Data," Information Systems Research, 10, 1999, pp. 134-149.

Holmstrom, B., and Roberts, J. The Boundaries of the Firm Revisited, in Malone, T.W., Laubacher, R., and Scott Morton, M.S. (eds*) Inventing the Organizations of the 21st Century*, The MIT Press: Cambridge. 2003.

Ito, K., and Rose, E. L. "An Emerging Structure of Corporations," *Multinational Business Review,* 12, 2004, pp. 63-83.

Ives, B., and Jarvenpaa, S. L. "Applications of Global Information Technology: Key Issues for Management," *MIS Quarterly,* 23, 1999, pp. 33-49.

Laudon, K. C. and Laudon, J. P. *Management Information Systems: Managing the Digital Firm*, 9th edition, Pearson Prentice Hall, Upper Saddle River, NJ. 2006.

Malone, T., Yates, J. and Benjamin, R. "Electronic Markets and Electronic Hierarchies," *Communications of the ACM*, 6, 1987, pp. 485-497.

Palvia, P. C., Palvia, S.C., and Whitworth, J. E. Global Information Technology Management Environment: Reresentative World Issues, in *Global Information Technology and Electronic Commerce*, Palvia, et al. (eds.), 2002, pp. 1-27.

Palvia, P. C. Strategic Applications of Information Technology in Global Buesiness: The "GLITS" Model and an Instrument, in Global Information Technology and Electronic Commerce, Palvia, et al. (eds.), 2002, pp. 100-119.

Pinsonneault, A., and Kraemer, K. "Exploring the role of Information Technology in Organizational Downsizing: A Tale of Two American Cities," *Organizational Science,* 13, 2002, pp. 191-208.

Rice, Jr., J. B., and Hoppe, R. M. "Supply Chain vs. Supply Chain: The Hype and the Reality," *Supply Chain Management Review,* September/October, 2001, pp. 47-54.

Roche, E. The Multinational Enterprise in An Age of Internet and Electronic Commerce, in *Global Information Technology and Systems Management Key Issues and Trends,* Palvia, et al. (eds.), 1996, pp. 424-440.

Schifrin, M. "Partner or Perish", *Forbes*, May 21, 2001, 26-28.

Tapscott, D. *Digital Economy - Promise and Peril in the Age of Networked Intelligence*. McGraw Hill, New York, New York. 1996.

Xie, F. T., and Johnson, W. F. "Strategic Alliances: Incorporating the Impact of e-Business Technological Innovations," *The Journal of Industrial Marketing*, 19, 2004, pp. 208-222.

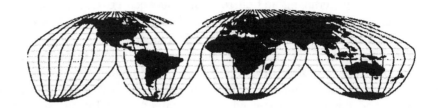

E-Government Concepts, Frameworks and Implementation: Worldwide Status and Challenges

Shailendra C. Jain Palvia
Long Island University, USA

Sushil S. Sharma
Ball State University, USA

CHAPTER SUMMARY

The evolution of the Internet has created the underlying infrastructure for electronic government (hereafter called e-government), both in information and service delivery; and, in fostering the exchange of information with an informed, aware citizenry. E-government generally refers to the delivery of national or local government information and services via the Internet or other digital means to citizens or businesses or other governmental agencies. The purpose of e-government is to develop a government e-portal, a one-stop Internet gateway to major government services. E-government provides efficient government management of information to the citizen; better service delivery to citizens; and empowerment of the people through access to information; improved productivity and cost savings in doing business with suppliers and customers of government; and participation in public policy decision-making. This chapter looks at the concepts, frameworks and implementation of e-government systems. As part of the discussion, it looks at the current status of e-government worldwide and identifies some future challenges for e-government systems.

INTRODUCTION

A very significant number of nations at all levels of government are already offering e-government services. Approaches to e-government program offerings and e-government readiness vary from country to country. The United Nations (UN) E-Government Survey 2005 conducted a study to assess the public sector e-government initiatives of 191 UN member states according to a weighted average composite index of e-readiness based on website assessment; telecommunication infrastructure and human resource endowment. It is expected that e-government will bring ultimately e-democracy that will allow governments to interact with the public directly on a one to one basis. This may pave the way for "direct democracy" because an individual will be able to interact with governments directly.

The e-government implementation will certainly provide greater opportunities for consultation and dialogue between government and citizens, and between government and businesses. Governments will use internet tools such as chat rooms, web boards and listservs to seek public feedback on their policies. Online consultations will be regular and frequent.

Notwithstanding the progress, there remains wide disparity in access to ICTs, and consequently to e-government offerings between, and among, regions and countries of the world. Most of the e-government implementations are still at an early stage of engaging citizens. There are many issues and challenges that need to be resolved for effective e-government implementation. Many believe that e-government implementation does not mean offering government services on a 24/7 basis, but meeting citizens' expectations for short response times, given that the potential volume of online activity represents a major challenge for governments in a world of resource constraints. The e-government will also require change in the roles and responsibilities of the institutions, governments and the public service. This chapter discusses e-government concepts and frameworks. The chapter also discusses current status of e-government implementation worldwide and future challenges that e-government has for its implementations. We start with key definitions to set the stage for detailed discussion.

E-GOVERNMENT DEFINITIONS

E-government is a generic term for web-based services from agencies of local, state and federal governments. In e-government, the government uses information technology and particularly the Internet to support government operations, engage citizens, and provide government services. The interaction may be in the form of obtaining information, filings, or making payments and a host of other activities via the World Wide Web (Sharma and Gupta, 2003, Sharma, 2004, Sharma 2006). E-government is defined by other sources as follows:

World Bank (www.worldbank.org) definition (AOEMA report): *"E-Government refers to the use by government agencies of information technologies (such as Wide Area Networks, the Internet, and mobile computing) that have the ability to transform relations with citizens, businesses, and other arms of government. These technologies can serve a variety of different ends: better delivery of government services to citizens, improved interactions with business and industry, citizen empowerment through access to information, or more efficient government management. The resulting benefits can be less corruption, increased transparency, greater convenience, revenue growth, and/or cost reductions."*

United Nations (www.unpan.org) definition (AOEMA report): *"E-government is defined as utilizing the Internet and the world-wide-web for delivering government information and services to citizens."*

Global Business Dialogue on Electronic Commerce - GBDe (www.gbde.org) definition (AOEMA report): *"Electronic government (hereafter e-Government) refers to a situation in which administrative, legislative and judicial agencies (including both central and local governments) digitize their internal and external operations and utilize networked systems efficiently to realize better quality in the provision of public services."*

The Gartner Group describes e-government as *"the continuous optimization of service delivery, constituency participation, and governance by transforming internal and external relationships through technology, the Internet and new media."*

The Working Group on E-government in the Developing World (www.pacificcouncil.org) defines e-government as follows: *"E-government is the use of information and communication technologies (ICTs) to promote more efficient and effective government, facilitate more accessible government services, allow greater public access to information, and make government more accountable to citizens. E-government might involve delivering services via the Internet, telephone, community centers (self-service or facilitated by others), wireless devices or other communications systems."*

While definitions of e-government by various sources may vary widely, there is a common theme. E-government involves using information technology, and especially the Internet, to improve the delivery of government services to citizens, businesses, and other government agencies. E-government enables citizens to interact and receive services from the federal, state or local governments twenty four hours a day, seven days a week.

E-government is in the early stages of development. Most governments have already taken or are taking initiatives offering government services online. However, for the true potential of e-government to be realized, government needs to restructure and transform its long entrenched business processes. According to Gartner, e-government involves the use of ICTs to support government operations and provide government services (Fraga, 2002). However, e-government goes even further and aims to fundamentally transform the production processes in which public services are generated and delivered, thereby transforming the entire range of relationships of public bodies with citizens, businesses and other governments (Leitner, 2003).

In the last few years, there has been much talk of mobile government or m-government. M-government refers to the use of wireless technologies like cellular/mobile phones, laptops and PDAs (Personal Digital Assistants) for offering and delivering government services. M-government is not a substitute for e-government, rather it complements it.

BENEFITS OF E-GOVERNMENT

Many governmental units across the world have embraced the digital revolution and have made available lots of information ranging from static publications to interactive databases. E-government offers many benefits to citizens, businesses and government organizations as listed below:
- Provide greater access to government information;
- Promote civic engagement by enabling the public to interact with government officials;
- Make government more accountable by making its operations more transparent, thus reducing the opportunities for corruption;
- Provide development opportunities, especially benefiting rural and traditionally underserved communities.
- Provide savings in time and cost
- Promote citizen empowerment
- Reduce redundancies in information resulting in improved productivity
- Reduce social and economic disparity
- Make government information and services available from anywhere globally anytime (24x365 basis)
- Provide "one stop" access to vast information and diverse services.

E-GOVERNANCE AND E-GOVERNMENT

E-Governance
E-governance, meaning 'electronic governance,' is using information and communication technologies (ICTs) at various levels of the government and the public sector and beyond, for the purpose of enhancing governance (Bedi, Singh and Srivastava, 2001; Holmes, 2001; Okot-Uma, 2000). Some authors contend that e-government constitutes only a subset (though a major one) of e-governance. According to these authors, e-governance is a broader concept and includes the use of ICT by government and civil society to promote greater participation of citizens in the governance of political institutions, e.g., use of the Internet by politicians and political parties to elicit views from their constituencies in an efficient manner, or the publicizing of views by civil society organizations

which are in conflict with the ruling powers (Howard, 2001 and Bannister and Walsh, 2002).

According to Keohane and Nye (2000): *"By governance, we mean the processes and institutions, both formal and informal, that guide and restrain the collective activities of a group. Government is the subset that acts with authority and creates formal obligations. Governance need not necessarily be conducted exclusively by governments. Private firms, associations of firms, nongovernmental organizations (NGOs), and associations of NGOs all engage in it, often in association with governmental bodies, to create governance; sometimes without governmental authority."* Clearly, this definition suggests that e-governance need not be limited to the public sector. It connotes managing and administering policies and procedures in the private sector as well.

The UNESCO definition (www.unesco.org) is: *"E-governance is the public sector's use of information and communication technologies with the aim of improving information and service delivery, encouraging citizen participation in the decision-making process and making government more accountable, transparent and effective. E-governance involves new styles of leadership, new ways of debating and deciding policy and investment, new ways of accessing education, new ways of listening to citizens and new ways of organizing and delivering information and services. E-governance is generally considered as a wider concept than e-government, since it can bring about a change in the way citizens relate to governments and to each other. E-governance can bring forth new concepts of citizenship, both in terms of citizen needs and responsibilities. Its objective is to engage, enable and empower the citizen."*

It is clear that considerable confusion exists in explaining e-government and e-governance. In what follows, we attempt to resolve the ambiguities and come up with clear and non-overlapping definitions. Our premise is simple: e-government's focus is on constituencies and stakeholders outside the organization, whether it is the government or public sector at the city, county, state, national, or international levels. On the other hand, e-governance focuses on administration and management within an organization, whether it is public or private, or large or small. A 2x2 matrix, shown in Table 1, summarizes the domains of e-government and e-governance.

		FOCUS	
		Outside	Inside
Type of Organization	Public Sector – Government Agency	e-Government (Extranet and Internet)	e-Governance (Intranet)
	Private Sector – MNCs or SMEs	Inter-Organizational Systems – IOS like CRM systems (Extranet and Internet)	e-Governance (Intranet)

Table 1. Palvia and Sharma Framework for e-Government versus e-Governance

Based on this classification, e-governance concerns internally-focused utilization of information and internet technologies to manage organizational resources – capital, human, material, machines – and administer policies and procedures (both for the public sector or private sector). The telecommunications network that facilitates e-governance is the Intranet. What has been generally termed as G2E (Government to Employee) will be now under the label of e-governance. E-governance deals with the online activities of government employees. The activities might include information to calculate retirement benefits, access to important applications, and content and collaboration with other government employees anytime, anywhere.

Any interaction of a governmental agency (G) with outside constituencies is called e-government. Outside constituencies can be citizens (C), businesses (B), or other governmental agencies (G) themselves. Government agencies should be held responsible and accountable for their actions in collecting taxes from its citizens in various forms and then using these revenues to provide diverse services to its constituents in the areas of defense, security, economic vitality, education, and health care. To perform all these activities efficiently and effectively, if the governmental agencies deploy information and Internet technologies, it is called e-government. The telecommunications network that provides these is the Extranet or the Internet itself. One special type of G2C is when elected representatives and political parties interact with the citizens nationally or in their constituencies. This type of G2C is also called e-democracy. In the next section, we will describe different categories of e-government services.

A TAXANOMY OF E-GOVERNMENT SERVICES

G2C – Government to Citizen
G2C are those activities in which the government provides one-stop, on-line access to information and services to citizens. G2C applications enable citizens to ask questions of government agencies and receive answers; file income taxes (federal, state, and local); pay taxes (income, real estate); renew driver's licenses; pay traffic tickets; change their address; and make appointments for vehicle emission inspections and driving tests. In addition, government may disseminate information on the web; provide downloadable forms online; conduct training (e.g., in California, drivers' education classes are offered online); help citizens find employment; provide tourism and recreation information; provide advice about health and safety issues; allow transfer of benefits like food coupons, file flood relief compensation (as in the case of Hurricane Katrina in New Orleans, USA) electronically through the use of smart cards; and the list goes on.

G2B – Government to Business
In G2B, the government deals with businesses such as suppliers using the Internet and other ICTs. G2B includes two two-way interactions and transactions: government-to-business and business-to-government (B2G). B2G refers to businesses selling products and services to government. Two key G2B areas are e-procurement and auctioning of government surpluses. Government buys large amounts of MROs (Maintenance, Repairs, and Operations) and other materials directly from suppliers. In many cases, RFQs are mandated by law. The tendering system is essentially a reverse auction (buy-side auction). The Hong Kong government provides some good examples of B2G services. The major projects of the Hong Kong government include: Electronic Service Delivery Scheme (ESD), Interactive Government Service Directory (IGSD), the Electronic Tendering System (ETS), the HKSAR Government Information Center (enables people to view news, government notices, information on leisure and cultural activities, and so on), and the HK Post e-Cert (this authority issues digital certificates to individuals and organizations). The ESD project provides 38 different public services through eleven agencies – transport department, immigration, tourist association, labor department, social welfare department, inland revenue department, registration and electoral office, trade and industry department, treasury department, rating and valuation department, innovation and technology commission.

In group purchasing, suppliers post group purchasing offers, and discount the price as more orders are placed. Government hospitals and public schools actively purchase in groups online. Many government agencies auction equipment surpluses ranging from vehicles to foreclosed real estate. The U.S., General Services Administration (GSA) launched a property auction site online www.auctionrp.com, where real-time auctions for surpluses and seized goods are conducted. Furthermore, businesses in the USA and other countries file income taxes and financial reports electronically. Electronic filing of taxes is now done in over 100 countries, from Finland to India to Thailand to United States. Even sales taxes and value added taxes can be paid online.

G2G – Government to Government
G2G deals with those activities that take place between different government organizations/agencies. Many of these activities are aimed at improving the efficiency and effectiveness of overall

government operations. Examples in the United States include Intelink (an intranet that carries classified information shared by different U.S. intelligence agencies), procurement at GSA (aggregating demand quantity for different units of the government), federal case registry (locating information about child support), and procurement marketing and access network (a searchable database that contracting officers in various government units use to find products and services sold by small, disadvantaged, or women-owned businesses).

Government to Constituents (E-Democracy)

E-democracy refers to online activities of governments, elected representatives, political parties and citizens for democratic processes. This includes political or current affairs discussion and online consultation between representatives and their constituents. During the 2004 U.S. presidential elections and 2006 midterm elections, both major party candidates had their own information portals and also sent e-mail messages to potential voters. In South Korea, since web surfers seldom read newspapers or watch TV, politicians have to rely on the Internet to recruit voters. Padaq, the Seoul-based over-the-counter stock exchange, offers an Internet game that allows players to buy "stocks" in a politician. This game resulted in over 500,000 members signing up in just one year. Yet another common use is the broadcasting of city council meetings, press conferences and public addresses.

Electronic voting is another important application within the domain of e-democracy. Manual voting processes are subject to error, manipulation, fraud, and rigging leading to losers calling for recounts. Voting faces a broad spectrum of technological and social problems that must be systematically addressed – voter registration to voter authentication to the casting of ballots to the counting and tallying of results. Such voting problems may result in major political crises, as happened in November 2004 in the Ukraine and the Gore-Bush presidential race in 2000 in the U.S. The first country to fully computerize balloting, as of 2000, was Brazil. Electronic voting machines were used successfully in Indian state elections in the 2004 parliamentary election. More than 600,000 electronic voting machines were used. The Election Commission of India used two similar voting machines made by Electronics Corporation of India and Bharat Electronics. These machines are battery-operated machines which are portable, 'easy to operate,' 'reliable,' 'tamper-proof and error free.' The machines were operated by supervised officials at polling stations. The illiterate voters were able to vote based on pictures and logos of the candidates and the party they represented. It not only greatly reduced the counting process time but also saved tons of ballot paper. There were hardly any complaints against the use of this system in India.

E-democracy involves 'electronic engagement' (*e-engagement*): engaging public in the policy process via electronic networks; 'electronic consultation' (*e-consultation*) which refers to interaction between public servants and the citizenry and interest groups; and 'electronic controllership' (*e-controllership*) consisting of the capability to manage the cost, performance, and services of an organization electronically (Riley, 2003).

E-GOVERNMENT SCOPE AND IMPLEMENTATION FRAMEWORKS

Like any other major innovation implementation, e-government implementation is evolutionary in nature involving multiple stages. This section presents five major frameworks; Layne and Lee's (2001) Four Stages model, United Nations/ASPA's Five Stages model, Gartner Group's Four Stages model, World Bank's Three Stages model, and finally Sharma and Gupta's Four Layers and Four Stages model. The source for the first four frameworks is Siau, K., Long, Y. (2005).

The Layne and Lee's Model of E-government Implementation

Layne and Lee (2001) proposed a framework for the evolutionary implementation of e-government involving four stages: cataloguing, transaction, vertical integration and horizontal integration. The cataloguing stage requires government agencies to create static web sites to gain 'online presence.' In the transaction stage the government offers users to transact online in a secure environment. Vertical integration requires the government to offer services fully integrated between local and central agencies that exist within the same function. The horizontal integration stage requires government to offer services across not only different levels of government but also integration across different functions of government. This stage of integration supports 'one-stop shopping.' The framework is illustrated in Figure 1 and Table 2.

The Layne & Lee Framework of E-Government

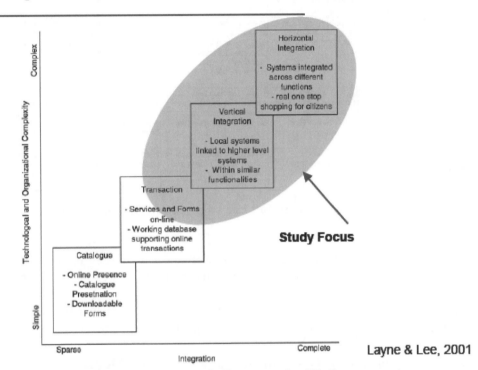

Figure 1. The Layne and Lee's Framework of E-Government

UN/ASPA Study: Five Stages of e-Government Implementation

The five stages of e-Government Implementation are: Emerging, Enhanced, Interactive, Transactional, and Fully Integrated.

Emerging: An emerging state is achieved through a few independent government websites which provide users with static organizational or political information. Sites may include contact information (i.e. telephone numbers and addresses of public officials). In rare cases, special features like FAQs may be found.

Enhanced: An enhanced stage is when a web site's content becomes more dynamic and the e-Government sites are linked to other official pages. Government publications, legislation, and newsletters are available. Search features and e-mail addresses are available. A site for the national or ruling government may also be present that links the surfer to ministries or departments.

Interactive: An interactive stage is when government web sites offer features that permit formal interactions between citizens and service providers. These interactions can be through e-mails, downloading and filling forms and applications and submitting them. Also, the content and information are regularly updated.

Dimensions of Business Process Change in E-Government

Business Process Change Project Dimensions	The Layne & Lee Framework of Electronic Government (2001)			
	Stage I - Cataloguing	Stage II - Transaction	Stage III - Vertical Integration	Stage IV - Horizontal Integration
Motives/Needs	Provide basic information services over the Web; Provide information quickly and conveniently	Extend services to online transaction; Reduce costs; Simplify service	Provide true one-stop service; Speed up and greatly improve government processes and services; Provide wide-scope integration	
Strategic Objectives	Create apublic image on the Web; Set up the evolutionary path for later stages	Make online transactions attractive; Link e-Gov systems and legacy systems; Establish standards for security and authentication	Integrate appropriate vertical and horizontal functions within meaningful constraints;Integrate and align business cultures; Merge e-Government and ICT systems;	
Focal Areas	Webified print content; Forms downloading; Fringe areas; Identification of potential future e-Gov areas	Legacy transaction systems in select areas; Other transactional services in fringe areas	Redesign busines core processes (in an evolutionary approach); Link sources of information; Newly design or redesign intra- & inter agency, intra- & inter-level, and intra- & inter-branch functions as appropriate	
Stakes and Stakeholders	Identifying salient stakeholders and their needs	Identifying and managing salient stakeholders and their needs	Identifying, managing, and involving salient stakeholders and their needs	

Table 2. The Layne and Lee's Framework of E-government

Transactional: A transactional stage is when the user can actually pay online for services such as parking fines, automobile registration fees, utility bills and taxes over complete secure environment.

Fully Integrated or Seamless: A fully integrated or seamless stage is when any government service is accessed instantly and automatically and all processing takes place without user intervention.

Gartner's Four Stages of E-Government Implementation Model

The four stages of the e-government implementation model are: Presence, Interaction, Transaction, and Transformation. These stages have similarities with the previous four stages model.

Presence: This phase simply consists of setting up a web site to post information such as agency mission, addresses, opening hours and possibly some official documents of relevance to the public. The web site is essentially an electronic brochure.

Interaction: This phase is characterized by web sites that provide basic search capabilities, host forms to download, and linkages with other relevant sites, as well as e-mail addresses of offices or officials.

Transaction: This phase is characterized by allowing constituents to conduct and complete entire tasks online on a 24/7 basis. The focus of this stage is to build self-service applications for the public to access online, but also to use the Web as a complement to other delivery channels. This is the current stage for several agencies and the most immediate target for many e-government initiatives worldwide.

Transformation: This phase is the ultimate goal of almost all national and local e-government initiatives. It is characterized by delivery of government services by providing a single point of contact to constituents that makes government organization totally transparent to citizens.

World Bank's Three Stage E-Government Implementation

The three stages of the World Bank's e-government implementation are: publish, interact and transact. They are similar to the first three stages of the previous two models.

Publish: This phase is characterized by publishing the government information online, beginning with rules and regulations, documents, and forms. This phase is targeted to disseminate information compiled by the government to various stakeholders.

Interact: This phase is characterized by engaging various users through web sites. Interactive e-government involves two-way communication and interactions may start with basic functions like email contact information for government officials or feedback forms that allow users to submit comments on legislative or policy proposals.

Transact: This phase is characterized by allowing users to conduct transactions online. A transact website offers a direct link to government services, available at any time.

Sharma and Gupta's Four Layer Model of E-Government Implementation

Sharma and Gupta's framework of e-government is more holistic and addresses both demand and supply sides of e-government implementation (Sharma and Gupta, 2003, Sharma, 2004, Sharma 2006). Their framework has four layers as shown in Figure 2. Their model addresses infrastructure and technology issues over and above the user-oriented evolutionary nature of the web sites as addressed by the previous four models. The details of each layer of this framework are explained below.

Layer 1 – Networks and Technical Infrastructure: The first layer consists of private and public data communication networks, servers, routers, gateways, communications processors, etc. A large number of local area networks (LANs) form intranets to interface with different government agencies and extranets to offer e-government services to its different constituencies.

Layer 2 –Digitization and Data Integration: Once the basic network infrastructure in the form of private and public data communication networks is in place, the next layer provides digitization and data integration, consisting of legacy data applications, ERP, workflow system, document management systems and data management systems. At this layer, the emphasis would be to convert data in paper (manual) form to digital form. At this layer, the digitization and integration of data may also lead to reengineering of various government processes (Miranda, 2000).

Layer 3 – Internet and Web-Enabled e-Government Service: At this layer, Internet enabled e-government allows citizens access to services, information, group discussions, decision making opportunities, and new ways to transact business with government anywhere and any time. At this layer various stages of e-government are offered. This layer essentially launches the various stages of services as described in the previous four models. For example: Stage 1 establishes web sites to provide static information of various government services. This stage focuses on the use of the web by governmental departments and agencies to offer information about themselves to citizens. Stage 2 extends the web site to full integration with intranet applications that facilitate the gathering, processing, and sharing of data within and across many federal and state governmental agencies. Stage 3 sets up extranet integration with the web site that connects governments to other business partners, suppliers and other public and private agencies. Stage 4 creates an e-portal for offering self-service e-government applications. This stage integrates various government web sites both at the federal and state level to facilitate formal exchange of information, and the establishment of a portal that combines all government services and offers a navigation path to them based on need or function.

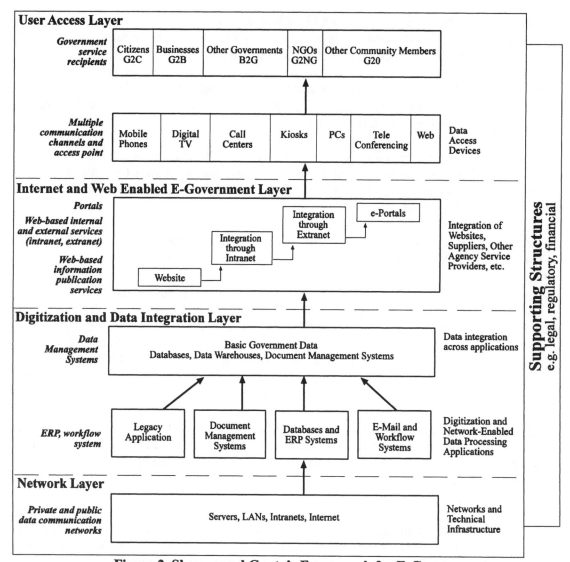

Figure 2. Sharma and Gupta's Framework for E-Government

At the e-government portal stage, the government delivers interactive services to citizens. This stage of e-government is increasingly interactive, allowing governments to use information technology tools to engage citizens in the development of policies, programs and services. Figure 3 illustrates the four stages.

<u>Layer 4 - User Access</u>: Although one might feel that once the Internet and web-enabled e-government service layer is complete, the e-government framework is complete, government should also be concerned about how various users of government services would receive these services. Citizens, businesses and other government service recipients can access various web-enabled e-government services through multiple communication channels and from multiple access points. While the web-enabled e-government service layer 3 creates different offerings to citizens through various systems, the user access layer opens these services to the public at any time from anywhere with the required security and trust. The user access layer should support all-purpose personal communication systems geared to societies "on the go" including multifunction cell phones, e-mail capability, PC, web surfing, fax, video-television, picture phone, AM/FM radio, call centers and global positioning systems.

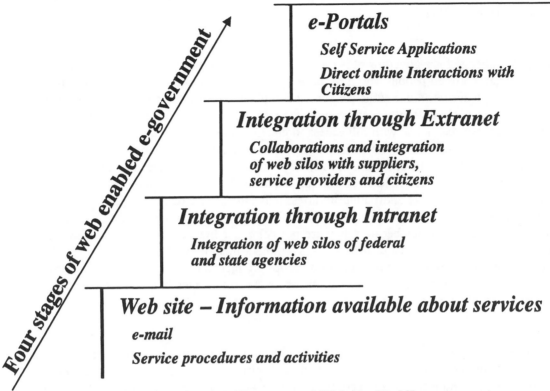

Figure 3. Four Stages of Internet and Web-Enabled E-government

Supporting Infrastructure: The framework for e-government is incomplete if it is not supported with the required legal and regulatory infrastructure. The support infrastructure includes an integrated network so that banks and financial institutions can serve as automatic clearing houses. The support infrastructure also includes a legal and regulatory framework to support payments on line and protect privacy. Security must be a top priority during the creation of a support infrastructure for e-government. The importance of support infrastructure for online payments can be exemplified with the personal frustration and anguish that one of the co-authors went through in dealing with the IRS and a state taxation authority. Online payments were not recognized by the support infrastructure for more than six months after the online payments were made by electronic checks and five months after the electronic checks were cashed by the respective governments.

FUTURE CHALLENGES FOR E-GOVERNMENT

Various governments who have implemented e-government frameworks have transformed relations with citizens, businesses and amongst various arms of government. There are, however, several remaining challenges.

Infrastructure Development
Many countries do not have the requisite infrastructure necessary to deploy e-government services throughout their territory. One of the key prerequisites for implementing e-government services is to have in place computer hardware, software, and reliable telecommunications services for connectivity. To ensure users' easy access to government information online, availability of the infrastructure should be coupled with availability of human resources with necessary skills to collect,

and process information in a timely manner. All these require political will and adequate commitment from top government officials.

Digital Divide

The biggest challenge for e-government is digital divide or disparities in computer access. The digital divide is the gap between people who have access to the Internet and computers and those who do not. Those without access and/or without essential computer skills cannot avail of the information that can provide economic opportunities, and cannot share in the benefits of e-government. Digital divide includes the gap between those with full access to electronic information and those without it due to such factors as socio-economic conditions, language barriers, physical situations, age, and education. Due to digital divide, not all citizens currently have equal access to computers and the Internet to access e-government services. Although various countries have taken initiatives to offer Internet-enabled computers in schools and public libraries, it is still not adequate. Even in countries where access to technological infrastructure is nearly ubiquitous, there are still marginalized groups who are unable to use the technologies because they are not computer literate. Unless the government takes enough measures to address this challenge, e-government benefits will be available to only a few. Governments must ensure that the marginalized groups are included in their e-government strategy to remove social and economic injustice. Governments must serve all members of society irrespective of their physical, social or economic capabilities.

Trust

To be successful, e-government projects must build trust within agencies, between agencies, across governments, with businesses, with NGOs and with citizens. The government must ensure that information the government collects about individuals and businesses will be fully protected and secured from any attack and misuse. Protecting the privacy of citizens' personal information stored on these databases while making effective use of the information contained in them is a vitally important issue. Policy makers must reciprocate with resources, if citizens are asked to entrust sensitive personal, financial and medical data to them in order to utilize e-government systems. Government websites and online services must adhere to the best practices of security and privacy. Also, government transparency should be embedded in the design of ICT systems.

Interoperability and Standardization

The e-government framework should develop systems and record formats that work together and across departments so that all government agencies could use the same online systems. In an increasingly flat global world, the requirement for this characteristic cannot be over-emphasized, especially for national governments to collaborate and for international organizations like the United Nations, World Health Organization, and World Bank to effectively utilize the Internet and other information technologies.

Education and Training of Users

E-government services are of no use unless the users are well educated and trained to use those services. People, especially if they are unfamiliar with technology, may be reluctant to try e-government services out of distrust or belief that online services will not meet their needs or due to lack of understanding of the technology. People must be trained and educated. Training such a large population requires substantial funding and effort which is a great challenge.

Business Process Reengineering

Computerization of existing manual processes can actually lead to higher levels of inefficiency and cost. It is essential to undertake process reengineering as an integral part of e-governance project implementation in order to ensure increased efficiency and reduced costs. This is a great challenge since there would be a great resistance from various stake holders for restructuring or reengineering due to their vested interests. Governments are generally entrenched in hierarchical bureaucracy. It is extremely tough to break through both hierarchical structure and bureaucracy. Nonetheless, if significant benefits have to be realized, reengineering of existing business processes is a pre-requisite.

Partnerships with Private Sectors and Other Agencies

Issues of public vs. private collaboration and competition are already part of international debate on governance. New rules may be needed to govern the relationship between public and private sectors. New partnerships and alliances can have unforeseen consequences, so it is important to be able to review new relationships frequently to ensure that both parties are pleased with the arrangement. Partnerships are prone to challenges, since interorganizational systems require that partners have equivalent IT infrastructure.

Adequate Funding

Another issue related to technology management is the funding of federal, state and local e-government projects. In order to implement a successful e-government program, policymakers must fight for and procure effective budgets that can meet the objectives of e-government. Providing more resources (dollars and staff) and making the budget process more transparent and effective are great challenges for public policy makers. Politicians from the legislative branch as well as the executive branch should take a proactive stance in implementing these initiatives. The funding is all the more important given the fact that public sector's IT infrastructure generally lags behind that of the private sector.

Performance Measures

Governments must create performance measures to evaluate and assess the progress and effectiveness of their e-government implementation. Calculating the value and progress of e-government investments is a difficult but necessary step if governments want to maintain support for projects. Performance measures can include: number of agencies and functions online, reduction in the average time for processing citizen requests or applications, reduction in the number of complaints about the level and quality of government services, increased voter registration and turnout, increased citizen participation in consultations and open proceedings, lower costs to government in delivering services, and increased revenue.

STATUS OF E-GOVERNMENTS AROUND THE WORLD

To assess e-government status, few indices have been developed. One of them is by the United Nations' Division for Public Economics and Public Administration. This index is an indicator of the progress the UN member countries have made in implementing e-government services. Several parameters and factors are taken into consideration. These include web presence measures (indicating stages of government websites), telecommunication infrastructure measures which define the capacity of a country's ICTs (indicators are Internet hosts per 10,000 people, percentage of a nation's population online, and PCs, telephone lines, mobile phones, and televisions per 1000 people); and human capital measures (using the UNDP Human Development Index, the Information Access Index, and urban/rural population ratio as indicators).

The assessment of e-government readiness index that included 191 countries was undertaken by the United Nations in 2001, 2003 and 2005. The 2001 study used the premise that the state of e-government readiness is a function of the combined level of a country's state of readiness, economic, technological development and human resource development. A final product of their analysis was the construction of a synthetic indicator named the *e-Government Index*. Two years later in 2003, a second survey slightly changed the definition of the e-government index and named it the *e-Government Readiness Index*.

The 2005 readiness index is a composite measurement of the *capacity* and *willingness* of countries to use e-government for ICT-led development. It is a composite index comprising the Web Measure Index, the Telecommunication Infrastructure Index and the Human Capital Index (The UN global E-Government Readiness Report 2005). A related index is the E-Participation Index. These are described below.

The Web Measure Index

Web Measure Index 2005 is based upon a five stage model of e-government framework. These five stages are; emerging, enhanced presence, interactive presence, transactional presence and networked presence. These stages are similar to those described in an earlier framework.

Emerging Presence is Stage I representing information which is limited and basic. The e-government online presence comprises a web page and/or an official website; links to ministries/departments of education, health, social welfare, labor and finance may/may not exist; links to regional/local government may/may not exist; some archived information such as the head of states' message or a document such as the constitution may be available on line; most information remains static with the fewest options for citizens.

Enhanced Presence is Stage II in which the government provides greater public policy and governance sources of current and archived information, such as policies, laws and regulation, reports, newsletters, and downloadable databases. The user can search for a document, there is a help feature and a site map is provided. A larger selection of public policy documents exists, such as an e-government strategy, policy briefs on specific education or health issues. Though more sophisticated, the interaction is still primarily unidirectional with information flowing essentially from government to the citizen.

Interactive Presence is Stage III in which the online services of the government enter the interactive mode with services to enhance convenience for the consumer such as downloadable forms for tax payment, and application for license renewal. Audio and video capability is provided for relevant public information. The government officials can be contacted via email, fax, telephone and mail. The site is updated with greater regularity to keep the information current and up to date for the public.

Transactional Presence is Stage IV that allows two-way interaction between the citizen and his/her government. It includes options for paying taxes; applying for ID cards, birth certificates/passports, license renewals and other similar C2G interactions by allowing him/her to submit these online 24/7. The citizens are able to pay for relevant public services, such as motor vehicle violation, taxes, fees for postal services through their credit, bank or debit card. Providers of goods and services are able to bid online for public contacts via secure links.

Networked Presence is Stage V representing the most sophisticated level in e-government. It is characterized by an integration of G2G, G2C and C2G services. The government encourages participatory deliberative decision-making and is willing and able to involve the society in a two-way open dialogue. Through interactive features such as the web comment form, and innovative online consultation mechanisms, the government actively solicits citizens' views on public policy, law making, and democratic participatory decision making. Implicit is the integration of public sector agencies with full cooperation and understanding of the concept of collective decision-making, participatory democracy and citizen empowerment as a democratic right.

Telecommunications Infrastructure Index

The Telecommunication Infrastructure Index is a composite weighted average index of six primary measures of a country's ICT infrastructure capacity. These are: PCs/1000 persons; Internet users/1000 persons; Telephone Lines/1000 persons; Online population; Mobile phones/1000 persons; and TV's/1000 persons.

Human Capital Index

The data for the Human Capital Index relies on the UNDP 'education index' which is a composite of the adult literacy rate and the combined primary, secondary and tertiary gross enrollment ratio with two third weight given to adult literacy and one third to gross enrollment ratio.

E-Participation Index

The E-Participation Index is used to assess the quality and usefulness of information and services provided by a country's government for the purpose of engaging its citizens in public policy issues. This index is indicative of both the capacity and the willingness of the country's government in encouraging the citizens in promoting deliberative and participatory decision-making and of the reach of its own socially inclusive governance program.

Current Status of E-government Implementations

Broad findings of the UN global E-Government Readiness Report 2005 are shown in Tables 2, 3 and 4. The index is on a 0-1 scale, with higher values representing higher e-readiness. Some comments are in order.

- Table 2 provides the indices for the top 50 countries with the United States of America (0.9062) being the world leader followed by Denmark (0.9058). Sweden (0.8983) has bypassed the United Kingdom (0.8777) to arrive at the 3rd global position. Among developing countries, the Republic of Korea (0.8727) leads with Singapore (0.8503), Estonia (0.7347), Malta (0.7012) and Chile (0.6963) close behind.
- According to Table 3, the regions of North America (0.8744) and Europe (0.6012) are in the leadership position on the e-government readiness index. In the rest of the world category (after North America and Europe), the rankings in descending sequence were: South and Eastern Asia (0.4922); and South and Central America (0.4643), Western Asia (0.4384); the Caribbean (0.4282); South and Central Asia (0.3448); Oceania (0.2888) and finally Africa (0.2642). The World e-government Readiness Index was 0.4267 in 2005.
- Table 4 depicts the e-government index information for fifteen countries in South and Eastern Asia. It reveals that the Republic of Korea, Singapore, and Japan are the top three with indices of 0.8727, 0.8503, and 0.7801. Myanmar, Timor-Leste, and Lao, P.D.R. are at the bottom of the list with indices of 0.2959, 0.2512, and 0.2421 respectively.

CONCLUSIONS

In this chapter, we have provided definitions of terms and concepts related to electronic government. We clarified the distinction between e-government and e-governance based on a parsimonious framework. We further described several categories of e-government – G2C, G2B, G2G, and e-democracy with examples given from different countries. This was followed by short descriptions of four evolutionary models of e-Government – each model having three or four evolutionary stages. Lastly, a comprehensive four layer model was described; the third layer of this model included four evolutionary stages for user information and interaction and transaction. In conclusion, we make the following recommendations:

1. E-government constituents such as citizens, businesses, and government agencies must be treated as customers and partners and not target groups.

Rank	Country	Index	Rank	Country	Index
1	United States	0.9062	26	Slovenia	0.6762
2	Denmark	0.9058	27	Hungary	0.6536
3	Sweden	0.8983	28	Luxembourg	0.6513
4	United Kingdom	0.8777	29	Czech Republic	0.6396
5	Republic of Korea	0.8727	30	Portugal	0.6084
6	Australia	0.8679	31	Mexico	0.6061
7	Singapore	0.8503	32	Latvia	0.6050
8	Canada	0.8425	33	Brazil	0.5981
9	Finland	0.8231	34	Argentina	0.5971
10	Norway	0.8228	35	Greece	0.5921
11	Germany	0.8050	36	Slovakia	0.5887
12	Netherlands	0.8021	37	Cyprus	0.5872
13	New Zealand	0.7987	38	Poland	0.5872
14	Japan	0.7801	39	Spain	0.5847
15	Iceland	0.7794	40	Lithuania	0.5786
16	Austria	0.7602	41	Philippines	0.5721
17	Switzerland	0.7548	42	United Arab Emirates	0.5718
18	Belgium	0.7381	43	Malaysia	0.5706
19	Estonia	0.7347	44	Romania	0.5704
20	Ireland	0.7251	45	Bulgaria	0.5605
21	Malta	0.7012	46	Thailand	0.5518
22	Chile	0.6963	47	Croatia	0.5480
23	France	0.6925	48	Ukraine	0.5456
24	Israel	0.6903	49	Uruguay	0.5387
25	Italy	0.6794	50	Russian Federation	0.5329

Table 2. E-government Readiness Index 2005: Top 50 Countries (Source: The UN Global E-Government Readiness Report 2005 "From E-Government to E-inclusion")

Region Year:	2005	2004	2003
North America	0.8744	0.8751	0.8670
Europe	0.6012	0.5866	0.5580
South and Eastern Asia	0.4922	0.4603	0.4370
South and Central America	0.4643	0.4558	0.4420
Western Asia	0.4384	0.4093	0.4100
Caribbean	0.4282	0.4106	0.4010
South and Central Asia	0.3448	0.3213	0.2920
Oceania	0.2888	0.3006	0.3510
Africa	0.2642	0.2528	0.2460
World Average	0.4267	0.4130	0.4020

Table 3. Regional E-Government Readiness Rankings (Source: The UN global E-Government Readiness Report 2005 "From E-government to E-inclusion")

Country	Index 2005	Global rank in 2005	Global rank in 2004	Change
Republic of Korea	0.8727	5	5	0
Singapore	0.8503	7	8	1
Japan	0.7801	14	18	4
Philippines	0.5721	41	47	6
Malaysia	0.5706	43	42	-1
Thailand	0.5518	46	50	4
China	0.5078	57	67	10
Brunei Darussalam	0.4475	73	63	-10
Mongolia	0.3962	93	75	-18
Indonesia	0.3819	96	85	-11
Viet Nam	0.3640	105	112	7
Cambodia	0.2989	128	129	1
Myanmar	0.2959	129	123	-6
Timor-Leste	0.2512	144	174	30
Lao, P.D.R.	0.2421	147	144	-3
Average	0.4922			

Table 4. E-government Readiness Rankings: South and Eastern Asia (Source: The UN global E-Government Readiness Report 2005 "From E-government to E-inclusion")

2. High-level leadership involvement is essential to ensure vertical e-government planning, to acquire the necessary resources, to motivate staff, to support dealings with external partners and stakeholders, and to ensure coordination across ministries and agencies. Strong leadership can speed the process of e-government implementation, promote coordination within and among agencies and help reinforce good governance objectives.

3. The government must prepare new principles, standards, and infrastructure that make it possible for all agencies to work in the new environment.

4. Radical changes are needed: new business processes, different information flows, changed policies, new kinds of records, advanced security measures, and new data management methods for e-government implementation. Also included are legal and policy infrastructure, telecommunications infrastructure, standards for data and technologies, rules and mechanisms for information use and sharing, and many new elements.

5. Integrated e-government requires data integration. Data integration requires new business processes, increases technical complexity, demands reliable security, and presents serious data privacy, quality, and ownership issues.

6. A strategy has to be developed to involve and reach all the people who need government services regardless of their age, income, language, or access to the Internet. It also needs to assure that all agencies and their private and nonprofit business partners are capable of engaging fully in using or delivering e-government applications.

7. Appropriate methods and strategy should be designed to inform and engage various stakeholders and make government more accountable by making processes and decisions more open and transparent. Given the diversity of players involved in delivering government services, effective e-government often requires coalitions of partners both within government and between government and the private and nonprofit sectors.

8. In order for e-government initiatives to be effective, leaders can take steps to evaluate customer demand of e-government services, and work closely with citizens and businesses to provide users with the services that are most useful to them.

9. Business process engineering, restructuring of government processes and clear documentation of all these need to be conducted. These efforts should be supplemented by continuous education and training of all e-government stakeholders.

MINICASE

People-Powered Politics: Call for Change Gets Out the Vote

Note: This case is provided to illustrate the use of e-government by an NGO. This is not an endorsement or criticism of any political party. The following is in the words of Eli Pariser, President of MoveOn.org.

As the Fall, 2006 homestretch approached it became clear that most Americans wanted a change of direction regarding the Iraq war. Each day, the news from Baghdad made Iraq the over-arching issue motivating voters for a change. We realized two important things about this election from the outset.

- First, we were facing a "turnout" rather than a "persuasion" election—our primary responsibility was helping to get voters who wanted change to actually show up at the polls.
- Second, we were facing a potential "change election" where a voter revolt could shake up the playing field and dramatically alter the political landscape in the final months.

Our early TV and grassroots mobilizations were designed to start that wave; our fall get-out-the-vote campaign had to be ready to put it over the top. We also realized that MoveOn's most powerful asset—our members—are scattered all over the country, and most of our densest concentrations were not in contested districts. We needed a plan to involve everyone, no matter where in the country they lived.

"Liquid" Phone Bank

I signed up to make calls because as a patriotic American I know that millions of tiny voices can drum the big money Republicans right out of Congress if we pull together as a team.
-William K., Old Fort, North Carolina, MoveOn member.

The core idea is fairly simple—a web-based "liquid phone bank" allowing MoveOn members to pour calls from wherever they live into wherever they are needed. We could then turn to any district in the country that needed extra attention, and keep the calls flowing until we reached all of our target voters. We tested our program in April in a California House special election and it worked. A Yale University study showed that our phone bank was the most effective volunteer calling program ever studied.

With the theory confirmed, we turned our attention to the larger 2006 campaign for mid-term election. We developed two ways for people to make calls. Individuals could call from home, using a cutting-edge online tool that walks the user through the script and records the results one call at a time. The design of this system was very user friendly with most permutations and combinations of possibilities planned out. And we even made changes on the go based on feedback from thousands of callers.

We also launched a weekly series of phone parties, where members gathered together to make calls on their cell phones. To recruit the volunteer army needed to make it work, we worked with our close partner, Grassroots Campaigns, to set up campaign offices in 40 cities. Each night

MoveOn members called other members in their region, asking them to sign up with the campaign. By the end of the program, MoveOn members recruited over 17,000 other members to join the volunteer team.

Phone Parties

For phone parties, members opened their homes and invited other members in their area to bring their cell phones (and chargers) and make calls to end one-party Republican rule in Washington. These parties proved to be a huge success, drawing in thousands of new volunteers and creating a real sense of local community around the program.

Because the program was based online, we were able to use "smart targeting" to direct members' calls to where they would have the highest impact. So volunteers living in or near competitive districts would automatically be directed to voters in their area. Volunteers in other parts of the country would be directed to whichever districts around the country needed the most urgent attention. The "liquid" internet technology we developed for the phone program made this possible.

We also wanted to make sure we were turning out the right voters. So we began an ambitious "micro-targeting" program, applying a grassroots twist to an approach Republicans have employed so successfully to get their supporters to the polls. In late October, the number of competitive races increased by the day and Call for Change was exactly the tool the moment required. It enabled us to send hundreds of thousands of turnout calls into the races where they were needed most as conditions changed. On October 19th, for example we saw a poll showing Tim Walz, the Democratic challenger in Minnesota, closing the gap. Within a few days calls were pouring into the district—making it a toss-up. When the dust settled, Call for Change involved more members in making more calls than even we had dared to dream. We exceeded all of our targets the night before Election Day. Here are some of the final numbers: 7492 house parties attended by 46,790 people; 51,719 people called from home; 7,001,102 total calls made; and 61 districts targeted.

And we did it all with small contributions from tens of thousands of members, proving once again the efficacy of the small donor approach, which offers candidates a way to win without becoming dependent on money from special interests. And we accomplished this amazing feat by utilizing Internet – e-mails and state-of-the-art online donation model while adhering to all relevant laws and regulations. Throughout the election year members responded to our repeated appeals to help finance the campaigns of candidates we supported and the work that MoveOn has done. In summary, $27,392,712 -- total raised; 608,727 -- number of individual contributions; $45.00 -- amount of average contribution; $6,040,420 -- amount bundled for 35 House and Senate candidates. Federal Election Commission data shows that MoveOn.org Political Action was one of the leading sources of financial support for Democratic candidates outside of the Democratic Party's committees.

Source: Adapted from "MoveOn.org Political Action – Election 2006 – People Powered Politics," a report sent in the 2nd week of November, 2006 to all MoveOn.org callers and supporters.

Discussion Questions
1. How does this case demonstrate the political power of ordinary folks in affecting the outcome of elections in a democracy?
2. Would such uses of Internet for grass roots movement usher in true people powered democracy and reduce the impact of lobbyists and interest-groups?
3. What is the "liquid phone bank" system? Please find out details of this MoveOn.org system and describe its positive and negative (if any) features.
4. What are phone parties?

KEY TERMS
E-government
E-services
E-democracy
E-governance
E-participation
Information and Communication Technologies (ICTs)
M-government

STUDY QUESTIONS
1. Define e-government, e-democracy and e-governance.

2. Describe various e-government implementation frameworks.

3. Select two of the first four implementation frameworks. What are the similarities and differences in these two? Develop an integrated framework combining the best features of both frameworks.

4. Compare and contrast the Layne and Lee's Model of E-government framework with Sharma and Gupta's framework.

5. What are the challenges of e-government implementation?

6. Comment on the current status of e-government implementation around the world. What measures are used for assessing the current status?

REFERENCES
Asia Oceania E-business Marketplace Alliance -AOEMA Report E-government from a User's Perspective, http://www.aoema.org/E-overnment/Definitions_and_Objectives.htm

Bertucci, G. *World Public Sector Report 2003: E-Government at the crossroads*, United Nations, New York, accessed March 2004, at
http://unpan1.un.org/intradoc/groups/public/documents/un/unpan012733.pdf . 2003.

Dawes, S. S., and Pardo, T. A. Building Collaborative Digital Government Systems. Systematic Constraints and Effective Practices. In W. J. McIver and A. K. Elmagarmid (Eds.), Advances in Digital Government, Technology, Human Factors, and Policy (pp. 259-273). Norwell, MA: Kluwer Academic Publishers. 2002.

de Bruijn, H. *Managing Performance in Public Sector*. London, U.K.: Routledge. 2002.

Detlor, B., and Finn, K. Towards a Framework for Government Portal Design: The Government, Citizen and Portal Perspectives, In Å. Grönlund (Ed.), Electronic Government: Design, Applications and Management. Hershey, PA: Idea Group Publishing. 2002.

Gant, J. P. Digital Government and Geographic Information Systems, In A. Pavlichev and G. D. Garson (Eds.), Digital Government: Principles and Best Practices. Hershey, PA: Idea Group Publishing. 2004.

Garson, G. D. The Promise of Digital Government, In A. Pavlichev and G. D. Garson (Eds.), Digital Government: Principles and Best Practices. Hershey, PA: Idea Group Publishing. 2004.

Heeks, R. *Most eGovernment-for-Development Projects Fail: How Can Risks be Reduced?* Paper No.14, iGovernment Working Paper Series, Institute for Development Policy and Management, University of Manchester, Manchester, U.K. 2003.

Ho, A. T. "Reinventing local governments and the e-Government initiative," *Public Administration Review*, (62:4), 2002, pp. 434-444.

Holden, S. H., Norris, D. F., and Fletcher, P. D. "Electronic Government at the Local Level. Progress to Date and Future Issues," *Public Performance and Management Review*, 26(4), 2003, pp. 325-344.

Holliday, I. "Building e-Government in East and Southeast Asia: Regional rhetoric and national (in) action," *Public Administration and Development*, 22, 2002, pp. 323-335.

Kaaya, J. "Implementing e-Government Services in East Africa: Assessing Status through Content Analysis of Government Websites," *Electronic Journal of E-government (EJEG)* 2(1), 2003, pp. 39-54.

Keohane, R. O. and Nye, J. S. "Introduction," In Nye, J. S. and Donahue, J.D. (editors), *Governance in a Globalization World*. Washington, D.C.: Brookings Institution Press. 2000.

Kettl, D. F. *The Transformation of Governance*, John Hopkins University Press, U.S.A. 2002.

La Porte, T. M., Demchak, C. C., and de Jong, M. "Democracy and bureaucracy in the age of the web." *Administration and Society*, (34:4), 2002, pp. 411-446.

Layne, K and Lee, J "Developing fully functional e-government: A four stage model," *Government Information Quarterly*, (18:2), 2001, pp. 122-36.

Moon, M. J. "The evolution of e-government among municipalities: Rhetoric or reality?" *Public Administration Review*, (62:4), 2002, pp. 424-33.

Netchaeva, I "E-Government and e-democracy: A comparison in the North and South. Gazette" *The International Journal for Communication Studies*, (64:5), 2002, pp. 467-477.

Saxena, K. B. C. "Informatization and Infocrats". *DATAQUEST*, (12:37), 1995, pp. 154-156.

Saxena, K. B. C. "Reengineering Public Administration in Developing Countries". *Long Range Planning*, (29:5), 1996, pp. 704-712.

Sharma, S.K. "Assessing E-government Implementations," *Electronic Government Journal*, 1(2), 2004, pp. 198-212.

Sharma, S. K. An E-Government Services Framework, , Encyclopedia of Commerce, E-Government and Mobile Commerce, Mehdi Khosrow-Pour, Information Resources Management Association, Idea Group Reference, USA, pp. 373-378. 2006.

Sharma, S. K. and Gupta, J. N. D. "Building Blocks of an E-government – A Framework", *Journal of Electronic Commerce in Organizations*, (1:4), 2003, pp. 34-48.

Siau, K., Long, Y. "Synthesizing e-government stage models – a meta-synthesis based on meta-ethnography approach," (105:4), 2005, pp. 443-458.

Silcock, R. 'What is e-Government?' *Parliamentary Affairs*, 54, 2001, pp. 88-101.

UN Global E-government Readiness Report. From E-government to E-inclusion, UNPAN/2005/14, United Nations publication, United Nations, 2005.

Thomas, C., Mbarika, V., LeBlanc, P., and Meso, P. "E-government in Africa: A New Era for Better Governance in Sub-Saharan Africa," *Proceedings of the Information Resource Management Association (IRMA 2004) International Conference*, 2004.

UN. UN Benchmarking e-Government: A global perspective – Assessing the progress of the UN member states, New York: United Nations, Division for Public Economics and Public Administration and American Society for Public Administration, 2002. http://unpan1.un.org/intradoc/groups/public/documents/un/unpan003984.pdf

Author Biographies

Murad Akmanligil

Murad Akmanligil has a Ph.D. in Management Information Systems from the University of Memphis. He has over 10 years of experience in the Information Technology industry. For the last 3 years, he has been working as a manager overseeing the testing of large projects at FedEx Services. Before that he worked as a software engineer and a consultant. His research interests are information systems development and global information systems management.

Yan Nee Ang

Yan Nee Ang is a PhD candidate in the School of Information Systems at the University of Tasmania, New Zealand. Her research has been presented at the Global IT Management Association Conference and the Cross-Cultural Meeting in Information Systems. She is currently researching the implementation of Enterprise Resource Planning systems in China with a particular emphasis on the cultural implications of those implementations.

Kallol Bagchi

Kallol Bagchi received his second Ph.D. in Business from Florida Atlantic University in 2001. He is an Associate Professor at the University of Texas at El Paso He has published in IS journals such as IJEC, JGITM, CAIS, CACM. His present research interests are in global information technology, adoption and diffusion of information technology, security, networking, and simulation. He is on the editorial board of JGITM. He is a member of the ACM, IEEECS, AIS, GITM, and DSI.

Naveed Baqir

Naveed Baqir is currently a doctoral scholar at University of North Carolina – Greensboro. He holds a masters degree in computer science, an MS in technology management and an MBA. His Ph.D. work is in the area of information system and operations management. He has over six years of corporate experience in professional software and IT systems development at international and national levels. He has served as editor of two IT publications: Computer News and CompuLink. He was instrumental in the design and implementation of a second generation agent platform funded by a consortium of Pakistani and Japanese organizations. He has taught at the University of Management and Technology, the National University of Sciences and Technology, Allama Iqbal Open University in Pakistan and the University of North Carolina – Greensboro in the United States. He has presented at many national and international conferences in North America, Europe and Asia along with publications in the *Economic Insight* and the *Journal of Knowledge Management*.

Charlie Chen

Charlie Chen is Assistant Professor in the Department of Information Technology & Operations Management at Appalachian State University. His research areas are e-learning effectiveness, mobile commerce, and knowledge management. He teaches data communications and networking, CASE tools, database concept, and e-commerce seminars. Prior to this position, he taught at California State University, Northridge. He has authored more than 10 referred articles and proceedings, presented at many professional conferences and venues. He has published in journals such as *Communications of Association for Information Systems, Journal of Knowledge Management Research Practice, and Journal of Information Systems Education*. He has authored a chapter on Global Information Systems in the *Encyclopedia of Information Systems*. He has reviewed papers for *MIS Quarterly*1, and HICSS, AMCIS and DSI conferences. Dr. Chen received his Ph.D. from the Claremont Graduate University and MAB from the American Graduate School of International Management (Thunderbird).

Elia Chepaitis

Elia Chepaitis is a Professor Emeritus of Information Systems at Fairfield University. She has had three research and teaching Fulbright Fellowships in Russia and Morocco. Dr. Chepaitis has been awarded numerous U.S. and international patents for an easy-to-use, scalable alternative to Braille and is interested in the development of a new electronic infrastructure for the blind.

R. Brent Gallupe

R. Brent Gallupe is Professor of Information Systems and Director of the Queen's Executive Decision Center at the School of Business, Queen's University at Kingston, Canada. His current research interests are in knowledge management systems, computer support for groups and teams, and global information management. His work has been published in such journals as *Management Science, Information Systems Research, MIS Quarterly, Academy of Management Journal, Sloan Management Review, and Journal of Applied Psychology.* Gallupe holds a B. Math (Hons.) from the University of Waterloo, an M.B.A. from York University and a Ph.D. from the University of Minnesota.

Rahul A. Gokhale:

Rahul Gokhale is a doctoral student of Information Systems in the department of Management at Clemson University. He holds a MS in Information Systems, and bachelors in Electrical Engineering. Prior to joining the doctoral program, he worked as a systems integration engineer with Johnson Controls. His primary interests are in studying problems such as, Control, Knowledge transfer, Theories of the firm and so forth.

Varun Grover

Varun Grover is a William S.Lee distinguished professor of Information Systems (Endowed by Duke Energy) in the department of Management at Clemson University. He holds a degree in electrical engineering from I.I.T., New Delhi, an MBA, and a Ph.D. from the University of Pittsburgh. Most of his work is on the business implications of Information technologies. Dr. Grover has published extensively in the IS field, with over 150 publications in refereed journals such as MISQ, JMIS, ISR, among others. He also serves as the senior editor of MISQ, JAIS, and Database, and the AE numerous others.

Albert L. Harris

Albert L. Harris is a Professor in the Department of Computer Information Systems at the John A. Walker College of Business, Appalachian State University and Editor-in-Chief of the *Journal of Information Systems Education*, the leading international journal on information systems education. Dr. Harris served as a Fulbright Scholar to Portugal in 2006. He is a Certified Information Systems Auditor (CISA), a Certified Computer Professional (CCP), and a Certified Management Consultant (CMC). He received his Ph.D. in MIS from Georgia State University, his M.S. in Systems Management from the George Washington University, and his B.S. in Quantitative Business Analysis from Indiana University. Dr. Harris teaches a variety of graduate and undergraduate classes in information systems. He is a member of the Board of Directors of the International Association of Information Management (IAIM) and the Education Special Interest Group (EDSIG) of AITP. He served for three years as Treasurer of EDSIG. He has more than 75 publications as book chapters, in journals, and in international and national conference proceedings. Prior to becoming an educator and researcher, he spent almost 15 years in IT consulting, the last five managing his own consulting firm. He served as an officer in the U.S. Marine Corps from 1966-1970.

Luca Iandoli

Luca Iandoli is an Associate Professor in the School of Engineering at the University Federico II of Naples, Italy), at the department of Business and Managerial Engineering (DIEG). He teaches Business and Management in Engineering degrees curricula and Research Methods at the PhD program in Science and Technology Management. His background is in Electronic Engineering and he has a PhD in Business and Management. His main research interests include: Decision support systems, Knowledge management and Organizational learning, Information Technology and Organizational Change. He is Vice President for Europe of the Global Information Technology Management Association and is on the editorial board of the *Journal of Global Information Technology Management, Journal of Information Technology Cases and Applications Research*, and *Fuzzy Economic Review*. Luca has published in several academic international journals such as *Human Resources Management Journal, Small Business Economics, Journal of Global Information Technology Management, Fuzzy Economic Review, J. of Artificial Societies and Social Simulation, Journal of Information Science and Technology*.

Brian D. Janz

Brian Janz is a Professor of MIS at the Fogelman College of Business and Economics and is Associate Director of the FedEx Center for Supply Chain Management at the FedEx Institute of Technology at the University of Memphis. Dr. Janz has over 25 years of experience in the information systems field working for The University of Minnesota, IBM, Honeywell, and General Motors, as well as consulting with Fortune 500 companies and governmental agencies. Dr. Janz earned a Ph.D. in MIS from the Carlson School of Management at the University of Minnesota. Dr. Janz's research interests focus on how information technologies affect organizational strategy, design, and knowledge worker behavior. Specifically, he is interested in the effects that knowledge management and information technologies have on organizational supply chain management, systems development, and overall business intelligence. Brian's research has been published in book chapters as well as many academic and practitioner journals including *MIS Quarterly, Decision Science, Journal of MIS, Personnel Psychology, Journal of Database Management, Journal of Information Technology Management, Information and Management, Journal of Global IT Management, Issues in Supply Chain Management, Communications of the AIS, Journal of Strategic Performance Measurement*, and the *Journal of Education for MIS*. In addition, Dr. Janz serves on the editorial review boards for numerous journals.

William R. King

William R. King holds the title of University Professor in the Katz Graduate School of Business of the University of Pittsburgh. He has served as Founding President of the Association for Information Systems (AIS), President of the Institute of Management Science (now INFORMS), as Editor-in-Chief of the *Management Information Systems Quarterly* and twice as Chair or Co-chair of the International Conferences on Information Systems. He has published 15 books and more than 300 research papers in the leading journals in management science, strategic planning and information systems. Recently, he was given the Leo Lifetime Exceptional Achievement Award by AIS.

Anil Kumar

Anil Kumar is an Associate Professor in the Business Information Systems Department at Central Michigan University. He has published several articles on global IT management and technology mediated learning in education. His current research focuses on global IT theories and frameworks, global IT management, and learning styles and technology mediated learning. Prior to his academic appointment, he spent several years working in the IS industry. He is active in several professional organizations and is on the editorial board of the *Journal of Global Information Technology Management*. Anil has published in several academic journals such as *Decision support systems, Journal of Global Information Technology Management, Industrial Management & Data Systems, Information Processing and Management: An International Journal, Journal of Computing in Teacher Education* and has presented papers at numerous international and national conferences.

Hans Lehmann

Hans Lehmann, Austrian by birth, is a management profession with some 25 years of business experience with information technology. After a career in data processing line management in Austria, he worked as an information technology manager in manufacturing and banking in South Africa. After completing an MBA, he joined Deloitte's and worked for some 12 years in their international management consultancy firm. Han's work experience spans continental Europe, Africa, the United Kingdom, North America, and Australasia. He specialized in the development and implementation management of international information systems for a number of blue chip multi-national companies in the manufacturing and financial sectors. IN 1991, Hans changed careers and joined the University of Auckland in New Zealand, where his research focuses on the strategic management of international information systems and electronic commerce.

Sharm Manwani

Sharm Manwani is Associate Professor and subject leader of the CIO Elective at Henley Management College where he completed his MBA and Doctorate. He has an executive background as a CIO with responsibility for business solutions, systems, services and program management in large global organizations. Now he researches and lectures in IT-Enabled Business Change and consults with leading companies on IT Strategy, Capability and Program Management. Professionally, Sharm is a Fellow of the British Computer Society, provides expert advice in business computing journals and is a member of the Executive Board of the Professionalism in IT program. He is a reviewer for the *Journal for IT Cases and Applications Research*, a member of the advisory panel of Computing Business and a judge for major awards. His research paper on 'Global IT Architecture: Who calls the tune' won the Henley Doctoral Research Paper Prize.

En Mao

En Mao is an Assistant Professor of MIS at Nicholls State University in Louisiana. Prior to Nicholls, she was at the University of Wisconsin-Milwaukee. She earned her Ph.D. from the University of Memphis. Her current research interests include information technology diffusion and acceptance, end-user behavior, knowledge management, global IT, and cross-cultural issues. She has published in the *Journal of Global Information Technology Management, Information and Management, Data Base*, and *Communications of the AIS*. Her work has also appeared as a book chapter in *Knowledge Mapping and Management*. Currently, she is serving as an associate editor on the editorial board of the *Journal of Information Privacy and Security*. She is also a member of the Editorial Review Board of the *Journal of Global Information Technology Management*.

F. Warren McFarlan

F. Warren McFarlan earned his AB from Harvard University in 1959, and his MBA and DBA from the Harvard Business School in 1961 and 1965 respectively. He has had a significant role in introducing materials on Management Information Systems to all major programs at the Harvard Business School since the first course on the subject was offered in 1962. Professor McFarlan's book, *Connecting the Dots* (coauthored with Cathleen Benko) appeared in 2003. *Corporate Information Strategy and Management: Text and Cases* (seventh edition), coauthored with Professors Lynda M. Applegate and Robert D. Austin appeared in 2006. He is the Albert H. Gordon Professor of Business Administration Emeritus and Baker Foundation Professor, Harvard Business School.

Ravi S. Narayanswamy:

Ravi Narayanswamy is a doctoral student of Information Systems in the department of Management at Clemson University. He holds a MS in Information systems, and an MBA in Marketing. Prior to pursuing his doctoral work, he worked in diverse areas with some of the leading multinational firms. His research focuses are in topics related to project management, organizational control, culture, and information security.

Nilay V. Oza

Nilay V. Oza is a senior researcher at the Software Business Laboratory, Helsinki University of Technology (HUT). His research interests include software business, global software outsourcing, business relationship management, trust in relationships, empirical software engineering and theories such as transaction cost economics, game theory, rational choice theory and social exchange theory. Nilay successfully defended his thesis at the School of Computer Science, Systems and Software Research Group, University of Hertfordshire, U.K. During the doctoral study of three years, Nilay conducted a large scale empirical investigation in Indian offshore software outsourcing companies. Earlier, Nilay undertook specialist masters degree in software engineering from the University of Hertfordshire. He also provides management and strategic consultation to software companies.

Prashant Palvia

Prashant Palvia is Joe Rosenthal Excellence Professor and Information Systems Ph.D. Program Director at the University of North Carolina at Greensboro (UNCG). He served as Department Head from 2000 to 2004. Prior to twenty four years in academics, he worked for nine years in industry. He received his Ph.D., MBA and MS from the University of Minnesota and BS from the University of Delhi, India. Prof. Palvia received UNCG's senior research excellence award in 2005. He is a leading authority in Global Information Technology Management (GITM) and chairs the annual GITMA world conferences. Professor Palvia is the Editor-in-Chief of *the Journal of Global Information Technology Management (JGITM)*, and is on editorial board of several journals. His research interests include global information technology, electronic commerce, media choice theory, trust in exchange relationships, and privacy & security. He has published 77 journal articles including in journal such as *MIS Quarterly, Decision Sciences, Communications of the ACM, Communications of the AIS, Information & Management, Decision Support Systems*, and *ACM Transactions on Database Systems*, and 136 articles in conference proceedings. Besides the current book, he also co-edited the previous three books on Global Information Technology Management.

Shailendra C. Jain Palvia

Shailendra C. Jain Palvia is Professor of Management Information Systems at the Long Island University, New York (USA). He received his Ph.D. from the University of Minnesota. He has published over 100 articles in referred journals and refereed proceedings. His research publications are in the areas of management of the systems development process, mode of use in problem solving, implementation issues for MIS/DSS, global information technology, software training methods, global electronic commerce, impact of ERP systems implementation and global IT outsourcing. His work has been published in refereed journals such as *Information Resource Management, Communications of the ACM, MIS Quarterly, Information & Management, Journal of Global Information Management,* JITCA, *International Information Systems, Industrial Management and Data Systems, Journal of Computer Information Systems,* and *Journal of Information Systems Education.* Dr. Palvia is the co-editor of three books on the theme of Global IT Management published in 1992, 1996, and 2002. Dr. Palvia is Editor-in-chief of the *Journal of Information Technology Cases and Applications Research (JITCAR)* since 1999 and an Associate Editor of the *Journal of Global Information Technology Management (JGITM)* since 1998. He chaired the five international outsourcing (ITO and BPO) conferences. He has been an invited speaker in Boston (USA), Stuttgart (Germany), Singapore, Mumbai (India), Bangalore (India), Anand (India), Napoli (Italy), St. Petersburg (Russia), Bangkok (Thailand), and Indore (India).

Praveen Pinjani

Praveen Pinjani is currently a fourth year Ph.D. student at the University of North Carolina at Greensboro. His research interests focus on global virtual teams and global information technology management. He has journal publications in *Information & Management,* and *Communications of the AIS.* He has presented refereed papers at various conferences, including AMCIS, GITMA and DSI. He holds a Master's degree from Texas Tech University and Post Graduate Diploma in Management from LBSIM, New Delhi. Additionally, he spent three years in business development with multinational financial corporations.

Carol Pollard

Carol Pollard is Associate Professor of Information Systems at Appalachian State University in North Carolina. Her research interests include decision support systems, impact of emerging technologies and technology transfer. Her current research focuses on the healthcare sector and small to medium-sized firms. Carol has published her research in *MIS Quarterly, Journal of Management Information Systems* and *Information and Management* and has presented at numerous national and international conferences. Carol is currently Research Director, Centre for Applied Research on Emerging Technologies (CARET) at Appalachian State University; Vice President, International of GITMA; Chair, ACIS Executive Committee and an Advisory Board member of Teradata University Network.

Pierluigi Rippa

Pierluigi Rippa received his Ph.D in Business and Managerial Engineering at the University of Napoli Federico II. Currently he works as researcher at the department of Business and Managerial Engineering, University of Napoli Federico II (Italy). His research interests include information technology adoption and organizational interaction, ERP systems development and adoption, Supply Chain Management, Statistical and Fuzzy application in Decision Support Systems. Referring to the above mentioned topics, he is author of several papers, published in international journal and presented in international conference.

Sushil K. Sharma

Sushil K. Sharma is an Associate Professor of Information Systems and Operations Management at Ball State University, Muncie, Indiana, USA. Co-author of two textbooks and co-editor of four books, Dr. Sharma has authored over 100 refereed research papers in many peer-reviewed national and international MIS and management journals, conferences proceedings and books. He serves on editorial boards of national and international journals and has also edited special issues. His primary teaching and research interests are in e-commerce, computer-mediated communications, community and social informatics, information systems security, e-government, ERP systems, database management systems, cluster computing, web services and knowledge management. He has a wide consulting experience in information systems and e-commerce and has served as an advisor and consultant to several government and private organizations including projects funded by the World Bank.

Yide Shen

Yide Shen is a doctoral student in the department of Computer Information Systems (CIS) at Georgia State University (GSU). She holds a BBA in Accounting from Wuahn University, P.R.China and a MS in MIS from University of Nebraska at Omaha. Her research interests include IT adoption and innovation, IT human resource issues, and software project management.

Barry Shore

Barry Shore is Professor of Decision Sciences at the Whittemore School of Business and Economics, the University of New Hampshire. He has published in the *Communications of the ACM*, the *Journal of Global Information Technology Management*, *Information and Management*, the *Journal of Strategic Information Systems* and the *International Journal of Technology Management*. He is the author of four textbooks, and is a recently elected fellow of the Global Information Technology Management Association. His BSEE is from Tufts University and PhD from the University of Wisconsin.

Steven John Simon

Steven John Simon is currently recalled to active duty with the US Navy serving as Chief Information Officer for US Strategic Command's Center for Combating Weapons of Mass Destruction and Editor-in-Chief of the *Journal of Information Science and Technology*. He received his Ph.D. from the University of South Carolina, specializing in MIS and International Business. Before entering the doctoral program he spent eighteen years in the private sector in management/computer operations and was owner/operator of seven McDonalds franchises. His current research interests include medical information systems, enterprise information systems, supply chain management, electronic commerce in the international environment, and determinants of information system ROI. He has extensive ERP experience having work with organizations such as IBM and the Defense Logistics Agency on implementation projects. Dr Simon, an officer in the United States Navy Reserve has been assigned as scientific liaison officer to the Office of Naval Research/Naval Research Labs, with past Navy assignments including serving as Director for Information Technology & Knowledge Management to the Commander of the United States Sixth Fleet, Information Resource Management Officer to the Commander of the Second Naval Construction Brigade, and the directorate of logistics for United States Atlantic Command. He has consulted and lectured extensively in Korea, Hong Kong, Malaysia, Singapore, and the People's Republic of China. He has previously published in journals such as *Information Systems Research, Journal of Applied Psychology, Communications of the CAM, Database, European Journal of Information Systems, The Journal of Global Information*

Technology Management, Journal of Global Information Management, Journal of Information Technology Cases and Applications Research, and *The Information Resources Management Journal.*

Detmar W. Straub

Detmar W. Straub is the J. Mack Robinson Distinguished Professor of Information Systems at Georgia State University. He has conducted research in the areas of Net-enhanced organizations (e-Commerce), computer security, technological innovation, and international IT studies. He holds a DBA (Doctor of Business Administration) in MIS from Indiana and a PhD in English from Penn State. He has published over 135 papers in journals such as *Management Science, Information Systems Research, MIS Quarterly, Organization Science, Communications of the ACM, Journal of MIS, Journal of AIS, Information & Management, Communications of the AIS, IEEE Transactions on Engineering Management, OMEGA, Academy of Management Executive,* and *Sloan Management Review.*

Eileen M. Trauth

Eileen M. Trauth is Professor of Information Sciences and Technology and Director of the Center for the Information Society at The Pennsylvania State University. Her research is concerned with societal, cultural and organizational influences on information technology and the information technology professions with a special focus on the role of diversity within the field. As a Fulbright Scholar in Ireland, Dr. Trauth investigated socio-cultural influences on the emergence of Ireland's information economy and published her results in *The Culture of an Information Economy: Influences and Impacts in the Republic of Ireland.* In the United States she has investigated cultural, economic, infrastructure and public policy influences on the development of information technology occupational clusters. Dr. Trauth has also conducted research on the under representation of women in the IT profession and is editor of the *Encyclopedia of Gender and Information Technology.* In addition, Dr. Trauth has published papers and books on qualitative research methods, global informatics, information policy, information management, and information systems skills. She is Associate Editor of *Information and Organization* and serves on the editorial boards of several international journals. Dr. Trauth received her Ph.D. and Masters degrees in information science from the University of Pittsburgh and her Bachelors degree in education from the University of Dayton.

Godwin J. Udo

Godwin J. Udo is the Chairperson of the Department of Information and Decision Sciences and the AT&T Professor of Business in the College of Business Administration at The University of Texas at El Paso. He holds a Ph.D. in Industrial Management from Clemson University. He teaches Information Systems courses at graduate and undergraduate levels. He is the author of over 100 research articles in the areas of technology transfer, computer security, IT adoption and management, and decision support systems. He is a member of DSI, IEEE, ISM, APICS, AIS, and INFORMS.

Vijay K. Vemuri

Vijay K. Vemuri is Assistant Professor of Information Systems at University of Bahrain, Kingdom of Bahrain. He previously taught at Long Island University and University of Illinois. He received his Ph.D. from the University of Illinois at Urbana-Champaign. His research interests include e-commerce, strategic implications of information technology and networking infrastructure. His research has been published in refereed journals such as *Electronic Markets, Information Resources Management Journal, European Journal of Operational Research,* and *Journal of IT Cases and Applications.*

Nicholas P. Vitalari

Nick Vitalari is Executive Vice President and co-founder of The Concours Group, and is an educator, author and advisor to the Global 1000. His work focuses on how people solve complex problems, how technology enables extraordinary corporate strategies, and the changing nature of sustainable corporate growth. At The Concours Group, he works with senior executives on the development of effective business operating models, strategic sourcing and negotiation, corporate self-renewal and sustainable corporate growth. As a former professor at the Paul Merage School of Business at the University of California, Dr. Vitalari co-founded Project NOAH -- a National Science Foundation funded program to assess the impact of microcomputers. Project NOAH predicted many of the technologies emerging today, including the information highway, work at home, consumer use of electronic networks and the rise of electronic commerce. He coined the term, "The Capable Enterprise," to describe how technology creates new distributed and flexible corporate structures and capabilities.

James C. Wetherbe

James Wetherbe is Stevenson Chaired Professor of Information Technology and Executive Director of the Institute for Internet Buyer Behavior at Texas Tech University. Internationally known as a dynamic speaker, author, and leading authority on the use of computers and information systems to improve organizational performance and competitiveness, Dr. Wetherbe is particularly appreciated for his ability to explain complex technology in straightforward, practical terms that can be strategically applied by both executives and general management. He is the author of 21 highly regarded books including *Information Technology for Management, god.online, The World On Time: 11 Management Principles That Made FedEx an Overnight Sensation, So, What's Your Point?* and *Systems Analysis and Design: Best Practices*. Quoted often in leading business and information system journals, Dr. Wetherbe has also authored over 200 articles, and is the first recipient of the MIS Quarterly Distinguished Scholar Award.

Giuseppe Zollo

Giuseppe Zollo is a professor of Business Economics and Organization at the Faculty of Engineering of University of Naples Federico II. During the years 1985-86 he was Visiting Research Associate at Dept. of Economics of Northeastern University, Boston (MA), USA. He has published in several journals and has presented papers at international conferences on innovation management, organization, small innovative firms and managerial application of fuzzy logic. In 1992, 1993 and 1995 he received the "Entrepreneurship Award" at the RENT-Research in Entrepreneurship Workshops organized by the European Institute for Advanced Studies in Management; in 1994 he received the "Best Paper Award" from FGF, Universitat Dortmund at the IntEnt '94 Conference. He is member of several editorial boards of international and Italian journals. He is Vice President of the International Association for Fuzzy-Set Management and Economy (SIGEF) and director of the University of Naples Center for Organizational Innovation and Communication.

Glossary

A

Acceptance Cycle: The part of the system development life cycle in which a user accepts a system or software product. The higher the Functional Quality, the higher the chance of Acceptance of the international information system by the business people; and the higher the Acceptance, the more it deepens the IT/Business Integration, which in turn facilitates higher Functional Quality of future enhancements. Thus the cycle enters another round.

Access Paradox: In the early days of Internet diffusion, the dominant view was that the internet was opening the market by lowering entry barriers to any industry. Anyone that was able to connect to the internet could become a global player. Later, facts and experience showed that this was not true for many reasons such as high costs for infrastructures and technology, skills shortage and high labor costs, necessity of deep organizational changes for companies going on-line, etc. This phenomenon is referred to as access paradox.

Alliance: More than just a joint venture between organizations, an alliance requires high levels of trust and information sharing between organizations for mutual benefit.

Arm's-Length Relationship (Model): An inter-organizational alliance characterized by: a competitive relationship between the focal firm and its suppliers; little relationship-specific investment; and minimal data sharing.

Artifact: A man-made object which carries information about the culture of its creator and users; product documentation like requirements, design, test plans of a software application (An IT Artifact refers to an IT-based object).

ATM Technology: ATM (asynchronous transfer mode) is a dedicated-connection switching technology that organizes digital data into fixed size cell units and transmits them over a physical medium using digital signal technology.

B

Bandwidth: A measure of a channel or communications capacity and speed. It is related to channel capacity for information transmission and refers to data (information) transmission rates when communicating over certain media or devices. The greater the bandwidth the more a community is equipped to exchange data with the rest of the world.

Basic Infrastructural Indicators: The level of infrastructure as reflected in the number of TV sets per 1000 people. One can also use electricity level (if data are available).

Best-in-Firm Software Adoption (BIF): A GIS development strategy which searches throughout the company for the global application which best fits the best experience of every unit then modifies into a single, common system to be implemented globally.

Best-of-Breed: A systems development strategy in which a single vendor strategy is rejected in favor of purchasing software modules from the best vendors in each module class. While this strategy assures the best modules for each functional area, integrating these modules to provide a seamless data environment over the entire the supply chain can be difficult.

Board of Directors: The management individuals charged with the conduct and management of a company's affairs. The Board of Directors may be comprised of inside directors (company officers) and outside directors (individuals who do not directly work for the company).

Bollywood: Nickname for India's film industry

BRIC Countries: BRIC is a term used to refer to the combination of Brazil, Russia, India, and China.

Broadband: Refers to a telecommunication signaling method which includes a relatively wide range of frequencies which may be divided into channels or frequency bins. Broadband Internet connection is commonly known as high speed Internet connection.

Business Process: A set of linked activities that create value by transforming an input into a more valuable output.

Business Process Oriented Integration: An application integration strategy in which a single logical model that spans many applications and data stores is created to provide a common business process to manage inter- or intra- company operations.

Business Process Outsourcing (BPO): The outsourcing of business functions, which include functions such as filing US tax returns, handling billing questions, and telemarketing at call centers.

Business Process Reengineering (BPR): A management approach that examines aspects of a business and its interactions, and attempts to improve the efficiency of the underlying processes. It is a fundamental and radical approach that either modifies or eliminates non-value adding activities.

Business-To-Business (B2B): The use of the Internet (or other computer networks) by a firm for transactions with other businesses (its suppliers, customers, distributors and other value chain partners).

Business-To-Commerce (B2C): The use of the Internet (or other computer networks) by a firm for transactions with its end customers/consumers.

Business-To-Employee (B2E): The use of the Internet (or other computer networks) by a firm for work activities and transactions with its employees.

Business-To-Government (B2G or G2B): Access to information and services using the Internet (or other computer networks) provided by the government to businesses.

C

C++: An object-oriented computer programming language.

Call Center: A centralized office used for the purpose of receiving and transmitting a large volume of requests by telephone. A call centre is operated by a company, many times at locations outside the U.S., to administer incoming product support or information inquiries from consumers. Outgoing calls for telemarketing, clientele, and debt collection are also made.

Caller-ID: A telecommunications technology that forwards caller information (i.e., name, location, phone number) to the call receiver at the time of call placement.

Central Development (CD): A GIS development strategy in which the system is developed at one site (usually at the headquarters) and then installed at the subsidiaries.

Charge Back: A system under which internal clients pay the IS department for its services in budgetary (but not cash) terms

Chief Executive Officer (CEO): The highest-ranking executive position in a company, organization or agency.

Chief Information Officer (CIO): The executive officer in charge of information processing in an organization. All systems design, development and datacenter operations fall under the CIO's domain.

CMM (Capability Maturity Model): A model, developed by the Software Engineering Institute at Carnegie Mellon University, to measure the maturity of the processes of an IS department or project. The CMM provides a framework for the continuous process improvement steps into five maturity levels: initial, repeatable, defined, managed, and optimizing.

Coase's Theorem: An interpretation of this theorem states that in economic transactions, efficiency will prevail as long as information among the transacting entities is perfect, cost of transactions is low, and negotiations are not too complicated or hindered.

Cocooning: Surrounding an existing legacy application with new and 'improved software that insulates the company from the obsolete legacy applications while providing the ability to interface with an organization's other applications.

Collectivism: Societies, in which people from birth onwards are integrated into strong, cohesive in-groups, often extended families (with uncles, aunts and grandparents) which continue protecting them in exchange for unquestioning loyalty.

Co-locate: To locate an organization's facility in close proximity to another organization in order to optimize logistics and reduce supply chain cycle times.

Co-sourcing: Outsourcing in which costs and benefits are shared by client and vendor

Commodity: Something that is widely available and more or less the same in kind and quality from whomever it is obtained

Competition Paradox: Traditional analysis would suggest that deregulation and opening of new markets should mean easier access for competitors and a reduction in market concentration. This however may not be true in all cases. Competing global companies often require large investments in innovation, technology infrastructures, and communication, etc. and this usually restricts the access to new markets. This contradiction is referred to as the competition paradox.

Connectivity: The property of a device, such as a PC, peripheral, PDA, mobile phone, etc., that enables it to be connected, generally to a network, PC, or another device without the need of an intervening device. Connectivity is a perception related to using computer networks to link to people and resources.

Connexity: One dictionary defines it as close interconnectedness, interrelatedness and interdependence. More knowledge about other lives, places and possibilities, boundaries and borders are more easily bypassed.

Common System: A common system is a computer-based application that utilizes the same software (and hardware) throughout an organization for the purpose of maintaining consistent and controllable applications.

Competing Values Framework: A framework used to study organizations that emphasize the competing tensions and conflicts inherent in groups.

Control: Process which brings about adherence to a goal or target through the exercise of power or authority. Attempt to achieve collaboration/coordination among a group of individuals who share only partially congruent objectives.

Control Mechanisms: Control mechanisms are the means used to implement control modes. For e.g. monitoring the output of a task (as in the number of function points completed during software development) and taking appropriate actions (rewards or sanctions) is an example of control mechanisms.

Control Modes: Control modes are the different kind of controls that an organization uses to ensure that its employees act in a manner that is consistent with the goals and objectives of the organization. There are two broad types: formal control modes and informal control modes. See below for more on these types

Control Portfolio: Usually one control mode is not enough for realizing organizational objectives. Organizations therefore employ a combination of control modes. For instance, formal control and informal control can form a total control portfolio. Similarly behavioral control combined with clan control can be seen as a mixed control portfolio involving both formal and informal modes

Coordination: Administrative tools used for achieving integration among different units within an organization

Core Competence: An area of specialized expertise of a firm that competitors cannot easily match or imitate; one of the things that a firm does better that most others

Core vs. Local Development (CL): A GIS development strategy where a large core is developed centrally while local variations are developed by the subsidiaries.

Critical Success Factor (CSF): Anything required for successful implementation or success of an organizational unit, project, or undertaking (widely used for information systems projects).

Cultural Barrier: Any barrier created by a culture in a country that obstructs the communications technology and the worldwide telecommunications infrastructure that carries data across country borders. Cultural barriers may include language and dialects, alphabets, and coding differences.

Cultural Heterogeneity: Refers to the differences between two cultures as gauged along different dimensions outlined by scholars like Hall, and Hofstede. In offshoring, cultural heterogeneity relates to the differences between the national culture of the client, and the national culture of the vendor.

Cultural Homogeneity: Opposite of cultural heterogeneity. Pure cultural homogeneity does not exist, but by and large some countries like USA and Canada (as measured by Hofstede's dimensions or other parameters to gauge culture) are culturally closer than other countries.

Culturalist: Those scholars or practitioners who argue that national (and other cultural forms) have a significant effect on organizational processes and outcomes. For example, a culturalist would suggest that national culture can impact project performance (an organizational phenomenon)

Culture: A collective programming of mind which distinguishes the members from one group or category of people from another. Culture is learned from the social environment, which causes cultural differences to exist both at the society level and the nation level

Culture Gap: The existence of behavioral asymmetries between international work groups.

Cybercriminals: Criminals who commit crimes on the Internet, using the Internet, and by means of the Internet.

D

Data Security: An organization's data is valuable corporate resource and must be secured against abuse advertently or inadvertently.

Data Warehouse: A computer system for archiving and analyzing an organization's historical data, such as sales, salaries, or other information from day-to-day operations. Normally, an organization copies information from its operational systems to the data warehouse on a regular schedule; after that, management can perform complex queries and analysis (such as data mining) on the information without slowing down the operational systems.

Databases: A database is an organized collection of information pertaining to a company. This information stored as records can be accessed electronically. In an MNC, a database will include information on worldwide customers, suppliers, vendors, competitors, products etc.

Database Management System: Software, such as Oracle, used to organize and manage a company's data for retrieval by managers to support their decision making functions.

Delphi Method: A method for obtaining opinions/forecasts from a panel of independent experts over several rounds. After each round, a summary of the forecasts is provided to the experts, possibly along with the reasons for them. When the forecasts change little between rounds, the process is stopped.

Digital Divide: The gap between those with regular, effective access to computers and Internet technologies and those without or the gap between Internet/technology "haves" and "have-nots". It also refers to the divergence of technology access between industrialized and developing societies.

Dimensions of Culture: Dimensions of culture are usually the parameters used to differentiate one culture from another. It might also be useful to think about dimensions as reflecting the idiosyncrasies of different cultural groups.

E

E-democracy: E-democracy is whereby e-government is involved in the development of direct forms of political deliberation and decision-making through electronic referendums and similar devices.

E-governance: E-governance is a broader concept, which includes the use of ICT internally by government and civil society to promote greater participation of citizens in the governance of political institutions.

E-government: E-government refers to any government functions or processes that are carried out in digital form over the Internet.

E-participation: E-participation is the process of engaging citizens and businesses via electronic channels for political deliberations and decision making.

E-payment: Making payment electronically while performing transactions over the Internet or other computer networks. Payment is made by direct credit, electronic transfer of credit card details, or some other electronic means, as opposed to payment by check or cash.

E-services: E-services refer to the provision of services using ICTs, especially the Internet and the World Wide Web.

Economic Commission for Latin America and the Caribbean (ECLAC): An organization made up of a set of 33 nations.

Economic Corruption: A type of corruption that occurs when economic uncertainty and controls is used to distort the facts.

Economic Indicators: GDP per capita, Inflation, Information technology (IT) expenditure as % of GDP

Economic Policies: Policies that intend to increase the wealth of entities or stakeholders.

Electronic Brokerage Effect: An effect of IT on transaction costs in which IT provides a better match for buyers' needs and sellers' offerings.

Electronic Commerce (EC or E-commerce): The distribution, buying, selling, marketing, and servicing of products or services over electronic systems such as the Internet and other computer networks.

Electronic Communication Effect: An effect of IT on transaction costs in which IT increases the rate of processing of transactions and reduces the cost per transaction,

Electronic Data Interchange (EDI): The computer-to-computer exchange of normal business documents, by agreed message standards, from one computer application to another by electronic means.

Electronic Integration Effect: An effect of IT on transaction costs in which IT enables integration of various processes and operations within a firm or across the value chain.

ELF Index: Quantifies ethno-linguistic fractionalization in countries and represents the probability that two individuals drawn randomly will be from different groups. Low value implies less ethnic fragmentation.

Enterprise Integration: The process by which business units from suppliers through headquarters and subsidiaries, including customers, are linked through information technology. The purpose of Enterprise Integration is to deliver, in a cost effective way, the right product or service at the right time to the right customer and at the right quality level.

Enterprise Resource Planning (ERP): An integrated computer based information system that helps support, enable and manage enterprise wide business processes. These systems help bind the different functional areas such as accounting, production, inventory management into an integrated system. An ERP system can also be used to extend the organization by electronically linking to customers and suppliers.

Ethnocentrism: Predisposition of a firm where all strategic decisions are guided by the values and interests of the parent.

European Union: A supranational and intergovernmental union of 27 independent, democratic member states. The European Union is the world's largest confederation of independent states, established under that name in 1992 by the Treaty on European Union (the Maastricht Treaty).

External Suppliers: Those suppliers that are not part of the legal corporate entity.

Extranet: A network that utilizes Internet technologies (i.e., web pages, browsers, etc.) for applications between organizations.

F

Factory Mode: One of the quadrants of the Strategic Impact Grid by F.W. McFarlan. In this quadrant, organizations have implemented systems with a strategic impact, but there are no new developments planned. This quadrant is usually comprised of service companies, who depend on a few information intensive activities.

Family Quadrant: A quadrant into which cultures are placed that are low in uncertainty avoidance and high in power distance.

Federal IS Structure: A structure for the IS function of an organization that combines a centralized corporate department with IT-competent sub-units.

Focal Firm: The central firm in the supply chain relationship that contracts with its suppliers and oversees all of the activities from its suppliers to the delivery of the goods or service to its final customer.

G

General Agreement on Trade in Services (GATS): A treaty negotiated by the WTO and signed by major trading countries that governs free trade in Services (services are considered trade items that are not tangible goods).

Geocentrism: Predisposition of a firm where it attempts to integrate the diverse subsidiaries through a global systems approach.

Geographic Tracking Systems: Satellite or cellular tracking devices most commonly used in trucks or trailers to ascertain position and feed the information to ancillary systems such as TMS, Routing or WMS.

GIGO (Garbage In Garbage Out): An aphorism referring to the fact that computers, unlike humans, will unquestioningly process the most nonsensical of input data and produce nonsensical output.

Global Arbitrage: Taking advantage of cost and price difference in different areas of the work

Global Business Strategy: A strategy that relies on a high degree of centralized decision making; decisions are made at headquarters. It is characterized by high control and low coordination from the headquarters.

Global Company: A company that manages production establishments or delivers services in countries around the world.

Global Culture: The mindset of a firm that seeks to promote the best people everywhere in the world and the standards for evaluation are usually universal but weighted to suit local conditions.

Global Information System (GIS): An information system that is used across one or more national borders to help support decision-making, manage organizational data, support and enable organizational business processes, facilitate organizational communications, and support global business strategy.

Global IT Architecture: The IT architecture of a multinational firm which has IT resources distributed in many countries.

Governance Policies: Policies that aim to create and sustain the environment for economic and social development, and maintain continued economic investments in national ICT.

Grounded Theory: A general research method (most often associated with qualitative research) developed by the sociologists Barney Glaser and Anselm Strauss. Grounded theory was developed as a systematic methodology, and its name underscores the generation of theory from data. A researcher using this approach will formulate a theory, either substantive (setting specific) or formal, about the phenomena they are studying that can be evaluated.

Groupware: Software applications that focus on providing productivity solutions for groups of people. Email, bulletin boards, chat rooms, file sharing, and electronic meetings, are all features of groupware.

Guanxi: A central concept in Chinese society that describes, in part, a personal connection between two people in which one is able to prevail upon another to perform a favor or service, or be prevailed upon.

H

Home Country Culture: The mindset of a firm which would most likely develop home country nationals for positions everywhere in the world and apply home standards for evaluation.

Host Country Culture: The mindset of a firm where people of local nationality would be developed for key positions in their own country with local standards for evaluation.

Hawthorne Study: The Hawthorne studies conducted between 1927 and 1932 by Elton Mayo were attempts to find out what conditions affect productivity of employees.

Hypertext Mark-Up Language (HTML): One of the programming or scripting languages used to develop World-Wide Web (WWW) web pages.

I

IBM AS/400: A mini-computer developed by IBM in the late 1980s.

IC Card (integrated circuit card or ICC): Also known as a smart card or chip card is any pocket-sized card with embedded integrated circuits. There are two broad categories of ICCs: memory cards which contain only non-volatile memory storage components and microprocessor cards which contain both memory and microprocessor components.

Identity Theft: The criminal abuse of consumers' "means of identification" to exploit someone's credit worthiness to commit loan fraud, mortgage fraud, lines-of-credit fraud, credit card fraud, commodities and services frauds, or other similar fraud.

Ideology: An organized collection of ideas. It is a comprehensive vision, a way of looking at things; a set of ideas proposed by the dominant class of a society to all members of its society.

Individualism: Societies in which the ties between individuals are loose: everyone is expected to look after him/herself and his/her immediate family.

Individualism-Collectivism: The degree to which each individual takes care of himself or herself or relinquishes some of this responsibility to the group.

Information and Communication Technologies (ICTs): Information and communication technologies include telecommunications technologies, such as telephony, cable, satellite and radio, as well as digital technologies, such as computers, information networks and software for the processing, storage and communication of digital information.

Information Architecture: A high level map of the information requirements of an organization. It is also called the enterprise model.

Information Culture: A set of information system values and practices shared by those members of an organization.

Information Flow Policies: Policies that either encourage or protect against the free flow of information.

Information Oriented Integration: An application integration strategy in which the objective is simple sharing of information between applications.

Information Systems Development (ISD) project: A project to build an information system for a company.

Information Technology (IT): The hardware and software technologies that permit information gathering, processing, and distribution.

Information Technology (IT) Architecture: The design of various IT elements (e.g., network topology, servers, software, users, internet, intranet, extranet, IT management structure, and IT organization) that work together to achieve organizational goals.

Information Technology (IT) Infrastructure: The current state of IT resources in the firm, and may or may not reflect the IT architecture. It may include components such as computers, telecommunication networks, databases, operating systems, systems software, and business applications.

Intellectual Property Rights (IPR): Similar to patents on material goods. IPR afford protection to the owners of intangible property.

Internal Suppliers: Those suppliers that are within the legal corporate entity but are considered separate and autonomous departments or divisions.

International Business Strategy: A strategy that relies on transferring and adapting a company's knowledge and expertise to foreign subsidiaries. It is characterized by high control and high coordination from the headquarters.

International Information System (IIS): An information system that is used by a multinational enterprise or company.

Internal Markets: Organizational formats in which departments offer services to clients within, and outside of, the organization.

Internet: The worldwide, publicly accessible network of interconnected computer networks that transmit data using the standard Internet Protocol (IP). It is a "network of networks" that consists of millions of smaller domestic, academic, business, and government networks.

Internet Host: A computer system that provides access to the Internet.

Interorganizational Alliance: The nature of the relationship between a focal firm and its suppliers, implying either a close collaborative relationship (partnership) or a limited and competitive one (arm's-length).

Interpenetration: The inner and outer aspects of a person, place or thing are understood to penetrate each other such that the quality of the inner state is always discernible by its outer appearance

Interpersonal Trust: The trust index value is generated from percentage of respondents in each nation who replied that "most people can be trusted". High value implies high trust

Intranet: A network that utilizes Internet technologies (i.e., web pages, browsers, etc.) for applications internal to the organization.

IS Disaster Recovery Plan: A response plan to be executed if an IS disaster occurs. It includes the data, hardware, and software critical for a business to restart operations in the event of a natural or human-caused disaster. It should also include how to cope with unexpected or sudden loss of key personnel.

IT Enabled Services (ITES): A form of outsourced service which has emerged due to involvement of IT in various fields such as banking and finance, telecommunications, insurance, etc. Some of the examples of ITES are medical transcription, back-office accounting, insurance claim, credit card processing and many more. This is also called Business Process Outsourcing.

J

Joint Application Design (JAD): A software application development methodology that employs the use of teams composed of both application developers and end-users throughout the systems development life cycle (i.e., systems planning, analysis, design, implementation, and follow-on support).

Joint Development with Vendor (JDV): A GIS development strategy where the application is developed jointly with a vendor. Also called strategic partnership, it requires heavy and committed participation of the vendor in one or more phases.

Joint Venture: An entity formed between two or more parties to undertake economic activity together. The parties agree to create a new entity by both contributing equity, and they then share in the revenues, expenses, and control of the enterprise. The venture can be for one specific project only, or a continuing business relationship.

K

Keirestu: The post World War II Japanese corporate structures in which a group of firms function as a long-term business alliance and avoid competition among themselves.

Knowledge Sharing: The process of sharing knowledge by employees in an organization. Knowledge includes both explicit and tacit knowledge. While corporate knowledge may be captured and stored in computer based knowledge systems that can be accessed by all, tacit knowledge resides in employees and is often difficult to capture in computer based systems.

L

Leapfrog Computing: A strategy in which an organization that lags its competitors in technology usage makes a quantum leap in the generation of technology used that surpasses the generation of technology used by the majority of organizations in their industry.

Legacy Systems: Old, typically obsolete computer applications that are typically large, complex, and expensive to maintain.

Legal Barrier: Any barrier created by laws or government regulations that obstructs the communications technology and the worldwide telecommunications infrastructure that carries data across country borders. Political barriers usually impact the privacy rights of individuals.

Legal Privilege: The use of political cronyism to create imperfect competition. It includes wasted financial, material & labor resources and obstacles to information access.

Lesser Developed Country (LDC): UN classification for developing countries.

Logistics: The process of obtaining inputs, storing goods, and moving items to their destination.

Long Term Orientation (LTO): A higher LTO score can be indicative of a culture that is perseverant and parsimonious. A low LTO ranking reflects a freedom in the culture from long-term traditional commitments, which allows greater flexibility and the freedom to react quickly to new opportunities.

M

M-government: Defined as when mobile and/or wireless technologies like cellular/mobile phones, and laptops and PDAs (personal digital assistants) are used for offering and delivering government services.

Machine Quadrant: A quadrant into which cultures are placed that are low in power distance and high in uncertainty avoidance.

Malware: Software designed to infiltrate or damage a computer system without the owner's informed consent. It is derived from the name "malicious software."

Market Quadrant: A quadrant into which cultures are placed that are low in uncertainty avoidance and low in power distance.

Masculinity (MAS) Vs. Femininity: In general, it refers to the distribution of roles between the genders and is a measure of the difference between the roles played by men and women in a society. Specifically, as Hofstede's cultural dimension, it refers to the degree to which people prefer values of success and competition to modesty and concern over others.

Mass Customization: The strategy of customizing a product or service to meet the unique needs of each of the organization's individual customers.

Mediation: An act of bringing two states, sides or parties in a dispute closer together toward agreement.

Medical Tourism: The act of traveling to other countries to obtain medical, dental, and surgical care. It is also called medical travel.

Middle Shore: Countries in West Europe, who have similar culture and similar economic status.

Moderating Effect/Variable: A moderating effect or variable is a term used in social sciences to reflect the condition where the effect of one variable on another variable is dependent upon the presence or absence of a third variable. In other terms the moderating variable softens or increases the impact between two variables

Modified Package Software Acquisition: A GIS development strategy where the purchased software is modified to fit the needs of the company.

Most Favored Nation (Status) (MFN): Special treatment allotted to nations within the GATS trade agreement.

Multinational Business Strategy: A strategy that relies on the management of its subsidiaries as a part of a larger portfolio. It is characterized by low control and low coordination from the headquarters.

Multinational Corporation (MNC): An organization that has operations in more than one country. A MNC operates and manages production facilities or delivers services to its customers in multiple nations.

Multinational Design Team Development (MDT): A GIS development strategy in which the development team is comprised of systems and user personnel from multiple international sites.

Multinational Enterprise (MNEs): An organization that has operations in more than one country. A MNE operates and manages production facilities or delivers services to its customers in multiple nations. It is also known as a Multinational Corporation (MNC).

Multi-sourcing: Outsourcing to numerous vendors.

N

National Culture: Shared values of a particular group of people that can affect the way people relate, work, and make decisions.

Network Topology: The different configurations that can be adopted in building networks, such as a ring, bus, star or meshed shape.

NEXTStep: An object-oriented application development environment created by the Next Computer Company, an organization started by Steven Jobs, the co-founder of Apple Computer.

Non-Culturalist: That segment of scholars or practitioners which argues that culture has no effect on organizational phenomena or processes, or at least has no direct visible impacts. A non-culturalist for instance might argue that culture only influences work styles of individuals which in turn may or may not be related to say project performance.

O

Offshoring or Offshore Outsourcing: Offshore outsourcing implies transferring the responsibility of performing business function to a non-employee group (vendor) based in another country.

Offshore Outsourced Information Systems Development (OOISD): Information systems development activities required by a client in one country are outsourced to a vendor in another country

Onshore outsourcing: Contrasted with offshore outsourcing, onshore outsourcing is the transfer of responsibility for an IT function from one company (or group) to another company (or a non-employee group), based in the same country or geographic location.

Open Source Software (OSS): Software for which the underlying programming code is available to the users so that they may read it, make changes to it, and build new versions of the software incorporating their changes.

Organization Culture: A pattern of basic assumptions that establishes the correct way to perceive, think and feel about organizational problems.

Organization for Economic Co-operation and Development (OECD): An international organization of those developed countries that accept the principles of representative democracy and a free market economy. It originated in 1948 as the Organization for European Economic Co-operation (OEEC).

Organizational Networks: Businesses networks used to communicate internally with employees and externally with business partners and the government. There are two types of networks that may exist in a MNC, formal and informal organizational networks.

Outsourced Custom Development (OC): A global information system development strategy where the system is developed by or acquired from an external company (i.e., a service provider.).

Outsourcing: The business model of taking internal company functions and paying an outside firm to handle them. Outsourcing is done to save money, improve quality, or free company resources for core business activities.

Outsourcer: The company or group that is transferring the responsibility of the IT function. Also known as the client.

Outsourcee: The company or group to which the responsibility of the IT function is transferred or outsourced to. Also known as the vendor.

P

Paradigm Shift: A drastic level of business change in which the nature of the business and the nature of the organization are reevaluated.

Parallel Development (PD): Where the requirements gathering and the construction of the system are done at local sites and the system is connected through bridges.

Partnership Model: An inter-organizational alliance characterized by a close working relationship; relationship-specific investments and data sharing.

Personal Data: Data about an individual.

Political Barrier: Any barrier created by political actions in a country that obstructs the communications technology and the worldwide telecommunications infrastructure that carries data across country borders. Political barriers usually restrict accessibility of citizens to technology.

Political Corruption: A type of corruption that occurs when a government controls the media. As such, politics is used to report the news rather than facts.

Polycentrism: Predisposition of a firm where strategic decisions are tailored to suit the cultures of the various countries in which the MNC operates

Portal: Primarily a simple web interface to consumer or business content. Consumer portals include such services as e-mail, forums, search engines, and on-line shopping malls. An example is AOL. Business portals provide such services as the ability for supply chain partners to communicate with each other and exchange data over the Internet in a secure environment.

Power Distance Index (PDI): The (perceived) degree of inequality among people. The extent to which the less powerful members of organizations and institutions (like the family) accept and expect that power is distributed unequally

Primary Activities: A term attributed to Porter, dividing the activities of the firm into inbound logistics, operations, outbound logistics, marketing and sales, and service.

Privacy: The claim of individuals, groups and institutions to determine for themselves, when, how and to what extent information about them is communicated to others.

Production Database: A database that is used in the daily processing of business transactions. For example, a MNC such as Dell may use a production database to capture and process customer order data.

Productivity Paradox: The introduction of computers, office automation, and information technology was thought to boost labor (or total factor) productivity, however, as new information technology is introduced, worker productivity seemed to go down, not up. This is called the productivity paradox. Often times it takes a while before employees become familiar with technology and this leads to a decrease in their productivity.

Prototyping: An iterative development process where applications are broken down into smaller modules that can be developed quickly, reviewed by the end-user, and enhanced to address the end-users' feedback.

Public ICT Policy: A governmental policy for managing computers, information technology, and other computer-related assets.

Public ICT Policy Stakeholder: A person or organization that has a legitimate interest in any governmental policy related to computers, information technology, and other computer-related projects or entities.

Pyramid Quadrant: A quadrant into which cultures are placed that are high in power distance and high in uncertainty avoidance.

Q

R

Radio Frequency Tag: Also known as an "electronic label," "transponder" or "code plate," is made up of an RFID (radio frequency identification) chip attached to an antenna. The tag supports wireless communication to read and transmit data.

Regiocentrism: Predisposition of a firm where it tries to blend the interests of both the parent and the subsidiaries at least on a regional basis.

Regional Culture: The mindset of a firm that performs the same way as the host country but uses regional standards in place of host country standards

Rejection Cycle: The part of the system development life cycle in which a user rejects a system of software product. System or software rejection leads to increased isolation of the IT people. This has a further negative effect on Functional Quality.

Relationship-Specific Investment: Investments made in information technology by suppliers to accommodate the information strategy of the focal organization.

S

Sarbanes-Oxley Act of 2002: Often shortened to *SOX*. Legislation enacted in response to the high-profile Enron and WorldCom financial scandals to protect shareholders and the general public from accounting errors and fraudulent practices in the enterprise.

Service Level Agreement (SLA): A contract between a firm and the provider of information technology services that specifies, usually in measurable terms, what services the provider will furnish.

Service Oriented Architecture (SOA): A software architecture that utilize loosely coupled software services to support the requirements of the business processes. Software services in a SOA environment communicate with each other across organizational boundaries without knowledge of their underlying platform implementation

Service Oriented Architecture Protocol (SOAP): An XML-based protocol for exchanging information between computers in a decentralized, distributed environment.

Service Oriented Integration: A high level of application integration which permits applications to share common business logic and methods.

Six-Sigma: An approach to total quality management that is widely used by international firms such as GE and Motorola

Social Divide: The gap between information rich and poor in a given nation.

Social Indicators: Income Inequality, Secondary Education Average, Illiteracy level, Interpersonal Trust, Urbanization Level, Ethno-linguistic Fractionalization (ELF)

Societal-human Equity Policies: Policies that aim to achieve equitable distribution of citizenship privileges.

Society for Information Management (SIM): An association of senior IT executives, prominent academicians, selected consultants, and other IT thought leaders built on the foundation of local chapters, who share and enhance their intellectual capital for the benefit of its member organizations.

Spamware: Software designed by or for spammers. Spamware varies widely, but may include the ability to import thousands of addresses, to generate random addresses, to insert fraudulent headers into messages, to use dozens or hundreds of mail servers simultaneously, and to make use of open relays.

Spyware: Software that collects personal information about users without their informed consent. The term is often used interchangeably with adware and malware (software designed to infiltrate and damage a computer). Personal information is secretly recorded with a variety of techniques, including logging keystrokes, recording Internet web browsing history, and scanning documents on the computer's hard disk.

Strategic Alliance: An activity performed jointly by two or more organizations

Strategic Impact Grid: Created by W. F. McFarlan, it identifies how important IT is to the firm, and tries to assess the level of attention needed to manage current and new IT systems. It created four quadrants by using importance of current IT applications on one axis and importance of future IT applications on the other axis.

Strategic Mode: One of the quadrants of the Strategic Impact Grid. In this quadrant, organizations are the most dependent on information. Planning is pro-active for firms that operate in this quadrant. Risks are high and IT is integrated into the firm's organizational functions and business activities.

Supply Chain Management (SCM): The management of activities associated with the flow of products and services from the beginning of the manufacturing or processing cycle through to the end-user. It is the integration and management of activities, materials flows, and information flows between suppliers and customers necessary to transform raw materials from suppliers to finished goods to customers or end-users.

Support Mode: One of the quadrants of the Strategic Impact Grid. In this quadrant, the organization is a well established manufacturing related firm. Success hinges on efficiency of operations.

Synchronization: A term used in supply chain management to suggest the integration of information and product flow from suppliers through to customers.

T

TCP/IP: Telecommunications Protocol/Internet Protocol. The original and de facto standard protocol used for data interchange on the Internet.

Technical Barrier: Any barrier of technology that obstructs the communications technology and the worldwide telecommunications infrastructure that carries data across country borders. Technical barriers may include restrictions due to bandwidth, connectivity, or security.

Teleradiology: The electronic transmission of radiological patient images, such as x-rays, CTs, and MRIs, from one location to another for the purposes of interpretation and/or consultation.

Third Party: Service Provider: An entity that provides services to other entities.

Ti: The "essence", the deeper, more fundamental, more internal, more important, or invisible aspects of something: any kind of being, organization, phenomenon, concept, event, etc. Its usage in the major East Asian thought systems is mainly centered in the realm of human affairs or human psychology--with *ti* referring to the human mind, especially the deeper, more hidden dimension of the human mind--the mind as it is before entering into the realm of activity. In the objective universe, *ti* is used to express the deeper, more fundamental or invisible aspect of things, the "principles" of things, as opposed to their more outwardly manifest, phenomenal aspects.

Ti-Yong: The "essence-function" concept; unity between two things, or two aspects, which might, from an unenlightened point of view be seen as distinctly separated, or of unclear relationship.

Time-Boxing: Breaking a large project down into more manageable sub-tasks with readily achievable time deadlines.

Transborder Data Flow (TBDF): The movement of personally identifiable data from one country to another.

Transfer Prices: Somewhat arbitrary accounting charges that are used to determine the amount of budget transfers in a "charge back" system for accounting for the providing of services to internal clients

Transaction Costs: The costs of gathering information, evaluating available options, negotiating, contracting, and the change of legal ownership of an object.

Transnational Business Strategy: A strategy that relies on a balance between global integration and local responsiveness. It is characterized by low control and high coordination from the headquarters.

Transportation Mode: The means of transportation, such as sea, land, or air, used by the supplier to move goods from the supplier's facilities to next level suppliers, the focal firm, or its customers.

Trust: The willing acceptance of one's power to affect another.

Turnaround Mode: One of the quadrants of the Strategic Impact Grid. This is a temporary category quadrant. Firms may move to Factory category if strategic developments are not followed up. If follow up occurs, the company may move into the Strategic category.

U

Uncertainty Avoidance (UA): The degree to which a society feels threatened by for uncertainty and ambiguity; it ultimately refers to man's search for Truth.

Universal Description, Discovery and Integration (UDDI): An XML-based specification to publish and discover information about remote services.

Unmodified Package Software Acquisition: A GIS development strategy where a software package is purchased from a vendor. The package is generally parameter driven and can be configured as needed.

V

Value Added Network (VAN): An intermediary organization in an EDI based network to which EDI encoded messages are sent, stored, and then sent to their final destination. VANs charge a fee usually on a per document basis. They also provide additional services including increased security measures and error checking.

Value Added Tax (VAT): System of taxation where goods are taxed at each stage of processing that the tax is passed to the final consumer.

Value Chain: A term introduced by Porter, suggesting the value added by a firm and including all those activities from suppliers to the final customer.

Vendor-Client Relationship: The working relationship between the vendor and the client.

Vendor-Managed Inventories: The responsibility taken by suppliers to manage the inventories maintained on the shelves of retailers. Requires the use of information technology to establish the links for the necessary monitoring of retail data.

Virtual Team: A group of individuals who work across time, space, and organizational boundaries with links strengthened by webs of communication technology. Also known as a Geographically Dispersed Team (GDT).

W

Web Services: Any services that are available over the Internet that use XML messaging system. They are also self-describing and discoverable via a simple find mechanism.

Web Services Description Language (WSDL): Using XML, WSDL specifies a public interface for available functions and data types of a web service.

Web Services Flow Language (WSFL): An XML language for the description of Web Services compositions. It specifies the usage and interaction patterns of a collection of Web services

Wi-Fi (WiFi): Originally licensed by the Wi-Fi Alliance®, Wi-Fi describes the underlying technology of wireless local area networks based on the Institute of Electrical and Electronics Engineers Inc. (IEEE) 802.11 specifications. It was developed for mobile computing devices, such as laptops.

Wireless LAN (WLAN): A wireless local area network is the linking of two or more computers without using wires. WLAN utilizes spread-spectrum technology based on radio waves to enable communication between devices in a limited area.

WLAN Authentication and Privacy Infrastructure (WAPI): A Chinese National Standard for Wireless LAN (GB 15629.11-2003). Although supposed to work on top of WiFi, compatibility with the security protocol used by the IEEE 802.11 standard is in dispute.

World Trade Organization (WTO): An organization that oversees global trade, free trade, and trade regulations.

X

XML (eXtensible Markup Language): A text-based markup language specification from the World Wide Web Consortium (W3C). XML is for the definition of portable structured data. It can be used as a language for defining data descriptive languages.

Y

Yong: A "function," "usage," "activity," or "means." Outwardly manifest phenomenal aspects.

Z

INDEX